lonely planet

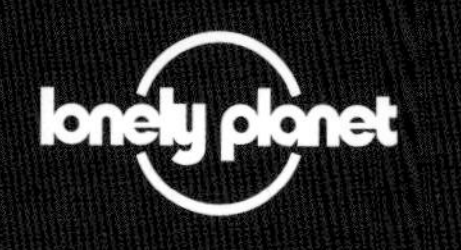

Mauritius, Réunion & Seychelles

Jan Dodd

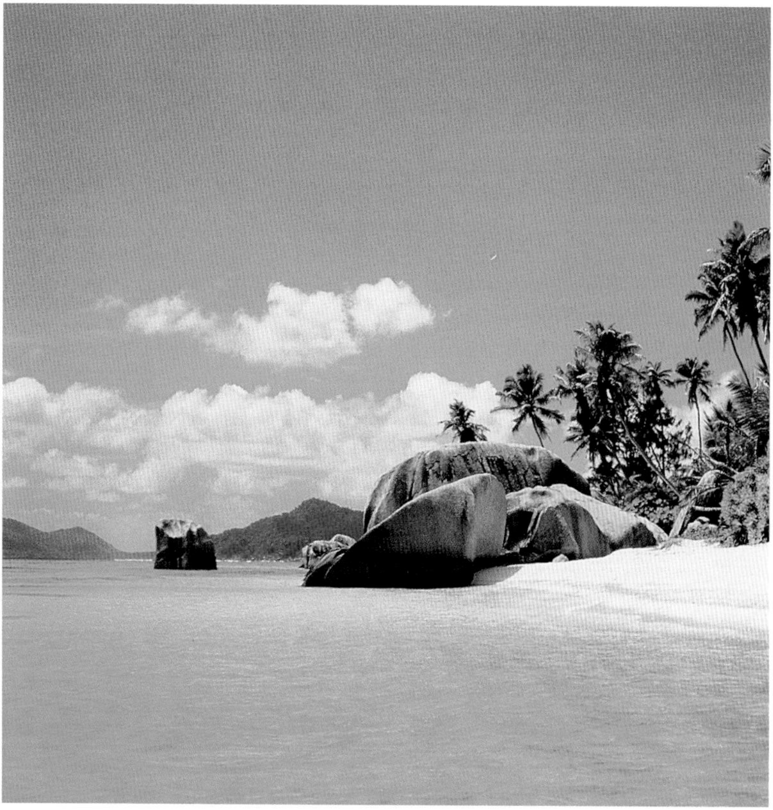

Contents

Highlights	7
Getting Started	13
Itineraries	17
The Authors	23
Snapshot	24
Food & Drink	26
Underwater Worlds	33
Mauritius	43
Réunion	145
Hiking in Réunion	224
Seychelles	237
Regional Directory	277
Regional Transport	286
Health	291
World Time Zones	296
Language	297
Glossary	304
Behind the Scenes	306
Index	308
Legend	316

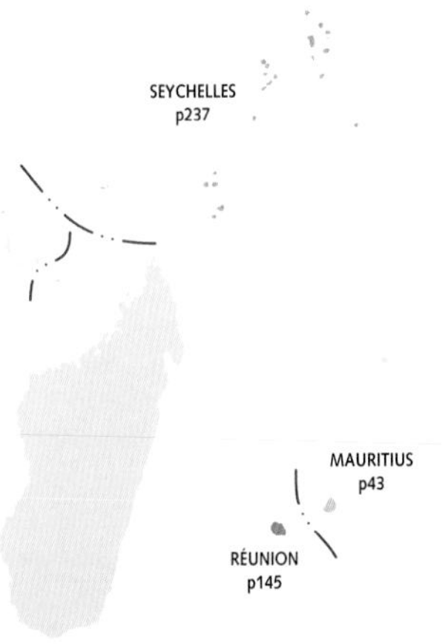

Lonely Planet books provide independent advice. Lonely Planet does not accept advertising in guidebooks, nor do we accept payment in exchange for listing or endorsing any place or business. Lonely Planet writers do not accept discounts or payments in exchange for positive coverage of any sort.

Lonely Planet réalise ses guides en toute indépendance et les ouvrages ne contiennent aucune publicité. Les établissements et prestataires mentionnés dans ce guide ne le sont que sur la foi du jugement et des recherches des auteurs, qui n'acceptent aucune rétribution ou réduction de prix en échange de leurs commentaires.

Destination Mauritius, Réunion & Seychelles

Just the names of these Indian Ocean islands evoke images of white sands, swaying palms, azure lagoons, romantic hideaways and exotic wildlife. But surprisingly, many people in the English-speaking world are unaware of the fabulous tropical delights on offer.

Not so the French, who used to rule all these islands and still own Réunion. Though the British took over temporarily, they never really warmed to the Indian Ocean, leaving the locals to pursue their own, French-influenced way of life and the islands to develop their own personalities.

For *the* ultimate tropical paradise, you can't beat the Seychelles, which boasts some of the most stunning islands on the planet. Paradise comes at a price, however, and only the extremely well heeled will be able to see the best the country has to offer.

Mauritius is more affordable and offers unusual cultural attractions in addition to its own gorgeous beaches. Aquatic activities abound, even walking under the sea!

Réunion is the surprise. Instead of beaches, its prime attractions are a smouldering volcano, world-class hiking in the mountainous interior, and endless other adventure activities.

Apart from their natural wonders, the islands offer a vibrant cultural mix. In Mauritius, Indian culture dominates; Réunion looks towards mainland France; and the Seychelles presents a Franco-African face to the world. The result is a flamboyant potpourri of people, cuisines, traditions and beliefs that should excite even the most experienced traveller.

OLIVIER CIRENDINI

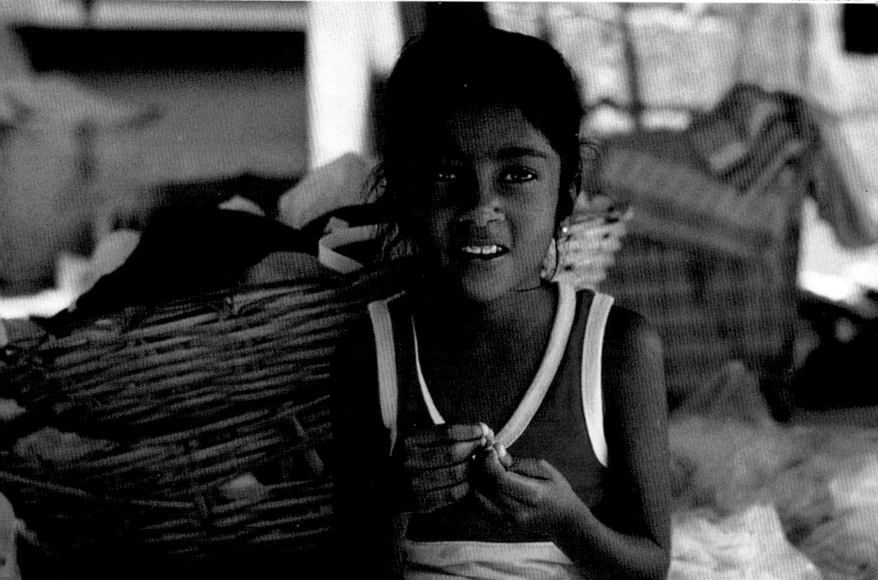

MAURITIUS

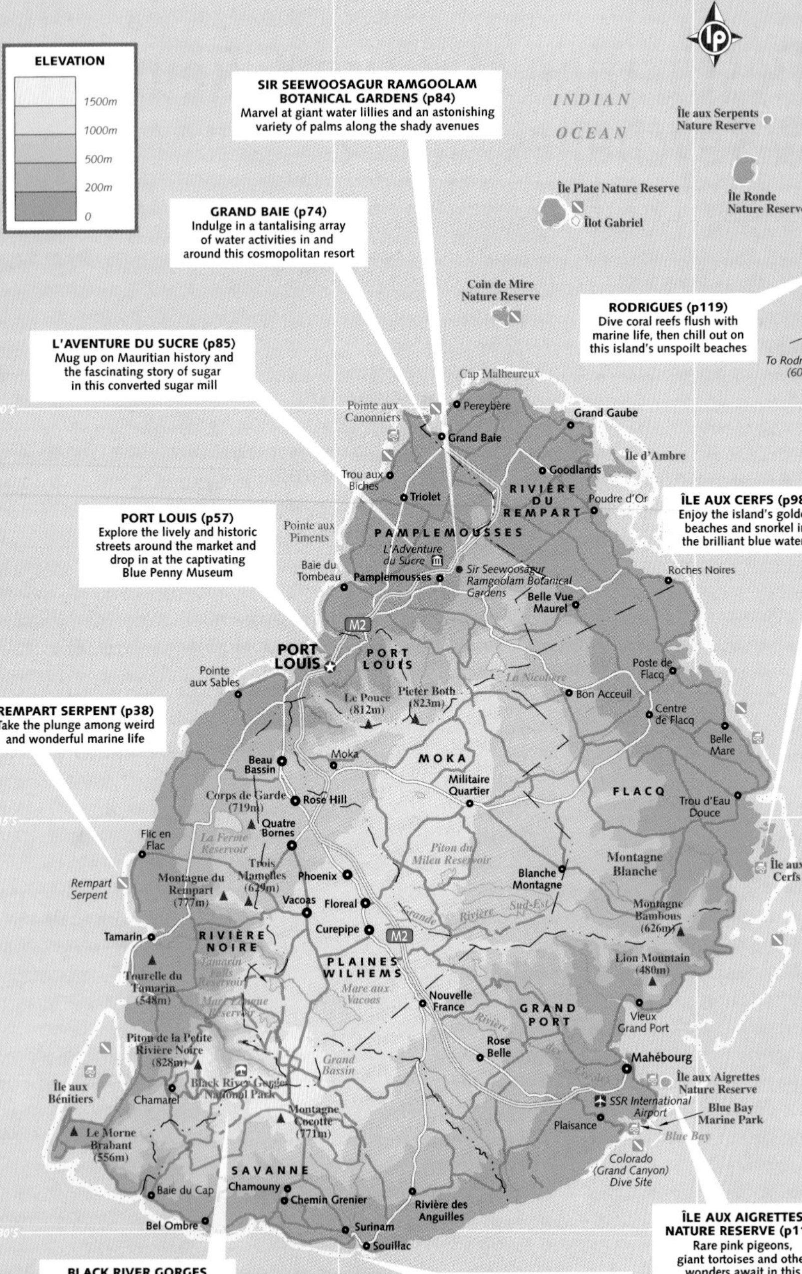

0 10 km
0 6 miles
ELEVATION
1500m
1000m
500m
200m
0
SIR SEEWOOSAGUR RAMGOOLAM BOTANICAL GARDENS (p84)
Marvel at giant water lillies and an astonishing variety of palms along the shady avenues
GRAND BAIE (p74)
Indulge in a tantalising array of water activities in and around this cosmopolitan resort
L'AVENTURE DU SUCRE (p85)
Mug up on Mauritian history and the fascinating story of sugar in this converted sugar mill
PORT LOUIS (p57)
Explore the lively and historic streets around the market and drop in at the captivating Blue Penny Museum
REMPART SERPENT (p38)
Take the plunge among weird and wonderful marine life
RODRIGUES (p119)
Dive coral reefs flush with marine life, then chill out on this island's unspoilt beaches
ÎLE AUX CERFS (p98)
Enjoy the island's golden beaches and snorkel in the brilliant blue waters
ÎLE AUX AIGRETTES NATURE RESERVE (p114)
Rare pink pigeons, giant tortoises and other wonders await in this island nature reserve
SOUTH COAST (p117)
Step back in time among traditional fishing villages along the south's rugged coastline
BLACK RIVER GORGES NATIONAL PARK (p86)
Hike through forested mountains past picturesque waterfalls and volcanic lakes
INDIAN OCEAN
Île aux Serpents Nature Reserve
Île Ronde Nature Reserve
Île Plate Nature Reserve
Îlot Gabriel
Coin de Mire Nature Reserve
To Rodrigues (600km)
Cap Malheureux
Pointe aux Canonniers
Pereybère
Grand Baie
Grand Gaube
Île d'Ambre
Goodlands
Trou aux Biches
Triolet
RIVIÈRE DU REMPART
Poudre d'Or
Pointe aux Piments
PAMPLEMOUSSES
L'Aventure du Sucre
Baie du Tombeau
Pamplemousses
Sir Seewoosagur Ramgoolam Botanical Gardens
Belle Vue Maurel
Roches Noires
M2
PORT LOUIS
PORT LOUIS
La Nicolière
Poste de Flacq
Pointe aux Sables
Le Pouce (812m)
Pieter Both (823m)
Bon Acceuil
Centre de Flacq
Belle Mare
Beau Bassin
Moka
MOKA
Militaire Quartier
FLACQ
Trou d'Eau Douce
Corps de Garde (719m)
Rose Hill
Quatre Bornes
20°00'S
20°15'S
20°30'S
Flic en Flac
La Ferme Reservoir
Trois Mamelles (629m)
Piton du Mileu Reservoir
Montagne Blanche
Île aux Cerfs
Rempart Serpent
Montagne du Rempart (777m)
Phoenix
Blanche Montagne
Vacoas
Floreal
Grande Rivière Sud-Est
Montagne Bambous (626m)
Tamarin
RIVIÈRE NOIRE
Curepipe
M2
Tamarin Falls Reservoir
PLAINES WILHEMS
Lion Mountain (480m)
Tourelle du Tamarin (548m)
Mare aux Vacoas
Mare Longue Reservoir
Nouvelle France
GRAND PORT
Vieux Grand Port
Rivière des Créoles
Piton de la Petite Rivière Noire (828m)
Rose Belle
Mahébourg
Grand Bassin
Île aux Aigrettes Nature Reserve
Île aux Bénitiers
Chamarel
Black River Gorges National Park
SSR International Airport
Blue Bay Marine Park
Montagne Cocotte (771m)
Plaisance
Blue Bay
Le Morne Brabant (556m)
Colorado (Grand Canyon) Dive Site
SAVANNE
Baie du Cap
Chamouny
Chemin Grenier
Rivière des Anguilles
Bel Ombre
Surinam
Souillac
57°15'E
57°30'E
57°45'E

RÉUNION

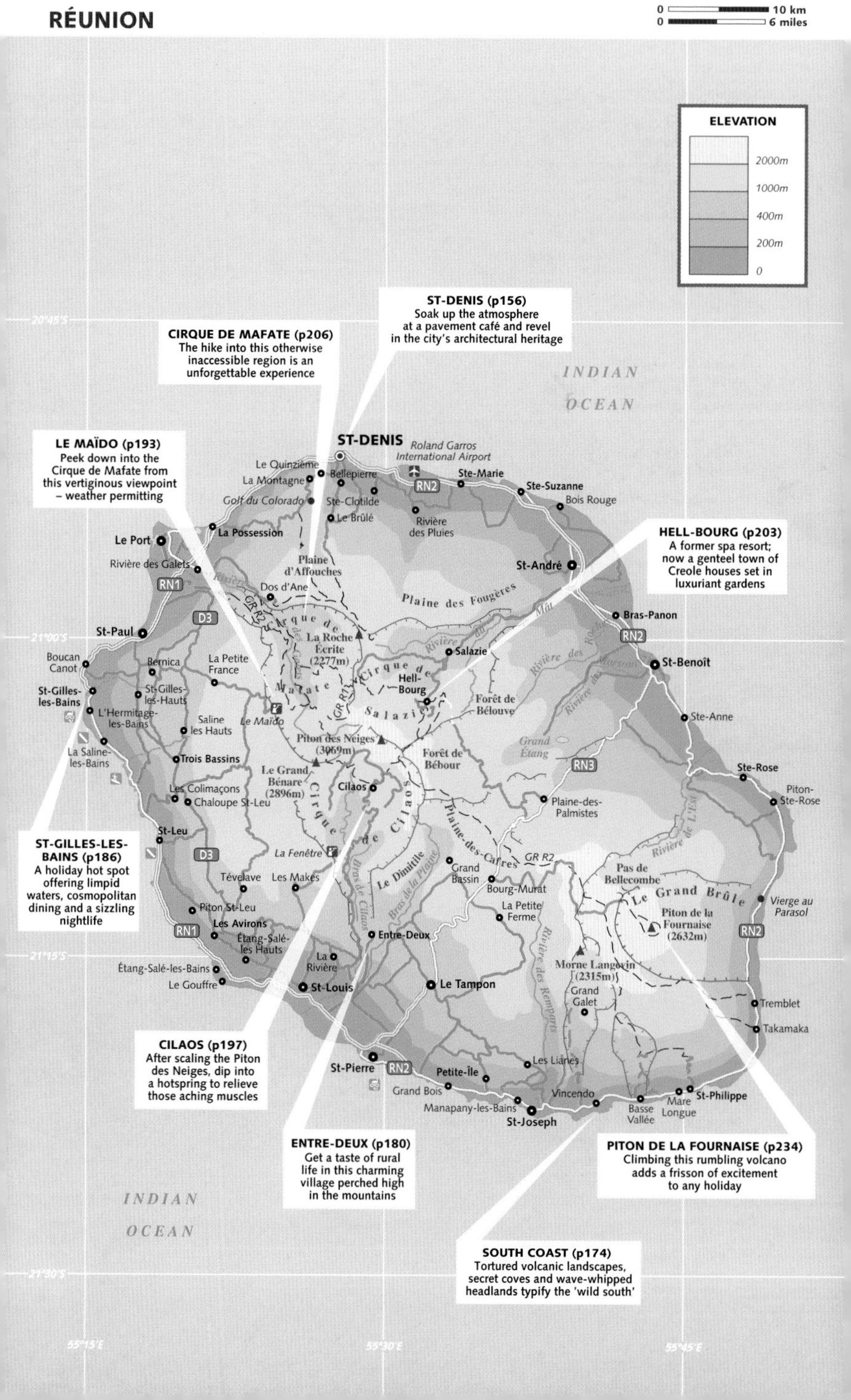

0 10 km
0 6 miles
ELEVATION
2000m
1000m
400m
200m
0
ST-DENIS (p156)
Soak up the atmosphere at a pavement café and revel in the city's architectural heritage
CIRQUE DE MAFATE (p206)
The hike into this otherwise inaccessible region is an unforgettable experience
LE MAÏDO (p193)
Peek down into the Cirque de Mafate from this vertiginous viewpoint – weather permitting
HELL-BOURG (p203)
A former spa resort; now a genteel town of Creole houses set in luxuriant gardens
ST-GILLES-LES-BAINS (p186)
A holiday hot spot offering limpid waters, cosmopolitan dining and a sizzling nightlife
CILAOS (p197)
After scaling the Piton des Neiges, dip into a hotspring to relieve those aching muscles
ENTRE-DEUX (p180)
Get a taste of rural life in this charming village perched high in the mountains
PITON DE LA FOURNAISE (p234)
Climbing this rumbling volcano adds a frisson of excitement to any holiday
SOUTH COAST (p174)
Tortured volcanic landscapes, secret coves and wave-whipped headlands typify the 'wild south'
INDIAN OCEAN
INDIAN OCEAN
20°45'S
21°00'S
21°15'S
21°30'S
55°15'E
55°30'E
55°45'E
ST-DENIS
Roland Garros International Airport
Le Quinzième
La Montagne
Bellepierre
Golf du Colorado
Ste-Clotilde
Le Brûlé
Rivière des Pluies
Ste-Marie
RN2
Ste-Suzanne
Bois Rouge
La Possession
Le Port
Rivière des Galets
RN1
Plaine d'Affouches
Dos d'Ane
St-André
Plaine des Fougères
Bras-Panon
RN2
D3
GR R2
Cirque de Mafate
La Roche Écrite (2277m)
St-Paul
Boucan Canot
Bernica
La Petite France
St-Gilles-les-Bains
St-Gilles-les-Hauts
L'Hermitage-les-Bains
Saline les Hauts
Le Maïdo
La Saline-les-Bains
Trois Bassins
Salazie
Cirque de Salazie
Hell-Bourg
GR R1
Rivière du Mât
Rivière des Roches
Rivière du Marsouin
St-Benoît
Forêt de Bélouve
Ste-Anne
Piton des Neiges (3069m)
Le Grand Bénare (2896m)
Cilaos
Cirque de Cilaos
Forêt de Bébour
Grand Étang
RN3
Ste-Rose
Piton-Ste-Rose
Les Colimaçons
Chaloupe St-Leu
Plaine-des-Palmistes
St-Leu
D3
La Fenêtre
Plaine-des-Cafres
GR R2
Rivière de l'Est
Bras de Cilaos
Le Dimitile
Bras de la Plaine
Grand Bassin
Pas de Bellecombe
Le Grand Brûlé
Vierge au Parasol
Tévelave
Les Makes
Bourg-Murat
Piton de la Fournaise (2632m)
Piton St-Leu
Les Avirons
RN1
Étang-Salé-les Hauts
Entre-Deux
La Petite Ferme
RN2
Rivière des Remparts
La Rivière
Morne Langevin (2315m)
Étang-Salé-les-Bains
Le Gouffre
St-Louis
Le Tampon
Grand Galet
Tremblet
Takamaka
St-Pierre
RN2
Petite-Île
Les Lianes
Grand Bois
Manapany-les-Bains
St-Joseph
Vincendo
Basse Vallée
Mare Longue
St-Philippe

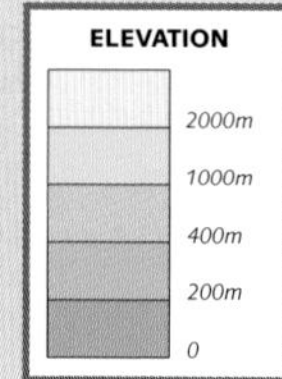

SEYCHELLES

0 16 km
0 10 miles

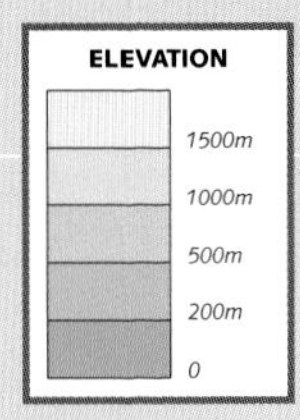

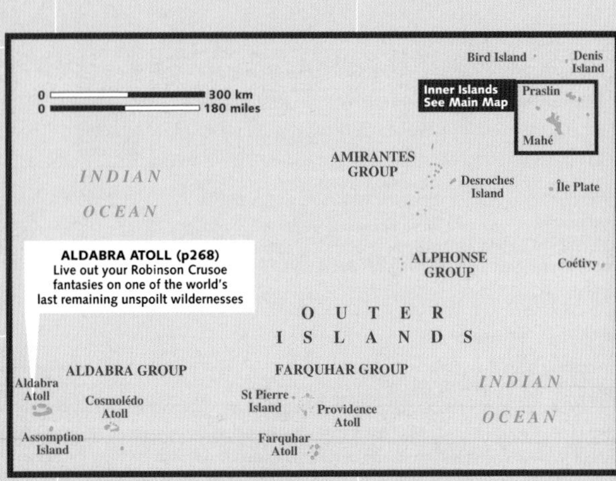

ALDABRA ATOLL (p268)
Live out your Robinson Crusoe fantasies on one of the world's last remaining unspoilt wildernesses

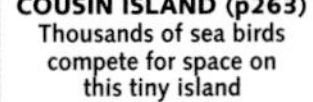

COUSIN ISLAND (p263)
Thousands of sea birds compete for space on this tiny island

ANSE LAZIO (p260)
Where winter fantasies of glorious white beaches lapped by crystal-clear waters come true

VALLÉE DE MAI (p258)
A steamy tropical forest, famous for its palm trees bearing amazingly voluptuous nuts

Aride Island
Curieuse Marine National Park
Curieuse Island
Praslin
Cousin Island
Grand Anse
Anse Volbert
Baie Ste Anne
Cousine Island
Petite Sœur
Grande Sœur
La Fouche
Cocos
Félicité Island
Round Island
La Passe
La Digue
Marianne
INNER ISLANDS
Île du Nord

LA DIGUE (p264)
Kick back on an island where life still moves at the pace of an ox cart

MAHÉ DIVE SITES (p41)
Explore the Seychelles' top dive sites: Shark Bank, Îlot & Brissare Rocks

Les Mamelles
La Passe
Silhouette Island
Brissare Rocks
Îlot Dive Site
Shark Bank Dive Site
Ste Anne Marine National Park
Ste Anne Island
Beau Vallon
Baie Ternay Marine National Park
VICTORIA
Cerf Island
Morne Seychellois National Park
Seychelles International Airport
Mahé
Port Launay Marine National Park
Île aux Récifs
Frégate Island
Îlot Frégate

ANSE SOURCE D'ARGENT (p264)
One of the world's most photographed beaches still retains its wow factor

INDIAN OCEAN

VICTORIA (p247)
The country's pint-sized capital has a very British atmosphere and splendid botanical gardens

BEAU VALLON (p251)
After sunning it up on a beautiful beach, indulge in a seafood extravaganza

4°15'S
4°30'S
4°45'S
55°15'E
55°30'E
55°45'E

Mauritius

Mauritius offers stunning tropical beaches, aquatic activities galore, excellent restaurants, bustling town markets, stunning architecture and much more. As well as the highlights on these pages, why don't you cruise the **Northern Islands** (p80), or count coloured earths at the **Vallée des Couleurs** (p118)? Unwind along the south coast and watch the waves roll in at **Souillac** (p117) or search for pink pigeons on **Île aux Aigrettes nature reserve** (p114). Dive with exotic marine life at the **Rempart Serpent dive site** (p38) or ogle the world's rarest stamps at the **Blue Penny Musem** (p61). Learn about sugar at the **L'Aventure du Sucre** (p85) then visit the unspoilt beaches of **Rodrigues** (p119).

JEAN ROBERT

Marvel at giant water lilies in the Sir Seewoosagur Ramgoolam Botanical Gardens (p84)

Eye-up exotic tropical produce in Port Louis' Central Market (p60)

JEAN-BERNARD CARILLET

Rent a boat and explore the Flic en Flac coast (p101)

JEAN-BERNARD CARILLET

OLIVIER CIRENDINI

Unwind on Grand Baie (p74)

Be a slave to the rhythm of the *séga* (p52)

SUSAN STORM

Hike the Black River Gorges (p86) for views over to Grande Rivière Noire

DEANNA SWANEY

JEAN-BERNARD CARILLET

Check out the latest fashions in the glitzy Caudan Waterfront (p66) complex, Port Louis

JEAN-BERNARD CARILLET

Try some snorkelling at the family-friendly Pereybère (p80)

HIGHLIGHTS Réunion

Hike through ravines and up precipitous peaks of Réunion's mountainous interior and be rewarded with breathtaking views. Potter around craft markets and gardens or simply enjoy the many beaches. Aside from the highlights here, explore the capital, **St-Denis** (p156), with its wealth of Creole architecture and fine dining opportunities. Devote some time to **Le Jardin d'Eden** (p187), a botanical garden packed with all sorts of weird and wonderful species. Learn about local life by staying in a *chambre d'hôte* (B&B) at **Entre-Deux** (p180), one of the prettiest mountain villages, and dropping by the fishing villages and crafts workshops along the little-visited **south coast** (p174).

JEAN-BERNARD CARILLET

Appreciate Creole architecture in Cilaos (p197), Cirque de Cilaos

Paraglide off a precipice at Le Maïdo (p193)

JEAN-BERNARD CARILLET

Take a hike up the lava-strewn slopes of Piton de la Fournaise (p234)

JEAN-BERNARD CARILLET

ARIADNE VAN ZANDBERGEN

Collapse on the beach at St-Gilles-les-Bains (p186)

JEAN-BERNARD CARILLET

Wander the charming streets of Hell-Bourg (p203), Cirque de Salazie

Don your hiking boots and discover the Cirque de Mafate (p206)

OLIVIER CIRENDINI

The Seychelles provides palm-fringed beaches galore and lagoons like liquid glass, with plenty to entertain botanists, bird-watchers and divers. Don't miss the morning markets of **Victoria** (p247) and indulge in all manner of water sports at **Beau Vallon Beach** (p251). **Praslin** (p258) is best known for its coco de mer palms and stunning beaches, including the crescent-curve of **Anse Lazio** (p260). Boat out to **Cousin Island** (p263), where the air is thick with sea birds. The relaxed and traditional La Digue has the magical **Anse Source d'Argent** (p265). To escape the crowds, head for one of the **Outer Islands** (p268) which provide the ultimate island hideaway.

JOHN HAY

Hike Mahé's (p247) forest-clad mountains

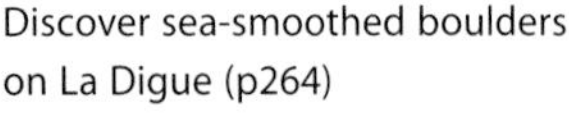

Discover sea-smoothed boulders on La Digue (p264)

LAWSON WOOD

Cast yourself adrift on Aldabra Atoll (p268)

RALPH LEE HC

Getting Started

Mauritius, Réunion and the Seychelles make for safe and easy travelling. There are no dreadful diseases or life-threatening animals; crime rates are extremely low; and standards of hygiene are generally high. Transport in and around the islands is reliable and comfortable. The main factors to bear in mind are that these are popular destinations, so don't leave planning to the last minute, and that they are not cheap. Budget travellers will have a hard time in the Seychelles. Réunion, on the other hand, is manageable with a bit of care, while Mauritius offers the best chance of dipping your toes in paradise without breaking the bank.

WHEN TO GO

For all three destinations you are advised to plan your travel well in advance, especially during the French holidays when hotels can be booked up months before. Ask your travel agent for advice on the dates of school holidays in France, which vary slightly from year to year. The Christmas to New Year period is also particularly busy. Airline reservations may be difficult to get at this time, so book well ahead to avoid disappointment. Keep in mind that many hotels hike up their room rates during the peak seasons.

See p279 for Climate Charts.

Sporting and leisure considerations may play a part in when you visit, and weather is another important factor. For instance, if you're planning a hiking trip to Réunion, the best time is during the dry season, which runs from late April through October.

The climate in all three destinations is broadly similar: a hot, rainy summer from December to April (October to April in the Seychelles) is followed by a cooler, drier winter from May to November (May to September in the Seychelles). Rainfall levels are much higher in the mountains, particularly in Réunion, which boasts a number of world records. Cilaos holds the world record for most rain in a single day – a total of 1870mm fell on 16 March 1952. The cyclone season lasts from December to March. Although direct hits are rare, cyclones way offshore can still bring grey days and strong winds, even to the Seychelles, which technically lies outside the cyclone belt.

Coastal temperatures rarely drop below 20°C in Mauritius and Réunion or below 24°C in the Seychelles, making these islands a truly year-round destination.

DON'T LEAVE HOME WITHOUT...

- Checking the visa situation (p285).
- Having your vaccinations (p293).
- A copy of your travel insurance policy details (p281).
- One smart outfit – beachwear is reserved for the beach, and shorts, T-shirts and flip-flops are banned from many nightspots and restaurants. High in the cirques of Réunion, however, temperatures can drop to freezing, so if you're heading that way you'll need warm clothing.
- Sunglasses, plenty of high-factor sunscreen, a torch, a pair of binoculars for bird-watching, a compass if you're hiking (and a stack of Band-Aids!) and light rainwear. You can buy almost everything you'll need on the spot, but the range is likely to be more limited and most things will certainly be cheaper at home.

For more information on the best times to travel, see p45 for Mauritius, p147 for Réunion, and p239 for the Seychelles.

COSTS & MONEY

The islands of the Indian Ocean are some of the world's most sought-after tropical destinations, but paradise comes at a premium and you'll need plenty of cash if you want to do more than loll on the beach. The Seychelles is the most expensive of the three destinations, with few options for the budget traveller. Réunion is also on the pricey side, while Mauritius offers easily the best opportunities for making the pennies stretch a bit further.

Throughout the region the major expense will be accommodation, followed by activities and excursions, car hire and the like. You can keep accommodation costs down by staying in self-catering apartments or small guesthouses and by basing yourself in one place; the longer you stay (and the more of you there are), the cheaper it becomes. It helps to travel off season as well: prices are generally discounted and there's more chance of being able to bargain.

On the positive side, it's possible to eat reasonably cheaply even in the Seychelles by patronising snack stands and getting takeaway meals – or, of course, by self-catering. Buses in all three destinations provide a cheap method of getting around.

It's also worth investigating package holidays, including flights and accommodation, since these can often work out cheaper than travelling independently.

'It helps to travel off season as well: prices are generally discounted and there's more chance of being able to bargain.'

Mauritius

As far as a daily budget is concerned, backpackers staying in the cheapest guesthouses and eating meals at street stands can expect to spend in the region of €25 to €30 per person. Opting for a mid-range hotel and smarter restaurants will push it up to at least €50. These costs are calculated on the basis of two people sharing a room; single travellers will need to budget extra.

Réunion

Prices in Réunion are slightly more expensive than in mainland France. The absolute minimum daily budget, possible if you're staying in youth hostels and the cheapest guesthouses and eating takeaway meals or self-catering, will be €40 per person on the basis of two people sharing a room. For a reasonably comfortable mid-range hotel, with a light lunch and dinner in a decent restaurant, you're looking at around €80 to €100 per person.

Seychelles

Budget visitors to the Seychelles will struggle to get by on less than €70 per person per day (on the basis of two people sharing a room). A more realistic budget, allowing you to stay at a moderately priced hotel and treat yourself to a few good restaurants, will come in at around €100 to €150 per day at the minimum. Island-hopping and indulging in excursions and activities jacks the price up considerably.

TRAVEL LITERATURE

Travel literature in English about these islands is surprisingly thin on the ground. One of the earliest accounts, written in 1773, is *Journey to Mauritius* by Bernadin de St-Pierre, who describes the country in detail and gives a fascinating insight into colonial society and the horrors of slavery.

In his funny and informative book *Golden Bats & Pink Pigeons*, naturalist Gerald Durrell tells of his time spent rescuing a number of Mauritian species from the brink of extinction.

Durrell was too late for the dodo, but Errol Fuller does the bird proud with his comprehensive and quirky *Dodo: From Extinction to Icon,* which covers the history and the myths surrounding this endearing creature.

Seychelles travel lit is best represented by Athol Thomas' *Forgotten Eden*. Though written in the 1960s and now out of print, it still paints a vivid picture of the beauty and magic of these islands.

Beyond the Reefs by William Travis takes a look back at the Seychelles of the 1970s, before conservation issues came to the fore, when Travis saw plenty of action as a shark fisher and latter-day adventurer.

Empires of the Monsoon by Richard Hall is the most informative and entertaining history of the Indian Ocean. It only touches briefly on Mauritius, Réunion and the Seychelles, it does place them in a broader context.

For a comprehensive guide to French words and phrases, you can't beat Lonely Planet's *French Phrasebook*. The basics of Creole are covered in *Speak Creole: A Tourist Guide* by James Burty David (Éditions de l'Océan Indien, Mauritius).

INTERNET RESOURCES

Birding Hotspots Around the World (www.camacdonald.com/birding) Comprehensive resource for bird-spotters.

Dive Global (www.diveglobal.com) Includes the lowdown on the best dive sites in the Seychelles.

livranoo.com (www.livranoo.com) Online bookshop specialising in Indian Ocean titles, including books published locally.

LonelyPlanet.com (www.lonelyplanet.com) Summaries on travelling in Mauritius, Réunion and the Seychelles, the Thorn Tree bulletin board, travel news and the subwwway section, with links to the most useful travel resources elsewhere on the web.

Mascareignes (www.mascareignes.com in French) Directory of Indian Ocean websites.

RESPONSIBLE TRAVEL

Tourism is vital to the economy of the region. All three destinations depend to varying degrees on tourism to supplement the agriculture, fishing and manufacturing sectors. Mauritius and Réunion in particular are keen to boost tourist income.

There's no question that this influx of visitors is putting additional pressure on the environment. Worst affected are the coasts and particularly the fringing lagoon, where areas of the coral reef and the fragile marine environment are seriously degraded (see p35). The sheer number

FAVOURITE FESTIVALS & EVENTS

Dipavali (Divali; late October or early November) Processions and dance displays mark the Tamil festival of light in Réunion (p170) and Mauritius (p134).

Festival Kreol (last week in October) Seychellois celebrate Creole culture with a week of music, dance and other jollifications (p244).

Maha Shivaratri (February or March) Mauritian Hindus turn out in force to make offerings at the holy lake of Grand Bassin (p93).

Teemeedee (December and January) Hindus and Tamils brave the heat during fire-walking ceremonies in Mauritius (p134) and Réunion (p216).

Grand Raid (October or November) In the aptly named 'cross-country for crazies', participants run across the island in just 18 hours (p212)!

TIPS FOR RESPONSIBLE TRAVEL

- Be careful not to cause damage to coral reefs and don't remove shells.
- Never buy souvenirs made from endangered species, notably turtleshell, shells and coral.
- Never drop litter, especially on beaches and in national parks. Take a bag and pick up trash others have left behind.
- Keep to marked paths in national parks and environmentally sensitive areas.
- Don't light fires and be careful when disposing of cigarette butts, particularly during droughts.
- Buy locally made souvenirs and day-to-day necessities, when possible.
- Budget your trip, and devote 10% (or more!) to environmental organisations working in the areas you visit.

of tourists also makes extra demands on water supplies, electricity and other resources; creates problems of waste management; and puts more vehicles on the roads.

Not that tourism can be blamed for all of the region's environmental woes of course, but there are positive steps that we as individual tourists can take to lessen our impact on the environment (see Tips for Responsible Travel above).

See Responsible Diving on p37 and Turtle Lore on p35 for further guidelines regarding the underwater world. For tips on the cultural aspects of responsible travel, see the boxed text on p48.

Itineraries

CLASSIC ROUTES

JAUNT AROUND MAURITIUS

Two Weeks

A fortnight is ideal to sample the many facets of Mauritian life. Because Mauritius is so small, it's possible to base yourself in one place and make day trips by bus, taxi or hire car.

Start with discovering the markets and museums of **Port Louis** (p57), then head north to **Trou aux Biches** (p70) or **Pereybère** (p80). Possible excursions include **Pamplemousses** (p84), **Grand Baie** (p74) and the **Northern Islands** (p80).

Admire the views at **Cap Malheureux** (p83), then laze on the beaches at **Belle Mare** (p99), which stretch long, white, sandy arcs south to **Trou d'Eau Douce** (p97). Make this your base for day trips to the **Île aux Cerfs** (p98) and the **Domaine du Chasseur** (p116).

After a couple of days, decamp to the laid-back town of **Mahébourg** (p109) or the sparkling azure lagoon of **Blue Bay** (p113); ecoexplore **Île aux Aigrettes** (p114).

Drive south along the glorious coast road via **Souillac** (p117) and **Baie du Cap** (p119) to make your next stop **Flic en Flac** (p101). Here you can delight in the underwater world, go hiking in the **Black River Gorges** (p86) and rummage for clothes around **Curepipe** (p90) and **Quatre Bornes** (p94) before heading back to Port Louis.

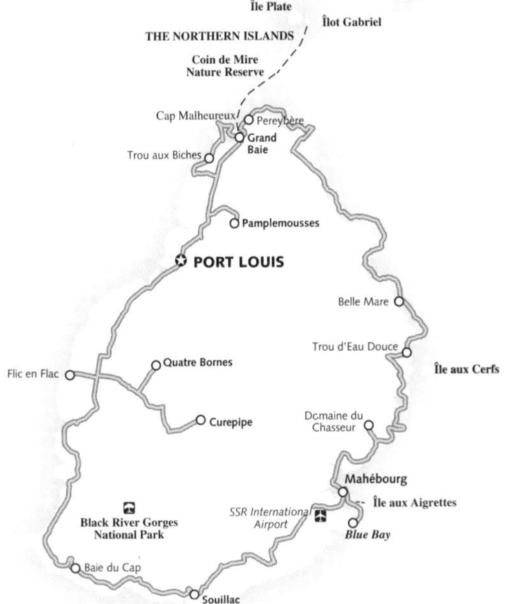

The two-week circuit of Mauritius will take you to sun-drenched beaches, botanical gardens, idyllic islands and lively market towns, all packed into just 300km.

TOUR OF RÉUNION

Two Weeks

In two weeks, you can loop around the island, take a couple of jaunts into the interior and even visit a bubbling volcano.

Spend the first day sampling cafè-culture and Creole architecture in the capital, **St-Denis** (p156). Set off clockwise via the Indian-influenced **St-André** (p169) to stay at least two nights in **Hell-Bourg** (p203), exploring the **Cirque de Salazie** (p202).

Heading back to the coast, spin south via **Ste-Anne** (p173) to **Ste-Rose** (p173), where lava laps at the door of a church and narrowly misses a Virgin. Stay the night near **St-Philippe** (p174) before making for the bright lights of **St-Pierre** (p177) – if possible, get here for the huge Saturday market.

The volcano awaits at **Piton de la Fournaise** (p234). Base yourself at the Gîte du Volcan, ready to make a dawn ascent for stunning views.

Backtrack to St-Pierre and turn inland along a spectacular road into the **Cirque de Cilaos** (p197). Allow at least two days to soak up the scenery and the laid-back atmosphere.

Finally, take time out on the beach at **L'Hermitage-les-Bains** (p186). Allow three days to make the most of the area's botanical gardens, museums and water sports, and to sample the infamous nightlife of **St-Gilles-les-Bains** (p186). From here, it's a short hop back up the coast to St-Denis.

From sophisticated beach resorts to mountain villages, art galleries to volcanoes, two weeks is perfect to sample the variety Réunion has to offer. Get hooked on the hiking, and you could easily fill a month. This tour covers around 400km.

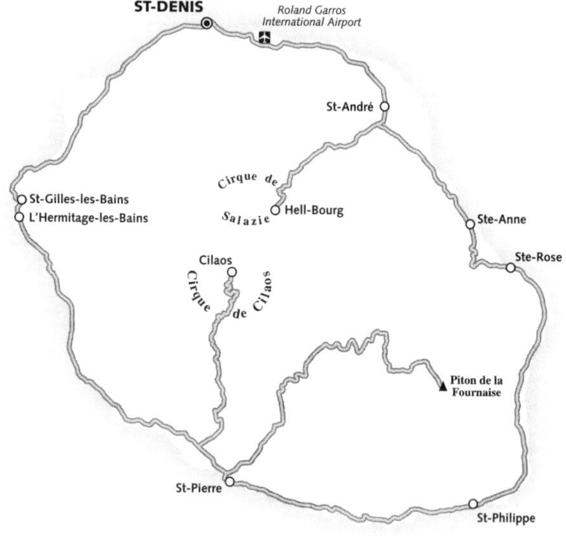

ESSENTIAL SEYCHELLES

Two Weeks

Two weeks is fine for a taster of the Seychelles' islands – even allowing for a few days sunning it up on the beach.

On the first day, tune into island life in the capital, **Victoria** (p247), checking out the market and strolling among the palm trees in the botanical gardens. Move on to **Beau Vallon** (p251), where three days can easily be spent messing around in and on the water – schedule in a day's diving or a boat trip to **Ste Anne Marine National Park** (p257). Devote the next two days to **South Mahé's** (p255) beaches and byways, and walking in the **Morne Seychellois National Park** (p254).

Next, cruise over to **Praslin** (p258). Ogle curvaceous coco de mer nuts in the **Vallée de Mai** (p258), before flaking out on the perfect, sugar-white sands at **Anse Lazio** (p260). Fill the next four days with snorkelling, diving and swimming off **Anse Volbert** (p260), getting up close and personal with giant tortoises on **Curieuse Island** (p263) and walking among cacophonous clouds of sea birds on **Cousin Island** (p263).

From Praslin, make sail for **La Digue** (p264). Three days is the perfect amount of time to lapse into La Digue's slow vibe. Visit **Anse Source d'Argent** (p265) – the archetypal paradise beach. Get there late afternoon for the best atmosphere. Take a snorkelling trip around nearby islands, then find solitude on the beaches of **Grand Anse** and **Petite Anse** (p265). All too soon, it will be time to tear yourself away for the trip back to Victoria.

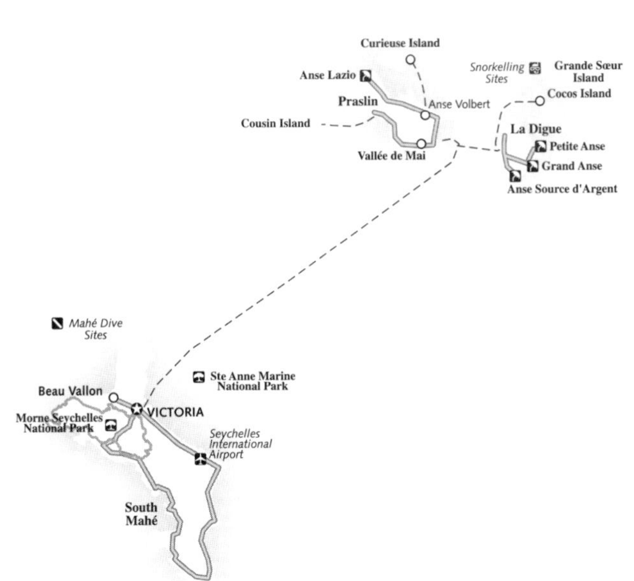

In just 200km and two weeks, this tour will cover the three main islands and a smattering of satellite islands, plus a sampler of marine parks, bird reserves and native forests. There's even time for boat trips and water sports.

ROADS LESS TRAVELLED

RODRIGUES – THE OTHER MAURITIUS

One Week

Escape the crowds of Mauritius' main island for **Rodrigues** (p119), a 1½-hour flight to the northeast and well off the tourist trail. A week is ample time to discover the delights of this small, mountainous island. Depending on the weather you can divide the days between walking, diving and taking boat trips to nearby islands.

First, though, spend half a day strolling the streets of **Port Mathurin** (p123). The island's endearingly sleepy 'capital' springs into life on Saturday morning when it seems the entire population descends for the weekly market. Then retire to the beach at nearby **Anse aux Anglais** (p124), which makes a good base.

The classic coastal hike starts at **St François** (p126), then heads south via a gem of a beach at **Trou d'Argent** (p126) to **Gravier** (p126), from where there are buses back to Port Mathurin. On a separate outing, climb **Mt Limon** (p126) for island-wide views.

You're spoilt for choice when it comes to diving. Top spots include the channel off St François, **La Passe St Francois** (p38), both on the edge of the lagoon, with more options beyond the reefs.

As for boat trips, first choice should be **Île aux Cocos** (p128) for its wealth of birdlife. There's good snorkelling around the little-visited **Île aux Chats** and **Île Hermitage** (p128) off the south coast.

On your last day, treat yourself to a seafood feast at one of the great family-run restaurants scattered around the island.

Leave behind the commercialism of Mauritius' main island for a week to discover a more traditional way of life among the fishing and agricultural communities of Rodrigues. Divers are in for a treat, too, exploring the underwater world of the massive, encircling lagoon.

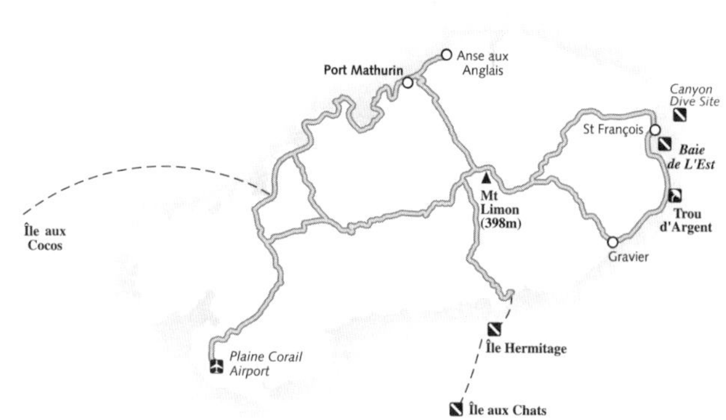

RÉUNION'S SUD SAUVAGE

One Week

Réunion's 'wild south' offers volcanic landscapes, massive ravines, wave-lashed cliffs and sensational hiking trails. You can discover the best of the region in a reasonably leisurely week.

Start at **Ste-Rose** (p173) and head south to find the first tongues of lava tumbling down to the sea. Pay a quick visit to the **Vierge au Parasol** (p173) before crossing the threatening lava fields of **Le Grand Brûlé** (p173), to spend a night or two near **St-Philippe** (p174) or **St-Joseph** (p176); stay up in the hills for a real taste of rural life. From here you can visit a spice garden, learn about vanilla and other local crafts or hike the spectacular **Rivière des Remparts** (p176).

Pass quickly through **St-Pierre** (p177) en route to the high plateau of **Plaine-des-Cafres** (p208) to visit the **Maison du Volcan** (p208). Take the magnificent forest road up to **Piton de la Fournaise** (p234), Réunion's restless volcano. Climb to the top at crack of dawn; circuit the crater rim to leave the crowds behind.

Now drop back down to Plaine-des-Cafres, where you could spend a couple of days hiking to **Grand Bassin** (p208), a village at the end of the world. Finally, head for **Plaine-des-Palmistes** (p206), where the hikes through the **Fôret de Bébour-Bélouve** (p207) and to **Trou de Fer** (p232) provide unforgettable experiences.

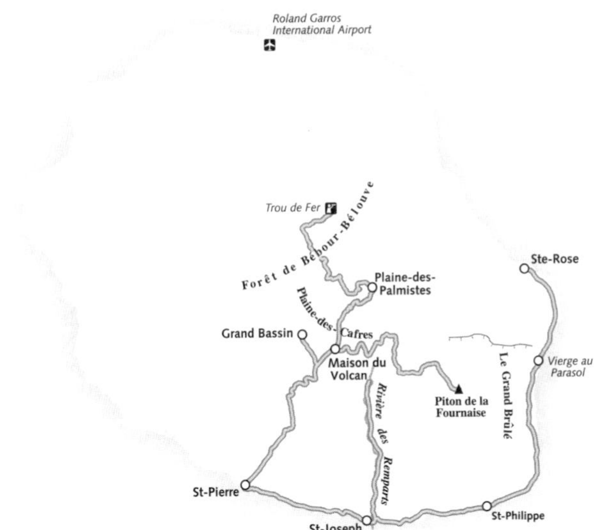

This one-week tour of southern Réunion takes you across lava fields, past breathtaking coastal scenery and up a volcano to gaze into the jaws of the giant. It ends 200km later among the quiet rural villages of the high plains.

TAILORED TRIPS

THE ADRENALIN RUSH

Réunion rightly markets itself as the 'intense isle'; almost every conceivable stomach-churning, heart-pumping activity is on offer. With a bit of planning – and a fair amount of cash – adventure-sports enthusiasts can test their stamina in an action-packed week. Check your insurance policy, take a deep breath and go for it!

Kick off day one in **St-Gilles-les-Bains** (p186) with an ear-popping helicopter ride, ducking and weaving around the three cirques. On landing, hotfoot it up to **Le Maïdo** (p193), grab a mountain bike and hurtle down to the coast again along vertiginous biking trails.

Later that day push on to **Cilaos** (p197). Make a crack-of-dawn start to scale the almost vertical **Piton des Neiges** (p231); to really enjoy the experience, spread the climb over two days. On day four, there's a choice between slithering down canyons, bouncing down rivers on a raft and testing your head for heights rock-climbing.

At the end of day four, up sticks for **St-Leu** (p184). Spend days five and six swooping high above the lagoon by paraglider, plunging off the reef to scuba dive with sharks, or surfing the world-famous left-hander at the mouth of the **Ravine des Colimaçons** (p186); less-experienced surfers will find thrills and spills aplenty riding the area's quieter waves.

Day seven? Definitely the day of rest!

DIVER'S DELIGHT

You could spend a lifetime diving the reefs and granite outcrops of the Seychelles, but a week is enough time to sample a range of sites, including some of the very best in the Indian Ocean.

Jump in at the deep end at **Shark Bank** (p41) off the northwest coast of **Mahé** (p247). No prizes for guessing what's in store here: sharks aplenty with their stingray sidekicks, barracuda and other bruisers. Off Mahe's north tip, **Îlot** (p41) offers an unbelievable variety of smaller fish in shimmering shoals. Nearby, **Brissare Rocks** (p41) is ablaze with fire coral.

On day four, head over to **Praslin** (p258) for a change of scene. The waters around **Curieuse Island** (p263) are teeming with fish life in dazzling, dizzying displays.

Spend your last day exploring the islands northwest of **La Digue** (p264). The rock formations around **Cocos** (p266), **Marianne** (p266) and the sisters, **Petite** and **Grande Sœur** (p266), are out of this world. Marine turtles are common, while stingrays, eagle rays and reef sharks add a touch of spice. Even the odd manta and whale shark cruise through from time to time.

The Authors

JAN DODD

Born in Africa, and having travelled widely in India and China and lived in France, it seemed logical – to Jan Dodd, at least – to put it all together and head for the Indian Ocean, where these cultures, plus British, fuse in the fascinating melting pots of Mauritius, Réunion and the Seychelles. She also nursed an inexplicable desire to stand on the easternmost part of Africa. Over many years, Jan has worked tirelessly at becoming a world expert on paradise beaches, sundowners and factor-60 sun cream. In her spare time she loves racing up mountains and throwing herself off cliffs. After thorough investigation, Jan's convinced these islands were heaven-sent.

My Favourite Trip

It's a tough call, but my favourite destination has to be Réunion. First of all, it's so delightfully quirky, being a slice of France sitting in the middle of the Indian Ocean. There's café culture side by side with African rhythms, and tropical palms waving over berets and baguettes. My first early-morning hike in the Cirque de Cilaos (p197) was an unforgettable experience, and the road up there is pretty amazing, too. The spice garden near St-Philippe (p187) is a treasure-trove, while Entre-Deux (p180) rates as my favourite mountain village. I relish the cosmopolitan atmosphere of St-Denis (p156), the laid-back vibe of the south, and the ancient, eerie Forêt de Bélouve (p207). All in all, Réunion's trump card is that it's never, ever boring.

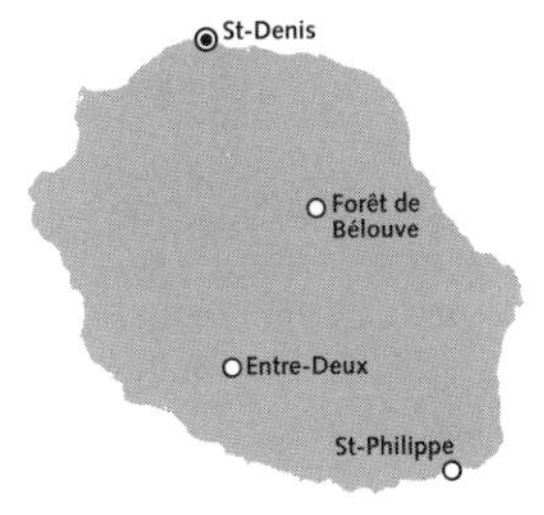

CONTRIBUTING AUTHORS

Madeleine and Clancy Philippe wrote the Food & Drink chapter. Madeleine was born in Mauritius and has been an Australian resident since 1982. A passionate cordon bleu chef and advocate for the cuisine of Mauritius, Réunion and Seychelles, she is the creator of the very popular website Recipes from Mauritius (http://ile-maurice.tripod.com). She is a leading authority on Mauritian cuisine. Clancy is an engineer by profession and a connoisseur of fine foods. He has extensively researched the cuisine of Mauritius, Réunion and Seychelles. Born in Mauritius and an Australian resident since 1982, he actively promotes the region for its heritage and unique cuisine.

Dr Caroline Evans wrote the Health chapter. She studied medicine at the University of London, and completed general practice training in Cambridge. She is the medical adviser to Nomad Travel Clinic, a private travel-health health clinic in London, and is also a GP specialising in travel medicine. She has been an expedition doctor for Raleigh International and Coral Cay expeditions.

Snapshot

In addition to their geographic isolation – adrift in the Indian Ocean off the east coast of Africa – Mauritius, Réunion and the Seychelles have much in common. To start with, their early history follows familiar themes. All three were colonised by the French and the British, who milked them as plantation economies based on slave labour. The majority of slaves came shackled from Africa, though after abolition their ranks were supplemented by indentured Indian and Chinese labourers. Times have changed, but it is the resulting rich ethnic, religious and cultural mix that gives these societies their distinct flavour.

That everyone manages to rub along reasonably harmoniously is something the locals are justifiably proud of. By and large, signs of racial tension have remained remarkably low key. Nevertheless, people are beginning to worry about the future, particularly in the current climate of a world increasingly riven along its religious fault lines. These concerns are even more acute when you're talking about small islands with relatively high levels of unemployment, with predominantly young populations and – even in the Seychelles – with a serious shortage of habitable land. As economies begin to falter and income levels fall, so poverty can exacerbate divisions within society. That's the all too familiar pattern, anyway. Whether these three islands can break the mould remains to be seen.

FILM TRIVIA

Apart from providing a seductive backdrop for numerous TV commercials, the Seychelles appear in a host of feature films. Recent movies shot there include *Castaway* (1986) and *Thunderbirds* (2004).

They all are suffering economic woes to some extent. It's tough going for an island with limited resources – which is therefore dependent on imports that have to be paid for in precious foreign exchange – to make its way in the modern world. Of the three, Mauritius has fared best by using its pool of cheap, skilled labour to develop an industrial sector based on textile and clothes manufacture. All was going swimmingly until 2003, when Southeast Asian factories began undercutting Mauritian output. Though the situation is by no means at crisis point, in an attempt to keep one step ahead, Mauritius is in the throes of reinventing itself as a wired-up, switched-on cyber island.

The Seychelles for its part relies on tuna to earn its daily bread. Exports have been holding steady, but the country's overriding problem is that it is mired in debt, to the tune of US$170 million – which is a lot of tuna, however you look at it. The government recently managed to reschedule the repayments, but the desperate scramble to accumulate foreign exchange to pay off its loans is pushing up inflation, putting off investors and making some tourists think twice. It's also causing a great deal of pain for local businesses, not to mention the Seychellois in the street.

In these circumstances, both the Seychelles and Mauritius regard Réunion with green-eyed envy. While Seychelles and Mauritius are now independent countries, Réunion chose to remain part of France. In many ways Réunion made a smart decision: the island is kept afloat by massive state subsidies. Furthermore, its economy, which is based almost entirely on sugar, appears healthier than it actually is, thanks to EU quotas and price guarantees. The chickens may come home to roost, however, when (if?) the EU finally manages to reform its Common Agricultural Policy and starts to tighten its purse strings.

For these and other reasons, all three islands have turned to tourism as a means of diversifying their economies. Interestingly, each has adopted a different approach. The Seychelles government took the top-dollar route, marketing itself extremely successfully as a luxury destination offering exclusivity at premium prices. Mauritius went for a broader base, although recent policies seem geared towards encouraging more free-spending, high-income visitors rather than budget travellers. The country's ace card has been to offer standards of service unequalled almost anywhere else on the planet; where else do hotels supply you with a personal beach butler, for example? Réunion has been able to rely on its own ready-made tourist market from mainland France. Until recently, that is. Now it is beginning to look further afield and is uniquely well positioned to tap into the growing demand for adventure holidays. It is also playing the ecotourism card.

In fact, Mauritius and the Seychelles are also keen to play up their environmental credentials. The upside of this is that environmental issues are receiving more serious attention throughout the region. Réunion is about to establish its first national park, somewhat belatedly it has to be said. But if all goes well, nearly half the total land mass will be protected by 2006. The Seychelles was ahead of the game, and environmentalists both here and in Mauritius have had some spectacular successes in rescuing endangered species from the brink. In both countries there have been recent examples of environmental concerns driving development policies. In Mauritius, it is Rodrigues which is leading the way, focusing on small-scale, community-based initiatives. In the Seychelles, 'bare-foot luxury' is the buzzword; in effect, the cost of restoring an island to its original habitat is being subsidised by wealthy tourists willing to pay for the privilege of staying in what is effectively a nature reserve. And why not? It's one way to reconcile the often conflicting demands of tourism with environmental conservation, and in the long run we all benefit.

Of course, tourism on its own won't provide all the answers. Another common theme emerging among local policy-makers is the need to develop closer ties not only with each other but also with mainland Africa. Rather than competing, they are increasingly looking for areas in which to cooperate and ways in which to build on their individual strengths. At the same time, all three are seeking to establish new trading partners, particularly in export markets; even now exports are heavily skewed towards Britain and France. It's all part of the long, painful process of breaking free from their colonial pasts.

CRAZY RACE

Every year some 2000 contestants attempt to run across the mountainous interior of Rèunion. They climb 7000m of altitude during the 130km-long race. The fastest usually take less than 18 hours.

Food & Drink

by Madeleine & Clancy Philippe

A passionate cordon bleu chef and advocate for the cuisine of Mauritius, Réunion and Seychelles, Madeleine is the creator of the website Recipes from Mauritius (http://ile-maurice.tripod.com). Clancy has extensively researched the unique cuisine of the region and actively promotes it and its heritage.

Your tastebuds will be captured by the food of Mauritius, Réunion and the Seychelles. The local cuisine is a unique combination of French, Indian, Chinese, African and British gastronomic delights. Whether it's the Creole *rougail* (spicy chutney popular in Réunion which forms the basis for a variety of dishes), feisty curries, *dhal puris* (thin pancakes served with beans and chilli sauce), seafood stir-fries or *bouillon crabes* (crabs cooked in broth) that take your fancy, there really is something for everyone.

Mauritius, Réunion and the Seychelles have similar historic backgrounds so the islands' cuisines, therefore, also strongly resemble one another. Influence from the French, African, and Indian and Chinese communities has led to an exciting blend of cuisines that have retained their distinct influences, and yet complement each other.

STAPLES & SPECIALITIES

Breakfast, usually eaten on the run, is decidedly European: bread and cheese, croissants, bacon and eggs and the like. Sometimes, it is leftovers. Rice is eaten for lunch and dinner, and is served with most dishes. Accompaniments such as *achard* (pickled vegetable salad), *chatini* (finely chopped tomato salad with onions, coriander and chillies) or other side-dishes with varying proportions of red or green chilli are always present.

The mainstay of the Creole cuisine is the *rougail*, a dish comprising, typically, sausages or *boucané* (smoked pork) cooked in a tomato and onion sauce. *Bouillon brêdes*, green vegetables cooked in a lightly spiced broth, is also ubiquitous. As you'd expect in an island paradise, a wide range of seafood dishes are available, including delicious seafood curries, fish vindaloo, seafood stir-fries and fish *bouillon* (broth). Pulses – usually either red or black lentils, split yellow peas or haricot beans – will be vegetarians' best friends, and are particularly common in Indian cooking. Desserts consist of Indian sweets, French pastries, mousses and fresh fruit. The only real variations between regions are the names of dishes and the manner in which they are served.

DID YOU KNOW?

Pipi and periwinkle *bouillon* (broth) is an aphrodisiac.

DRINKS

Whisky is the socially preferred drink, but you will also find local beers (including Seybrew beer in the Seychelles and the award-winning Phoenix Pilsner Beer in Mauritius), imported and local wines and a wide range of excellent local rums (including the renowned Green Island Rum in Mauritius and Rum Charrette in Réunion). Famous for its high quality, flavour and spicy character is the *rhum arrangés* (mixture of rum, fruit juice, cane syrup and a blend of herbs and berries)

TRAVEL YOUR TASTEBUDS

The gastronomically brave might consider trying one of these local delicacies:

- **Carri sauve souris** Bat curry
- **Octopus vindaloo** Octopus in turmeric and mustard seed sauce
- **Wild boar curry** Wild boar in a rich curry sauce

HIDDEN COSTS – TAXES & TIPPING

- **Mauritius** 15% government tax; tips appreciated but not expected
- **Réunion** 10% tip expected if service not charged
- **Seychelles** 7% government tax; tips appreciated but not expected

of Réunion. The Isautier-prepared rums, liqueurs and punches and coco rum in the Seychelles are also popular. The locally manufactured wines served in taverns or village bars can be potent, so drink with caution! Imported whiskies, gins and other spirits are available at a price. Remember to drink in moderation – disorderly and drunken behaviour is frowned upon.

Local lemonades and dairy drinks abound. Enjoy the thirst-quenching *alouda* (sweet, milky drink) from the Port Louis market in Mauritius; beautifully prepared fresh fruit drinks in the Seychelles; and the famous vanilla-flavoured teas throughout Réunion. During Hindu and Muslim festivals, deliciously flavoured drinks such as *lassi* (Indian yoghurt drink) and almond milk (almond- and cardamom-flavoured milk) are prepared.

'The local wines served in taverns or village bars can be potent, so drink with caution!'

CELEBRATIONS

There's a plethora of celebrations observed in Mauritius, Réunion and the Seychelles, ranging from the religious (such as Christmas and Eid al-Fitr) to the cultural (including New Year's Eve, the various Independence days and France's Bastille Day). The celebrations for the Indian Divali festival of light and the Chinese New Year are renowned for their culinary delicacies.

Religious festivals are celebrated in great traditional style with special meals prepared to mark the occasions. The most famous are Chinese New Year (January/February), Cavadee (February), Maha Shivaratree (February/March), Good Friday (March/April), the Divali festival of light (October-November), All Saints' Day (November) and the end of Ramadan (celebrated after the ninth month on the Muslim calendar).

In Réunion, local produce festivals are also held: Mango and Green Honey Festivals in January, the Fête du Café (Coffee Festival) in June, Fête de l'ail (Garlic Festival) in October and the Curcuma Festival in November. In the Seychelles, a Sunday of Bygone days (January) celebrates old traditions and foods, Dekouver Vye Marmit (August) rediscovers traditional recipes, and Coconut Evening (September) features an open-air buffet comprised entirely of dishes made from coconut.

WHERE TO EAT & DRINK

There is a wide choice of eating options on the islands, ranging from the most sophisticated restaurants to local eateries. There is resort dining, à la carte, restaurants specialising in a specific cuisine, local eateries and snack bars. Of course, prices vary enormously and it pays to make a few inquiries before sitting down to eat.

Although the more upmarket restaurants serve fabulous food (often at a hefty price), what you eat won't always be particularly traditional. Some establishments, however, do pride themselves on providing local specialities. Your best bet is to ask for advice – you will be directed to the best spots. But the best way to sample traditional fare is to eat with the locals. An inviation to experience a home-cooked Creole dinner is priceless.

Opening hours are varied. Most restaurants serve lunch and dinner daily, but do check to avoid disappointment. And it's best not to leave it too late in the evening, since kitchens tend to close early. Many smaller places have set meals available all day. Bars and pubs are open until late, and sometimes serve food. Most places are friendly, and even lone dinners will find wonderful company.

Quick Eats

Places to enjoy quick eats on the run are in plentiful supply on the islands. Street vendors are at every bus station and town square, and takeaway shops can be found in numerous shopping centres and markets; both offer inexpensive local treats, including Indian, French and Chinese delicacies. Almost all restaurants, except the most upmarket, will do takeaway. In Mauritius, roadside food stalls serving dinner dishes such as *biryani* (curried rice), Indian rotis, *dhal puris* and *farattas* (unleavened flaky flour pancakes) are popular. In Réunion, camion restaurants (trucks converted into mobile snack bars) offer takeaway snacks, including Creole dishes, sandwiches and pizzas. In the Seychelles, you will find mobile canteens selling fast food, and roadside fruit stalls. Not surprisingly, the quality of this food varies, but can be excellent.

The atmospheric markets are worth visiting for the popular *gâteaux piments* (deep-fried balls of lentils and chilli), known as *bonbons piments* in Réunion, which are cooked on the spot. You should also try the delicious *dhal puris*, rotis, samosas and *bhajas* (fried balls of besan dough with herbs or onion).

DID YOU KNOW?

Chilli causes the brain to release endorphins.

Indian and Chinese restaurants offer quick and inexpensive meals and snacks. Remember to buy some Indian savouries such as *caca pigeon* (an Indian nibble) or the famous Chinese *char siu* (barbecue pork).

VEGETARIANS & VEGANS

You'll struggle to find many vegetarian restaurants on the islands, although all Indian and Chinese restaurants have some good vegetarian dishes. Bear in mind, though, that much of this cooking uses meat or seafood stocks. Most hotels and restaurants will prepare special meals if you give them plenty of notice. Nonetheless, your best option is to opt for accommodation with self-catering facilities. Fresh vegetables and fruits are in plentiful supply in shops, markets and supermarkets almost all year round. Arrangements can be made for maid service – the maids are usually very good cooks, and you'll enjoy tasty Creole or Indian vegetarian meals. Enquire about the service, including your vegetarian or vegan preferences, when you make your booking.

WHINING & DINING

Children are very welcome on the islands, and most establishments are happy to accept them as long as they don't disturb other diners. Some establishments will provide smaller meals for children.

You'll probably find Chinese dishes such as fried noodles or fried rice are a good option for the kids; some of the spicy and highly flavoured Creole and Indian dishes are somewhat of an acquired taste and may be too much for children. The lightly-spiced Creole *rougail* should be more popular. Fast foods and snacks that will delight children are readily available, in particular sweet Indian *jalebies* (fried batter spirals in syrup), French cakes such as the famous Gâteau Napolitaine (butter biscuits with jam and icing), and pastries. A glass of the thirst-quenching *alouda* at the Port Louis market in Mauritius will be a pleasant experience for the kids. Where possible, infants should maintain their normal eating habits and avoid very hot dishes. Baby-food products are available at reasonable prices in Mauritius and Réunion, but if you are staying on the Seychelles it is recommended you bring these from home as availability is limited (see p271).

HABITS & CUSTOMS

Eating habits vary across ethnic groups. Some groups eat with their fingers, others don't eat meat on Fridays and some abstain from eating pork – it's hard to generalise across the community.

Breakfasts are normally very quick and informal. Lunch is also a fairly casual affair, although at the weekend it tends to be more formal, when family and friends gather to share the pleasures of the table. In restaurants, special menus are offered for weekend lunches. Before dinner, which is a very formal occasion, *gajacks* (predinner snacks) and predinner drinks are commonly served; during the meal, wine may also be served.

As eating and drinking are important social activities, behaviour at the table should be respectful. Locals can be strict about table manners, and it's considered rude to pick at your food or mix it together. You are also expected to be reasonably well dressed. Unless you are in a beach environment, wearing beachwear or other skimpy clothing won't be well received – casual but neat clothing is the norm. When invited to dine with locals, bring a small gift; perhaps some flowers or a bottle of whisky or wine.

If you are attending a traditional Indian or Chinese meal or a dinner associated with a religious celebration, follow what the locals do. Generally, your hosts will make you feel comfortable, but if you are unsure, ask about the serving customs and the order of dishes. Definitely attend an Indian or a Chinese wedding if you get the opportunity – these celebrations are true culinary feasts.

Ask permission before you smoke at meals, and try to be discreet if you do smoke. Smoking in restaurants is generally tolerated, but bear in mind that some places don't allow smoking in the dining areas.

DID YOU KNOW?

To make a 'millionaire's salad' you must cut down a whole palm tree, just to use the edible heart of palm. Once the heart of palm is removed, the plant dies.

Exotic Seafood of Seychelles, by Flavien Joubert, teaches you all you need to know about seafood in the Seychelles.

EAT YOUR WORDS

French and Creole are spoken throughout Mauritius, Réunion and the Seychelles (see p297). Although English is less widely spoken, people working in hotels and restaurants generally have at least a smattering. You should therefore be able to communicate in a mix of French and English. To start you off, a few basic phrases are given here.

Useful Phrases

Do you speak English?
Parlez-vous anglais? — par-lay voo ong-glay?

Are you still serving food?
On peux toujours passer des commandes? — om per too-zhoor pa-say day ko-mond?

A table for ..., please.
Une table pour ... personnes, s'il vous plaît. — ewn taa-ble poor ... pair-son seel voo play

Do you accept credit cards?
Est-ce qu'on peux payer avec une carte de crédit? — es-kom per pay-yay a-vek ewn kart der kray-dee?

I'm a vegetarian.
Je suis végétarien/ne. — zher swee vay-zhay-tay-ryun/ryen

Can I see the menu?
Est-ce que je peux voir la carte, s'il vous plaît? — es-ker zher per vwa la kart seel voo play?
What do you recommend?
Qu'est-ce que vous conseillez? — kes ker voo kon-say-yay?
I'll have what they're having.
Je prendrai la même chose qu'eux. — zher pron-dray la mem shoz ker
Not too spicy, please.
Pas trop épicé, s'il vous plaît. — pa tro ay-pee-say seel voo play
That was delicious!
C'était délicieux! — say-tay day-lee-syer
Please give me the bill.
L'addition, s'il vous plaît. — la-dee-syon seel voo play

Menu Decoder

Genuine Cuisine of Mauritius (Éditions de L'Océan Indien; eoibooks@intnet.mu; 1998), by Guy Fèlix, is a great Mauritian recipe book.

achards – pickled vegetable salad
alouda – sweet, milky drink, popular in Mauritius
baie rose – pink pepper
bhajas – fried balls of besan dough with herbs or onions
bibasse – medlar fruit
bichiques – sprat-like seafood delicacy
biryani – curried rice; sometimes known as briani
bois de songe – local vegetable
bol renversé – rice with various toppings, such as chicken, beef or mixed vegetables
bonbons piments – see *dhal puris*
boucané – smoked pork
bouillon brêdes – green vegetables cooked in a lightly spiced broth
bouillon crabes – crabs cooked in broth
brêdes – leafy green vegetables similar to Chinese cabbage
cabri massalé – goat curry
caca pigeon – Indian nibbles (literally 'pigeon droppings')
camarons d'eau douce – freshwater shrimps
carri coco – mild meat curry with coconut cream
carri poulet/poulpe/poisson – chicken/octopus/fish curry
carri sauve souris – bat curry
cassoulet – thick stew of duck meat and haricot beans
catless – Indian snack (cutlet in breadcrumbs)
char siu – barbecue pork
chatini – finely chopped tomato, onion, chilli and coriander appetiser
chou chou – green, squash-like vegetable
combava – a knobbly lime
confit de canard – duck meat preserved in its own fat
dhal puris – Indian snack (thin pancakes served with beans and chilli sauce)
dosa masala – Indian snack (thin bread with spicy potato filling)
faratta – unleavened flaky flour pancakes
foie gras – fattened duck liver
gajacks – predinner snacks
Gâteau Napolitaine – butter biscuits with jam and icing
gâteaux piments – Indian snack (deep-fried balls of lentils and chilli)
jalebies – fried batter spirals in syrup
lassi – Indian yoghurt drink
mazavaroo – chilli and prawn paste cooked in oil
mine frit – fried Chinese noodles
mojito – refreshing alcoholic drink made with mint, lemon, sugar and rum
murg dopiaza – chicken in an onion and tomato sauce
murg makhani – chicken with a tomato and cream sauce

octopus vindaloo – octopus in turmeric and mustard seed sauce
pain fouré – filled bread rolls
pasanda – curry laced with almonds and sesame seeds
phad thai – mixed fried noodles
porc à la sauce grand-mère – dish of pork with chilli sauce (literally 'pork in grandma's sauce')
pression – draft beer
rhum arrangés – mixture of rum, fruit juice, cane syrup and a blend of herbs and berries
riz/bol renversé – rice dish with various toppings
rogan josh – spiced lamb
rosenberghis – tiger prawns
rougail – spicy chutney popular in Réunion
rougail saucisses – sausages in tomato and onion sauce
salade ourite – octopus salad, with seasoning including oil, vinegar and sliced onions
samosa – Indian snack (triangle of pastry with various fillings)
sauce rouge – brandy sauce
tarte tatin – apple tart
tom yum thalay – citronella-laced seafood soup
vindaye – turmeric-flavoured sauce with mustard seeds and vinegar
waaria – spicy vegetable snack

Food Glossary

BASICS

beurre butter
carri curry
céréale cereal
gâteau cake
piment chilli
poivre pepper
sel salt

MEAT

agneau lamb
bœuf beef
calamar squid
camarons prawns
crevettes shrimps
fruit de mer seafood
langouste lobster
mourgatte squid
poisson fish
porc pork
poulet chicken
poulpe octopus
truites trout

FRUITS & VEGETABLES

ananas pineapple
banane banana
chou chou choko (squash)
goyave guava
noix de coco coconut
piment chilli
pomme apple
pomme de terre potato

Les Délices de Rodrigues (in French), by Françoise Baptiste, presents recipes from Rodrigues.

COOKING TERMS

bouilli	boiled
frit	fried
fumé	smoked
grillé	grilled
rôti	roasted

DRINKS

bière	beer
café	coffee
jus de fruit	fruit juice
thé	tea
vin (rouge/blanc)	wine (red/white)

Underwater Worlds

The Indo-Pacific region is one of the world's richest realms of marine flora and fauna. Snorkelling and scuba diving the fringing coral reefs of Mauritius, Réunion and the Seychelles opens the door to this magical world inhabited by delicate corals, tiny translucent shrimps and clouds of rainbow-coloured fish.

MARINE LIFE

Diving and snorkelling allow you to glimpse the marine ecosystem at work and to marvel at its complexity. Below is a brief introduction to the more common species you are likely to encounter.

Coral

Coral comes in a myriad of shapes and sizes. What you actually see is only the outer layer, a thin crust of living organisms (polyps) on the skeletons of older corals. The reef is thus constantly changing in shape and structure as the environment changes around it. Almost all polyp skeletons are white – it's the living polyps that give coral its colourful appearance. During the day, most polyps retract to the protection of their hard skeleton, so it's only at night that the full beauty of the hard corals can be seen.

The Indian Ocean's shallow-water reefs were badly hit by 'coral bleaching' in 1997 and 1998. This occurs when the surface water overheats and most experts blame global warming. Unnaturally high temperatures cause the polyps to expel the symbiotic algae that give them their colour. If the temperature does not drop quickly enough, the coral eventually dies from the loss of the protective algae.

In parts of the Seychelles, up to 90% of hard corals (the reef-building corals) were wiped out. They are still struggling, but there are encouraging signs of new growth. Fortunately, the fish and other reef creatures don't appear to have been affected. Everyone's hoping that there's no reoccurrence before the reefs have had a chance to recover.

For identification of tropical fish and corals, refer to *Reef Fishes & Corals* and *More Reef Fishes & Nudibranchs*, by Dennis King, or the *Indian Ocean Reef Guide*, by Helmut Debelius.

Echinoderms

This widely varied group of creatures includes sea urchins, starfish (or sea stars), brittle-stars, feather stars and sea cucumbers. Most share basic structural features, such as five 'arms' and a spiny skin.

Starfish are highly visible as they have few natural enemies and do not hide away during the daytime. Sea cucumbers are also commonly seen.

In Mauritius, look out for the *Field Guide to Corals of Mauritius*, by Ruby Moothien Pillay, Hiroaki Terashima, Atmanun Venkatasami and Hiro'omi Uchida, and the *Field Guide to Coastal Fisheries of Mauritius*, by Hiroaki Terashima, Javed I Mosaheb, Chiranjiwa N Paupiah and Vishwamitra Chineah, available in local bookshops.

Eels

Moray eels are very common around Mauritius and the Seychelles. They lurk in crevices looking menacing and can in fact give a nasty bite, although they aren't normally aggressive towards humans. The largest, the giant moray, can grow up to 3m long. The peppered moray is perhaps the most common around the Seychelles. It is active by night and is quite easily approached. Another night forager is the snake eel, distinguished by a fin along the length of its back.

Fish

The Indian Ocean is home to several thousand fish species. These include everything from tiny diamond fish, the smallest backboned animals, to

DANGEROUS MARINE LIFE

A number of Indian Ocean species are poisonous or may sting or bite. Watch out for sea urchins, for the gaudy lion-fish with their poisonous spined fins, and for the cleverly camouflaged – and exceptionally poisonous – stonefish. Some shells, such as the cone shell, can fire out a deadly poisonous barb. The species of fire coral (in fact a type of jellyfish) packs a powerful sting if touched. Shark attacks are extremely rare but seek advice from locals before plunging in (see Les Dents du Mer on p214).

huge whale sharks. Some fish are seen in the day, while others shelter in crevices and caverns only to emerge at night. Some are grazers, others are hunters. Some huddle together in groups for protection while others are more solitary. Territorial species guard their own patch of reef fiercely, while others range freely.

Among the most common and colourful fish you're likely to see darting around the reefs are clownfish, parrotfish, angelfish, emperor-fish, butterfly-fish and various types of grouper.

Pelagic fish – larger beasts that live in the open sea, such as tuna and barracuda – sometimes cruise quite close to the reef in search of prey. Of the shark species inhabiting these waters, the most common are the white-tipped reef shark, the hammerhead shark and the reasonably docile nurse shark, the latter distinguishable by its small mouth and the two barbels on the top of its lip.

SYMBIOSIS

A number of fish and other reef species engage in interesting symbiotic relationships, where two unrelated species team up for their mutual good. Such relationships are crucial to the maintenance of the marine ecosystem.

Cleaner fish are a particularly interesting example. The small cleaner wrasse set themselves up at 'cleaner stations' on the reef. When a customer approaches, they perform a short 'dance' to indicate that they're ready for action and then zip around the larger fish, nibbling off their fungal growth, dead scales, parasites and the like. They even swim directly into the mouths of much larger fish to clean their teeth! Some fish travel considerable distances for a clean and brush-up.

Certain varieties of shrimps, including most of those found in the Seychelles, also act as fish cleaners, and the reef has 'false cleaners' too. These are tiny fish that masquerade as cleaners and then quickly take a bite out of the deceived prey. They've even been known to take a nip at swimmers!

A somewhat one-sided relationship is that between the anemone and the anemone fish. These tiny, brightly coloured fish become acclimatised to living among the stinging tentacles of anemones, which provide them with protection. The most common anemone fish is the skunk anemone fish, which is creamy-brown in colour with a horizontal white line from the tip of the nose to the tip of the tail.

In a similar vein, the remora (or suckerfish) attaches itself by hitching a ride on manta rays, sharks and turtles, and eats any scraps left behind by its host.

Molluscs

Like echinoderms, molluscs are a very varied group which share similar structures such as a shell or a muscular 'foot'. Molluscs include snails, slugs and nudibranchs (all gastropods); oysters, scallops and clams (bivalves); and octopus and squid (cephalopods).

Nudibranchs, or sea slugs, are snails that have abandoned their shells and put on their party clothes. They're some of the most graceful and colourful reef creatures you can see. The fleshy mantles of clams can also be seen in a spectacular array of colours.

Rays

The most common species of ray found around the Seychelles and Mauritius is the manta ray, the wingspan of which can reach over 6m.

The spotted eagle ray is a large ray with a snout somewhat like a pig's, which it uses to dig and forage beneath the sand for crustaceans and molluscs.

The electric or torpedo ray is much smaller, and grows to a length of around 50cm. Its rounded body has two electrical organs with which it stuns its prey. It should be treated with respect – the electrical charge is between 14V and 37V.

The blue-spotted stingray grows to a maximum length of 50cm and is quite common in the sandy areas between the granite boulders of the Seychelles. It is circular in shape and covered in bright blue spots, and has a strong tail and a venomous spine.

One of the larger stingray species, often encountered at Shark Bank off Mahé, is the brissant (or round ribbon-tailed) ray. It can grow up to 2m across.

Turtles

Turtles still occur throughout the region, albeit in dwindling numbers. Species include the loggerhead, green, leatherback and hawksbill turtles. The best place to see turtles in the wild is the Seychelles, where there are a number of important breeding grounds for hawksbill and green turtles.

According to the Convention on International Trade in Endangered Species (CITES), marine turtles are among the world's most endangered species, threatened by pollution and human exploitation. Their downfall has been their edible flesh and eggs, highly prized by local fishermen, and their shell, which is used for jewellery and ornaments.

MARINE CONSERVATION

The underwater world represents one of the richest and most complex ecosystems and one which is still relatively poorly understood. For this reason, much of the work in marine conservation consists of research and monitoring programmes. Many organisations are also active in protecting endangered species and in raising environmental awareness.

The main pressures on the marine environment are pollution, over-exploitation and inappropriate activities, such as the use of drag anchors and of explosives for fishing.

In recent years Mauritius, Réunion and the Seychelles have all introduced laws banning destructive practices, such as shell and coral

TURTLE LORE

Help ensure turtles have a future by following a few simple rules:

- Do not eat turtle meat or soup.
- Do not buy souvenirs made from turtleshell (often known as tortoiseshell).
- Do not disturb nesting turtles or hatchlings by shining torches or car headlights on the beach.

collection and spear-fishing. Each has also established marine reserves to protect at least some of their coral reefs. A major problem is the lack of resources (or political will) to ensure adequate policing.

Réunion has been the most successful so far in bringing about improvements in the marine environment. This is partly thanks to the relatively small extent of its lagoon. Other factors include its integrated approach to conservation issues, the active participation of the local community and access to fairly generous funding. As a result, the lagoon is now markedly cleaner than a few years back. The diversity of fish life is beginning to improve and there are signs of new coral growth.

Environmentalists in the Seychelles and Mauritius have also registered notable successes, such as the recent ban on whale-shark hunting in the Seychelles, but it is going to be a long haul. For the moment there is an enormous amount of work to be done in assessing the impact of various activities on the marine environment. With this information it will be possible to draw up strategies for the sustainable use of marine resources.

Visitors have a crucial role to play too. We strongly urge you not to buy or collect seashells, and not to buy any seashell or turtleshell products. As far as possible, divers should give their business to the more responsible operators and should report those that continue destructive practices.

'We strongly urge you not to buy or collect seashells, and not to buy any seashell or turtleshell products.'

Mauritius

The most active groups are the **Mauritius Marine Conservation Society** (MMCS; ☎ 696 5368; http://pages.intnet.mu/mmcs in French; c/o MUG, Railway Rd, Phoenix) and the **Mauritius Underwater Group** (MUG; ☎ 696 5369; http://pages.intnet.mu/mug; Railway Rd, Phoenix), both of which were founded by concerned local divers. They run education, research and monitoring programmes, campaign for the control of water pollution and reef destruction and the installation of pavement mooring buoys, and have created 13 artificial reefs (the wrecks along the west coast) to enhance the marine environment. Both groups are also pushing for more marine parks.

In Rodrigues, **Shoals** (☎ 831 1225; www.shoals-rodrigues.org) is campaigning for the installation of 'environmentally friendly' mooring buoys and working with local authorities to establish marine reserves as part of a sustainable fisheries project.

Supported by the **Mauritius Scuba Diving Association** (MSDA; ☎ 454 0011; msda@intnet.mu), an increasing number of dive operators now regularly clean 'their' stretch of lagoon. If you find an operator polluting or destroying the reef, report them to the MSDA.

Réunion

The **Association Parc Marin de la Réunion** (☎ 0262 346444; http://perso.wanadoo.fr/parcmarin.reunion in French; 7 Rue de la Compagnie des Indes, St-Leu) is charged with managing and protecting the lagoon. The association's wide-ranging responsibilities include patrolling the marine park, running educational and scientific programmes, monitoring water quality and the health of the reefs, and advising on coastal development. It is currently campaigning for the park to be upgraded to a nature reserve, which would give the association greater legal powers.

Seychelles

The **Marine Conservation Society Seychelles** (MCSS; www.mcss.sc; PO Box 1299, Victoria, Mahé) is monitoring and promoting marine habitats and biodiversity. Current projects include installing ecofriendly mooring buoys and

RESPONSIBLE DIVING

Consider the following tips when diving to help preserve the ecology and beauty of reefs:

- Avoid touching or standing on living marine organisms or dragging equipment across the reef. Polyps can be damaged by even the gentlest contact. If you must hold on to the reef, only touch exposed rock or dead coral.
- Be conscious of your fins. Even without contact, the surge from fin strokes can damage delicate organisms. Clouds of sand can smother them.
- Practise and maintain proper buoyancy control. Major damage can be done by descending too fast and colliding with the reef.
- Spend as little time as possible in underwater caves as air bubbles caught under the roof can leave organisms high and dry. Take turns to inspect the interior of a small cave.
- Minimise your disturbance of marine animals in their natural environment: never ride on the backs of turtles; do not feed fish.

assessing the impact of coral bleaching. As a result of MCSS's whale-shark monitoring programme, in 2003 the government declared whale sharks to be protected within Seychelles' territorial waters. The goal is to have them listed as an endangered species worldwide. MCSS now also monitors turtles as part of a project to develop a nationwide turtle management strategy and is working with the Banyan Tree Resort to protect nest sites at Anse Intendance. Visitors are welcome to participate in the monitoring programmes. To add to the fun, you can also adopt a whale shark or a turtle through MCSS.

Nature Seychelles (☎ 225097; www.nature.org.sc; PO Box 1310, Victoria) also works to improve biodiversity. Its conservation projects include the restoration of island ecosystems and it recently embarked on a wide-reaching project to investigate the effects of coral bleaching on fish life.

Seychelles Island Foundation (☎ 321755; www.sif.sc; 305 Premier Bldg, Albert St, Victoria) concentrates its efforts on studying and protecting Aldabra, a marine biodiversity hot spot.

DIVING

Safety

The majority of dive operators in Mauritius, Réunion and the Seychelles are members of one or more internationally recognised organisations, such as Professional Association of Diving Instructors (PADI), National Association of Underwater Instructors (NAUI) or Confédération Mondiale des Activités Subaquatiques (CMAS), and have high standards of safety. Accidents do happen, however, and emergency treatment should be sought immediately. There are decompression chambers in all three destinations.

You may be asked for a recent medical certificate (less than a year old) before being allowed to dive. Some operators will also ask to see your logbook. For tips on safe diving, see Safety Guidelines for Diving on p39.

Mauritius

As an Indian Ocean diving destination, Mauritius has been largely overshadowed by the popularity of the Maldives and the Seychelles. However, the dive industry here is well developed, and offers plenty of interest for beginners and advanced divers.

TOP THREE DIVE SITES OF MAURITIUS

- **Rempart Serpent** (Snake Rampart) This is the signature site of the west region. Located a 15-minute boat trip from Flic en Flac, it takes its name from the sinuous rock lying about 25m below the surface, which attracts perhaps the greatest concentration in the world of weird and wonderful scorpion fish, stonefish, moray eels and lion-fish. For experienced divers only.
- **La Passe St François** Off the east coast of Rodrigues, this kilometre-long channel is a vortex of tuna, barracuda, parrotfish, swirling shoals of big-eye kingfish, even turtles and the occasional small shark. Just one of many superb sites in the 200-km sq lagoon surrounding the island.
- **Colorado** (Grand Canyon) This 400m-long canyon off Blue Bay is an underwater version of the famous American valley. The scenery here is just as breathtaking and the adventure even more exhilarating. Sightings of barracuda, kingfish, tuna and turtles are pretty regular, while black-tip sharks cruise by on occasion. However, it's a deep, difficult dive and is inaccessible in rough weather.

Mauritius is almost entirely surrounded by a barrier reef, within which turquoise lagoons provide great possibilities for snorkellers, swimmers and novice divers. Dynamic fish action and prolific coral density are only found on reefs close to the barrier and beyond. Here lie some of the best dive sites in the Indian Ocean.

Some of the most popular sites lie off the west coast, particularly around Flic en Flac and Trou aux Biches. Sites here offer abundant fish life and spectacular underwater scenery. Further north, there's an excellent chance of diving with sharks around Île Plate and Coin de Mire. Even more thrilling dive sites are in store off Belle Mare and Blue Bay on the east coast, though you need luck with the weather. Divers looking for virgin sites are heading to Rodrigues; diving only started here in 1996 and the diversity of coral and fish life is outstanding.

WHEN TO DIVE

Mauritius is a year-round dive destination. The most favourable periods are October to December, March and April (January and February are peak months for cyclone activity). During July and August, when the southeast trade winds are at their strongest, the seas are too rough and murky for diving all along the east coast and around Rodrigues.

OPERATORS

Many dive centres in Mauritius are hotel-based, but those listed below welcome walk-in clients. There are also a number of independent operators, particularly in and around Grand Baie. Most belong to the **Mauritian Scuba Diving Association** (MSDA; ☎ 454 0011; msda@intnet.mu), which is affiliated with CMAS and makes regular and rigorous checks. Divers must take out MSDA insurance, which costs Rs 100 per person, lasts two months and is valid at all MSDA registered centres.

The cost of a dive (including gear) is around Rs 750 per person (slightly more on Rodrigues). A first-level certificate course costs between Rs 8000 and Rs 10,000.

Dive operators in Mauritius:

Angelo Diving (Map p76; ☎ 263 3227; angelodive@intnet.mu; Royal Road; Grand Baie)
Atlantis Diving (Map p71; ☎ 265 7172; atlantis_divers@yahoo.co.uk; Trou aux Biches)
Blue Water Diving (Map p71; ☎ 265 7186; www.bluewaterdivingcenter.com in French; Mont Choisy)

SAFETY GUIDELINES FOR DIVING

Before embarking on a scuba diving or snorkelling trip, consider the following points to ensure a safe and enjoyable experience:

- Possess a current diving certification card from a recognised scuba diving agency, such as PADI, NAUI or CMAS.
- Be sure you are healthy and feel comfortable diving.
- Obtain reliable information about physical and environmental conditions at the dive site from a reputable local operator.
- Be aware of local laws, regulations and etiquette about marine life and the environment.
- Dive only at sites within your realm of experience; engage the services of a competent, professionally trained dive instructor or dive master.
- Be aware that underwater conditions vary significantly from one region, or even site, to another. Seasonal changes can significantly alter dive conditions. These differences influence what equipment divers need and the techniques they use.

Bouba Diving (Map p120; ☎ 832 3063; ebony@intnet.mu; Hotel Mourouk Ebony, Port Sud-Est, Rodrigues)
Coral Diving (Map p110; ☎ 631 9505, 604 1000; www.coraldiving.com) Blue Bay (Blue Lagoon Beach Hotel); Pointe d'Esny (Le Preskîl Hotel)
Cotton Dive (Map p120; ☎ 831 8001; diverod@intnet.mu; Cotton Bay Hotel, Pointe Coton, Rodrigues)
Dive Dream (Map p71; ☎ 257 2848; www.divedream.net; Trou aux Biches)
Exploration Sous-Marine (Map p104; ☎ 453 8450; szalay@intnet.mu; Villas Caroline, Flic en Flac)
Nautilus Diving (Map p71; ☎ 265 5495; www.nautilusdivers.com; Trou aux Biches Hotel, Trou aux Biches)
Neptune Diving (www.neptunediving.co.za) Grand Baie (Map p76; ☎ 263 3768, 251 4152 Royal Rd); Belle Mare (Map p96; ☎ 515 0936; Emeraude Hotel)
Ocean Spirit Diving (Map p81; ☎ 563 0376; gringospirit@yahoo.com; Pereybère)
Pro-Dive (Map p71; ☎ 265 6213; www.geocities.com/padgraphics/prodive; Casuarina Hotel, Trou aux Biches)

Réunion

The diving on offer in Réunion is mostly aimed at the amateur diver, with a wide choice of shallow dives inside the lagoon and deeper dives (mostly 20m to 25m) just outside. Most dive sites are located off the west coast between St-Gilles-les-Bains and St-Pierre.

Pointe au Sel, south of St-Leu, is widely regarded as Réunion's best all-round dive site. In addition to great scenery, it offers a fabulous array of fish life. Other popular options include La Maison Verte, also south of St-Leu, with good coral and fish aplenty, and the aptly named Coral Garden, off St-Pierre. There are also a number of wrecks in the lagoon.

Experienced divers seeking something more challenging should contact one of the operators below to arrange a custom package. For general dive inquiries, call the **Comité Régional de Sports Sous-Marins** (☎ 0262 330095).

WHEN TO DIVE

While it is possible to dive all year, the best time is October to April, when the water is at its warmest. However, you might want to avoid February through March, which is the cyclone season.

OPERATORS

The dive centres are concentrated around St-Gilles-les-Bains and St-Leu. Rates start at about €45/40 per dive (including gear) for first-time/experienced divers. Some centres offer night dives and most offer the full range of certification courses; the bigger centres usually have English-speaking instructors. You'll pay in the region of €250 for a first-level certificate course.

Dive operators in Réunion:

Abyss Plongée (☎ 0262 347979; www.abyss-plongee.com; 7 Blvd Bonnier, St-Leu)
Atlantis (☎ 0262 347747; atlantis@oceans.fr; 3 Impasse des Plongeurs, Pointe des Châteaux, St-Leu)
B'Leu Océan (☎ 0262 349749; www.bleuocean.fr in French; Route National 1, St-Leu)
Bleu Marine Réunion (Map p188; ☎ 0262 242200; www.bleu-marine-reunion.com; Port de Plaisance, St-Gilles-les-Bains)
Corail Plongée (Map p188; ☎ 0262 243725; www.corail-plongee.com; Port de Plaisance, St-Gilles-les-Bains)
L'Excelsus (Map p182; ☎ 0262 347365; www.chez.com/excelsus in French; 1 Impasse des Plongeurs, Pointe des Châteaux, St-Leu)
Ô sea Bleu (Map p188; ☎ 0262 331615; www.reunion-plongee.com in French; Port de Plaisance, St-Gilles-les-Bains)
Réunion Plongée (Map p182; ☎ 0262 347777; clubrp@wanadoo.fr in French; 13 Impasse des Plongeurs, Pointe des Châteaux, St-Leu)

DIVING TIP

Make sure you allow 24 hours between diving and taking a flight.

Seychelles

With over 900 species of fish, 100 types of shells and 50 varieties of coral, the Seychelles is a diver's paradise and an underwater photographer's dream. The main group of islands, including Mahé, Praslin and La Digue, are granite formations with a fringing coral reef. In contrast, the outer islands, such as Desroches, Cosmolédo and Aldabra, number among the world's largest coral atolls. Although extensive areas of reef were devastated by bleaching in 1997 and 1998 (see p33), new growth is beginning to reappear. Fortunately, the fish life is as abundant as ever.

There is a wide variety of diving options, from wrecks and wall dives to the increasingly popular 'adventure dives'. Most are boat dives, though shore diving is available in a number of locations. Few dives go below 20m and decompression dives are not permitted.

The Sub Indian Ocean Seychelles (SUBIOS) underwater festival, held each October, is a mecca for divers. It combines diving with an underwater photography competition and film presentations. For current programme information, rules and entry form, check the festival's website (www.subios.sc).

WHEN TO DIVE

The best visibility and calmest seas are from March to May and September to November. Visibility can drop dramatically during November with the rise in the plankton which sweeps across the Indian Ocean, bringing with it manta rays and whale sharks. During the monsoon season, rainwater runoff can affect visibility.

Because of the variety of sites, however, every season offers something sensational, whether it's clear waters with occasional sightings of big fish, or poor visibility with an excellent chance of diving with whale sharks.

The outer islands are more susceptible than the main islands to offshore winds and the might of the Indian Ocean swell. Tidal variations and currents can be punishing.

TOP THREE DIVE SITES OF THE SEYCHELLES

- **Shark Bank** As the name suggests, sharks are a fairly common sight around this 30m-tall granite pillar 9km off Beau Vallon (Mahé) – generally reef sharks, but also whale sharks between February and November. Expect to encounter brissant rays the size of mini mokes, eagle rays, barracuda, and teeming yellow snapper and big eyes. The pillar is covered with bright orange sponges and white gorgonians. There is nearly always a strong current at this site. For experienced divers only.
- **Îlot** This granite outcrop just off north Mahé consists of several large boulders topped by a tuft of palm trees. The current in the channel can be quite strong, but the cluster of boulders yields one of the highest densities of fish life in the Seychelles. Golden cup coral festoons the canyons and gullies, and gorgonians and other soft corals abound. You're sure to see yellow-spotted burr fish, anemones and clownfish, peppered moray eels, Spanish dancer nudibranchs and thousands of hingeback shrimps. Îlot is a 15-minute boat ride from Beau Vallon. It's suitable for all levels and is a popular night dive.
- **Brissare Rocks** About 5km north of Mahé, and accessed from Beau Vallon, this is another granite pinnacle. It is characterised by abundant fire coral and great concentrations of yellow snapper, wrasse, parrotfish and fusiliers, as well as groupers and eagle rays. Reef sharks and whale sharks are also known to visit. For experienced divers only.

OPERATORS

Most dive centres are in the big hotels, though there are a few independent operators on Mahé and Praslin. All offer equipment and services of the highest standards. Most are dedicated five-star PADI centres with multilingual staff, and offer the full range of certification courses.

The cost of a dive is around €50 (including gear), while PADI beginner courses start at upwards of €450. If you dive in a marine park, there's an additional park fee of €10 per person. Live-aboard excursions are also available through yacht-charter companies (p274) and the *Indian Ocean Explorer* (p274), which offers dive packages to Aldabra.

Other Seychelles dive operators:

Azzurra Pro-Dive (Map p265; ☎ 234232; www.ladigue.sc; La Digue Island Lodge, Anse Réunion, La Digue)
Big Blue Divers (Map p252; ☎ 261106; www.bigbluedivers.net; Beau Vallon, Mahé)
Bleu Marine (Map p259; ☎ 515765; www.bleumarine-seychelles.com in French; La Vanille Hotel, Anse La Blague, Praslin)
Island Ventures (Map p252; ☎ 247165; www.dive-seychelles.com; Berjaya Beau Vallon Bay Beach Resort, Beau Vallon, Mahé)
Octopus Diving Centre (Map p259; ☎ 232350; www.octopusdiving.com, Anse Volbert, Praslin)
Underwater Dive Centre (Map p252; ☎ 345445; www.diveseychelles.com.sc; Coral Strand Hotel, Beau Vallon, Mahé)
Whitetip Divers (Map p259; ☎/fax 232282; Paradise Sun Hotel, Anse Volbert, Praslin)

SNORKELLING

Snorkelling is a great way to explore the underwater world with minimal equipment and without the costs associated with diving. Even the shallowest reefs are home to many colourful critters. In all three destinations, rental gear is widely available from dive centres; in Mauritius, you can buy your own set quite cheaply in the big supermarkets.

In Mauritius, top spots include the marine park at Blue Bay and along the west coast off Flic en Flac and Trou aux Biches, not forgetting the lagoon around Rodrigues. Companies running trips on glass-bottomed boats will often include snorkelling in the deal.

SNORKELLING TIPS

- Clean your mask by wetting it and rubbing saliva into it before rinsing. This should prevent the mask from fogging.
- Wear a T-shirt and use water-resistant sunscreen to prevent sunburn.
- Wear fins or plastic shoes to protect your feet.
- Never snorkel alone.

In Réunion, the lagoon along the west coast between St-Gilles-les-Bains and St-Pierre offers great snorkelling, with particularly good marine life off L'Hermitage-les-Bains. Take advice before leaping in as the currents can be dangerous.

In the Seychelles, the sheltered lagoons provide safe havens for swimming and snorkelling. The Ste Anne and Port Launay marine parks are firm favourites in the waters around Mahé. Around Praslin, try off Anse Lazio and Anse Volbert beaches, or take a boat trip from Anse Volbert to St Pierre islet. Close to La Digue, the submerged granite boulders around Coco, Grande Sœur and Marianne islands are teeming with fish life.

Mauritius

JEAN-BERNARD CARILLET

Mauritius

CONTENTS

Highlights	45
Climate & When to Go	45
History	46
The Culture	48
Religion	51
Arts	51
Environment	54
Port Louis	**57**
Around Port Louis	67
North Mauritius	**68**
Balaclava & Baie de l'Arsenal	70
Trou aux Biches & Around	70
Grand Baie	74
Northern Islands	80
Pereybère	80
Cap Malheureux	83
Grand Gaube	84
Pamplemousses	84
Central Mauritius	**86**
Hiking the Central Plateau & Black River Gorges	86
Curepipe	90
Around Curepipe	93
Quatre Bornes	94
Rose Hill	94
Moka & Around	95
East Mauritius	**95**
Trou d'Eau Douce	97
Île aux Cerfs	98
Belle Mare & Around	99
Centre de Flacq	100
West Mauritius	**101**
Flic en Flac & Around	101
Tamarin	105
La Preneuse	106
Grande Rivière Noire	107
La Gaulette & Around	107
Le Morne Peninsula	108
South Mauritius	**109**
Mahébourg	109
Around Mahébourg	113
Vieux Grand Port to Bambous Virieux	115
Mahébourg to Baie du Cap	117
Rodrigues	**119**
Port Mathurin	123
Around Rodrigues	126
Offshore Islands	128
Mauritius Directory	**129**
Transport in Mauritius	**139**

FAST FACTS

- **Area** 2040 sq km
- **Capital** Port Louis
- **Country code** ☎ 230
- **Main religion** Hinduism
- **Major exports** textiles, clothing, sugar, cut flowers
- **Money** rupee; €1 = Rs 30
- **Official languages** English and French
- **Official name** Republic of Mauritius
- **Population** 1.2 million
- **Unemployment** 10%

In 1896, Mark Twain wrote that God modelled Mauritius on Paradise. That may be overselling it a touch nowadays, but Mauritius is still a stunning tropical destination where you can laze on some of the finest beaches in the Indian Ocean and indulge in all manner of wild and wonderful water activities in the encircling aquamarine lagoons. Add to that the country's dramatic mountains and its vibrant cultural mix, matched by a truly irresistible range of culinary creations, and it's not surprising that the number of visitors to these relaxed and varied islands is constantly on the rise.

Many people come to Mauritius on all-inclusive packages to stay in the fabulous beach hotels, several of which rate among the best in the world. There's no shortage, however, of cheap-and-cheerful guesthouses, apartments and small, family-run hotels for the independent traveller. Similarly, there are eating options to suit all pockets. These range from street-corner snack stalls and beachfront cafés to gourmet restaurants where the country's heritage of Creole, French, Indian and Chinese cuisines is combined to sublime effect.

With around half the population Hindu, Mauritius has a distinct Indian flavour. This is most vividly highlighted during the many festivals celebrated throughout the year and in the eye-catching temples. Cheek-by-jowl with the temples stand mosques, churches and Buddhist pagodas – evidence of the extraordinary tolerance which underpins this multicultural society and gives Mauritius its special allure.

HIGHLIGHTS

- **Dining** Tuck in at the cosmopolitan restaurants of Port Louis (p64)
- **The open road** Go hiking in the Black River Gorges National Park (p86)
- **Natural wonders** Spot pink pigeons on Île aux Aigrettes (p114)
- **Adrenaline rush** Dive off the coast of Flic en Flac (p38)
- **Chill-out spot** Relax on the beaches of Île aux Cerfs (p98)
- **Scenic drive** Explore the rugged south coast (p117)
- **Off-beat experience** Take an undersea walk at Grand Baie (p75)
- **Green spaces** Stroll among palms in the Sir Seewoosagur Ramgoolam Botanical Gardens (p84)
- **Fascinating facts** Learn all about sugar at L'Aventure du Sucre (p85)
- **Remote adventure** Explore the byways of Rodrigues (p119)

CLIMATE & WHEN TO GO

Mauritius experiences a hot, humid summer from December to April and a cooler, drier period from May to November. However, there is considerable variation from one part of the island to another.

Coastal temperatures range between 25°C and 33°C in summer and between 18°C and 24°C in winter. On the plateau it will be some 5°C cooler. The highlands are also the wettest part of the island – it can rain here at any time of year and even when it's not raining, the area can be cloaked in low cloud.

Under the influence of the prevailing southeasterly winds, the east coast is slightly cooler and wetter than the west. When the winds are at their strongest in July and August, it can be blustery on the east coast, though the breeze brings welcome relief in summer.

The cyclone season lasts from December to March. Although a direct hit happens rarely, cyclones way out at sea can bring days of squally rain. Rodrigues is more prone to cyclones than Mauritius.

Apart from the Christmas–New Year peak, Mauritius doesn't really have high and low seasons. The situation is more

HOW MUCH?

- Cup of coffee Rs 25
- Sandwich Rs 30-50
- Meal in a cheap restaurant Rs 150-200
- Meal in an upmarket restaurant Rs 350-600
- Scuba dive (including gear) Rs 750

LONELY PLANET INDEX

- Litre of petrol Rs 20
- Litre of bottled water Rs 10
- Small bottle of Phoenix beer Rs 35
- Souvenir T-shirt Rs 150
- Street snack – *dhal puris* Rs 5

dependent on outside factors (such as the French school holidays) than on the weather, though divers and other water-sports enthusiasts should avoid the peak cyclone season in January and February.

See p279 for the climate chart for Port Louis.

HISTORY

Mauritius has a long colonial history. It experienced four changes of 'ownership' between the arrival of the first European settlers in 1598 and independence in 1968. The colonisers brought with them African slaves and, later, indentured labourers from India and China, resulting in the rich cultural and ethnic mix that exists today.

The First Colonisers

Although Arab traders knew of Mauritius – which they called Dina Arobi (Isle of Desolation) – perhaps as early as the 10th century, the first Europeans to discover these uninhabited islands were the Portuguese around 1507. They, too, were more interested in trade, however, and never attempted to settle.

In 1598, a group of Dutch sailors landed on the southeast coast of the island, claimed it for the Netherlands and named it after Prince Maurits of Nassau. For the next 40 years the Dutch used Mauritius as a supply base for Batavia (Java), before deciding to settle near their original landing spot. Settlement ruins can still be seen at Vieux Grand Port, near Mahébourg.

The colony never really flourished, however, and the Dutch abandoned it in 1710. Nevertheless, they left their mark: the Dutch were responsible for the extinction of the dodo and for the introduction of slaves from Africa, deer from Java, wild boar, tobacco and, above all, sugar cane.

Île de France

Five years later it was the turn of the French, when Captain Guillaume Dufresne d'Arsel sailed across from what is now Réunion and claimed Mauritius for France. The island was rechristened Île de France, but nothing much happened until the arrival in 1735 of the dynamic governor, Bertrand François Mahé de Labourdonnais, Mauritius' first hero. He not only transformed Port Louis into a thriving seaport, but also built the first sugar mill and established a road network.

It was around this time that Mauritius' best-known historic event occurred when the *St Géran* went down during a storm off the northeast coast in 1744. The shipwreck inspired Bernardin de St-Pierre's romantic novel *Paul et Virginie*, an early bestseller (see Paul & Virgine on p85 for more details of the event).

As the English gained the upper hand in the Indian Ocean in the late 18th century, the Compagnie des Indes Orientales collapsed. Port Louis became a haven for pirates and slightly more respectable corsairs – mercenary marines paid by a country to prey on enemy ships. The most famous Franco-Mauritian corsair was Robert Surcouf, who wrought havoc on British shipping.

In 1789, French settlers in Mauritius recognised the revolution in France and got rid of their governor. But they refused to free their slaves when the abolition of slavery was decreed in Paris in 1794.

British Rule

In 1810, during the Napoleonic Wars, the British moved in on Mauritius as part of their grand plan to control the Indian Ocean. Things started badly when they were defeated at the Battle of Vieux Grand Port, the only French naval victory inscribed on the Arc de Triomphe in Paris. Just a few months later, however, British forces landed at Cap Malheureux on the north coast and took over the island.

The new British rulers renamed the island Mauritius, but allowed the Franco-Mauritians to retain their language, religion, legal system and the all-important sugarcane plantations, on which the economy depended. The slaves were finally freed in 1835, by which time there were over 70,000 on the island. They were replaced or supplemented by labour imported from India and China. As many as 500,000 Indians took up the promise of a better life in Mauritius, often to find themselves living and working in appalling conditions on minimum pay.

By sheer weight of numbers, the Indian workforce gradually achieved a greater say in the running of the country. Their struggle was given extra impetus when the Indian political and spiritual leader Mahatma Gandhi visited Mauritius in 1901 to push for civil rights. However, the key event was the introduction of universal suffrage in 1959, and the key personality Dr (later Sir) Seewoosagur Ramgoolam. Founder of the Labour Party in 1936, Seewoosagur Ramgoolam led the fight for independence, which was finally granted in 1968.

Independence

The prime minister of newly independent Mauritius was, not surprisingly, Sir Seewoosagur Ramgoolam. He remained in office for the next 13 years and continued to command great reverence until his death in 1986; a host of public buildings has been named in his honour.

Since then the political landscape has largely been dominated by the duo of Anerood Jugnauth, the Indian leader of the Mouvement Socialiste Mauricien (MSM), and the Franco-Mauritian Paul Bérenger with his leftist Mouvement Militant Mauricien (MMM). The two parties formed their first coalition government in 1982, with Jugnauth as prime minister and Bérenger as finance minister. In the years that followed, the two men were in and out of government, sometimes power-sharing, at other times in opposition to each other, according to the complex and shifting web of allegiances which enlivens Mauritian politics.

On the economic front meanwhile, Mauritius was undergoing a minor miracle. Up until the 1970s the Mauritian economy could be summed up in one word – sugar. Sugar represented more than 90% of the country's exports, covered most of its fertile land and was its largest employer by far. Every so often, a cyclone would devastate the cane crop, or a world drop in sugar prices would have bitter consequences.

From the 1970s the government went all out to promote textiles, tourism and financial services, much of it based on foreign investment. Soon Mauritius was one of the world's largest exporters of textiles, with Ralph Lauren, Pierre Cardin, Lacoste and other famous brands all manufactured on the island. Income from tourism also grew by leaps and bounds as the government targeted the luxury end of the market.

The strategy paid off. The 1980s and 1990s saw the Mauritian economy grow by a remarkable 5% a year. Unemployment fell

KAYA

It was a black day for Mauritius, and a blacker one still for the Creole community. On 21 February 1999, the singer Joseph Topize (aka Kaya) was found dead in his police cell, seemingly a victim of police brutality, after being arrested for smoking cannabis at a prolegalisation rally.

As the pioneer of *seggae*, a unique combination of reggae and traditional *séga* beats, Kaya provided a voice for disadvantaged Creoles across the country. His death in the custody of Indian police split Mauritian society along racial lines, triggering four days of violent riots that left several people dead and brought the country to a standstill.

An autopsy cleared the police of wrongdoing, but the events have forced the Indian-dominated government to acknowledge *la malaise Créole*, Creoles' anger at their impoverished status in a country that has been dominated by Indians since independence.

In contrast to the violent scenes, Kaya's music is full of positive energy. The classic album *Seggae Experience* is a tribute to the singer's unique vision.

from a whopping 42% in 1980 to less than 6% by 2000 and overall standards of living improved. Even so, rates of unemployment and poverty remained high among the Creole population, many of whom also felt frustrated at their lack of political power in the face of the Indian majority. These tensions spilled out on to the streets of Port Louis in 1999, triggered by the death in police custody of the singer Kaya, an ardent campaigner for the rights of the disadvantaged Creole population, people of mixed Afro-European origin. The riots brought the country to a standstill for four days and forced the government to make political concessions.

Mauritius Today

While there have been no more major riots, the economic situation today isn't quite so rosy. By the end of 2003 growth had slipped back and unemployment shot up to around 10%. The main cause of the downturn is competition from cheap textiles from Southeast Asia. At the same time, the sugar industry continues its long, slow decline. Plant closures combined with mechanisation have led to thousands of unskilled cane workers losing their jobs. There are no welfare payouts, but the government provides free health care, family planning and other social services for cane workers.

Though this has taken the shine off Mauritius' 'economic miracle', it's not all doom and gloom. The number of tourist arrivals continues to grow (nearly 700,000 in 2002), and thousands of Mauritians are employed in the sector.

The other major plank in the government's strategy is to encourage foreign investment in telecoms. The latest talk is of Mauritius becoming a 'cyberisland', fully wired up with all the latest technology and ready to become a key player in the region's information networks.

On the political front, Paul Bérenger made headlines in 2003 when he became the country's first non-Indian prime minister thanks to a deal made with Jugnauth during the 2000 election campaign, in which Jugnauth promised to hand over power to Bérenger if their coalition won. Jugnauth, meanwhile, became president. Though this is a nonpolitical position, he is still very much behind the scenes. His son, Pravind, is not only leader of the MSM, but also deputy prime minister.

THE CULTURE

Mauritius is often cited as an example of racial and religious harmony, and compared with most other countries it is. On the surface, there are few signs of conflict. However, racial divisions are still apparent, more so than in the Seychelles or Réunion. Tensions between the Hindu majority and Muslim and Creole minorities persist despite the general respect for constitutional prohibitions against discrimination, and constitute one of the country's few potential political flashpoints.

The National Psyche

Despite being a relatively young country (less than 40 years old) with a diverse population, there is a surprisingly strong sense of national identity in Mauritius

RESPONSIBLE TRAVEL

The people of Mauritius have a well-deserved reputation for being exceptionally tolerant. That said, there are a few 'rules' of behaviour to abide by.

Although beachwear is fine for the beaches, you will cause offence and may invite pestering if you dress skimpily elsewhere. Nude bathing is forbidden, while women going topless is tolerated around some hotel pools, but not on the beaches.

Mauritius has many temples and mosques. You are welcome to visit, but should dress and behave with respect: miniskirts and singlet tops are a no-no, and it is normal to remove your shoes – there's usually a sign indicating where to leave them. Many temples and mosques also ask you not to take photos, while some Hindu temples request that you remove all leather items, such as belts. At mosques, you may be required to cover your head in certain areas, so remember to take along a scarf. Never touch a carving or statue of a deity. If at any time you're unsure about protocol, the best thing is to ask.

that transcends racial and cultural ties. Of the various forces binding Mauritians together, the most important is language. Not the official languages of English and French, but Creole, which is spoken by 70% of the population and understood by virtually all Mauritians. Another common bond is that everyone is an immigrant or descended from immigrants. Food and music are also unifiers, as is the importance placed on family life. Mauritius is a small, close-knit community. Living in such close proximity breaks down barriers and increases understanding between the different groups. Respect for others and tolerance are deeply engrained in all sectors of society.

Mauritians place great importance on education – not just to get a better job, but as a goal in its own right. Lawyers, doctors and teachers are regarded with tremendous respect. The pinnacle of success for many is to work in the civil service, though this is beginning to change as salaries rise among artisans and businesspeople.

As individuals, Mauritians live up to their reputation of being friendly, laid-back, hospitable and generous. Many go out of their way to help strangers, and there's nothing a Mauritian likes more than a good chat. They're gentle people, more likely to make a joke about something than get angry. Cultural differences do occur, however: the Chinese tend to be more reserved than the happy-go-lucky Creoles, who work hard but do love a good party.

Lifestyle

In general, each ethnic group maintains a way of life similar to that found in their countries of origin, even if they are second- or third-generation Mauritian. Several generations typically live together under one roof and the main social unit is the extended family – as witnessed by the size of family parties on a Sunday picnic. Mauritians are usually married by the age of 25. The majority of wives stay home to raise the family, while the husband earns the daily bread. Arranged marriages are still the norm among Indian families, while the Hindu caste system has also been replicated to some degree. Among all groups, religion and religious institutions continue to play a central role in community life.

As elsewhere, this very traditional pattern is starting to break down as the younger generation grows more individualistic and more Westernised. They are far more likely to socialise with people from other communities, and intermarriage is on the rise. Other forces for change are the rise in consumerism and the emergence of a largely Indian and Chinese middle class. Middle-class couples are more likely to set up their own home and to have fewer children, while the wife may even go out to work. Statistics also show a slight decline in the number of marriages, while the divorce rate has doubled over the last decade.

Women's equality still has a long way to go in Mauritius. Many women have to accept low-paid, unskilled jobs, typically in a textile factory or as a cleaner. Even highly qualified women can find it hard to get promotion in the private sector, though do better in public service. This may be set to change, however, as in 2003 the government passed a Sex Discrimination Act and set up an independent unit to investigate sex discrimination cases, including sexual harassment at work. The unit is also charged with raising awareness levels and educating employers about equal opportunities.

There is little evidence of discrimination against gays and lesbians in Mauritius. Nevertheless, it's a very macho society, and gays and especially lesbians tend to keep a low profile. Outward signs of affection by same-sex couples make some people uneasy, but it's more likely to result in teasing than anything more serious.

Despite the fact that all forms of discrimination are illegal under the Mauritian constitution, it is widely recognised that the Creole minority has been socially, economically and politically marginalised. It's a vicious circle. Creoles find it harder to get work, partly because of low levels of literacy, but few Creole children complete secondary school because they're needed to help support the family. Expectations are also lower – and so it goes on.

As a result of the economic boom, overall living standards have improved in recent years and the majority of houses now have piped water and electricity. However, the gap between rich and poor is widening. It is estimated that the top 20% of the

THE CHAGOS ISLANDERS

As inhabitants of the Chagos Archipelago of the British Indian Ocean Territory, at least 1000 Chagos islanders, or Îlois, were evicted from their homes when Diego Garcia, the largest of the islands, was leased to the Americans as a military base in 1965 on a 50-year lease. The islanders were resettled in Mauritius between 1965 and 1973. Some 5000 now live in abject poverty in the slums of Port Louis, where they continue to fight for their right to return home.

The islanders won compensation of £4 million from the British in 1982. This was largely paid through the Mauritian government, however, and little went directly to the islanders.

In 2000 the High Court in London ruled that the Îlois had been evicted illegally and upheld their right to be repatriated. Nothing happened, so the Îlois went back to court. In October 2003 the judge rejected their claim for further compensation, though he acknowledged that the British government had treated the islanders 'shamefully' and that the compensation had been inadequate. The Îlois are now preparing yet another appeal.

The Mauritian government has also waged a long-running campaign regarding ownership of the archipelago, largely motivated by the islands' tourist potential. The issue has been pushed into the background in recent years, but is likely to be revived as the 2015 deadline for the renewal of the lease approaches.

Peter Benson describes the forced removal of the Îlois to Mauritius in his novel *A Lesser Dependency*.

population earns 44% of the total income and that 10% lives below the poverty mark. A labourer's wage is just Rs 6000 per month, while a teacher might earn Rs 12,000. There is minimal social-security provision in Mauritius; people rely on their family in times of need. You'll find a few beggars around the markets and mosques, but it's very low-key.

Crime levels also remain relatively low, though petty crime is on the rise. It mostly involves burglaries, but tourists can be a target for thieves (see p133). While drug use is even less of a problem, it too is increasing. Small amounts of heroin are smuggled in from South Africa en route to Réunion and elsewhere; some is consumed locally, along with minor amounts of locally produced cannabis.

One thing that is rife is corruption, though the only form likely to affect tourists is the commission system prevalent among taxi drivers (see p143). Local drivers fume about police 'fines'; connections are used to the maximum; and newspapers are full of financial scandals in the cosy, closed world of the Hindu-dominated administration. But after years of inaction, the present government seems serious about tackling the problem. In 2002 it set up the Independent Commission Against Corruption, which has already unearthed some pretty dirty dealings. Among a number of high-profile cases, two senior bank officials were arrested for embezzling Rs 866 million and a former cabinet minister for accepting Rs 4.5 million in bribes.

Population

The population of Mauritius is made up of four ethnic groups: Indo-Mauritian (68%), Creole (27%), Sino-Mauritian (3%) and Franco-Mauritian (2%). Another small group you might come across are the Chagos islanders (see The Chagos Islanders, above).

Although the population growth rate (currently 0.9%) is now quite low, a quarter of Mauritians are under 15 years of age. The country also has one of the world's highest population densities, with an average of nearly 600 people per sq km, rising to a staggering 3000 per sq km in urban areas. Worst are Port Louis and the Central Plateau towns, which developed in the wake of the malaria epidemics that hit the coast in the 1860s (p59). Even more people are drifting to urban areas in search of work as the sugar factories mechanise or close down altogether. The vast majority of Mauritians now work in construction, industry and the service sector – all very urban activities.

The Indian population (the majority of which is Hindu) is descended from the labourers who were brought to the island to work the cane fields. Nowadays, Indians form the backbone of the labouring and agricultural community and own many of the island's small- and medium-sized businesses, typically in manufacturing and the retail trade. The Central Plateau towns such as Rose Hill have a strong Indian flavour.

Indians also tend to be prominent in civic life. Because they are in the majority, Hindus always win elections. The present prime minister, the Franco-Mauritian Paul Bérenger, is the first non-Indian at the helm in the country's history, and he's only there because of a deal struck with his predecessor, the Indian Anerood Jugnauth (see p47).

After the Indo-Mauritians, the next largest group are Creoles, descendants of African slaves, with varying amounts of European blood. Creoles as a whole form the most disadvantaged sector of society. The majority work in low-paid jobs or eke out a living from fishing or subsistence farming, most notably on Rodrigues, where Creoles make up 98% of the population.

The 30,000 Sino-Mauritians are involved mostly in commerce. Despite their small numbers, the Chinese community plays a disproportionate role in the country's economy, though they tend to avoid politics. Most came to the country as self-employed entrepreneurs and settled in the towns (particularly Port Louis), though most villages have at least one Chinese store.

Franco-Mauritians, the descendants of the *grands blancs* (rich whites), have their hands on Mauritius' purse strings. Most of the sugar mills, banks and other big businesses are still owned by Franco-Mauritians, who tend to screen themselves off from their former labourers in palatial private residences in the hills around Curepipe, and own almost all the luxurious holiday homes along the coast. Many others have decamped completely to live in South Africa and France.

RELIGION

There is a close link between religion and race in Mauritius and a remarkable degree of religious tolerance. Mosques, churches and Hindu temples can be found within a stone's throw of each other in many parts of the country. For tips on visiting places of worship, see Responsible Travel on p48.

Over half the population is Hindu, all of whom are of Indian origin. Festivals play a central role in the Hindu faith and the calendar is packed with colourful celebrations. See p134 for a rundown of the most important.

There's a certain amount of resentment against the Hindus in Mauritius; not for religious reasons but because the Hindu majority dominates the country's political life and its administration. Up until now, with the economy in full swing, this has merely resulted in grumbling about discrimination and 'jobs for the boys', but there's a fear this might change if the economy really begins to falter.

Nearly a third of the population is Roman Catholic. Catholicism is practised by most Creoles, and it has picked up a few voodoo overtones over the years. Most Franco-Mauritians are also Catholic and a few Chinese and Indians have converted, largely through intermarriage.

Muslims, followers of Islam, make up roughly a fifth of the population. Like the Hindus, Mauritian Muslims originally came from India. In Mauritius, where Islam coexists in close proximity to other religions, it tends to be fairly liberal, though attendance at mosque is high and many Muslim women wear the veil.

Sino-Mauritians are the least conspicuous in their worship. The one big exception is Chinese New Year, which is celebrated in Port Louis with great gusto. There are a few Chinese temples in Port Louis.

ARTS

Mauritian architecture, literature and fine arts are all firmly based in the French tradition. The country's music, however, is African in origin and is very much alive and kicking.

Literature

Mauritius' most famous contribution to world literature – one that has become entangled in the island's history – is the romantic novel *Paul et Virginie* by Bernardin de St-Pierre, which was first published in 1788 (see Paul & Virginie, p85). An English translation of the novel is widely available in Mauritius. The author captures the landscapes beautifully, though his ultramoralistic tear-jerker is less likely to appeal to modern tastes.

Those who want to read a 20th-century Mauritian novel should try something by

Malcolm de Chazal, whose most famous works are *Sens Plastique*, available in translation, and *Petrusmok*. Chazal was an eccentric recluse, but he inspired a whole generation of local writers. His works are a highly original blend of poetry and philosophy, and are peppered with pithy statements, such as 'Avoid clean people who have a dirty stare' and 'The seed is the plant's handbag'.

Of living writers, perhaps the best-known internationally is Carl de Souza. In his novel *Le Sang de l'Anglais* he looks at the often ambivalent relationship between Mauritians and their countries of origin, while *La Maison qui Marchait Vers le Large*, set in Port Louis, takes intercommunity conflict as its theme. *Les Jours Kaya* is a coming-of-age book set against the violence following Kaya's death (see p47).

Other contemporary novelists to look out for include Ananda Devi, Shenaz Patel and Natacha Appanah-Mouriquand. Unfortunately, their works as yet are only available in French, regarded as the language of culture.

Joseph Conrad's semi-autobiographical short story, *A Smile of Fortune*, is set in Mauritius, and his love story *Twixt Land and Sea* takes place in Port Louis. In more recent times, the French author JMG Clézio, whose father was Mauritian, has also set a number of novels in Mauritius, of which *Le Chercheur d'Or* (The Prospector) has been translated into English.

Music & Dance

You'll hear *séga* everywhere nowadays, but in the early 20th century it fell seriously out of fashion. Its revival in the early 1950s is credited to the Creole singer Ti-Frère, whose song 'Anita' has become a classic. Though he died in 1992, Ti-Frère is still the country's most popular *séga* star. More recent Creole groups and singers with a wide following include Cassiya, Fanfan and the prolific Jean-Claude Gaspard.

Séga evolved slightly differently in Rodrigues. Here the drum plays a more prominent role in what's known as *séga tambour*. The island's accordion bands are also famous for their surprising repertoire, which includes waltzes, polkas, quadrilles and Scottish reels. Over the years these were learned from passing European sailors and gradually absorbed into the local folk music. They're now an essential part of any Rodriguan knees-up.

A new Mauritian musical form was invented by Creole musician Kaya in *seggae*, which blends elements of *séga* and reggae. With his band Racine Tatane, Kaya gave a voice to dissatisfied Creoles around the island. Tragically, the singer died in police custody in February 1999. Following in Kaya's footsteps, Ras Natty Baby and his Natty Rebels are one of most popular *seggae* groups; sales gained an extra boost when Ras Natty Baby was imprisoned for heroin trafficking in 2003.

SÉGA!

The national dance of Mauritius was originally conceived by African slaves as a diversion from the injustice of their daily existence. At the end of a hard day in the cane fields, couples danced the *séga* around campfires on the beach to the accompaniment of drums.

Because of the sand (some say because of the shackles), there could be no fancy footwork. So today, when dancing the *séga*, the feet never leave the ground. The rest of the body makes up for it and the result, when the fire is hot, can be extremely erotic. In the rhythm and beat of *séga*, you can see or hear connections with the Latin American salsa, the Caribbean calypso, and the African origins of the people. It's a personal, visceral dance where the dancers let the music take over and abandon themselves to the beat.

The dance is traditionally accompanied by the beat of the *ravanne*, a primitive goatskin drum. The beat starts slowly and builds into a pulsating rhythm which normally carries away performers and onlookers alike. You may be lucky enough to see the dance being performed spontaneously at beach parties or family barbecues. Otherwise, you'll have to make do with the less authentic *séga* soirees offered by some bars and restaurants and most of the big hotels, often in combination with a Mauritian buffet. Nonresidents are usually welcome, though may have to pay (generally around Rs 200/100 per adult/child, which is then deducted from your food or drink bill).

RECOMMENDED LISTENING

- *Île Maurice* Ti-Frère (Ocora; 1991) The best of Ti-Frère, with lyrics translated into English.
- *Île Maurice: Séga Ravanne*, Fanfan (Ocora; 1999) *Séga* taken from the oral tradition.
- *Album d'Or*, Cassiya (Cassiya Productions; 2000) Modern *séga* interpretations.
- *Makoutia: Chants et Danses de Rodrigues*, Racines. Good introduction to Rodriguan music, with English text.
- *Seggae Experience*, Kaya (Meli-Mela; 1999) Kaya's classic album is still widely available in Mauritius.

Recently, *ragga*, a blend of house music, traditional Indian music and reggae, has been gaining a following. Up-and-coming Mauritian *ragga* groups include Black Ayou and the Authentic Steel Brothers.

Architecture

Caught up in the need to develop its economy, Mauritius paid little attention to its architectural heritage until recently. As a result many splendid colonial mansions and more humble dwellings have been lost under the sea of concrete. Those still standing may be luckier. In 2003 the government set up a National Heritage Fund charged with preserving the country's historic buildings.

Those which have fared best are the plantation houses dating from the 18th and 19th centuries which you'll still see standing in glorious isolation amid the cane fields. Many are privately owned and closed to the public, such as Le Réduit, near Moka, which is now the President's official residence. Others have been converted into museums and restaurants, including Eureka, a beautifully restored mansion also near Moka. But rescuing these houses is expensive and time-consuming. Many of the raw materials, such as tamarind wood, are in short supply. It's easier and cheaper to rip down the old timber frames, and throw up brand new concrete blocks on the sturdy foundations beneath.

The majority of Mauritians now live in nondescript concrete apartment blocks in the towns and cities. Middle-class families might possibly afford a seaside apartment or villa. The coast around Trou aux Biches and Flic en Flac is lined with these uninspiring boxes, all cheek-by-jowl. A few more enlightened developers are beginning to add traditional flourishes,

THE ARCHITECTURAL HERITAGE

The first French settlers naturally brought with them building styles from home. Over the years the architecture gradually evolved until it became supremely well suited to the hot, humid tropics. It's for this reason that so many of the grand plantation houses have survived the ravages of time.

Flourishes that appear to be ornamental – vaulted roofs and decorative pierced screens, for example – all serve to keep the occupants cool and dry. The most distinctive feature is the shingled roof with ornamental turrets and rows of attic windows. These wedding-cake touches conceal a vaulted roof which allows the air to circulate. Another characteristic element is the wide, airy *varangue* (veranda), where raffia blinds, fans and pot plants create a cooling humidity.

The roofs, windows and overhangs are usually lined with delicate, lace-like *lambrequins* (decorative wooden borders), which are purely ornamental. They vary from simple, repetitive floral patterns to elaborate pierced friezes; in all cases a botanical theme predominates.

Lambrequins, shingle roofs and verandas or wrought-iron balconies are also found in colonial-era town houses. The more prestigious buildings were constructed of brick, or even stone, and so are better able to withstand cyclones and termites. In Port Louis, Government House and other buildings lining Place S Bissoondoyal are all fine examples.

At the other end of the scale, traditional labourers' houses typically consist of two rooms (one for sleeping, one for eating) and a veranda; because of the fire risk the kitchen is usually separate. Nowadays they are built of corrugated iron rather than termite-resistant hardwood, but are still painted in eye-catching colours which offset the white *lambrequins*. The garden overflowing with edible and ornamental plants is almost as important as the house itself.

such as *lambrequins* (decorative wooden borders) and bright paintwork. Hotels and restaurants are also getting better at incorporating a bit of local colour.

As for major civic projects, the most prestigious in recent times has been Port Louis' Caudan Waterfront development. Given its location at the very heart of the capital, the architects decided to incorporate elements of the traditional architecture found around nearby Place S Bissoondoyal. Further inspiration came from the nearby stone-and-steel dockyard buildings to provide another link with the past.

Visual Arts

Historically, Mauritian artists took their lead from what was happening in Europe and, particularly, France. Some of the 18th- and 19th-century engravings and oils of Mauritian landscapes you see could almost be mistaken for Europe. The classical statue of Paul and Virginie in Port Louis' Blue Penny Museum and the one of King Edward VII in the city's Champ de Mars were both created by Mauritius' best-known sculptor, Prosper d'Épinay.

In the 20th century, the surrealist writer and painter Malcolm de Chazal injected a bit of local colour into the scene. Inspired by the island's prolific nature, his paintings are full of light and energy. You'll see numerous copies of the *Blue Dodo* and other Chazal works around, but originals are extremely rare.

Contemporary Mauritian art tends to be driven by the tourist market. One artist you'll find reproduced everywhere is Vaco Baissac, instantly recognisable from the blocks of colour outlined in black, like a stained-glass window. His gallery is in Grand Baie (p79).

Other commercially successful artists include Danielle Hitié, who produces minutely detailed renderings of markets as well as rural scenes, and Françoise Vrot, known for her very expressive portraits of women fieldworkers. Both artists are exhibited in galleries in Port Louis (p67) and Grand Baie, where Vrot also has her studio (p79).

Keep an eye out for exhibitions by more innovative contemporary artists such as Hervé Masson, Serge Constantin, Henri Koombes and Khalid Nazroo. All have had some success on the international scene, though are less visible locally.

ENVIRONMENT

Tourist arrivals have been increasing at a rate of 9% a year for the last 20 years and there's little sign of a slow down. If anything, the government is keen to encourage even more tourists – at least, the rich ones – to plug the gap left by a declining sugar industry. However, the expansion of tourist facilities is straining the island's infrastructure and causing problems such as environmental degradation and excessive demand on services such as electricity, water and transport.

The Land

Mauritius is the peak of an enormous volcanic chain which also includes Réunion, though it is much older and therefore less rugged than Réunion.

The island's highest mountains are found in the southwest, from where the land drops slightly to a central plateau before climbing again to the chain of oddly shaped mountains behind Port Louis and the Montagne Bambou range to the east. Beyond these mountains, a plain slopes gently down to the north coast.

Unlike Réunion, Mauritius has no active volcanoes, although remnants of volcanic activity abound. Extinct craters and volcanic lakes, such as the Trou aux Cerfs crater in Curepipe and the Grand Bassin holy lake, are good examples. Over the aeons, the volcanoes generated millions of lava boulders, much to the chagrin of the indentured farm labourers, who had to clear the land for sugar cane. Heaps of boulders dot the landscape. Some that have been piled into tidy pyramids are listed monuments!

Mauritius also includes a number of widely scattered inhabited islands, of which the most important is Rodrigues, 600km to the northeast. Rodrigues is another ancient volcanic peak and is surrounded by a lagoon twice the size of the island itself.

Wildlife

Mauritius is a haven for the botanist, zoologist, ornithologist and other 'ologists'. To experience some of what's on offer in the way of flora and fauna, the visitor must go to the botanical gardens at Pamplemousses and Curepipe, to Casela Nature Park and the Black River Gorges National Park in the southwest, and to Île aux Aigrettes and the Domaine du Chasseur in the south.

The best source of information is the **Mauritian Wildlife Foundation** (MWF; ☎ 631 2396; www.ile-aux-aigrettes.com/pages/mwf.htm), which was founded in 1984 to protect and manage the country's many rare species. The MWF vigorously supports the creation of national parks and reserves, and the monitoring of whales, dolphins and turtles. It has had significant success in restoring the populations of several endangered bird species and in conserving endemic vegetation. Nevertheless, there is still a long way to go.

For information on marine life, see p33.

ANIMALS

The first wild animals that visitors to Mauritius are likely to meet are the bands of macaque monkeys which hang out around Grand Bassin and the Black River Gorges. Mongooses are also common. They were introduced from India in the late 19th century to control plague-carrying rats. The intention was to import only males, but some females slipped through and soon there were mongooses everywhere. Java deer, imported by the Dutch for fresh meat, and wild pigs roam the more remote forests.

Native reptiles include the beautiful turquoise and red Ornate Day Gecko and Telfair's skink, a clawed lizard, both of which can be seen on Île aux Aigrettes. There are no dangerous species, however, in Mauritius.

As for bird life, the best-known representative was the dodo, the pigeon that found its docility rewarded with extinction (see Dead as a Dodo, below). Several other local bird species looked as doomed as the dodo until a few years back. Thanks to phenomenal conservation efforts, however, some now have a chance of survival.

The Mauritius kestrel was the victim of pesticide poisoning, habitat destruction and hunting. By 1974 just six birds remained: four in the wild and two in captivity. A captive breeding programme established in 1973 has led to an amazing recovery, with numbers now over 800. With luck, you might see kestrels in the Black River Gorges and at the Domaine du Chasseur, north of Mahébourg.

The lovely pink pigeon has also been pulled back from the brink thanks to captive breeding. From a mere 10 or so individuals in 1990 there are now around 400. A colony has now been established on Île aux Aigrettes, off Mahébourg, safe from egg-stealing rats and monkeys and human poachers.

Similar captive breeding programmes are helping to preserve the echo parakeet, found mainly in the Black River Gorges, and the Rodrigues fruit bat (see p122), among other endangered species.

The birds you're most likely to see, however, are the introduced songbirds, such

DEAD AS A DODO

Illustrations from the logbooks of the first ships to reach Mauritius show hundreds of plump flightless birds running down to the beach to investigate the newcomers. Lacking natural predators, these giant relatives of the pigeon were easy prey for hungry sailors, who named the bird *dodo*, meaning 'stupid'. It took just 30 years for passing sailors and their pets or pests – dogs, monkeys, pigs and rats – to drive the dodo to extinction; the last confirmed sighting was in the 1660s.

Just as surprising as the speed of the dodo's demise is how little evidence remains that the bird ever existed. A few relics made it back to Europe during the 18th century – a dried beak ended up at the University of Copenhagen in Denmark, while the University of Oxford in England managed to get hold of a whole head and a foot – but until recently our knowledge of the dodo was mainly based on sketches by 17th-century seamen.

However, in 1865 local schoolteacher George Clark discovered a dodo skeleton in a marshy area on the site of what is now the international airport. The skeleton was reassembled by scientists in Edinburgh, and has formed the basis of all subsequent dodo reconstructions, one of which is on display in the Natural History Museum in Port Louis.

For the full story of the dodo's demise, read Errol Fuller's fascinating book *Dodo: From Extinction to Icon*.

as the little red Madagascar fody, the Indian mynah (its yellow beak and feet giving it a cartoon-character appearance) and the most common bird of all on Mauritius – the red-whiskered bulbul. Between October and May the Terre Rouge estuary north of Port Louis provides an important wintering ground for migratory water birds such as the whimbrel, the grey plover and the common and curlew sandpipers.

PLANTS

Almost one-third of the 900 plant species found in Mauritius are unique to these islands. Many of these endemic plants have fared poorly in competition with introduced plants, especially guava and privet, and have been depleted by introduced deer, pigs and monkeys. General forest clearance and the establishment of crop monocultures have exacerbated the problem, so that less than 1% of Mauritius' original forest is intact.

Mauritius' forests originally included the tambalacoque tree, which is also known as the dodo tree and is not far from extinction itself. It's a tall tree with a silver trunk and a large, tough seed that supposedly only germinated after being eaten by and passing through the stomach of a dodo. Scientists are sceptical about this rumour, but there's no denying the tree is extremely difficult to propagate. The easiest place to find this and other rare plant species is in the botanical gardens at Pamplemousses.

For a tropical island, Mauritius is not big on coconut palms. Instead, casuarinas (also known as *filaos*) fringe most of the beaches. These tall, wispy trees act as useful windbreaks and grow well in sandy soil. Along with casuarinas, eucalyptus trees have been widely planted to help stop erosion.

Other impressive and highly visible trees are the giant Indian banyan and the brilliant red flowering flamboyant, or royal poinciana.

Staying with shades of red, one flower you will see in abundance is anthurium, with its single, glossy petal and protruding yellow spadix. The plant originated in South America and was introduced to Mauritius in the late 19th century. The flower, which at first sight you'd swear was plastic, can last up to three weeks after being cut and is therefore a popular display plant. Now grown in commercial quantities for export, it is used to spruce up hotels and public meeting places.

National Parks

Since 1988, several international organisations have been working with the government to set up conservation areas in Mauritius. About 3.5% of the land area is now protected either as national parks, managed mainly for ecosystem preservation and for recreation, or as nature reserves. The latter cover areas containing some outstanding or representative ecosystem or areas of particularly rich biodiversity, which are also suitable for ecotourism and educational purposes. The most important and interesting reserves open to the public are listed in the following table.

The largest park is the Black River Gorges National Park, established in 1994 in the southwest of the island. It covers some

IMPORTANT NATIONAL PARKS

Park	Features	Activities	Best time to visit
Black River Gorges National Park (p86)	forested mountains, Mauritius kestrel, black ebony trees, macaque monkeys	hiking, bird-watching	Sep-Jan for flowers
Blue Bay Marine Park (p113)	lagoon, corals, fish life	snorkelling, diving, glass-bottomed boat tours	all year
Île aux Aigrettes Nature Reserve (p114)	coral island, coastal forests, pink pigeons, giant Aldabra tortoises	ecotours	all year

68 sq km and preserves a wide variety of forest environments, from pine forest to tropical scrub, and includes the country's largest area of native forest. Two of the most important nature reserves are Île aux Aigrettes and Île Ronde, both of which are being restored to their natural state by replacing introduced plants and animals with native species.

In 1997 two marine parks were proclaimed at Blue Bay, near Mahébourg, and Balaclava on the west coast. As yet only the Blue Bay park is functioning in any way, but the number of visitors to the area makes it difficult to establish rigorous controls and there is a need to encourage local fishermen to use less destructive techniques. It is hoped to establish a third marine park off Port Sud-Est in Rodrigues to prevent further coral damage caused by octopus gatherers. (See p35 for more about marine conservation in Mauritius.)

Environmental Issues

The environment of Mauritius has paid a heavy price for the country's rapid economic development. For many species it is already too late, but there is a growing awareness of the need for conservation among decision makers and the general public. The difficulty is to achieve a balance between protecting the immensely fragile island ecosystems and easing the ever-increasing pressure on land and other natural resources.

One area of particular concern is the amount of new development along the coast, much of it tourist related. There are plans for hotels along the unspoilt south coast of Mauritius and on Rodrigues, leading to local opposition. A proposal for a hotel on Île des Deux Cocos in Blue Bay, for example, met with such fierce resistance that it has been pushed back indefinitely.

The government now requires an environmental impact assessment for all new building projects, including coastal hotels, marinas and golf courses, and even for activities such as undersea walks. Planning regulations for hotel developments on Rodrigues are particularly strict: they must be small, single storey, built in traditional style and stand at least 30m back from the high-tide mark. Since water shortages are a problem on Rodrigues, new hotels must also recycle their water.

To combat littering and other forms of environmental degradation, the government has established a special environmental police force charged with enforcing the legislation and educating the local population. To report wrongdoers, there is even a **hotline** (☎ 210 5151).

If anything, the marine environment is suffering even more from overexploitation. The coast off Grand Baie is particularly affected by too many divers and boats concentrated in a few specific locations. In addition, silting and chemical pollution are resulting in extensive coral damage and falling fish populations. For more information on marine conservation in Mauritius, see p35.

The Mauritian Wildlife Foundation is heavily involved in raising awareness of conservation issues among the local population and tourists. A visit to see MWF's work on Île aux Aigrettes (p114) is highly recommended.

PORT LOUIS

pop 172,000

With bustling shopping streets and a modern business district complete with sky-scrapers, Port Louis (the final 's' is silent) forms the administrative and commercial hub of Mauritius. It is home to one of the country's most rewarding museums and offers an enticing variety of restaurants, bars and cafés. Shopping opportunities abound, from vibrant street markets to a flashy waterfront complex full of trendy boutiques.

Port Louis is the most multicultural town in Mauritius, with distinct Islamic, Hindu, Christian, Chinese and Creole neighbourhoods and an accompanying array of mosques, Hindu temples, Chinese pagodas and Christian churches.

Even in the centre, a surprising number of colonial-era buildings remain. Though these old mansions and town houses are slowly giving way to modern concrete blocks, for now, at least, the city strikes a healthy balance between old and new, and the government has acknowledged the need to preserve its architectural heritage.

Nevertheless, Port Louis is not an immediately attractive city, despite its seafront location and a backdrop of encircling

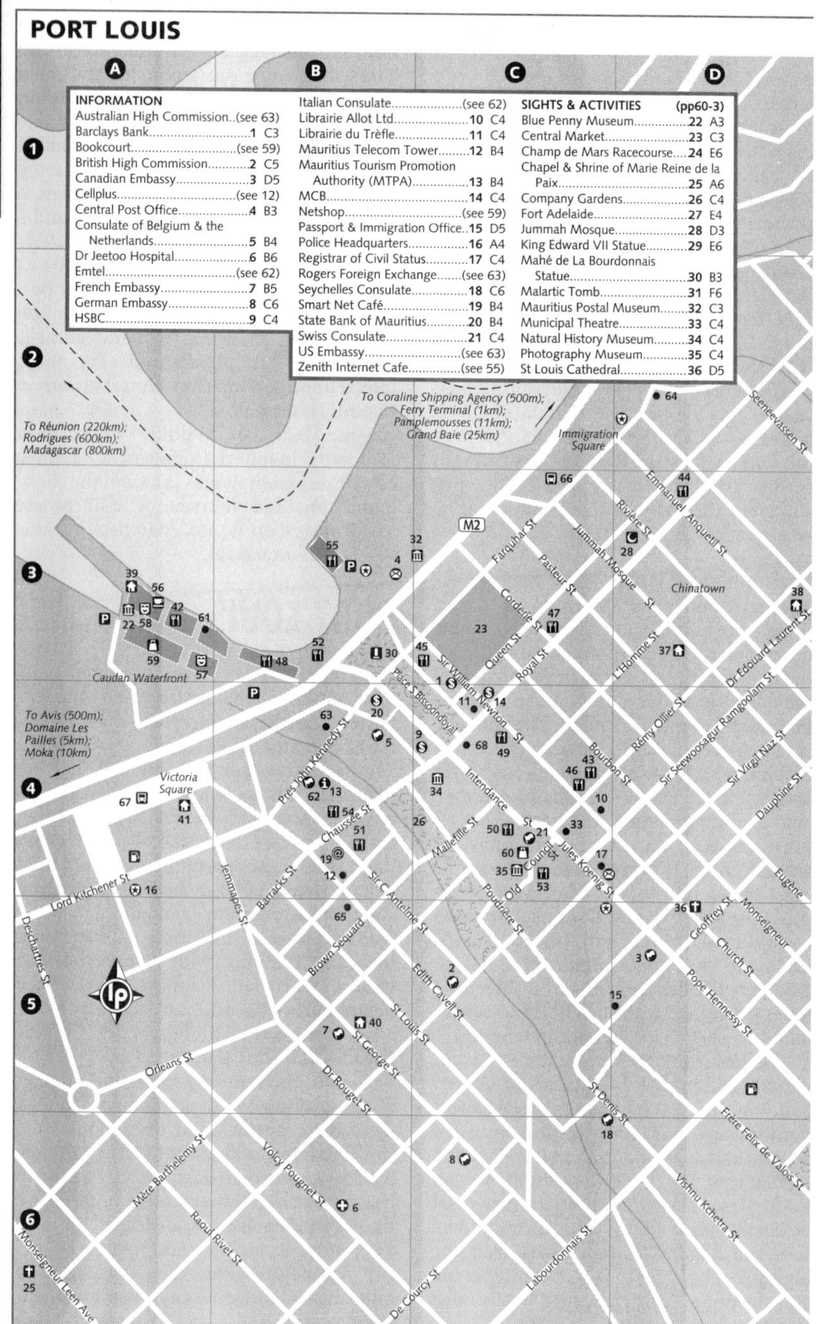
PORT LOUIS
A
B
C
D
1
2
3
4
5
6
INFORMATION
Australian High Commission..(see 63)
Barclays Bank............................1 C3
Bookcourt.............................(see 59)
British High Commission............2 C5
Canadian Embassy.....................3 D5
Cellplus.................................(see 12)
Central Post Office....................4 B3
Consulate of Belgium & the Netherlands..........................5 B4
Dr Jeetoo Hospital.....................6 B6
Emtel....................................(see 62)
French Embassy.........................7 B5
German Embassy.......................8 C6
HSBC.......................................9 C4
Italian Consulate...................(see 62)
Librairie Allot Ltd.....................10 C4
Librairie du Trèfle.....................11 C4
Mauritius Telecom Tower.........12 B4
Mauritius Tourism Promotion Authority (MTPA)...............13 B4
MCB..14 C4
Netshop...............................(see 59)
Passport & Immigration Office..15 D5
Police Headquarters................16 A4
Registrar of Civil Status............17 C4
Rogers Foreign Exchange.......(see 63)
Seychelles Consulate................18 C6
Smart Net Café........................19 B4
State Bank of Mauritius............20 B4
Swiss Consulate.......................21 C4
US Embassy..........................(see 63)
Zenith Internet Cafe..............(see 55)
SIGHTS & ACTIVITIES (pp60-3)
Blue Penny Museum................22 A3
Central Market........................23 C3
Champ de Mars Racecourse....24 E6
Chapel & Shrine of Marie Reine de la Paix..................................25 A6
Company Gardens..................26 C4
Fort Adelaide..........................27 E4
Jummah Mosque.....................28 D3
King Edward VII Statue............29 E6
Mahé de La Bourdonnais Statue................................30 B3
Malartic Tomb.........................31 F6
Mauritius Postal Museum........32 C3
Municipal Theatre...................33 C4
Natural History Museum..........34 C4
Photography Museum.............35 C4
St Louis Cathedral..................36 D5
To Coraline Shipping Agency (500m); Ferry Terminal (1km); Pamplemousses (11km); Grand Baie (25km)
To Réunion (220km); Rodrigues (600km); Madagascar (800km)
To Avis (500m); Domaine Les Pailles (5km); Moka (10km)
Immigration Square
Caudan Waterfront
Victoria Square
Chinatown
M2
Place S Bissoondoyal
Seeneevassen St
Emmanuel Anquetil St
Rivière St
Jummah Mosque St
Pasteur St
Farquhar St
Corderie St
Queen St
Royal St
L'Homme St
Dr Edouard Laurent St
Sir Seewoosagur Ramgoolam St
Rémy Ollier St
Sir Virgil Naz St
Dauphine St
Bourbon St
Sir William Newton St
Intendance St
Pres John Kennedy St
Chaussée St
Mallefille St
Old Council St
Jules Koenig St
Poudrière St
Barracks St
Jemmapes St
Lord Kitchener St
Deschartres St
Sir C Antelme St
Brown Sequard
Edith Cavell St
St Louis St
St George St
Dr Rouget St
Orleans St
Eugène
Geoffrey St
Monseigneur
Church St
Pope Hennessy St
St Denis St
Frère Felix de Valois St
Vishnu Kchetra St
Mère Barthelemy St
Volcy Pougnet St
Raoul Rivet St
Monseigneur Leen Ave
De Courcy St
Labourdonnais St

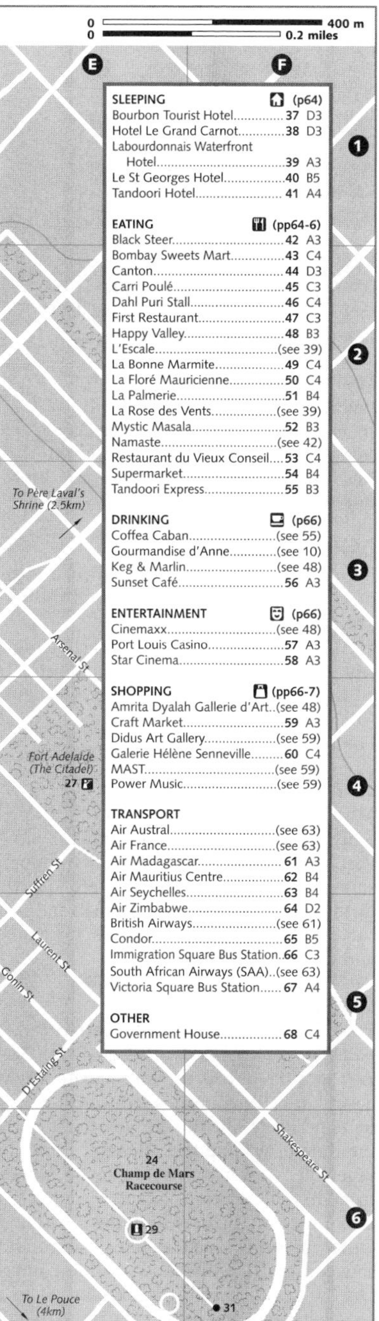

hills. By day, it is noisy and overcrowded and its roads clogged with traffic, while after hours the centre can seem deathly quiet. Add to this the lack of accommodation options and it's not surprising that many visitors tend to bypass the Mauritian capital and head straight for the beaches to the north and west. This is a shame because, once you get under its skin, the city can be an appealing place and deserves at least a day or two's exploration.

HISTORY

Port Louis was first settled in the 17th century by the Dutch, who called it Noordt Wester Haven. It was the French governor Bertrand François Mahé de Labourdonnais, however, who took the initiative and developed it into a busy capital and port after 1736. Labourdonnais is commemorated by a much-photographed statue at the seaward end of Place S Bissoondoyal (formerly Place d'Armes), the square which marks the city centre.

Few cities have bounced back from as many natural disasters as Port Louis. Between 1773 and 1892 a series of fires, plagues and tropical storms all tried, and failed, to level the town. In 1819 cholera arrived from Manila on the frigate *Topaz*, killing an estimated 700 Port Louis residents. Things quietened down until 1866, when malaria suddenly appeared on the scene, causing a further 3700 fatalities. Around this time people started heading for the cooler (and healthier) central plateau, so the town's population was mercifully small when the 1892 cyclone whipped through, destroying 3000 homes. The city recovered in terms of prosperity, but not in terms of population; most people working in Port Louis commute from the central plateau towns.

ORIENTATION

Built on a grid pattern and sloping gently down towards the harbour, the centre of Port Louis is easy to find your way around. The only disorienting thing can be the street names. Road signs mix English and French at random – terms such as 'rue' and 'street', or 'route' and 'road', are used interchangeably. Pedestrians should also beware of names that sound similar. For example, there are three E Laurent Sts (Eugène Laurent St, Dr Edouard Laurent St and Edgar Laurent St) within a few blocks of each other in the town centre. To complicate matters further, there's a tendency to change road names to reflect the current political mood.

The city centre is marked by Place S Bissoondoyal, a picturesque palm-lined avenue which runs from the harbour to Government House. From here nearly all the sites of interest are within easy walking distance. The main banks have their offices around this square or along nearby Sir William Newton St, while Royal St, which runs northeast through Chinatown, is also of interest to travellers.

Port Louis' two main bus stations are located either side of the city centre, each a few minutes' walk from Place S Bissoondoyal. Arriving from the airport, you'll be dropped at the more southerly, Victoria Square bus station.

INFORMATION

Bookshops

Bookcourt (☎ 211 9262; Caudan Waterfront) The country's best bookshop sells a broad range of English and French books, including guidebooks. Also good for newspapers and magazines.

Librairie Allot Ltd (☎ 212 7132; Happy World House, Sir William Newton St) Usually stocks the IGN map of Mauritius.

Librairie du Trèfle (☎ 212 1106; 5 Royal St)

Emergency

Ambulance (☎ 114)

Fire services (☎ 995)

Police (emergency ☎ 999; headquarters ☎ 203 1212; Line Barracks, Lord Kitchener St)

Internet Access

Netshop (☎ 213 1913; Caudan Waterfront)

Smart Net Café (☎ 210 2177; Ramphul Bldg, Chausée St)

Zenith Internet Café (Astrolabe, Port Louis Waterfront; 🕑 10am-8pm Mon-Thu, 10am-10pm Fri & Sat, 10am-4pm Sun) Open outside normal office hours.

Medical Services

Dr Jeetoo Hospital (☎ 212 3201; Volcy Pougnet St) Provides 24-hour medical and dental treatment and a 24-hour pharmacy. Staff speak English and French.

Money

All the major banks have ATMs and are open standard banking hours (9am-3.15pm Mon-Thu, 9am-5pm Fri).

Barclays (☎ 207 1800; Sir William Newton St)

HSBC (☎ 203 8333; Pl S Bissoondoyal)

State Bank (☎ 202 1111; State Bank Tower, Pl S Bissoondoyal)

MCB (☎ 202 5000; 9-15 Sir William Newton St)

Rogers Foreign Exchange (☎ 202 6608; Rogers House, 5 President John Kennedy St; 🕑 8.30am-4.15pm Mon-Fri, 9am-noon Sat) Exchange bureau (cash only) open slightly longer than standard banking hours.

Post

Central Post Office (☎ 208 2851; Place du Quai; 🕑 8.15am-4pm Mon-Fri, 8.15-11.45am Sat) The last 45 minutes before closing are for stamp sales only.

Tourist Information

Mauritius Tourism Promotion Authority (MTPA; ☎ 208 6397; Air Mauritius Centre, President John Kennedy St; ☎ 9am-4pm Mon-Fri, 9am-noon Sat) Distributes maps of Port Louis and Mauritius plus a limited range of brochures.

DANGERS & ANNOYANCES

Beware of pickpockets in the crowded alleys of Port Louis market and around the bus stations.

All travellers, but particularly single women, should stick to well-lit main streets at night and avoid Company Gardens, which after dark becomes a venue for Port Louis' low-key red-light district.

SIGHTS & ACTIVITIES

Most of Port Louis' sights are scattered around the waterfront and southeast along Poudrière St and Intendance St. Although some, such as Fort Adelaide, are slightly further out, the distances are small and you can easily hop around the shops, museums and the market in a day.

Central Market

Port Louis' much-touted **Central Market** (🕑 5.30am-5.30pm Mon-Sat, 5.30am-11.30pm Sun) isn't as authentic as the tour agents would have you believe, but it's still worth a visit to experience the hustle and bustle. At the time of writing the colourful fruit and vegetable market was about to be moved from its old location, along Farquhar St, into a new multistorey building next door. Other sections, such as the T-shirt and souvenir stalls, will follow in due course. On the seaward side of Farquhar St is a somewhat pungent meat and fish market.

OLIVIER CIRENDINI

Sea turtle (p35), Réunion

MICHAEL AW

Blue striped snapper (p33), Mauritius

Spotfin lionfish (p33), Mauritius

MICHAEL AW

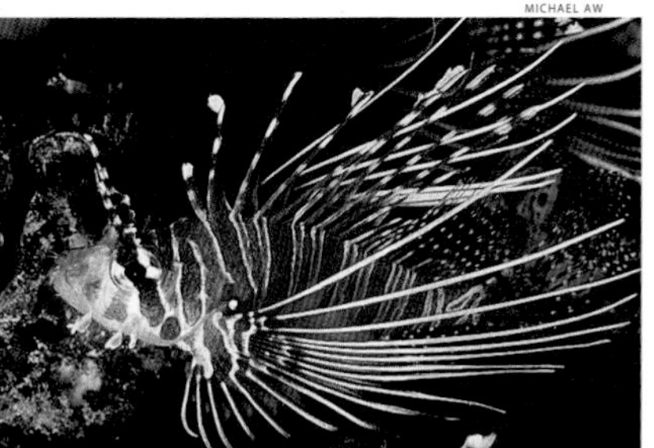

Whale shark (p41), Seychelles

LAWSON WOOD

MICHAEL AW

Giant moray (p33), Mauritius

LAWSON

Scuba diving (p40), Seychelles

Golden-cup coral (p33), Seychelles

LAWSON

PORT LOUIS IN TWO DAYS

Kick-start your day – and your senses – with a stroll through the **Central Market** (p60) to ogle the rainbow array of fruits and vegetables. Take breakfast on the hop, snacking on *dhal puris* (thin pancakes served with beans and chilli sauce) or *gâteaux piments* (deep-fried balls of lentils and chilli), washed down with a glass of *alouda* (a toothsome concoction of milk, fruit syrup and agar, a jelly-like substance made from seaweed). Pay your respects to the dodo at the **Natural History Museum** (p61), then head north via the eye-catching **Jummah Mosque** (p62) to lunch at one of **Chinatown's** (p62) top-class restaurants. Devote the afternoon to the fascinating **Blue Penny Museum** (p61) and a spot of shopping in the impressive **Caudan Waterfront** (p66) complex, before treating yourself to seafood feast and a night of luxury at the **Labourdonnais Waterfront Hotel** (p64).

On your second day step back in time with a visit to the **Photography Museum** (p62); climb to **Fort Adelaide** (p63) for a bird's-eye view of the city; and watch the world go by in the **Company Gardens** (p62). As the sun sets grab a ringside seat at one of bars and cafés on the waterfront, then tuck in to one of the cuisines on offer – Indian, Chinese, Creole? Take your pick.

For herbal cures and aphrodisiacs, head for the fruit and vegetable section, where a couple of vendors sell traditional herbal medicines, which they claim cure everything from obesity to stuttering. The cures are based on traditional Indian *ayurvedic* (herbal) medicine, and most take the form of leaves which you brew up into a tea. A one-month course of 'slimming herbs', for example, costs Rs 125.

If you're looking for souvenirs, a wide variety of Malagasy handicrafts are available, along with souvenir T-shirts of varying quality. The level of hustling here can be tiresome, however, and you'll have to bargain hard; start by slashing the price quoted by about 30%.

Blue Penny Museum

The star attractions of this ultramodern **museum** (☎ 210 8176; www.bluepennymuseum.com; Caudan Waterfront; adult/child Rs 120/80; 🕒 10am-4.30pm Mon-Sat) are two of the world's rarest stamps: the red one-penny and blue two-pence 'Post Office' stamps issued in 1847 (see Stamp of Approval, right). To preserve the colours, they are only lit up for 10 minutes at a time: every hour, on the half-hour.

You'll need an hour anyway to do the rest of the museum justice. Using original maps and documents, it traces the history of Mauritius from the island's discovery to the present day. There's a particularly good section on Port Louis, where 19th-century engravings make interesting comparisons with contemporary photos. Pride of place goes to a superbly lifelike statue by the Mauritian sculptor Prosper d'Épinay, carved in 1884. Based on Bernadin de St-Pierre's novel *Paul et Virginie* (Paul & Virginie, p85), it shows the young hero carrying his sweetheart across a raging torrent.

Natural History Museum

Most people visit this **museum** (☎ 212 0639; Chaussée St; admission free; 🕒 9am-4pm Mon, Tue, Thu & Fri, 9am-noon Sat) to see the famous – though somewhat grubby – reconstruction of a dodo. The curious looking bird was assembled by

STAMP OF APPROVAL

Philatelists (stamp collectors to the rest of us) go weak at the knees at the mention of the Mauritian 'Post Office' one-penny and two-pence stamps. Issued in 1847, these stamps were incorrectly printed with the words 'Post Office' rather than 'Post Paid'. They were recalled upon discovery of the error, but not before the wife of the British governor had mailed out a few dozen on invitations to one of her famous balls!

These stamps now rank among the most valuable in the world. The 'Bordeaux cover', a letter bearing both stamps which was mailed to France, was last sold for a staggering US$3.8 million. In 1993 a consortium of Mauritian companies paid US$2.2 million for the pair of unused one-penny and two-pence stamps now on display in Port Louis' Blue Penny Museum. This is the only place in the world where the two can be seen together on public view.

Scottish scientists in the late 19th century, using the only complete dodo skeleton in existence (see p55).

The rest of the museum features a missable collection of stuffed birds, including the solitaire and red rail, both also now extinct, and marine creatures.

Photography Museum

This small but engaging **museum** (☎ 211 1705; Old Council St; admission Rs 100; 10am-3pm Mon-Fri), down a lane opposite the Municipal Theatre, is the labour of love of local photographer Tristan Bréville. He's amassed a treasure trove of old cameras and prints, including several daguerreotypes (the forerunner of photographs) produced in Mauritius in 1840, just a few months after the technique was discovered in France. The museum also contains a vast archive of historical photos of the island, only a tiny fraction of which are on display.

Jummah Mosque

The **Jummah Mosque** (Royal St; 8am-noon & 2-4pm Mon-Thu, Sat & Sun), the most important mosque in Mauritius, was built in the 1850s, and is a delightful blend of Indian, Creole and Islamic architecture – it would look equally at home in Istanbul, Delhi or New Orleans! Visitors are welcome in the peaceful inner courtyard except on Fridays and during the month of Ramadan. (For more information on etiquette, see Responsible Travel, p48.)

Chinatown

The Chinese have traditionally occupied a quietly industrious position in the life of Port Louis. The region between the two 'friendship gates' on Royal St forms the centre of Port Louis' Chinatown. Though it's far less exuberant than, say, those of New York or London, you'll find a few Chinese temples and grocers here, and the streets echo with the unmistakable clatter of mah jong tiles (used in a game similar to dominos). It's here, too, that you'll find some of Port Louis' best Chinese restaurants.

Place S Bissoondoyal

This major thoroughfare is lined with royal palms and leads up to Government House, a beautiful French colonial structure which dates from 1738, though it was added to later. The statue of **Mahé de Labourdonnais** at the quayside end of the avenue is to Port Louis as the Little Mermaid is to Copenhagen.

Company Gardens

Beside the National History Museum on Chaussée St, this small park was once the vegetable patch of the French East India Company. Today it is home to some truly enormous banyan trees, providing a shady retreat for lovers, strollers and statues, including that of local sculptor Prosper d'Épinay and the much-loved musician Ti-Frère (see p52). The area is best avoided at night when it takes on a rather seedy air.

Municipal Theatre

This appealing theatre on Jules Koenig St has changed little since it was built in 1822, making it the oldest in the Indian Ocean. Decorated in the style of the classic London theatres, it seats about 600 on three levels, and has an exquisitely painted dome ceiling with cherubs and chandeliers. Photos of Margot Fonteyn, who danced here in 1975, adorn the foyer. If rehearsals are taking place, ask if you can go inside for a quick peek.

Mauritius Postal Museum

This two-room **museum** (☎ 208 2851; Pl du Quai; admission free; 9am-3.45pm Mon-Fri, 9-11.30am Sat) beside the central post office houses a mishmash of commemorative stamps and other postal paraphernalia. These include copies of the famous 'Post Office' stamps of 1847 (see Stamp of Approval, p61), though you can now see the originals in the Blue Penny Museum. The museum shop sells replica first-day covers of the famous stamps, which make unusual souvenirs.

Cathedrals & Churches

Notable places of worship include the **St James Cathedral** (Poudrière St) and **St Louis Cathedral** (Sir William Newton St). Inaugurated in 1850, St James has a peaceful, wood-panelled interior with plaques commemorating local worthies. The more austere, but also busier, St Louis dates from 1932.

The modern **chapel and shrine of Marie Reine de la Paix** (Monseigneur Leen Ave) is a popular spot for prayers, and the ornamental gardens offer views over the city. The most important place of pilgrimage for Mauritian Christians is the shrine of Père Laval on the city's northern outskirts (p68).

Fort Adelaide

Fort Adelaide, also known as the Citadel, resembles a Moorish fortress. Built by the British, the fort sits high on the crown of the hill, offering splendid views over the city and its harbour. The quickest route up is via Suffren St. Allow around 10 minutes for the climb.

Champ de Mars Racecourse

This racecourse was a military training ground until the **Mauritius Turf Club** (☎ 208 6047) was founded in 1812, making it the second oldest racecourse in the world. Mauritian independence was proclaimed here in 1968. Within the racecourse stands a statue of **King Edward VII** by the sculptor Prosper d'Épinay, and the **Malartic Tomb**, an obelisk to a French governor.

The racing season lasts from May to late November, with meetings usually held on a Saturday. The biggest race of all is the Maiden Cup in September. If you're here on a race day, it's well worth joining the throng of betting-crazy locals. Tickets for the stands cost Rs 150, but admission to the rest of the ground is usually free. For dates of meetings, contact the Mauritius Turf Club or check the local press.

WALKING TOUR

WALKING TOUR

Distance: 3.5km
Duration: 2hr

Starting at the seaward end of **Place S Bissoondoyal** (**1**; p62), walk inland towards **Government House** (**2**; p62), in front of which a decidedly imperious statue of Queen Victoria still stands guard. Turn right along Chausée St to pay a quick visit to the dodo in the **Natural History Museum** (**3**; p61), then cut up through **Company Gardens** (**4**; p62), which provides a rare patch of green in the city centre. A short way along Poudrière St, a cobbled lane, Old Council St, leads gently uphill to one of Port Louis' most attractive corners. Here you'll find a clutch of colonial buildings, one of which contains the **Photography Museum** (**5**; p62) while the **Restaurant du Vieux Conseil** (**6**; p65) occupies the courtyard of another. At the end, you

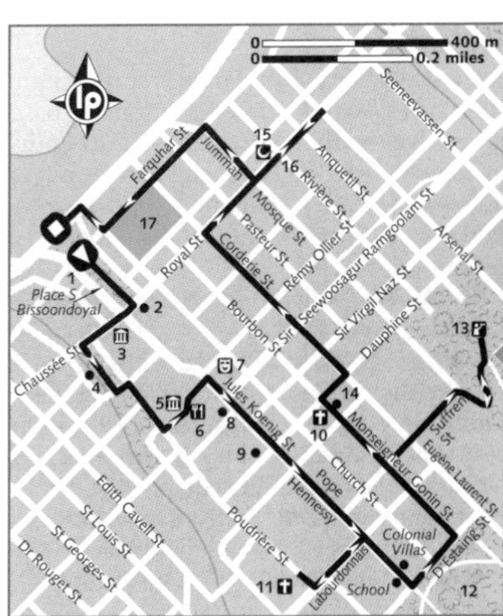

emerge in front of the neoclassic **Municipal Theatre** (**7**; p62).

Turning inland again, busy Jules Koenig St takes you past the modern and unprepossessing **City Hall** (**8**) and the more appealing **Supreme Court** (**9**), built in 1780, with its ornate gates and shady courtyard. A little further on, **St Louis Cathedral** (**10**; p62) lies off to your left (visible across an open square). You're now on Pope Hennessy St, from where you could take a short detour south along Labourdonnais St to **St James Cathedral** (**11**; p62).

A row of striking, colonial-era bungalows and a grey-stone secondary school, built in 1893, mark the top end of Pope Hennessy St. Beyond lies the **Champs de Mars racecourse** (**12**; p63), though outside the race season there's nothing particular to see. Better to save your energy for the climb to **Fort Adelaide** (**13**; p63) for expansive views.

From the fort, drop back down to Monseigneur Gonin St to see the grand, colonnaded **archbishop's residence** (**14**), then head north westwards along Corderie St, lined with cloth merchants, to Royal St. A right turn here brings you to the delightful **Jummah Mosque** (**15**; p62) and then to the first of the 'friendship gates' which marks the entrance to **Chinatown** (**16**; p62). When you've had your fill exploring, head down Jummah Mosque St to Farquhar St, turn left and you'll soon find yourself in the pell-mell of the **Central Market** (**17**; p60). Finally, take one of the underpasses to the waterfront for some well-earned refreshment.

SLEEPING

For a capital city, Port Louis is surprisingly short of accommodation. Most tourists base themselves on the coast and visit Port Louis on day trips. There's a clutch of budget hotels which are just about acceptable, one mid-range business hotel and one very plush option. That's it.

Le St Georges Hotel (☎ 211 2581; www.blue-season-hotels.com; 19 St Georges St; s/d incl breakfast Rs 1680/2160;) Popular with business-people, the St Georges is a fairly modern, multistorey place on a quiet street within easy walking distance of the centre. Spacious if characterless rooms are equipped with TV, phone and bathroom. There's a small business centre as well as a restaurant and bar.

Bourbon Tourist Hotel (☎ 240 4407; fax 242 2087; 36 Jummah Mosque St; s/d Rs 660/800;) Though it's expensive for what you get and has a distinctly institutional feel, this is the most appealing of the budget options. The rooms are large and clean, and come with a bathroom and TV as standard.

Hotel Le Grand Carnot (☎ 240 3054; 17 Dr Edouard Laurent St; s/d incl breakfast Rs 350/450) This is another OK budget option, consisting of tiny, fan-cooled cubicles. The front door's locked at 9.30pm; if you're back any later, you'll have to wake the owners to get inside.

Labourdonnais Waterfront Hotel (☎ 202 4000; www.labourdonnais.com; Caudan Waterfront; s/d incl breakfast US$260/400, turret rooms Rs 8500/12,250;) Right on the harbour, Port Louis' only luxury hotel caters primarily to business visitors. Around a vast atrium, the rooms are equipped to five-star standards. Best are the corner turret rooms with panoramic views. Facilities include three restaurants (p65), a piano bar, a health centre and childcare services. There are free boat transfers to the Maritim Hotel (p70) four days a week and sunset harbour cruises. Ask about discount rates at weekends.

Tandoori Hotel (☎ 212 0031; Jemmapes St; s/d Rs 300/400) The Tandoori is run down but popular for its cheap prices and friendly welcome. The rooms, all with fan and bathroom, are of dubious cleanliness and cop a bit of noise from the bus station right outside.

AUTHOR'S CHOICE

First Restaurant (☎ 212 0685; cnr Royal & Corderie Sts; mains Rs 85-450, dim sum per plate Rs 35 ; lunch & dinner Tue-Sun; dim sum lunch only;) At the top of a narrow stairwell, this unusually stylish Chinese restaurant offers good-quality food at affordable prices. At lunch it's hard to resist the dim sum trolley, though there's no shortage of tempting fare on the menu, from standard fried rice and noodle dishes to delicacies such as whole steamed fish with ginger and a broad range of vegetarian choices. Or treat yourself to roast duck from among the pricier house specials. The food is fresh, filling and tasty and the service excellent. Reservations are a must for Saturday and Sunday lunch.

EATING

While short on hotels, Port Louis offers a decent variety of eating options. The city is spiced with small, cheap establishments ranging from street stalls to canteen-style outlets. There's also a good choice of more expensive restaurants serving Indian, Chinese, Creole or European fare, though little specifically for vegetarians. The main drawback is that many places close in the evening and on Sunday; those in the waterfront complex are a useful exception.

Budget

Canton (☎ 241 4911, 15 Emmanuel Anquetil St; mains from Rs 60; 10am-8pm Mon-Sat;) Plastic tablecloths and floral wallpaper give this Chinese restaurant a homey feel, matched by the hearty portions of sweet-and-sour chicken, prawn chop suey and a bewildering variety of noodle dishes. Quick service and cheap prices draw a mainly local crowd.

La Bonne Marmite (☎ 212 4406; 18 Sir William Newton St; set menus around Rs 110; lunch only Mon-Fri;) While it looks smart, with its fountain and cane chairs, this bright little restaurant offers surprisingly good-value Indian, Creole and Chinese set lunches. There's always one vegetarian option. Upstairs is a more formal restaurant serving Indian, Creole and French dishes from Rs 300.

Tandoori Express (☎ 210 9898; Astrolabe Bldg, Port Louis Waterfront; mains Rs 65-180, set menus Rs 120-160; lunch & dinner, closed Sun and dinner Mon) This cheap and cheerful canteen offers authentic Indian food – such as Goan fish curry, rice and naan bread, and vegetarian platters – to take away or eat at tables on the waterfront.

Mystic Masala (Port Louis Waterfront; set menus Rs 60-110 lunch & dinner) Tasty Indian snacks and light meals are the order of the day at this harbourfront kiosk with its handful of trestle tables. Portions aren't huge but a side order of samosas or a *dosa masala* (pancake-like bread with a spicy potato filling) and a glass of *lassi* (yoghurt drink) or *alouda* (sweet, milky drink) will round things off nicely.

Mid-Range

La Flore Mauricienne (212 2200; 10 Intendance St; mains Rs 150-450; 7.30am-5pm Mon-Fri, 8.30am-1pm Sat;) Best for its bustling terrace (though there's also a more formal, air-con dining area inside), this café-restaurant near Government House is something of an institution; a popular lunch spot for office workers and tourists alike. Plump for a quick quiche and salad, take pot luck with the daily special (which might be pork chops with mustard) or perhaps opt for a Creole curry. Vegetarians are well catered for with salads and Indian set meals. Afterwards, indulge yourself at the bakery counter.

Restaurant du Vieux Conseil (211 0393; Old Council St; mains Rs 200-300; lunch Mon-Sat) There's no better refuge from the city streets than the quiet and shady courtyard of this old Creole villa. The menu features a limited range of Creole-French dishes such as octopus salad with Rodrigues lemon or palm heart with smoked marlin for starters, followed by hare with mustard or fish vindaloo. The service is efficient and friendly and the food perfectly acceptable, though don't expect any fireworks.

Carri Poulé (212 1295; Place S Bissoondoyal; vegetarian dishes from Rs 115, meat dishes from Rs 230; lunch Mon-Sat, dinner Fri & Sat;) While lacking in ambience, Carri Poulé arguably dishes up some of the best Indian fare in town. There's a vast range of curries and tandoori favourites to choose from, not to mention naan breads, samosas and other side orders. The lunch-time buffet (Rs 350) offers good value for those with a hearty appetite.

Happy Valley (210 1228; Port Louis Waterfront; mains Rs 80-250; lunch & dinner, closed lunch Sun;) A friendly place on the 2nd floor serving reasonable Chinese fare, including delicacies such as jellyfish salad as well as more mainstream choices. Portions are generous and the balcony tables perfect for people-watching.

La Palmeraie (212 2597, 7 Sir Célicourt Antelme St; mains from Rs 150; lunch Mon-Fri;) Among the street stalls, this cool, soft-lit cavern comes as a surprise. The speciality is seafood served French or Creole style: prawns with white butter, for example, or seafood omelette. It's all very fresh and tasty.

Black Steer (211 9147; Caudan Waterfront; burgers Rs 150-200, grills from Rs 250; lunch & dinner;) This popular steakhouse overlooks the harbour and offers great steaks, mixed grills, combos and the like. It's now added a few dishes for non-carnivores, such as baked spuds and vegetable curries.

Top End

Namaste (211 6710; Caudan Waterfront; meat dishes from Rs 230, vegetarian dishes from Rs 135; lunch & dinner, closed lunch Sun;) Upmarket Indian restaurant with a solid reputation for its North Indian cuisine. The Saturday lunch buffet (Rs 460) is worth a splurge. Otherwise, portions are a touch small, but well prepared, and the service is suitably attentive. At night the two-person balcony tables offer romantic harbour views.

L'Escale (202 4000; Labourdonnais Waterfront Hotel, Caudan Waterfront; mains from around Rs 200; 6.30am-11pm;) Situated in the lobby of the Labourdonnais Waterfront Hotel (p64), this is the place to come for a dose of pampering. The broad menu includes Thai, Moroccan and European dishes and covers everything from salads, pizzas and burgers to local curries. It's strong on desserts, too – treat yourself to a lemon cheesecake or banana crumble.

La Rose des Vents (202 4000; Labourdonnais Waterfront Hotel, Caudan Waterfront; mains Rs 300-800; lunch & dinner, closed Sat lunch & Sun;) The Labourdonnais Waterfront Hotel (p64) also boasts an upmarket seafood restaurant, with goodies such as steamed lobster with lemon grass and ginger, followed perhaps by a trilogy of *crème brûlée*. Nonresidents should book ahead.

Quick Eats

Port Louis is a snackers' paradise. The Central Market and bus stations provide happy hunting grounds, but you'll find stalls all over town peddling samosas and *gâteaux piments*, sandwiches or more substantial curries. To spot the best just look for the queues from mid-morning onwards. A perennial favourite is the *dhal puris* **stall** (cnr Sir William Newton & Rémy Ollier St). Nearby, **Bombay Sweets Mart** (7 Rémy Ollier St) is famous for the Indian nibbles colourfully known as *caca pigeon* (literally, 'pigeon droppings'). It also sells other sweet and savoury snacks. If you'd rather sit down to eat, head for Tandoori Express or Mystic Masala (see p65).

Self-Catering

Self-caterers should head for the Central Market. There's also a handy **supermarket** (Sir Célicourt Antelme St). Most restaurants, apart from the very expensive ones, do takeaway.

DRINKING

Port Louis' café and bar life centres on the waterfront complex. This is very much the place to be seen, and at weekends places are packed with well-heeled Mauritian families, expats, tourists and visiting sailors.

Keg & Marlin (☎ 211 6821; Port Louis Waterfront; noon-midnight Mon-Thu, to 3am Fri, to 1am Sat & Sun;) Port Louis' most popular watering hole is a passable copy of an English pub, complete with traditional bar food and screenings of major sports events. Phoenix is the beer of choice, but it also stocks a decent range of imported brews.

Coffea Caban (☎ 210 5376; Astrolabe Bldg, Port Louis Waterfront; 9.30am-9.30pm;) Caffeine addicts lusting after a cappuccino, mocaccino or café latte will find relief on the harbour's north side. Coffea Caban also serves teas, hot chocolate and milk shakes, and the waterside tables make a pleasant place to hang out.

Sunset Café (☎ 211 9137; Caudan Waterfront; 9am-10pm Mon-Thu, to midnight Fri & Sat, to 11pm Sun;) A rather pricey French-style café, but a nice spot to linger while the sun goes down.

Among the few cafés scattered around the rest of town, **La Flore Mauricienne** (☎ 212 2200; 10 Intendance St; 7.30am-5pm Mon-Fri, 8.30am-1pm Sat;) and **Gourmandise d'Anne** (☎ 208 0606; Happy World House, Sir William Newton St; 9am-5pm Mon-Fri, 9am-noon Sat;) are worth seeking out.

ENTERTAINMENT

While the opening of the Caudan Waterfront complex transformed Port Louis' nightlife, don't expect to be dancing till dawn. The best on offer are the bars (see left) – including just one live-music venue – and cinemas, or you can chance your luck at the casino. On the cultural side, it's worth checking what's on at the Municipal Theatre.

Casino

Port Louis Casino (☎ 210 4203; Caudan Waterfront; 10am-4am, gaming tables 8pm-4am;) If you're feeling lucky, head for the incongruous ship-shaped building on the waterfront. There are slot machines downstairs and blackjack and American roulette on the 1st floor. Smart-casual dress is required.

Cinemas

Star Cinema (☎ 211 5361; Caudan Waterfront; tickets Rs 120;) This is Port Louis' biggest and best cinema, with three screens offering mainstream international releases. Films are generally dubbed into French and there are usually four or five performances a day.

Cinemaxx (☎ 210 7416; Port Louis Waterfront; tickets Rs 100;) The two-screen Cinemaxx usually shows one Hindi or Tamil film and one international release daily. Again, most films are dubbed into French, though occasionally you'll find one with English subtitles.

Live Music

Keg & Marlin (☎ 211 6821; Port Louis Waterfront; noon-midnight Mon-Thu, to 3am Fri, to 1am Sat & Sun,) Friday night sees this pub packed to the gills as the house band lets rip. The music's as eclectic as the crowd. Smart-casual dress is required.

Theatre

Municipal Theatre (Jules Koenig St) There are frequent plays – in French, English and Creole – as well as jazz and classical music recitals at Port Louis' principal theatre. Ticket prices vary, but most events cost around Rs 100. Look for announcements in the local press or call the tourist office to find out what's on.

SHOPPING

Port Louis **Central Market** (5.30am-5.30pm Mon-Sat, 5.30am-11.30pm Sun) has a wide selection of T-shirts, basketry, spices and other souvenirs; you'll need to bargain to get a decent price. Less fun but also less hassle, the **Craft Market** (☎ 210 0139) in the Caudan Waterfront offers more upmarket souvenirs, such as Mauritius glass (p93) and essential oils from the Domaine de l'Ylang Ylang (p116). The model ship manufacturer **MAST** (☎ 211 7170) also has an outlet here.

The Caudan Waterfront is also the place to go for trendy knick-knacks and designer boutiques, including Floreal, Maille St, Shibani, IV Pl@y and Habit (for more information see p137). **Bookcourt** (☎ 211 9262) boasts the city's best choice of books and magazines, while **Power Music** (☎ 211 9143) has a good selection of CDs by local artists.

Works of art make evocative souvenirs. Port Louis is home to several galleries featuring local artists, notably **Didus Art Gallery** (☎ 210 7438; Caudan Waterfront), **Amrita Dyalah Galerie d'Art** (☎ 213 1551; Port Louis Waterfront) and **Galerie Hélène Senneville** (☎ 212 8339; Old Council St).

GETTING THERE & AWAY

Air

All of the major airlines have offices in Port Louis.

Air France (☎ 208 7070; Rogers House, 5 President John Kennedy St, Port Louis)
Air Madagascar (☎ 203 2156; IBL House, Caudan Waterfront, Port Louis)
Air Zimbabwe (☎ 241 1573; IKS Bldg, Farquhar St, Port Louis)
British Airways (☎ 202 8000; IBL House, Caudan Waterfront, Port Louis)
Condor (☎ 207 3034; 18 Edith Cavell St, Port Louis)
South African Airways (☎ 213 0700; Rogers House, 5 President John Kennedy St, Port Louis)

Bus

Port Louis' two bus stations are both located in the city centre. Buses for northern and eastern destinations, such as Trou aux Biches, Grand Baie and Pamplemousses, leave from Immigration Square, northeast of the Central Market.

Buses for southern and western destinations, such as Mahébourg, Curepipe and Quatre Bornes, use the Victoria Square terminus just south of the centre.

The first departure on most routes is at about 6am; the last leaves at around 6pm.

Car

Car rental is expensive in Port Louis. You'll find better rates in the major tourist centres such as Grand Baie, Flic en Flac or Mahébourg.

Ferry

Ferries to Rodrigues and Rèunion dock beside the new passenger terminal on Quai D of Port-Louis harbour, about 1km northwest of town. For further information about boats to and from Rodrigues see p140, and p139 for Réunion.

GETTING AROUND

To/From the Airport

There are no special airport buses, but regular services between Port Louis and Mahébourg call at the airport; the stop is near the roundabout, roughly 300m from the terminal buildings. Heading to the airport from Port Louis, allow two hours to be on the safe side and make sure the conductor knows where you're going, as drivers occasionally skip the detour down to the airport.

Expect to pay around Rs 650 to Rs 700 for a taxi ride from Port Louis to the airport.

Car

Given the number of traffic snarls, it's not worth trying to drive around Port Louis. Day-trippers are advised to leave their car in one of the car parks in the waterfront complex. These are open from 7am to 11pm and cost Rs 25 for the first four hours plus Rs 25 for each additional hour.

Cars can be parked on the street for a maximum of two hours at a time in any one place and the appropriate number of parking coupons must be displayed on the dashboard. See p142 for more about street parking.

Taxi

Expect to pay around Rs 50 for a short taxi ride across town, and slightly more at night. As usual, make sure you agree a price before setting off. It's best to avoid using taxis during the morning and evening rush hours, when you'll probably end up just sitting in a queue. See p143 for more information on taxis.

AROUND PORT LOUIS

Domaine Les Pailles

About 5km south of Port Louis, the former sugar estate of **Domaine Les Pailles** (Map p87;

(☎ 286 4225; www.domainelespailles.net; ⏲ 10am-5pm) has been transformed into a cultural and heritage centre which provides for an enjoyable day or half-day excursion. The facilities include rides in horse-drawn carriages, a miniature railway, a working replica of a traditional ox-driven sugar mill, a rum distillery producing the estate's own brew, a spice garden and a children's playground. A quad-biking circuit has also recently been added.

Visitors can choose to tour the site by train, horse carriage or jeep, with the cost of entry varying accordingly. The cheapest options are one-hour tours by train at Rs 245/135 per adult/child and by horse-drawn carriage at Rs 265/145. A jeep safari costs Rs 555/280 and more expensive packages including lunch are also available. Quad biking costs from Rs 400 for 30 minutes.

On weekdays it's also possible to trek around the estate. Call the riding centre, **Les Écuries du Domaine** (☎ 286 4240; ⏲ 8am-5.30pm Mon-Fri, 8am-noon Sat), to make a reservation. An hour's trekking costs Rs 770 per person.

The Domaine also has a selection of upmarket restaurants. Best of the bunch are the **Clos St Louis** (mains Rs 280-450; ⏲ lunch Mon-Sat, dinner Fri & Sat), in a replica colonial villa, which offers top-notch Creole and French cuisine, and **Indra** (mains from Rs 250; ⏲ lunch & dinner Mon-Sat), which serves excellent Indian fare.

To get to the Domaine, take any bus running between Port Louis and Curepipe and ask to be let off at the turning for Domaine Les Pailles (it's clearly signposted). From the main road it takes less than half an hour on foot to the reception centre. Alternatively, it's a 10-minute taxi ride from Port Louis or Moka.

Père Laval's Shrine

The **shrine** (☎ 242 2129; ⏲ 8.30am-noon & 1-4.45pm Mon-Sat, 10am-noon & 1-4pm Sun) of the Catholic French priest and missionary Père Jacques Désiré Laval is something of a Lourdes of the Indian Ocean, with many miracles attributed to visits to the priest's grave. The padre died in 1864 and was beatified in 1979 during a visit by Pope John Paul II. He is credited with converting 67,000 people to Christianity during his 23 years in Mauritius.

Today Père Laval is a popular figure for Mauritians of all religions. Pilgrims come here from as far afield as South Africa, Britain and France to commemorate the anniversary of his death on 9 September. The coloured plaster effigy of the priest that lies on top of the tomb has been rubbed smooth in places by pilgrims touching it in the hope of miracle cures.

At other times of year the shrine is fairly quiet, though the services held on Friday at 1pm and 5pm attract a reasonable crowd. In the same complex is a large modern church and a shop with a permanent exhibition of Père Laval's robe, mitre, letters and photographs.

To get to the shrine, take a bus signed 'Cité La Cure' or 'Père Laval' from the Immigration Square bus station in Port Louis.

NORTH MAURITIUS

Rocky headlands and long, white-sand beaches fringe the northwest coast of Mauritius. This coast is also one of the more heavily developed, with a vast array of hotels, apartments and guesthouses, and numerous activities for tourists. The lagoon, sheltered from the prevailing winds, offer a host of water sports and is particularly good for snorkelling and diving. Yacht cruises to the offshore islands are also popular, as are trips in glass-bottomed boats and even undersea walks – a bizarre experience not to be missed.

All these facilities combined with good transport links makes the northwest coast a convenient place to base yourself. The big hotels start with a bang in the south around the attractive Baie de l'Arsenal, while further north Trou aux Biches marks the start of a terrific beach stretching as far as Mont Choisy, where several luxury hotels have sprung up. Trou aux Biches is developing fast – too fast for some – but for now it's still pleasantly quiet and relaxed, and relatively cheap.

Continuing north, Grand Baie is a bustling holiday centre, which even boasts a clutch of bars and discos for those hankering after some nightlife. Others will prefer to base themselves in the quieter town of Pereybère on a much better, cleaner beach a few kilometres up the coast.

Beyond Pereybère the beaches and hotels largely peter out and the scenery gets wilder as you round Cap Malheureux, offering uninterrupted views of Coin de Mire, and

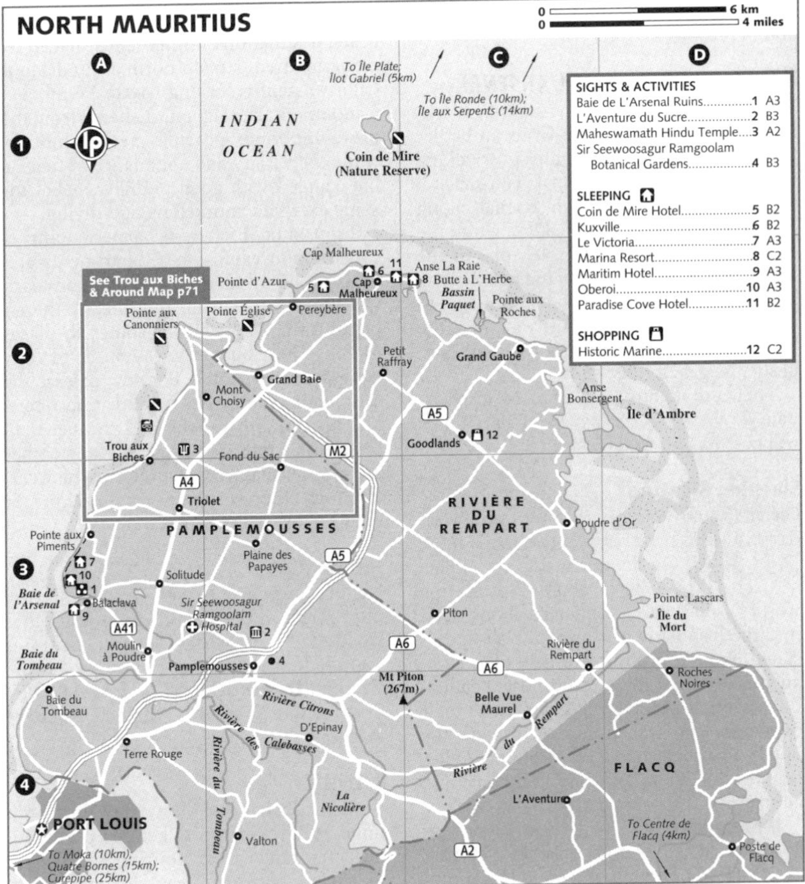

come onto the windward side of the island. There is equally scant development on the northeast coast. For those wanting to get away from it all, Grand Gaube has one appealing hotel on a crescent of sugar-white sand.

In the interior, a plain of sugar-cane fields, pocked with piles of volcanic boulders, slopes gently down to the sea. The area is home to two major attractions near the town of Pamplemousses: the Sir Seewoosagur Ramgoolam Botanical Gardens and a fascinating museum dedicated to sugar.

Getting There & Around

The most useful bus routes in and around this area are those running from Port Louis' Immigration Square bus station up the coast to Trou aux Biches, Grand Baie, Pereybère and Cap Malheureux. There are also express services direct from Port Louis to Grand Baie. Port Louis is also the starting point for buses via Pamplemousses to Grand Gaube.

To reach this area from the airport you'll need to change buses in Port Louis. Alternatively, a taxi to towns along the northwest coast should cost in the region of Rs 800. Count on around Rs 1000 to Grand Gaube.

Many hotels and guesthouses have bikes for rent and can help organise car rental. Otherwise, you can approach the rental agencies direct. The largest concentration is in Grand Baie, and there are a smattering of outlets in and around Trou aux Biches and Pereybère.

BALACLAVA & BAIE DE L'ARSENAL

Balaclava is named after the region's black-lava rocks, rather than the Crimean battlefield. It is an attractive wild area overlooking the secluded Baie de l'Arsenal. You can still see the **ruins** of the French arsenal, along with a flour mill and a lime kiln, within the grounds of the Maritim Hotel, one of the more sympathetic of several big hotels along here. Nonresidents can obtain permission to visit the ruins from the security guard at the hotel entrance; the track begins about 30m inside the gate to the right.

There are no bus services to Balaclava or Baie de l'Arsenal. A taxi from Port Louis will cost Rs 250 to Rs 300.

Sleeping & Eating

Oberoi (☎ 204 3600; www.oberoihotels.com; Pte aux Piments; d from Rs 21,000, with private pool from Rs 37,500;) On the north side of the Baie d'Arsenal, the Oberoi counts among the world's great hotels. Wooden pavilions blend into the lush gardens. Inside it's all understated luxury, an inventive mix of African and Asian design, making the most of natural light. More expensive villas come with their own pool and walled garden, though the hotel's two main pools are stunning. Other facilities include a top-class health spa and all manner of sports activities.

Maritim Hotel (☎ 204 1000; www.maritim.de; Balaclava; s/d incl breakfast from Rs 5400/8000;) Though older and less sumptuous than the Oberoi, the Maritim deserves its five stars nonetheless. Its main plus points are a 25-hectare park, complete with a nine-hole golf course, tennis courts and riding stables. It has a great beach where guests can indulge in everything from snorkelling to water-skiing, and a choice of three restaurants.

Le Victoria (☎ 204 2000; www.levictoria-hotel.com; Pte aux Piments; s/d half board from Rs 4250/6250;) This relaxed four-star hotel is popular with families and water-sports enthusiasts. Guests can also make use of facilities at other Beachcomber hotels.

TROU AUX BICHES & AROUND

About 20km north of Port Louis, Trou aux Biches (Hole of the Does) is rapidly becoming one of Mauritius' most popular beach destinations. White sands shaded by casuarina trees stretch north around Mont Choisy's gently curving bay to Pointe aux Canonniers. The lagoon, sheltered from the prevailing winds, provides great swimming, while the variety and abundance of marine life coupled with good visibility makes for some excellent snorkelling and diving.

Trou aux Biches is experiencing a construction explosion as apartments and villas go up all along this stretch of coast. On the positive side, this means there's plenty of choice when it comes to places to stay, from budget guesthouses to fully equipped resort hotels. For now, at least, the area retains some of its relaxed atmosphere, and it's certainly quieter and cheaper than Grand Baie to the north. Even the beaches are pleasantly uncrowded during the week, although there's fierce competition for picnic spots at weekends.

Information

Neither Trou aux Biches or Mont Choisy offer much in the way of shops and other facilities. There are a few grocery stores scattered around and a branch of the **Mauritius Commercial Bank** (MCB; Royal Rd, Mont Choisy), with a 24-hour ATM and a **bureau de change** (9am-5pm Mon-Fri, 9am-noon Sat).

Activities

Trou aux Biches and Mont Choisy are both important water-sports centres. Activities on offer range from touring the lagoon in a glass-bottomed boat to parasailing, water-skiing, deep-sea fishing and diving. Nondivers can experience the next best thing with a ride in a submarine. Most hotels and guesthouses can help organise excursions. Alternatively, contact one of the tour agents in Grand Baie (p75).

Snorkelling equipment (Rs 150 per day) can be rented at the **boat house** (☎ 728 4335; 9am-5pm) on Trou aux Biches public beach. The latter also rents out pedalos and kayaks (Rs 300 per hour) and offers a variety of other activities, including glass-bottomed boat tours (Rs 300 per hour per person), water-skiing (Rs 500 for 12 minutes) and parasailing (Rs 800 for 10 minutes).

Prices are similar at the **Casuarina Hotel boat house** (☎ 759 1127; Mont Choisy; 9am-5pm). In addition, they also offer windsurfing

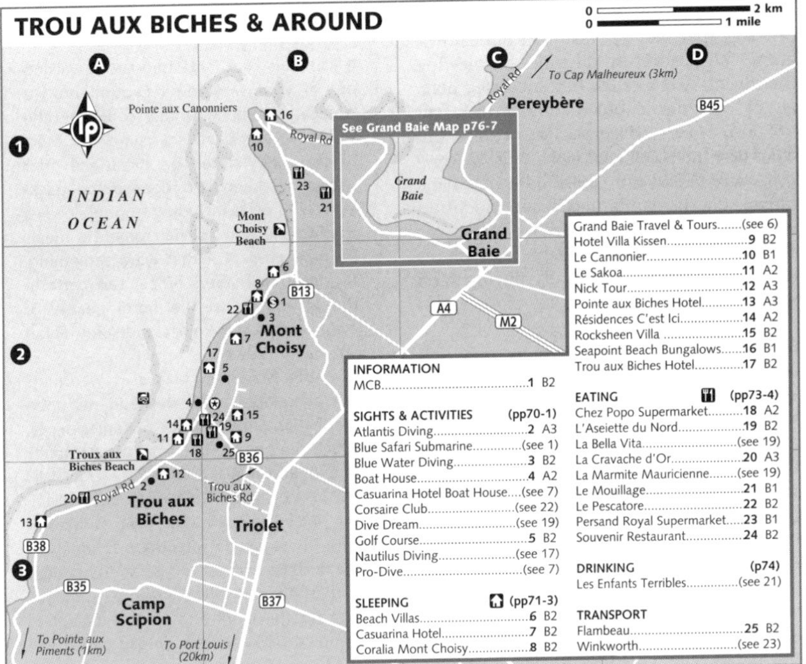

(Rs 300 per hour) and catamaran outings to the Northern Islands (p80).

DEEP-SEA FISHING

Deep-sea anglers should head for the **Corsaire Club** (☎ 265 5209; fax 265 6267; 🕑 9am-5pm) beside Le Pescatore restaurant in Mont Choisy. A half-day's boat charter costs around Rs 11,000, and a full day will set you back Rs 12,000.

DIVING

Dive centres consistently recommended for their professional and friendly service are **Nautilus Diving** (☎ 265 5495; ricana@intnet.mu; 🕑 10am-4pm Mon-Sat) at the Trou aux Biches Hotel and **Atlantis Diving** (☎ 265 7172; atlantis_divers@yahoo.co.uk; 🕑 8am-5pm) further south along the main road.

Other good options in the area include **Pro-Dive** (☎ 265 6213; www.geocities.com/padgraphics/prodive; 🕑 8.30am-6.30pm Mon-Sat) at the Casuarina Hotel, **Dive Dream** (☎ 257 2848; www.divedream.net; Trou aux Biches; 🕑 9am-5pm) and **Blue Water Diving** (☎ 265 7186; www.bluewaterdivingcenter.com; Mont Choisy; 🕑 8.30am-4.30pm).

Dives start at around Rs 750 to Rs 800, rising to Rs 1000 or so for a night dive.

GOLF

The nine-hole **golf course** (☎ 204 6565; 🕑 7am-6pm; green fee Rs 600, club hire Rs 275) at the Trou aux Biches Hotel is one of the few public-access courses in Mauritius.

SUBMARINE RIDES

If you fancy diving but don't want to get wet, **Blue Safari Submarine** (☎ 263 3333; www.blue-safari.com; Mont Choisy; adult/child Rs 2650/1400; 🕑 9am-4pm) takes you down among the coral and fishes to a depth of 35m. The ride lasts roughly two hours, of which 40 minutes are spent underwater, with departures every hour according to demand. Reservations are recommended at least a day in advance. The company also maintains an **office** (Map p76-7; Royal Rd, Grand Baie; 🕑 8am-6pm) in Grand Baie.

Sleeping

It seems almost every building along this stretch of coast is available for rent in some shape or form. Much of the accommodation is in the mid-range and consists of self-catering apartments, villas and bungalows, often with terraces or balconies for viewing the sunset. A few of the best are listed here.

For a wider choice, contact **Nick Tour** (☎ 265 5279; nicktour@intnet.mu; Trou aux Biches) and **Grand Baie Travel and Tours** (GBTT; ☎ 265 5261; www.gbtt.com; Beach Villas; Mont Choisy); both manage a range of well-maintained accommodation in the area.

Book well in advance as the best places fill up in a flash – especially during high season.

BUDGET

Rocksheen Villa (☎ 265 5043; www.rocksheenvilla.com; 161 Morcellement Jhuboo, Trou aux Biches; s/d incl breakfast Rs 500/600, studio from Rs 600;) Down a quiet side street about 300m back from the beach is this homely guesthouse run by an unfailingly helpful Scottish-Mauritian couple. Well run and spotlessly clean, the place receives consistently good reports from travellers. You need to book well ahead, although if it's full, the owners can usually suggest alternatives.

Hotel Villa Kissen (☎ 265 5523; sandonna@intnet.mu; Trou aux Biches; s/d incl breakfast Rs 450/600) This friendly guesthouse on the main road is a good budget option. Unfussy but decent-sized rooms come with private bathroom. The front rooms can be a bit noisy.

MID-RANGE

Le Sakoa (☎ 265 5242; www.lesakoa.com; Trou aux Biches; d incl breakfast from Rs 2500;) Prices at this intimate and stylish hotel are surprisingly affordable. Well-proportioned rooms are decked out with great attention to detail, including a fully equipped kitchenette and generous verandas. There's a good restaurant – the candlelit Mauritian buffet on Wednesday night (Rs 450; reservations required for nonguests) is worth a splurge – and it's on a decent stretch of beach.

Résidences C'est Ici (☎ 265 5231; c.ici@intnet.mu; Trou aux Biches; studio/apt from Rs 1350/1500;) This hotel has spruce, well-equipped self-catering accommodation at very reasonable prices. From two-person studios to apartments for up to five, each has its own terrace. It's set among coconut palms right on the beach.

Beach Villas (☎ 265 5261; www.gbtt.com; Mont Choisy; studio/apt from Rs 1600/2650;) This little group of self-catering studios (for two persons) and apartments (for up to four) stands out for its friendly and efficient service. The accommodation itself is perfectly comfortable, if unexciting. The rental agency Grand Baie Travel and Tours is based here.

Coralia Mont Choisy (☎ 265 6070; mont_choisy@intnet.mu; Mont Choisy; s/d incl breakfast Rs 3865/5150; half board Rs 4620/6665;) The strong points of this three-star hotel are the variety of free sports on offer (including tennis, water-skiing and windsurfing), the facilities available for children and its location on a good beach. The bright, cheery rooms are furnished to a reasonable standard.

Casuarina Hotel (☎ 265 6552; casuarina@intnet.mu; Trou aux Biches; s/d half board from Rs 2660/4000, apt from Rs 4450;) Whitewashed walls, archways and fountains lend a vaguely Moorish air to this attractive hotel set in well-established gardens. Facilities include three restaurants, two pools, a kids' club and free water sports for guests. A small minus point: you have to cross the road to reach the hotel beach.

WEDDING BELLS

If you have ever fantasised about walking out of your wedding reception onto a tropical beach, Mauritius could be the venue you've been searching for. Most of the luxury hotels on the island offer special wedding and honeymoon packages, with perks including tropical flowers, champagne and special romantic meals for newlyweds. For that extra something, the local civil status officer can perform the ceremony on the hotel beach, or even underwater courtesy of Blue Safari Submarine (see p71).

Under Mauritian law, civil weddings can be celebrated by nonresidents upon production of a certificate of nonresidency, which can be obtained from the **Registrar of Civil Status** (Map p58; ☎ 201 1727; civstat@intnet.mu; Emmanuel Anquetil Bldg, Jules Koenig St, Port Louis). The application process takes at least 10 days, and requires two copies of the birth certificates and passports of both parties. Alternatively, you can let someone else do the work and book a complete wedding package from abroad direct with the hotel or through a travel agent.

Other recommendations:

Seapoint Beach Bungalows (☎ 696 4804; www.seapointbungalows.com; Pte aux Canonniers; studio Rs 2000, apt from Rs 2400) A secluded complex of self-catering studios and apartments on the beach.

Pointe aux Biches Hotel (☎ 265 6297; pabhotel@intnet.mu; Pte aux Piments; s/d incl breakfast from Rs 925/1600;) A slightly cramped but comfortable and inexpensive three-star hotel. Half-board deals available.

TOP END

Le Canonnier (☎ 263 7000; www.lecanonnier-hotel.com; Pte aux Canonniers; s/d half board from Rs 5300/7050;) Lush gardens complete with an old fort, cannons and a humungous banyan tree give a real lost-world feel to this five-star Beachcomber hotel. The grounds are unusually spacious – with no less than three beaches – so it's possible to find a quiet corner even at peak times. Beautifully appointed rooms, impeccable but friendly service and a whole array of land- and water-based activities round out the picture.

Trou aux Biches Hotel (☎ 265 6562; www.trouauxbiches-hotel.com; Trou aux Biches; s/d half board from Rs 7800/11,300;) The sister hotel of Le Canonnier boasts even bigger grounds (40 hectares), a superb 2km-long beach and everything you could want in the way of facilities, including a golf course and a casino. Some may find it overwhelming, though it's great for families and anyone looking for a bit more action. The standards of maintenance aren't always what they should be at this price, however.

Eating

As ever more restaurants set up along here, there is an increasingly broad selection of outlets catering for most tastes.

Self-caterers should head for the well-stocked **Chez Popo Supermarket** (Royal Rd) in Trou aux Biches. Around Mont Choisy, **Persand Royal Supermarket** (Royal Rd) is your best bet.

BUDGET & MID-RANGE

Souvenir Restaurant (☎ 265 7047; Trou aux Biches; mains Rs 45-125; 7am-9pm Mon-Sat 7am-2pm Sun) This unpretentious little place just behind Trou aux Biches public beach is one of the best eating joints around for a cheap and cheerful feed. It attracts a constant stream of hungry customers in search of sustenance such as *mine frit* (fried noodles) or octopus curry. The only downside is its location on a fairly busy junction.

L'Assiette du Nord (☎ 265 7040; Trou aux Biches; mains around Rs 125-200; lunch & dinner) A popular mid-range option where you can opt for the terrace or a slightly smarter dining area behind the fish tank partition. Seafood features strongly, served in Chinese, Indian and Creole style. Try fish cooked in banana leaf with madras sauce or perhaps prawns in garlic butter.

La Bella Vita (☎ 265 6534; Trou aux Biches; pizzas from Rs 125, mains around Rs 180; lunch & dinner;) This pretty little Italian has all the classics – tasty pizza and pasta dishes – plus local takes such as Paul & Virginie pizza (ham and eggs) and pasta with smoked marlin. It also offers standard Mauritian fare.

Le Marmite Mauricienne (☎ 265 7604; Trou aux Biches; mains from around Rs 65; lunch & dinner) If the Souvenir Restaurant is full, you could try this place around the corner. It serves everything from sandwiches, salads and omelettes to fish curries and chicken and chips.

TOP END

La Cravache d'Or (☎ 265 7021; Trou aux Biches; grilled fresh fish Rs 575; lunch & dinner Mon-Sat) Treat yourself to a seafood feast at one of the island's top restaurants. The place is pleasantly relaxed, with just a few tables on a seafront terrace, while the food is both inventive and exquisitely presented. Dishes such as king prawns with a fennel fondue, using only the freshest of ingredients, are to be lingered over. Reservations are recommended, especially at weekends.

Le Pescatore (☎ 265 6337; Mont Choisy; mains around Rs 700, set menu Rs 1840; lunch & dinner) It's hard to beat this stylish seafood restaurant for sheer atmosphere. By day, the shady veranda provides a grandstand view of the bustle at the next-door jetty. Later, as the sun sets, candles and fairy lights make this the perfect spot for a romantic dinner. The food is on the pricey side, but worth it for such novelties as crispy shellfish with sea urchin cream.

Le Mouillage (☎ 263 8766; Pte aux Canonniers; mains around Rs 500; dinner;) With its cosy wood-panelled interior and seascapes, 'The Mooring' makes the most of its nautical theme. House specials include prawn salad with zest of paw paw, grilled

St-Brandon lobster and plenty of fresh crab, typically teamed with palm heart. It offers a good range of wines and occasional live jazz. Reservations are recommended at weekends.

Drinking

As far as bars go, about the only option outside the hotels is **Les Enfants Terribles** (☎ 263 8117; Pte aux Canonniers; 6pm-3am;) a very chilled-out place beside Le Mouillage (p73). It attracts a mixed crowd of tourists and well-heeled locals and offers free transport within the northern region.

Getting There & Around

Trou aux Biches and Mont Choisy are served by nonexpress buses running between Port Louis' Immigration Square bus station and Cap Malheureux via Grand Baie. There are bus stops about every 500m along the coastal highway.

A taxi to Grand Baie costs around Rs 150, to Port Louis Rs 250 and to the airport Rs 800. A return trip to Pamplemousses, including waiting time, should be in the region of Rs 500.

To hire a car, contact **Flambeau** (☎ 262 6357; Trou aux Biches) or the slightly more expensive **Winkworth** (☎ 263 4789; persand@intnet.mu), beside the Persand Royal Supermarket in Pointe aux Canonniers.

The latter also rents out 100cc motorbikes and 50cc scooters for Rs 520 per day and pedal bikes at Rs 150 per day. In Trou aux Biches, the Souvenir Restaurant (p73) has bicycles at Rs 125 per day, while Flambeau charges around Rs 180 per day.

GRAND BAIE

pop 2800

Once a tiny fishing village on an idyllic horseshoe bay, Grand Baie these days resembles a mini St-Tropez, with expensive boutiques, dozens of restaurants and practically everything in town catering to tourists. It even boasts a thriving nightlife. People either love or loathe the commercialism and the crowds.

Grand Baie was called De Bogt Zonder Eyndt (Bay, or Bend, Without End) by the Dutch in the 17th century. The bay is still remarkably picturesque, but unfortunately the beach is poor and the water not as clean as it once was. Nevertheless, all sorts of water activities are on offer, including diving, glass-bottomed boat trips and undersea walks. Grand Baie is also the main departure point for cruises to the Northern Islands (p80).

There are few other attractions in the area; most people come here to eat, drink and unwind in the company of other visitors. It's not a bad place to base yourself, however. Public transport connections are good and there's a wide choice of accommodation from cheap apartments to top-notch luxury resorts.

Orientation

Orientation in Grand Baie is easy, as almost everything is strung out along the coastal highway. The centre point of the town is the Sunset Boulevard shopping complex (including the jetty) at the junction of the coastal highway, known here as Royal Rd, and the road inland to Goodlands and the M2 motorway via the Super U Hypermarket.

The terminus for express buses to and from Port Louis is on Royal Rd about 100m north of the town centre. Nonexpress services via Trou aux Biches stop every few hundred metres along the coast road.

Information

Papyrus (☎ 263 0012; Richmond Hill Bldg, La Salette Rd; 9am-7pm Mon-Sat, 9.30am-noon Sun)
A reasonably well-stocked bookshop with a range of local and foreign magazines and newspapers as well as books and postcards.

Netshop (☎ 263 0820, Super U Hypermarket, La Salette Rd; 9am-8.30pm Mon-Sat, 9am-1.30pm Sun) You can log on to the Internet here.

MONEY

Mauritius Commercial Bank (MCB; Royal Rd; exchange bureau 8am-6pm Mon-Sat, 9am-noon Sun)

State Bank (Royal Rd; exchange bureau 8am-6pm Mon-Sat, 9am-noon Sun)

Thomas Cook (8am-8pm)

POST

Central Post Office (Richmond Hill Bldg; 8.15am-4pm Mon-Fri, 8.15am-11.45pm Sat) Out near the Super U Hypermarket; the last 45 minutes before closing are for stamp sales only.

Sights & Activities

Grand Baie's prime attraction is the range of water-based activities on offer. Otherwise, the only specific sights are a couple of vividly colourful Tamil temples: **Surya Oudaya Sangam** (admission Rs 25; 8am-5pm Mon-Sat) at the west end of town, and the older **Shiv Kalyan Vath Mandir** towards Pereybère. Both are dedicated to Shiva. Visitors are welcome but should behave with respect (p48).

CRUISES

Cruises are a popular activity in Grand Baie. Perhaps the most interesting is that offered by **Yacht Charters** (263 8395; www.island-adventures.org; Royal Rd; 8am-7pm). Its magnificent sailing ship, the *Isla Mauritia*, was built in 1852 and is claimed to be the world's oldest active working schooner. Today the *Isla Mauritia* offers day cruises with snorkelling, lunch and traditional music for Rs 1950, and sunset cruises from Rs 1450. It's best to book at least two days in advance.

Other companies offer cruises on modern catamarans. The most popular options are the day trips around the Northern Islands (p80), including a barbecue lunch and stops for swimming and snorkelling. You can also take a sunset cruise, with the option of dinner on board. Prices start at around Rs 1200 per adult (Rs 500 for children under 12) for a day trip around the Northern Islands, and Rs 600 per person for a sunset cruise (excluding dinner).

One of the biggest operators is **Croisières Australes** (670 4301; www.mttb-mautourco.com), which owns the two luxury 'Harris Wilson' boats; bookings can be made through MauriTours or any other Grand Baie tour agent (right). **Centre Sport Nautique** (CNL; 263 8017; Sunset Boulevard, Royal Rd) also owns a couple of catamarans. Boats depart from the Sunset Boulevard jetty.

DEEP-SEA FISHING

Based beside the Sunset Boulevard jetty, **Sportfisher** (263 8358; www.sportfisher.com; Royal Rd; half/full day Rs 10,000/12,000 per boat; 6am-6pm) has three boats, each taking up to six people (three anglers and three companions). Most tour agents can also arrange trips.

DIVING

The focus of dive activity is gradually shifting south to Mont Choisy and Trou aux Biches, but a number of operators still maintain a base in Grand Baie. Among these, **Neptune Diving** (263 3768; www.neptunediving.co.za; Royal Rd; 8.30am-4.30pm Mon-Sat) and **Angelo Diving** (263 3227; angelodive@intnet.mu; Royal Rd) both get consistently good reports. A dive costs around Rs 850.

UNDERSEA WALKS

For nondivers, **Captain Nemo's Undersea Walk** (263 7819; www.captainemo-underseawalk.com; Royal Rd; per person Rs 870; 8.30am-5pm) provides the unique experience of walking underwater wearing a diver's helmet and weight belt. Solar-powered pumps on the boat above feed oxygen to you during the 25-minute 'walk on the wet side'. In general, there's a minimum age requirement of seven years, but it depends on the size of the child, so check before to be sure. There are trips every few hours from 9am to 3pm. In peak season it's advisable to book a day in advance.

SEMISUBMERSIBLES

A number of semisubmersible vessels offer coral-viewing tours. *Le Nessee* (adult/child Rs 750/375) is a distinctive yellow semi-submarine run by Croisières Australes (left). It departs from Grand Baie's Sunset Boulevard jetty several times daily and the trip lasts just under two hours, with 30 minutes snorkelling for those that wish. Tickets are available from hotels and tour agents.

SWIMMING

The beach at Grand Baie is nothing special and the bay here is congested with boats. Instead, you're better off heading for La Cuvette public beach beside the Veranda Hotel on the bay's north side. It's not huge, but the sand is good and the water clean.

Tours

Grand Baie's numerous tour agents can provide information on things to do in the area with the aim, naturally, of signing you up for this cruise package or that coach trip. While prices tend to be similar, the details may vary, so make sure you know exactly what is included. Most agents sell tickets for glass-bottomed boat trips, undersea walks, *Le Nessee* (above) and the Blue Safari Submarine (p71). Many also offer car hire services and airport transfers and can organise accommodation.

Tour agents with a reliable reputation:

Grand Baie Travel & Tours (GBTT; 263 8771; www.gbtt.com; Royal Rd)

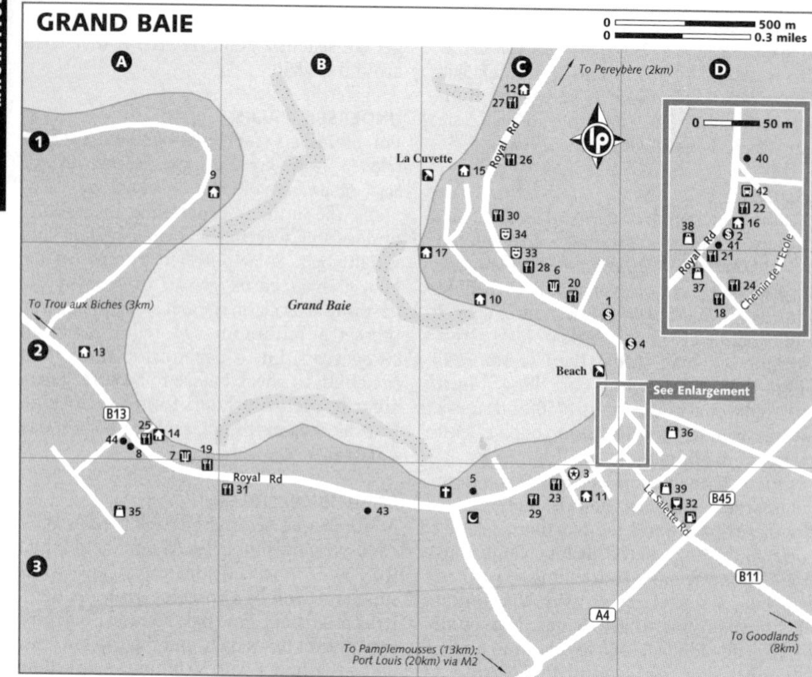

Ebrahim Travel & Tours (☎ 263 7845; gbccar@intnet.mu; Ebrahim Flats, Royal Rd)

Keiffel Tours (☎ 263 8226; keiffeltour@intnet.mu; Royal Rd)

Maurisun Adventure & Tours (☎ 263 0192; www.maurisun.com; Royal Rd) A cut above the competition, thanks to its range of adventure tours, including sea kayaking.

MauriTours (☎ 263 6056; www.mauritours.net; Sunset Boulevard, Royal Rd) Upmarket all-round travel agency selling air tickets, excursions, accommodation, island tours and cruises.

Sleeping

Much of the budget and mid-range accommodation in Grand Baie takes the form of self-catering studios and apartments. There are some excellent deals around, especially if you arrive at a quiet time of the year and with three friends in tow. A clutch of luxury hotels occupy the east side of the bay.

BUDGET

Residence Peramal (☎ 263 8109; residenceperamal@intnet.mu; Royal Rd; studio Rs 740-870, apt Rs 1120) Excellent value self-catering accommodation on a little promontory plum in the centre of Grand Baie. The fan-cooled units (for up to four people) are modern, spacious and well maintained. Not surprisingly, it gets booked up well in advance.

Ti Fleur Soleil (☎ 563 0380; www.tifleursoleil.com; Royal Rd; s/d incl breakfast from Rs 650/850; ❄) You can't miss this sunshine-yellow and sea-blue hotel just across from Grand Baie public beach. Inside, the welcome and the rooms – all with terrace – are equally cheerful. There's a choice of fan-cooled or air-con rooms.

Filao Village Hotel (☎ 263 7482; www.filaosvillage.8k.com; Pte aux Canonniers; studio incl breakfast from Rs 1250; ❄ 💻) Friendly, family-run place on a small beach just west of Grand Baie. It consists of 12 self-catering studios with a small kitchen, terrace, TV and phone. A good option if you're looking for somewhere out of the thick of things.

MID-RANGE

Les Orchidées (☎ 263 8780; www.mauritius-island.com/orchidees; Rte de la Colline; s/d incl breakfast from

INFORMATION
Barclays Bank.....1 C2
HSBC.....(see 37)
MCB.....2 D1
Netshop.....(see 39)
Papyrus.....(see 32)
Police.....3 C3
Post Office.....(see 32)
State Bank.....(see 20)
Thomas Cook Exchange Bureau.....4 D2

SIGHTS & ACTIVITIES (pp74-5)
Angelo Diving.....5 C3
Blue Safari Submarine.....(see 8)
Captain Nemo's Undersea Walk.....(see 20)
Centre Sport Nautique.....(see 38)
Neptune Diving.....(see 8)
Shiv Kalyan Vath Mandir Temple.....6 C2
Sportfisher.....(see 38)
Surya Oudaya Sangam Temple.....7 A2
Yacht Charters.....8 A2

SLEEPING (pp76-7)
Filao Village Hotel.....9 A1
Le Mauricia.....10 C2
Les Orchidées.....11 C3
Merville Beach Hotel.....12 C1
Ocean Villas.....13 A2
Residence Peramal.....14 A2
Royal Palm.....15 C1
Ti Fleur Soleil.....16 D1
Veranda Hotel.....17 C2

EATING (pp77-9)
Alchemy.....18 D2
Coolen Restaurant.....19 A3
Don Camillo.....20 C2
Food Court.....(see 37)
Grand Baie Store.....21 D2
Hong Kong Tower.....(see 29)
L'Épicerie Gourmand.....(see 28)
La Jonque.....22 D1
La Méditerranée.....23 C3
La Vieille Rouge.....24 D2
Le Capitaine.....25 A2
Le Tanjore.....26 C1
Lotus on the Square.....27 C1
Luigi's.....28 C2
Sakura.....29 C3
Store 2000.....30 C1
Vegetable Shop.....31 B3

DRINKING (p79)
Banana Café.....(see 20)
Funky Monkey.....(see 21)
Keg & Marlin.....32 D3
La Rhumerie.....(see 16)
Sunset Café.....(see 38)

ENTERTAINMENT (p79)
El Diablo.....33 C2
Star Dance.....34 C1
Zanzibar.....(see 20)

SHOPPING (p79)
Galerie Françoise Vrot.....35 A3
Galerie Vaco Baissac.....(see 1)
Grand Baie Bazaar.....36 D2
Sunset Boulevard.....37 D2
Sunset Boulevard.....38 D1
Super U Hypermarket.....39 D3

TRANSPORT
Avis.....40 D1
Budget.....(see 38)
Contract Cars.....41 D1
Express Buses to Port Louis.....42 D1

OTHER
Ebrahim Travel & Tours.....(see 41)
Grand Baie Travel & Tours.....(see 40)
Keiffel Tours.....43 B3
Maurisun Adventure & Tours.....44 A2
MauriTours.....(see 38)

Rs 1220/1540;) This small hotel in an up-and-coming area behind the main drag stands out for its colourful contemporary décor and high-quality furnishings. It's not on the sea, but it does have a pool and offers excellent value for money. Half-board deals are available.

Veranda Hotel (263 8015; www.verandagroup.com; Royal Rd; s/d half board from Rs 4070/5830;) Popular thanks to a good range of facilities – including two pools, a dive centre, water sports and kids' club – and its location on one of Grand Baie's better beaches. The garden setting adds a nice tropical touch, while the rooms are comfortable and well equipped.

Ocean Villas (263 6788; www.ocean-villas.com; Royal Rd; d incl breakfast from Rs 1280, apt from Rs 1600;) Recommended for its broad range of accommodation, from straightforward hotel rooms to self-catering units for up to eight people, with half-board options. Facilities include a pool plus a small strip of beach (with limited water sports on offer) a restaurant and scooter rental.

Merville Beach Hotel (263 8621; www.naiade.com; s/d half board from Rs 4000/6000;) This friendly and relaxed three-star hotel offers a good beach and sports facilities to match, including a dive centre. The gardens are a bit bare and the standard rooms are in an unsympathetic block, but inside they are nicely decked out in candy colours; more expensive rooms occupy thatched chalets.

TOP END

Le Mauricia (209 1100; www.lemauricia-hotel.com; s/d half board from Rs 5500/7400;) One of the more affordable four-stars, Le Mauricia sits in spacious grounds on a prime stretch of palm-fringed beach. It's big and efficient, and has two good-sized pools and all the activities you'd expect: everything from a kids' club to a raft of water and land sports. Cheerful and airy rooms come with sea-view terraces.

Royal Palm (209 8300; www.royalpalm-hotel.com; r incl breakfast from Rs 28,900;) The flagship hotel of the Beachcomber group has the atmosphere of an exclusive club. Guests come here to be cocooned and cosseted. The rooms are impeccable and the service and facilities top-notch. The health spa even boasts its own restaurant serving low-calorie cuisine.

Eating

The centre of Grand Baie is packed with restaurants, snack stalls and fast-food outlets. Standards and service can be pretty erratic, however, and places tend to come and go.

BUDGET

La Vieille Rouge (518 0579; La Salette Rd; mains Rs 80-200; 10am-midnight) It doesn't ooze atmosphere, but this is one of Grand Baie's more reliable budget eateries. You'll find a standard selection of Creole curries, Chinese dishes, fresh fish and so forth. It's all tasty and comes in decent portions.

BUT I ORDERED THE LOBSTER!

Before you order the most expensive seafood dish on the menu, you should note that there is no strict convention for the names used. The normal translation for shrimps is *crevettes*, but prawns *(camarons)* may also be *crevettes*, except when they are *crevettes géantes* (in which case they shouldn't be confused with *camarons d'eau douce*, which are freshwater shrimps unless they're tiger prawns, which are also known as *rosenberghis*). Confused?

Other seafood to watch out for includes squid, which is *mourgatte* or *calamar*, and octopus, which is *poulpe*. The word *langouste* (lobster) covers everything from langoustines and crayfish to rock lobsters – ask someone to explain what you're getting before you commit to a meal!

Coolen Restaurant (Chez Ram; ☎ 263 8569; Royal Rd; mains Rs 80-125; ⌚ closed Wed) Recently revamped but as popular as ever with locals and tourists alike for its cheap prices and typically Mauritian atmosphere. The food is equally homey, focusing on curries and fresh fish. Specials such as lobster are more pricey.

Food Court (Royal Rd; fried rice/noodles Rs 50, meal Rs 75; ⌚ lunch only Mon-Sat) Squeaky clean canteen-style takeaway offering fried rice and noodles and a daily selection of main dishes, such as beef in satay sauce or fish with lashings of garlic, served with rice and haricot beans. You can eat at the nearby trestle tables.

MID-RANGE

Don Camillo (☎ 263 8540; Royal Rd; pizzas Rs 140-255, pasta Rs 150-220; ⌚ lunch Mon-Sat, dinner daily; ❄) If you're craving something other than curry, this relaxed Italian hits the spot with its lip-smacking pizzas and pasta dishes. It's not in the most promising location, beside the Caltex petrol station, but it's shielded by pot plants. In the evening it's positively buzzing – either get there early or reserve.

Hong Kong Tower (☎ 263 5288; Royal Rd; Peking duck Rs 500, steamboat Rs 350 per person; ⌚ dinner, closed Tue; ❄) Though a bit out of the way, this place stands out among Grand Baie's Chinese restaurants for its original cuisine. House specials include Peking duck, served in all manner of guises, and steamboat, a lavish do-it-yourself feast of fish, meat and vegetables – you simmer them over a table-stove, then drink the flavour-filled soup.

La Jonque (☎ 263 8729; Royal Rd; mains Rs 120-280; ⌚ lunch & dinner; ❄) A long-established Chinese restaurant offering an exceptional range of dishes. Though you'll find sweet-and-sour squid, shrimp chop suey and all the old favourites, its speciality is sizzling dishes, such as sizzling fish in oyster sauce or duck in black pepper sauce.

Le Tanjore (☎ 263 6030; Royal Rd; mains around Rs 140; ⌚ lunch & dinner) This large, open restaurant on the main road may not look much, but it serves good-value Indian fare such as chicken or lamb *pasanda* (a curry laced with almonds and sesame seeds).

Luigi's (☎ 269 1125; Royal Rd; pizzas & pasta Rs 125-180, mains Rs 250; ⌚ Mon-Sat noon-11pm, Sun 6-9.30pm) Classic little trattoria serving authentic pizza and pasta dishes plus a range of daily specials, such as seafood gnocchi and *daurade* (sea bream) with a tapenade of chives and tomato. Make sure you leave room for one of the scrumptious deserts.

Le Capitaine (☎ 263 8108; Royal Rd; mains Rs 260-400; ⌚ lunch & dinner) Le Capitaine is a moderately upscale restaurant in a pleasant seaside setting. Despite its reputation for serving ultrafresh seafood, it continues to gets mixed reports from travellers. At the bottom of the price range there's fish fillet cooked in Madeira sauce, while fresh lobster comes in at around Rs 800 for 500g.

Other recommendations:

Alchemy (☎ 263 5314; grills Rs 260-290; La Salette Rd; ⌚ lunch & dinner) Tuck in to a juicy steak with green pepper or mushroom sauce and other grilled dishes.

La Méditerranée (☎ 263 8019; Royal Rd; mains around Rs 160-250; ⌚ lunch & dinner) A simple and inexpensive little restaurant serving well-prepared French and Mauritian food.

Lotus on the Square (☎ 263 3251; Royal Rd; ⌚ lunch Mon-Sat) This garden café serves light lunches such as salads and crêpes.

Sakura (☎ 263 8092; Royal Rd; mains around Rs 300-400; ⌚ lunch Mon-Sat, dinner daily; ❄) A passable rendition of a Japanese restaurant, with dishes such as sushi and tempura.

SELF-CATERING

The **Super U Hypermarket** (La Salette Rd; ⌚ 9am-8.30pm Mon-Sat, 9am-1.30pm Sun) sells almost everything self-caterers could want. You can also buy groceries and other essentials at **Grand Baie Store** (Royal Rd) and **Store 2000** (Royal Rd), and there's a good **vegetable shop** (Royal Rd) at the west end of town.

For a real treat, **L'Épicerie Gourmand** (Royal Rd; ⏰ 9.30am-7pm Mon-Sat, 9am-noon Sun) is a treasure-trove of imported delicacies including cheese, ham and pâté. It also sells luscious cakes and pastries and artisanal ice cream.

Drinking

Banana Café (☎ 263 0326; Royal Rd; ⏰ 10am-3am Mon-Sat, 5pm-3am Sun) While not actually on the beach, Grand Baie's most popular drinking hole gives a fair impression with its sand-strewn floor and palm trees. A laid-back place to sip your local rum or pina colada. There's live music most Fridays.

Lotus on the Square (☎ 263 3251; Royal Rd; ⏰ 9.30am-5pm Mon-Sat) The garden of this small, arty café on the road to Pereybère makes a nice place to linger over a latte or cappuccino. It also does refreshing fruit juices and home-made sorbets in unusual flavours such as tamarind, basil and cinnamon.

Alchemy (☎ 263 5314; La Salette Rd; ⏰ 8am-midnight) A convivial little bar attracting a mixed crowd of locals and tourists with its cheap prices and retro soundtrack. Saturday is *séga* night – this is a good place to catch a performance outside the big hotels.

Sunset Café (☎ 263 9602; Sunset Boulevard, Royal Rd; ⏰ 8.30am-7.30pm Mon-Sat, 8.30am-6pm Sun) Slightly pricey, but one of the few places overlooking the bay.

Other recommendations:

La Rhumerie (☎ 263 7664; ⏰ 7am-midnight) Friendly bar with wicked selection of *rhum arrangés* (flavoured rums); Rs 70 a shot or Rs 300 for five.

Funky Monkey (☎ 269 1141; ⏰ 7.30am-midnight) Can get loud(ish) and lively after dark.

Keg & Marlin (☎ 269 1591; Richmond Hill Bldg, La Salette Rd; ⏰ noon-midnight) A fair rendition of an English-style pub, albeit in rather soulless surroundings, with live music on a Saturday.

Entertainment

DISCOS

El Diablo (☎ 263 7664; Royal Rd; admission free Wed, Rs 200 Fri & Sat; ⏰ 11.30pm-5am Wed, Fri & Sat; ⌘) Grand Baie's top nightspot positively sizzles on a Friday and Saturday night when all three dance floors are packed. On Wednesday only Le Lounge is open, offering a mostly '80s playlist. Smart-casual dress is required.

Star Dance (☎ 263 6388; Royal Rd; admission free Wed, Rs 150 Fri & Sat; ⏰ Wed, Fri & Sat 11pm-5am; ⌘) El Diablo's close rival also has three floors with a choice of techno, tropical and '60s to '80s music. Again, only one floor is open on a Wednesday and the dress code is smart-casual, though Star Dance tends to be slightly less selective.

Zanzibar (☎ 263 3265; Royal Rd; admission Rs 100; ⏰ 11.30pm-5am Mon-Sat) There's a nicely intimate, clubby atmosphere to this small bar-disco which is decked out with sofas and African artefacts.

SÉGA

Most major hotels in Grand Baie provide entertainment such as live music and theme evenings, including at least one *séga* night per week (see p52).

Alternatively, the Alchemy bar-restaurant (left) hosts *séga* performances every Saturday night at 7pm. There's no admission charge, but you're expected to at least buy a drink.

Shopping

The shopping complex, **Sunset Boulevard** (Royal Rd) is home to chic boutiques including knitwear specialists Floreal, Maille St and Shibani; Harris Wilson for menswear; and Hémisphère Sud for fabulous leather goods. Cheaper clothing stores, such as Red Snapper and IV Pl@y, concentrate in and around the Super U Hypermarket.

A broad range of Mauritian and Malagasy crafts are available at the **Grand Baie Bazaar** (⏰ 9.30am-4.30pm Mon-Sat, 9am-noon Sun) craft market off Royal Rd. Prices aren't fixed, but it's not expensive and there's minimal hassling from vendors.

To purchase some original art, visit the studio of **Françoise Vrot** (☎ 263 5118; galerievrot@tropicscope.com; Reservoir Rd; ⏰ 10am-1pm & 3-6.30pm) to see her expressive portraits of women fieldworkers; or buy one of Vaco Baissac's instantly recognisable works at his gallery, **Galerie Vaco Baissac** (☎ 263 3106; Dodo Square, Royal Rd, Grand Baie; ⏰ 9.30am-7pm Mon-Sat).

Getting There & Away

Express buses run directly between Immigration Square in Port Louis and Grand Baie every half-hour, terminating beside Le Jonque restaurant. Nonexpress buses en route to Cap Malheureux will also drop you in Grand Baie. Buses between

Pamplemousses and Grand Baie leave roughly every hour.

For taxi rides from Grand Baie, expect to pay around Rs 150 to Trou aux Biches, Rs 350 to Port Louis and Rs 700 to the airport. A return trip to Pamplemousses, including waiting time, should set you back Rs 400 or so.

Getting Around

CAR

There are numerous car-rental companies in Grand Baie, so you should be able to bargain, especially if you're renting for several days. Prices generally start at around Rs 800 for the smallest hatchback on the basis of one week's rental. Find out whether the management of your hotel or guesthouse has a special discount agreement with a local company. Otherwise, try one of the agents listed here.

Contract Cars (☎ 263 7845; gbccar@intnet.mu; Royal Rd)
Keiffel Tours (☎ 263 8226; keiffeltour@intnet.mu; Royal Rd)
Avis (☎ 263 7600; avis@ibl.intnet.mu; Royal Rd)
Budget (☎ 263 6056; Royal Rd)

MOTORCYCLE

Motorbikes of 50cc and 100cc are widely available in Grand Baie; rental charges hover at around Rs 400 to Rs 450 per day, less if you rent for several days. Both Contract Cars Ltd and Keiffel Tours (see above) should be able to help, or try one of the numerous tour agents along Royal Rd.

BICYCLE

Many hotels and guesthouses can arrange bicycle hire. Rates vary, but expect to pay between Rs 100 and Rs 150 per day, or less if you hire for several days. Most of the local tour operators have bikes for rent; just walk down Royal Rd and see what's on offer.

NORTHERN ISLANDS

Coin de Mire, Île Plate & Îlot Gabriel

The islands closest to the northern tip of Mauritius – Coin de Mire, Île Plate and Îlot Gabriel – are popular day trips from Grand Baie.

The distinctive Coin de Mire (Gunner's Quoin), 4km off the coast, was so named because it resembles the quoin or wedge used to steady the aim of a cannon. The island is now a nature reserve and home to a number of rare species, such as the red-tailed tropicbird and Bojer's skink. It is likely that it will be closed to visitors in the near future. In any case, landing here can be tricky, so most operators take you to Île Plate, 7km further north, which offers good snorkelling.

Îlot Gabriel is a pretty island lying within the coral reef just east of Île Plate and is a popular lunch stop for day cruises.

Boats to the islands depart from Grand Baie. You can book through almost any local tour agent or direct with the cruise companies (p75). Prices start at Rs 1000 per person, including lunch. Dive centres in Grand Baie also offer dive trips around these islands.

Île Ronde & Île aux Serpents

Île Ronde (Round Island) and Île aux Serpents (Snake Island) are two significant nature reserves about 20km and 24km res-pectively from Mauritius. It is not possible to land on them. Ironically, Île Ronde is not round and has snakes, while Île aux Serpents is round and has no snakes; the theory is that an early cartographer simply made a mistake.

Île Ronde covers roughly 170 hectares and scientists believe it has more endangered species per square kilometre than anywhere else in the world. Many of the plants, such as the hurricane palm (of which one lonely tree remains) and the bottle palm, are unique to the island.

The endemic fauna includes the keel-scaled boa and the burrowing boa (possibly extinct), three types of skink and three types of gecko. Among the sea birds that breed on the island are the wedge-tailed shearwater, the red-tailed tropicbird and the gadfly (or Round Island) petrel. Naturalist Gerald Durrell, gives a very graphic description of the island in his book *Golden Bats & Pink Pigeons*.

The smaller Île aux Serpents (42 hectares) is a renowned bird sanctuary. The birds residing on the island include the sooty tern, the lesser noddy, the common noddy and the masked (blue-footed) booby. Nactus geckos and Bojer's skinks are also found here.

PEREYBÈRE

Pereybère (peu-ray-bear) is a rapidly expanding seaside town a couple of kilometres north

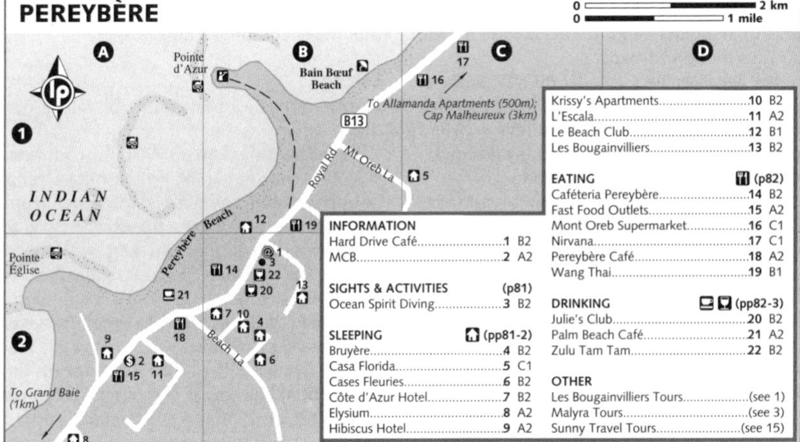

of Grand Baie. It has a fine, white-sand beach and everything you need in the way of banks, tour agents and restaurants. Nevertheless, Pereybère is still relatively quiet compared to Grand Baie and, since accommodation also tends to be cheaper, many people prefer to stay here instead.

Information

Pereybère boasts an efficient Internet café, the **Hard Drive Café** (☎ 263 1076; Royal Rd; 10am-6.30pm Mon-Sat, 10am-5.30pm Sun). The **Mauritius Commercial Bank** (MCB; Royal Rd) has an **exchange bureau** (8am-6pm Mon-Sat, 9am-noon Sun) open outside regular banking hours.

Activities

Most people come to Pereybère simply to unwind beside the beautiful azure lagoon. The swimming is good here and the roped-off area is particularly safe for children. When the weekend crowds get too much, there are quieter beaches a short stroll away at Pointe d'Azur.

There's also good snorkelling offshore. The best coral can be found directly off the public beach (but watch out for glass-bottomed boats and water-skiiers).

Divers can organise expeditions through **Ocean Spirit Diving** (☎ 563 0376; Royal Rd; gingospirit@yahoo.com; 8am-8pm Mon-Sat, 8am-noon Sun).

Tours

Pereybère tour agents sell the standard range of tours, including cruises and coach trips.

Les Bougainvilliers Tours (☎ 269 1632; lesbougainvilliers@hotmail.com; Royal Rd)

Malyra Tours (☎ 263 6274; www.villamalyra.com; Royal Rd)

Sunny Travel Tours (☎ 263 5359; info@sunnyrental.com; Royal Rd)

Sleeping

Accommodation in Pereybère consists mainly of self-catering studios and apartments. Though few places are actually on the beach, most are only a short walk away.

BUDGET

Bruyère (☎ 263 7316, dod.chettiar@intnet.mu; Beach Lane; 1/2 r apt from Rs 600/800;) Spruce, well-run and well-equipped one- and two-bedroom apartments in the home of a delightful Scottish-Mauritian couple. It's in a quiet residential area close to the beach and town centre.

Cases Fleuries (☎ 263 8868, casefle@intnet.mu; Beach Lane; studio from Rs 900; apt from Rs 1000;) A variety of studios and apartments for up to six people set in a flower-filled garden. The atmosphere is slightly snooty, but it's popular nonetheless, so be sure to book ahead.

Krissy's Apartments (☎ 263 8859, limfat@bow.intnet.mu; Beach Lane; studio/apt from Rs 600/Rs 1000;) This friendly place consists of simple but clean studios and two-bedroom apartments in a block tucked off the main road.

L'Escala (☎ 263 7379; fax 240 0117; Royal Rd; studio/apt from Rs 500/Rs 800;) A small garden and warm welcome make up for the slightly jaded décor in this complex of studios and apartments behind the arcade at the southern end of town.

Les Bougainvilliers (☎/fax 263 8807; studio/apt Rs 750/Rs 900;) Swathed in bougainvillea flowers, this homely place offers a broad range of spick-and-span studios and apartments with up to three bedrooms.

Allamanda (☎ 263 8110; www.allamanda.mu; Royal Rd; studio/apt from Rs 200/Rs 400) The area's cheapest accommodation is located about 1.5km north of town towards Cap Malheureux. It consists of basic but cheery studios and two-bedroom apartments.

MID-RANGE

Elysium (☎ 269 1102; www.hotelelysium.com; Royal Rd; s/d incl breakfast from Rs 1250/1950;) Don't be put off by the scrubby approach; inside this stylish boutique-hotel all is Zen-like calm. The rooms are fashionably uncluttered, but equipped to unusually high standards, including air-conditioning and mini-bar, and decked out with natural fabrics. The quality of service is also a cut above the norm.

Casa Florida (☎ 263 7371; www.casaflorida.net; Mont Oreb Lane; s/d incl breakfast Rs 865/1005, apt from Rs 1285;) Set in spacious gardens, Casa Florida is an efficient and popular place. It offers a broad choice of accommodation, from standard hotel rooms to two-bedroom self-catering apartments, all with the option of half board. There's a bar and restaurant, with *séga* on a Saturday night.

Le Beach Club (☎ 263 5104; www.le-beachclub.com; Royal Rd; studio incl breakfast from Rs 1200, apt from Rs 3100;) This complex of studios and two-bedroom apartments feels slightly hemmed in but it is one of the few places on the seafront. The units are furnished in bright tropical colours. It's worth paying a bit extra for a balcony and sea views.

Côte d'Azur Hotel (☎ 263 8165; www.hotelcotedazur.com; Royal Rd; d/studio/apt from Rs 1200/1350/1650;) A choice of extremely well-equipped hotel-style rooms and one- and two-bedroom apartments in a modern block on the main road. All come with air-con, private safe, satellite TV and phone, while some boast a CD player, jacuzzi and a washing machine.

Hibiscus Hotel (☎ 263 8554; www.hibiscushotel.com; Royal Rd;) This pleasant and popular hotel at the south end of Pereybère beach was being renovated at the time of writing, but should be worth a look. The hotel restaurant (below) is still operating.

Eating

Pereybère has a broad range of eating options.

Pereybère Café (☎ 263 8700; Royal Rd; mains Rs 80-90, set menus from Rs 280; lunch & dinner) This popular restaurant across the road from the public beach serves up excellent-value Chinese fare such as chicken with bean sprouts and calamari in *sauce rouge* (brandy sauce). Reservations are a must for dinner.

Nirvana (☎ 262 6711; Royal Rd; tandoor dishes from Rs 250, vegetarian curries from Rs 170; dinner only Mon-Sat;) Arguably the best restaurant on the north coast, Nirvana is 1km north of central Pereybère and offers spectacular Indian food in stylish surroundings. Dishes from the tandoori oven include *murg makhani* (chicken with tomato and cream sauce) and grilled white prawns.

Wang Thai (☎ 263 4050; Royal Rd; mains Rs 200-450; dinner daily, lunch Tue-Sun;) Buddha statues and raw silks set the scene in this surprisingly affordable Thai restaurant. Treat you tastebuds to such classics as *tom yum thalay* (citronella-laced seafood soup), green curries and *phad thai* (mixed fried noodles).

Hibiscus Hotel (☎ 263 8554; Royal Rd; mains Rs 300-500; lunch & dinner) The hotel's restaurant, on an open terrace overlooking the sea, serves fresh seafood as well as more unusual dishes such as venison carpaccio with melon. *Séga* nights (usually Sunday) include a substantial buffet (Rs 620) and dancing on the beach.

Caféteria Pereybère (☎ 263 8539; Royal Rd; mains Rs 120-220 10.30am-10pm) This friendly all-day café-restaurant behind the public beach offers grilled fish, octopus curry and steak and chips from an extensive menu. Portions are on the small side.

For a cheap beach munch, there are snack stands in the car park behind the public beach and several fast-food **outlets** (Royal Rd) serving pizza and fried chicken. Self-caterers have to make do with the small **Mont Oreb Supermarket** (Royal Rd) at the north end of town.

Drinking & Entertainment

Pereybère has a very low-key bar and café scene. There's just one nice beachfront café, though Caféteria Pereybère is close to the sea. Entertainment consists of live music or perhaps a karaoke night at one of the bars and *séga* performances at the Hibiscus Hotel – nonguests are welcome as long as they buy a drink or some food (reservations required).

Julie's Club (☎ 269 0320; Royal Rd; 11am-midnight) Relaxed and friendly bar with live music or some other event most Friday and Saturday nights.

Zulu Tam Tam (☎ 263 0883; Royal Rd; 7.30am-2am) This upbeat bar-cum-pizzeria is popular with a younger crowd. Local bands, including the occasional big name, perform most nights from 9pm.

Palm Beach Café (☎ 263 5821; Royal Rd; 11.30am-8pm Tue-Sun) The place to sip a coffee or fresh juice lulled by the sound of the waves. It also serves snacks and light meals.

Getting There & Around

Buses between Port Louis and Cap Malheureux stop in Pereybère as well as Grand Baie. Services run roughly every 30 minutes.

You can rent cars, motorbikes and bicycles through the three local tour agents (p81). Cars start at Rs 600 per day and motorbikes at Rs 400 for a 50cc or 100cc bike. Pedal bikes cost upwards of Rs 100 per day. Most of Grand Baie's car-hire companies will also drop off and pick up cars in Pereybère.

CAP MALHEUREUX

Cap Malheureux marks the most northerly point of the Mauritian mainland. It was named the 'Cape of Misfortune' for the number of ships that foundered on the rocks. This was also where the English invasion force landed in 1810 and launched their successful attack against the French. Nowadays the cape is a peaceful spot with superb views of Coin de Mire island.

A little further on lies the minuscule fishing village also known as Cap Malheureux, with its much-photographed church, the red-roofed Notre Dame Auxiliatrice. It's worth a quick peek inside for its intricate woodwork and a holy-water basin fashioned out of a giant clam shell.

Heading around the coast the landscape becomes wilder and more rugged. In between the rocky coves and muddy tidal creeks a clutch of hotels occupy the few decent beaches. They offer a perfect hideaway for those who want to get away from it all.

Sleeping

Coin de Mire Hotel (☎ 262 7302; www.coindemire-hotel.com; s/d half board from around Rs 2300/3200, superior rooms Rs 2700/4000;) Set in mature gardens roughly 1km west of Cap Malheureux Point, this is an attractive and well-run hotel. The rooms are comfortable, though for air-con you'll need to upgrade to the more spacious superior rooms. There are two pools, a restaurant, a bar (with live entertainment, including *séga*) and a range of water activities.

Kuxville (☎ 262 7913; www.kuxville.de; gardenside/seaside studio from €29/58, apt from €52/87) A very popular apartment complex with a strong German flavour about 1.5km west of Cap Malheureux village. Accommodation is in impeccably clean studios or apartments sleeping up to four people; 'gardenside' units are in a newer compound across the road. There's a fine little beach and a small dive centre as well as various other water sports.

Marina Resort (☎ 204 8800; www.marina-resort.com; s/d full board from Rs 3710/5300;) Set in tropical gardens on a small beach to the east of Cap Malheureux, the Marina is an efficient, family-friendly hotel offering bright, spacious rooms with terraces or balconies. Full board rates include all drinks, transport to Grand Baie and most of the sports facilities (tennis, water-skiing and sailing, but not diving).

Paradise Cove Hotel (☎ 204 4000; www.paradisecovehotel.com; s/d half board from Rs 9200/16,000;) This luxurious hotel built around an idyllic little cove lives up to its name. It's all very peaceful and terribly understated, with fountains and hammocks slung between the palm trees. The rooms are equally tasteful, mixing Asian antiques and modern art to great effect, and the service impeccable. There are two restaurants, a health centre, tennis courts and a multitude of water activities, including free catamaran cruises to the Northern Islands.

Eating

Outside the hotel restaurants, this area is short on eating options. Snack stands are set up beside Cap Malheureux church at weekends and there are picnic spots all along the coast.

Otherwise, the best bet is **Le Coin de Mire** (☎ 262 8070; mains from Rs 110; lunch & dinner) opposite the church in Cap Malheureux village. It offers a huge range of dishes, from omelettes and fried rice to wild-boar curry. The food is average, but friendly service and the view from the upstairs dining room compensate.

Getting There & Away

Buses run roughly every half hour between Port Louis' Immigration Square bus station and Cap Malheureux.

A taxi to Port Louis will cost at least Rs 500; Rs 1000 to the airport.

GRAND GAUBE

Grand Gaube is a sleepy fishing village with a good hotel and beach about 6km east of Cap Malheureux. Small bays protected by rocky headlands typify this northeast coast. These can be treacherous waters. In 1744 the *St Géran* foundered off Grand Gaube in a storm. The disaster inspired the famous love story *Paul et Virginie*, by Bernadin de St-Pierre (see Paul & Virginie, p85).

Inland from Grand Gaube, the landscape is open and windswept, the cane fields rapidly being built over with modern housing estates. There's nothing specific to see in the area, but it has a distinctly Mauritian atmosphere, a world away from the tourist developments on the west coast.

Sleeping & Eating

Paul & Virginie (☎ 288 0215, http://paul-et-virginie-hotel.com; s/d half board from Rs 2625/3750) Grand Gaube's one hotel is a pleasant surprise. It's small enough not to be overwhelming, yet offers all the services and comforts required: two pools, a couple of restaurants, plenty of entertainment and activities, a kids' club and so forth. The faintly colonial décor picks up on the Paul and Virginie theme, which even runs to a small reading room-cum-museum. The rooms are nicely fitted out and spacious, all with sea views, and there's a small but attractive beach.

Getting There & Away

Buses run every 15 minutes or so between Port Louis' Immigration Square bus station and Grand Gaube.

A taxi to Port Louis will cost around Rs 500, to Grand Baie Rs 300 and to the airport Rs 1000.

PAMPLEMOUSSES

This small village was named for the grapefruit-like citrus trees that the Dutch introduced to Mauritius from Java. It's home to the Sir Seewoosagur Ramgoolam Botanical Gardens (occasionally referred to as the Royal Botanical Gardens), which feature a stunning variety of endemic and foreign plant species. Nearby, the decommissioned Beau Plan sugar factory has been converted into a fascinating museum.

Sir Seewoosagur Ramgoolam Botanical Gardens

These attractive **gardens** (admission free; 8.30am-5.30pm) are one of the most popular tourist attractions in Mauritius. Named after Sir Seewoosagur Ramgoolam, the first prime minister of Mauritius after independence, the gardens also house the funerary platform where he was cremated. His ashes were scattered on the Ganges in India.

If you are not botanically minded, you probably will be after a visit here. If you *are* so minded, you won't want to leave. The plants are gradually being labelled and map-boards installed, but the gardens are really best seen with a guide (Rs 50 per person for an hour's tour), as you'll miss many of the most interesting species if you go alone. Alternatively, you can buy an excellent guidebook (Rs 125) at the **booths** (8.30am-5.30pm Mon-Fri) located just inside the two entrances, or from tourist shops all over the island.

The gardens were started by Mahé de Labourdonnais in 1735 as a vegetable plot for his Mon Plaisir Château, but came into their own in 1768 under the auspices of the French horticulturalist Pierre Poivre. Like Kew Gardens in England, the gardens played a significant role in the horticultural espionage of the day. Poivre imported spice plants from around the world in a bid to end France's dependence on Asian spices. The gardens were neglected between 1810 and 1849 until British horticulturalist James Duncan transformed them into an arboretum for palms and other tropical trees.

Palms still constitute the most important part of the horticultural display, and they

PAUL & VIRGINIE

Mauritius' most popular folk tale tells the story of two lovers, Paul and Virginie, who encounter tragedy when the ship that is carrying Virginie founders on the reef. Although Paul swims out to the wreck to save her, Virginie modestly refuses to remove her clothes to swim ashore, and drowns; Paul dies of a broken heart shortly after.

The story was written by Bernardin de St-Pierre in the 18th century, but was inspired by a real-life tragedy that took place some years earlier. In 1744, the ship *St Géran* was wrecked during a storm off Île d'Ambre, to the southeast of Grand Gaube, with almost 200 lives lost. Among them were two female passengers who refused to undress to swim ashore and were dragged down by the weight of their clothes. The true story is more a tragedy of social mores than one of romance!

The *St Géran* was carrying a horde of Spanish money and machinery from France for the island's first sugar refinery. A French dive expedition explored the wreck in 1966 and many of their finds are on display in Mahébourg's National History Museum and the Blue Penny Museum in Port Louis.

You'll run into Paul and Virginie everywhere in Mauritius. The statue by Prosper d'Épinay is perhaps the most famous memorial. The original is in the Blue Penny Museum and there's a copy near the town hall in Curepipe.

come in an astonishing variety of shapes and forms. Some of the more prominent are the stubby bottle palms, the tall royal palms and the talipot palms, which flower once after about 40 years and then die. Other varieties include the raffia, sugar, toddy, fever, fan and even sealing-wax palms. There are many other curious tree species on display, including the marmalade box tree, the fish poison tree and the sausage tree.

The centrepiece of the gardens is a pond filled with giant Victoria amazonica water lilies, native to the Amazon region. Young leaves emerge as wrinkled balls and unfold into the classic tea-tray shape up to 2m across in a matter of hours. The flowers in the centre of the huge leaves open white one day and close red the next. The lilies are at their biggest and best in the warm summer months, notably January.

Various international dignitaries have planted trees in the gardens, including Nelson Mandela, Indira Gandhi and a host of British royals.

The gardens have two entrances, both on the west side. The main gate (supposedly sent all the way from Crystal Palace in London) is the more southerly, opposite the church. The second is in the northwest corner beside the car park.

After working up an appetite exploring the gardens, treat yourself to a slice of home-made Sachertorte (rich chocolate cake) or apple pie at the **Wiener Walzer Café** (☎ 243 8465; cakes Rs 80, tuna salad Rs 80; 🕑 9am-6pm) behind the church. It also does a great coffee and rustles up light meals along the lines of salads and crêpes.

L'Aventure du Sucre

Just across the motorway from the botanical gardens, the former Beau Plan sugar factory now houses this excellent **museum** (☎ 243 0660; adult/child Rs 250/125; 🕑 9am-6pm). It not only tells the story of sugar in fascinating detail, but along the way covers the history of Mauritius, slavery, the rum trade and much, much more. Allow at least a couple of hours to do it justice.

The factory was founded in 1797 and only ceased working in 1999. Most of the machinery is still in place and former workers are on hand to answer questions about the factory and the complicated process of turning sugar cane into crystals. There are also videos and interactive displays as well as quizzes for children. At the end of the visit you can taste four of the fifteen different varieties of unrefined sugar, two of which were invented in Mauritius.

If all that's set your taste buds working, you could sup a glass of sugar cane juice at **Le Fangourin** (☎ 243 0660; mains Rs 150-480; 🕑 9am-6pm), a stylish café-restaurant in the grounds of the museum. It specialises in sophisticated Creole cuisine and all sorts of sugary delights.

Getting There & Away

Pamplemousses can be reached by bus from Grand Baie, Trou aux Biches, Grand Gaube and Port Louis. Services from Grand Baie and Trou aux Biches run approximately every hour and stop near the sugar museum on the way to the botanical gardens.

Buses from Port Louis' Immigration Square bus station and Grand Gaube operate every 10 to 15 minutes. These buses only stop at the botanical gardens, from where it takes about 10 minutes to walk to the museum.

CENTRAL MAURITIUS

Although Mauritius is primarily seen as a beach destination, the island's interior offers some great mountain scenery and good hiking opportunities for those seeking a change from sun, sea and sand. The hiking may not be as extensive or challenging as on Réunion, but it still takes you into some surprisingly wild and unspoilt areas, notably in the Black Forest Gorges National Park.

This park covers an area of deep gorges and forested mountains, including Mauritius' highest peak, which mark the southwestern boundary of the island's Central Plateau. The Moka mountain range fringes the plateau to the north, where Le Pouce provides another popular half-day hike.

By contrast, the Central Plateau itself is a rather bleak area. Nothing but sugar-cane fields stretch to the north and east. The west comprises a series of towns practically running into each other from Curepipe north to Port Louis. No less than half the island's population live in this corridor, drawn by a climate that is cooler and less humid (at around 500m above sea level) than down on the coast.

These plateau towns hold few specific sights, but merit a visit if only to get a flavour of the Mauritian way of life away from the tourism-driven settlements of the coast. For many visitors the prime attraction is a little 'retail therapy' in the cheap clothing stores. Curepipe is traditionally the first stop, though the market at Quatre Bornes can yield some amazing bargains. Floréal's textile museum provides an interesting detour – not to mention more shopping opportunities. Phoenix, on the other hand, is synonymous with Mauritius' biggest brewery.

Southwest of Curepipe lies a more appealing region of lakes and natural parkland. The Mare aux Vacoas reservoir is the island's largest lake. It is flanked to the west by the Mare Longue and Tamarin Falls reservoirs – the latter named after a spectacular series of seven waterfalls immediately north of the lake – and to the south by Grand Bassin. This crater lake is one of the most important pilgrimage sites in the country.

There are few places to stay on the Central Plateau. Instead, most visitors come here on day trips. A popular excursion is to combine Curepipe or Floréal, for example, with a drive through the Black River Gorges National Park, and then drop down to the sea via Chamarel or Baie du Cap to explore the southwest coast.

Getting There & Around

The Central Plateau towns are served by frequent bus connections with Port Louis. Other useful routes include the direct services between Quatre Bornes and Flic en Flac, on the west coast, and between Curepipe and Mahébourg, to the southeast; the latter service passes via the airport.

If you don't have your own transport, the easiest way to get around is by taxi, though there's a risk of being stuck in traffic jams.

There are no bike or motorbike rental outlets in the area. As for cars, companies elsewhere on the island will always deliver to your hotel.

HIKING THE CENTRAL PLATEAU & BLACK RIVER GORGES

The mountain ranges fringing the Central Plateau offer a variety of rambles and longer hikes. One of the most popular is the excellent but steep ascent of Le Pouce, on the plateau's northern edge. To the west, Corps de Garde is more of a challenge but equally rewarding.

The most varied hiking, however, is to be found in the beautiful highland area southwest of Curepipe, where the Black River Gorges National Park offers a range of environments from dry lowlands to the wet, forest-cloaked peaks. Surrounded by casuarina and conifer trees and tumbling waterfalls, it is like no other part of Mauritius. Of several hikes traversing the park, the

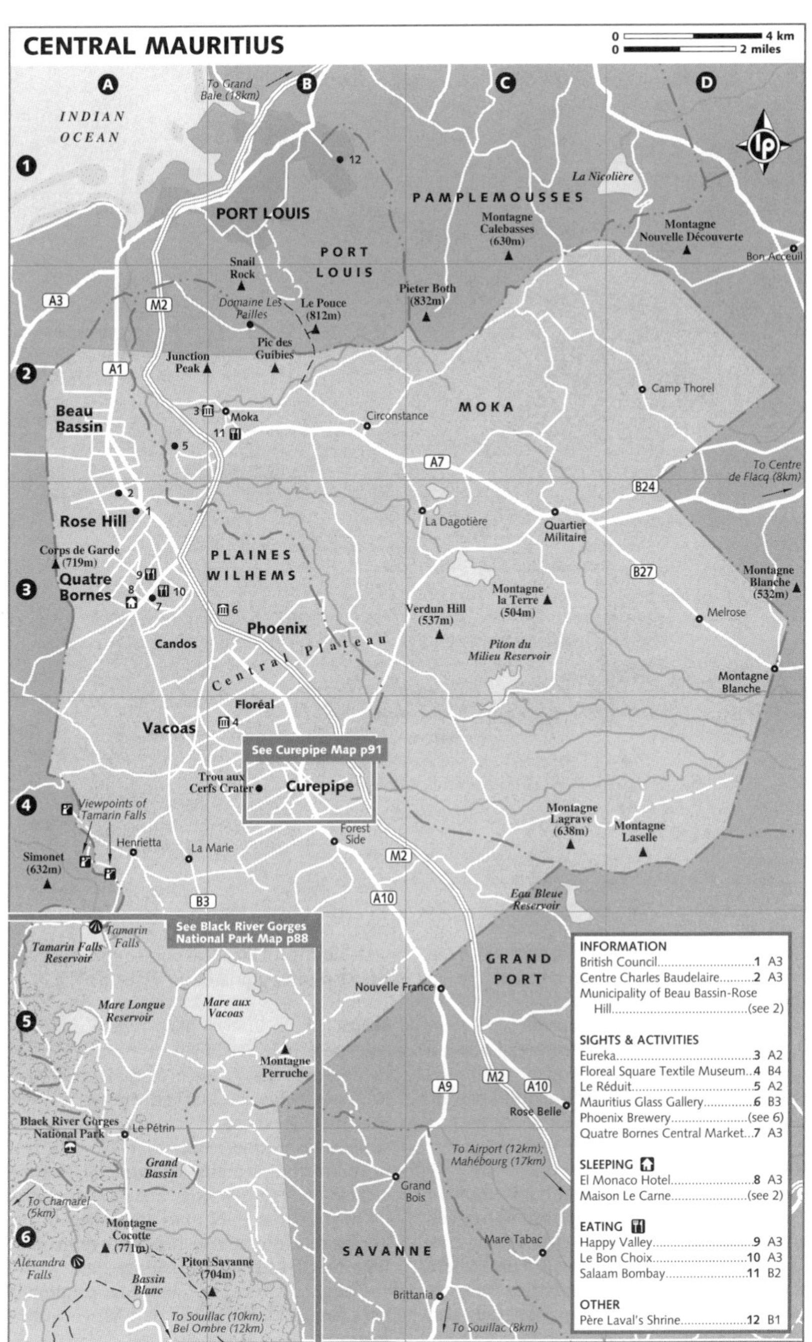
CENTRAL MAURITIUS
0 4 km
0 2 miles
A
B
C
D
1
2
3
4
5
6
INDIAN OCEAN
To Grand Baie (18km)
12
La Nicolière
PAMPLEMOUSSES
PORT LOUIS
Montagne Calebasses (630m)
Montagne Nouvelle Découverte
Bon Acceuil
Snail Rock
PORT LOUIS
Pieter Both (832m)
A3
M2
Domaine Les Pailles
Le Pouce (812m)
Pic des Guibies
Junction Peak
A1
Camp Thorel
Beau Bassin
3
Moka
MOKA
Circonstance
11
5
A7
To Centre de Flacq (8km)
B24
2
1
Rose Hill
La Dagotière
Quartier Militaire
Corps de Garde (719m)
PLAINES WILHEMS
9
Quatre Bornes
8
10
7
B27
Montagne Blanche (532m)
Montagne la Terre (504m)
6
Verdun Hill (537m)
Melrose
Phoenix
Candos
Central Plateau
Piton du Milieu Reservoir
Montagne Blanche
Floréal
Vacoas
4
See Curepipe Map p91
Trou aux Cerfs Crater
Curepipe
Viewpoints of Tamarin Falls
Forest Side
Montagne Lagrave (638m)
Montagne Laselle
Henrietta
La Marie
Simonet (632m)
M2
B3
A10
Eau Bleue Reservoir
See Black River Gorges National Park Map p88
Tamarin Falls
Tamarin Falls Reservoir
GRAND PORT
Mare Longue Reservoir
Mare aux Vacoas
Nouvelle France
Montagne Perruche
A9
M2
A10
Rose Belle
Black River Gorges National Park
Le Pétrin
Grand Bassin
To Airport (12km); Mahébourg (17km)
To Chamarel (5km)
Grand Bois
Montagne Cocotte (771m)
Mare Tabac
Alexandra Falls
Piton Savanne (704m)
SAVANNE
Bassin Blanc
Brittania
To Souillac (10km); Bel Ombre (12km)
To Souillac (8km)
INFORMATION
British Council....1 A3
Centre Charles Baudelaire....2 A3
Municipality of Beau Bassin-Rose Hill....(see 2)
SIGHTS & ACTIVITIES
Eureka....3 A2
Floreal Square Textile Museum..4 B4
Le Réduit....5 A2
Mauritius Glass Gallery....6 B3
Phoenix Brewery....(see 6)
Quatre Bornes Central Market...7 A3
SLEEPING
El Monaco Hotel....8 A3
Maison Le Carne....(see 2)
EATING
Happy Valley....9 A3
Le Bon Choix....10 A3
Salaam Bombay....11 B2
OTHER
Père Laval's Shrine....12 B1

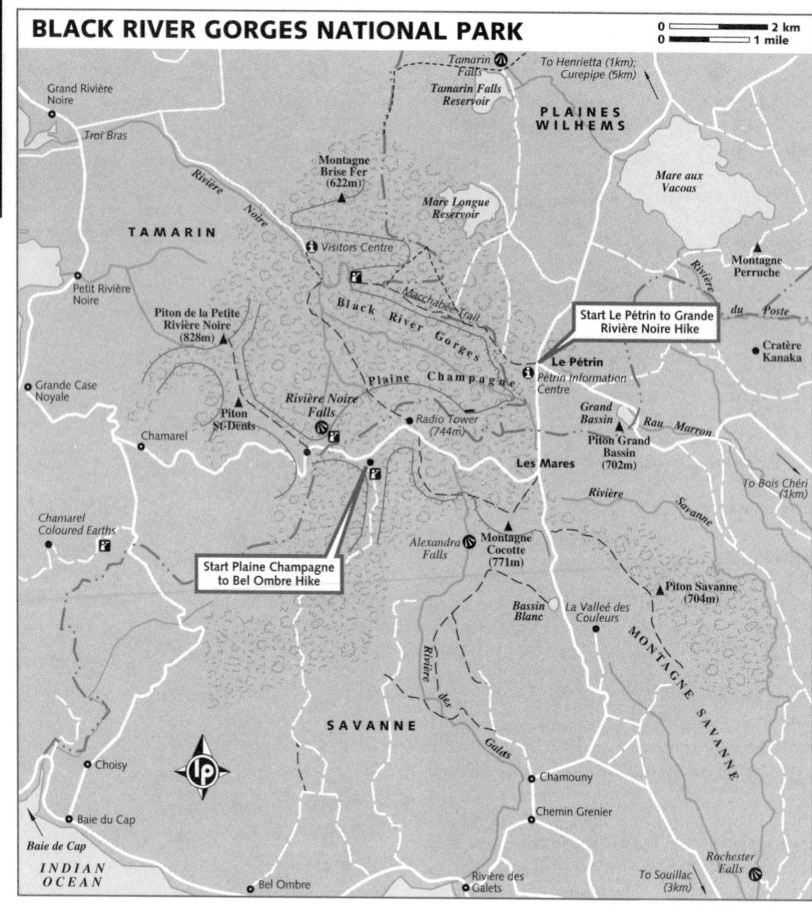

classic route follows the Macchabée Trail down the Black River valley to emerge on the west coast.

While Le Pouce and Corps de Garde can be reached by bus either from the plateau towns or Port Louis, accessing the trailheads within the national park will require private transport or a taxi ride.

Information

In general, hiking information is thin on the ground. Your best option is to seek advice from local people before setting out. The exception is the national park, where wardens at the two information centres (see p89) can give advice on the trails and sometimes act as guides.

A handful of local adventure-tour specialists also offer guided hikes (see p131).

Maps

The IGN map (p135) isn't completely up to date but shows most of the tracks and footpaths. Roads marked in yellow on this map are generally just rough tracks, sometimes passable only to 4WD vehicles, but perfectly acceptable as footpaths. They're all easy enough to follow, but smaller tracks (shown on the IGN map as dashed lines) are more difficult and may be overgrown, requiring a little bush-bashing.

Rough, photocopied maps of the national park are available at the park's two information centres (see p89).

Central Plateau

On the northern edge of the Central Plateau, the prominent thumb-shaped peak known as Le Pouce makes a great introduction to walking in Mauritius. It's an easy hike, offering a splendid half-day outing with stunning views over the plateau, and north to Port Louis and the coast. Corps de Garde, to the southwest of Rose Hill, is an impressive peak that also makes for an exhilarating half-day hike.

LE POUCE

The ascent of Le Pouce (812m) is best tackled from the south, near the town of Moka (p95).

The path starts northeast of Moka. To get there by public transport, hop on a bus heading to Nouvelle Découverte from Curepipe, Rose Hill or Port Louis' Victoria Square bus station and ask the driver to drop you off at the trailhead; services run roughly every half hour. Travelling by car, follow signs for Eureka from the motorway, then take the right turn signed to Le Pouce. After roughly 3km, where the road bends sharply to the right, a dirt track (also signed to Le Pouce) heads off east through the sugar cane fields.

After about 700m the path starts zig-zagging steeply uphill. A 30-minute climb brings you out on a saddle, from where you get your first views over Port Louis. From there it takes another 20 minutes or so walking east along the ridge to reach the base of the 'thumb'. The final ascent is almost vertical in places; if you don't feel up to it, never mind – even from the base you get sweeping views over the whole island.

Rather than returning the same way, you can head down to Port Louis. The path leads steeply down the north side of the ridge from the saddle. Allow about an hour for the descent.

CORPS DE GARDE

The wedge-shaped massif dominating Rose Hill (p94) offers a very rewarding ascent, though it's not for anyone with vertigo.

To reach the start of the trail from central Rose Hill, follow Dr Maurice Curé St northeast from the junction with Royal Rd. After about 1km, take a right turn into Surverswarnath St (you'll pass a Tamil temple on your left) and continue until you hit a staggered junction with the main road. On the far side, follow St Anne St up to a second staggered junction near the Hart de Keating stadium and follow Cretin Ave, which leads out into the fields.

The easiest trail to follow begins just beyond the football ground and Hindu crematorium. It runs straight up to the red-and-white radar antenna at the top of the ridge. From here, the main track follows the ridge south, passing a huge perched boulder before reaching a tricky cliff over which you'll need to scramble. There are several more hair-raising sections to test your courage before you reach the nose (719m), which offers amazing views over the plains.

Allow about three hours for the walk if you're starting from the centre of Rose Hill; 1½ hours if you drive up to the trailhead.

TAMARIN FALLS

These falls, roughly 8km southwest of Curepipe (p90), are awkward to reach but it's worth the effort for a beautiful, deep, cool bathe at the bottom of the series of seven falls. They are only accessible via a challenging trail that begins near the Tamarin Falls reservoir, south of the village of Henrietta, but you will have to explore to find it. It's best to take one of the local guides usually waiting around Henrietta bus station.

There are buses to Henrietta from Curepipe every 20 minutes or so and from Port Louis roughly every hour. From Henrietta, it's about a 2km walk to the falls.

Black River Gorges National Park

A network of hiking trails crisscross the wild and empty Black River Gorges National Park. Unfortunately, they're not always well marked and on occasion, walkers have become seriously lost. You should check the route and the current state of the trails at the information centres before setting off. Alternatively, you may want to hire a guide.

The main **visitors centre** (🕑 9am-4pm Mon-Fri, 9am-5pm Sat & Sun) is at the park's western entrance, about 5km southeast of Grande Rivière Noire (p107). The alternative is the **Pétrin Information Centre** (☎ 507 0128; 🕑 9am-3pm Mon-Fri) at the eastern entrance to the park. Staff at both can advise on the different trails and hand out fairly sketchy maps. They also sometimes act as guides. You should make the arrangements at least a day or two in advance. Rates start at Rs 500 a day.

All the trailheads are clearly marked and are accessed from one of the two roads running through the park. The main road runs north–south along the park's eastern boundary, past the Pétrin Information Centre, then swings westward at Les Mares to climb up onto the Plaine Champagne. The road's highest point (744m) is marked by a radio tower. About 2km further west is the Rivière Noire viewpoint, affording a spectacular view of waterfalls and Piton de la Petite Rivière Noire. After another 10km the road drops to the coast at Grande Case Noyale.

The second road branches south at the Les Mares junction. After 3km it passes Bassin Blanc, a classic crater lake surrounded by forest. Beyond the lake the road zigzags down the valley to Chamouny and Chemin Grenier.

Getting to the trailheads is difficult without your own transport. The best option is to get a taxi to drop you off and then pick up a bus at the lower end; the coast road is well covered by buses travelling between the main towns.

Note that there is nowhere to buy food or drinks in the park. Make sure you bring plenty of water and energy-boosting snacks. You'll also need insect repellent, wet-weather gear and shoes with a good grip.

The best time to visit the park is during the flowering season between September and January. Look for the rare tambalacoque or dodo tree, the black ebony trees and the wild guavas (see Guavas, right). Bird-watchers should keep an eye out for the Mauritius kestrel, pink pigeon, echo parakeet and Mauritius cuckoo-shrike, among other rarities; park wardens can indicate the most likely viewing spots.

LE PÉTRIN TO GRANDE RIVIÈRE NOIRE

This is a superb 15km hike that takes you through some of the finest and most scenic countryside in Mauritius. It begins beside the Pétrin Information Centre and traverses the national park, passing tiny pockets of indigenous vegetation dispersed through acacia and other introduced forest. Though steep in parts, it's moderately easy and reasonably fit walkers should be able to do it in four to five hours.

The first part of the walk follows the Macchabée Trail, a forestry track heading west from Le Pétrin along the ridge to a viewpoint overlooking the Grande Rivière Noire valley. From here the route descends precipitously along a steep and devilishly slippery track for about 1km, emerging on a wider path which continues down to the river and, eventually, to the visitors centre.

Most people arrange for a taxi to meet them at the visitors centre. If not, the last 5km is a less interesting but easy stroll along a sealed road which brings you out on the coast beside the Jade Pavilion restaurant and supermarket at the Trois Bras junction in Grande Rivière Noire. From here you can pick up buses to Quatre Bornes and Port Louis.

GUAVAS

During the guava season, from February to June, you will see hundreds of Mauritian families scrumping the fruit from wild guava trees all over Mauritius. The small red fruits resemble tiny apples and have a tart skin but a delicious soft interior with hard seeds; they taste like fresh strawberries! In case you are worried about picking the wrong thing, you'll see vendors selling bags of the fruit throughout the season for next to nothing. Try them the Indian way, with salt and chilli.

PLAINE CHAMPAGNE TO BEL OMBRE

The trailhead for this 16km walk is on the Curepipe–Chamarel road, just under 1km west of the radio tower which marks the road's highest point. The trail heads due south to Bel Ombre, passing through lovely mixed forests and plantations. After 10km you leave the park and start to cross private land. The last stretch meanders along some rather confusing tracks, but a reasonably good sense of direction will get you to the coast road without too much difficulty. From Bel Ombre, there are buses to Curepipe and Rivière des Galets.

Allow about four hours for this moderately easy walk.

CUREPIPE

pop 80,000

Located between Port Louis and Mahébourg, Curepipe is a fairly prosperous and lively place with good shopping, and some moderately interesting sights. These include

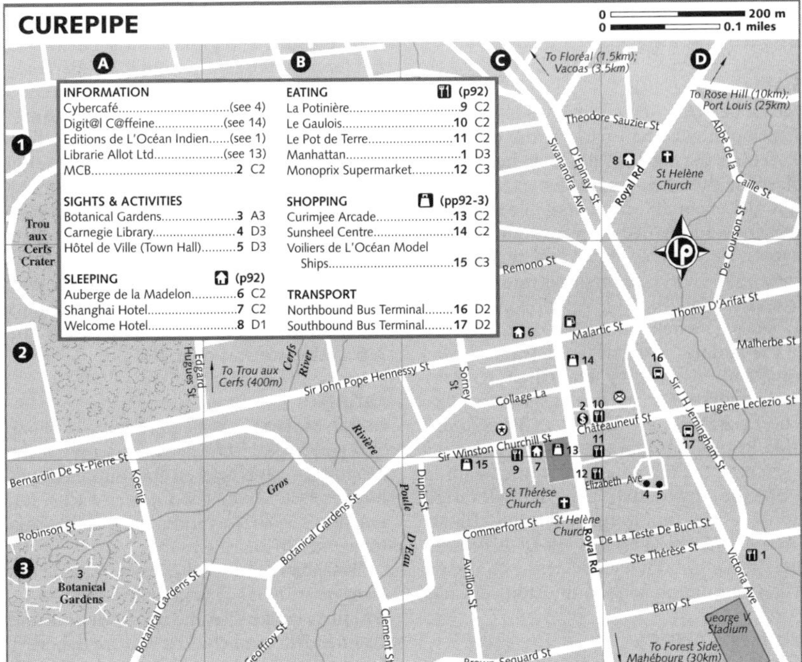

handsome buildings from the colonial era and a perfectly formed mini volcanic crater.

Curepipe is the highest of the plateau towns. At 550m above sea level, temperatures are refreshingly cool in summer, but the town is often swathed in cloud. The damp climate gives the buildings an ageing, mildewed quality. Bring an umbrella, as it can rain without warning at any time of year. According to lowlanders, Curepipe has two seasons: the little season of big rains and the big season of little rains.

Curepipe owes its size and prominence to the malaria epidemic of 1867, which caused thousands of people to flee infested Port Louis for the healthier uplands. Some claim that the name Curepipe originates from the days when soldiers from the Quartier Militaire would stop here to smoke and 'cure' (clean) their pipes. According to another theory, it's named after a village in southwest France.

Orientation

Curepipe is bisected by Royal Rd which runs approximately north–south. Most of the banks, shops and restaurants are on this street around the junction with Châteauneuf St. Head east along Châteauneuf St for the bus station. Most of the sights, such as the Trou aux Cerfs crater and the botanical gardens, are within easy walking distance of the centre.

Information

BOOKSHOPS

Editions de L'Océan Indien (☎ 674 9065; Manhattan Mall, Victoria Ave) Outlet of local publisher, with a number of titles on Mauritius.

Librairie Allot Ltd (☎ 676 1253; Curimjee Arcade, Royal Rd) Books, papers and magazines in French and English.

INTERNET ACCESS

Cybercafé (☎ 670 4897; Carnegie Library, Elizabeth Ave; per min Rs 1; 9am-6pm Mon-Fri, 9am-3pm Sat) Municipal cybercafé offering cheap access.

Digit@l C@ffeine (☎ 670 5335; Sunsheel Centre, Royal Rd; 9.30am-7pm Mon-Sat, 9.30am-3pm Sun)

MONEY

The major banks, most with ATMs, are located on Royal Rd. Among them is the

Mauritius Commercial Bank exchange bureau (9am-5pm Mon-Sat).

Sights

TOWN CENTRE

Overlooking a small park in the centre of Curepipe, the **Hôtel de Ville** (town hall) is one of Mauritius' best surviving examples of colonial-era architecture. Its gable windows, veranda and the decorative wooden friezes known as *dentelles* are typical of the style (see p53). The building was moved here from Moka in 1903.

The park's main draw is a copy in bronze of the famous statue of the fictitious lovers Paul and Virginie by Mauritian sculptor Prosper d'Épinay (see Paul & Virginie p85). The original is on display in Port Louis' Blue Penny Museum (p61).

Next to the town hall, the stone building with the distinctive neoclassical porch houses the municipal **Carnegie Library** (674 2278; 9.30am-6pm Mon-Fri, 9.30am-3pm Sat). Its collection includes rare books on Mauritius dating back to the 18th century.

TROU AUX CERFS

About 1km west of central Curepipe, the **Trou aux Cerfs** (p87) is an extinct volcanic crater some 100m deep and 1km in circumference. The bowl is heavily wooded, but from the road around the rim – a favourite spot for joggers and walkers – you get lovely views of the plateau. There are benches for rest and reflection, and a radar station for keeping an electronic eye on cyclone activity.

BOTANICAL GARDENS

These well-kept and informal **gardens** (admission free; May-Sep 8am-6pm, Oct-Apr 7am-7pm), with their lakes and lawns, provide another pleasant spot for some quiet contemplation. They were created in 1870 to grow plants in need of a more temperate climate than exists at the Sir Seewoosagur Ramgoolam Botanical Gardens in Pamplemousses (p84).

Sleeping

At the time of writing, the choice of accommodation in Curepipe was limited to a couple of acceptable budget hotels. Things should improve, however, when the town's only mid-range option reopens after its refit.

Auberge de la Madelon (676 1520; madelon@intnet.mu; 10 Sir John Pope Hennessy St; s/d incl breakfast Rs 500/550;) By far the best option is this spruce and friendly place on a quiet road not far from the centre. Simple but perfectly comfortable rooms come with private bathroom, air-con, TV, fridge and phone.

Welcome Hotel (675 3265; fax 674 7292; 196 Royal Rd; d incl breakfast Rs 500, without toilet Rs 400) The welcome is certainly warm, and the fan-cooled rooms are clean and functional, with iron bedsteads. There are shared toilets for the cheaper rooms.

Shanghai Hotel (676 1965; fax 674 4267; Sir Winston Churchill St) This mid-range business hotel should be worth a look when the renovation work is completed.

Eating

Le Pot de Terre (676 2204; mains Rs 50-125; 7.30am-8pm Mon-Sat, 7.30am-2pm Sun) Opposite the Mono-prix supermarket, this unpretentious local's place serves good value snacks and lunches. The choice ranges from sandwiches to grilled fish and fried rice.

Manhattan (674 0594; 2F Manhattan Mall, Victoria Ave; mains Rs 120-350; lunch Tue-Sun, dinner Tue-Sat;) Juicy steaks, ribs and combos (steak and calamari, ribs and chicken etc) are the order of the day at this ranch-style steakhouse, alongside burgers and Mexican dishes. Noncarnivores can opt for veggie enchilada or fajita, and there's a good kids' menu.

La Potinière (676 2648; Sir Winston Churchill St; mains from around Rs 200, crêpes Rs 100-200; lunch only Mon-Sat;) Curepipe's most upmarket restaurant hides in an unassuming concrete block, but inside all is starched linen and gleaming tableware. It serves predominantly French cuisine, with a choice of sweet and savoury crêpes (pancakes) as well as more substantial dishes, and excellent home-made deserts.

Le Gaulois (675 5674; Dr Ferrière St; mains around Rs 190; lunch only Mon-Sat) This small and unfussy restaurant does unusual takes on local dishes, such as spaghetti Creole and prawn tagliatelle, as well as more mainstream curries and French fare.

Shopping

There are several shopping malls around the central crossroads. Of these, the **Curimjee Arcade** (Royal Rd) contains a collection of upmarket duty-free shops selling clothes and souvenirs. Further north, the glitzy new **Sunsheel Centre** (Royal Rd) is also worth a

OLIVIER CIRENDINI

Fishing boat in Riviere du Rempart, Grand Baie (p74)

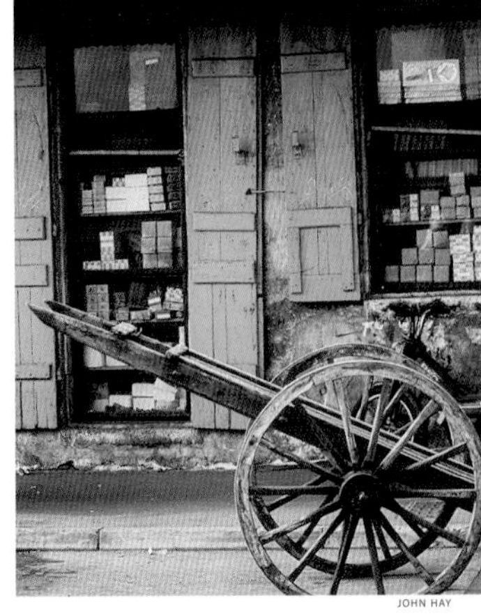

JOHN HAY

Shops, Port Louis (p57)

Local fisherman, Mauritius (p50)

JOHN HAY

JO

Séga musician with *ravanne* (p52), Mauritius

OLIVIER CIRENDINI

Waterfall, Trois Roches (p229)

Fried fish patties at Port Louis market (p60), Mauritius

SUSAN

GRAND BASSIN

According to legend, Shiva and his wife Parvati were circling the earth on a contraption made from flowers when they were dazzled by an island set in an emerald sea. Shiva, who was carrying the Ganges River on his head to protect the world from floods, decided to land. As he did so a couple of drops of water sprayed from his head and landed in a crater to form a lake. The Ganges expressed unhappiness about its water being left on an uninhabited island, but Shiva replied that dwellers from the banks of the Ganges would one day settle there and perform an annual pilgrimage, during which water from the lake would be presented as an offering.

The dazzling island is, of course, Mauritius; the legendary crater lake is known as Grand Bassin (or Ganga Talao). It is a renowned pilgrimage site, to which up to 500,000 of the island's Hindu community come each year to pay homage to Shiva during the Maha Shivaratri celebrations. This vast festival takes place over three days in February or March (depending on the lunar cycle) and is the largest Hindu celebration outside India.

The most devoted pilgrims walk from their village to the sacred lake carrying a *kanvar*, a light wooden frame or arch decorated with paper flowers. Others make their way by coach or car. Once there they perform a *puja*, burning incense and camphor at the lake shore and offering food and flowers.

Visitors are welcome to attend Maha Shivaratri, but should do so with respect; dress modestly, and remove your shoes before entering temples and holy places.

look. There's a lovely Indian fabric shop on the ground floor and outlets of Habit and Café Cotton.

Curepipe is a centre for model-ship showrooms and workshops. One such is **Voiliers de L'Océan** (☎ 676 6986; voiliers@intnet.mu; Sir Winston Churchill St; 🕓 9am-6pm), which has a good selection. You can see the ships being made between 8am and 5pm Monday to Friday.

Getting There & Away

Curepipe is an important transport hub, with frequent bus services to Port Louis (Victoria Square), Mahébourg, Centre de Flacq, Moka and surrounding towns such as Floréal, Phoenix, Quatre Bornes and Rose Hill. The terminals for north- and southbound buses lie on either side of Châteauneuf St, at the junction with Victoria Ave.

Expect to pay around Rs 400 for a taxi ride from Curepipe to the airport and Rs 350 to Port Louis.

AROUND CUREPIPE

Floréal

This slightly posh suburb northwest of Curepipe has become synonymous with the high-quality knitwear produced by the Floreal Knitwear Company. Of particular interest is the **Floreal Square Textile Museum** (☎ 698 7959; Swami Sivananda Ave; admission free; 🕓 9.30am-5.30pm Mon-Fri, 9.30am-4pm Sat) and shopping mall on the main road from Curepipe. Some of the workers who painstakingly put the clothes together will take you step by step through the commercial knitwear business. There's also a short video presentation and displays outlining the history not only of knitwear but of clothes and textiles in general. Although it's all to the greater glory of the Floreal Knitwear Company, it may open your eyes to how much work goes into making your favourite sweater!

You can buy Floreal knitwear in the shop below the museum; prices are good and there's a wider choice than in Floreal's other outlets around the island. The mall contains several equally upmarket clothes boutiques, and there's even a café on hand should you need sustenance. It serves slightly pricey but good quality cakes and light lunches such as salads and home-made quiche.

Phoenix

This industrial centre is the home of the **Phoenix Brewery**, located beside the M2 Motorway, which brews Phoenix Beer and Blue Marlin. While Phoenix doesn't hold much of interest for visitors, the **Mauritius Glass Gallery** (☎ 696 3360; admission free; 🕓 8am-5pm Mon-Sat), beside the brewery, produces unusual – and environmentally sound – souvenirs made from recycled glass. You can see them being made using traditional methods in the workshop, which also doubles as a small museum.

Black River Gorges National Park

This national park, some 10km southwest of Curepipe, is a favourite haunt of hikers. It also provides two spectacular drives. Perhaps the more stunning road, but only by a whisker, is that cutting west across Plaine Champagne before corkscrewing down to the coast; at each bend the view seems better than the last. The other road takes you plunging steeply down to the south. For more information, see p86.

QUATRE BORNES

pop 78,000

The bustling commercial centre of Quatre Bornes is best known for its twice-weekly clothes market. It takes place on Thursday and Sunday in the Central Market, located opposite the town hall on St Jean Rd, the main thoroughfare running southwest to northeast through Quatre Bornes. Locals flock here from miles around to rummage the stalls, where it's possible to find top-quality garments with almost imperceptible flaws selling at knock-down prices; check carefully though, since quality varies enormously.

Sleeping & Eating

Quatre Bornes' one decent hotel and the recommended restaurants are strung out along St Jean Rd.

El Monaco Hotel (☎ 425 2608, elmo@bow.intnet.mu; St Jean Rd; s/d incl breakfast Rs 805/920, half board Rs 1035/1380;) About 500m southwest of the town hall, this hotel is set off the street in a quiet courtyard with a pool and attractive garden. It offers functional but perfectly acceptable rooms with fan, bathroom, TV and telephone.

Happy Valley (☎ 454 6065; 79 St Jean Rd; mains Rs 160-350, dim sum from Rs 50 for 4 pieces; lunch & dinner, closed Wed;) This Chinese restaurant 200m or so northeast of the town hall is not strong on décor, but popular for its reasonable prices and tasty and well-prepared food. House specials include Peking duck, spicy squid and the aptly named Three Marvels Hot Pot, a seafood and vegetable steamboat. At Sunday lunch time it's packed with local Chinese families tucking into dim sum.

Le Bon Choix (☎ 465 3856; 76 St Jean Rd; mains Rs 130-350; lunch & dinner) Across the road from the Happy Valley is this cheerful and bustling place catering largely to tourists, though it's not expensive. In addition to hearty Creole curries, it serves meat and seafood grills and a selection of Indian and Chinese dishes.

Getting There & Away

Frequent bus services operate between Rose Hill, Port Louis and the bus station in Quatre Bornes beside the town hall. Buses for Curepipe, Floréal and Flic en Flac stop at regular intervals along St Jean Rd.

ROSE HILL

pop 106,000

Mauritius' second largest town after Port Louis sits at the foot of the impressive Corps de Garde mountain (see p89 for more about tackling this peak). Rose Hill retains a few interesting old buildings and is home to two major cultural centres. It also has a reputation as a cheap place to shop, particularly for imported Indian textiles.

Most places of interest are strung out along St Jean Rd, which is Rose Hill's main thoroughfare. The intersection of St Jean Rd and Vandermeersch St marks the town centre, where you'll find the bus station and the main shopping malls as well as numerous basic restaurants and food stalls. For tiptop Indian snacks, you can't beat the *dhal puris* sold by **Dewa & Sons** (Arab Town market, Royal Rd) to the south of centre; they're reputed to be the best on the island.

Cultural Centres

Two of the most important cultural centres in Mauritius are located in Rose Hill. The **British Council** (☎ 454 9550; general.enquiries@mu.britishcouncil.org; St Jean Rd; 11am-5pm Tue-Fri, 9am-2.30pm Sat) is across the main road from the bus station. It has a regular programme of events in English and a good library.

Behind Maison Carne is the **Centre Charles Baudelaire** (☎ 454 7929; ccb@intnet.mu; 15/17 Gordon St; 10am-5.30pm Tue-Fri, 9am-3pm Sat), which puts on an impressive schedule of plays, concerts and other events promoting French culture.

Creole Buildings

There are several impressive buildings in the centre of Rose Hill. The **Municipality of Beau Bassin-Rose Hill** on St Jean Rd is housed in an unusual Creole building which was constructed in 1933 as a theatre. Next door, **Maison Le Carne** is a more attractive old Creole mansion. It now houses the Mauritius Research Council.

Getting There & Away

There are regular buses from Port Louis and Curepipe to Rose Hill, and from Rose Hill to Centre de Flacq on the east coast.

MOKA & AROUND

pop 8500

Waterfalls, valleys, towering mountains and some wonderful mansions make the area around the town of Moka pleasant and picturesque. Only 10km south of Port Louis, Moka is the country's centre of academia, home to both the University of Mauritius and the Mahatma Gandhi Institute, which promotes Indian culture.

The ridge of mountains north of Moka provide some excellent walking. The most popular hike is to the summit of Le Pouce (812m), which provides stunning views over the central plateau and north to Port Louis (see p89 for more about climbing Le Pouce).

Le Réduit

Close to the university is Le Réduit, a superb mansion surrounded by an extensive park. It was built in 1778 for the French governor Barthélémy David, who succeeded Mahé de Labourdonnais. Now the President's official residence, it is sadly closed to the public.

Eureka

This renowned **Creole mansion** (☎ 433 4951; house only Rs 175, house & garden Rs 300; 9am-5pm Mon-Sat, 9am-3.30pm Sun), built in the 1830s, stands in woodland on the northwest edge of Moka. A masterpiece of tropical construction, the house boasts 109 doors, which keep the interior deliciously cool during the hot summers.

Inside is an unusually fine collection of period furniture imported by the French East India Company. There's also a Chinese room and a music room and, the height of sophistication in those days, a colonial shower contraption. Lining the staircase are some fine antique maps of Asia and Africa.

The courtyard behind the house is surrounded by stone cottages, which were once the staff quarters and kitchen. There is also an attractively landscaped garden containing ebony trees and other rare indigenous species, as well as a river and mini waterfalls.

Entry includes optional guided tours. Allow 30 minutes for the house alone and an extra hour for the gardens.

To get to Eureka, take a bus from Curepipe or Victoria Square in Port Louis and get off at Moka. Eureka is signed about 1km north of the bus stop.

Eating

Salaam Bombay (☎ 433 1003; Royal Rd; dishes Rs 80-280; lunch & dinner Tue-Sun) Just up the road from the Mahatma Gandhi Institute, this new restaurant is getting a reputation for its authentic Indian cuisine. Beautifully prepared tandoor and tikka dishes take pride of place, though there's also a wide choice of vegetarian dishes – the vegetarian thali (Rs 120) provides a good value sampler. The location, on a busy roundabout as you come into Moka from the motorway, is unpromising, but great food, attentive staff and the colourful contemporary décor more than compensate.

Eureka (☎ 433 4951; set menu Rs 575; lunch) Though somewhat pricey, lunch on the veranda of the colonial mansion is an experience to be savoured, both for the quality of the surroundings and the traditional Creole cuisine. The daily set menu consists of three courses plus coffee or tea.

EAST MAURITIUS

The east coast of Mauritius is relatively quiet and undeveloped. This is surprising since it's here that you'll find some of the island's best beaches, if not *the* best. As elsewhere, many of the prime stretches have been grabbed by the large hotels, notably around Trou d'Eau Douce and Belle Mare, but there's more than enough sand to go around. Even the public beaches here are quieter than almost anywhere else in Mauritius. The one exception is the hugely popular Île aux Cerfs, which offers several fine beaches and an alluring sandy-bottomed lagoon.

The village of Trou d'Eau Douce, with the only budget accommodation in the area, makes a good base. Towards Belle Mare it's largely big, luxury hotels, but further north

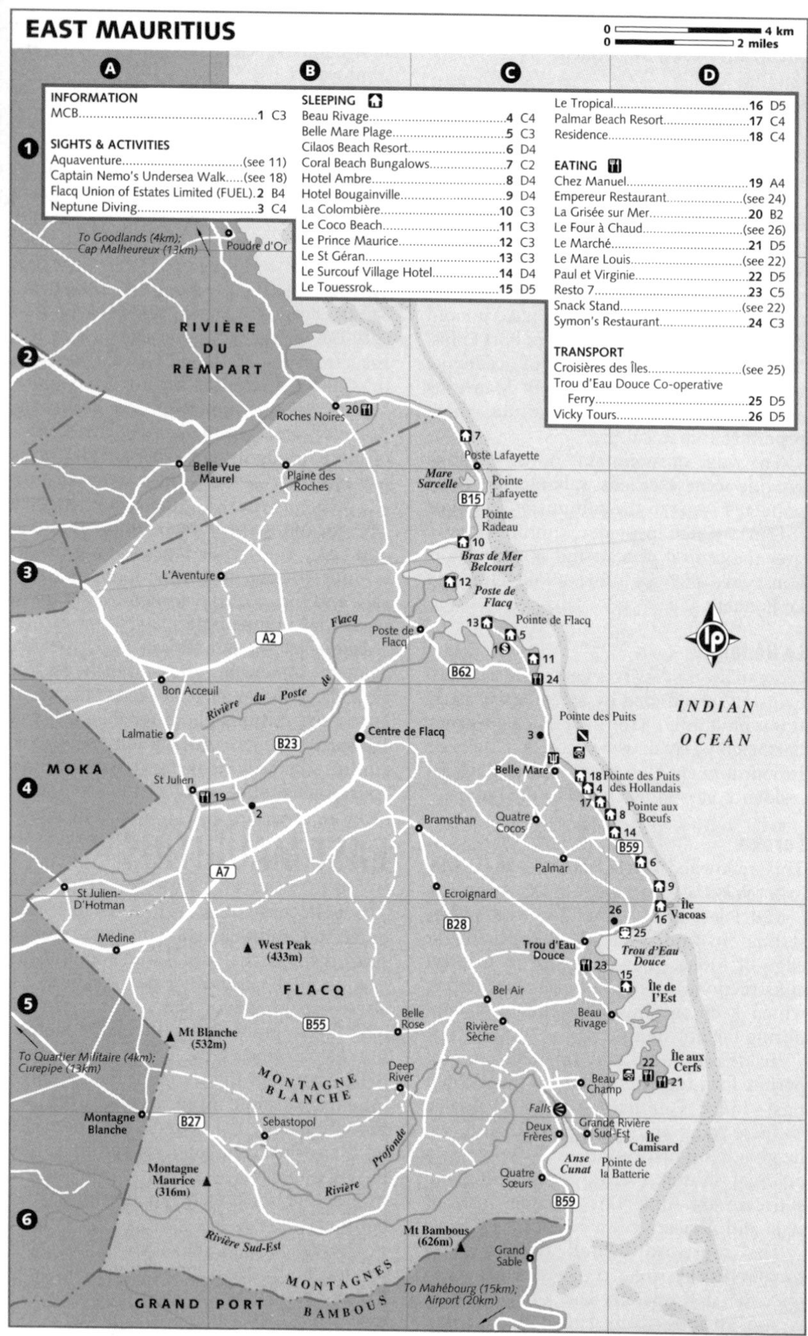
EAST MAURITIUS
0 4 km
0 2 miles
A
B
C
D
1
2
3
4
5
6
INFORMATION
MCB....1 C3
SIGHTS & ACTIVITIES
Aquaventure....(see 11)
Captain Nemo's Undersea Walk....(see 18)
Flacq Union of Estates Limited (FUEL)....2 B4
Neptune Diving....3 C4
SLEEPING
Beau Rivage....4 C4
Belle Mare Plage....5 C3
Cilaos Beach Resort....6 D4
Coral Beach Bungalows....7 C2
Hotel Ambre....8 D4
Hotel Bougainville....9 D4
La Colombière....10 C3
Le Coco Beach....11 C3
Le Prince Maurice....12 C3
Le St Géran....13 C3
Le Surcouf Village Hotel....14 D4
Le Touessrok....15 D5
Le Tropical....16 D5
Palmar Beach Resort....17 C4
Residence....18 C4
EATING
Chez Manuel....19 A4
Empereur Restaurant....(see 24)
La Grisée sur Mer....20 B2
Le Four à Chaud....(see 26)
Le Marché....21 D5
Le Mare Louis....(see 22)
Paul et Virginie....22 D5
Resto 7....23 C5
Snack Stand....(see 22)
Symon's Restaurant....24 C3
TRANSPORT
Croisières des Îles....(see 25)
Trou d'Eau Douce Co-operative Ferry....25 D5
Vicky Tours....26 D5
To Goodlands (4km); Cap Malheureux (13km)
Poudre d'Or
RIVIÈRE DU REMPART
Roches Noires
Belle Vue Maurel
Plaine des Roches
Poste Lafayette
Mare Sarcelle
Pointe Lafayette
B15
Pointe Radeau
Bras de Mer Belcourt
Poste de Flacq
Pointe de Flacq
L'Aventure
Flacq
Poste de Flacq
A2
B62
Bon Acceuil
Rivière du Poste de Flacq
Lalmatie
B23
Centre de Flacq
Pointe des Puits
INDIAN OCEAN
MOKA
St Julien
Belle Mare
Pointe des Puits des Hollandais
Pointe aux Bœufs
Bramsthan
Quatre Cocos
B59
A7
Palmar
St Julien-D'Hotman
Ecroignard
Île Vacoas
B28
Medine
West Peak (433m)
Trou d'Eau Douce
FLACQ
Île de l'Est
Bel Air
Belle Rose
B55
Rivière Sèche
Beau Rivage
Mt Blanche (532m)
To Quartier Militaire (4km); Curepipe (13km)
MONTAGNE BLANCHE
Deep River
Île aux Cerfs
Beau Champ
Falls
Montagne Blanche
B27
Sebastopol
Deux Frères
Grande Rivière Sud-Est
Île Camisard
Rivière Profonde
Anse Cunat
Pointe de la Batterie
Montagne Maurice (316m)
Quatre Sœurs
B59
Rivière Sud-Est
Mt Bambous (626m)
Grand Sable
MONTAGNES BAMBOUS
To Mahébourg (15km); Airport (20km)
GRAND PORT

again there are a few pleasant mid-range options for those seeking sun, sand and solitude.

Inland from the coast, fields of sugar cane interspersed with vegetable gardens slope gently up towards the mountains. It's an attractive scene, and makes a pleasant change from the beaches, though the area offers nothing particular in the way of sights. The main town, Centre de Flacq, has a good market and is also useful for its banks, shops and transport connections.

Getting There & Around

The main transport hub for east Mauritius is Centre de Flacq. You'll have to change here coming by bus from Port Louis, the Central Plateau towns or from Mahébourg in the south. There are onward connections from Centre de Flacq to villages along the east coast, although some services are pretty infrequent.

Most hotels and guesthouses have bikes for rent. Otherwise, you can rent bikes in Trou d'Eau Douce. Car rental can either be arranged through your hotel or through one of the big agencies (p142).

TROU D'EAU DOUCE

pop 5400

The first major settlement you reach travelling up the east coast is the attractive fishing village of Trou d'Eau Douce; the name (Hole of Sweet Water) refers to a sea pool fed by a freshwater underground stream. Its main claim to fame is as the jumping-off point for Île aux Cerfs. The majority of visitors come here on day trips, but Trou d'Eau Douce has enough in the way of accommodation and restaurants to make it worth considering as a base.

Trou d'Eau Douce is built on a sheltered bay. It's pretty much a one-road town, with almost everything strung out along the coast-hugging Royal Rd. The centre is marked by a church, near which you'll find the post office, police station and a small petrol station.

Internet access is available during restricted hours at the restaurant Sous le Manguier (see p98).

Sleeping

With its mix of guesthouses, self-catering apartments and hotels, Trou d'Eau Douce offers the broadest range of accommodation available on this stretch of coast. Prices are a touch higher than in Grand Baie and Mahébourg, for example, but this may change as the new hotels and apartment blocks going up immediately north of town begin to come on stream.

Le Dodo Apartments (☎ 480 0034; Royal Rd; apt from Rs 600) Four neat and very spacious apartments in a modern block set back from the main road, about 300m north of the church. All have a fan, TV and balcony or terrace. Bike hire is available.

Cilaos Beach Resort (☎ 480 2985; www.cilaos.mauritius.as; Royal Rd; studio/apt from Rs 900/1300) If you want to be right on the beach, try this small complex of studios and apartments about 1km north of Trou d'Eau Douce. They're not oozing character, but offer good value for money and are well kept and run by a very helpful family.

Le Tropical (☎ 480 1300; tropical@naiade.com; Royal Rd; s/d full board from Rs 3390/5100;) This three-star Naïade hotel is on a good beach about 500m north of town. It's a pretty place, with pleasant gardens and modern, comfortable rooms occupying seafront duplexes. Rooms are on a full-board basis only, but this includes all drinks, free boat trips to Île aux Cerfs and a number of water sports. Guests can also use the facilities at other Naïade hotels.

Le Touessrok (☎ 402 7400; www.oneandonlyletouessrok.com; s/d full board from Rs 12,150/18,000;) Ranked as one of the world's top hotels, this five-star combines an idyllic location with top-notch facilities and irreproachable service – you even get your own 'beach butler'. The rooms themselves are the last word in contemporary chic. The hotel owns not only Île aux Cerfs (p98), but also the totally exclusive, Robinson Crusoe-style hideaway, Îlot Mangénie. Other facilities include worldclass restaurants, a health spa, three pools, a kids' club and a recreational centre for teenagers. You will find it 3km south of town.

Other recommendations:

Auberge Etiennette (☎ 480 0497; etienet@bow.intnet.mu; Royal Rd; d/studio Rs 400/600) Friendly little place near the police station offering basic double rooms and studios (for up to three people) with fan and kitchenette.

Hotel Bougainville (☎ 480 2206; resa.bougainville@apavou-hotels.com; Royal Rd; s/d half board from

Rs 2220/3480;) Attractive and comfortable hotel squeezed on to a narrow strip of beach 800m north of town.

Resto 7 (480 2766; Sept Croisées; d/apt from Rs 400/900) Basic rooms below the restaurant (see below) plus good value apartments in a modern block nearby.

Sous le Manguier (419 3855, slm@intnet.mu; Royal Rd; studio Rs 400, apt Rs 600-1100;) The owners of this restaurant (p97) rent out two tidy self-catering apartments (for up to four people) and a small studio.

Eating

Sous le Manguier (419 3855; Royal Rd; snacks Rs 70-100, curry lunch Rs 150, dinner including drinks Rs 350; lunch, dinner on reservation only) Excellent home cooking is on offer at this combined snack and *table d'hôte* (where you eat with the family) opposite the church. At midday, you can tuck into a good-value curry lunch at the downstairs snackbar. In the evening, the owners invite you to join them for a veritable feast of local specialities on their upstairs terrace.

Resto 7 (480 2766; Sept Croisées; mains Rs 70-250; lunch & dinner) Signed 1km south of town, this friendly, family-run place specialises in seafood and local dishes such as lobster and octopus curry as well as more snacky options, like baguettes. It also offers well-priced boat trips to Île aux Cerfs.

Chez Tino (480 2769; Royal Rd; mains around Rs 160-250; lunch daily, dinner Mon-Sat) An attractive little place just north of the village centre, with reasonably priced food and a terrace overlooking the sea. Tasty Mauritian dishes include such staples as squid with lemon or *camarons* in garlic butter.

La Case la Paille (480 2821; Royal Rd; dishes Rs 75-125; 7am-8pm Mon-Sat, 7am-1pm Sun) Join the locals at this tiny, traditional restaurant across the road from Chez Tino. The menu consists of fried noodles or rice, grilled fish and perhaps chicken or octopus curry. It's all fresh and comes in generous portions. A simple bread-and-jam breakfast costs under Rs 50.

Le Four à Chaud (480 1036; Royal Rd; mains Rs 260-725; closed for dinner Sun-Fri) This upscale seafood restaurant at the north end of Trou d'Eau Douce is worth a splurge for a romantic candlelit dinner. Artfully presented dishes such as prawns with palm-heart salad and braised fish in banana leaf feature on the limited menu.

For self-caterers, there are grocers and small supermarkets along Royal Rd.

Getting There & Around

There are no direct buses from Port Louis to Trou d'Eau Douce. You'll need to change at Centre de Flacq, from where onward services to Trou d'Eau Douce run every half-hour. Taxis cost around Rs 250 from Centre de Flacq and Rs 1000 from the airport.

Vicky Tours (760 0254; Royal Rd; 9am-7pm), at the north end of town, rents bicycles for Rs 125 a day.

ÎLE AUX CERFS

Day-tripping tourists long ago replaced the *cerfs* (stags) on this low-lying island with its stunning, casuarina-shaded beaches, which now constitutes one of the top tourist sites in Mauritius. Don't expect splendid isolation, but the further you go from the boat jetty, the more likely you are to find a patch of sand between the sun-bronzed bodies. At low tide you can also wade across to the smaller and quieter Île de l'Est, which is joined to Île aux Cerfs by a picturesque sand bar. In winter, the beaches on the island's west side provide sheltered sunbathing spots.

Île aux Cerfs belongs to the plush Le Touessrok Hotel. The majority of water sports on offer are reserved for hotel guests, although the magnificent 18-hole golf course is also open to outsiders as long as they book in advance.

Many visitors bring picnics to the island, but there are two restaurants on Île aux Cerfs. The **Paul et Virginie restaurant** (mains from Rs 250; noon-3pm) on the beach offers expensive seafood while **Le Marché** (noon-3pm) offers Mauritian fare. Alternatively, beside the jetty is a **snack stand** (burgers, fried rice Rs 100; 11.30am-4.30pm).

Getting There & Away

Despite what the signs say, there is no public ferry to Île aux Cerfs. Guests of Le Touessrok get whisked over to the island for free on the hotel launch. Lesser mortals have to use one of the private operators in Trou d'Eau Douce. Those with a reliable reputation include **Vicky Tours** (754 5597; Royal Rd; 9am-5pm), **Trou d'Eau Douce Co-operative Ferry** (519 0452; Royal Rd; 8.15am-5pm) and **Croisières des Îles** (519 0876; Royal Rd; 8am-5pm), all at the north end of town. You can also arrange boats through Resto 7 and Chez Tino (see p98) or through your hotel or guesthouse.

Prices tend to be fairly standard, at around Rs 200 per person for the return trip by ordinary boat (15 minutes each way) and Rs 400 by speedboat (five minutes). Depending how busy it is, boats leave roughly every 30 minutes between 9am and 4pm, with the last boat back at 5pm at the latest.

Most operators also offer various combinations of Île aux Cerfs with glass-bottomed boat trips, snorkelling and a barbecue lunch. Another popular option is to include a side trip to the waterfall near the mouth of the Grande Rivière Sud-Est. For a package including Île aux Cerfs, the waterfall and lunch, expect to pay in the region of Rs 800 per person.

BELLE MARE & AROUND

North from Trou d'Eau Douce as far as Pointe de Flacq, a 10km-long beach includes some of the best white sand and azure ocean in Mauritius. The stretch around Belle Mare is generally regarded as one of the island's finest; Palmar beach, just to the south, is not far behind. North of Belle Mare, the scenery begins to change, becoming almost wild in places with creeks and marshy lagoons.

Information

Mauritius Commercial Bank (MCB; 9am-5pm Mon-Sat, 9am-noon Sun) has a useful branch with exchange facilities near the Belle Mare Plage hotel, but no ATM.

You'll find a few supermarkets in Belle Mare village, but for other services the closest town is Centre de Flacq.

Activities

The east coast's most famous dive site, 'the Pass', is located off Belle Mare. To explore this and other local sites, contact **Neptune Diving** (☎ 515 0936 or 251 4152; www.neptunediving.co.za; 8.30am-4.30pm Mon-Sat) at the Emeraude Hotel.

Nondivers can stroll among the fishes off Belle Mare. **Captain Nemo's Undersea Walk** (☎ 263 7819; www.captainemo-underseawalk.com; Rs 870; 8.30am-5pm), the long-established Grand Baie operation (p75), operates from beside the Residence hotel. Or try **Aquaventure** (☎ 729 7953; Poste de Flacq; adult/child Rs 800/600; 9am-4.30pm), based at Le Coco Beach hotel. In both cases bookings are required.

Sleeping

Not surprisingly, the coast around Belle Mare is the preserve of some of the most exclusive hotels in Mauritius. However, there are a few mid-range options scattered around. Those seeking solitude should head north along the road towards Poste Lafayette.

MID-RANGE

Le Surcouf Village Hotel (☎ 415 1800; fax 415 1860; Palmar; s/d half board from Rs 1900/3000;) Smaller than most along here, this family-friendly hotel offers 40 or so clean and comfortable if unexciting rooms, all with sea-view balconies. Rates include glass-bottomed boat trips and the use of canoes and pedalos.

Palmar Beach Resort (☎ 415 1041; www.palmar-beach-resort.com; Palmar; s/d half board from Rs 3900/5580;) A small-scale and efficient three-star on a stunning beach with a good range of all-inclusive water sports. The rooms are nicely designed with lots of natural wood and muted colours. There are two restaurants, a fitness centre, a kids' club and a dive centre.

Le Coco Beach (☎ 415 1010; www.lecocobeach.com; Poste de Flacq; s/d half board from Rs 4500/6600;) No-one could accuse the Coco Beach of subtlety; some will love the over-the-top décor and the carnival atmosphere, while others may find it way too much. It's a big place, with more than 300 rooms – brightly decorated, of course – set in spacious grounds on a 1km-long beach. The hotel boasts an immense pool and an excellent programme of kids' activities. Adults aren't forgotten either, with a disco and all sorts of boisterous entertainment, including a '*séga* initiation'.

Coral Beach Bungalows (☎ 423 9229; www.coralbeachbungalows.com; Poste Lafayette; studio Rs 1900;) This complex of six, two-person studios sits on a lovely, quiet stretch of beach and is run by a German-Mauritian couple. Each with a kitchenette and terrace, the studios are small but cheerful and absolutely spotless.

La Colombière (☎ 410 5248; www.colombiere-sur-mer.com; Poste Lafayette; studio/apt from Rs 1500/3000;) A broad range of self-catering studios and apartments (for up to seven people) in a great location, across the lagoon from the Prince Maurice hotel. Most units are in a rather unattractive block and are a bit cramped at the cheaper end, but clean and well equipped. There are two small pools and a tennis court.

TOP END

Belle Mare Plage (☎ 415 1083; www.bellemareplagehotel.com; Poste de Flacq; s/d half board from Rs 5940/8580;) A golfer's dream with no less than two championship-level courses and a well-respected golf academy. You can also indulge in water sports, tennis and squash, or flop by one of the three pools. Recently revamped, the hotel offers good value, with a broad range of accommodation and all the five-star comforts you'd expect. It's set in a 15-hectare park at the north end of Belle Mare beach.

Beau Rivage (☎ 402 2000; brivage@naiade.com; Belle Mare; s/d half board from Rs 7890/11,700;) Run by the reliable Naïade chain, this is another affordable five-star. The three-storey thatched villas, grouped around a huge pool, blend fairly successfully among the palm trees. Inside, imaginative use of sophisticated, tropical colours gives the rooms character.

Residence (☎ 401 8888; www.theresidence.com; Belle Mare; s/d half board from Rs 11,220/16,440;) The Residence stands out from its rivals by evoking 1930s colonial elegance, from the cane chairs, potted palms and Oriental antiques to the rooms with their light, natural fabrics and tropical woods – not to mention a personal butler.

Other recommendations:

Hotel Ambre (☎ 401 8000, resa.ambre@apavou-hotels.com; Palmar; s/d incl breakfast from Rs 3210/5400;) Large, moderately priced four-star in spacious grounds. Generous pool and good water-sports facilities.

Le Prince Maurice (☎ 413 9130; www.princemaurice.com; Poste de Flacq; s/d incl breakfast from Rs 12,150/16,200;) Surprisingly relaxed deluxe hotel in a superb location. Guests have access to facilities at the Belle Mare Plage.

Le St Géran (☎ 401 1688; www.oneandonlylesaintgeran.com; Poste de Flacq; s/d half board from Rs 16,000/23,700;) Ultimate luxury with a hint of colonial-era elegance, three ultra-sophisticated restaurants, outstanding spa facilities and a nine-hole golf course.

Eating

Outside the big hotels, the eating options along this stretch of coast are surprisingly thin on the ground.

Symon's Restaurant (☎ 415 1135; Belle Mare; mains Rs 100-250; 10am-10pm;) Tasty food at reasonable prices, a touch of ambience and professional service make this stand out. The Indian dishes in particular hit the spot, but it's a difficult choice from a huge selection of Indian, Creole and Chinese fare. It's just a shame it doesn't have a sea view.

Empereur Restaurant (☎ 415 1254; Belle Mare; mains Rs 50-130; 10am-10pm;) Next door to Symon's, and also looking west to the mountains, this somewhat cavernous restaurant offers cheap if unexciting Chinese standards such as fried noodles and sweet-and-sour squid.

La Grisée sur Mer (☎ 411 5622; Roches Noires; mains Rs 275-600; lunch & dinner) Though it's a touch pricey, this little seafood restaurant is one of the few places to eat along the coast north of Belle Mare. For something different, you can opt for sushi (from Rs 100 for eight pieces) or tuna sashimi (Rs 260) from the Japanese menu.

Getting There & Around

There are very occasional buses to Palmar from Centre de Flacq, but none to Belle Mare. At least one bus an hour runs from Centre de Flacq north via Poste Lafayette to Rivière du Rempart.

A taxi from Centre de Flacq to Belle Mare or Palmar costs about Rs 250.

CENTRE DE FLACQ

pop 16,700

The major settlement in east Mauritius is Centre de Flacq, a lively market town with a distinct Indian influence. There's nowhere to stay, but it's worth a visit just for the general hubbub and atmosphere. If you're heading to or from Trou d'Eau Douce, Palmar or Poste Lafayette by bus, you will have to change here.

Five kilometres west of Centre de Flacq, the **Flacq Union of Estates Limited** (FUEL; ☎ 413 2583) sugar mill is the largest and most modern on the island. Tours of the plant, which usually take place during the cane harvest (July to late November) have been suspended following a change in management, but may be resumed; phone to find out the current situation.

Eating

For a quick bite, there are numerous Indian snack stands and canteens in the town centre around the market and bus station. The main market days are Wednesday and Sunday.

In the village of St Julien, 1km northwest of the FUEL sugar mill, **Chez Manuel** (☎ 418 3599;

mains Rs 140-230; ⏰ lunch & dinner Mon-Sat) is a well-known Chinese restaurant. Try their 'Peking chicken' or treat yourself to a cracking seafood hot-pot. Reservations are recommended and transport is provided to and from eastcoast hotels.

Getting There & Away

Buses run between Port Louis' Immigration Square bus station and Centre de Flacq. Centre de Flacq is also linked by bus to Rose Hill, Curepipe, Mahébourg (via the coast road), Trou d'Eau Douce, Palmar and Poste Lafayette.

Taxis leave from near the market in Centre de Flacq and charge around Rs 250 to go to Belle Mare or Trou d'Eau Douce.

WEST MAURITIUS

Heading down the west coast of Mauritius from Port Louis, the cane fields gradually give way to pasture and then forest as the mountains encroach on the coastal plain. It's these mountains, together with Le Morne Brabant, an isolated crag jutting into the ocean, which give the region its distinctive character, providing a dramatic backdrop to the beaches and fishing villages.

There are few major settlements along this coast. Flic en Flac, in the north, is the biggest place around, but even it retains a village atmosphere, despite the number of holiday villas going up. Flic en Flac marks the start of a splendid strip of beach running south to Wolmar, with its clutch of luxury hotels. There's some excellent diving to be had along here, while further south Tamarin boasts a small surfing scene and Grande Rivière Noire is a centre for big-game fishing. Recently, this area has also become known as a good place for dolphin-watching, with a number of operators offering boat trips.

South of Grande Rivière Noire the beaches are replaced by mangrove swamps, but come back with a bang at Le Morne village. The 4km-long beach along the peninsula's west coast rivals that at Belle Mare (p99). The hotels here are also some of the best in the country.

Not that this region is just about beaches and water sports. The most visited sight in the southwest is Chamarel's famous coloured earths, in the hills east of Le Morne. There's also Casela Nature Park, near Flic en Flac, and an old watchtower – now a museum – at La Preneuse, north of Grande Rivière Noire. The Black River Gorges National Park (p89) is also within easy striking distance; the park's western entrance is only a few kilometres inland from Grande Rivière Noire.

Getting Around

The main bus routes in West Mauritius are those from Port Louis down to Grande Riviére Noire, and from Quatre Bornes to Baie du Cap. There is also an infrequent service between Quatre Bornes and Chamarel.

Your hotel or guesthouse should be able to arrange bike and car hire. Otherwise, one of the outlets in Flic en Flac or La Gaulette should be able to help.

FLIC EN FLAC & AROUND

pop 1800

Presiding over an immense beach and lying well away from the main coastal highway, Flic en Flac has a lot going for it. There's a decent range of places to stay and eat, and the town has all the essential services such as banks and a post office, yet is still small enough to feel comfortably laid-back. It remains to be seen how long this will last. All along this coast the cane fields are being ploughed up for new housing developments. There's now a glitzy supermarket complex and even a casino. Some argue that Flic en Flac is in danger of being spoilt, but for the moment it's still an appealing place to spend a few days. For those in search of a more exclusive beach holiday, Wolmar, 2km to the south, has a number of impressive luxury resorts. As to its delightful name, Flic en Flac is thought to be a corruption of the old Dutch name Fried Landt Flaak (meaning 'Free and Flat Land').

Orientation

The centre of Flic en Flac is dominated by the Spar supermarket complex. Most of the tour agents and car rental outlets and a number of hotels and guesthouses are located north of here along Flic en Flac's main road. There's another, older shopping mall, with a bank and a couple of restaurants, where this road turns sharply east, heading inland to the Port Louis-Tamarin highway.

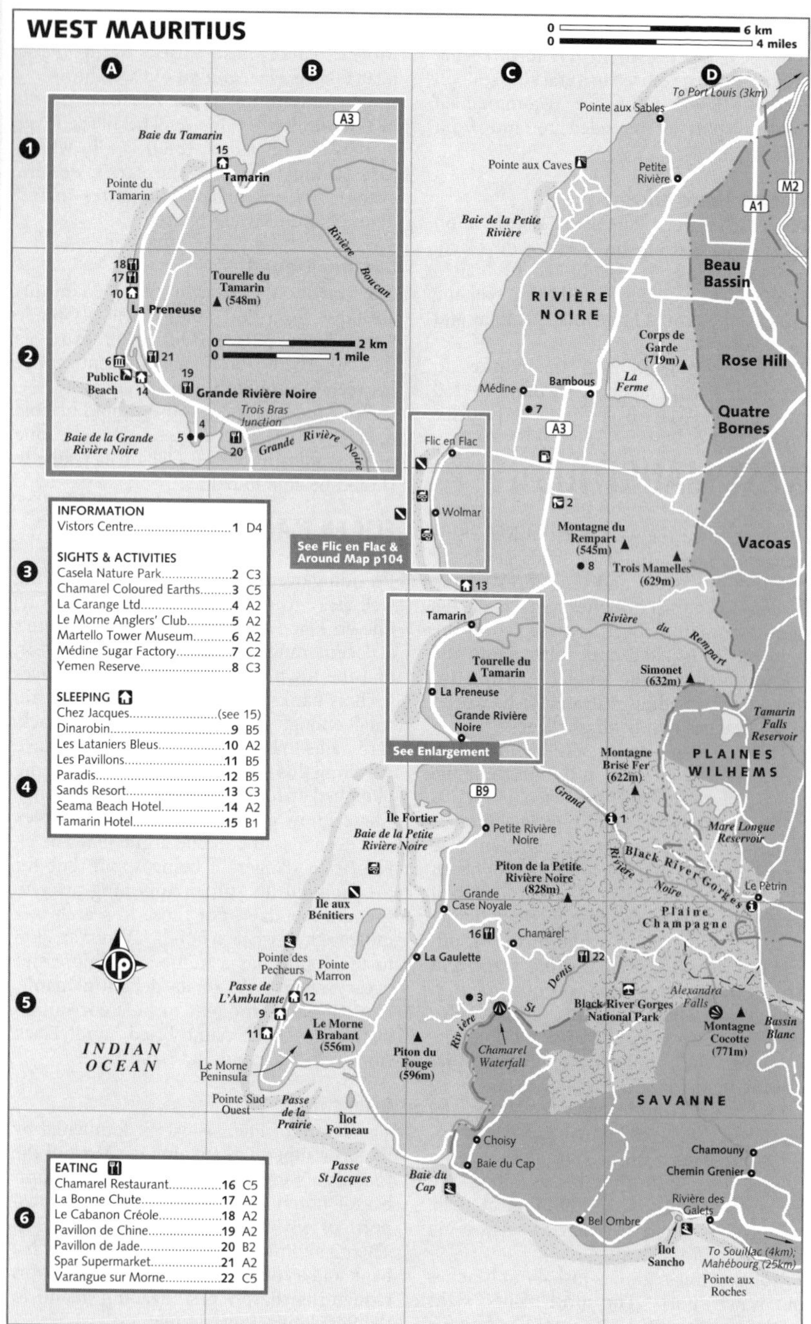
WEST MAURITIUS
0 6 km
0 4 miles
INFORMATION
Vistors Centre 1 D4
SIGHTS & ACTIVITIES
Casela Nature Park 2 C3
Chamarel Coloured Earths 3 C5
La Carange Ltd 4 A2
Le Morne Anglers' Club 5 A2
Martello Tower Museum 6 A2
Médine Sugar Factory 7 C2
Yemen Reserve 8 C3
SLEEPING
Chez Jacques (see 15)
Dinarobin 9 B5
Les Lataniers Bleus 10 A2
Les Pavillons 11 B5
Paradis 12 B5
Sands Resort 13 C3
Seama Beach Hotel 14 A2
Tamarin Hotel 15 B1
EATING
Chamarel Restaurant 16 C5
La Bonne Chute 17 A2
Le Cabanon Créole 18 A2
Pavillon de Chine 19 A2
Pavillon de Jade 20 B2
Spar Supermarket 21 A2
Varangue sur Morne 22 C5
Baie du Tamarin
Tamarin
Pointe du Tamarin
Rivière Boucan
Tourelle du Tamarin (548m)
La Preneuse
0 2 km
0 1 mile
Public Beach
Grande Rivière Noire
Trois Bras Junction
Baie de la Grande Rivière Noire
Grande Rivière Noire
To Port Louis (3km)
Pointe aux Sables
Pointe aux Caves
Petite Rivière
Baie de la Petite Rivière
Beau Bassin
RIVIÈRE NOIRE
Corps de Garde (719m)
Rose Hill
Médine
Bambous
La Ferme
Quatre Bornes
Flic en Flac
Wolmar
See Flic en Flac & Around Map p104
Montagne du Rempart (545m)
Trois Mamelles (629m)
Vacoas
Rivière du Rempart
Simonet (632m)
Tourelle du Tamarin
Tamarin Falls Reservoir
See Enlargement
Montagne Brise Fer (622m)
PLAINES WILHEMS
Île Fortier
Baie de la Petite Rivière Noire
Petite Rivière Noire
Grand Rivière Noire
Black River Gorges
Mare Longue Reservoir
Piton de la Petite Rivière Noire (828m)
Le Pétrin
Île aux Bénitiers
Grande Case Noyale
Plaine Champagne
Chamarel
Pointe des Pecheurs
Pointe Marron
La Gaulette
Passe de L'Ambulante
Le Morne Brabant (556m)
Denis
St Denis
Alexandra Falls
Black River Gorges National Park
Montagne Cocotte (771m)
Bassin Blanc
INDIAN OCEAN
Le Morne Peninsula
Piton du Fouge (596m)
Rivière
Chamarel Waterfall
Pointe Sud Ouest
Passe de la Prairie
Îlot Forneau
SAVANNE
Choisy
Baie du Cap
Chamouny
Passe St Jacques
Baie du Cap
Chemin Grenier
Rivière des Galets
Bel Ombre
Îlot Sancho
To Souillac (4km); Mahébourg (25km)
Pointe aux Roches

Information

The police station and post office are both on Royal Rd.

Flic en Flac Tourist Agency (☎ 453 9389; www.fftourist.com; 8.30am-5pm Mon-Sat, 8.30am-1pm Sun) Offers tours and cruises, car, bike and motorbike rental and can help find accommodation.

Le Resh Tourist Agency (☎ 453 9616; www.leresh.intnet.mu)

Mauritius Commercial Bank (MCB; exchange bureau 8am-6pm Mon-Sat, 9am-noon Sun)

Smartnet Café (8.30am-8pm Mon-Sat, 8.30am-6pm Sun) You'll find this Internet café in the Spar supermarket.

Sights & Activities

CASELA NATURE PARK

This 14-hectare **nature park** (☎ 452 0694; www.caselayemen.com; adult/child Rs 135/40; 9am-5pm May-Sep, 9am-6pm Oct-Apr) is on the main road 1km south of the turn to Flic en Flac. It is beautifully landscaped and has sweeping views over the coastal plain. The park houses some 1500 birds, representing species from around the world – some in rather small cages – including rare pink pigeons. There are also tigers, zebras, monkeys and deer living in a semi-reserve, and giant tortoises, one of which is 180 years old. Children are well catered for with a petting zoo, playground and mini golf.

Casela also offers 'safaris' by jeep, mountain bike or on foot around the nearby Yemen reserve (45 sq km), where deer, wild pigs, fruit bats and monkeys can be seen in their natural habitat; prices vary according to the different packages. Quad biking (around Rs 1000 per hour) and rock climbing (half/full day Rs 1200/1500) are also on offer.

The park has a pleasant **restaurant** (mains Rs 180-300; 10am-4pm) serving drinks, snacks and more substantial meals.

DIVING

The lagoon off Flic en Flac is good for swimming and snorkelling, and some of the best and most varied diving in Mauritius is to be found off the coast here; see Underwater Worlds (p38) for more information.

The dive centre **Exploration Sous-Marine** (☎ 453 8450, szalay@intnet.mu; 9-9.30am, 11-11.30am, 2-2.30pm & 4-4.30pm Mon-Fri, 9-9.30am, 11-11.30am, 1-1.30pm & 3-3.30pm Sat), based at Villas Caroline, has a particularly good reputation.

The majority of big hotels in Wolmar also have dive centres.

MÉDINE SUGAR FACTORY

During the cutting season (July to November) it's possible to take a guided tour (1½ hours) of this **sugar factory** (☎ 452 0401; adult/child Rs 135/60; 9am-2pm Mon, Wed, Fri Jul-Nov) 6km north of Flic en Flac. The factory is the second biggest in Mauritius after the FUEL refinery (p100) and the largest producing brown – rather than white – sugar. The guide takes you around the mill, explaining the whole complicated production process, and also the distillery, where the 'waste' molasses are turned into rum. The visit ends with a tasting session.

Sleeping

Flic en Flac has a good spread of apartments, hotels and guesthouses. All the luxury hotels, plus one or two mid-range places, are concentrated at Wolmar, 2km to the south.

Agents offering self-catering accommodation in the area, among other things, include **Flic en Flac Tourist Agency** (☎ 453 9389; www.fftourist.com) and **Jet's Villa Ltd** (☎ 453 9600; www.jet-7.com).

BUDGET

Little Acorn (☎ 453 5277; studio Rs 550) This friendly little place in the centre of Flic en Flac has a handful of neat and tidy studios. Though nothing fancy, they're okay for the price.

La Désirade (☎ 453 8520; apt from Rs 900;) Two large, homely and well-equipped apartments for up to four people hidden from the main road behind a small, flowery garden. The upstairs apartment has air-con and is slightly more expensive.

Easy World Hotel (☎ 453 8557; fax 464 5233; r Rs 500, apt from Rs 600) Set back a little from the main road, this three-storey block contains a range of rather aged rooms and self-catering studios and apartments. Ask to see several since standards vary.

MID-RANGE

Villas Caroline (☎ 453 8411; caroline@intnet.mu; s/d half board from Rs 2800/3600, superior Rs 3100/3800, apt Rs 4500;) This comfortable and colourful three-star is one of the few places right on Flic en Flac beach. All rooms are nicely appointed, but it's worth paying extra for the more spacious superior rooms, or you can opt for a bungalow-apartment. There is a great restaurant, entertainment most nights (including *séga* on Saturday) and a well-regarded dive centre.

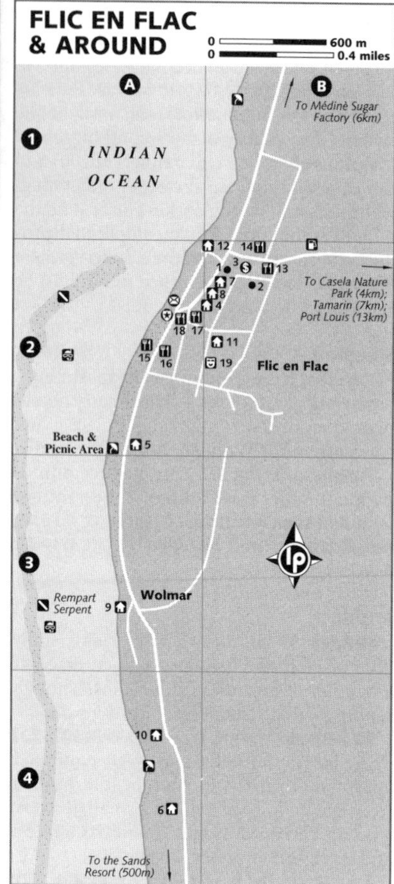

INFORMATION
Flic en Flac Tourist Agency....1 B2
Jet's Villa Ltd....2 B2
MCB exchange bureau....3 B2
Smartnet Café....(see 18)

SIGHTS & ACTIVITIES (p103)
Exploration Sous-Marine....(see 12)

SLEEPING (pp103-5)
Easy World Hotel....4 B2
Escale Vacances....5 A2
Hilton....6 A4
La Désirade....7 B2
Little Acorn....8 B2
Pearle Beach Hotel....9 A3
Sugar Beach Resort....10 A4
Villa Paul & Virginie....11 B2
Villas Caroline....12 B2

EATING (p105)
Casa Pizza....(see 11)
Le Bois Noire....13 B2
Le Papayou....(see 13)
Leslie Restaurant....14 B2
Mer de Chine....15 A2
Moti Mahal....(see 12)
Ocean Restaurant....16 A2
Sea Breeze....17 A2
Spar Supermarket....18 A2

DRINKING (p105)
Bar....(see 18)

ENTERTAINMENT (p105)
Casino....(see 18)
Kenzibar....19 B2

TRANSPORT
Sixt Car Rental....(see 4)

Escale Vacances (☎ 453 9389; www.fftourist.com; apt Rs 1500;) Justifiably popular modern apartment complex across the road from Flic en Flac beach. The fully-equipped, one-bedroom duplexes represent excellent value for money; those on the front get sea views, though cop some road noise. It's well run and friendly.

Villa Paul & Virginie (☎ 453 8537; csoobhany@hotmail.com; s/d incl breakfast Rs 1200/1500;) Owned by a jovial artist-musician, this guesthouse behind the Spar supermarket is full of suitably artistic clutter. The rooms don't have a lot of character, and are a touch expensive for what you get, but they meet all the basic requirements. It has an attractive courtyard and a great Italian restaurant, Casa Pizza.

Pearle Beach Hotel (☎ 453 8428; pearle@intnet.mu; s/d half board from Rs 2700/3600;) This is a friendly place right on Wolmar beach, with plain but perfectly decent rooms – all with air-con, phone and TV – in small bungalows or in a newer block behind. It has the usual water sports, including a good dive centre.

TOP END

Sands Resort (☎ 403 1200; www.thesands.info; s/d half board from Rs 4200/6960;) This reasonably priced and intimate four-star is a welcome addition to Wolmar's luxury hotel scene. The whole place has an airy, tropical elegance, from the open, timber-frame lobby to the bedrooms with their subtle, earthy tones, generous bathrooms and sea-view balconies or terraces. There are two restaurants, a spa and plenty of sports activities, including a dive centre.

Hilton (☎ 403 1000; www.mauritius.hilton.com; s/d half board from Rs 8800/12,100;) Set in luxuriant gardens, the Hilton exudes exotic atmosphere. The rooms are designed with equal flair, occupying small villas scattered discretely among the palm trees. There are no less than four restaurants, two bars, a top-class spa and a full range of sports activities.

Sugar Beach Resort (☎ 453 9090; info@oneandonlyresorts.mu; s/d half board from Rs 7580/11,230;) A plush hotel built to a colonial theme, with rooms in plantation-style houses surrounded by manicured lawns. If you can drag yourself off the beach, there are all manner of activities, from aerobics and bike rides to Creole language classes, cookery and cricket. The kids' club is also excellent.

Eating

Casa Pizza (☎ 453 8537; pizzas Rs 100-300; dinner) In the evening, the vine-covered terrace of Villa Paul & Virginie makes a nicely laid-back place for a pizza. There's live jazz on Friday and Saturday.

Leslie Restaurant (☎ 453 8172; mains Rs 75-150; lunch & dinner Tue-Sun) This sweet little Creole place at the north end of town is on the main road; it's friendly, and serves tasty curries and Chinese dishes in decent portions.

Le Papayou (☎ 453 9826; mains Rs 100-230; 9am-10pm) Upbeat café-restaurant opposite Leslie Restaurant, which attracts locals and tourists with its cheap prices and eclectic menu. It also does good breakfast deals.

Sea Breeze (☎ 453 9241; mains Rs 130-550; lunch & dinner, closed Wed;) This cheerful Creole-style place in the centre of town is popular for its reliable Chinese cuisine. There's a good range of seafood dishes – for a splurge, try the grilled lobster.

Moti Mahal (☎ 435 8411; mains around Rs 200-300; dinner only Tue-Sun) Treat yourself to some cracking north Indian cuisine such as *murg dopiaza* (chicken in an onion and tomato sauce) and the classic *rogan josh* (spiced lamb) in this refined restaurant in Villas Caroline.

Spar supermarket (Royal Rd; 8am-8pm Mon-Sat, 8am-1pm Sun) This supermarket is stocked full of goodies for self-caterers.

Other recommendations:

Le Bois Noire (☎ 453 8820; mains from Rs 100; lunch & dinner) Inexpensive Chinese-influenced food and seafood specials are on offer at this homely little place near Le Papayou.

Ocean Restaurant (☎ 453 8627; mains Rs 90-300; 10am-10pm;) This revamped restaurant across from Flic en Flac beach is best for its well-prepared Chinese dishes.

Mer de Chine (☎ 453 8208; mains from Rs 80; lunch & dinner) Cheap snacks on the beach.

Entertainment

Flic en Flac's entertainment scene largely revolves around the big hotels, to which outsiders are usually welcome if they phone ahead; there's generally an entry fee of around Rs 200 which is discounted against the bar or food bill.

Kenzibar (☎ 453 5259; 6pm-midnight Mon-Sat) Beside Villa Paul & Virginie, this laid-back bar is the best in town. It has flaming torches and African ambience, not to mention a mean *rhum arrangé*.

At the other extreme, there's a very sophisticated **bar** (11am-4am) – all low lights and fountains – in the Spar complex at the entrance to the **Casino** (☎ 453 8022; slot machines 10am-2am; gaming tables 9pm-4am).

Getting There & Away

There is a bus from Port Louis to Flic en Flac and Wolmar every 20 minutes or so. A taxi from Port Louis to Flic en Flac will cost you around Rs 300 to Rs 400, and Rs 800 to the airport.

Getting Around

The big hotels usually offer bicycle and car hire. However, you'll probably find cheaper prices at the switched-on **Flic en Flac Tourist Agency** (☎ 453 9389; www.fftourist.com) in the centre of Flic en Flac, or **Le Resh Tourist Agency** (☎ 453 9616; leresh.intnet.mu), up at the north end of town; count on Rs 150 to Rs 200 per day for bikes and upwards of Rs 1000 for the smallest car. The former also rents out 100cc bikes from Rs 500 a day.

Other car rental outlets include the following:

Easy World Hotel (☎ 453 8557; fax 464 5233)
Sixt (☎ 453 8475; sixtcar@intnet.mu)

TAMARIN

pop 3500

Tamarin rode high on the wave of surfing enthusiasm that swept the island in the 1970s. The scene is very low-key these days, but from May to September you'll still find young locals and the occasional tourist eyeing up the surf. Other than surfing and an OK beach, Tamarin doesn't have a great deal to offer, unless you're looking for somewhere cheap to kick back for a few days off the beaten track.

The surrounding landscape is drier and harsher than elsewhere in Mauritius. Salt production is a major industry in the area; Tamarin is encircled by salt evaporation ponds.

Sleeping & Eating

There are a couple of budget guesthouses on the road down to the beach from the church and a three-star hotel just along the seafront.

Chez Jacques (☎ 483 6445; fax 483 6252; s/d incl breakfast Rs 500/800;) There is something of a travellers' scene at this laid-back guesthouse, which is down on the left as you head for the beach. The rooms come with private bathrooms and are bright and cheerful after a renovation. The owner organises boat trips and has surfboards and bikes for hire.

Tamarin Hotel (☎ 483 6387; resa.tamarins@blue-season-hotels.com; s/d half board from Rs 2250/3000;) Set back from Tamarin beach, this revamped hotel goes in for kitsch, art-deco ambience. Facilities include a restaurant, bar, sauna and fitness centre, as well as kids' club and tour desk.

Getting There & Around

Buses headed for Tamarin leave Port Louis roughly every hour and Quatre Bornes every 20 minutes.

A taxi from Port Louis or Curepipe costs around Rs 500; from the airport it's about Rs 900.

Bicycles are available for hire at Chez Jacques (above), where you should also be able to arrange dolphin-watching and other boat trips.

LA PRENEUSE

A few kilometres south of Tamarin, the quiet village of La Preneuse merits a quick stop to visit the Martello Tower, which formed part of the old coastal fortifications and now houses an informative museum. La Preneuse was named after a French ship involved in a naval battle with the English in the area in the late 18th century.

Martello Tower Museum

In the 1830s the British built five Martello towers – copies of the tower at Martello in Corsica – to protect their young colony. They were trying to abolish slavery on the island in the face of fierce opposition from local French planters, who believed the lack of cheap labour would destroy the sugar cane industry. The coastal defences were built as a precaution in case the French navy came to support the feared rebellion.

While the other towers have either disappeared or are in ruins, the one at La Preneuse has been opened as a **museum** (☎ 583 0178; adult/child Rs 50/10; 9.30am-4.30pm Tue-Sat, 9.30am-1.30pm Sun). After a short video presentation, the guide points out the tower's ingenious design. With walls over 3m thick in places and topped by a cannon with a 2km range, it certainly seems impregnable, though in this case it was never put to the test.

Sleeping & Eating

La Preneuse offers a couple of places to stay – one of them excellent – and two interesting restaurants. Self-caterers can stock up in the big Spar supermarket on the main road.

Les Lataniers Bleus (☎ 483 6541; leslataniersbleus.com; d incl breakfast from Rs 2650, dinner Rs 400;) This delightful haven offers spick-and-span villas in a garden fronting onto the beach. The villas have up to five bedrooms and a communal kitchen; you can rent one room or the whole villa. The evening meals (by reservation only) are highly recommended.

Seama Beach Hotel (☎ 483 5506; s/d incl breakfast Rs 500/800) Simple, clean rooms are on offer at this friendly place close to the Martello tower and La Preneuse beach (if you take a dip, be careful of strong currents offshore).

Le Cabanon Créole (☎ 483 5783; mains around Rs 90; lunch & dinner) Friendly service and authentic and inexpensive Creole home-cooking make this traditional family-run place a perennial favourite. It serves a limited range of daily dishes such as *rougail saucisses* and chicken curry; specials, like lobster or whole fresh fish, can be ordered in advance. It's best to reserve in the evenings as there's only a handful of tables.

La Bonne Chute (☎ 483 6552; mains Rs 160-300; lunch & dinner Mon-Sat) Behind the wall next to the Caltex petrol station lurks this attractive garden-style restaurant. The food is upmarket, but not overly expensive. It serves seafood and Creole cuisine, with unusual dishes such as prawn bisque (soup) with cognac and roast wild boar. But make sure you leave room for one of the wicked desserts.

Getting There & Away

La Preneuse is on the same bus route as Tamarin, with services from Port Louis roughly every hour and Quatre Bornes every 20 minutes.

A taxi from Port Louis or the Central Plateau towns costs in the region of Rs 500. From the airport count on around Rs 900.

GRANDE RIVIÈRE NOIRE

pop 2200

Two kilometres on from La Preneuse, the otherwise sleepy community of Grande Rivière Noire is a major centre for big-game fishing. Just offshore from the mouth of the estuary, the ocean bottom plunges to 700m, providing the perfect environment for jacks and other bait fish. These small fry attract big predators such as tuna, shark and marlin. If you're after more gentle pursuits, you can also arrange cruises and dolphin-watching expeditions from here, and one of the two main entrances to the Black River Gorges National Park (p89) lies just 5km inland.

Activities

Deep-sea fishing is the main activity here between November and March. A number of local fishermen offer fully equipped boats. Many of them congregate at **Le Morne Anglers' Club** (☎ 483 6528; 6.30am-8.30pm), signed off the main road. You can also arrange trips through **La Carange Ltd** (☎ 729 9497; 6am-5pm) nearby. Prices vary between around Rs 6000 and Rs 9000 for a half-day trip (six hours) and Rs 9000 to Rs 13000 for a full nine hours. For further information, see p130.

Le Morne Anglers' Club also offers boat charter and catamaran cruises (Rs 1700 per person) along the coast, for a spot of dolphin-watching combined with snorkelling and a barbecue lunch.

Eating

Pavillon de Jade (☎ 483 6630; dishes Rs 70-250; lunch & dinner;) You'll find this appealing restaurant, with its bright and breezy room and views of the mountains, above a supermarket on the Trois Bras junction just south of Grande Rivière Noire.

Pavillon de Chine (☎ 483 5787; mains from Rs 150; closed Thu) Further north, this restaurant is more upmarket but opens onto the highway.

Getting There & Away

The Quatre Bornes to Baie du Cap service covers Grande Rivière Noire, with departures every 20 minutes or so. There are also buses every one to two hours from Port Louis. Taxi fares should be the same as for Tamarin.

LA GAULETTE & AROUND

pop 2000

South of Grande Rivière Noire, the mountains draw ever closer to the coast. There are pine woods and mangroves along the shore, but little in the way of habitation, beyond some down-at-heel hamlets, until you reach the fishing village of La Gaulette 8km or so later. La Gaulette boasts a couple of restaurants and a well-stocked supermarket, as well as a good guesthouse where **Ropsen Chawan** (☎ 451 5763, ropsen@intnet.mu; studio from Rs 900;) offers boat trips to the nearby Île aux Bénitiers, to swim and picnic on the beach (Rs 700 per person), and to watch the dolphins (Rs 900). There's even an **Internet café** (☎ 451 5910; 10am-10pm Mon-Sat) on the main road, beneath the Pointe Pecheur restaurant.

The reason most people come to this area, however, is to visit the famous 'coloured earths' of Chamarel, in the hills 9km east of La Gaulette. Chamarel features on almost every tour itinerary, though you'll find more colours and fewer people at the rival site near Souillac (p118). From Chamarel, a spectacular mountain road climbs onto the Plaine Champagne in the Black River Gorges National Park, while another, almost as scenic, heads south to Baie du Cap. This latter road is less well-maintained and may be impassable after heavy rains.

Sights

The much-vaunted **Chamarel coloured earths** (☎ 483 8298; admission Rs 60; 7am-5.30pm), 4km south of the quiet village of Chamarel, are interesting rather than amazing. The colours – there are said to be seven different shades of brown – are believed to be the result of uneven cooling of molten rock. In fact, there is a surprising amount of variation, particularly in bright sunlight.

About 3km down the road from the entrance gate to the earths, it's worth stopping off at the viewpoint over the

Chamarel waterfall, which plunges more than 100m in a single drop.

Both sites lie in the grounds of a private estate that once belonged to Charles de Chazal de Chamarel, who entertained Matthew Flinders during Flinders' captivity in Mauritius during the Napoleonic Wars (p119).

Sleeping & Eating

There isn't much choice for a place to stay around La Gaulette, but there's more when it comes to eating, with a couple of places in La Gaulette and two very fancy restaurants up in the hills. Self-caterers will find the essentials at the supermarket beneath La Gaulette Restaurant.

Guesthouse Ropsen Chawan (☎ 451 5763; ropsen@intnet.mu; studio from Rs 900;) The only accommodation in La Gaulette is provided by a local taxi driver who has a range of tidy self-catering studios and apartments for up to six people. He also provides evening meals on request (Rs 150 for a main course) and organises boat trips.

Pointe Pecheur (☎ 451 5910; mains mostly Rs 120-230; 10am-10pm Mon-Sat;) Above the Internet café, this cheerful little place offers some unusual dishes, with the emphasis on seafood, at reasonable prices. To start you could try *waaria*, a spicy vegetarian snack, or crab soup followed by tuna vindaloo, or perhaps grilled chicken with honey.

La Gaulette Restaurant (☎ 451 5116; dishes from Rs 100; lunch & dinner Tue-Sun;) The pink colour-scheme of this Chinese-Creole restaurant across the road from Pointe Pecheur won't be to everyone's taste, but the food is perfectly acceptable and not expensive.

Chamarel Restaurant (☎ 483 6937; set menu Rs 665; lunch Mon-Sat) Perched on the hillside 1km west of Chamarel, the prime attraction here is the stunning view rather than the overpriced food. Nevertheless, it's best to reserve since it's popular with tour groups and visiting dignitaries. Between 3pm and 4pm you can stop by just for a drink.

Varangue sur Morne (☎ 483 5710; mains from Rs 360; 11am-4.30pm) This former hunting lodge set in landscaped gardens 3km above Chamarel lives up to its reputation as one of the island's top restaurants. The views are pretty impressive, too. House specials include wild boar and venison, while the dessert menu features a lip-smacking coconut mousse with strawberry coulis. Afterwards, you can walk it off around the grounds. Reservations are advised.

Getting There & Around

Buses between Quatre Bornes and Baie du Cap stop in La Gaulette, with services every 20 minutes or so. There are no direct buses from Port Louis. Instead you have to go via Quatre Bornes, or take the bus from Port Louis to Grande Riviére Noire and change.

There are infrequent buses from Quatre Bornes to Chamarel, which drop you by the entrance to the estate.

A taxi from the Port Louis to La Gaulette will cost around Rs 600; from the airport, Rs 900. Expect to pay Rs 600 or so for the return fare from La Gaulette to Chamarel.

You can rent cars (from Rs 900 per day), bicycles (Rs 100 per day) and 50cc motorbikes (Rs 500) from Ropsen Chawan in La Gaulette.

LE MORNE PENINSULA

Le Morne, one of Mauritius' most alluring beaches, stretches uninterrupted for 4km along the coast of the 'hammerhead' peninsula on the southwest tip of the island. A number of exclusive hotels have taken advantage of the spectacular setting here, but there are still some stretches of unclaimed beach.

Reminiscent of the Rock of Gibraltar in shape, Le Morne Brabant (556m) is very imposing. The cliffs are said to be unscaleable, but, in the early 19th century, escaped slaves managed to hide out on top. The story has it that the slaves, ignorant of the fact that slavery had been abolished, panicked when they saw a troop of soldiers making their way up the cliffs one day. Believing they were to be recaptured, the slaves flung themselves from the cliff tops. Hence the name Le Morne (Mournful One).

Sleeping & Eating

Les Pavillons (☎ 401 4000; pavillons@naiade.intnet.mu; s/d half board from Rs 5650/8300;) In the midst of the big five-star hotels is this small and friendly member of the Naïade group. The rooms are in attractive plantation-style pavilions and the whole place has a nicely upbeat atmosphere. There are three restaurants, clubs for children and teenagers, and decent sports facilities. Not surprisingly, you'll need to book well ahead.

Dinarobin (☎ 401 4900; www.dinarobin-hotel.com; s/d half board from Rs 11,300/17,200; ⊠ ⁘ 🖳 🏊) It's difficult to fault this classy new five-star. From its beautifully conceived and airy rooms opening onto generous terraces, to the three top-class restaurants and the superb health spa, guests are cosseted all the way. The hotel boasts two big pools and an impressive bar, offering nightly entertainment, as well as a range of sports facilities. Guests also have access to the facilities at the Paradis next door.

Paradis (☎ 401 5050; www.paradis-hotel.com; s/d half board from Rs 9600/13,800; ⊠ ⁘ 🖳 🏊) The sister hotel to the Dinarobin is a mecca for sports enthusiasts. In addition to all the usual water sports, there's a championship golf course, six floodlit tennis courts and a high-tech gym; kids are equally well looked after. When it all gets too much, you can collapse in the health spa for a sports massage or even a special 'after-golf' massage. The rooms are suitably luxurious and the views arguably the best on the peninsula.

Getting There & Away

Buses en route between Quatre Bornes and Baie du Cap stop on the main road by the junction for Le Morne. These buses run roughly every hour. A taxi from Port Louis to the Le Morne hotels will cost in the region of Rs 800 and from the airport Rs 1000.

SOUTH MAURITIUS

The southern region of Mauritius includes some of island's wildest landscapes. Exploring the rocky, windswept south coast is one of the highlights of any visit to the country. You'll also find some impressive areas of preserved forest on the slopes of the aptly named Lion Mountain which dominates the southeast corner of Mauritius. Sun lovers, meanwhile, can soak up the rays and indulge in the usual water sports at the peaceful resort of Blue Bay. In general, however, this region is refreshingly free from tourist developments, which greatly adds to its appeal. Indeed, the only settlement of any size in the south is Mahébourg.

Getting There & Around

Mahébourg is the main transport hub in this region, with buses departing from here for destinations along both the east and south coasts. Mahébourg is also the best place to arrange car hire and about the only one offering bicycles and motorbikes for rent.

Towns along the south coast have slightly better bus connections than those in the east. Useful services include those from Souillac to Curepipe and Port Louis, and from Baie du Cap up the west coast to Quatre Bornes.

MAHÉBOURG

pop 16,000

Despite being the closest town to the international airport, Mahébourg retains an old-fashioned charm and provides a pleasant introduction to Mauritius. Many people spend just the first or last days of their trip here, but Mahébourg also makes a good base from which to explore the south and west coasts.

Founded in 1805, Mahébourg (pronounced my-bor) was named after the famous French governor Mahé de Labourdonnais. It started life as a busy port, but these days it's something of a backwater, with a small fishing fleet and a relaxed and friendly atmosphere. All that may change if the government's much-delayed plan to develop the waterfront Port Louis–style progresses any further. It's been mercifully slow-going. So far they've built a rather kitsch Chinese-style market hall and a more attractive seafront esplanade, where locals come for an evening stroll and to admire the view: Lion Mountain stands guard to the north while out to sea a smattering of islands mark the far side of the lagoon, which changes from one intense colour to another at great speed.

Mahébourg's most famous site is a small but interesting museum of naval history. The church also merits a quick look in passing and, if time allows, it's worth venturing just north of town to visit a delightful old biscuit factory. There are no beaches here, but Blue Bay is within easy reach as well as Pointe d'Esny, from where boats leave for Île aux Aigrettes.

Orientation

There's a decidedly French air to Mahébourg's grid of tree-lined streets which spread north and east from the butter-coloured Catholic church. The main commercial area is found to the northeast, focused on the market and nearby bus

SOUTH MAURITIUS

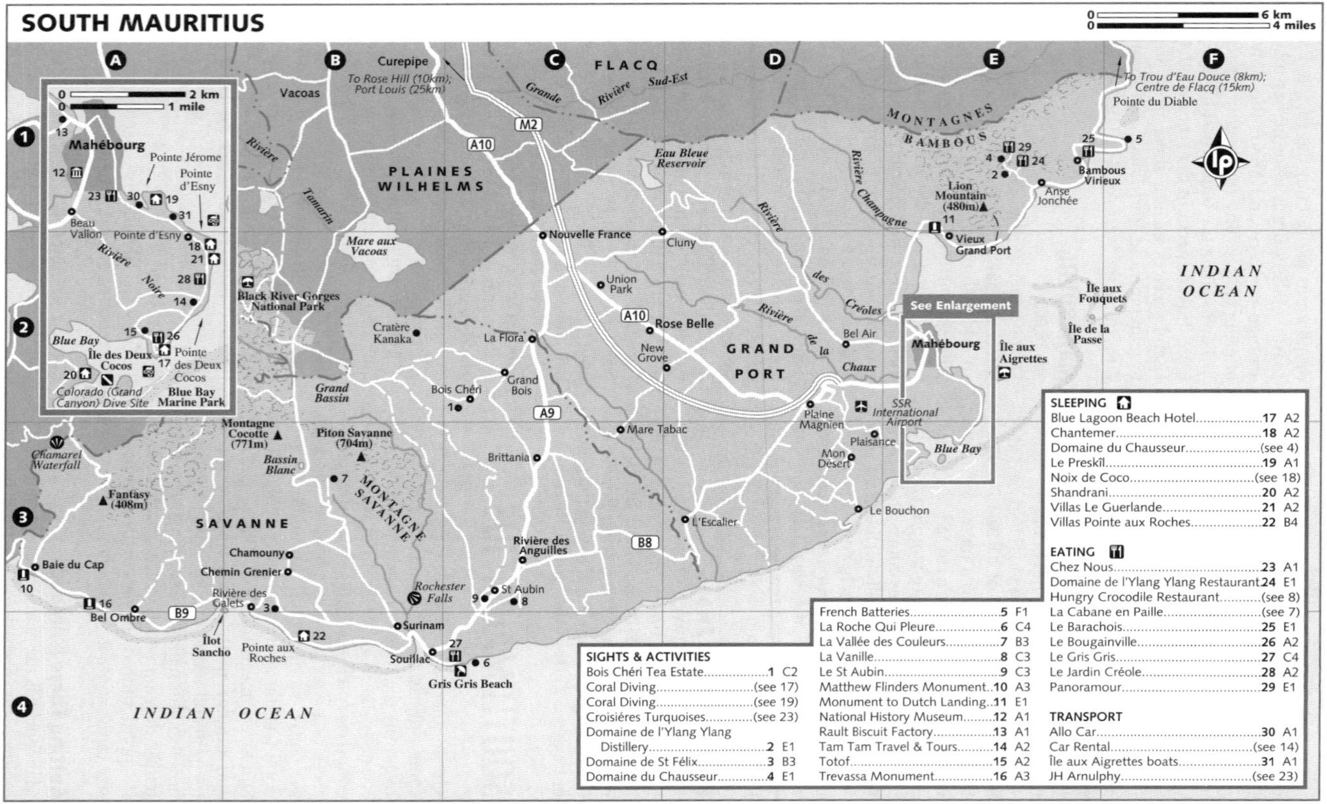

SIGHTS & ACTIVITIES

Bois Chéri Tea Estate	1	C2
Coral Diving	(see 17)	
Coral Diving	(see 19)	
Croisiéres Turquoises	(see 23)	
Domaine de l'Ylang Ylang Distillery	2	E1
Domaine de St Félix	3	B3
Domaine du Chausseur	4	E1
French Batteries	5	F1
La Roche Qui Pleure	6	C4
La Vallée des Couleurs	7	B3
La Vanille	8	C3
Le St Aubin	9	C3
Matthew Flinders Monument	10	A3
Monument to Dutch Landing	11	E1
National History Museum	12	A1
Rault Biscuit Factory	13	A1
Tam Tam Travel & Tours	14	A2
Totof	15	A2
Trevassa Monument	16	A3

SLEEPING

Blue Lagoon Beach Hotel	17	A2
Chantemer	18	A2
Domaine du Chausseur	(see 4)	
Le Preskîl	19	A1
Noix de Coco	(see 18)	
Shandrani	20	A2
Villas Le Guerlande	21	A2
Villas Pointe aux Roches	22	B4

EATING

Chez Nous	23	A1
Domaine de l'Ylang Ylang Restaurant	24	E1
Hungry Crocodile Restaurant	(see 8)	
La Cabane en Paille	(see 7)	
Le Barachois	25	E1
Le Bougainville	26	A2
Le Gris Gris	27	C4
Le Jardin Créole	28	A2
Panoramour	29	E1

TRANSPORT

Allo Car	30	A1
Car Rental	(see 14)	
Île aux Aigrettes boats	31	A1
JH Arnulphy	(see 23)	

station. Hotels and guesthouses are scattered among the quiet residential streets lying between Royal Rd and the seafront.

Information

Cybersurf (☎ 631 4247; Rue de Labourdonnais; ⏲ 9am-8.30pm Mon-Sat, 9am-noon Sun)
HSBC (☎ 631 9633; Royal Rd)
Mauritius Commercial Bank (MCB; ☎ 631 2879; Royal Rd)
Post office (⏲ 8.15am-4pm Mon-Fri, 8.15am-11.45pm Sat) The last 45 minutes before closing are for stamp sales only.
Man Ramdhayan (☎ 631 5638) Offers minibus tours of the island; prices start at Rs 300 per person. Book by phone (there's no office) and he'll come and pick you up at your hotel.

Sights

You can easily cover Mahébourg's smattering of sights in a day, leaving plenty of time to wander the back streets and take a stroll along the seafront. Everything can be tackled on foot, though you might want to hire a bike to get out to the biscuit factory.

NATIONAL HISTORY MUSEUM

The colonial mansion housing this **museum** (☎ 631 9329; Royal Rd; admission free; ⏲ 9am-4pm except Tue) just south of the Mahébourg centre used to belong to the Robillard family and played an important part in the island's history.

It was here in 1810 that the injured commanders of the French and English fleets were taken for treatment after the Battle of Vieux Grand Port, the only naval battle in which the French got the upper hand over their British foes. The story of the victory is retold in the museum, along with salvaged items – cannons, grapeshot and the all-important wine bottles – from the British frigate *Magicienne*, which sank in the battle.

Also on display are the bell and part of the cargo of Spanish coins from the wreck of the *St Géran*. The sinking of the ship in 1744, off the northeast coast of Mauritius, inspired the famous love story *Paul et Virginie* by Bernardin de St-Pierre (p85).

Other exhibits include early Dutch and Portuguese maps of Mauritius; china and beautiful seafaring instruments from assorted wrecks; a pistol supposedly belonging to the legendary corsair Robert Surcouf; the furniture of Mahé de Labourdonnais; and portraits of these and other figures pivotal in the history of Mauritius.

NOTRE DAME DES ANGES

The butter-coloured tower of Notre Dame des Anges church provides a focal point in Mahébourg. The original church was built in 1849, but it has been restored several times over the years, most recently in 1938. Take a quick peek inside at the baronial roof timbers. Local people visit throughout the day to make offerings to Père Laval (p68), whose statue stands to your right immediately inside the door.

RAULT BISCUIT FACTORY

In 1870 the Rault family started producing manioc biscuits at their little **biscuit factory** (☎ 631 9559; adult/child Rs 100/70; ⏲ 9.30am-3pm Mon-Fri) on the northern outskirts of Mahébourg. It has changed hardly a jot since. The crispy, square cookies are made almost entirely by hand, using a secret recipe passed down the generations, and baked on hotplates over stoves fuelled with dried sugar cane leaves. The short guided tour ends with a chance to sample the end result – with a nice cup of tea of course.

The factory is about 1km north of Cavendish Bridge; follow signs to 'Biscuiterie Rault'.

Sleeping

Mahébourg has a small number of guesthouses catering to independent travellers. Another possibility is to stay down the road in Blue Bay.

Auberge Aquarella (☎ 631 2767; aquarellamu@email.com; 6 Rue Sivananda; s/d incl breakfast from Rs 800/900) The best option all round is this well run and recently renovated guesthouse overlooking the bay. The rooms are very stylish. All have private bathrooms, and those on the front boast unbeatable sea views. Evening meals (Rs 350 per person) are available on request and are highly recommended.

Pensionnat Orient (☎ 631 2111; orient@intnet.mu; Rue des Hollandais; s/d from Rs 400/500) Another welcoming place to stay, with a range of unfussy but good value rooms. They're spruce and spacious and come with a TV and bathroom.

Nice Place Guest House (☎ 631 9419; niceplace55@hotmail.com; Rue de Labourdonnais; s/d from Rs 300/400, studio from Rs 500) This guesthouse run by a lovely

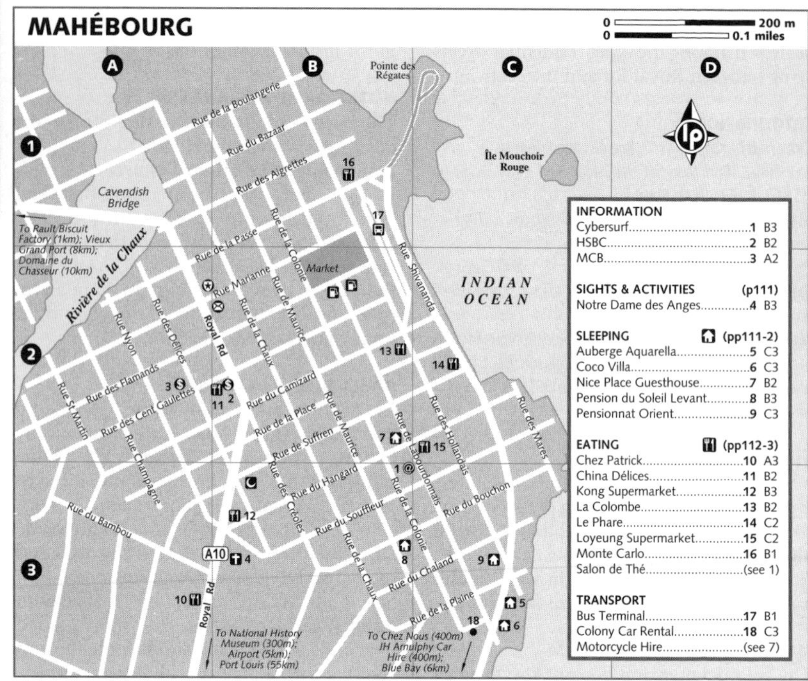

Indian couple has slightly faded rooms (with shared showers, toilets and basic kitchen facilities) and new self-catering studios.

Other recommendations:

Coco Villa (☎ 631 2346; cocovilla20@hotmail.com; s/d from Rs 600/750;) Overpriced but a possibility if everywhere else is full.

Pension du Soleil Levant (☎ / fax 631 9665; Rue Maurice; s/d Rs 300/350) Large and clean if boxy rooms above the owners' store.

Eating

Chez Nous (☎ 631 8906; Barachois; mains Rs 125-200; lunch & dinner, except Sat lunch & Wed;) Though it's a bit of a trek to this restaurant on Mahébourg's southern outskirts (on the coast road towards Blue Bay), the reward is a friendly atmosphere combined with delicious, well-prepared and very reasonably priced food; the sea views are an added bonus. In addition to fresh seafood and Creole dishes such as vanilla chicken, it offers quiche, grills, vegetarian lasagne and similar European fare.

Monte Carlo (☎ 631 7449; Rue de la Passe; mains from Rs 160; lunch & dinner;) Not the best location, overlooking the bus station, but pretty enough inside. It serves reliable Creole, Chinese and more pricey French cuisine. If you're counting the rupees, a dish of fried rice or noodles (around Rs 80) won't break the bank.

La Colombe (☎ 631 8594; 5 Rue Hollandais; mains Rs 170-300; lunch & dinner) This cheerful little restaurant offers an interesting variety of Creole and Chinese food as well as European staples such as burger and chips. House specials include venison and wild boar with honey. Things liven up a bit on Saturday, when it's *séga* night.

Chez Patrick (☎ 631 9298; Royal Rd; mains around Rs 100; lunch & dinner;) Patrick's is hugely popular with locals and tourists for its traditional atmosphere and authentic Creole cooking. Portions are on the small side, however, and when it's busy service can be excruciatingly slow. It's advisable to reserve in the evening.

For a quick bite, there are several lunch places and snack stands around the market and along Royal Rd. The best supermarkets are two Chinese stores: **Kong** (Royal Rd), beside the church; and **Loyeung** (Rue de Labourdonnais) across from Nice Place Guest House.

Other recommendations:

China Delices (☎ 631 7731; Rue des Cent Gaulettes; mains Rs 75-160; 🕑 10.30am-9pm, closed Thu) Cheap and cheerful Chinese, popular for its takeaway service.

Le Phare (☎ 631 9728; mains around Rs 450; 🕑 lunch & dinner) Mahébourg's swishest restaurant offers expensive seafood. The day we visited the service was a bit frosty.

Drinking

Mahébourg is not for party animals. The best that's on offer is the occasional *séga* night at La Colombe restaurant or perhaps a few drinks at the bar of Chez Nous.

Salon de Thé (Rue de Labourdonnais; 🕑 8am-5pm Mon-Sat, 8am-noon Sun) Near Nice Place Guest House, this is a perfect spot for a quiet cup of tea or coffee. It also does good pastries and will rustle up a coffee and croissant for breakfast.

Getting There & Away

Mahébourg is an important transport hub. There are express buses every half hour to and from Port Louis and at least every 15 minutes from Curepipe. Most but not all these buses stop at the airport en route; check before boarding. The shuttle to Blue Bay runs every 30 minutes.

Buses running north from Mahébourg go to Centre de Flacq via Vieux Grand Port every 20 minutes or so. Heading south, there are less frequent services to Souillac via Rivière des Anguilles.

A taxi for the 15 minute hop from SSR international airport to Mahébourg costs around Rs 300. From Port Louis expect to pay Rs 450.

Getting Around

For car hire, **Colony Car Rental** (☎ 631 7062; Rue de la Colonie) not only offers some of the lowest rates on the island, but the owner is exceptionally helpful. He also does competitively priced airport pick-ups. Otherwise, most guesthouses can help, or try **JH Arnulphy** (☎ 631 9806, ste.arnulphy@intnet.mu) beside Chez Nous restaurant. Arnulphy can also help with bicycle hire; rates start at Rs 75 per day. Blue Bay makes a leisurely excursion by bicycle.

Nice Place Guest House hires out 100cc motorcycles for Rs 500 a day.

AROUND MAHÉBOURG

While Mahébourg itself is short of sand, the beaches begin only a couple of kilometres south, at Pointe d'Esny, and continue down the coast for 4km to the hugely picturesque Blue Bay, aptly named for its brilliant blue lagoon. In 1997 the Blue Bay Marine Park was established to protect the relatively unspoilt coral reef. Just offshore, rare endemic animal and plant species are being reintroduced to the Île aux Aigrettes Nature Reserve.

Pointe d'Esny & Blue Bay

The coast from Pointe d'Esny to Blue Bay is lined with holiday villas. The area has a prosperous feel and is as popular with Mauritians as foreign visitors. At weekends in particular Blue Bay beach is crowded with picnickers, but during the week it can be blissfully quiet. Gently sloping and protected, the beach is excellent for children. There are a couple of good restaurants and some fine places to stay in the area, and visitors can indulge in the usual array of water sports.

ACTIVITIES

Blue Bay is the main centre for water-based activities in southern Mauritius. Options vary from snorkelling and diving to cruising around the offshore islands.

The main dive operator is **Coral Diving** (☎ 631 9505, 604 1000; www.coraldiving.com; 🕑 9am-5pm Mon-Sat, 9am-1pm Sun) with centres at both the Blue Lagoon Beach Hotel in Blue Bay, and Le Preskîl at Pointe d'Esny.

Totof (☎ 637 6342, 751 1772; 🕑 9.30am-4pm) is run by a young couple who get lots of recommendations for their glass-bottomed boat trips around the bay (Rs 200 per person for an hour's outing). They also offer longer excursions to the offshore islands; a day trip costs from Rs 900 per person including lunch. They operate out of a small green hut in the parking lot directly behind Blue Bay beach; beware rivals around Blue Bay who try to pass themselves off as Totof.

Another reliable outfit is **Tam Tam Travel & Tours** (☎ 631 8642; tamtnt@intnet.mu) on the road from Mahébourg. In addition to glass-bottomed boat trips in the bay (Rs 250 per person for 90 minutes), it organises longer excursions to nearby islands and up the coast to Île aux Cerfs (from Rs 850 per person).

Croisières Turquoises (☎ 631 8347; croistur@intnet.mu; 🕑 8am-4.30pm Mon-Fri & 8am-noon Sat), near Chez

Nous restaurant on the southern outskirts of Mahébourg, specialises in luxury catamaran cruises. Boats sail up to Île aux Cerfs (Rs 1500 per person) several days a week from Pointe Jérome near Le Preskîl hotel.

SLEEPING

Blue Bay is a popular place to stay, particularly with families. One slight disadvantage is the rumble of early-morning departures from the nearby airport; there aren't that many, but some people find them intrusive.

There are a few hotels in the area, but many people opt for self-catering apartments, which stretch along the coast as far as Pointe d'Esny. In addition to the places listed, Tam Tam Travel & Tours and the car rental outlets in Mahébourg (p113) can help find rental accommodation.

Chantemer (☎ 631 9688; www.chantemer.mu; d incl breakfast from Rs 1600) With only five rooms, you'll need to book well ahead for this attractive and well run private guesthouse with a lovely garden leading down to the beach. It's all tastefully decorated with family heirlooms and artworks. The owner goes out of her way to be helpful.

Villas Le Guerlande (☎ 631 9882; fax 631 9225; studio half board Rs 3100, seaside/gardenside apt from Rs 3680/3100;) This is a complex of bright and breezy self-catering one-bedroom studios and bungalow-apartments for up to four people. The cheaper, gardenside bungalows are across a quiet road from the beach.

Shandrani (☎ 603 4343; www.shandrani-hotel.com; s/d half board from Rs 6300/8700;) On the south side of Blue Bay, this relaxed and family-friendly five-star stands in lush gardens on its own private peninsula. It has no less than three beaches and all the facilities you would expect including four restaurants, a golf course, tennis courts a dive centre and more. The only slight hiccup is the location under the flight path.

Noix de Coco (☎ 631 9987; noixdecoco@intnet.mu; s/d incl breakfast from Rs 1000/1200;) A welcoming guesthouse with a handful of cheerful fan-cooled rooms grouped around a communal living/kitchen area. There's also a pleasant breakfast terrace and a garden.

Other recommendations:

Le Preskîl (☎ 604 1000; www.lepreskil.com; s/d half board from Rs 3480/4650;) Cramped but dazzlingly colourful Creole-style three-star built on a tiny promontory just south of Mahébourg. Numerous activities include *séga* nights and dive trips.

Blue Lagoon Beach Hotel (☎ 631 9529; www.bluelagoonbeachhotel.com; s/d incl breakfast from Rs 1730/2700;) An excellent location on Blue Bay, a good range of activities and reasonable prices compensate for the rather ordinary rooms.

EATING

Le Jardin Créole (☎ 631 5801; mains around Rs 200, pizzas Rs 95-155; lunch & dinner;) The plant-filled courtyard of this sophisticated little restaurant at Pointe d'Esny is just the place for a romantic candlelit dinner. Pizzas go down a storm, though it's a shame to miss out on luscious Creole mains such as seafood and palm-heart pancake, or grilled tuna with honey, lime and sesame. Reservations are recommended.

Le Bougainville (☎ 631 8199; mains Rs 170-250, pizzas Rs 135-165; 10am-10pm) In a shady spot behind Blue Bay beach, Le Bougainville attracts a constant stream of customers in search of refreshment. The menu ranges from salads and pizzas to dishes such as chicken with Rodrigues lemon.

GETTING THERE & AROUND

Buses to and from Mahébourg run every 30 minutes. A taxi there will cost Rs 50.

Car rental is available from **Allo Car** (☎ 631 1810; allocarltd@intnet.mu) and Tam Tam Travel & Tours at Pointe d'Esny. The latter also rents bicycles for Rs 75 per day and 50cc motorbikes for Rs 550.

Île aux Aigrettes

This island nature reserve lies roughly 1km off the coast. It preserves very rare remnants of the coastal forests of Mauritius and provides a sanctuary for animal and plant species unique to these islands.

Over most of the island, introduced invasive plants have now been replaced with native species. Rats, shrews and other imported animals, which cause damage to rare plant species and threaten indigenous animal species, are slowly being eradicated. At the same time, native species known to have existed on the island in the past – including pink pigeons, giant Aldabra tortoises and Telfair's skinks (a clawed lizard) – are being reintroduced. This is the only place in the world where you are almost certain to see pink pigeons in the wild; the population now numbers over 90 birds.

All this has been achieved by the **Mauritian Wildlife Foundation (MWF)** (☎ 631 2396; www.ile-aux-aigrettes.com; adult/child Rs 500/250), which now manages the reserve and conducts tours of the island; revenues are ploughed back into its conservation work. There are at least two departures daily from Pointe Jérome, near Le Preskîl hotel. Bookings should be made a couple of days in advance either by phoning MWF or through a tour agent. The 90-minute tour of the island involves a good deal of walking; wear comfortable shoes and bring a hat, sunscreen, water and insect repellent.

VIEUX GRAND PORT TO BAMBOUS VIRIEUX

North of Mahébourg, the main road hugs the coast as it winds around the base of Lion Mountain and the Montagne Bambous range. This area was the first settled by the Dutch early in the 17th century, and was one of the first parts of the country to lose its native ebony forest to the burgeoning sugar cane industry. Nevertheless, dense forest still cloaks the mountains. Hunting is a popular activity here, but the vast hunting estates also provide a valuable habitat for many native animal and plant species. One such estate is open to the public and nearby you can visit another where essential oils are distilled using traditional methods. Further north again, nature trails meander through an area of mangrove forest.

There are a few restaurants in the area, but the choice of places to stay is limited. With your own transport, the places described below can easily be covered on a day's outing from Mahébourg or Blue Bay, or from Trou d'Eau Douce to the north. Travelling by bus will involve a fair bit of walking.

Vieux Grand Port

pop 2900

About 5km north of Mahébourg, a small monument on the banks of the Rivière Champagne commemorates the first landing by Dutch sailors, which took place on 9 September 1598 under the command of Wybrandt Van Warwyck. The Dutch later built a fort 3km further north again in what is now the town of Vieux Grand Port. It was the local headquarters of the Dutch East India Company until 1710, when the Dutch abandoned the island. The site was then taken over by the French.

The battered ruins of Fort Frederik Hendrik stand in a park near the church at the northern end of Vieux Grand Port. A few clay pipes, wine bottles and other items left behind by the Dutch and French occupants are now on display in the **Frederik Hendrik Museum** (☎ 634 4319; admission free; 9am-4pm Mon-Sat, 9am-noon Sun) beside the entrance gate. The museum also outlines the history of the Dutch in Mauritius.

Vieux Grand Port is perhaps more famous as the site of the only French naval victory to be inscribed on the Arc de Triomphe in Paris. Relics of the 1810 battle with the English are on display at the National History Museum in Mahébourg.

> **REPLANTING THE MANGROVES**
>
> Following the 1866 malaria epidemic, in which nearly 3700 people died, the British colonial administration correctly identified the mangrove swamps around the coast of Mauritius as the main breeding ground for malaria-carrying mosquitoes. As part of a campaign of eradication, huge tracts of mangrove were uprooted or burned and swamps were filled in with volcanic boulders. Eucalyptus trees were even brought in from Australia to dry up areas of marshy ground.
>
> As an antimalarial strategy, the programme was very successful. It was only later that scientists discovered the important role that mangrove swamps play in the breeding cycles of many of the tropical fish that the islanders depend on for food.
>
> Today the Mauritian government is taking steps to preserve the remaining swamps and to re-establish mangroves, for example, at Bambous Virieux on the southeast coast of Mauritius. Of course, what is good news for tropical fish will also be good news for mosquitoes!

Lion Mountain

Overlooking Vieux Grand Port is Lion Mountain (480m), immediately recognisable from its sphinx-like profile. The mountain offers a splendid half-day hike with stunning views over the coast. It's a very challenging but rewarding walk that climbs up the lion's 'back' to finish at an impressive viewpoint on the 'head'.

The trail begins beside the police station at the north end of Vieux Grand Port. From there an easy to find 4WD track heads inland through the sugar cane; turn right at the first junction and follow the trail up towards the ridge. A set of concrete steps begins on the right just after you reach the start of the forested area. The steps lead to a bunker, from where a footpath climbs through the forest to the top of the lion's back. Once here you can detour to the right for a view out over the coast before heading inland to the peak itself.

The main trail is very obvious and runs straight along the ridge and up over a rocky area to the peak. There are a few hairy scrambles over the rocks before you reach the flat area on the lion's head. From here you can see right across the interior of the island. Return the same way you came up.

Allow around three to four hours for the return trip.

Domaine du Chasseur

As its name suggests, **Domaine du Chasseur** (Estate of the Hunter; ☎ 634 5097; www.dchasseur.com; admission Rs 170) is primarily a hunting reserve for wild boar and deer. The 950 hectares of forested mountain terrain also act as a reserve for many endemic bird species, including the Mauritius kestrel – one of the world's rarest birds of prey.

If there are no hunters around, visitors can walk up to the restaurant viewpoint or hop on a jeep (Rs 290) for the 1km ride; if you are eating, the entry fees are deducted from your bill. Better still is the guided two-hour forest walk (Rs 290) to a lookout 800m above sea level.

The estate's highly regarded restaurant, **Panoramour** (mains around Rs 150-600, 3-course menu Rs 860; 🕑 8.30am-4.30pm, dinner by reservation), is perched 500m up on top of a hill with wonderful views to the coast. It's a picturesque place to try delicacies such as estate-raised venison flamed in brandy and roast wild boar with yams; true gourmets may want to sample the pan-fried deer brains. If none of that appeals, you can have an afternoon tea or coffee and banana cake for Rs 170.

Accommodation is provided near the restaurant in thatched **bungalows** (inc breakfast d Rs 2500). It's a great spot if you fancy a splurge away from the beach.

Domaine du Chasseur is 3km inland from the coast road; the turn is signed just before the village of Anse Jonchée, about 12km from Mahébourg. If you phone ahead, someone will usually pick you up from the main road.

Domaine de l'Ylang Ylang

This small **estate** (☎ 634 5668; 🕑 9.30am-4.30pm) on the road up towards Domaine du Chasseur contains the only surviving commercial perfume distillery in Mauritius. Flowers and plants grown for their essential oils include the heady ylang-ylang flower, lemongrass, camphor, *baie rose* (pink pepper) and eucalyptus.

A basic tour of the gardens and traditional, wood-fired distillery where the plant oils are extracted costs Rs 75 per person; walking tours of the plantation also cost Rs 75. A tour of the plantation, distillery and forest with lunch costs Rs 550 per person, or Rs 600 by 4WD.

Also on the estate is a nicely rustic **restaurant** (mains around Rs 300; 🕑 9.30am-3pm) serving dishes such as venison curry and a few vegetarian options, washed down with the domain's own fruit juice.

To get to the restaurant, take the Domaine du Chasseur road for nearly 2km until you find the turn signposted to the right. The distillery is another 200m further on, signed to the left.

Bambous Virieux

This small settlement is the site of a pioneering project to restore the mangroves that were destroyed by the British following the malaria epidemic of 1866 (see Replanting the Mangroves, p115).

A short nature trail has been created through the mangroves at **Le Barachois** (☎ 634 5643; mains Rs 125-500; 🕑 10am-4pm, dinner by reservation), a restaurant that offers tasty seafood in small, rustic huts overlooking the water.

Getting There & Around

Buses between Mahébourg and Centre de Flacq ply the coast road, passing through Vieux Grand Port, Anse Jonchée and

Bambous Virieux. There are departures every 20 minutes or so.

A taxi from Mahébourg will cost around Rs 800 for a day trip taking in the Domaine du Chasseur and Domaine de l'Ylang Ylang.

MAHÉBOURG TO BAIE DU CAP

The south coast of Mauritius, from Mahébourg west to Baie du Cap, contains some of the country's wildest and most attractive scenery. Here you'll find basalt cliffs and sheltered sandy coves, waterfalls and traditional fishing villages where fisherfolk sell their catch at roadside stalls. Behind the coast, sugar cane fields and forests clothe the hillside in a patchwork of intense greens.

The region's prime tourist sites – a moderately interesting crocodile park and a tea plantation – are concentrated around Rivière des Anguilles and Souillac. Further west there's an area of 'coloured earths' to visit, but in general the scenery is the star attraction. While there are a number of beaches, few are suitable for swimming; in most cases the lagoon is too shallow or the current too strong.

This area is also the least developed for tourism. At the moment there is just one hotel along the whole coast and only a few restaurants. There are plans to build a clutch of hotels around Bel Ombre, but whether they will materialise is another question.

Rivière des Anguilles & Around

pop 10,000

The town of Rivière des Anguilles, 26km west of Mahébourg, holds no particular interest in its own right, but there are a number of sights in the countryside around.

LA VANILLE

Part zoo, part nature reserve and part crocodile farm, **La Vanille** (☎ 626 2503; crocpark@intnet.mu; Mon-Fri adult/child Rs 65/165, Sat & Sun adult/child Rs 125/50; 🕑 9.30am-5pm) is clearly signed 2km south of Rivière des Anguilles. The park has a successful breeding programme for giant Aldabra tortoises. There is also a variety of other reptiles and wildlife on display, and special activities for children, though the commercially raised Nile crocodiles are the main attraction.

Crocodile products are on sale in the park shop; personally we feel that crocodiles look better without handles, but there's no strong environmental reason not to buy.

Allow at least an hour for the visit. Should you feel peckish, or curious, try the **Hungry Crocodile Restaurant** (crocodile meat curry Rs 432, fritters Rs 247, croc & chips Rs 98). It also does more conventional dishes.

BOIS CHÉRI TEA ESTATE

This 250-hectare **tea estate** (☎ 617 9109; lesaintaubin@intnet.mu; adult/child Rs 75/150; 🕑 8.30am-3.30pm Mon-Fri, 8.30am-1.30pm Sat) is located about 12km north of Rivière des Anguilles. Visitors are taken on an hour-long tour of the tea-processing plant, before visiting a rather dusty museum to learn about the history of tea. More appealing is the tea-tasting which takes place in the company lodge, in the midst of the plantation with panoramic views of the coast. The estate produces seven different sorts of black tea, including the ubiquitous vanilla tea and a coconut-flavoured brew called Dodo tea.

ST AUBIN

The Bois Chéri tea company also owns **Le St Aubin** (☎ 626 1513; lesaintaubin@intnet.mu; adult/child Rs 150/75; 🕑 8.30am-4pm Mon-Sat), an elegant plantation house which dates back to 1819, in the village of St Aubin, 2km west of Rivière des Anguilles. The estate no longer produces sugar, but in the gardens of the house there is a traditional rum distillery and a nursery growing anthurium flowers and vanilla; the guide explains all about the fascinating history of vanilla production (see Vanilla Unveiled, p171).

The best vanilla pods are exported, while the remainder are used in the **restaurant** (including admission set menu Rs 690; 🕑 lunch Mon-Sat) of Le St Aubin, along with palm heart, pineapple, mango, chilli and other produce from the gardens. The traditionally furnished house makes a splendid setting for a meal featuring typical Mauritian dishes, including classics such as palm-heart salad or vanilla chicken. Reservations are recommended.

Souillac & Around

pop 4200

Continuing west along the coast, the next major settlement you come to is Souillac, 7km from Rivière des Anguilles. Again, the town is of little interest, but the coast here is impressively rugged and there are a few interesting places dotted around. Souillac is named after the Vicomte de Souillac, the island's French governor from 1779 to 1787.

SIGHTS

Robert Edward Hart Museum

Robert Edward Hart (1891–1954) was a renowned Mauritian poet, appreciated by the French and the English alike. He lived out the last 13 years of his life at Le Nef, in a coral-stone cottage just below the bus station which marks the centre of Souillac.

The cottage was opened to the public as a **museum** (☎ 625 6101; free admission; 🕒 9am-4pm Mon, Wed & Fri, 9am-noon Sat & Sun) in 1967. On display are some originals and copies of Hart's letters, plays, speeches and poetry, as well as his fiddle, spectacles and pith helmet. One of his speeches, on love and marriage, was delivered at the Curepipe hôtel de ville in 1914 for the benefit of English and French war victims.

Gris Gris & La Roche qui Pleure

Continue east along the road past the Robert Edward Hart Museum and you come to a grassy cliff top, which affords a view of the black rocky coastline where the reef is broken. A path leads down to the wild and empty Gris Gris beach; a wooden sign warns of the dangers of swimming here. The term *gris gris* traditionally refers to 'black magic', and looking at the tortuous coastline, you can see how the area got its name.

Right at the end of the next headland, 600m further on, La Roche qui Pleure (The Crying Rock) resembles a crying man. In fact it looks a lot like the profile of Robert Edward Hart. Two pictures in the Robert Edward Hart Museum show the comparison in case you need help spotting the actual rock.

La Vallée des Couleurs

In 1998, workers clearing new land for sugar cane 10km north of Souillac discovered an area of multi-hued soil similar to the coloured earths of Chamarel on the west coast. Analysis revealed that, instead of a mere seven different colours, here there were 23! To emphasise the point, in one section of **La Vallée des Couleurs** (☎ 622 8686; adult/child Rs 75/150; 🕒 9am-4.30pm) the earths have been separated into their different colours.

Not only do you get more colours for your money here, but the site receives surprisingly few visitors. A nature trail of sorts leads to the coloured earths past small waterfalls and picnic kiosks with views down to the coast. It takes about an hour to complete the circuit.

There's also a rustic café-restaurant, **La Cabane en Paille** (☎ 723 3115; mains around Rs 250; 🕒 10.30am-3pm), serving drinks and slightly pricey but well-prepared local dishes.

Domaine de St Félix

The St Félix **sugar estate** (☎ 622 6538; saintfelix@intnet.mu; adult/child Rs 200/100; 🕒 9.30am-5pm Mon-Fri, 9.30am-3pm Sat), 8km west of Souillac, was founded in the 1770s. It is the oldest working factory in Mauritius, and during the cutting season (mid-June to November) you can visit the plant to watch the steaming, clanking machinery in operation. The power to run the machines comes from burning the fibrous residue of the cane, known as *bagasse*, making the factory self-sufficient in energy.

SLEEPING

Villas Pointe aux Roches (☎ 625 6111; paroches@intnet.mu; s/d half board Rs 1380/2530, apt from Rs 2020;) If you want to get away from it all, Villas Pointe aux Roches is perfect. About 6km west of Souillac on the coast road, the villas here are fairly unappealing white boxes in need of maintenance, but the beachfront location and the setting among the palms are ample compensation. Facilities include a mediocre restaurant (though the breakfast buffet is good), kayaks, tennis and bikes (Rs 200 per day).

EATING

For a meal on the hop, try the snack stands around the bus station in Souillac.

Le Gris Gris (aka Chez Rosy; ☎ 625 4179; mains Rs 150-180; 🕒 noon-5pm) This smart restaurant beside the Gris Gris car park is a friendly place serving no-nonsense home-cooking.

Le Batelage (☎ 625 6083; mains Rs 300-500; 🕒 lunch & dinner) An upscale restaurant with a lovely shady terrace beside the river mouth in Souillac. It serves ultra-fresh seafood, such as whole steamed fish with curry sauce, and is well worth a splurge.

GETTING THERE & AROUND

There are buses roughly every half hour from Mahébourg to Souillac via the airport and Rivière des Anguilles. From Port Louis, buses run hourly, calling at Rivière des Anguilles en route. There are also frequent services to and from Souillac to Curepipe, with three buses a day taking the coast road via Pointe aux Roches. Buses heading along the coast to Baie du Cap depart hourly.

A taxi from Souillac to Villas Pointe aux Roches costs around Rs 100; Rs 450 to the airport.

Baie du Cap

pop 2300

In spite of a great variety of coastal scenery, this area has not yet been developed (though hotel developments are planned). You'll find some marvellous stretches of casuarina-lined sand west of Baie du Cap and there's good surf at Macondé Point, on the east side of the bay.

The only real sights in the area are a couple of low-key monuments. The first is the **Trevassa Monument**, about 1km beyond Bel Ombre village, which commemorates the sinking of the British steamer *Trevassa* in 1923. She went down 2600km off Mauritius. Sixteen survivors were eventually washed ashore at Bel Ombre having survived 25 days in an open lifeboat.

The second is the **Matthew Flinders monument** which stands on the shore 500m west of Baie du Cap. It was erected in 2003 in honour of the arrival here 200 years earlier of the English navigator and cartographer Matthew Flinders. He was less warmly received at the time; the poor bloke didn't know that England and France were at war and he was imprisoned for more than six years. For an interesting read on the subject, take a look at Huguette Ly-Tio-Fane Pineo's book *In the Grips of the Eagle: Matthew Flinders at the Île de France, 1803-1810.*

There are a couple of cheap and cheerful restaurants beside the junction in Baie du Cap village. **Chand Snack** (mains around Rs 90; 7am-10pm;) is the slightly smarter and offers the wider choice.

Bus services along here are limited. Baie du Cap is the terminus for buses from Souillac, and from Quatre Bornes via Tamarin. In both cases buses run approximately every 20 minutes.

RODRIGUES

The rocky volcanic island of Rodrigues, 600km northeast of mainland Mauritius, can seem dry and rugged after the tropical lushness of the main island, but most people very quickly warm to the friendly and laid-back atmosphere. As well as having some magnificent deserted beaches, the island is surrounded by extensive coral reefs with some of the best diving in Mauritius. There are also attractive walks in the rugged interior.

Although it measures only 8km by 18km, Rodrigues supports a population of about 37,000 people, almost all of African descent. Most speak Creole rather than French or English, and over 90% are Roman Catholic. After the abolition of slavery in Mauritius, many freed slaves chose to begin a new life here, away from their oppressors.

The economic mainstays of Rodrigues are fishing and agriculture, with tourism and handicrafts playing an increasingly important role. The fisheries around the island are exceptionally rich, though the lagoon itself is suffering from overfishing; the octopus catch in particular is dwindling rapidly. Pressure on agricultural land is also causing problems. Much of the island has been stripped of its tree cover, resulting in serious erosion. The cyclones that periodically rage across the island don't help either; in 2003 Cyclone Kalunde, which produced wind speeds of up to 250km/h, caused tremendous damage.

Long-term overfishing coupled with silting (from erosion in the hills) is placing severe stress on the marine ecosystem, with particular concern for the lagoon. **Shoals Rodrigues** (☎ 831 1225; www.shoals-rodrigues.org), an NGO working with local fishing communities, warns that large areas of coral have been damaged, mainly through destructive fishing practises associated with octopus gatherers, who go out on foot to prise the octopus from their shelters. At the same time, fishing with seine nets, which remove young as well as mature fish, is depleting fish stocks. The number of fishing licences has been cut substantially and Shoals is also working to establish a network of marine reserves, which will replenish fish populations throughout the lagoon.

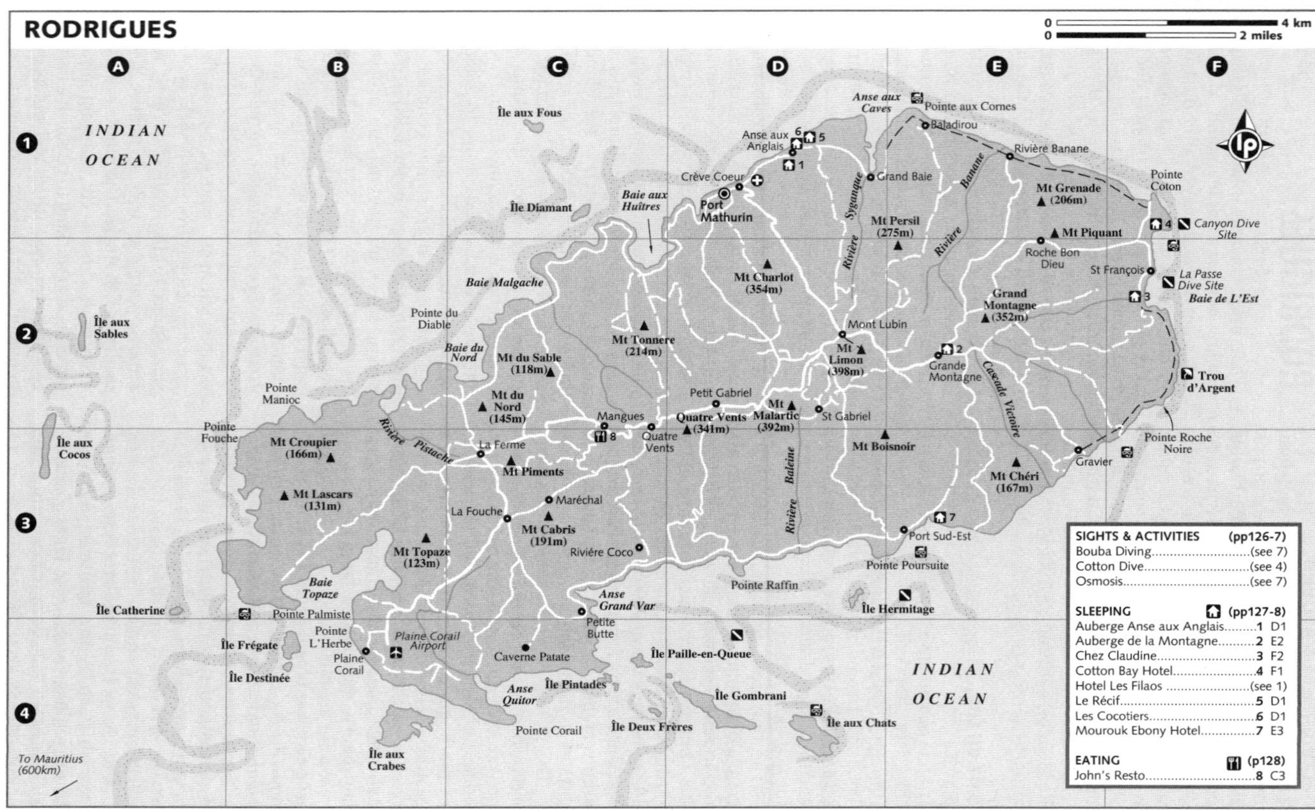
RODRIGUES
0 4 km
0 2 miles
A B C D E F
1 2 3 4
INDIAN OCEAN
Île aux Fous
Île Diamant
Baie aux Huîtres
Baie Malgache
Pointe du Diable
Baie du Nord
Pointe Manioc
Pointe Fouche
Île aux Sables
Île aux Cocos
Île Catherine
Île Frégate
Île Destinée
Île aux Crabes
To Mauritius (600km)
Anse aux Caves
Pointe aux Cornes
Baladirou
Anse aux Anglais
Crève Coeur
Port Mathurin
Rivière Sygangue
Grand Baie
Rivière Banane
Mt Grenade (206m)
Mt Piquant
Mt Persil (275m)
Mt Charlot (354m)
Mt Tonnere (214m)
Mt du Sable (118m)
Mt du Nord (145m)
Mt Croupier (166m)
Mt Lascars (131m)
Rivière Pistache
La Ferme
Mt Piments
Mangues
Quatre Vents
Quatre Vents (341m)
Petit Gabriel
Mt Malartic (392m)
St Gabriel
Mt Limon (398m)
Mont Lubin
Grande Montagne
Grand Montagne (352m)
Roche Bon Dieu
St François
Pointe Coton
Canyon Dive Site
La Passe Dive Site
Baie de L'Est
Trou d'Argent
Cascade Victoire
Pointe Roche Noire
Gravier
Mt Chéri (167m)
Mt Boisnoir
Rivière Baleine
Port Sud-Est
Pointe Poursuite
Pointe Raffin
Île Hermitage
La Fouche
Maréchal
Mt Cabris (191m)
Rivière Coco
Mt Topaze (123m)
Baie Topaze
Pointe Palmiste
Pointe L'Herbe
Plaine Corail
Plaine Corail Airport
Caverne Patate
Anse Grand Var
Petite Butte
Anse Quitor
Île Pintades
Pointe Corail
Île Paille-en-Queue
Île Deux Frères
Île Gombrani
Île aux Chats
SIGHTS & ACTIVITIES (pp126-7)
Bouba Diving (see 7)
Cotton Dive (see 4)
Osmosis (see 7)
SLEEPING (pp127-8)
Auberge Anse aux Anglais 1 D1
Auberge de la Montagne 2 E2
Chez Claudine 3 F2
Cotton Bay Hotel 4 F1
Hotel Les Filaos (see 1)
Le Récif 5 D1
Les Cocotiers 6 D1
Mourouk Ebony Hotel 7 E3
EATING (p128)
John's Resto 8 C3

As fishing and agriculture begin to wane, so the local authorities are looking to tour-ism to boost the island's economy and provide much-needed employment. Rodrigues is receiving heavy promotion as an 'anti-stress destination' for holiday-makers from throughout the region, particularly Réunion. The government seems keen to go the route of sympathetic, small-scale development, with the emphasis on B&B accommodation, and there is much talk of ecotourism. How this squares with the planned construction of hotels along the largely unspoilt east coast remains to be seen.

For now, however, Rodrigues still provides something of a retreat after the commercialism of Mauritius. Shops here are not nearly so well stocked and prices are slightly higher. It's not a bad idea to bring supplies of any special items you may need, especially medicines, just to be on the safe side.

History

Rodrigues is named after the Portuguese navigator, Don Diégo Rodriguez, who was the first European to discover the uninhabited island in 1528. Dutch sailors were the next to pay a call, albeit very briefly, in 1601, followed a few years later by the French.

At first Rodrigues was simply a place where ships could take refuge from storms and replenish their supplies of fresh water and meat. Giant tortoises were especially prized since they could be kept alive on board for months. Over the years thousands were taken or killed until they completely died out. Rodrigues also had a big flightless bird, the solitaire, which went the same sorry way as its distant cousin, the dodo.

The first serious attempt at colonisation occurred in 1691 when the Frenchman François Leguat and a small band of Huguenot companions fled religious persecution in France in search of a 'promised land'. They made a good stab at it. Crops grew well and the island's fauna and flora was a source of wonder. Even so, after two years life on a paradise island began to pall, not least due to the lack of female company. Having no boat of their own (the ship they arrived on failed to return as promised), Leguat and his friends built a craft out of driftwood and eventually made it to Mauritius.

The next group to arrive were far more determined. In 1735, the French founded a permanent colony on Rodrigues as part of a European power-struggle to control the Indian Ocean. They established a small settlement at Port Mathurin, but a lack of leadership coupled with the difficult climate meant the colony never really prospered. When the British – who wanted a base from which to attack Mauritius – invaded in 1809, they met with little resistance.

One of the more important events under British rule was the arrival of telecommunications in 1901. Rodrigues was one of the staging posts for the undersea cable linking Britain and Australia. The old Cable & Wireless offices are still to be seen at Pointe Canon above Port Mathurin.

Then, in 1967, Rodriguans distinguished themselves by voting against independence by a whopping 90% (the rest of Mauritius voted strongly in favour). It was a dramatic illustration of the difference in outlook between the two islands. Following independence, Rodriguans continued to argue that their needs were significantly different from the rest of the country and that, in any case, they were being neglected by the central government. What they wanted was a greater say in their own future.

The campaign was led by Serge Clair and his Organisation du Peuple de Rodrigues (OPR), founded in 1976. His patience and political skill eventually paid off. In 2001 it was announced that Rodrigues would be allowed a degree of autonomy, notably in socioeconomic affairs and in the management of their natural resources. The following year 18 counsellors were elected; the Regional Assembly was formally inaugurated in 2002 with Serge Clair as Chief Commissioner. The assembly is now trying to tackle the overriding problems of population growth and poverty.

Almost as momentous for many islanders was the visit of Pope John-Paul II in 1989. Nearly the entire population turned out to celebrate Mass at La Ferme.

Two good books about the history and culture of Rodrigues are *The Island of Rodrigues*, by Alfred North-Coombes, and *L'Île Rodrigues: Memoires et Temoignages*, by André Létio Roussetty. The latter is a very personal account of the island in the 1940s.

Wildlife

Over the centuries, the thick forest that covered Rodrigues has been destroyed by felling and intensive grazing. Much of the vegetation you see today consists of introduced species. Of the 38 or so native plant species remaining, all but two are considered endangered, vulnerable or rare.

The government, in collaboration with the MWF, is acting to protect areas of critical importance by clearing them of introduced plants (which grow much more quickly) and replanting native species. It is hoped that these areas will act as refuges for the island's rare endemic fauna, such as the Rodrigues warbler and the Rodrigues fody. The warbler population has made a shaky recovery from virtual extinction in the 1960s to an estimated 70 pairs today. The fody population has also increased from a low of 60 pairs in 1983 to approximately 300 pairs.

Another species under threat is the Rodrigues fruit bat. The population of these large, brown bats had reached critically low levels of just 75 individuals in 1974. With the help of strict laws and conservation measures, the population had inched its way up to 5000 or so before Cyclone Kalunde struck in 2003. It's estimated that some 2000 survived, and the numbers are on the rise again. You can see them gliding over Port Mathurin at dusk to reach their feeding grounds.

The small islands surrounding Rodrigues support important colonies of sea birds. Fairy terns and noddys nest on Île aux Cocos and Île aux Sables, off the northwest coast.

> **WATER**
>
> Rodrigues' water is generally neither chlorinated nor filtered. Instead, it is advisable to drink bottled water, which is widely available.
>
> The island experiences frequent water shortages. Visitors are asked not to waste water.

Getting There & Away

AIR

The main **Air Mauritius office** (☎ 831 1632; fax 831 1959; ADS Bldg, Rue Max Lucchesi) is in Port Mathurin. There is also an office at the **airport** (☎ 832 7700) which is open for all arrivals and departures.

Air Mauritius operates at least two daily flights to Rodrigues from Mauritius which take 1½ hours one way. The return fare is Rs 3210/3610 in low/high season for a stay of between three days and one month. You will need your passport.

There is a luggage limit of 15kg per person, with excess charged at Rs 35 per kilo. When checking in at the Mauritius end, you may be asked how much you weigh. Don't worry, you won't have to go through the indignity of being weighed like a sack of potatoes – an approximation is fine.

Air Mauritius also now flies direct from Réunion to Rodrigues twice a week. Return fares start at €350 from Réunion.

All passengers are required to reconfirm their return tickets either immediately on arrival at Rodrigues (there is an Air Mauritius counter in the baggage hall) or at least three days before departure. It's a good idea to phone the airline the day before you leave anyway, just to make sure there's been no change to the schedule.

SEA

The *Mauritius Pride* and the *Mauritius Trochetia* make the voyage from Port Louis to Rodrigues four times a month, docking at the passenger terminal on Rue Wolfert Harmensz in Port Mathurin. The outbound trip takes about 36 hours and back to Mauritius 25 hours, depending on sea conditions. Non-Mauritians pay Rs 3300 return for a seat or Rs 4800 for a cabin (Rs 6450 on the *Trochetia*), including meals. The boats are popular with locals, so book well ahead.

Information and tickets are available from travel agents or direct from the Mauritius Shipping Corporation. Contact **Coraline Shipping Agency** (Map p58; ☎ 217 2285; msc@coraline.intnet.mu; Nova Bldg, Military Rd, Port Louis) and the **Mauritius Shipping Corporation** (Map p125; ☎ 831 0640; Rue François Leguat, Port Mathurin). Tickets should be reconfirmed two days before departure.

Getting Around

TO/FROM THE AIRPORT

Flights arrive at **Plaine Corail Airport** (☎ 831 6301) at the southwest tip of the island. Public bus No 206 runs between the airport and Port Mathurin roughly every 40 minutes from 5.30am to 4.30pm. The private **Supercopter bus service** (☎ 831 1859; one-way Rs 100) meets all flights and drops off at hotels in Port Mathurin and Anse aux Anglais; phone ahead to be sure of a seat.

For destinations elsewhere on the island, you can either take the bus to Port Mathurin and then get an onward connection, or arrange for your hotel or a tour operator to pick you up. Prices start at around Rs 250 per person for a round trip.

A taxi to or from Port Mathurin costs Rs 300; to Pointe Coton Rs 600; and to Port Sud-Est Rs 500. Fares are slightly more expensive at night.

BUS

The main bus terminal is in Port Mathurin. In addition to the airport bus, the most useful bus routes are those to Grand Baie and Pointe Coton in the east of the island, and to Gravier, Port Sud-Est and Riviére Coco on the south coast. All apart from the Grand Baie buses pass through Mont Lubin in the centre of the island.

Buses operate every 30 to 45 minutes from about 6am to 5.30pm Monday to Saturday on most routes. The Sunday service is fairly sporadic.

CAR

The road system in Rodrigues has improved enormously and sealed roads now lead to most parts of the island. Though 4WD vehicles are no longer strictly necessary, most hire cars are still sturdy pick-ups.

Car rental can be arranged through most hotels and guesthouses and local tour operators (p124), who will deliver all over the island. Expect to pay at least Rs 1000 per day.

Make sure you have sufficient petrol before setting off for the day. The island's only **petrol station** (Rue Max Lucchesi; 6am-6.30pm Mon-Sat, 6am-3pm Sun) is in Port Mathurin.

BICYCLE & MOTORCYCLE

If your hotel or guesthouse doesn't offer bike or motorcycle rental, contact one of the outlets in Port Mathurin (p126). The going rate is around Rs 200 per day for a bike and at least Rs 500 for a 125cc motorbike.

TAXI

Most taxis on Rodrigues are 4WD pick-ups. The fare from Port Mathurin to Pointe Coton costs Rs 300 and to Port Sud-Est Rs 400, slightly more at night. You can also hire taxis by the day for an island tour; expect to pay in the region of Rs 1500.

PORT MATHURIN

pop 6000

As the administrative, commercial and industrial hub of the island, Port Mathurin is a lively little town. On Saturday morning it's particularly busy as people come from all over to shop – and socialise – in the weekly market. The market apart, there are no particularly compelling sights, but it's worth wandering the streets of weather-beaten wood or corrugated-iron buildings to soak up the atmosphere.

The new regional authorities are in the midst of replacing Port Mathurin's British-era street names. However, many people still use the old names, so we give both versions on the town map.

Information

EMERGENCY

Hospital (☎ 831 1628) The island's main hospital is at Crève Coeur, immediately west of Port Mathurin.

Port Mathurin Pharmacy (☎ 831 2279; Rue de la Solidarité, Port Mathurin; 7.30am-4.30pm Mon-Fri, 7.30am-3pm Sat, 7.30am-11pm Sun) The only pharmacy on the island.

INTERNET ACCESS

Rodnet Cybercafé (☎ 831 0747; Rue Johnston; 9am-5pm Mon-Sat) Rodrigues' sole Internet café is at the Putt-Putt mini golf.

MEDIA

You can buy the national dailies in Port Mathurin, but no international papers.

MONEY

The banks all have offices where you can change money and withdraw cash from the ATMs.

Barclays (☎ 831 1553; Rue de la Solidarité, Port Mathurin)

Mauritius Commercial Bank (MCB; ☎ 831 1833; Rue Max Lucchesi)

State Bank (☎ 831 1642; Rue Max Lucchesi, Port Mathurin)

POST

Central post office (☎ 831 2098; Rue de la Solidarité; 8.15-11.45am & noon-4pm Mon-Fri, 8.15-11.45pm Sat)

TELEPHONE

There are plenty of public phones on Rodrigues.

Mauritius Telecom office (☎ 831 1816; Rue Johnston, Port Mathurin; 8am-8.30pm Mon-Sat) You can buy *télécartes* (phonecards) here, and there is a cardphone outside for international calls.

TRAVEL AGENCIES

These agencies also have desks at the airport, which are open for flight arrivals.

Ecotourisme (☎ 831 2801; www.rodrigues-island.org/ecotourisme.html; Rue Max Lucchesi)

RodTours (☎ 831 2249; www.rodrigues-island.org/rodTours.html; Camp du Roi) Part of MauriTours.

Rotourco (☎ 831 0747; site.voila.fr/rotourco; Rue François Leguat)

Rodrigues 2000 Tours (☎ 831 1894; 2000trs@intnet.mu; Rue Max Lucchesi)

TOURIST INFORMATION

There is no tourist office on Rodrigues. If you're lucky you might find a copy of *Rodrigues: Le Guide*, produced annually by the Mauritius Tourist Promotion Authority, which contains a brief overview of the island and handy listings.

Otherwise, your best bet for information is your hotel or guesthouse or one of the tour agents listed above. You could also try contacting the **Association of Rodriguan Tourism Operators** (ARTO; ☎ 831 3350, 831 4607; www.rodrigues-island.org/arto.html), a grouping of hotel operators which can also provide more general information.

Sights & Activities

One of the oldest buildings still standing in Port Mathurin, **La Résidence** (Rue de la Solidarité) dates from 1897, when it provided a fairly modest home for the British Chief Commissioner. It is now used as function rooms for the new Regional Assembly.

On the south side of town, **Craft Aid** (☎ 831 1766; Camp du Roi; admission free; 8am-4pm Mon-Fri) is a non-profit association providing training, work and accommodation for the handicapped and young unemployed. Around 50 people work at the centre producing various crafts and some delicious, award-winning honey. Visitors are welcome and are given a guided tour of the workshops. There's also a small shop here and another on Rue de la Solidarité.

For fine views over Port Mathurin and the lagoon, there's an easy 1km-walk from the end of Rue Mamzelle Julia to a lookout atop Mt Fanal. At dusk this is a good place to see Rodrigues fruit bats.

Sleeping

Port Mathurin makes a convenient base if you are travelling by bus, or want all the facilities on your doorstep. A popular alternative is to stay just along the coast at Anse aux Anglais.

Escale Vacances (☎ 831 2555; www.rodrigues-island.org/escalesVacances.html; Rue Johnston; s/d incl breakfast from Rs 1475/2450, half board Rs 1675/2750;) A delightful small hotel with a relaxed tropical atmosphere. Squeaky-clean rooms and a decent restaurant make this the best address in town. The half board deals represent excellent value.

Hébergement Fatehmamode (☎ 831 1551; mahmood@intnet.mu; Rue Max Lucchesi; s/d from Rs 150, apt from Rs 500;) Bargain-basement accommodation in cell-like single rooms (with communal bathroom) and slightly more comfortable apartments.

Pension Ciel d'Été (☎ 831 1587; fax 831 2004; Rue François Leguat; s/d incl breakfast Rs 500/800, half board Rs 700/1200) A cheerful little guesthouse with spick-and-span rooms and a small garden. Though it suffers a bit from road noise, it is often full.

Le Flamboyant (☎ 831 2784; fax 831 2785; Rue Victoria; s/d incl breakfast Rs 900/1900, half board Rs 1050/2100;) This recently renovated hotel offers slightly boxy rooms with bathroom, TV and minibar. There's a restaurant-bar and a tiny pool squeezed in at the back.

Eating

For quick eats, outlets on Rue de la Solidarité sell *pain fouré* (filled rolls), noodles and the like for a handful of rupees. There's also a clutch of restaurants offering traditional local cuisine. Specialities are octopus (in curries and salads), succulent ham and chicken, and dishes featuring the famous Rodrigues chillies, lemons and honey.

Restaurant du Quai (☎ 831 2840; Rue Wolfert Harmensz; mains Rs 70-300; lunch & dinner, closed

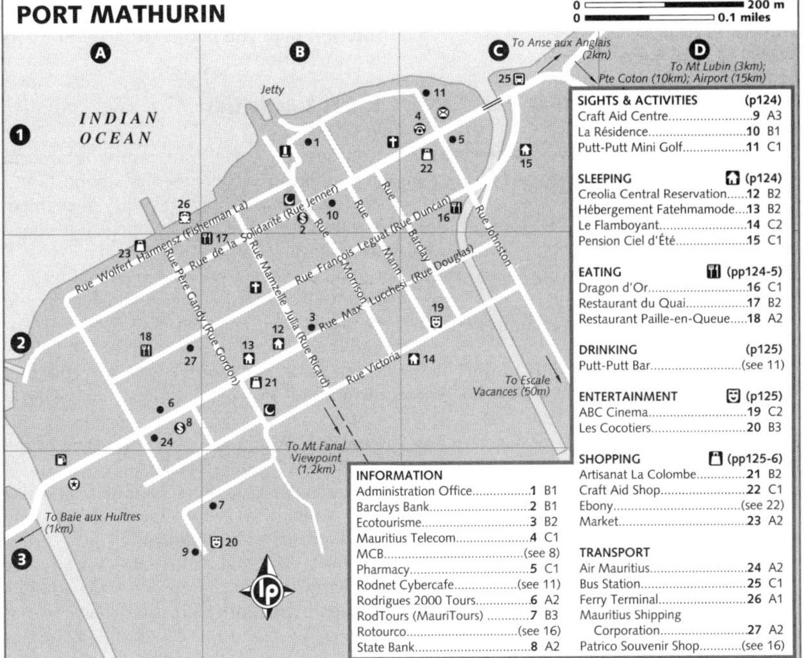

lunch Tue-Sun;) The service can be a tad slow, but this jolly little restaurant cooks up great fish and seafood curries plus a smattering of Chinese, European and vegetarian dishes.

Restaurant Paille-en-Queue (831 0561; Rue François Leguat; mains Rs 85-300; lunch & dinner) This place is popular with locals and tourists for its broad menu of hearty local as well as Chinese fare, including such Rodriguan classics as honey chicken and octopus curry.

Dragon d'Or (831 0541; Rue François Leguat; mains Rs 75-100; lunch & dinner, closed dinner Wed) A friendly place serving cheap and cheerful Chinese and Creole fare. Portions are small, but the food is tasty.

Self-caterers will find several small grocery stores on Rue de la Solidarité and Rue Mamzelle Julia. You can buy fresh fruit from stalls near the post office (mornings only from Monday to Saturday). On Saturday there is an excellent **street market** (Rue Wolfert Harmensz) down by the ferry terminal, with a smaller version on Wednesday.

Entertainment

ABC Cinema (831 1216; Rue Victoria) Screens films at least once a day.

Putt-Putt Bar (4pm-midnight Tue-Sun) It's elbow-room only at the bar at the Putt-Putt mini golf on Wednesday and Saturday when local musicians run through their repertoire of *séga* and folk.

Les Cocotiers (831 1877; Camp du Roi) There's occasionally something on at weekends at this open-air disco. Look out for adverts posted around town.

Putt-Putt mini golf (831 2356; Rue Johnston; adult/child Rs 75/50; 10am-midnight) The epicentre of Port Mathurin's entertainment scene boasts floodlit mini/crazy golf, a cafe and a bar.

Shopping

Rue de la Solidarité and Rue Mamzelle Julia are the main shopping streets. Here you'll find a number of outlets selling handicrafts, especially baskets and hats made from dried vacoa leaves. Items made from coconut fibres and coconut-shell jewellery are also popular souvenirs. Look out, too, for local foodstuffs such as preserved lemons, chillies and honey. The Saturday market is reasonably cheap and a pleasantly relaxed place to shop.

Other recommendations:

Artisanat La Colombe (☎ 831 0430; Rue Max Lucchesi) Specialises in preserved foodstuffs and basketware.

Ebony (Rue de la Solidarité) A good range of vacoa hats and bags.

Craft Aid (Rue de la Solidarité) Sells coconut-shell items, honey and model boats made by handicapped people (p124).

Getting There & Away

For information about getting to and from the airport, see p122.

For information about travelling by boat, see p122.

You can rent bikes and motorbikes from **Hébergement Fatehmamode** (☎ 831 1551; mahmood@intnet.mu; Rue Max Lucchesi). Tour agent **Rotourco** (☎ 831 0747; http://site.voila.fr/rotourco; Rue François Leguat) also has a few motorbikes for rent, as does the nearby **Patrico souvenir shop** (☎ 831 2044; Rue François Leguat). Count on Rs 200 per day for a bike and at least Rs 500 for a 125cc motorbike.

Ask your hotel or guesthouse about car hire, or contact a local tour agent. Rates start at around Rs 1000 per day.

Port Mathurin's well-organised bus station (p123) is across the river on the east side of town.

AROUND RODRIGUES

Rodrigues is reasonably small, so most places are only a short drive away, but walking is by far the best way to explore this glorious island.

The finest beaches are on the east coast from Pointe Coton around to Port Sud-Est. Top of the list is the immaculate beach at **Trou d'Argent**, only accessible by boat or on foot. **St François** and the small cove at **Gravier** are also magical spots. **Anse aux Anglais**, where the first British troops landed, has a decent beach – albeit with grey sand – and is a popular place to stay.

One of the most dramatic roads on the island descends from Mont Lubin to Port Sud-Est, offering great views of the island-spattered lagoon. This south coast is also where you'll find Rodrigues' very own cave system.

The west is dry and rather dull, though just offshore the Île aux Cocos represents Rodrigues' single most popular tourist attraction.

Last but not least, it's in the mountainous interior that you'll find Rodrigues at its most traditional.

Sights & Activities

WALKING

Rodrigues is perfect for rambling around at your leisure. There are few signposts and the less popular trails are pretty ill-defined, but the landscape is fairly open so it's hard to get lost.

You can begin the classic coastal walk at Pointe Coton or St François, which takes you south to the gorgeous beach at Trou d'Argent and then around the coast to Gravier. Allow about three hours for the walk, not counting swimming and picnic stops. Both Pointe Coton and Gravier are accessible by bus from Port Mathurin; check the time of the last bus back before you set off.

The walk from Port Mathurin or Anse aux Anglais to Pointe Coton is another good half-day's excursion.

The uplands around Mt Limon and Mt Malartic, which represent the island's highest points, offer great all-round views. The easy way up Mt Limon (398m) is to take a bus to the village of Mt Lubin. Then walk east along the road to Grande Montagne for 400m to find the path signed up to the right; it takes just five minutes to reach the top.

WATER SPORTS

There are many excellent dive locations around Rodrigues. In general, the marine environment is still remarkably well-preserved and there's a tremendous variety of dives on offer. The best sites lie off the east and south coasts.

So far, the number of divers coming to Rodrigues remains relatively small. The two main dive centres are **Cotton Dive** (☎ 831 8001; diverod@intnet.mu; 🕑 8am-4pm Sun-Fri, closed Jul & Aug) at the Cotton Bay Hotel and **Bouba Diving** (☎ 832 3063; ebony@intnet.mu; 🕑 7am-5pm) at the Mourouk Ebony Hotel. In both cases, nonguests should ring ahead to make an appointment. A dive costs around Rs 900.

For more about diving in Rodrigues, see Underwater Worlds p38.

Other water sports are available through **Osmosis** (☎ 832 3051; osmosis@intnet.mu; 🕑 7am-5pm), which is also based at the Mourouk

Ebony Hotel. An hour's windsurfing costs Rs 550 or so with all the equipment; kite surfing, Rs 1500 for one descent.

CAVERNE PATATE

Caverne Patate, in the southwest corner of the island, is a moderately impressive cave system with a few stalagmite and stalactite formations. The guide points out formations with uncanny resemblances to a dodo, Buckingham Palace and even Winston Churchill!

The requisite permit is issued in the **Administration Office** (Map p125; ☎ 831 2058; Rodrigues Regional Assembly, Rue Morrison, Port Mathurin; 8am-noon Mon-Fri). It costs Rs 200 for up to 30 people.

There are four guided tours daily, usually at 9.30am, 11.30am, 1.30pm and 3.30pm. You should arrive at the cave entrance on the day and time specified on your permit. The 600m tunnel is an easy walk, but gets slippery in wet weather; wear shoes with a good grip and take a light jacket or pullover.

The track to the caves is signed off the road from La Ferme to Petite Butte. Buses en route between La Ferme and Rivière Cocos will drop you off at the turn; coming from Port Mathurin, you'll have to change buses at one of these two towns.

Tours

Local tour agents (p124) offer a variety of excursions; the efficient Ecotourisme and Rodrigues 2000 Tours have reliable reputations. Most hotels and guesthouses can also help.

The most popular outing is a day trip to Île aux Cocos (from Rs 600 per person including picnic lunch), followed by various minibus tours of Rodrigues itself (from around Rs 450/1000 for a half/full day). Other options include a boat trip to Île aux Chats (Rs 800 including barbecue lunch) and a variety of guided walks and bike rides.

Sleeping

The main concentration of hotels and guesthouses is found 2km east of Port Mathurin at Anse aux Anglais. Other options are scattered along the east and south coasts and in the interior. There are a couple of upmarket hotels, but the nicest choice is a *chambre d'hôte* (family-run B&B). *Chambres d'hôte* only have a handful of rooms and the best fill up quickly, so book ahead.

Tour agents (p124) can help book accommodation, or contact **Creolia Central Reservation** (Map p125; ☎ 831 0783; www.ilerodrigues.com; Rue Max Lucchesi, Port Mathurin).

Camping is possible just about anywhere on the island. The beaches around Pointe Coton and Grand Baie are good places to start.

The list following starts in Anse aux Anglais, then heads up into the interior, before dropping down to the east and then south coasts.

Auberge Anse aux Anglais (☎ 831 2179; aubergehung@intnet.mu; s/d half board from Rs 850/1300;) Tucked off the road in Anse aux Anglais, with a pretty garden, this is a popular choice. Clean, simple rooms come with private bathroom, phone and either fan or air-con.

Hotel Les Filaos (☎ 831 1644; filaos@intnet.mu; s/d incl breakfast from Rs 600/900;) Right beside the Auberge Anse aux Anglais, this hotel is friendly and well maintained. The rooms are gradually being upgraded and a pool and restaurant have recently been added.

Les Cocotiers (☎ 831 1058; lescocotiers@intnet.mu; s/d half board from Rs 2000/3100, s/d with sea views Rs 2375/3650;) A stylish complex on the beach at Anse aux Anglais, with attractive gardens and cheerful, spacious rooms. More expensive rooms come with balcony and sea views. It has two pools, a good restaurant and traditional Rodrigues folk music several times a week.

Le Récif (☎ 831 1804; www.lerecif.com; s/d half board from Rs 950/1500;) Perched on the cliff above Anse aux Anglais, this hotel-restaurant has a handful of big, airy rooms with balconies to match. Be warned that at weekends the dining room below transforms into a disco. Guests can use the facilities of the Mourouk Ebony Hotel which is under the same ownership.

Auberge de la Montagne (☎ 831 4607; www.rodrigues-island.org/aubergeDeLaMontagne.html; s/d half board from Rs 600/1200) A welcoming *chambre d'hôte* up in the hills at Grande Montagne. There are just six immaculate rooms, the cheapest of which share communal facilities. The owner, Françoise Baptiste, is a mine of information and a splendid cook.

Cotton Bay Hotel (☎ 831 8001; cottonb@intnet.mu; s/d half board from Rs 3700/5700;) Rodrigues' most luxurious hotel is tucked away at Pointe Coton on an excellent beach. There's a good swimming pool to splash in, a kids' club and a restaurant. If you fancy a trot around the island, horse riding is available for Rs 450 per hour. There's also a highly rated dive centre.

Chez Claudine (☎ 831 8242; cbmoneret@intnet.mu; s/d half board Rs 900/1800) Standing in splendid isolation on one of the island's best beaches at St François, this *chambre d'hôte* offers a perfect retreat. There are just five spruce rooms with communal facilities in a chalet-style building. It's possible to arrange snorkelling and dive trips and you're well placed for walks along the east coast.

Mourouk Ebony Hotel (☎ 832 3350; www.mouroukebonyhotel.com; s/d half board from Rs 2610/3960;) A pleasantly relaxed mid-range hotel in an isolated position near Port Sud-Est. Accommodation is in comfortable Creole-style bungalows (each with a shocking-red roof). There's a smallish pool, a bar and a pleasant restaurant. Island tours and activities such as diving, windsurfing and cycling are also available.

Eating

If you're out on a day trip or fancy a change from eating at your hotel or guesthouse, there are a few good places dotted around the island. For self-caterers, most villages have some sort of grocers or general store.

John's Resto (☎ 831 6306; meals Rs 90-350; lunch) Rodrigues' best seafood restaurant is up in the hills in the village of Mangue, between Quatre Vents and La Ferme. This is the place to treat yourself to fresh lobster (a bargain at Rs 350 for 500g) or crab.

Auberge de la Montagne (☎ 831 4607; meals Rs 200; lunch & dinner by reservation) Françoise Baptiste, the delightful owner of this *chambre d'hôte* and author of a book on Rodriguan cooking, prepares lip-smacking local specialties. You should reserve at least a day in advance.

Chez Claudine (☎ 831 8242; cbmoneret@intnet.mu; meals Rs 250-300; lunch & dinner by reservation) If you're walking to Trou d'Argent, phone in advance to reserve lunch at this *chambre d'hôte* at St François. The specialty is seafood grilled on an open wood fire.

Entertainment

Apart from a couple of places in Port Mathurin, nightlife on the island is virtually nonexistent. The exception is live folk music performances. Rodriguans are known as skilled accordionists, who play versions of old colonial ballroom and country dances such as the 'scottish', the waltz and the mazurka. They also play a distinctive version of the *séga*, known as *séga tambour*, where the drum is unusually prominent. Popular groups include Racines, Cardinal Blanc, Cascavelles and Ambience Tropicale. They often perform at the big hotels, all of which have folk evenings to which nonguests are welcome (it's a good idea to phone ahead).

Le Récif (☎ 831 1804; women/men Rs 85/175; 10pm-2am Fri & Sat) In Anse aux Anglais, this is another good place to hear local music. On Friday, the first part of the evening features live folk music, followed by a disco. Saturday night is all disco, though they play a fair amount of local hits.

OFFSHORE ISLANDS

There are many small islands dotted around Rodrigues. Commonly visited islands include Île aux Cocos, to the west, and Île aux Chats and Île Hermitage off the south coast.

Île aux Cocos nature reserve, barely 1km in length, is a nature reserve and bird sanctuary populated by small colonies of noddys and lesser noddys. It is only possible to visit Île aux Cocos on a guided tour (from Rs 600 per person including picnic lunch), which can be arranged through hotels and tour agents. The boat trip takes at least an hour each way; take a jacket as it can be very windy.

Île Hermitage, a tiny island renowned for its beauty (and for its possible hidden treasure), and **Île aux Chats** are both accessible by boat from Port Sud-Est. The latter is an unremarkable island, but is surrounded by a healthy coral reef, which makes it a popular destination for snorkelling and diving.

You can arrange excursions to all these islands through hotels and tour agents. Another option is to try asking local fishermen in Port Sud-Est, who are usually willing to ferry people out to one of the nearby islands and pick them up later.

MAURITIUS DIRECTORY

The following section contains practical information for visitors to Mauritius arranged in alphabetical order. For information relevant to the entire region, see the Regional Directory (p277).

ACCOMMODATION

Mauritius offers the full range of accommodation, from budget rooms to super-luxury suites. The main options are self-catering apartments, guesthouses and hotels, from small family-run places to luxury beach hotels. The vast majority are located around the coast.

The budget traveller is perhaps least well-served as regards choice, quality and value for money, though there are some notable exceptions. The most important thing to remember is that the more of you there are and the longer you stay, the cheaper it is; rates should drop by around 20% to 30% if you stay for more than a week. It's perfectly possible to base yourself in one place and see all of Mauritius, especially if you hire a car.

For a double room, you should expect to pay under Rs 1000 at the budget end; Rs 1000 to 5000 in a mid-range hotel; and over Rs 5000 at the top end.

Many mid-range and all top end hotels apply seasonal rates. This chapter quotes low-season rates (generally May to July), unless otherwise stated. These rates increase considerably (by up to 45% for a double room, for example) during the Christmas–New Year peak.

Camping

There are no official camping grounds, but also no restrictions – within reason – about camping on public land. Few shoestring travellers or outdoor enthusiasts bring a tent, but the opportunity to use one exists. Probably the best places to camp are the public beaches, such as Blue Bay near Mahébourg, Flic en Flac, Pointe des Puits near Belle Mare, Mont Choisy, and the ones on Le Morne Peninsula. Casuarina trees provide shade and shelter. There are well-maintained public toilets on the most popular beaches. The main drawback to camping, apart from the lack of facilities, is the lack of security.

Guesthouses

Guesthouses are a popular budget choice. Most are near the beach and offer rooms in a family home. They make a good alternative to hotels, as you can learn a lot about local life through the owners – the atmosphere tends to be more down-to-earth. Guesthouses are springing up in the main tourist destinations, particularly along the west coast.

Hotels

Most travellers to Mauritius are looking for that perfect combination of sun, surf and sand. Some of the beach hotels in Mauritius are absolutely world-class, and offer every luxury from golf courses to swish restaurants, evening dinner shows and fabulous spas. These are the places to look at for the honeymoon trip or the once-in-a-lifetime splurge. Rates are high, but still comparative with those of other luxury resorts around the world. Some hotels offer good half-board deals and a variety of free activities. Most of the chains, such as Naïade and Beachcomber, also offer the opportunity to interchange accommodation with other members in the group. Given the large number of beach hotels competing for customers, you should have no qualms about shopping around for the best deal and requesting discounts if you stay longer than a week.

For those with less extravagant budgets, there are numerous smaller, more homely beach hotels, with fewer facilities. The best of the sand has been snapped up by the big hotel chains, so these cheaper places tend to be relegated to the less impressive stretches of beach.

You'll also find a handful of business hotels in Port Louis and on the Central Plateau.

Self-Catering

If you're staying more than a few days, self-catering accommodation is usually the best bargain. The options are a studio, apartment or bungalow. The definitions are a little blurred, but in general studios consist of a combined bedroom, kitchen and living room, with a separate bathroom. Apartments have a separate kitchen and lounge in addition to one or more bedrooms and bathrooms.

A bungalow (sometimes referred to as a villa), is the same as an apartment but in a stand-alone unit.

In theory they are all fully furnished. The best are equipped to the nines with air-con, microwaves and all mod-cons. Others are poorly maintained, noisy and provide limited cooking facilities; if possible, ask to see the place before making a decision.

Most self-catering accommodation is concentrated along the west coast, particularly around Grand Baie and Flic en Flac. They are not always signed, so you may have to go looking. Local tour agents can usually help and there are now a number of dedicated letting agents. Security can be a problem, so make sure the place you rent has a caretaker, a safe or security alarms – or all three.

In most cases you'll be asked for a deposit when you make a booking. Maid-service is sometimes included in the price or can be arranged for an additional charge. Most maids will also shop and cook for you – again, for an extra fee.

ACTIVITIES

Many visitors come to Mauritius for the water sports, though there's also excellent hiking. Most activities can be booked through your hotel or through a local tour operator. Major hotels have tennis courts and gyms and provide items such as windsurfers and kayaks for guests' use. Some also make them available to nonresidents (for a fee), or it's sometimes possible to rent equipment at the public beaches. Grand Baie, Trou aux Biches, Flic en Flac and Blue Bay are particularly good for messing around on – and in – the water.

Coral Viewing

A number of operators offer coral-viewing tours for non-divers. Most impressive is Blue Safari Submarine, a proper submarine which operates out of Mont Choisy (p71). It goes down 35m below sea level for a close encounter with reef-life.

Next comes the yellow semisubmersible *Le Nessee*, which cruises the lagoon off Grand Baie, followed by a whole flotilla of glass-bottomed boats. These can be arranged through tour agents and hotels, or you can go direct to the boat owners in Grand Baie, Blue Bay and Trou aux Biches among other places.

Cycling

Cycling is a great way to explore the coast and to reach some of the more remote beaches. Most hotels and guesthouses have bikes for rent. You'll also find rental outlets in the main tourist centres such as Grand Baie, Flic en Flac and Mahébourg.

A few specialist operators now offer escorted mountain-biking tours. The Black River Gorges (p89) area is a popular destination. Rodrigues is also a great place to get the wind in your hair. Expeditions can be arranged through **Yemaya Adventures** (☎ 752 0046; www.yemayaadventures.com) or through **Maurisun Adventure & Tours** (☎ 263 0192; www.maurisun.com; Royal Rd) in Grand Baie. On Rodrigues, contact **Osmosis** (☎ 832 3051; osmosis@intnet.mu; 🕑 7am-5pm), based at the Mourouk Ebony Hotel.

Deep-Sea Fishing

The fisheries around Mauritius support large predators such as marlin, wahoo, tuna and sharks, luring big-game fishermen from around the world. November to April is the prime season for marlin, when the water is at its warmest. Tuna, wahoo and sharks can be found year-round. Annual fishing competitions are held at Grande Rivière Noire in November and February.

Game fishing has far less environmental impact than commercial fishing, but the weight and the number of fish caught has shown a marked decline since its heyday in the 1970s. It's now rare to catch anything over 400kg. Using the practise of 'tag-and-release' is an option for those who want the thrill without depriving the ocean of these magnificent creatures.

Anglers get to take home a trophy such as the marlin's nose spike, or a couple of fillets, but the day's catch belongs to the operator, who sells it to be served up at local restaurants.

Most of the big hotels run boats, and there are several private operators based at Grande Rivière Noire, Trou aux Biches and Grand Baie. Most outfits have a minimum hire time of around six hours, and each boat can normally take three anglers and three guests. Expect to pay upwards of Rs 12,000 per boat.

TOP TIPS FOR HIKERS

Special conditions apply to hiking in tropical conditions. First of all, it's thirsty work, so make sure you drink plenty of liquids. The damp conditions also provide a fertile breeding ground for mosquitoes; apply a strong repellent if you're hiking through forested areas.

The majority of the walks in Mauritius start on the Central Plateau, which is prone to tropical downpours at any time of year, butespecially from December to March. Since rainfall is most likely in the afternoon, you're best starting early in the morning. Trailscanbecometreacherouslyslipperyafter rain, so good footwear is essential.

There are few serious dangers to hikers in Mauritius. If you do any bush-bashing, you should watch out for spiny acacias, aloé cactuses and *framboise* bushes (thorny local shrubs). As in other mountainous areas, you should also beware of sudden drop-offs, which may be hidden by undergrowth. It's generally unwise to try and forge your own path without knowing the terrain.

Diving & Snorkelling

Mauritius offers a huge variety of dive sites to suit all abilities, and has plenty for snorkellers to ogle at. The main dive centres are located in and around Grand Baie, Flic en Flac, Blue Bay and Belle Mare. Rodrigues also has some superb sites and fewer divers. For detailed information on diving and snorkelling in Mauritius, see p37.

Hiking

For those interested in more than the usual beach activities, Mauritius offers some attractive hikes. Most are in the Central Plateau area around the Black River Gorges National Park; see p86 for detailed descriptions. Lion Mountain (north of Mahébourg) is another popular climb, while a day exploring the east coast of Rodrigues is a must for anyone wanting to get away from it all.

As a general rule when hiking, you should pay attention to 'Entrée Interdit' (Entry Prohibited) signs – they may mean you're entering a hunting reserve. 'Chemin Privée' (Private Road) signs are generally there for the benefit of motorists; most landowners won't object to the odd pedestrian. It's best to ask if you're unsure about where you should and shouldn't walk.

One possibility is to go with a guide. **Yemaya Adventures** (☎ 752 0046; www.yemayaadventures.com) and **Maurisun Adventure & Tours** (☎ 263 0192; www.maurisun.com; Royal Rd) in Grand Baie both offer escorted hikes, or you could try Krishna Peramal at the Résidence Peramal (p76), also in Grand Baie. On Rodrigues, contact **Osmosis** (☎ 832 3051; osmosis@intnet.mu; 7am-5pm), based at the Mourouk Ebony Hotel.

Horse Riding

There are opportunities for horse and pony riding at Domaine Les Pailles, an estate run as a tourist attraction (see p67 for details). Some hotels, particularly the upmarket ones, may also be able to arrange horse riding.

Surfing

A small scene led by Australian and South African surfers built up in the 1970s around Tamarin on the west coast (the surf movie *The Forgotten Island of Santosha* was made here), but the wave crashed during the 1980s.

These days, the scene around Tamarin comprises a small community of local and Réunionnais surfers. You can plug into what's happening and rent surfboards from Chez Jacques guesthouse in Tamarin.

The surf at Tamarin itself is fairly tame; better breaks in the area include Le Morne and One Eye's (named after the one-eyed owner of Le Morne estate), both at the northern end of Le Morne Peninsula. There are also good surfing locations near Baie du Cap. Lefts and Rights is further south by Îlot Sancho, and there's a tricky break opposite the public gardens in Souillac.

The surfing season lasts from around May to September.

Undersea Walks

This novel activity has caught on in a big way in Mauritius as it allows non-divers the chance to experience life below the waves. Participants don a weight-belt and a diving helmet and stroll along the sea bed feeding the fish in a sort of Jules Verne journey beneath the sea. Oxygen is piped down from the surface – using solar-powered compressors, no less – and divers are on hand in case there are any problems. Many travellers rate the experience as a highlight of their trip.

The two prime spots for an underwater ramble are Grand Baie and Belle Mare. The main operator is Captain Nemo's Undersea Walk (p75).

Yacht Cruises

The main centre for cruises is Grand Baie, from where luxury catamarans depart regularly for day trips to the Northern Islands, sunset cruises and the like. Perhaps the most interesting outing is a trip on the *Isla Mauritia*, a classy old schooner run by Yacht Charters in Grand Baie (p75). On the east coast, a couple of companies offer cruises from Pointe d'Esny to Île aux Cerfs.

All of these cruises can be booked through tour agents. Most of the big hotels also arrange cruises for their guests. Packages usually include lunch and snorkelling. Whether there's actually enough wind to fill the sails is in the hands of the gods.

BOOKS

For a historical overview of Mauritius, you can't beat Sydney Seldon's *A Comprehensive History of Mauritius* – despite the title, the book is 600 pages long.

Fortunately, there are plenty of more portable history books around. In *They Came to Mauritius*, Derek Hollingworth presents lively portraits of men and women who shaped the island's history or simply recorded their impressions as they passed by, from Mahé de Labourdonnais to Charles Darwin and Joseph Conrad.

Another interesting account of visitors to the island is *Prisoners in Paradise* by Sheila Ward. She recounts the lives of five personalities who were imprisoned in Mauritius before independence. These colourful characters include the British explorer Matthew Flinders, a Malagasy prince and Dr Stoyanovitch, a former prime minister of Yugoslavia.

For a more detailed account of Matthew Flinders' time in Mauritius, get hold of a copy of *In the Grips of the Eagle: Matthew Flinders at Île de France* by Huguette Ly-Tio-Fane Pineo.

In the late 18th century Bernadin de St-Pierre, author of the tropical tear-jerker *Paul et Virginie* (see p85), spent two years in Mauritius. He later published his keen – and often critical – observations on colonial life in *Journey to Mauritius*. The book, which has recently been re-published, had a huge impact at the time and is still a fascinating read today.

For a more contemporary look at local culture, try local humourist Yvan Lagesse's wry assessment of Mauritian life in *Comment vivre à l'île Maurice en 25 leçons* (How to Live in Mauritius in 25 Lessons).

Among the best-loved Mauritian folk-tales are those which were published in 1888 in *Sirandann Sanpek: Zistwar an Créole* by Charles Baissac. The collection has been reprinted with English translations by Ledikasyon pu Travayer. The same company also publishes *Mauritian Creole in Seven Easy Lessons* by Mark Frew, which lives up to its name if you're interested in learning the local lingo. For a basic phrasebook, *Speak Creole* published by **Éditions de L'Océan Indien** (EOI; eoibooks@intnet.mu), is a popular choice.

You can learn more about preserving Mauritian wildlife in naturalist Gerald Durrell's amusing and informative book *Golden Bats & Pink Pigeons*. Another excellent read is *Last Chance to See* by Douglas Adams and Mark Carwardine, in which the authors wander the globe in search of endangered species; the chapter 'Rare or Medium Rare' deals with Mauritius. For identifying local bird life, get a copy of *Birds of Mauritius* by Claude Michel published locally by Éditions de l'Océan Indien.

For coverage of Mauritian fiction, see p51. For books about coral and fish life, see p33; and for cookery books, pp29–32.

When shopping for books locally, remember that a bookshop is *un librairie*; a library is *un bibliothéque*.

BUSINESS HOURS

Banks in Mauritius are generally open from 9.15am to 3.15pm Monday to Thursday, and 9am to 5pm Friday.

Government offices are usually open from 9am to 4pm Monday to Friday and 9am to noon Saturday.

Shops are typically open from 8am to 4pm Monday to Friday, and 9am to noon on Saturday. Some close on Thursday or Saturday afternoons. However, on Rodrigues in particular, shops and offices close much earlier than 4pm; to be on the safe side it's best to do all your business in the morning.

CHILDREN

Travelling with children in Mauritius presents no particular problems. In fact, kids generally have a ball. The main attraction is undoubtedly the seaside. The beaches at Pereybère, Belle Mare, Blue Bay and Flic en Flac are particularly child-friendly. The domestic and wild animals on display at Casela Nature Park near Flic en Flac and La Vanille to the west of Mahébourg should also go down a treat. Older children might be interested in the interactive displays and machinery at L'Aventure du Sucre, the sugar museum at Pamplemousses. Domain Les Pailles near Port Louis offers activities to suit all ages, from pony and train rides for the little ones to quad-biking and full-blown trekking for teenagers.

To put their holiday in context, there's a wonderful series of cartoon books by Henry Koobes (published locally by Editions Vizavi Ltd). The English-language titles include *In Dodoland*, *SOS Shark* and *Meli-Melo in the Molasses*.

For more about travelling with children in the region, see p278.

DANGERS & ANNOYANCES

Though Mauritius is safer than many other countries, there are still a few things to be aware of.

Petty theft can be a problem in the main tourist areas, particularly on Île aux Cerfs and around Port Louis' Central Market, though you should be vigilant everywhere. There have also been reports of break-ins at self-catering apartments around the Grand Baie area (see p129).

Taxi drivers in Mauritius can earn up to 30% commission from certain shops, hotels, restaurants and other businesses to which they take clients. Bear this in mind if a taxi driver tells you that the place you want to go to is full or closed or more expensive than one he knows. Insist first on going to your chosen destination.

If a hotel or some other security guard tries to discourage you from entering a beach area, it's worth knowing that the beach between the high and low tide lines is public property. You are therefore legally entitled to use the beach, though not to venture on to private land above the high tide mark.

ELECTRICITY

The power supply throughout Mauritius is 220V. British-style three-pin sockets are most common, though you'll also find the continental two-pin variety. In most cases an adaptor is provided.

EMBASSIES & CONSULATES

Mauritian Embassies & Consulates

Mauritius has diplomatic representation in the following countries:

Australia (☎ 06-281 1203; mhccan@cyberone.com.au; 2 Beale Crescent, Deakin Canberra, ACT 2600)
Belgium (☎ 02 740 1930; ambmaur@skynet.be; 68 rue des Bollandistes, Etterbeek, 1040 Brussels)
Canada (☎ 0514-393 9500; fax 0514-393 9324; 606 Cathcart St, Suite 200, Montréal, Québec H3B 1K9)
France (☎ 01 42 27 30 19; ambassade.maurice@online.fr; 127 Rue de Tocqueville, 75017 Paris)
Germany (☎ 030-263 9360; mu.embln.3@t-online.de; Burgraf Centre, 84 Kurfurstenstrasse, 10787 Berlin)
New Zealand (☎ 0649-276 3789; gwullrich@uacl.co.nz; 33-37 Great South Rd, Otahuhu, Auckland)
Seychelles (☎ 225097; birdlife@seychelles.net; PO Box 1310, Aarti Chambers, Mont Fleuri, Mahé)
UK (☎ 020-7581 0294; londonmhc@bintnernet.com; 32-33 Elvaston Place, London SW7 5NW)
USA (☎ 202-244 1491; mauritius.embassy@prodigy.net; Suite 441, 4301 Connecticut Ave NW, Washington, DC, 20008)

Embassies & Consulates in Mauritius

Countries with diplomatic representation in Mauritius include the following:

Australian High Commission (Map p58; ☎ 208 1700; www.ahcmauritius.org; Rogers House, 5 President John Kennedy St, Port Louis)
Belgium & the Netherlands (Map p58; ☎ 202 7225; fbg@ibl.intnet.mu; 10 Dr Ferrière St, Port Louis; 9am-noon Mon-Fri)
British High Commission (Map p58; ☎ 202 9400; bhc@intnet.mu; Les Cascades Bldg, Edith Cavell St, Port Louis; 8.15am-3.45pm Mon-Thu 8.15am-1.30pm Fri)
Canada (Map p58; ☎ 212 5500; canada@intnet.mu; 18 Jules Koenig St, Port Louis; 10am-noon Mon-Fri)
France (Map p58; ☎ 202 0100; www.ambafrance-mu.org; 14 St Georges St, Port Louis; 8am-1pm)
Germany (Map p58; ☎ 211 4100; hgkdeutsch@intnet.mu; 32 St Georges St, Port Louis; 9am-noon Mon-Fri)
Italy (Map p58; ☎ 207 7844; fax 202 3215; Air Mauritius Building, John Kennedy St, Port Louis)

New Zealand (Map p58; ☎ 286 4920; nzconsulatemtius@hotmail.com; Anchor Bldg, Les Pailles)
Seychelles (Map p58; ☎ 211 1688; gfok@intnet.mu; 616 St James Ct, St Denis St, Port Louis)
Switzerland (Map p58; ☎ 208 8763; swiss.consul@intnet.mu; 2 Jules Koenig St, Port Louis; 9am-noon Mon-Fri)
USA (Map p58; ☎ 202 4400; mauritius.usembassy.gov; Rogers House, 5 President John Kennedy St, Port Louis; 7.30am-4pm Mon-Fri)

See the Regional Directory (p277) for information about what to expect from embassies and consulates.

FESTIVALS & EVENTS

Given the range of beliefs and customs in Mauritius, hardly a week goes by without some celebration. You can usually find out about the latest *cavadee*, *teemeedee* or other ceremonies from the Mauritius Tourism Promotion Authority in Port Louis (p60).

On Rodrigues, the main cultural event is the Festival Kréol, which takes place over three days at the end of October. Concerts, crafts exhibitions and other events – including lots of eating – break out all over the island.

The Fête du Poisson, held on Rodrigues in the first week of March, marks the opening of the fishing season. It is celebrated with all sorts of festivities including fishing expeditions – and lots more eating.

Regattas featuring traditional wooden fishing boats are popular in Rodrigues. Most take place in the lagoon off Port Sud-Est between January and December, but the most prestigious event of the year is the regatta held off Pointe de l'Herbe in May.

Hindu Festivals

CAVADEE

One of the more unusual Mauritian festivals, the Thaipoosam Cavadee takes place in January or February each year at most Hindu temples, and features acts of self-mutilation by devotees. Honouring a vow to Subramanya, the second son of Shiva, pilgrims pierce their tongues and cheeks with skewers. They then march from their chosen temple to the banks of a river carrying the *cavadee* (a wooden arch decorated with flowers and palm leaves, with pots of milk suspended from each end of the base) on their shoulders.

The Thaipoosam Cavadee is a public holiday, but other small *cavadees* occur during the rest of the year at selected temples.

TEEMEEDEE

This is a Hindu and Tamil fire-walking ceremony in honour of various gods. The ceremonies occur throughout the year, but mostly in December and January. After fasting and bathing, the participants walk over red-hot embers scattered along the ground. The Hindu temples in Quatre Bornes, Camp Diable (near Rivie‘re des Anguilles) and The Vale (near Goodlands) are noted for this event. A feat along similar lines is sword climbing, seen mostly between April and June. The best demonstrations occur at Mont Choisy and the towns of Triolet and Solitude (between Port Louis and Trou aux Biches).

OTHER HINDU FESTIVALS

Each year, most of the island's Hindus make a pilgrimage to Grand Bassin, a crater lake in the south of the island, for the festival Maha Shivaratri. For information about the celebration, see the boxed text on p93.

Hindus also celebrate the victory of Rama over the evil deity Ravana during Divali, which falls in late October or early November. To mark this joyous event, countless candles and lamps are lit to show Rama (the seventh incarnation of Vishnu) the way home from his period of exile.

Holi, the festival of colours, is known for the exuberant throwing of coloured powder and water, and tourists are not exempt from the odd dousing. The festival symbolises the victory of divine power over demonic strength. On the night before Holi, bonfires are built to symbolise the destruction of the evil demon Holika. This festival is held in February or March.

Other major public festivals include Pongal (January or February), Ougadi (March or April) and Ganesh Chaturti (August or September). The latter celebrates the birthday of Ganesh, the elephant-headed god of wisdom and prosperity.

Muslim Festivals

Muslims celebrate Eid al-Fitr to mark the end of the fasting month of Ramadan, which is the ninth month of the lunar year. Eid al-Fitr is always a public holiday.

Chinese Festivals

The Chinese New Year is celebrated with the Chinese Spring Festival, which is a public holiday and falls in late January or early February. On new year's eve, homes are spring-cleaned and decked in red, the colour of happiness, and firecrackers are let off to ward off evil spirits. On the following day, cakes made of rice flour and honey are given to family and friends. No scissors or knives may be used in case someone is hurt and begins the new year with bad luck.

Christian Festivals

The most important date for many Mauritian Christians is 9 September, Père Laval Feast Day, which marks the anniversary of the priest's death. Pilgrims from around the world come to his shrine at Ste-Croix to pray for miracle cures (p68).

FOOD

A meal in a budget restaurant in Mauritius should cost less than Rs 200. Moving up a notch, you can expect to pay between Rs 200 and Rs 350 in a mid-range place, while the bill at a classy, top-of-the-range establishment will be at least Rs 350 per head. For information about just some of the culinary delights in store in Mauritius, see p26.

HOLIDAYS

The following public holidays are observed in Mauritius:

New Year 1 & 2 January
Thaipoosam Cavadee January/February
Chinese Spring Festival January/February
Abolition of Slavery 1 February
Maha Shivaratree February/March
Ougadi March/April
National Day 12 March
Labour Day 1 May
Assumption of the Blessed Virgin Mary 15 August
Ganesh Chaturti September
Divali October/November
Arrival of Indentured Labourers 2 November
Eid al-Fitr November/December
Christmas Day 25 December

INTERNET RESOURCES

Acres of web space are devoted to Mauritius, both in English and French. A selection of the more useful sites for planning your trip are as follows.

www.mauritius-info.com Very user-friendly site offering business and tourism listings.
www.mauritius.net Good site from the MTPA, where you can download brochures about the country.
www.rodrigues-island.org Great portal for everything Rodrigues-related.
www.tropicscope.com Excellent broad overview, listings and links.

MAPS

The best and most detailed map of Mauritius is that published by the **Institut Géographique Nationale** (IGN; www.ign.fr). The Globetrotter travel map is good for its detailed insets including Port Louis, Curepipe and the botanical gardens at Pamplemousses. Both are available from local bookstores and supermarkets.

There are no decent maps of Rodrigues. The best available are very broad-brush road maps on sale for Rs 75 in tourist shops in Port Mathurin. But it's a small place and difficult to get lost.

MEDIA

Newspapers & Magazines

The main daily papers are *L'Express* and *Le Mauricien*, both in French, with the occasional article in English. The *News on Sunday* and the *Mauritius Times* are English-language weeklies which print a smattering of international news.

Weekly magazines, all in French, include *Le Weekend*, with good news coverage, and *Weekend Scope*, *Cinq Plus* and *Cinq Plus Dimanche*, all concentrating on cinematic and political glitterati.

Maurice Passion is a good bilingual quarterly magazine that's worth picking up for its articles on history, culture and other features with a tourist focus.

A selection of foreign-language papers and magazines are available in the main tourist centres and some of the larger hotels. The French media are best represented, though you'll also find English-language publications such as the *International Herald Tribune*, *Sunday Times*, *Daily Mail* and *Time*.

On Rodrigues, there are three local weekly papers published in French and Creole: the OPR-backed *Le Vrai Rodrigues*; the opposition's *Ici Rodrigues*; and the new and independent *Tribune*.

TV & Radio

There are three national TV channels, run by the Mauritius Broadcasting Corporation (MBC): MBC 1 offers a broad mix of programmes in English and French; MBC 2 is the Hindi channel; MBC 3 shows BBC World, Sky News, sports and other imported fare. Newspapers publish programme schedules.

The alternative is Télé Réunion (RFO) beamed across from Réunion, though reception isn't great everywhere on the island. The presentation is slicker and it's all in French. There are also several pay-TV stations. Top hotels offer a variety of foreign-language satellite stations.

MBC operates a radio service which broadcasts in French, Creole, Hindi, Chinese and English.

MONEY

The Mauritian unit of currency is the rupee (Rs), which is divided into 100 cents. There are coins of 5, 20 and 50 cents, and Rs 1, Rs 5 and Rs 10. The banknote denominations are Rs 25, Rs 50, Rs 100, Rs 200, Rs 500, Rs 1000 and Rs 2000.

ATMs

Armed with your PIN, it's perfectly possible to travel on plastic in Mauritius since ATMs are widespread. Even Rodrigues has a smattering of them. They're mostly located outside banks, though you'll also find them at the airports, at larger supermarkets and in some shopping malls. The majority of machines accept Visa and MasterCard, or any similar cards in the Cirrus and Plus networks, while Amex now has a tie-in with MCB.

Credit Cards

Visa and MasterCard are the most useful cards to carry, though Amex is catching up. Nearly all tourist shops and the more upmarket restaurants and hotels accept payment by credit card, as do car hire companies, tour agents and so forth. Anywhere outside the main tourist haunts and small businesses still expect payment in cash.

A few places add on an extra fee, typically 3%, to the bill to cover 'bank charges'. The cheaper car hire companies are the worst offenders. To be on the safe side, always ask.

A SHOPAHOLIC'S TOP FIVE

Quatre Bornes (p94) Rummage for brand-name bargains in the twice-weekly clothes market

Port Louis Central Market (p60) Mug up on tropical botany among the fruit and veg stalls

Caudan Waterfront (p66) There's something for everyone in Port Louis' temple to consumerism

Port Mathurin Market (p125) Get here early to see the market at its best

Voiliers de L'Océan (p93) The model ships on sale here are as much works-of-art as souvenirs

Cash advances on credit cards are available from most major banks, including MCB, Barclays, the State Bank and HSBC. Just remember to take your passport.

Moneychangers

Major currencies and travellers cheques can be changed at the main banks, exchange bureaus and the larger hotels. Exchange bureaus sometimes offer slightly better rates than banks, but there's usually little difference. Hotels tend to have the worst rates and may add an additional service commission. As a general rule, travellers cheques bring a better rate than cash. There is no black market in Mauritius.

Banks don't charge commission on changing cash. As for travellers cheques, the system varies. Some banks, such as HSBC, charge 1% of the total, with a minimum of Rs 200, while MCB and the State Bank levy Rs 50 for up to 10 cheques. Don't forget to take along your passport when changing money. And make sure you hang on to the encashment form, which will have to be presented if you want to change Mauritian rupees back into foreign currency at the end of your stay.

Taxes

Most items apart from unprepared food are subject to 15% VAT. There is no hard and fast rule about whether this tax is included in prices quoted for meals, rooms and activities. If it's not clear, be sure to ask or you might

WILL THE REAL RALPH LAUREN PLEASE STAND UP?

It all began back in 1992 when a local garment company registered the Ralph Lauren trademark and logo in Mauritius. It then licensed the mark to another company which began churning out shirts, sweaters and other apparel, each bearing a discrete polo-rider logo and an uncanny resemblance to clothes by a certain American designer: Polo Ralph Lauren.

By the time the real Ralph Lauren realised what was happening, it was too late. An epidemic of look-alike 'outlet stores' had spread through Mauritius. Business boomed as tourists flocked to the stores. Under pressure from Ralph Lauren and other aggrieved companies, however, in 2003 the Mauritian government finally beefed up its intellectual property laws. This was followed by a surprise ruling in February 2004 in which the Supreme Court ordered the 'fake' outlet stores closed. What happens next remains to be seen.

be in for a nasty shock. Top end hotels and restaurants sometimes add a service charge.

SHOPPING

If the beaches begin to pall, you can shop till you drop in Mauritius. From fake Ralph Lauren T-shirts and Adidas shoes to faultless Floreal knitwear; from dodo fridge magnets to hand-crafted model sailing ships, there's something for everyone.

Given such a wide choice, there is no reason to purchase items made from endangered species. For information about shells, coral and turtle products, which should not be purchased, see Underwater Worlds, p33.

Bargaining is very much part of life in Mauritius. It's usual to bargain in markets and anywhere where prices aren't marked, sometimes even on marked prices if you're a big spender. As a tourist, however, you'll need well-honed bargaining skills to get much of a discount.

Clothing

The textile industry is one of Mauritius' biggest earners. Many of the brand-name clothes on sale in Europe, Australia and America are produced in the factories around Curepipe, Floréal and Vacoas. Shoppers can save by buying at the source, and many of the bigger suppliers have outlet stores where you can snap up items at a fraction of their usual retail price. Those really watching the rupees can opt for convincing – and not so convincing – copies of well-known designer brands. Until recently, Ralph Lauren was flavour of the month, with 'outlet shops' popping up like mushrooms (see Will the Real Ralph Lauren Please Stand Up?, right). One of the best places to picks up genuine seconds is the market at Quatre Bornes (p94). Other vendors tend to congregate on President John Kennedy St in Port Louis, and in the Rose Hill and Curepipe markets in Central Mauritius. Check carefully for minor flaws and dodgy stitching.

Floreal Knitwear in Floréal is renowned for its stylish sweaters and other knitted garments. The company supplies Gap, Next and other international outfitters, but you can buy the same items before the branded labels have been added for a fraction of the final cost at their Floréal emporium.

Shibani and Maille St are two other local companies producing high quality knitwear. Maille St specialises in cashmere sweaters in colours to die for. For kids there's Gecko, while Habit and the fetchingly named IV Pl@y target teens with up-to-the minute streetwear. You'll find branches of all these shops in Port Louis' Caudan Waterfront complex, Sunset Boulevard in Grand Baie and other upmarket shopping malls.

Handicrafts & Souvenirs

Locally produced basketry, essential oils, sugar, spices, teas and T-shirts all make very port-able souvenirs. The Craft Market in Port Louis' Caudan Waterfront complex offers perhaps the widest choice and the quality is high. Other good places to browse are Port Louis' Central Market and the Grand Baie Bazaar. Vendors at both also sell Malagasy handicrafts, including leather belts and bags, embroidery and semiprecious-stone solitaire sets.

From Rodrigues you can take home a very natty vacaos-leaf hat or basket. The island is also famous for its honey and lemon and chilli preserves. Jewellery and other items made from coconut shell by handicapped people are available from Craft Aid.

Model Ships

Whether or not you could conceive of having one at home, it is difficult not to be impressed by the skill that goes into producing Mauritius' famous model ships. Small-scale shipbuilding has become a huge business and you'll see intricate replicas of famous vessels, such as the *Bounty, Victory, Endeavour, Golden Hind* and even the *Titanic*, for sale all over the island; it's hard to believe that shipbuilding dates back to only 1968, when an unknown Mauritian carved a model ship for fun and launched a whole new industry.

The models are made out of teak or mahogany (cheaper camphor wood is liable to crack), and larger ships take up to 400 hours to complete. Men usually work on the structure and the women do the rigging and sails, which are dipped in tea to give them a weathered look.

If you're thinking of buying, shop around to compare prices, which range from Rs 2400 up to Rs 80,000 or more. One of the best model ship-builders is **Voiliers de L'Océan** (☎/fax 676 6986; Sir Winston Churchill St, Curepipe; 🕑 7.30am-6pm); the company also has an outlet, MAST, in the Caudan Waterfront complex. The biggest factory is **Historic Marine** (☎ 283 9404; 🕑 8am-5pm Mon-Fri, 9am-noon Sat & Sun) in Goodlands, in the north of the island. In both cases the staff will be happy to show you around the workshop (weekdays only) without any pressure to buy.

To get your goods home safely, shops will pack the models for carry-on luggage or in sturdy boxes to go in the hold, and deliver them to your hotel or the airport at no extra charge.

TELEPHONE

The telephone service has received massive investment over the last few years. Calls no longer get lost or misrouted and there are public phones on almost every street corner.

The state-controlled Mauritius Telecom has a virtual monopoly on land lines. The mobile network has been opened up to competition, though so far there's only one other operator, Emtel, in the market.

Coin-operated phones can only be used for calls within Mauritius. You need to feed in a minimum of two Rs 1 coins to make a call, which buys you about two minutes' phone time. They also accept Rs 5 coins.

You can dial abroad using IDD from private phones and public card-phones. Some public phones now accept credit cards, though they're few and far between.

The rate for a call to Australia, Europe or the USA is about Rs 20 per minute. These rates fall by around 25% during off-peak hours (10pm to 6am from Monday to Friday and noon on Saturday to 6am the following Monday).

When phoning Mauritius from abroad, you'll need to dial the international code for Mauritius (230), followed by the local number minus the first 0. There are no area codes in Mauritius.

NEW PHONE NUMBERS

Mauritius Telecom has announced plans to increase all phone numbers in Mauritius to eight digits in order to meet increased demand. At the time of writing no decision had been made as to the new num-bering system.

Mobile Phones

Coverage on Mauritius is generally excellent. If you have a GSM phone and it has been 'unlocked', you can keep costs down by buying a local SIM card from either **Cellplus (Mauritius Telecom)** (☎ 203 7649; Mauritius Telecom Tower, Edith Cavell St, Port Louis) or **Emtel** (☎ 203 7649; Mauritius Telecom Tower, Edith Cavell St, Port Louis). A starter pack costs around Rs 600 including Rs 125-worth of calls. To top-up your credit you can buy prepaid cards almost anywhere.

Local calls are charged at between Rs 1.50 and Rs 5 per minute depending if you're calling someone on the same network or not. International calls cost a couple of rupees per minute on top of the standard Mauritius Telecom rates.

Because Rodrigues uses a different mobile phone system from the mainland, SIM cards purchased in Mauritius will not work here. You will have to buy a new card.

Phonecards

Télécartes (phonecards) are on sale at Mauritius Telecom offices, bookstores, news-vendors, supermarkets and the like. They come in denominations of Rs 50, Rs 100, Rs 250 and Rs 500. A Rs 50 card gives you roughly three minutes to Australia, Europe or the USA.

TOURIST INFORMATION

Independent travellers in Mauritius are a fairly rare species, which partly accounts for the very limited tourist information services on the ground. Fortunately, you'll find most shopkeepers, bus drivers, police officers and bar staff are happy to help.

The **Mauritius Tourism Promotion Authority** (MTPA; ☎ 208 6397; www.mauritius.net) runs a friendly if sometimes uninformed tourist office in Port Louis , where you can pick up basic maps and a reasonably useful guide covering the main sights and activities.

MTPA also has a desk in the arrivals hall at the **SSR airport** (☎ 637 3635), though it's only open from the first flight until 1pm.

More useful is Mauritius Telecom's 24-hour phone service, **Tourist Info** (☎ 152). At any time of day or night you can speak to someone (in English) who will at least try to answer your questions.

VISAS

You don't need a visa to enter Mauritius if you are a citizen of the European Union, the USA, Australia, Canada, Japan, New Zealand or a number of other countries. You can find more information on this website (http://pmo.gov.mu/dha/ministry/novisa.htm). Initial entry is granted for a maximum of one month. If you change your departure plans, make sure you don't exceed your permitted stay.

Extensions for a further three months as a tourist are available from the **Passport & Immigration Office** (☎ 210 9312; fax 210 9322; Ster-ling House, Lislet Geoffrey St, Port Louis). Applications must be submitted with one form, two passport-size photos, your passport, an onward ticket and proof of finances. Two letters may also be necessary – one from you explaining why you want to stay longer, and one by a local 'sponsor' (it can be someone providing accommodation).

Providing you can satisfy these demands there should be no further problems, but since the police are responsible for passport control, and quite a few visitors overstay their entry permits, there are 'get tough' periods.

TRANSPORT IN MAURITIUS

GETTING THERE & AWAY

The following section covers transport between the three islands of Réunion, Mauritius and the Seychelles. For information about getting to the region from elsewhere, see the Regional Transport Directory (p286).

Air

Air Mauritius and Air Austral between them operate several flights a day from Réunion to Mauritius. Return fares start at around €250 in low season. Air Mauritius also has two weekly flights to Rodrigues; a one-month return fare costs €350. From the Seychelles, there's a choice between Air Mauritius and Air Seychelles, which between them operate four to five flights a week. Tickets cost between €400 and €550 for a three-month return in low season. All three carriers have a good safety record.

AIRPORTS

Mauritius now boasts two international airports: the **Sir Seewoosagur Ramgoolam International Airport** (SSR; code MRU; ☎ 603 3030; http://mauritius-airport.intnet.mu) on the main island; and the spanking new **Plaine Corail Airport** (RRG; ☎ 831 6301) on Rodrigues.

AIRLINES

Air Austral (airline code UU; ☎ 202 6677; www.air-austral.com; Rogers House, 5 President John Kennedy St, Port Louis; hub Roland Garros International Airport, Réunion)

Air Mauritius (airline code MK; ☎ 207 7070; www.airmauritius.com; Air Mauritius Centre, President John Kennedy St, Port Louis; hub SSR International Airport, Mauritius)

Air Seychelles (airline code HM; ☎ 202 6655; www.airseychelles.net; Rogers House, 5 President John Kennedy St, Port Louis; hub Seychelles International Airport, Mahé)

Sea

The Mauritius Shipping Corporation operates two boats between Réunion and Mauritius, with several sailings each month. The one-way journey takes about 11 hours. The newer and more comfortable boat is the *Mauritius Trochetia*. The return fare from Réunion in low/high season starts at roughly €165/200 for a berth in a 2nd-class cabin. From Mauritius, the price is Rs 3750/4350.

The sister ship, *Mauritius Pride* is slightly cheaper. For a reclining seat in low/high season, you'll pay around €135/160 return from Réunion and Rs 3000/3600 from Mauritius. The equivalent fares for a berth in a two-person cabin are €195/230 and Rs 4350/5250.

Tickets and information are available through travel agents or direct from the Mauritius Shipping Corporation representative **Coraline Shipping Agency** (☎ 217 2285; msc@coraline.intnet.mu; Nova Bldg, Military Rd, Port Louis).

GETTING AROUND

Air

The only domestic carrier is Air Mauritius which operates at least two flights per day to Rodrigues – this rises to five flights during the Christmas peak season. The return fare costs Rs 3210/3610 in low/high season for a stay of between three days and one month. The journey between the two islands takes 1½ hours.

Air Mauritius also offers helicopter tours and charters from SSR International Airport and a number of major hotels. A full one-hour island tour costs Rs 22,000 for up to four passengers; a quick 15-minute jaunt will set you back Rs 8800. For information and reservations, contact **Air Mauritius Helicopter Services** (☎ 637 3552; helicopter@airmauritius.com).

Bicycle

Cycling isn't really a practical means of long-distance transport in Mauritius – there is simply too much traffic – but bikes are fine for short hops along the coast. Given that the coast is pleasantly flat, it's amazing how much ground you can cover in a day without killing yourself or getting saddle-sore. The coast roads are also quieter than those in the interior, so you can relax and take in the landscape.

In general, the roads are well maintained, but look out for potholes along country lanes. Avoid cycling anywhere at night, as most roads are poorly lit and traffic can be erratic.

You can rent bikes (usually mountain bikes) from most hotels and guesthouses and also from some tour agents and car-rental outlets in the main tourist centres such as Grand Baie, Flic en Flac and Trou d'Eau Douce. The cheapest deals will start at around Rs 100 per day. You'll usually be asked for a deposit of Rs 5000, either in cash or by taking an imprint of your credit card. Most bikes are in pretty reasonable condition, but be sure to check the brakes, gears and saddle (some are mighty uncomfortable) before riding off into the blue-beyond. The bike should have a lock. Use it, especially if you leave your bike at the beach and outside shops; attach it to a tree, fence railings or some other immovable object.

Boat

The only scheduled domestic passenger services are between Port Louis and Rodrigues. The *Mauritius Trochetia* and the older *Mauritius Pride* between them sail four times a month in each direction; the outward journey takes about 36 hours and the return to Port Louis roughly 25 hours. Tickets and information are available through travel agents or direct from the Mauritius Shipping Corporation: contact **Coraline Shipping Agency** (☎ 217 2285; msc@coraline.intnet.mu; Nova Bldg, 1 Military Rd, Port Louis) or, on Rodrigues, the **Mauritius Shipping Corporation** (☎ 831 0640; Rue François Leguat, Port Mathurin). Return fares cost Rs 3300/4800 for a seat/cabin in the *Mauritius Pride* and Rs 6450 for a 2nd-class cabin in the *Mauritius Trochetia*. These are popular services, so it is advised that you book ahead.

Various private operators offer cruises to offshore islands, or snorkelling and fishing excursions. See p130 and the listings under individual towns for more information about these services.

Bus

Bus services are cheap and easy to use, and can take you just about anywhere. It's best to stick to express buses whenever possible, as standard buses seem to stop every few metres and can take up to twice as long to reach the same destination. To give an idea of journey times, it takes approximately an hour by standard services from Mahébourg

MAIN BUS COMPANIES IN MAURITIUS

Company name	Contact details	Main routes
Mauritius Bus Transport	☎ 245 2539	Pamplemousses to Crève Coeur
National Transport Corporation (NTC)	☎ 426 1859; cnt.bus@intnet.mu	Port Louis to Centre de Flacq, Curepipe, Flic en Flac, Floréal, Grande Rivière Noire, Pamplemousses, Quatre Bornes, Rose Hill, Souillac; Quatre Bornes to Baie du Cap; Curepipe to Baie du Cap, Floréal, Quatre Bornes, Souillac, Flic en Flac
Rose Hill Transport	☎ 464 1221	Port Louis to Rose Hill
Triolet Bus Service (TBS)	☎ 261 6516	Port Louis to Cap Malheureux, Grand Baie, Mont Choisy, Pereybère, Trou aux Biches; Pamplemousses to Cap Malheureux, Grand Baie, Grande Gaube, Mont Choisy
United Bus Service (UBS)	☎ 212 2026	Port Louis to Curepipe, Mahébourg, Ste Croix

to Curepipe, an hour from Curepipe to Port Louis and an hour from Port Louis to Grand Baie.

Long-distance buses run from around 6am to 6.30pm, though there is a late service between Port Louis and Curepipe until 11pm. Generally there are buses every fifteen minutes or so on the major routes, with less frequent buses on the express services. Buses in country areas can be few and far between.

As an indication, fares range from Rs 9 for a short trip up to a maximum of Rs 21 for the run from Port Louis to Mahébourg. Air-con express buses may be a couple of rupees extra. Tickets are available from the conductor; keep some small change handy. Retain your tickets, as inspectors often board to check them. Press the buzzer when you want to get off.

The buses are single-deck vehicles bearing dynamic names such as 'Road Warrior', 'Bad Boys' and 'The Street Ruler'. It's perhaps not surprising that some drivers harbour Formula One racing fantasies; fortunately, the frequent stops slow things down a touch. Though the buses are in varying states of disrepair, the fleet is gradually being upgraded.

The buses are almost always packed, especially on the main routes, but turnover is quick at all the stops. If you start the trip standing, you're likely to end up sitting.

Be warned that you could have problems taking large bags or backpacks on a bus. If it takes up a seat, you will probably have to pay for that extra seat. A few travellers have even been refused entry to a full bus if they have a large bag.

There is no country-wide bus service for Mauritius. Instead there are five large regional bus companies (see the table) and scores of individual operators. Unfortunately, there are no published timetables available. Your best source of information is to phone the company or the umbrella body, the **National Transport Authority** (☎ 202 2800; www.ncb.intnet.mu/mpi). Locals also usually know the best way to get from A to B.

Car & Motorcycle

If you're short on time or want to be truly independent, then renting a car or motorcycle is the way to go. Prices aren't as low as they could be, considering the numbers of visitors who rent vehicles, but you should be able to negotiate a discount if you're renting for a week or more.

Mauritian roads range from an excellent motorway – running from SSR International Airport to Port Louis and Grand Baie – to heavily potholed minor roads. However, a greater danger are other drivers, not the roads. Mauritian drivers tend to have little consideration for each other, let alone for motorbikes. Buses are notorious for overtaking and then pulling in immediately ahead of other vehicles to pick up or drop off passengers; always show extra caution when a bus comes in sight. Night driving should be avoided unless you enjoy an assault course of ill-lit oncoming vehicles, totally unlit bikes and weaving pedestrians. Motorcyclists should also be prepared for the elements, as sudden rain showers can come out of clear skies.

CAR

Generally, drivers must be more than 23 years of age (some companies require a minimum age of 21) and have held a driving licence for at least one year, and payment must be made in advance. You can pay by credit card (Visa and MasterCard are the most widely accepted), though small companies might add a 3% 'processing fee' for this service.

All foreigners are technically required to have an international driving licence. Few rental agencies enforce this, but it's safest to carry one as the police can demand to see it.

Rates for the smallest hatchback start at around Rs 1000 a day (including insurance and unlimited mileage) with one of the independent operators; add Rs 150 or so for air-con. International chains such as Hertz and Sixt charge from Rs 1400 a day. On top of that you will be required to pay a refundable deposit, usually Rs 15,000; most companies will take an imprint of your credit card to cover this. Policies usually specify that drivers are liable for the first Rs 10,000 of damage in the event of an accident.

While there are dozens of rental outlets in Mauritius, during the peak Christmas holiday season cars can be hard to come by. It's best to book several weeks in advance, especially if you don't want to pay the earth.

All the major international car-rental companies listed below have airport desks or can deliver to the airport. Some reliable local companies are given under the individual towns.

ADA (☎ 675 2626; www.ada.fr in French)
Avis (☎ 208 1624; www.avis.com)
Budget (☎ 467 9709; www.budget.com)
Hertz (☎ 670 4301; www.hertz.com)

MOTORCYCLE

There are only a few places where you can rent motorbikes, which is a shame as this is a great way to explore the quiet coastal roads. While you'll occasionally find a 125cc bike, most are 100cc or under; the smaller models are sometimes referred to as scooters.

Whatever the engine size, most places charge upwards of Rs 450 a day including a helmet. As with car rental, payment is requested in advance along with a deposit of Rs 5000 or so.

Most of the bikes are fairly well worn, but parts are widely available should anything fail. Beware of 'imitation' parts, which are copies of genuine manufacturer spares, cast in inferior metal.

Towns offering motorcycle hire include Grand Baie, Flic en Flac, Mahébourg and Port Mathurin. You should be aware that most motorcycle hire is 'unofficial' so you may not be covered in case of a collision.

PARKING

Parking is free and not a problem in most of Mauritius, though it's best not to leave your car in an isolated spot. City parking requires payment. There are supervised car parks in Port Louis, but elsewhere you'll have to park on the street, which involves buying parking coupons. These are available from petrol stations and cost from Rs 50 for 10 coupons, with each coupon valid for 30 minutes. The same coupons can be used all over the island. Street parking is generally free at night and at weekends; the exact hours, which vary from one town to another, are indicated on signposts.

ROAD RULES

Local motorists seem to think they'll save electricity by not switching on their headlights and the police are better at people control than traffic control.

Traffic congestion is heavy in Port Louis. There are many pedestrian zebra crossings, but cross with care. Don't expect courtesy and don't expect drivers to be worried about insurance – you'll get knocked over.

Driving is on the left and the speed limit varies from 30km/h in town centres to 80km/h on the open road and is clearly signed. Even so, not many people stick to these limits and the island has its fair share of accidents.

Drivers and passengers are required to wear seat belts. For lack of sufficient breathalysers, the alcohol limit (legally 0.5 grams per litre) is defined by the police as one glass of beer.

Hitching

Hitching is never entirely safe in any country in the world, and we don't recommend it. Travellers who decide to hitch should understand that they are taking a small but potentially serious risk. People who choose to hitch will be safer if they travel in pairs and let someone know where they are planning to go.

Getting a lift in Mauritius is subject to pretty much the same quirks of luck and fate that you experience hitching anywhere. The only place where it really does come in handy is Rodrigues. Since few people there own cars, hitching is a popular way to get around, especially on Sundays, when buses are few and far between.

Taxi

Taxis are the quickest and most convenient method of getting around the country, but you'll need to be savvy if you don't want to end up paying over the odds. Mauritian taxis have meters, but few drivers are willing to use them. You *must* agree on the price before getting into the taxi, and make sure there is no doubt about it. During the journey most cabbies will also tout for future business; if you aren't careful you may find that you've agreed to an all-day island tour. If you aren't interested, make this very clear, as many drivers won't take no for an answer.

Many guesthouse managers/owners have attempted to mitigate their guests' constant frustration with rip-offs by arranging prices with local taxi drivers. The quotes given under such arrangements, particularly those from small guesthouses, are often acceptable; they can usually arrange competitively priced airport pick-ups as well. Once you've got a feel for the rates, you can venture into independent bargaining.

Taxis charge slightly more at night and may ask for an extra fee if you want the comfort of air-con. It's also worth remembering that some taxis charge around Rs 1 per minute waiting time. It seems minimal, but it adds up if you stop for lunch or do some sightseeing on foot. Your best bet is to negotiate a fare with the driver that includes waiting time. As a rough bargaining guide, here are some of the fares you can expect to pay for one-way trips.

From	To	Cost
Flic en Flac	Port Louis	Rs 300
Mahébourg	Blue Bay	Rs 50
SSR airport	Mahébourg	Rs 300
SSR airport	Flic en Flac	Rs 800
SSR airport	Port Louis	Rs 650
SSR airport	Grand Baie	Rs 700
Trou aux Biches	Grand Baie	Rs 150
Trou aux Biches	Port Louis	Rs 250

For between Rs 1200 and Rs 2000, you can hire a taxi for a full-day tour of sights around the island (the fare varies with how much ground you intend to cover). You can cut costs by forming a group – the price should *not* be calculated per person. If you want to squeeze a tour of the whole island into one day, keep in mind that this won't leave much time for sightseeing. You're better off splitting the island tour into two days. Once you've agreed a price and itinerary, it helps to get the details down in writing.

Although most drivers can speak both French and English, double-check before setting off to ensure you won't face a day-long communication barrier. If you're lucky, you'll get an excellent and informative guide, but note that most cabbies work on a commission basis with particular restaurants, shops and sights. If you want to go to a restaurant of your choice, you may have to insist on it. Again, small guesthouses can usually recommend a reliable driver.

SHARE TAXI

When individual fares are hard to come by, some cabs will cruise around their area supplementing the bus service. For quick, short-haul trips they pick up passengers waiting at the bus stops and charge just a little more than the bus. Their services are called 'share taxis' or 'taxi trains'. Mind you, if you flag down a share taxi, you'll only be swapping a big sardine can for a small one, and if you flag down an empty cab, you may have to pay the full fare.

Réunion

JEAN-BERNARD CARILLET

Réunion

CONTENTS

Highlights	147
Climate & When to Go	147
History	148
The Culture	150
Religion	151
Arts	151
Environment	153
St-Denis	**156**
Around St-Denis	166
East Coast	**167**
Ste-Suzanne & Around	168
St-André & Around	169
Bras-Panon	171
St-Benoît & Around	172
Ste-Anne	173
Ste-Rose & Around	173
South Coast	**174**
St-Philippe & Around	174
St-Joseph & Around	176
St-Pierre	177
Around St-Pierre	180
West Coast	**181**
Étang-Salé-les-Bains & Around	183
Tévelave	183
St-Leu	184
Around St-Leu	185
La-Saline-les-Bains & Around	186
St-Gillies-les-Bains & L'Hermitage-les-Bains	186
Boucan Canot	192
St-Gilles-les-Hauts & Around	192
Le Maïdo & Around	193
St-Paul	194
The Interior	**195**
Cirque de Cilaos	197
Cirque de Salazie	202
Cirque de Mafate	206
Les Hautes Plaines	206
Réunion Directory	**209**
Transport	**220**

FAST FACTS

- **Area** 2510 sq km
- **Capital** St-Denis
- **Country code** ☎ 33
- **Main religion** Catholicism
- **Major export** Sugar
- **Money** euro
- **Official language** French
- **Official name** Department of Réunion
- **Population** 750,000
- **Unemployment** 30%

It's hard to get your head around Réunion. With its pavement cafés where casually chic businessmen breakfast on coffees and croissants, its French postal vans and its beret-clad bowls players, it's as though a slice of mainland France has been relocated lock, stock and wine barrel to an island in the middle of the Indian Ocean.

And what an island! Sheer and lush, it appears to have risen dripping wet from the deep blue sea. Like Hawaii, Réunion has breathtaking natural landscapes, a live volcano and a subtly tropical climate – but on arrival, you're likely to be offered a baguette and a cup of strong black coffee rather than a palm skirt and a garland of flowers!

The island is run as an overseas department of France, making it one of the last colonial possessions in the world. French culture dominates every facet of life, and the Réunionnais are proudly French speaking, almost to the exclusion of all other languages.

The French atmosphere of the island, however, has a firmly tropical twist, with subtle traces of Indian, African and even Chinese cultures. All of these traditions are blended in Réunion's unofficial language, Creole, and in the island's cuisine, a sort of 'Paris meets Mumbai by way of Beijing' experience.

Historically, the French have kept the secret of this beautiful island firmly to themselves. But news of Réunion's dramatic natural wonders, its world-class hiking trails and its intriguing cultural heritage is beginning to seep out.

HIGHLIGHTS

- **Café life** People-watch while you pause in a pavement café in St-Denis (p164)
- **The open road** Explore the wild and woolly south coast (p174)
- **Scenic lookout** Get an eye-full of the vertiginous views at Le Maïdo (p193)
- **Party place** Get into the groove at St-Gilles-les-Bain (p186)
- **Scenic drive** Zigzag up to Cilaos (p197)
- **Hot spot** Hike up the smouldering Piton de la Fournaise volcano (p234)
- **Green spaces** Check out the the so-called Garden of Eden (Jardin d'Eden) (p187)
- **Creole culture** Stroll the streets of Hell-Bourg (p203)
- **Remote adventure** Test your stamina in the Cirque de Mafate (p228)
- **Rural retreat** Experience traditional life in Entre-Deux (p180)

CLIMATE & WHEN TO GO

Because of the high mountains, Réunion's climate varies more than that of Mauritius. It still, however, experiences only two distinct seasons: the hot, rainy summer from December to April and the cool, dry winter from late April to October. The east coast is considerably wetter than the west, but wettest of all are the mountains above the east coast – around Takamaka, Plaine-des-Palmistes and the northern and eastern slopes of the volcano. As with Mauritius, the cyclone season is roughly December to March.

Temperatures on the coast average 22°C during winter and 27°C in summer. In the mountains, they drop to 11°C and 18°C respectively. The southeast trade winds blow all year round and can make hiking at high altitude uncomfortably cold in winter.

Clouds generally cover the peaks and high plains from mid-morning. The best time for viewing the landscape is at first light and during the drier winter months. The dry season is also the most favourable for hiking (see p225 for more information on when to hike).

The peak tourist seasons are April, May and during the French school holidays from

HOW MUCH?

- Espresso coffee €1.50-2
- Sandwich €2-4
- Meal in a cheap restaurant €8-10
- Meal in a good restaurant €20-30
- Scuba dive (including gear) €40

LONELY PLANET INDEX

- Litre of petrol €1.10
- Litre and a half of bottled water €1.10
- Small bottle of Dodo beer €2.50
- Souvenir T-shirt €15
- Street snack – samosa €0.20

late July to early September. You are strongly advised to book accommodation well in advance during these months. From October through to the New Year holidays is also reasonably busy, but after this everything eases down during cyclone-prone February and March. The weather normally changes for the better in April, which isn't a bad time to a visit.

See p279 for the climate chart (detailing temperature and rainfall) for St-Denis.

HISTORY

Réunion has a history similar to that of Mauritius. It was colonised by the French after the mid-17th century but later fell briefly under British rule. As in Mauritius, the colonisers introduced plantation crops and African slaves. Later came Indian indentured labourers and Chinese merchants, creating an ethnic diversity which is one of these islands' most distinctive characteristics. While Mauritius gained its independence in 1968, however, Réunion remains a department of France.

The First Colonisers

The first visitors to the uninhabited island were probably Malay, Arab and European mariners, none of whom stayed. Then in 1642, the French took the decision to settle the island, which at the time was called Mascarin, when the French East India Company sent its ship, the *St-Louis*, to investigate. The first settlers arrived four years later, when the French governor of Fort Dauphin in southern Madagascar banished a dozen mutineers to the island. The mutineers landed at what is now St-Paul and lived in a cave for three years. This Grotte des Premiers Français (Cave of the First French) still exists on the outskirts of St-Paul but is currently closed to visitors.

On the basis of enthusiastic reports from the mutineers, the King of France officially claimed the island in 1649 and renamed it Île Bourbon.

However appealing it seemed, there was no great rush to populate and develop the island and, from around 1685, Indian Ocean

CYCLONE WARNING

Réunion's cyclone warning system is based on three levels of alert.

Level one is known as a *vigilance cyclonique* (cyclone watch), and goes into effect whenever a cyclone is detected; this usually gives you a couple of days' warning, though the cyclone may equally well veer off on another course. A level-one warning requires people to make sure they have enough supplies (food, batteries, candles, water etc) to last at least four or five days, to cancel all hiking and boating (you should be able to get a refund, but check when booking), and to pay attention to news bulletins regarding the storm's path.

The *alerte orange* (orange alert) denotes an important threat in the next 24 hours. Schools and day nurseries are closed, but businesses remain open. As a preventive measure, the population is urged to bring indoors any objects or animals that might be carried away, and to protect all doors and windows. And, of course, to listen to news broadcasts.

The *alerte rouge* (red alert) is announced when danger is imminent. It entails a ban on driving, and the population is advised to obey the instructions broadcast by radio or other means. Use of the telephone is also restricted.

After the cyclone has passed, it is not recommended to drink untreated tap water. Mains water supplies can become contaminated by dead animals and other debris washed into the system.

pirates began using Île Bourbon as a trading base. The 260 settlers benefited from these illicit dealings until the French government and the French East India Company clamped down on them and took control at the beginning of the 18th century.

The Planters Arrive

Until 1715, the French East India Company was content to provide only for its own needs and those of passing ships, but then coffee was introduced, and between 1715 and 1730 it became the island's main cash crop. The island's economy changed dramatically. As coffee required intensive labour, African and Malagasy slaves were brought by the shipload despite French East India Company rules which forbade the use of slave labour. During this period, grains, spices and cotton were also introduced as cash crops.

Like Mauritius, Réunion came of age under the governorship of the visionary Mahé de Labourdonnais, who served from 1735 to 1746. However, Labourdonnais treated Île de France (Mauritius) as a favoured sibling, and Île Bourbon was left in a Cinderella role. As a result of poor management and the rivalry between France and Britain during the 18th century, as well as the collapse of the French East India Company, the government of the island passed directly to the French crown in 1764.

After the French Revolution, Île Bourbon came under the jurisdiction of the Colonial Assembly. It was at this time that the island's name was changed to La Réunion ('Joining' or 'Meeting'), for reasons known only to the Colonial Assembly. Certainly, the name didn't find favour with the planters, who later rechristened their home Île Bonaparte after you-know-who.

The late 18th century saw a number of slave revolts, and many *marrons* (escaped slaves) took refuge in the mountainous interior, organising themselves into villages run by democratically elected chiefs. These tribal chieftains were the true pioneers of the settlement of Réunion, but most ultimately fell victim to bounty hunters such as François Mussard who were employed to hunt them down. The scars of this period of the island's history are still fresh in the population's psyche; there are numerous monuments around the island celebrating the achievements of French Réunionnais, but little record of the island's Creole pioneers except the names of several peaks (Dimitile, Enchaing, Cimandef) where they were hunted down and killed.

A Brief British Interlude

The formerly productive coffee plantations were destroyed by cyclones very early in the 19th century, and in 1810, during the Napoleonic Wars, Bonaparte lost the island to the *habits rouges* (redcoats). They didn't stay long: just five years later, under the Treaty of Paris, the spoil was returned to the French as Île Bourbon. The British, however, retained their grip on Mauritius, Rodrigues and the Seychelles.

Under British rule, sugar cane had been introduced to Réunion and quickly became the primary crop. It resulted in the dispossession of many small farmers who were forced to sell out to those with capital to invest in the new monoculture. The supplanted farmers migrated to the interior to find land and carry on with their agricultural activities. During this period, the Desbassyns brothers rose to success as the island's foremost sugar barons. The vanilla industry, introduced in 1819, also grew rapidly.

The French Return

In 1848, the Second Republic was proclaimed in France, slavery was abolished and Île Bourbon again became La Réunion. At the time, the island had a population of over 100,000 people, mostly freed slaves. Like Mauritius, Réunion immediately experienced a labour crisis, and like the British in Mauritius, the French 'solved' the problem by importing contract labourers from India, most of them Hindus, to work the sugar cane.

Réunion's golden age of trade and development lasted until 1870, with the country flourishing on the trade route between Europe, India and the Far East. Competition from Cuba and the European sugar beet industry, combined with the opening of the Suez Canal (which short-circuited the journey around the Cape of Good Hope), resulted in an economic slump – shipping decreased, the sugar industry declined, and land and capital were further concentrated in the hands of a small French elite. Some small planters brightened their prospects by turning to geranium oil.

After WWI, in which 14,000 Réunionnais served, the sugar industry regained a bit of momentum, but it again suffered badly through the blockade of the island during WWII.

Réunion Becomes a DOM

Despite a certain amount of opposition, notably from the big plantation owners and industrialists who feared losing their privileged status, Réunion became a Département Français d'Outre-Mer (DOM; French Overseas Department) in 1946. The island is administered by a Préfet (prefect), who is appointed by the French Prime Minister, and an elected council in charge of local affairs. It is represented in the French National Assembly by five deputies, and in the French Senate by three councillors.

Since 1946 there have been feeble independence movements from time to time but, unlike those in France's Pacific territories, these have never amounted to anything. While the Réunionnais seemed satisfied to remain totally French, general economic and social discontent surfaced in dramatic anti-government riots in St-Denis in 1991 which left 10 people dead.

Réunion Today

As a French department, Réunion suffers from some of the same ills affecting mainland France. Réunion's unemployment rate, for example, currently hovers around 30%, way above the national average, but at least it's down from the peak of 38% in 1998. And Réunion sees a continual tide of would-be immigrants: with a system of generous welfare payments for the unemployed (nearly a quarter of the population depend on income support), the island is seen as a land of milk and honey by those from Mauritius, Seychelles and some mainland African countries. In recent years there has been significant immigration from neighbouring Comoros and Mayotte Islands.

On the economic front, 2003 saw a slight downturn after a period of modest growth. Réunion imports around 60% of its needs from *la métropole* (mainland France). In turn, mainland France accounts for some 70% of Réunion's exports. The vast majority of this (almost 90%) is sugar, with other agricultural and marine products coming a distant second.

For the present, Réunion's sugar producers have managed to hang on to their European quotas and guaranteed prices, but following EU enlargement and with the reform of the Common Agricultural Policy looming, they may not be able to do so for much longer. As a result, the movers and shakers of Réunion's economy are increasingly looking to closer ties with Mauritius and the rest of Africa for their financial future.

One of the greatest immediate concerns, however, is how to cope with all the people. Recent estimates suggest that the population of Réunion will reach one million by 2030, if not before. Already there is tremendous pressure on building land. Most of the population is concentrated on the coastal strip, where the towns are gradually beginning to merge into one continuous urban 'ring'. Houses are also spreading slowly up the hillsides and traffic congestion is becoming a major headache.

To relieve some of this pressure, the government is investing in an ambitious new expressway, the Route des Tamarins, between St-Paul and Étang-Salé-les-Bains, which will open a big swathe of mountainside to new development. At the same time the government is in the throes of creating a national park, which will go some way to protecting the island's unique cultural and environmental heritage.

THE CULTURE

The National Psyche

The physical and cultural distinctions between the various ethnic groups are far less apparent in Réunion than in Mauritius. In Réunion there has been much more interracial mixing over the years. Ask the Réunionnais how they see themselves and the chances are they'll say 'Creole' – not in the narrow sense of having Afro-French ancestry, but simply meaning one of 'the people'. That is, someone who speaks Creole, who was born and bred on the island and is probably – but not necessarily – of mixed ancestry. This sense of community is the gel which holds society together.

While the Réunionnais do also regard themselves as French, they don't particularly identify with people from the mainland. There is even a slight undercurrent of resentment towards the 100,000 or so mainlanders who dominate the island's administration and economy. They are seen as somewhat aloof and privileged, having access to higher paid jobs and thus better schools and housing. The locals refer to them very slightly derogatorily as Z'oreilles (the Ears); the usual explanation is that they are straining to hear what's being said about them in the local patois.

Lifestyle

As in Mauritius, society is changing fast and the older generation worry that the traditions are being lost. One of the strongest bonds unifying society, after the Creole language, is the importance placed on family life. At the weekend there's nothing the Réunionnais like better than bundling off to the seaside or the mountains for a huge family picnic.

Perhaps because of the enclosed, mountainous terrain in which they live, the Réunionnais tend not to be as immediately open and friendly as the Mauritians or Seychellois. They are in general more reserved, but within this overall pattern there are local differences: southerners are reckoned to be more relaxed and friendly, while perhaps not surprisingly the people living in the cirques are the most introverted.

Another noticeable characteristic is that people of all ages retain an old-fashioned politeness. For example, you'll get a better reception and find people more willing to help if you start a conversation with a formal '*bonjour, monsieur/madam*' rather than launching straight in. By the same token, great importance is placed on showing respect for others, no matter what their race or religion. People are also relatively tolerant towards homosexuality, though by no means as liberal as in mainland France; open displays of affection may be regarded with disdain, especially outside St-Denis. (See p48 for some pointers on how not to cause offence).

Not that it's all hunky-dory. Réunion suffers from the same problems of a disaffected younger generation as in mainland Europe, with growing rates of petty crime and graffiti-strewn streets. But on the whole it's a society that lives very easily together, and the Réunionnais are quietly but justifiably proud of what they have achieved.

Population

Réunion has the same population mix of Africans, Europeans, Indians and Chinese as Mauritius, but in different proportions. Creoles (people of Afro-French ancestry) are the largest ethnic group, comprising around 40% of the population. Europeans (ie the French) make up the second-largest group, at about 6%. Malabars (Hindu Indians) comprise about 25% of the population, the Chinese 3%, and Z'arabes (Muslim Indians) make up about 2%. Because the birth rate has been high for the past 25 years, the island's population is weighted in favour of youth, with a third of the population under 20 years of age.

RELIGION

An estimated 70% of the population belongs to the Catholic faith, which dominates the island's religious character. It is visible in the shrines along every highway and byway, in caves and on cliff tops (many of these shrines were constructed for family members killed in accidents on those sites), and evidenced in the many saints' days and holidays. St-Denis shuts down on Sunday, when half the city goes to *the* beach (Boucan Canot).

Hindus (roughly 25%) and Muslims (2%) follow their religions freely, and most large towns have both a temple and a mosque. Traditional Hindu rites such as *teemeedee,* which features fire-walking, and *cavadee,* which for pilgrims entails piercing the cheeks with skewers, often take place. (For more information on these rites, see p134).

Interestingly, a great deal of syncretism between Hinduism, Islam and Catholicism has evolved over the years. In fact, many of the Malabar-Réunionnais participate in both Hindu and Catholic rites and rituals.

Apart from celebrating the Chinese New Year, the Sino-Réunionnais community (making up about 3% of the population) is not very conspicuous in its religious or its traditional practices.

ARTS

One of the greatest pleasures of visiting Réunion is experiencing Creole-flavoured French culture or French-flavoured Creole culture, depending on how you look at it. For news of cultural activities on the island, keep an eye on the local press and visit local tourist offices, where you can pick up flyers, theatre programmes and a number of free events guides such as the bimonthly *Insomniak,* which gives details of forthcoming theatre performances, concerts and exhibitions.

Literature

Few Réunionnais novelists are known of outside the island and none are translated into English. One of the most widely recognised and prolific contemporary authors is the journalist and historian Daniel Vaxelaire, who has written a number of evocative historical novels. His *Chasseurs des Noires,* an easily accessible tale of a slave-hunter's life-changing encounter with an escaped slave, is probably the best to start with.

Jean-François Sam-Long, a novelist and poet who helped relaunch Creole literature in the 1970s, also takes slavery as his theme. *Madame Desbassyns* was inspired by the remarkable life-story of a sugar baroness (p192). In *La Nuit Cyclone* he explores the gulf between Whites and Blacks in a small village against a backdrop of black magic and superstition.

Other well-established novelists to look out for are Axel Gauvin *(Train Fou, L'Aimé* and *Cravate et Fils)* and Jules Bénard.

There are several up-and-coming writers who deal with contemporary issues. Joëlle Ecormier spins her first novel, *Plus Légér que l'Air,* around a young islander living in France who returns to Réunion to face her past. *Les Chants des Kayanms* by Agnès Gueneau also revolves around métro-Réunion relationships, in this case a love affair between a local woman and a man from the mainland. It's a lyrical tale, evoking the rhythms of *maloya* (traditional slave music), and one which breaks a few clichés along the way.

Music & Dance

Réunion's music mixes the African rhythms of reggae, *séga* (traditional slave music) and *maloya* with French, British and American rock and folk sounds. Like *séga, maloya* is derived from the music of the slaves, but it is slower and more reflective, its rhythms and words heavy with history, somewhat like New Orleans blues; fans say it carries the true spirit of Réunion. *Maloya* songs often carry a political message and up until the 1970s the music was banned for being too subversive.

It is interesting to see how the dance accompanying *séga* differs here from the versions in Mauritius, the Seychelles and Madagascar. As elsewhere, the slaves in Réunion adapted the dances of the White settlers, particularly the quadrille, to their own African rhythms, but more variations have survived in Réunion because freed slaves went on to form the majority of the island's population. The *séga* is now danced by everyone in Réunion in the manner of a shuffling rock step.

Instruments used to accompany the *séga* and the *maloya* range from traditional home-made percussion pieces, such as the hide-covered *houleur* drum and the maraca-like *caïambe,* to the accordion and modern band instruments.

The giants of the local music scene, and increasingly well known in mainland France, are Danyel Waró, the group Ziskakan and rastaman Michel Fock. The latter, known professionally as Ti-Fock, adds a synthesised touch to the traditional *maloya* and *séga* rhythms.

Waró and Ziskakan are superb practitioners of *maloya*. Favourite subjects for them are slavery, poverty and the search for cultural identity.

As for Creole-flavoured modern grooves, the Réunionnais leave those to their tropical cousins in Martinique and Guadeloupe, although they make popular listening in Réunion. It's all catchy stuff, and you'll hear it in bars, discos and vehicles throughout the islands of the Indian Ocean.

Architecture

The distinctive 18th-century Creole architecture of Réunion is evident in both the grand villas built by wealthy planters and other *colons,* (settlers/colonists) and in the *ti' cases,* the homes of the common folk.

The Service Départemental de l'Architecture et du Patrimoine (Departmental Office of Architecture and Patrimony) is actively striving to preserve the remaining examples of Creole architecture around the island. You can see a number of beautifully restored houses along Rue de Paris in St-Denis and in the towns of Cilaos and

Hell-Bourg, among other places. The authorities in Hell-Bourg have been particularly active; they are in the throes of establishing an eco-museum and have published a guide to the best of the local *cases créoles* (Creole homes). The Maison de la Montagne in St-Denis has also put together a guide to 12 villages *créoles*, including Cilaos, Hell-Bourg and Entre-Deux, chosen for their particularly rich architectural heritage and traditional way of life.

(For more information about this exotic type of architecture, see Architectural Heritage, p53).

Visual Arts

Unlike Seychellois artists, whose artistic style is a direct response to the environment, most Réunion artists have tended to take their inspiration from European styles. French influences dominate and the imposing landscape of the island can make for interesting subject matter, though much of the work on offer could be considered either too bright and gaudy, too ordered and dull, or too much like Gauguin! For a sampler of what's on offer, visit the Musée Léon Dierx in St-Denis.

Contemporary art in Réunion received a huge boost with the opening in 1991 of both the École des Beaux-Arts (Fine Arts School) in Le Port and L'Artothéque in St-Denis. Alongside a number of well-regarded métro artists who have settled in Réunion, there are now also a handful of local artists, many of whom are self-taught, producing innovative work as part of a broad movement to define their Creole identity.

Some of the island's most visible and well-known artists are its sculptors. You'll see Henri Maillot's distinctive ballerina figures and Éric Pongérard's monumental artworks adorning the island's highways and byways: watch out for the red-skirted dancer and the *Cathédral,* a 'forest' of decapitated tree trunks inspired by the damage wrought by Cyclone Dinah in 2002, as you come into St-Denis from the airport. Alain Padeau's massive ironwork sculpture of open manacles on the seafront in St-Paul commemorates the abolition of slavery.

Other sculptors to look out for are Gilbert Cain and the self-taught Jean-Daniel Refoulma, who produces highly polished, mystical wooden figures. Catherine Boyer creates wonderfully soft, sensual pieces. Her most famous to date consisted of 1000 miniature penises made out of pink chewing gum, which caused a scandal when it was unveiled at L'Artothéque in 2001.

A less controversial artist you're likely to come across is the sculptor and printmaker Philippe Turpin, who etches on copper and then rolls the prints off the inky plates. The effect, like the technique, has little to do with Creole tradition. Instead, Turpin captures the wonder of Réunion in a fantastical, almost medieval way; his renditions of the cirques resemble illustrations of fairy kingdoms. Turpin's studio is in the mountain spa village of Cilaos.

The work of these and other artists can be seen at several places around the island including Le Cadre Noire and La Caze in St-Denis, and Galerie Noir et Blanc in L'Éperon, above St-Gilles-les-Bains.

Theatre

The island has several excellent professional theatre groups, of which **Théâtre Vollard** (☎ 02 62 21 25 26; www.vollard.com; contact address is Ste-Clotilde, a suburb of St-Denis) is the most established. Other professional troupes include **Théâtre Talipot** (☎ 02 62 25 99 39) in St-Pierre and St-Leu's innovative **Compagnie Nektar** (☎ 06 92 05 40 31).

The main venues for theatre around the island are the Théâtre de Champ-Fleuri and Théâtre du Grand Marché in St-Denis; the Théâtre Luc Donat and Bato Fou in Le Tampon; Le Séchoir near St-Leu; and the Théâtre Les Bambous in St-Benoît.

ENVIRONMENT

Réunion lies about 220km southwest of Mauritius, at the southernmost end of the great Mascareignes volcanic chain. Réunion's volcano, Piton de la Fournaise, erupts with great regularity, spewing lava down its southern and eastern flanks. The last major eruption occurred in 1986, when lava flows reached the sea and added another few square metres to the island. Since 1998 there have been smaller but still spectacular eruptions almost every year.

The Land

There are two major mountainous areas on Réunion. The older of the two covers most of the western half of the island.

The highest mountain is Piton des Neiges (3069m), an alpine-class peak. Surrounding it are three immense and splendid amphitheatres: the cirques of Cilaos, Mafate and Salazie. These long, wide, deep hollows are sheer-walled canyons filled with convoluted peaks and valleys, the eroded remnants of the ancient volcanic shield that surrounded Piton des Neiges.

The smaller of the two mountainous regions lies in the southeast and is still evolving. It comprises several extinct volcanic cones and one that is still very much alive, Piton de la Fournaise (2632m). This rumbling peak still pops its cork relatively frequently in spectacular fashion, and between eruptions quietly steams and hisses away. No-one lives in the shadow of the volcano, where lava flowing down to the shore has left a remarkable jumbled slope of cooled black volcanic rock. Piton de la Fournaise is undoubtedly the island's most popular and intriguing attraction.

These two mountainous areas are separated by a region of high plains, while the coast is defined by a gently sloping plain which varies in width. Numerous rivers wind their way down from the Piton des Neiges range, through the cirques, cutting deeply into the coastal plains to form spectacular ravines.

Wildlife

ANIMALS

Because it was never part of a continental land mass, Réunion has relatively few animal species. Those that did exist have not fared well since the arrival of humans. The island had solitaires (a type of bird) and giant tortoises when it was first settled, but the early colonists and their animals made short work of them. The tortoises were boiled down for the oil in their skins; 500 individuals were needed to produce just one barrel of oil.

Réunion's only indigenous mammal species are two types of bat, both of which can sometimes be seen around the coast at night. The mammals you're far more likely to see are introduced hares, deers and rats.

During the rainy season, many of Réunion's roads are paved with squashed frogs! Tenrecs, which resemble hedgehogs, were introduced from Madagascar and don't seem to find the roads as much of a challenge as the frogs. The tenrecs, however, are fewer in number.

The most interesting creepy crawlers are the giant millipedes – some as long as a human foot – which loll around beneath rocks in more humid areas. Another oversized creature is the yellow-and-black *Nephila* spider whose massive webs are a common sight.

The mosquitoes that plague Réunion during the rainy season can be tenacious. Oddly enough, they seem to be at their worst in St-Denis. The higher into the hills you go, the less evident the little bloodsuckers become. On the bright side, there are no poisonous or toothy nasties of any description.

As far as birdlife is concerned, of the original 30 species endemic to the island, only nine remain. The island's rarest birds are the *merle blanc* or cuckoo shrike – locals call it the *tuit tuit,* for obvious reasons – and the black petrel. Probably the best chance of seeing – or, more likely, hearing – the *tuit tuit* is directly south of St-Denis, near the foot of La Roche Écrite. Only an estimated 160 pairs remain. No-one knows how many black petrel still survive; estimates vary between 40 and 400 pairs.

Bulbuls, which resemble blackbirds (with yellow beaks and legs, but grey feathers), and are locally known as *merles,* are also common. The Mascarene paradise flycatcher is a pretty little bird with a small crest and a long, flowing red tail. It is also known as *la vierge* because its blue head and white breast reminded early settlers of the Virgin Mary.

Birds native to the highlands include the *tec-tec* or Réunion stonechat (again, the name is onomatopoeic), which inhabits the tamarind forests. There's also the *papangue,* or Maillardi buzzard, a protected hawklike bird which begins life as a little brown bird and turns black and white as it grows older. It is Réunion's only surviving bird of prey and may be spotted soaring over the ravines.

The best-known sea bird is the white *paille-en-queue* or white-tailed tropicbird, which sports two long tail plumes. It can often be seen riding the thermals created by the Piton de la Fournaise volcano. Other sea birds include visiting albatrosses and shearwaters.

Mynahs, introduced at the end of the 18th century to keep the grasshoppers under control, are common all over the island, as are the small, red cardinal-like birds known as fodies.

The best spots to see birdlife are the Forêt de Bélouve above Hell-Bourg, and the wilderness region of Le Grand Brûlé at the southern tip of the island. Bird-watchers may want to hunt down a copy of the field guide *Oiseaux de la Réunion* by Nicolas Barré and Armand Barau. The text is in French, but there are accurate colour illustrations of all species present on the island, identified by their Latin, English, French and local names. You'll also find information on local birds and (where to spot them) on the website of the **Société d'Études Ornithologiques de la Réunion** (SEOR; ☎ 02 62 20 46 65; www.seor.fr in French), an organisation working to save some of the island's rarest species.

PLANTS

Thanks to an abundant rainfall and marked differences in altitude, Réunion boasts some of the most varied plant life in the world. Parts of the island are like a grand botanical garden. Between the coast and the alpine peaks you'll find palms, screw pines (also known as pandanus or *vacoa*), casuarinas *(filaos)*, vanilla, spices, other tropical fruit and vegetable crops, rainforest and alpine flora.

Réunion has no less than 700 indigenous plant species, 150 of which are trees. Unlike Mauritius, large areas of natural forest still remain. It's estimated that 30% of the island is covered by native forest; some areas – particularly in the ravines – have never been touched by man.

Nearly all the forests (some 1000 sq km) are managed by the large and active forestry division, the **Office National des Forêts** (ONF; www.onf.fr in French), which is more concerned with preserving than chopping down the forests; it has established 130 sq km of natural reserves and plans to increase this to 300 sq km. Afforestation has been carried out mainly with the Japanese cryptomeria, the *tamarin des Hauts* (mountain tamarind tree), the casuarina and various palms.

Gnarled and twisted and sporting yellow, mimosa-like flowers, the *tamarin des Hauts,* a type of acacia, is endemic to Réunion. Locals compare them to oak trees because the timber is excellent for building. One of the best places to see these ancient trees is in the Forêt de Bélouve east of the Cirque de Salazie.

At the other extreme, the lava fields around the volcano exhibit a barren, moonlike face. Here the various stages of vegetation growth, from a bare new lava base, are evident. The first plant to appear on lava is the heather-like plant the French call branle vert (*Philippia montana*). Its leaves contain a combustible oil. Much later in the growth cycle come tamarind and other acacia trees.

Like any tropical island, Réunion has a wealth of flowering species, including orchids, hibiscus, bougainvillea, frangipani and jacaranda. To appreciate the sheer wealth of plant life on the island, a trip to one of the several excellent botanical gardens is in order. There's the Conservatoire Botanique National de Mascarin and the Jardin d'Eden near St-Gilles-les-Bains and the Jardin des Parfums et des Épices just outside St-Philippe.

Environmental Issues

As in Mauritius, the central problem confronting Réunion is how to reconcile environmental preservation with a growing population in need of additional housing, roads, jobs, electricity, water and recreational space – not to mention the increasing numbers of tourists putting pressure on fragile marine and upland ecosystems.

Unlike Mauritius, however, the authorities here have access to greater financial resources, backed up by all sorts of European rules and regulations. In general, they have been able to adopt a more coordinated approach, introducing measures to improve water treatment and reduce nitrate use by farmers, for example, at the same time as cleaning up the lagoon.

It is estimated that nearly a third of the 25km-long lagoon along the west coast from Boucan Canot south to Trois-Bassins has already suffered damage from a variety of causes: sedimentation, agricultural and domestic pollution, cyclones, fishermen and divers. To prevent the situation deteriorating even further, a marine park was set up in 1997. In addition to educating local people on the need to keep the beaches and the water clean, the **Association**

Parc Marin Réunion (☎ 02 62 34 64 44; www.chez.com/parcmarin; 7 Rue de la Compagnie des Indes, St-Leu) has been working with local fishermen and various water-sports operators to establish protection zones. The next step is to establish a fully fledged nature reserve, which it is hoped will be in place by 2006.

There are big plans afoot to protect the interior of the island, too. If the proposed **Parc National des Hauts** (www.parc-national-reunion.prd.fr in French) gets prime ministerial approval nearly half of Réunion's total land area will be protected starting from 2006. The plan is for a tightly regulated core area of 1,000 sq km, including the volcano, the mountain peaks and the areas around Mafate and Grand Bassin, surrounded by a buffer zone of some 700 sq km to encompass most of the ravines. It envisages a totally integrated approach, not only to protect the animal and plant life, but to preserve traditional ways of life and to encourage sustainable development, including green tourism initiatives.

Despite all these positive signs, however, there are a few flies in the ointment. Two massive engineering works are currently under way.

The 'smaller' is the Route des Tamarins, a 34km expressway which will slice across the hills above St-Gilles and require more than 100 bridges over the ravines; the road is due for completion sometime in 2007. Local environmentalists, such as the Société Réunionnaise pour la Protection de l'Environnement (SREPEN), and even the government's own **Direction Régionale de l'Environnement** (DIREN; www.reunion.environnement.gouv.fr in French) have raised objections to the scheme, which cuts across the only remaining savannah habitat on the island and will force displaced farmers onto areas of marginal land.

No-one is betting any money on the end date for the second major engineering project, which has been dubbed 'the building works of the century' – last century, that is. The idea behind this incredible scheme is to transfer water from the east coast, where supply exceeds demand, to the dry and heavily populated west coast. The solution someone came up with was to drill a tunnel 30km long and 3.5m high right through the island! Tunnelling began in 1989, but needless to say they hit a few hitches along the way. Work stopped in the Cirque de Salazie in 2002 because the tunnels became flooded. Locals staged demonstrations, but the government seems determined to continue despite spiralling costs.

(For tips on responsible travel see p16).

ST-DENIS

pop 140,000

With its brasseries, bistros and café culture, St-Denis (san-de-*nee*) is a perfect reproduction of metropolitan France, down to the sprawling suburbs which surround the historic centre. Though more akin to a laid-back provincial town than a buzzing capital, St-Denis nevertheless presents a prosperous and cosmopolitan face to the world. It also dominates island life. It's here that you'll find the main business and financial centre, the administrative offices, the university and Réunion's most important museums, galleries and theatres.

With most of Réunion's tourist attractions located elsewhere on the island, many tourists only stay long enough to book *gîtes de montagne* (mountain lodges). But there's plenty to see and do in St-Denis, from exploring its historic buildings to soaking up some atmosphere along the seafront promenade. For fine dining and varied nightlife, the capital of Réunion is unparalleled in the Indian Ocean.

HISTORY

St-Denis was founded in 1668 by the governor Regnault, who named the settlement after a ship that ran aground here. But St-Denis didn't really start to develop until the governor Mahé de Labourdonnais moved the capital here from St-Paul in 1738: the harbour was in general more sheltered and easier to defend, and water more abundant, though attempts at constructing a port at Le Barachois were foiled by a succession of cyclones.

The 19th century ushered in St-Denis' golden age. As money poured in from their sugar plantations, the town's worthies built themselves fine mansions, some of which can still be seen along Rue de Paris and in the surrounding streets. But in the late 1800s the bottom dropped out of the sugar market and the good times came to a stuttering end. St-Denis' fortunes only began to revive when it became the new departmental capital in 1946. To cope with the influx of civil servants, financiers and office workers, the city expanded rapidly eastwards along the coast and up the mountains behind. Even today the cranes are much in evidence as St-Denis struggles to house its ever-growing population.

ORIENTATION

The centre of St-Denis is built on a grid pattern on a coastal plain dropping gently northwards towards the sea. Life revolves around the seafront Barachois, with its cafés and bars, and Ave de la Victoire, the main thoroughfare heading inland. It's along this avenue and its extension, Rue de Paris, that you'll find many of St-Denis' grandest colonial edifices.

The main shopping area stretches along the semi-pedestrianised Rue Maréchal Leclerc, which strikes east from Ave de la Victoire, and spills over into the surrounding streets. Continue along Rue Maréchal Leclerc towards the ocean and you'll eventually reach L'Océan bus terminal, the main *gare routière* (bus station).

INFORMATION

Bookshops

La Bouquinerie (☎ 02 62 41 31 46; bouquinerie.reunion@wanadoo.fr; 5 Rue Laferrière) Second-hand bookshop with a few English-language titles.

Librairie L'Entrepôt (☎ 02 62 20 94 94; entrepot@sa-autremont.com; 82-88 Rue Juliette Dodu) Friendly and helpful staff, a good selection of predominantly French-language books, newspapers and magazines and a great cybercafé make this the best bookshop in town.

Librairie Papeterie Gerard (☎ 02 62 20 08 15; 5 Rue de la Compagnie)

Le Rallye Presse (☎ 02 62 20 34 66; 3 Ave de la Victoire; 🕓 6.30am-11pm) Small newsagent with a big range of newspapers and magazines in French and English.

Emergency

Ambulance (☎ 15)

Fire services (☎ 18)

Police (emergency ☎ 17, headquarters ☎ 02 62 90 74 74; 133 Rue Jean Chatel)

Internet Access

B@bookcafé (☎ 02 62 20 94 94; babookafe@sa-autrement.com; 82-88 Rue Juliette Dodu) Pleasant atmosphere and great coffee upstairs in the Librairie L' Entrepôt.

BC-Jeux (☎ 02 62 21 50 10; www.bc-games.com; 79 Rue Félix Guyon; 🕓 9am-6.30pm Mon-Sat) The biggest and cheapest of St-Denis' Internet cafés.

La C@se À Hello (☎ 02 62 94 19 55; la-case-a-hello@wanadoo.fr; 68 Rue Juliette Dodu; 🕓 10am-8pm Mon-Sat)

Medical Services

Centre Hospitalier Bellepierre (☎ 02 62 21 24 90; Allées des Topazes, Bellepierre) To the southwest of the centre, Réunion's main hospital has 24-hour medical and dental treatment, a pharmacy open round the clock and English-speaking staff.

Money

All the main banks and the central post office have ATMs. Changing money is more difficult. At the time of writing only the main branches of Crédit Agricole and BNP Paribas had any exchange facilities and those were under review after a spate of bank robberies. You can change sterling and US dollars at the central post office but not travellers cheques.

BNP Paribas (☎ 02 62 40 30 30; 67 Rue Juliette Dodu) Exchange desk open from 8am to 12.45pm and 1.45pm to 4pm on Tuesday and Thursday.

Crédit Agricole (☎ 02 62 90 91 00; 14 Rue Felix Guyon; 🕓 8am-5pm Mon-Wed & Fri, 8am-3.45pm Thu)

Post

Central post office (☎ 02 62 21 21 12; 60 Rue Maréchal Leclerc; 🕓 7.30am-6pm Mon-Fri, 7.30am-noon Sat)

Tourist Offices

Office du Tourisme (☎ 02 62 41 83 00; fax 02 62 21 37 76; 53 Rue Pasteur; 🕓 8.30am-6pm Mon-Sat) The St-Denis tourist office has English-speaking staff and can provide plenty of information, maps and brochures.

Point d'Information Touristique (☎ 02 62 48 81 81; Roland Garros Airport; 🕓 for all arrivals)

Maison de la Montagne (☎ 02 62 90 78 78; www.reunion-nature.com in French; 10 Pl Sarda Garriga; 🕓 9am-5pm Mon-Thu, 9am-4pm Fri, 9am-noon Sat) For hiking information and booking *gîtes de montagne*.

DANGERS & ANNOYANCES

The city centre by night is by no means as rough as it used to be, but it's wise to avoid the seafront and to keep to the well-lit main streets.

SIGHTS

St-Denis' most important sights are concentrated along the main road running

ST-DENIS

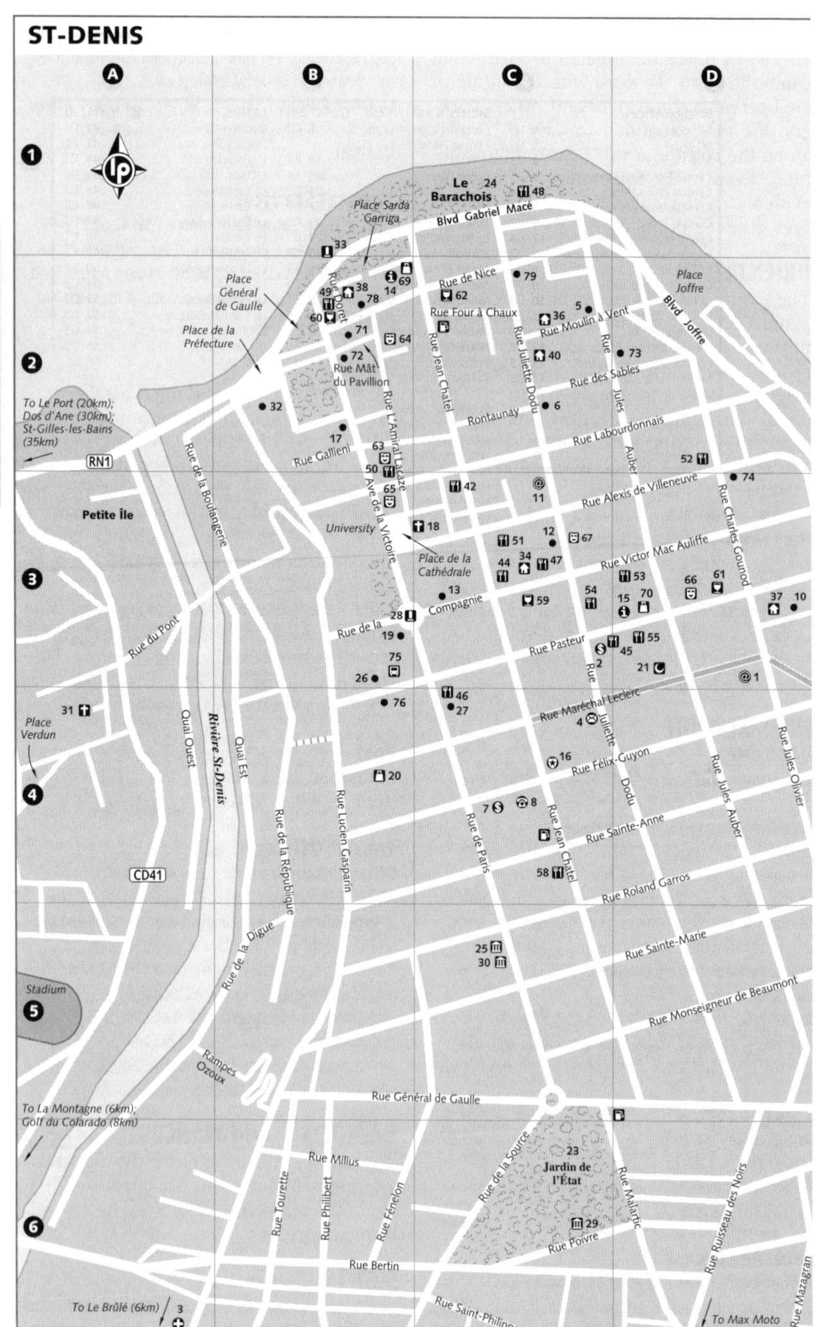

Le Barachois
Blvd Gabriel Macé
Place Sarda Garriga
Place Général de Gaulle
Place de la Préfecture
Rue Doret
Rue de Nice
Rue Four à Chaux
Rue Moulin à Vent
Rue Mât du Pavillion
Rue Jean Chatel
Rue Juliette Dodu
Rue Jules Auber
Rue des Sables
Rontaunay
Rue Labourdonnais
Place Joffre
Blvd Joffre
To Le Port (20km); Dos d'Ane (30km); St-Gilles-les-Bains (35km)
RN1
Rue Gallieni
Rue L'Amiral Lacaze
Ave de la Victoire
Rue de la Boulangerie
Petite Île
University
Place de la Cathédrale
Rue Alexis de Villeneuve
Rue Victor Mac Auliffe
Rue Charles Gounod
Rue de la Compagnie
Rue du Pont
Rue Pasteur
Rue Maréchal Leclerc
Place Verdun
Quai Ouest
Rivière St-Denis
Quai Est
Rue Félix-Guyon
Rue Jules Olivier
Rue de Paris
Rue Sainte-Anne
Rue Lucien Gasparin
Rue de la République
CD41
Rue Roland Garros
Rue de la Digue
Rue Sainte-Marie
Stadium
Rue Monseigneur de Beaumont
Rampes Ozoux
Rue Général de Gaulle
To La Montagne (6km); Golf du Colarado (8km)
Rue Millius
Rue de la Source
Jardin de l'État
Rue Malartic
Rue Ruisseau des Noirs
Rue Tourette
Rue Philibert
Rue Fénelon
Rue Poivre
Rue Bertin
Rue Saint-Philippe
To Le Brûlé (6km)
To Max Moto
Rue Mazagran

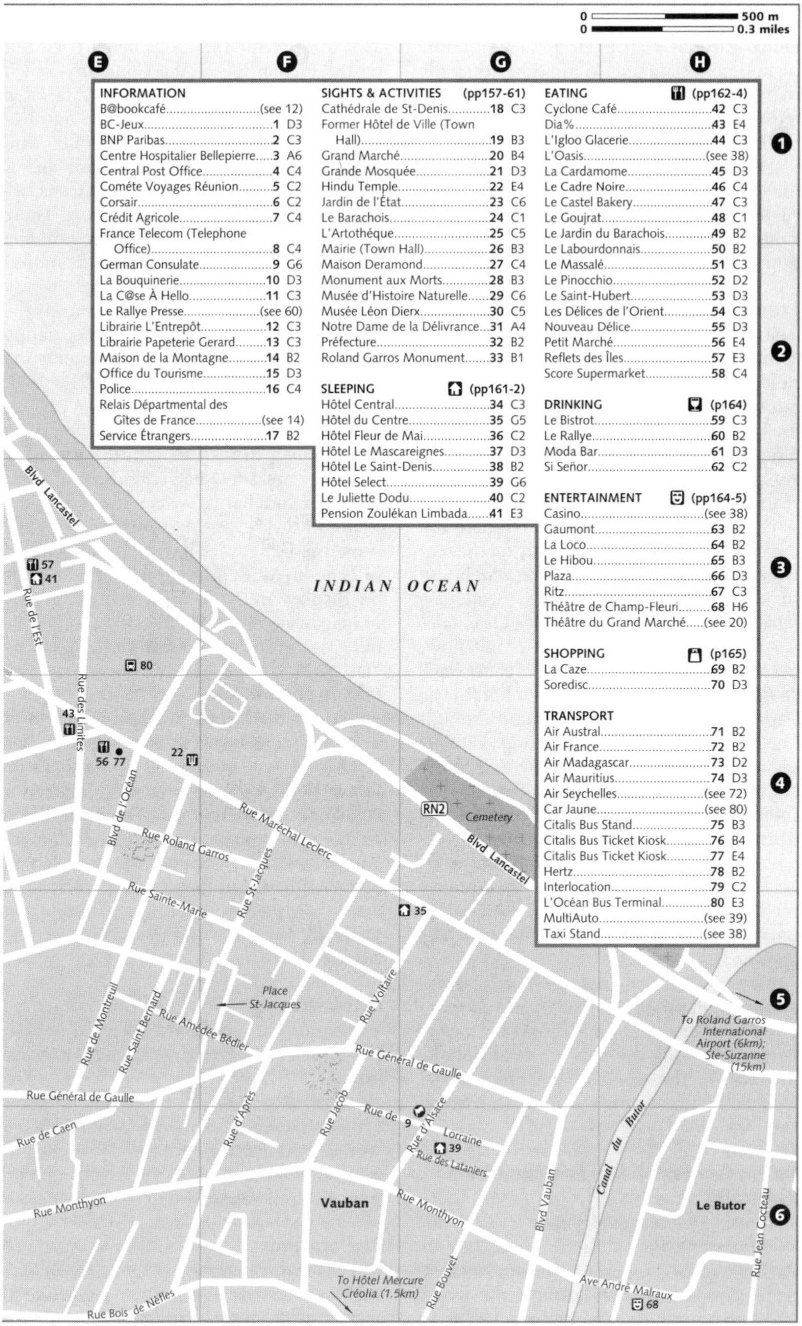

0 500 m
0 0.3 miles

E F G H

INFORMATION
B@bookcafé (see 12)
BC-Jeux 1 D3
BNP Paribas 2 C3
Centre Hospitalier Bellepierre 3 A6
Central Post Office 4 C4
Cométe Voyages Réunion 5 C2
Corsair 6 C2
Crédit Agricole 7 C4
France Telecom (Telephone Office) 8 C4
German Consulate 9 G6
La Bouquinerie 10 D3
La C@se À Hello 11 C3
Le Rallye Presse (see 60)
Librairie L'Entrepôt 12 C3
Librairie Papeterie Gerard 13 C3
Maison de la Montagne 14 B2
Office du Tourisme 15 D3
Police 16 C4
Relais Départmental des Gîtes de France (see 14)
Service Étrangers 17 B2

SIGHTS & ACTIVITIES (pp157-61)
Cathédrale de St-Denis 18 C3
Former Hôtel de Ville (Town Hall) 19 B3
Grand Marché 20 B4
Grande Mosquée 21 D3
Hindu Temple 22 E4
Jardin de l'État 23 C6
Le Barachois 24 C1
L'Artothéque 25 C5
Mairie (Town Hall) 26 B3
Maison Deramond 27 C4
Monument aux Morts 28 B3
Musée d'Histoire Naturelle 29 C6
Musée Léon Dierx 30 C5
Notre Dame de la Délivrance 31 A4
Préfecture 32 B2
Roland Garros Monument 33 B1

SLEEPING (pp161-2)
Hôtel Central 34 C3
Hôtel du Centre 35 G5
Hôtel Fleur de Mai 36 C2
Hôtel Le Mascareignes 37 D3
Hôtel Le Saint-Denis 38 B2
Hôtel Select 39 G6
Le Juliette Dodu 40 C2
Pension Zoulékan Limbada 41 E3

EATING (pp162-4)
Cyclone Café 42 C3
Dia% 43 E4
L'Igloo Glacerie 44 C3
L'Oasis (see 38)
La Cardamome 45 D3
Le Cadre Noire 46 C4
Le Castel Bakery 47 C3
Le Goujrat 48 C1
Le Jardin du Barachois 49 B2
Le Labourdonnais 50 B2
Le Massalé 51 C3
Le Pinocchio 52 D2
Le Saint-Hubert 53 D3
Les Délices de l'Orient 54 C3
Nouveau Délice 55 D3
Petit Marché 56 E4
Reflets des Îles 57 E3
Score Supermarket 58 C4

DRINKING (p164)
Le Bistrot 59 C3
Le Rallye 60 B2
Moda Bar 61 D3
Si Señor 62 C2

ENTERTAINMENT (pp164-5)
Casino (see 38)
Gaumont 63 B2
La Loco 64 B2
Le Hibou 65 B3
Plaza 66 D3
Ritz 67 C3
Théâtre de Champ-Fleuri 68 H6
Théâtre du Grand Marché (see 20)

SHOPPING (p165)
La Caze 69 B2
Soredisc 70 D3

TRANSPORT
Air Austral 71 B2
Air France 72 B2
Air Madagascar 73 D2
Air Mauritius 74 D3
Air Seychelles (see 72)
Car Jaune (see 80)
Citalis Bus Stand 75 B3
Citalis Bus Ticket Kiosk 76 B4
Citalis Bus Ticket Kiosk 77 E4
Hertz 78 B2
Interlocation 79 C2
L'Océan Bus Terminal 80 E3
MultiAuto (see 39)
Taxi Stand (see 38)

RÉUNION

from Le Barachois in the north to the botanical gardens (Jardin de l'État) a couple of kilometres inland. With time to spare, there are a few second-tier attractions dotted around the city, but even so they can all be explored on foot in an energetic day.

The tourist office runs tours (in French only) of St-Denis that take in historic sights such as the Jardin de l'État and the mansions of Rue de Paris. The tour lasts 1½ hours and costs €4.

Creole Mansions & Historic Buildings

There is a variety of impressive Creole mansions in St-Denis, a number of which have now been declared historic monuments and are being slowly restored. The larger ones are mainly strung out along Rue de Paris. Since few are open to the public, you'll have to content yourself with peering through the railings.

One of the grandest is the **Préfecture** (Blvd Gabriel Macé), which stands proudly on the seafront. It began life as a coffee warehouse in 1734 and later served as the headquarters of the Compagnie des Indes Orientales (French East India Company). Many, however, consider the neoclassical **Former Hôtel de Ville (Town Hall)**, at the north end of Rue de Paris, to be the city's most beautiful building; it's certainly more imposing, with its regimented columns, balustrades and jaunty clock-tower. By contrast, the Tuscan-style **Cathédrale de St-Denis** (Rue de Paris) standing nearby is a much more sober affair.

Also of interest is **Maison Deramond** (15 Rue de Paris), which was the family home of former French prime minister Raymond Barre and the birthplace of the poet and painter Léon Dierx.

Many of these palatial residences feature elaborate verandas and intricate *lambrequins* (ornamental window and door borders). The roof shingles are traditionally made from the wood of the *tamarin des Hauts*. (For more on traditional architecture, see p53.)

Jardin de l'État & Musée d'Histoire Naturelle

The attractive **botanical garden** (admission free; 7am-6pm), at the southern end of Rue de Paris features numerous perfume plants, tropical oddities from around the world and lots of orchids. The original Jardin de l'État was established near the river in 1764 as a nursery for the crops being tried out by the French East India Company, but it moved to its present location a decade later. In the gardens is a monument to agronomist Joseph Hubert from St-Benoît, who brought many useful agricultural specimens – including cloves, mangosteens, lychees and breadfruit – to Réunion. There is also a statue commemorating botanist Pierre Poivre, who performed a similar service for nearby Mauritius.

At the far end of the gardens stands the somewhat austere Palais Législatif, dating from 1834, which houses the interesting **Musée d'Histoire Naturelle** (02 62 20 02 19; admission €2; 10am-5.30pm Tue-Sun). Very little of Réunion's natural history survived long enough to make it into the museum, but there are a few displays of extinct and nearly extinct native species, including the Réunion owl, kestrel, parrot and ibis. The museum also covers Indian Ocean wildlife in general. Many of the birds and animals on display are – or were – from nearby Madagascar, although the dodo and solitaire also make an appearance.

Musée Léon Dierx

Housed in the former bishop's palace, built in 1845, the **Musée Léon Dierx** (02 62 20 24 82; 28 Rue de Paris; admission €2; 9.30am-5.30pm Tue-Sun) contains Réunion's most important collection of modern art. The more high-profile works include paintings, sculptures and ceramics by Picasso, Renoir, Gaugin and Vlaminck, but the majority are by local artists such as the poet and painter Léon Dierx (1838–1912) and the ultra-romantic Adolphe Leroy.

L'Artothéque

The handsome pale yellow villa next door to the Musée Léon Dierx contains **L'Artothéque** (02 62 41 75 50; 26 Rue de Paris; admission free; 9.30am-5.30pm Tue-Sun). This contemporary art gallery hosts changing exhibitions of works by local artists and those from neighbouring countries. It's always worth popping in to see if there's anything of interest.

Le Barachois

This seafront park, lined by cannons facing out to sea, is *the* place to promenade in St-Denis. The park has an area set aside for

MAIL ORDER MIRACLE

St Expédit is one of Réunion's most popular saints, though some scholars argue there never was a person called Expédit. Instead, they attribute the origins of this 'saint who ain't' to a box of religious relics that were shipped from Rome in a parcel bearing the Italian word *espedito* (expedited). When the box arrived in Paris, the nuns mistakenly assumed that this was the saint's name and christened their new chapel La Chapelle de St Expédit.

Whatever the truth, the idea was brought to Réunion in 1931 when a local woman erected a statue of the 'saint' in the Notre Dame de la Délivrance church in St-Denis in thanks for answering her prayer to return to Réunion. Soon there were shrines honouring St Expédit all over the island, where people prayed for his help in the speedy resolution of all sorts of tricky problems.

Over the years, however, worship of the saint has taken on the sinister overtones of a voodoo cult: figurines stuck with pins are left at the saint's feet; beheaded statues of him are perhaps the result of unanswered petitions. The saint has also been adopted into the Hindu faith, which accounts for the brilliant, blood-red colour of many shrines. As a result the Catholic Church has tried to distance itself from the cult, but the number of shrines continues to grow.

pétanque (a game similar to bowls), cafés and a **monument** to the Réunion-born aviator Roland Garros, leaning nonchalantly on a propeller. Garros was the first pilot to cross the Mediterranean and also the inventor who worked out a way of timing machine-gun fire so it could be directed through a turning propeller. Shady Pl Sarda Garriga, across the road, was named after the governor who abolished slavery in Réunion in 1848.

On Sundays the section of the highway that passes through Le Barachois is closed to traffic, and the park positively heaves with promenading local families.

Notre Dame de la Délivrance

This attractive church dates from 1893 and sits on the hillside across the usually dry Rivière St-Denis. It's noteworthy for the statue of St Expédit just inside the door, dressed as a young Roman soldier. He is permanently decorated with red flowers, ribbons and other offerings either from petitioners or in thanks for prayers answered. See Mail Order Miracle (above) for more information about this unusual saint.

Hindu Temple

St-Denis' small but wildly colourful **Hindu temple** (Rue Maréchal Leclerc) stands out among the shops east of the centre, opposite Rue de Montreuil. If you wish to visit, remember to remove your shoes and any leather items. (For more information on etiquette, see p48). Photography is not allowed.

Grande Mosquée

The cool white-and-green interior of the **Grande Mosquée** (121 Rue Maréchal Leclerc; 🕑 9am-noon & 2-4pm), also known as the Noor-E-Islam mosque, is a haven of peace. The Islamic community in St-Denis is very traditional, so if you wish to visit, dress and behave with respect (see p48 for more).

SLEEPING

There is high demand throughout the year for accommodation, especially in the budget and mid-range categories, in St-Denis, so advance booking is highly recommended. At the bottom of the scale, there are some very rough and ready guesthouses, usually known as *pensions*, catering to students and overseas workers. Most are best avoided, though the *pension* listed is secure, central and well maintained. There's a better choice of budget and mid-range hotels scattered around the city but surprisingly little in the way of upmarket accommodation.

AUTHOR'S CHOICE

Hôtel Le Mascareignes (☎ 02 62 21 15 28; www.hotelmascareignes.com; 3 Rue Lafferière; s/d from €29/34; ❄) All round best budget choice for its friendly, English-speaking owners, city-centre location and well-priced rooms. The Creole murals and a sunny breakfast terrace are guaranteed to put you in a holiday mood. It offers simple but well-scrubbed rooms; the three on the 1st floor with their own terrace are a popular choice.

Budget

Hôtel du Centre (☎ 02 62 41 73 02; www.runweb.com/hotelducentre; 272 Rue Maréchal Leclerc; s/d from €23/28) Not to be confused with the Hôtel Central, St-Denis' cheapest hotel is popular with overseas workers and makes a convenient place to crash near the main bus station. Boxy, brightly painted rooms come with TV, fan, washbasin and a tiny shower cubicle, but no toilets at the cheaper end.

Pension Zoulékan Limbada (☎ 02 62 41 05 00; 35 Rue de l'Est; d €20) One of the better private guesthouses, this Indian-run *pension* offers a handful of spotlessly clean twin rooms with communal washing facilities. Guests are asked to be quiet all the time and respect prayer times.

Mid-Range

Hôtel Fleur de Mai (☎ 02 62 41 51 81; hotelfleurdemai@wanadoo.fr; 1 Rue Moulin à Vent; s/d €36/40; ❄) This sweet little hotel lives up to its name with a small, flower-filled garden. The rooms are bright and gleaming, with private bathroom, TV and phone as standard. It's also very central.

Hôtel Central (☎ 02 62 94 18 08; central.hotel@wanadoo.fr; 37 Rue de la Compagnie; s/d from €45/59; P ❄) This efficient and welcoming hotel is a popular mid-range option right in the centre. It offers a broad choice of well-appointed rooms and the added benefit of English-speaking staff.

Hôtel Select (☎ 02 62 41 13 50; www.runweb.com/hotelselect; 1 Rue des Lataniers; s/d from €30/40; ❄ 🏊) The sister hotel of the Hôtel du Centre is a slightly more upmarket establishment and a little further from the centre. Though perfectly comfortable, with private bathroom, satellite TV and telephone, the rooms are nothing to write home about.

Top End

Le Juliette Dodu (☎ 02 62 20 91 20; www.hotel-jdodu.com; 31 Rue Juliette Dodu; s/d from €75/91; ❄ 💻 🏊 P) Easily the nicest place in the upper price bracket is this lovely hotel in a stylish colonial building with intricately carved woodwork and other Creole flourishes. The rooms have less local character but are cosy and equipped with all the three-star comforts you'd expect.

Hôtel Le Saint-Denis (☎ 02 62 21 80 20; resa.stdenis@apavou-hotels.com; 2 Rue Doret; s/d from €103/135; ❄ 🏊) Overlooking Le Barachois, this grey, concrete business hotel is better inside than out. The bar and other communal areas have recently been given a zen make over. The rooms themselves are fairly ordinary, but well equipped, with a minibar and DVD player as standard. The hotel restaurant, L'Oasis, is recommended.

Hôtel Mercure Créolia (☎ 02 62 94 26 26; H1674-GM@accor-hotels.com; 14 Rue du Stade Montgaillard; d from €90; ❄ 💻 🏊) A huge, modern hotel set up above St-Denis to the southeast with commanding views over the city. Creole embellishments liven up the lobby and public areas, though the rooms could do with a bit more character; it's worth upgrading for a sea view. Facilities include a a tennis court, a bar and a fine restaurant.

EATING

Thanks to the French passion for *la gastronomie* (gastronomy), there's a restaurant or café around virtually every corner in St-Denis. Rue Pasteur is a good place to browse, as is the south end of Ave de la Victoire. Around the corner, the snack bars on Le Barachois sell fast eats for people on the run.

Lunch is something of a sacred institution for the Réunionnais and this is especially evident in St-Denis. Getting a table between noon and 1.30pm can be tricky.

You should be able to get a reasonable *plat du jour* (dish of the day) at lunch time for between €8 and €12, but to experience *haute cuisine* (high-class cuisine) in St-Denis, you'll have to bid *adieu* (goodbye) to a pile of euros. All cafés, bars and restaur-ants have a menu and price list on display, which makes life easier.

Chinese

Nouveau Délice (☎ 02 62 21 92 00; 62 Rue Pasteur; mains €7-10; 🕐 lunch Mon-Sat, dinner Mon & Thu-Sat) Small, friendly and inexpensive place specialising in dishes cooked and presented in traditional metal *marmites* (cooking pots). It's all fresh, very tasty and the portions are generous.

Les Délices de l'Orient (☎ 02 62 41 44 20; 59 Rue Juliette Dodu; mains from €8; 🕐 lunch & dinner Tue-Sat; ⊠ ❄) No points for décor in this big, bright Cantonese restaurant, but the food more than makes up for it. The vast menu covers classics such as *riz renversé*, a bowl of rice with various toppings, and *porc à la sauce grand-mère* (pork with chilli sauce).

AUTHOR'S CHOICE

Cyclone Café (☎ 02 62 20 00 23; 24 Rue Jean Chatel; mains around €11; ⏲ lunch Mon-Fri, dinner Mon-Sat; ❄) This trendy café with its wooden floorboards and art house décor offers great food in chilled-out surroundings. The daily specials such as tuna tartare or quiche and salad are popular at lunch time with shoppers and briefcase-toting workers; the evenings pull in a younger, hipper crowd. There's always a selection of Creole curries and cheese or cold-meat platters, followed by profiteroles, brownies or perhaps apple crumble for those with hearty appetites. Later in the evening the restaurant transforms into a popular bar.

Creole, French & European

Reflets des Îles (☎ 02 62 21 73 82; 27 Rue de l'Est; mains €12-15; ⏲ lunch & dinner Mon-Sat; ⊠ ❄) Locals and tourists rub shoulders in this traditional restaurant serving cracking Creole cuisine. Thanks to an annotated menu and helpful staff, it's the perfect place to try out local fare such as the ubiquitous *rougail saucisses* (sausages in a tomato sauce) with *grains* (lentils or haricot beans) and a side-dish of *brêdes* (a leafy vegetable). Other country dishes include rabbit and vermouth stew or variations on duck. The waiters play the tropical-island card with their snazzy shirts.

Le Jardin du Barachois (☎ 06 92 21 07 94; Rue Doret; mains €14-20; ⏲ lunch Mon-Sat, dinner daily; ⊠ ❄) Resembling the garden of a Creole house, this sunny little restaurant is earning a big reputation for its innovative takes on local dishes. This is sophisticated fare with a métro twist, with dishes such as a swordfish curry laced with *combava* (an aromatic citrus fruit) or a duo of red snapper and salmon with mango. There's a good range of salads and a lunch time *plat du jour* for €12.

Le Saint-Hubert (☎ 02 62 21 95 95; 4 Rue Victor Mac Auliffe; mains €10-12; ⏲ lunch & dinner; ❄) A classic French brasserie serving métro treats such as trout with almonds and *tarte tatin* (a sort of apple tart) and a big choice of salads. You'll need to get here early to be sure of a table, particularly one on the pavement terrace.

L'Oasis (☎ 02 62 21 80 20; Le Barachois; mains €12-20; ⏲ lunch & dinner) The restaurant of the Hôtel Le Saint-Denis is best in fine weather when you can sit out under the flamboyant trees. It offers a varied menu of Creole and métro fare such as curries, *confit de canard* (succulent preserved duck meat) and big, fresh salads.

Le Labourdonnais (☎ 02 62 21 44 26; 14 Rue L'Amiral Lacaze; mains €15-25, 3-course menu €30; ⏲ lunch Mon-Fri, dinner Mon-Sat; ⊠ ❄) One of the town's top restaurants, using the best of local ingredients to create traditional Creole curries and more refined métro dishes, from *foie gras* (fattened duck liver) flavoured with local vanilla to sole stuffed with prawns. It also offers an unusually good wine list. The décor blends rustic beams and stone walls with colonial-era elegance.

Other recommendations:

B@bookcafé (☎ 02 62 20 94 94; 82-88 Rue Juliette Dodu; dishes €6-9; ⏲ 9am-6.30pm Mon-Sat) The Internet café in L'Entrepôt Librairie is a popular lunch spot, with five or so daily dishes to choose from and all-day drinks and cakes.

Le Cadre Noire (☎ 02 62 21 44 88; 11 Rue de Paris; www.cadre-noir.com in French; 2-course lunch €10; ⏲ 11am-7pm Tue-Sat; ❄) Art-gallery setting for a light lunch comprising a main dish (vegetarian on Tuesday and Thursday) and dessert, all home-made. Also does great afternoon tea and cakes.

Le Pinocchio (☎ 02 62 41 75 00; 65 Rue Alexis de Villeneuve; pasta €9-11, mains €13-15; ⏲ lunch Tue-Sat, dinner Mon-Sat; ❄) Popular trattoria patronised by St-Denis' Italian community.

Indian

La Cardamome (☎ 02 62 21 25 46; 48 Rue Pasteur; mains €10-14; ⏲ lunch & dinner; ❄) This cheerful little restaurant is packed out on Friday and Saturday evenings when it offers a buffet for just €11. It also does a more limited weekday lunch buffet for €8, or you can choose from the standard menu. There's no alcohol.

Le Goujrat (☎ 02 62 21 60 61; Blvd Gabriel Macé; mains €11-14; ⏲ lunch & dinner Tue-Sat; ❄) Not the greatest location, above the municipal swimming pool, but the food's tasty and comes in decent-sized portions. Vegetarians are well-catered for and there are some well-priced lunch deals.

Quick Eats

Le Massalé (☎ 02 62 21 75 06; 30 Rue Alexis de Villeneuve; ⏲ 10am-8.30pm Mon-Sat, 11am-8.30pm Sun) For more than 30 years this tiny outlet has been selling a mouthwatering array

RÉUNION

of Indian snacks and sweets to eat in or take away. Perennial favourites include samosas – fish, crab or chicken in pastry parcels – for around €0.50 each, as well as *catless* (cutlets in breadcrumbs) from €1.20. Wash it down with a glass of refreshing cardamom tea.

L'Igloo Glacerie (☎ 02 62 21 34 69; 67 Rue Jean Chatel; 11am-midnight;) This is *the* place to indulge in a wild and wonderful ice-cream concoction. The melon with chocolate dip is to die for. Cornets cost from €1.80 for one scoop; sit-down sundaes cost from €5 but are a meal in themselves. Soft-serve ice cream is sold in the annex opposite. You can also get light lunches such as omelettes and salads here.

Le Castel (☎ 02 62 21 27 66; 43 Rue de la Compagnie; 6.15am-2pm & 3.30-7pm Tue-Sat, 7am-noon Sun;) St-Denis' best bakery has a small seating area were you can get a drink to go with one of their luscious pastries. It also sells sandwiches, salads and a range of prepared dishes at lunch time to eat in or take away.

Self-catering

Self-caterers are best off heading to the **Score supermarket** (Rue Jean Chatel) or **Dia%** (Rue Maréchal Leclerc). For fresh fruit and vegetables, there is a wide range of cheap produce at the **Petit Marché** (Rue Maréchal Leclerc; 6am-6pm Mon-Sat, 6am-noon Sun).

DRINKING

Cyclone Café (☎ 02 62 20 00 23; 24 Rue Jean-Chatel; 5pm-2am Mon-Sat;). After the kitchen shuts down, this atmospheric watering hole is usually buzzing, with regular live bands and other events, and the kind of friendly atmosphere you'd normally associate with your local pub. Most people opt for the draft Bière Bourbon (commonly known as Dodo after the label); a small *pression* (draft beer) costs €2.

Le Rallye (☎ 02 62 21 34 27; 3 Ave de la Victoire; 6am-midnight;) A trendily downbeat bar (with local DJs) and café that is a popular hang-out with the university crowd. There are jazz and blues concerts on Friday and Saturday nights, plus the occasional themed evening.

Si Señor (☎ 02 62 21 80 06; 24 Rue de Nice; 7pm-1am Tue-Sun;) This chic music bar gets going around 11pm as people gather for a pre-disco warm-up. Wednesday is karaoke night, Thursday salsa and there's a DJ on Friday and Saturday. It also runs salsa and Afro-Caribbean dance classes three nights a week.

Also recommended:

Moda Bar (☎ 02 62 21 68 29; 72 Rue Pasteur; 6pm-2am Mon-Sat;) Ultra-modern bar which serves a mean *mojito* (refreshing alcoholic drink made with mint, lemon, sugar and lots of rum). There are events most nights, including salsa evenings on Friday, and dance classes on Monday and Wednesday.

Le Bistrot (☎ 02 62 21 14 26; 34 Rue de la Compagnie; 10am-2am Mon-Sat;) Popular with students for its cheap prices, funky playlist and live sports screenings.

ENTERTAINMENT

For information about cultural activities ask in the tourist office, or contact the **Office Départemental de la Culture** (☎ 02 62 41 93 00; www.odcreunion.com in French). It's also worth checking the local newspapers to see what's happening in town. Discos and live music events are detailed in the free, monthly *Les Pages Noires*.

Casino

Casino de St-Denis (☎ 02 62 41 33 33; Le Barachois; slot machines 10am-1am Sun-Thu, 10am-3am Fri & Sat, gaming tables from 9.30pm;) located beside the Hôtel Le Saint-Denis, offering slot machines and rather more upmarket gambling. Admission to the slot machines is free, but entry to the gaming room (for American roulette, blackjack and poker) costs €10. You'll need some form of identification and smart clothes to get past security at the door.

Cinemas

St-Denis has three cinemas, which show a mix of French films and mainstream international blockbusters dubbed into French. Very occasionally you might get an English-language film. The **Gaumont** (☎ 02 62 41 20 00; Rue L'Amiral Lacaze;) and the **Plaza** (☎ 02 62 21 04 36; 79 Rue Pasteur;) both have two screens, while the **Ritz** (☎ 02 62 20 09 52; 53 Rue Juliette Dodu;) has three. Tickets cost between €4 and €7, depending on the time of day.

Nightclubs

Most of Réunion's discos are down the coast at St-Gilles-les-Bains, but there are a couple of OK nightspots in the centre of St-Denis (see also Drinking, left).

La Loco (☎ 02 62 21 07 45; 7 Rue L'Amiral Lacaze; admission free Tue-Thu, women/men including one drink €10/16 Fri & Sat; ⏰ 10pm-5am Tue-Sat; ✖) Classic mirrored disco with a mixed clientele and music to match. Friday and Saturday are theme nights.

Le Hibou (☎ 02 62 20 00 66; Rue Labourdonnais; admission including one drink €16; ⏰ 11.30pm-5am Fri & Sat; ✖) An intimate dance floor and lots of seating space give more of a clubby feel to this place catering to an older age group. The music ranges from salsa to *séga* with a touch of techno.

Theatre

There are two main theatres in St-Denis.

Théâtre de Champ-Fleuri (☎ 02 62 41 93 00; www.odcreunion.com in French; Ave André Malraux) A modern theatre located on the southeast side of town. It puts on an excellent programme of theatre, music and dance between March and December. Ticket prices vary.

Théâtre du Grand Marché (☎ 02 62 20 96 36; www.cdoi-reunion.com in French; 2 Rue Maréchal Leclerc; adult/child €18/10) Appropriately enough this theatre is beside the Grand Marché. It offers contemporary theatre, including a fair number of children's events, lectures and the occasional film screenings sometimes in the original language.

You can pick up programmes at the theatres or at the tourist office.

SHOPPING

The main shopping streets are the semi-pedestrianised Rue Maréchal Leclerc and Rue Juliette Dodu.

At the west end of Rue Maréchal Leclerc, the **Grand Marché** (☎ 02 62 21 09 02; 2 Rue Maréchal Leclerc; ⏰ 8am-6pm Mon-Sat) is the city's principal handicraft market. It has a mishmash of items for sale, including Malagasy wooden handicrafts, fragrant spices, woven baskets, embroidery, T-shirts, furniture and a jumble of knick-knacks. The prices are rather inflated, so it's certainly worth trying to bargain.

The **Petit Marché** (Rue Maréchal Leclerc), on the east side of town, is mainly a fresh produce market, but you can buy herbs and spices and local *rhums arrangés* (flavoured rums) here at competitive prices.

Down on Le Barachois, **La Caze** (☎ 02 62 21 55 47; 10 Pl Sarda Garriga) stocks a good range of Réunionnais crafts and gifts, from vanilla, herbs and soaps to Cilaos wine.

For tapes and CDs of *maloya*, *séga* and other local music, **Soredisc** (☎ 02 62 21 68 29; 61 Rue Pasteur) has by far and away the biggest selection.

GETTING THERE & AWAY

Air

The vast majority of flights come in to **Roland Garros International Airport** (code RUN; ☎ 02 62 28 16 16; www.reunion.aeroport.fr in French) about 10km east of St-Denis. For further information regarding air travel see p286.

Bus

The main long-distance bus station is the L'Océan bus terminal to the east of centre between Rue Maréchal Leclerc and Blvd Lancastel.

From here **Car Jaune** (☎ 02 62 08 10 12 39 74) operates two express services: Line A heads west to St-Pierre via St-Paul, St-Leu, Étang-Salé-les-Bains and St-Louis; Line F goes east to St-Benoît via Ste-Suzanne and St-André. There are also nonexpress services on these two routes with additional stops in the smaller towns.

Information for Car Jaune regarding all their routes around the island and the airport bus service is available from the kiosk at the bus terminal between 4.30am and 7.45pm Monday to Friday and from 6.45am to noon and 1pm to 5.45pm Saturday and Sunday. Tickets can be bought on the bus or from the kiosk from 6.30am to 5.45pm Monday to Friday and to 5pm on Saturday. You can also pick up timetables at the tourist office.

For more information on buses around the island, see p221.

Car & Motorcyle

There's not much point in having a car in St-Denis unless you're using it as a base to explore the rest of the island. If that's the case, you can either pick a car up at the airport or avoid paying the airport surcharge (around €15) by having it delivered to your hotel. Whichever you opt for, it's a good idea to book ahead, especially for the smallest, cheapest cars.

For contact details of the main car rental agencies see p221. Most of the big international firms and a number of local outfits have representatives at the airport and most offer delivery. Alternatively, you could try

Interlocation (☎/fax 02 62 21 08 42; 36 Rue de Nice), **MultiAuto** (☎ 0262 290166; multiauto@wanadoo.fr; Hôtel Select, 1 Rue des Lataniers) or **Hertz** (☎ 02 62 21 22 52; www.hertzreunion.com; Rue de Nice) in St-Denis.

Motorbikes (from 125cc up to 750cc) can be rented from **Max Moto** (☎ 02 62 21 15 25; fax 02 62 21 45 66; 10 Ave Gaston Monerville). Again, advance reservations are recommended. Max will pick you up from the airport.

Ferry

St-Denis' ferry terminal is at Le Port located 16km west of St-Denis. For further information see p220.

GETTING AROUND

To/From the Airport

Taxis between St-Denis and Roland Garros International Airport cost around €18 during the day and €20 at night. Cheaper and almost as convenient is the regular Navette Aéroport service, which runs from L'Océan bus terminal to the airport about once an hour between 7am and 7.45pm (between 7.30am and 7.15pm coming from the airport). The fare is €4 and the journey takes a minimum of 15 minutes.

To get the regular bus into St-Denis from the airport, you need to cross the car park outside the terminal building, walk under the expressway overpass and follow the road uphill towards Rivière des Pluies. The stop is just up from the roundabout on the right-hand side, about 800m from the airport in total. The bus you're looking for is the St-Benoît to St-Denis service (Line G) and it will cost €1.60 into town. To reach the airport from St-Denis, take Line G heading towards St-Benoît from the L'Océan bus terminal and ask to be let off at the airport.

To/from the Port

The terminal for passenger ferries to Mauritius is at Port Est in Le Port, 16km west of St-Denis. There are no bus services direct to the terminal. All nonexpress and some express buses between St-Denis and St-Pierre stop at the bus station in Le Port, from where local buses operated by **Bus Fleuri** (☎ 02 62 75 22 22) depart roughly every 30 minutes for the Gare Maritime, Port Est. Unless you're really watching the pennies, you're better off splashing out on a taxi (€30 from St-Denis).

There is a small information desk at the ferry terminal, open for arrivals, but no other facilities for tourists. And there's no bank – make sure you change some money into euros before you arrive. If you want a taxi in Le Port, call **Taxi Auber** (☎ 06 92 65 19 68) which operates 24 hours a day.

Public Transport

St-Denis is relatively small and getting around the centre on foot is a breeze, but there is nevertheless a good and comprehensive city bus service, run by **Citalis** (☎ 08 00 65 56 55; 🕑 7.30am-6pm Mon-Fri, 8am-5pm Sat).

Bus stops are well marked. The main bus stands are on Rue Pasteur near the Hôtel de Ville and on Rue Maréchal Leclerc near L'Océan bus terminal. The kiosks (same hours as the phone service) near both these stands can provide you with a free route-map *(Plan du Réseau de Bus)* and timetables. You can also pick these up at the tourist office.

The city is divided into three zones. Tickets are slightly cheaper if you buy them at the kiosks than from the driver – one zone (€1), two zones (€1.40) and all three zones (€1.60). You can also buy a *carnet* (booklet) of 10 tickets for €7.60, €10 and €12.20, respectively. Remember to validate the ticket by punching it in the machine by the door as you board, and hang onto it, as random checks are common. Various weekly and student passes are also available.

Taxi

Taxis around town are generally expensive. The minimum fare is €2.50 and a trip across town will set you back at least €8.

During the day you should have no problem finding a taxi, but if you're having trouble, try the stand outside the Hôtel Le Saint-Denis. It gets more difficult at night, when you might have to phone for one. A reliable company offering a 24-hour service is **Taxis Paille-en-Queue** (☎ 02 62 29 20 29).

AROUND ST-DENIS

Le Brûlé & La Montagne

These hill districts behind St-Denis offer great views over the town and are starting points for hikes to Plaine d'Affouches, La Roche Écrite and even over the mountains into the Cirque de Salazie.

From Le Brûlé, there are some pleasant walks along the Route Forestière de la Roche Écrite (a forestry road). Another possibility is Bassin du Diable, a wild and isolated valley accessible from upper Bellepierre, the first village downhill from Le Brûlé. The track turns off to the right (headed uphill) where the bus turns around at Bassin Couderc (the last stop in Bellepierre village). Allow about an hour each way.

LA ROCHE ÉCRITE

Like the higher Piton des Neiges, this 2277m peak is often obscured by clouds by about 10am. Although it isn't technically in the Cirque de Mafate, it does offer a spectacular view of the cirque and it's conveniently close to St-Denis. From the summit it's possible to drop down via a precipitous path to Grand Îlet in the Cirque de Salazie and cross over into Mafate via the Col des Bœufs.

There are several possible routes to the peak. The most popular option takes you along the GR R2 from Le Brûlé to the *gîte de montagne* at Plaine des Chicots (three hours), then on to Caverne des Soldats, through huge slabs of lava and limestone, and up the summit (1½ hours). You can then either return the same way or strike west from the *gîte de montagne* along the cirque rim to Dos d'Ane (p195); allow four hours for the descent.

An alternative route departs from Le Quinzième hamlet on the La Montagne road by footpath (at least four hours) or along the GR R2 variant from the kiosk overlooking the upper Rivière St-Denis to the Plaine d'Affouches (two hours) and on to join the Le Brûlé route at the *gîte de montagne* (two hours). From there, it's at least 1½ hours to the summit.

SLEEPING & EATING

Mme Jacqueline Lepée (Les Hortensias; ☎ 02 62 23 02 32; jeanpaullepee@minitel.net; 15 Chemin des Frangipaniers; s/d €38/46, gîte from €183, dinner €17) Right on the GR R2 in Le Brûlé, Madame Lepée offers a *chambre d'hôte* (family-run B&B) and two self-contained *gîtes* (self-catering accommodation) in an attractive garden setting.

Gîte de la Plaine des Chicots (☎ 02 62 43 99 84; dm €13.50, breakfast/dinner €4.50/14.50) This *gîte de montagne* is high above St-Denis near the base of La Roche Écrite and is only accessible on foot. Bookings must be made through the Maison de la Montagne (p225).

Domaine des Jamroses (☎ 02 62 23 59 00; www.ilereunion.com/domainejamroses in French; 6 Chemin du Colorado; s/d from €93/130;) A charming, family-run hotel in La Montagne. The rooms are kitted out with period furniture and most have magnificent views of the coast. There's a squash court and a fine restaurant; many of the spices and fruits come from the hotel gardens.

GETTING THERE & AWAY

Access to these areas is by taxi or bus up the steep, winding roads. To reach Le Brûlé, take bus No 12 from Rue de Paris or L'Océan bus terminal in St-Denis to the end of the route (at Bassin Couderc, in Bellepierre), then change for the minibus to Le Brule. Again, get off at the last stop, Au Banc. For the trip to La Montagne, take bus No 21 or 22.

EAST COAST

The east coast from St-Denis around to Ste-Rose is Réunion's farming belt. The main produce of the area is sugar cane, but the region is also known for its vanilla plantations and fruit orchards. The completion of the dual carriageway between St-Denis and St-Benoît is bringing much new development, particularly around St-André, where the cane fields are rapidly giving way to housing estates. Further south, a more relaxed rural atmosphere prevails.

While this coast lacks the beaches of the west, the region makes up for it with spectacular waterfalls and lush tropical vegetation. South of St-Benoît, the landscape becomes more open and less populated as the road hugs the coast around Piton de la Fournaise, the volcano which regularly spews lava down its eastern flanks. The most recent flows of 1986 and 2002 are clearly visible across the eerie volcanic plain known as Le Grand Brûlé.

The region isn't particularly well endowed with accommodation and eating options. St-André and Ste-Rose provide the greatest choice; either would make a good base for exploring the region.

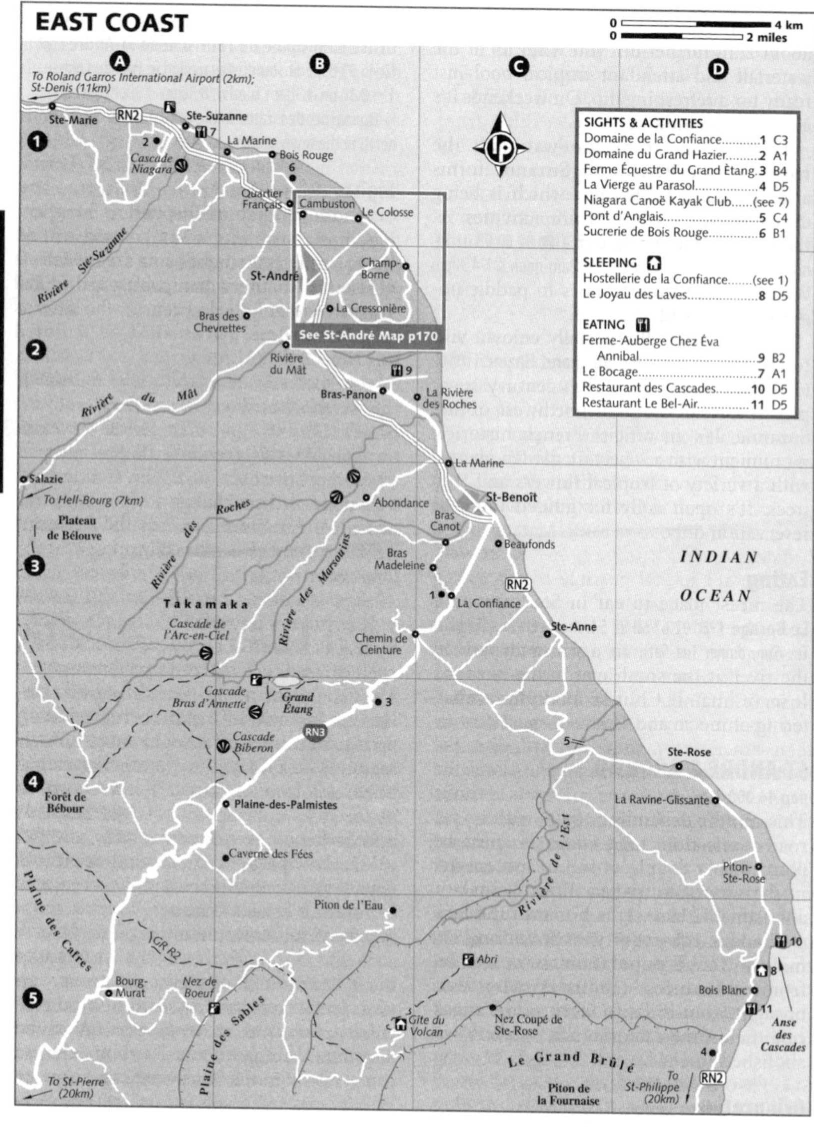

STE-SUZANNE & AROUND

pop 20,000

The seaside village of Ste-Suzanne is worth a quick stop on the route down the coast. The coastline here is fairly uninspiring and the rocky beach is unsuitable for swimming, although there is an imposing lighthouse on the town's northern edge.

Ste-Suzanne is served by Car Jaune bus routes F and G running between St-Dennis (€1.90) and St-Benoît (€2.20).

Sights & Activities

Just beyond the church towards the southern end of town is a road signposted inland to **Cascade Niagara**, a 60m waterfall on the

Rivière Ste-Suzanne. At the end of the road, about 2km further on, you wind up at the waterfall and attendant tropical pool just ready for a refreshing dip. On weekends it's a popular picnic site.

Downstream from the waterfall, the mouth of the Rivière Ste-Suzanne forms a natural lake, Le Bocage, which is being developed for various leisure activities. At the **Niagara Canoë Kayak Club** (☎ 02 62 98 02 31; nckc@ool.fr; half/full day €8/16; 🕑 8am-noon & 1-4.30pm Mon-Sat) you can rent canoes to paddle upstream to Cascade Niagara.

Garden fans will especially enjoy a visit to the classic **Domaine du Grand Hazier** (☎ 02 62 52 32 81; tours €5.50) an 18th-century sugar planter's residence 3km northwest of Ste-Suzanne. It's an official French historical monument with a 2-hectare garden planted with a variety of tropical flowers and fruit trees. It's open daily for guided tours by reservation only.

Eating

The nicest place to eat in Ste-Suzanne is **Le Bocage** (☎ 02 62 52 21 54; mains €8-20; 🕑 lunch Tue-Sun, dinner Tue-Sat), in a tranquil park by the river at the south end of Ste-Suzanne. It serves mainly Chinese food plus a smattering of métro and Creole dishes.

ST-ANDRÉ & AROUND

pop 44,000

This rapidly expanding town, with its fast road connections to St-Denis, is a pleasant place with a couple of sights and enough in the way of tourist facilities to make it a reasonable base. It is home to the largest Indian community in Réunion. The mainly Tamil population is descended from indentured labourers who were brought from India to work in the sugar-cane fields and factories after slavery was abolished in 1848.

Orientation

St-André is very spread out. In the centre, Ave de l'Île de France and Ave de la République are the main shopping streets; the *gare routière* (bus station) is next to the shopping mall at the east end of Ave de la République. Since the sights, sleeping and eating options are also widely scattered, you really need your own transport to get about.

Information

Office Municipale du Tourisme de St-André (☎ 02 62 46 91 63; omt.standre@wanadoo.fr; Parc du Colosse; 🕑 8.30am-4.30pm Tue-Fri, 8.30am-3.30pm Sat) This is inconveniently located in the coastal leisure park 3km north of the town centre.

Sights

St André's Indian atmosphere is most apparent in the Hindu temples dotted around the town. The most imposing are the **Temple of Colosse** (Chemin Champ-Borne) and **Kali Temple** (Ave de l'Île de France); the latter is open to visitors (shoes must be removed before entering).

Apart from the temples, the main attraction is the **Maison de la Vanille** (☎ 02 62 46 00 14; 466 Rue de la Gare; admission adult/child €5/2; 🕑 9am-noon & 2-6pm Tue-Sat), an elegant Creole mansion set amid gardens and a small vanilla plantation. Visitors learn the elaborate process of hand pollination necessary to coax the vanilla orchid to produce those gloriously aromatic beans we know and love (see Vanilla Unveiled p171). Guided tours last about 45 minutes and can be conducted in English if required.

Also worth a look are **Maison Valliamé** (Rue Lagourgue), a handsome colonial villa a short walk northeast of centre, and the massive **Banyan tree** in front of the **town hall**. These unusual native trees are known locally as *élastiques* because of the elastic, rubber-like gum in their bark. A huge seafront leisure park, the **Parc du Colosse**, is being developed on the former sugar-cane fields on St-André's eastern outskirts.

The **Sucrerie de Bois-Rouge** (☎ 02 62 58 59 74; www.bois-rouge.fr in French; refinery and distillery adult/child €8/5.50, distillery €3.50/2.50; 🕑 9am-5.30pm Mon-Fri, closed 20 Dec-20 Jan) is on the coast 3km north of St-André. During the cane harvest (roughly July to late November) visitors are shown around the huge, high-tech plant, following the process from the delivery of the cut cane to the final glittering crystals. The two-hour tour also includes the neighbouring distillery, where the by-products (cane juice and molasses) are transformed into rum. Nothing is wasted: the remaining fibres are burnt to produce electricity. Outside the harvest season, you can visit the distillery alone. Note that children aged under seven years are not allowed into the refinery. English-language tours are available on request.

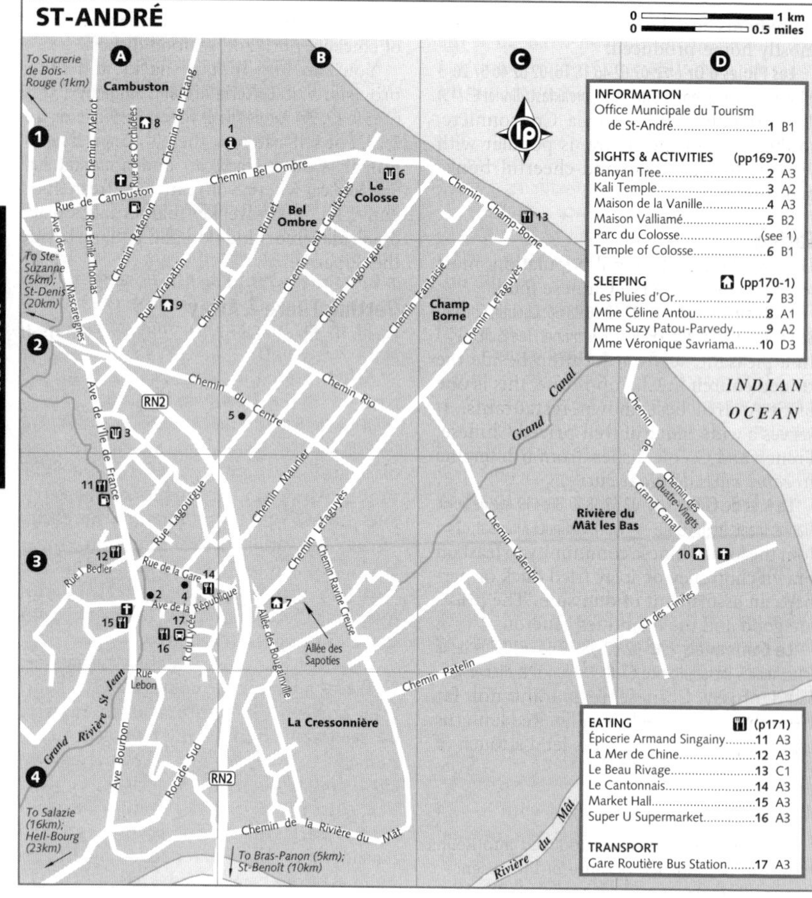

Festivals & Events

Tamil fire-walking ceremonies are normally held during January. Participants enter a meditative state and then walk over red-hot embers as a sign of devotion to various deities. The **cavadee** festival usually takes place in January or February. Dancers and decorated floats process through the town centre during **Divali** (aka Dipavali), the Festival of Light, in October or November. Contact the tourist office for specific dates.

For more about these festivals, see p134.

Sleeping

Mme Céline Antou (L'Adour; ☎ 02 62 46 57 52; adourgite@wanadoo.fr; 620 Ruelle des Orchidées; s/d €38/48, gîte per week/weekend €379/150;) By far the nicest option is this very comfortable and stylish place on the northeast edge of town. It has one *chambre d'hôte* and two *gîtes* for up to four people in lovely little Creole-style bungalows surrounded by gardens.

Mme Véronique Savriama (☎ 02 62 46 69 84; auberge-savriama@wanadoo.fr; 1084 Chemin Quatre-Vingt; s/d €30/43, dinner €14-18) In the hamlet of Rivière du Mât les Bas on the coast southeast of St-André, a welcoming Indian family offers six unfussy *chambres d'hôte* and good *table d'hôte* (meal served at a *chambre d'hôte*) meals.

Mme Suzy Patou-Parvedy (Au P'tit Coin Exotique; ☎ 02 62 46 46 07; 460 Rue Virapatrin; s/d €33/38, dinner €19) A *chambre d'hôte* with three pretty rooms surrounded by luxuriant gardens.

Ingredients for the *table d'hôte* meals are mostly home-produced.

Les Pluies d'Or (☎ 02 62 46 18 16, 02 62 46 57 26; 3 Allée des Sapoties; dm/d €18/34.50, breakfast/dinner €3/15) This friendly *pension* in La Cressonnière, to the south of the centre, is popular with walkers for its cheap-and-cheerful bunk-bed rooms.

Eating

Despite the largely Tamil population, most local restaurants serve Chinese food.

Le Beau Rivage (☎ 02 62 46 08 66; Chemin Champ-Borne; mains €10-30; lunch & dinner Tue-Sun;) In a pleasant, seafront location beside the ruined church in Champ Borne, this is one of St-Andrés best-known restaurants. It serves a wide range of well-priced Chinese, French and Creole dishes, from fish terrine to *cabri massalé* (goat curry).

La Mer de Chine (☎ 02 62 58 77 80; 419 Ave de Île de France; mains from €6.50; lunch & dinner Mon-Sat;) Join the local Chinese community to feast on prawn chop suey or spicy fried duck or perhaps an assortment of dim sum. The prices are good and the quantities generous.

Le Cantonnais (☎ 02 62 58 39 13; 620 Rue de la Gare; mains including rice €7-8; lunch & dinner Tue-Sat) Unfussy Chinese restaurant not far from the Maison de la Vanille. Red lanterns and rampant dragon motifs lend a touch of atmosphere to go with the standard selection of chicken, pork and seafood dishes.

You can buy Indian snacks and other provisions at **Épicerie Armand Singainy** (☎ 02 62 58 05 62; 951 Ave de l'Île de France; 9am-noon & 2-7pm). For self-caterers, there's a **Super U supermarket** (Ave de la République) and a **market hall** (Ave Bourbon) where you can buy fresh food daily. The main weekly market takes place on Friday mornings on the square beside the Super U.

Getting There & Away

Buses from St-Denis (€2.70) to St-Benoît (€1.10) pass through St-André. If you're travelling to Salazie by bus (€1.60), you will have to change here; there are seven buses daily in each direction (three on Sunday). See p203 for onward connections from Salazie to Hell-Bourg.

BRAS-PANON

pop 9800

Bras-Panon is Réunion's vanilla capital, and most visitors come here to see (and smell!) the fragrant vanilla processing plant. The town is also associated with a rare sprat-like delicacy known as *bichiques*. In early summer (around November or December) these are caught at the mouth of the Rivière des Roches as they swim upriver to spawn.

VANILLA UNVEILED

The vanilla orchid was introduced into Réunion from Mexico around 1820, but early attempts at cultivation failed because of the absence of the Mexican bee that pollinates the flower and triggers the development of the vanilla pod. Fortunately for custard lovers everywhere, a method of hand-pollination was discovered in Réunion in 1841 by a 12-year-old slave, Edmond Albius. Vanilla was highly prized in Europe at the time and Albius's discovery ushered in an economic boom, at least for the French 'vanilla barons'. Albius was freed, but died in poverty.

The vanilla bubble burst, however, when synthetic vanilla – made from coal – was invented in the late 19th century. Réunion's vanilla industry was almost wiped out, but in recent years the growing demand for natural products has led to something of a revival. You'll now find vanilla 'plantations' hidden in the forests from St-Suzanne south to St-Philippe.

Vanilla still rates as one of the world's most costly spices. This isn't so surprising when you learn that the flowers are still hand-pollinated, and the workers need nimble fingers since the blooms only last a matter of hours. It then takes eight to 10 months before the pods can be harvested (generally around November) and another year or more of carefully controlled drying to bring out their full, complex flavour and aroma.

The majority of Réunion's crop is exported (Coca Cola is the world's single biggest buyer), but vanilla is still a firm favourite in local cuisine. It crops up in all sorts of delicacies, from cakes and pastries to coffee, liqueurs, even vanilla duck and chicken. Best of all is the sublime flavour of a vanilla-steeped *rhum arrangé* (a mixture of rum, fruit juice, cane syrup and a blend of herbs and berries).

Car Jaune buses (Lines F and G) stop outside the vanilla cooperative en route between St-André and St-Benoît (both €1.10).

Sights

The Coopérative de Vanille (☎ 02 62 51 70 12; 21 Route Nationale; admission €5; 8.30am-noon & 2-5pm Mon-Sat), a working vanilla processing plant, offers an introduction to the process of producing Réunion's famous Vanille Bourbon. After the 40-minute guided tour, visitors are welcome to walk around the small museum and pick up a few samples in the factory shop. It's worth a visit just for the dreamy smell.

Sleeping & Eating

There's not much in the way of accommodation in Bras-Panon. Restaurants are easier to find.

Ferme-Auberge Chez Éva Annibal (☎ 02 62 51 53 76; fax 02 62 51 52 01; Chemin Rivière du Mât; d €25; meals €18;) The main attraction here is the traditional home-cooking. Set meals (by reservation only) include such delights as duck with vanilla and swordfish curry. There are also three functional but clean rooms with communal facilities in a separate building.

Le Vani-La (☎ 02 62 51 56 58; 21 Rue Nationale; mains €10-15; lunch Mon-Fri) No guessing the main ingredient at this little restaurant beside the Coopérative de Vanille. It turns up in both savoury and sweet dishes, and you can round things off with a vanilla-flavoured coffee.

Le Bec Fin (☎ 02 62 51 52 24; 66 Route Nationale; mains from €11; lunch daily, dinner Thu-Sat) Scrumptious Creole, métro and Chinese dishes and a friendly welcome make Le Bec Fin a popular choice. On weekdays it lays on an excellent buffet lunch for just €11.

Le Beauvallon (☎ 02 62 50 42 92; mains €10-32; lunch daily, dinner Thu-Sun) Beside the mouth of the Rivière des Roches, this is a nice, airy place to try local specialties such as *carri bichiques* (a curry made from tiny sprat-like fish).

ST-BENOÎT & AROUND

pop 31,500

St-Benoît is another big agricultural and fishing centre. It specialises in fruit (especially lychees, mangos and pineapples), rice, spices, coffee, maize and sugar. Much of the town was destroyed in a fire in 1950 and holds little of interest. The hills and valleys to the west, however, are worth exploring. The Rivière des Marsouins valley in particular is a delight, with its plunging waterfalls and luxuriant vegetation.

Sights & Activities

TAKAMAKA

North of St-Benoît the D53 strikes southwest, following the Rivière des Marsouins 15km upstream to end beside the Takamaka hydroelectricity station. Despite the power plant, the overwhelming impression is of a wild, virtually untouched valley, its walls cloaked with impenetrable forests. Here and there the dense green is broken by a silver ribbon of cascading water. Where the road ends a footpath plunges down to a bathing pool (allow at least 1½ hours one way). From here you can continue to the Forêt de Bébour and eventually to Hell-Bourg or Cilaos.

GRAND ÉTANG

Around 12km southwest of St-Benoît along the road towards Plaine-des-Palmistes, is the 3km road to Grand Étang (Big Pond). This pretty picnic spot lies at the bottom of an almost vertical ridge separating it from the Rivière des Marsouins valley. Most people simply walk around the lake. It's muddy in places, but shouldn't take more than a couple of hours, including a side-trip to the Bras d'Annette waterfalls.

FERME ÉQUESTRE DU GRAND ÉTANG

This **riding centre** (☎ 02 62 50 90 03; riconourry@wanadoo.fr; half/full day €40/100), just beyond the turn-off to Grand Étang, offers treks to Grand Étang; the full-day trek includes lunch. It's also possible to arrange longer excursions to the cirques and around Piton de la Fournaise.

DOMAINE DE LA CONFIANCE

About 6km from St-Benoît along the road towards Plaine-des-Palmistes is **Domaine de la Confiance** (☎ 02 62 50 90 72; http://perso.wanadoo.fr/laconfiance), a once grand 18th-century Creole mansion surrounded by a 3-hectare garden of lush tropical vegetation. At the time of writing, the domaine was undergoing extensive renovations and was closed to visitors; see the website for the latest situation.

Sleeping & Eating

Hostellerie de la Confiance (☎ 02 62 50 90 50; fax 02 62 50 97 27; s/d from €53/63; main dishes €11-25; lunch Sun-Fri, dinner daily;) The old stable block of the Domaine de la Confiance has been transformed into this charming hotel with just eight tastefully decorated rooms surrounded by quiet gardens. The restaurant is equally refined, serving such delicacies as scallops with vanilla and duck in a lychee sauce.

Getting There & Away

From St-Benoît a scenic road (the RN3) cuts across the Plaine-des-Palmistes to St-Pierre and St-Louis on the far side of the island. Alternatively, you can continue south along the coast road, passing through Ste-Anne, Ste-Rose, St-Philippe and St-Joseph to reach St-Pierre.

St-Benoît is an important bus terminus. Services to and from St-Denis (€3.30) run approximately every half hour. There are also two services linking St-Benoît and St-Pierre: Line H (€7.60) follows the RN3 over the Plaine-des-Palmistes; Line I (€7.10) takes the coast road via Ste-Philippe and St-Joseph. In both cases there are two to three buses daily.

STE-ANNE

The village of Ste-Anne, about 5km south along the coast from St-Benoît, is noted for its unusual **church**. The façade of the building is covered in extravagant, stucco depictions of fruit, flowers and angels. The overall effect is flamboyant rather than tasteful, and is reminiscent of the Mestizo architecture of the Andes in South America. Credit goes to Father Daubemberger from Alsace, who rebuilt the tower and began to decorate the original plain church in the 1920s. He died in 1948 and was laid to rest inside the church.

In the **Maison de l'Artisanat complex** next to the church, is a little shop selling handmade soaps, shampoos and more than 100 different perfumes. Local vanilla, geranium and vetiver are top sellers.

Between Ste-Anne and Ste-Rose is the graceful **Pont d'Anglais** suspension bridge over the Rivière de l'Est, now bypassed by the main highway but open to pedestrians. It was claimed to be the longest suspension bridge in the world at the time of its construction in the late 19th century.

Ste-Anne is a stop on the coastal bus route from St-Benoît (€1.10) to St-Pierre (€6.50).

STE-ROSE & AROUND

pop 6600

The small fishing community of Ste-Rose has its harbour at the inlet of La Marine. There's a monument here to the young English commander Corbett, who was killed in 1809 during a naval battle against the French off the coast.

South of Ste-Rose the first tongues of lava from Piton de la Fournaise start to make their appearance.

RÉUNION

Sights & Activities

Notre Dame des Laves is in Piton Ste-Rose, 4.5km south of Ste-Rose. The lava flow from a 1977 eruption went through the village, split when it came to the church and reformed again on the other side. Many people see the church's escape as a miracle of divine intervention. A wooden log 'washed up' by the lava now forms the lectern inside the church, while the stained glass windows depict various stages of the eruption.

Anse des Cascades, a shady picnic spot, is beside the sea about 3km south of Piton Ste-Rose. The water from the hills drops dramatically into the sea near a traditional little fishing harbour. There's a pleasant café-restaurant here.

Beyond Anse des Cascades, the main road continues south along the coast, climbs and then drops down to cross the 6km-wide volcanic plain known as Le Grand Brûlé. Where the road starts to cross the lava flows stands **La Vierge au Parasol**, a statue of the Virgin Mary optimistically holding an umbrella as protection against the volcano! A local planter set it up at the turn of the century in the hope of protecting his vanilla pods from volcanic hellfire and brimstone.

In 2002, however, the Virgin had to be rescued when lava threatened to engulf her. She was later replaced a few metres from the original spot, beside a looming lava wall.

Sleeping & Eating

While there's nowhere particular to stay or eat in Ste-Rose itself, there are a few options along the national highway heading south.

Le Joyau des Laves (☎ 02 62 47 34 00; www.joyaudeslaves.com in French; d from €35; menus €10-25;

(lunch daily except Fri, dinner daily except Sun) On the headland at Piton-Cascade, 7km south of Ste-Rose, this is a very comfortable *chambre d'hôte* run by a delightful young couple. Even if you're not staying, it's worth phoning ahead to eat in the restaurant. This is a good place to try local specialties such as palm hearts and *baba figues* (banana flowers) from the surrounding gardens.

La Cayenne (☎ 02 62 47 23 46; s/d from €35/40, dinner €18) Perched above the sea in La Ravine-Glissante, 1.5km south of Ste-Rose, this welcoming and well-run guesthouse offers six rooms, of which the cheapest share communal toilets. The owner, Mme Narayanin, also produces excellent meals using mostly home-grown ingredients (reservations required). The only downside is the Roz d'Zil disco on the main road just behind La Cayenne; it can be a bit noisy on Friday and Saturday nights.

Restaurant des Cascades (☎ 02 62 47 20 42; mains €10-25, set-lunch €14; 9.30am-5.30pm daily except Fri) At lunch time this rustic little place under the trees at Anse des Cascades serves fresh fish and Creole dishes as well as sandwiches to eat in or take away.

Restaurant Le Bel-Air (☎ 02 62 47 22 50; mains €12-13; lunch) Venison stew, beef with ginger and vanilla chicken feature on the Creole menu at this roadside restaurant overlooking Le Grand Brûlé. The two-course set-lunch (Monday to Saturday) represents good value.

Getting There & Away

Buses running from St-Benoît (€2.70) to St-Pierre make handy stops near Notre Dame des Laves, Anse des Cascades and La Vierge au Parasol.

SOUTH COAST

The south coast of Réunion sits in the shadow of Piton de la Fournaise and is known as *le sud sauvage* (the wild south). The tortured landscape here is the result of thousands of years of volcanic activity; great tongues of black lava slice through the forest and even reach the ocean at several points. Not surprisingly, very few Réunionnais tempt providence by living in the path of the lava flows!

As a result the southeast coast in particular has very few settlements and places to stay or eat are thin on the ground. It's a region that sees few visitors, but which repays exploration with some wonderfully wild coastal scenery and villages which still move to the rhythm of rural life.

The towns and villages along the coast are served by Car Jaune buses plying between St-Benoît and St-Pierre two to three times a day.

ST-PHILIPPE & AROUND

pop 5000

This small, quiet town on the south coast is the first population centre you hit after leaving the arid, eerie landscape of Le Grand Brûlé, formed by the main lava flow from the volcano. The steep slopes above, known as Les Grandes Pentes, have funnelled lava down to the coast for thousands of years. Because of the lack of population, this area forms an important nature reserve for native birds.

In 1986, in one of the most violent eruptions in recent years, the lava unusually flowed south of Le Grand Brûlé to reach the sea between Pointe du Tremblet and Pointe de la Table. This eruption added over 30 hectares to the island's area, and more than 450 people had to be evacuated and several homes were lost.

Buses between St-Benoît (€4.90) and St-Pierre (€2.70) stop at the town hall in St-Philippe and at Le Baril and Basse Vallée among other places.

Information

Cybercase (☎ 02 62 37 83 57; 2-6pm Mon, 9am-noon & 1-6pm Tue, Wed & Fri, 9am-4pm Sat) In Le Baril village 5km west of St-Philippe, at the time of writing this was the only Internet café on this stretch of coast.

Office du Tourisme de St-Philippe (☎/fax 02 62 37 10 43; 9am-5pm Mon-Fri, 9am-4pm Sat & Sun) On the main road beside the town hall you can pick up information on the entire southeast coast of the island, including leaflets detailing recommended walks.

Sights & Activities

The 3-hectare garden **Le Jardin des Parfums et des Épices** (☎ 02 62 37 06 36; www.jardin-parfums-epices.fr in French; adult/child €3.05/6.10; tours at 10.30am & 2.30pm) contains over 1500 species in a natural setting in the Mare Longue forest, 3km west of St-Philippe. Knowledgeable and enthusiastic guides present the island's history, economy and culture through the plants;

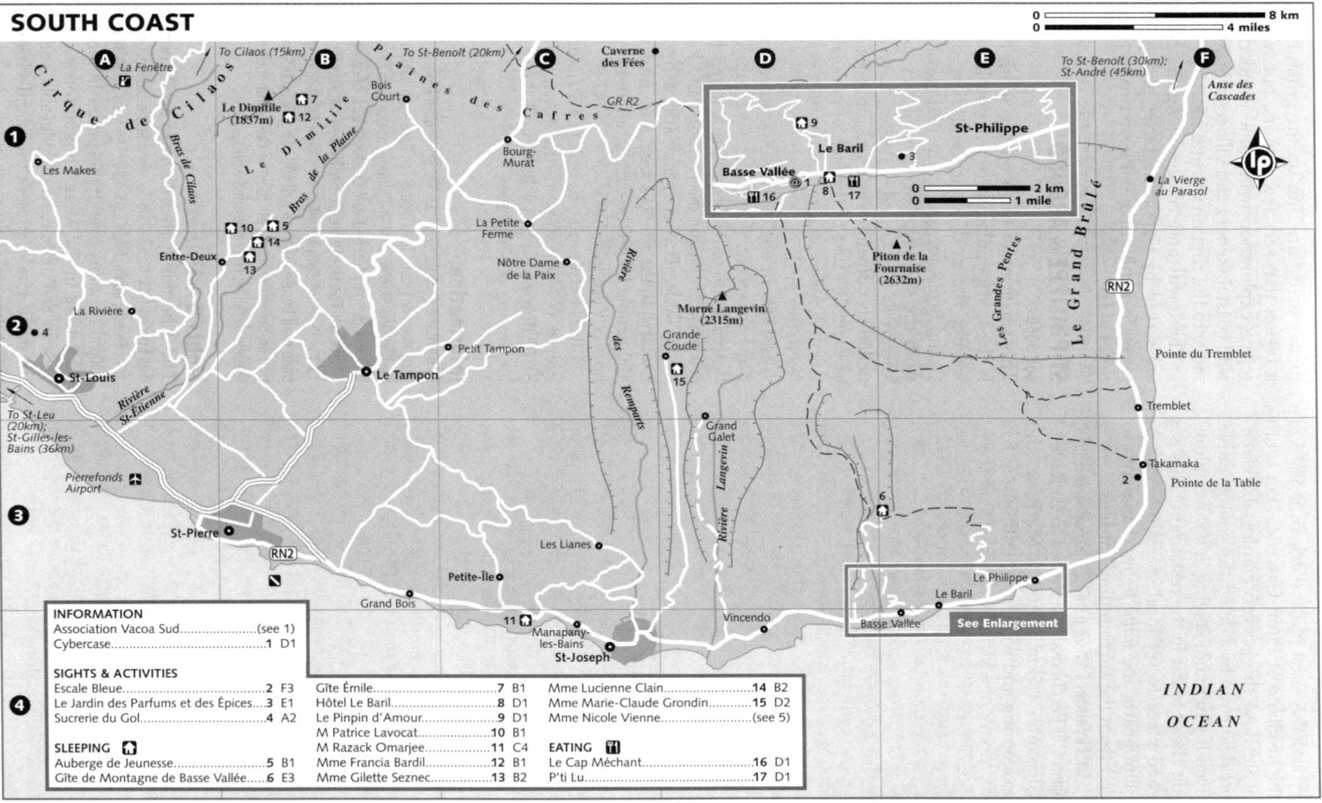
SOUTH COAST
0 8 km
0 4 miles
A B C D E F
1 2 3 4
To Cilaos (15km)
To St-Benoît (20km)
To St-Benoît (30km); St-André (45km)
To St-Leu (20km); St-Gilles-les-Bains (36km)
La Fenêtre
Cirque de Cilaos
Bras de Cilaos
Les Makes
Le Dimitile (1837m)
Le Dimitile
Bras de la Plaine
Bois Court
Plaines des Cafres
Caverne des Fées
GR R2
Bourg-Murat
La Petite Ferme
Nôtre Dame de la Paix
Entre-Deux
La Rivière
St-Louis
Rivière St-Étienne
Pierrefonds Airport
Petit Tampon
Le Tampon
St-Pierre
RN2
Grand Bois
Petite-Île
Les Lianes
Manapany-les-Bains
St-Joseph
Rivière des Remparts
Morne Langevin (2315m)
Grande Coude
Grand Galet
Rivière Langevin
Vincendo
Piton de la Fournaise (2632m)
Les Grandes Pentes
Le Grand Brûlé
Basse Vallée
Le Baril
Le Philippe
See Enlargement
St-Philippe
0 2 km
0 1 mile
Pointe du Tremblet
Tremblet
Takamaka
Pointe de la Table
La Vierge au Parasol
Anse des Cascades
INDIAN OCEAN
INFORMATION
Association Vacoa Sud.....(see 1)
Cybercase.....1 D1
SIGHTS & ACTIVITIES
Escale Bleue.....2 F3
Le Jardin des Parfums et des Épices.....3 E1
Sucrerie du Gol.....4 A2
SLEEPING
Auberge de Jeunesse.....5 B1
Gîte de Montagne de Basse Vallée.....6 E3
Gîte Émile.....7 B1
Hôtel Le Baril.....8 D1
Le Pinpin d'Amour.....9 D1
M Patrice Lavocat.....10 B1
M Razack Omarjee.....11 C4
Mme Francia Bardil.....12 B1
Mme Gilette Seznec.....13 B2
Mme Lucienne Clain.....14 B2
Mme Marie-Claude Grondin.....15 D2
Mme Nicole Vienne.....(see 5)
EATING
Le Cap Méchant.....16 D1
P'ti Lu.....17 D1

RÉUNION

tours (in French only) must be booked at least one day in advance.

The quaint **Eco-Musée de St-Philippe** (☎ 02 62 37 16 43; adult/child €5/2; 9am-noon & 2-4.30pm Mon-Sat), a few doors down from St-Philippe's town hall, is also known as Au Bon Roi Louis after the French king who encouraged the settlement of the area. The little Creole house is stuffed with an eclectic assortment of antiques and agricultural equipment. Visitors receive a very detailed tour (in French) from the owners.

The area around St-Philippe is known for its production of baskets, bags, hats and other items from *vacoa* fronds. You can see them being made and learn more about this versatile palm at **Association Vacoa Sud** (☎ 02 62 37 16 97; admission free; 9am-5pm) in Le Baril, 5km west of St-Philippe.

In Tremblat village, 6km north of St-Philippe, the vanilla producer **Escale Bleue** (☎ 02 62 37 03 99; admission free; 9.30am-5.30pm Mon-Fri) welcomes visitors to its workshop. The vanilla plants here are trained around trees in the traditional manner rather than the stakes used in intensive cultivation.

Sleeping & Eating

There's nowhere to stay in St-Philippe and nowhere particularly to eat, but there are a few options around the villages of Le Baril and Basse Vallée a few kilometres to the west.

Le Pinpin d'Amour (☎ 02 62 37 14 86; 56 Chemin Paul Hoareau; s/d €40/45, dinner €20) Named after the artichoke-like fruit of the *vacoa* palm, this genteel place in the hills above Le Baril offers cheerful *chambres d'hôte*. Pinpin and *vacoa* heart also feature strongly in the *table d'hôte* meals (reservations required).

Hôtel Le Baril (☎ 02 62 37 01 04; www.anthurium.com; s/d from €48/54; mains €10-20;) A small and somewhat faded hotel set above the rocky shoreline. The rooms suffer from damp, but those on the front have the attraction of the waves crashing right below. The restaurant is one of the few places open in the evening. House specials include local dishes such as rabbit stew and pork curry with palm heart.

Gîte de Montagne de Basse Vallée (☎ 02 62 37 36 25; dm €13.50, breakfast/dinner €4/13.5) This *gîte de montagne* is about 8km above the village of Basse Vallée, along the Route Forestière de Basse Vallée (the GR R2 variant). Bookings must be made through the Maison de la Montagne (p225).

Le Cap Méchant (☎ 02 62 37 00 61; mains €10-30; lunch Tue-Sun) In a pleasant location on the seafront in Basse Vallée, this place is hugely popular for its cracking Creole and Chinese cuisine. There's a large choice of dishes and an unusually good-value wine list.

P'ti Lu (☎ 02 62 86 22 09; meals from €7; lunch daily except Thu) This friendly little restaurant attracts a local crowd with its well-priced sandwiches, snacks and hot meals. Though no great shakes from the outside, it's nicely situated beside the tidal swimming pool to the north of Le Baril.

ST-JOSEPH & AROUND

pop 13,000

St-Joseph, at the mouth of the magnificent valley of the Rivière des Remparts, is a rather dull town. It does, however, boast amenities such as banks and a post office and there are some decent places to stay and eat in the vicinity.

For walkers, the classic hike is along the Rivière des Remparts, though the gentler Langevin valley to the east is also well worth exploring. The latter is accessible by car, as is the narrow ridge dividing the two valleys; at one point the ridge is little wider than the road itself.

East of St-Joseph it's possible to swim at the black-sand beach below the village of Vincendo. There's also a protected tide pool at Manapany-les-Bains, a few kilometres to the west of town. This charming spot lies at the mouth of an impressive ravine.

Information

Maison du Tourisme du Sud Sauvage (☎ 02 62 37 37 11; pat.sudsauvage@wanadoo.fr; 3 Rue Paul Demange; 9am-5pm Mon-Fri, 10am-4pm Sat, 9am-1pm Sun) Near the *gare routière* in the centre of St-Joseph, this office provides information for the whole region. Ask for the leaflets detailing local walks and sights.

Sleeping

M Razack Omarjee (Veremer; ☎ 02 62 31 65 10; www.chambre-gite-veremer.com; 40 Chemin Sylvain Vitry; s/d from €31/36;) Two very comfortable *chambres d'hôte* in a little Creole building with a fantastic garden and great views. It's about 10km west of St-Joseph, signed off the main road just beyond the turning for Petite-Île.

Mme Marie-Claude Grondin (Eucalyptus; ☎ 02 62 56 39 48; 24 Chemin de la Croisure; s/d €31/39; meals from €16) This *chambre d'hôte* with two sparkling rooms is way up in the hills at Grand Coude. The farm produces venison and wild boar, which feature in Mme Grondin's excellent *table d'hôte* meals (reservations required).

Eating

La Case (☎ 02 62 56 41 66; 31 Rue Leconte Delisle; mains €13-30; lunch daily, dinner Tue-Sun;) St-Joseph's top restaurant is a good place for a splurge. It presents refined dishes, such as ostrich carpaccio and grilled langoustine flambéed in whisky, in elegant surroundings. Though it's on a busy main road in the town centre, inside the pretty Creole house all is calm.

L'Ambroisie (☎ 02 62 31 51 99; 306 Rue Raphaël Babet; mains €12-24; lunch daily, dinner Tue & Thu-Sat;) Greek gods and horns of plenty adorn the walls of this cheerful place up the hill from the St-Joseph bus station. Instead of ambrosia, however, the menu features a more mundane – though perfectly tasty – selection of curries and métro staples.

Le Tagine (☎ 02 62 37 32 51; 23 Chemin de la Marine; mains from €11; lunch daily, dinner Thu-Sat) In Vincendo, by the turn-off for the beach, have a change from the usual with couscous, tagine and other Moroccan fare. The dining room is a bit soulless, but a warm welcome and authentic flavours more than make up for it.

Chez Jo (☎ 02 62 31 48 83; 143 Blvd de l'Océan; mains from €11; winter 9am-6pm daily except Thu, summer to 8pm) If you're down in Manapany-les-Bains, try this relaxed place overlooking the tide pool. It rustles up sandwiches, snacks and main meals to eat in or take away.

Getting There & Away

St-Joseph lies on Car Jaune's coastal bus route between St-Benoît (€6) and St-Pierre (€1.60). In addition to the central bus station, buses stop in Vincendo, Manapany and Petite-Île.

ST-PIERRE

pop 26,000

Regarded as the 'capital' of the south, St-Pierre is Réunion's third-largest *commune* after St-Denis and St-Paul and is developing fast on the back of a largely agro-industrial economy. The town centre has a nice workaday atmosphere and an attractive seafront, while its sandy but exposed beach is popular with local holidaymakers. Some visitors choose to spend a night or two here on their way to the high plains and Piton de la Fournaise. St-Pierre's weekly market is one of the most important in the island.

Orientation

The centre of St-Pierre consists of a compact grid of streets. Most places are easily walkable, though the *gare routiére* for the long-distance buses, at the junction of Rue de Presbytère and Rue Luc Lorion, is a bit of a hike. The main shopping street is Rue des Bons Enfants.

Information

There are ATMs at the central post office and at most banks in the town centre.

Centre Hospitalier de St-Pierre (☎ 02 62 35 90 00; RN2, Terre Sainte) The main hospital for the southern region located 2km east of town.

Central post office (Rue des Bons Enfants; 7.30am-5.30pm Mon-Fri, 7.30am-noon Sat) This lies on the town's main shopping street. Can change foreign currency (only US dollars and sterling notes).

Crédit Agricole (Rue du Four à Chaux; 8am-4.15pm Mon-Wed & Fri, 8am-3.30pm Thu) Accepts American Express travellers cheques and can change US dollars and sterling notes.

Librairie Cazal (☎ 02 62 35 35 35; Rue Désiré Barquisseau) This is the best place to find newspapers, maps and guides.

Office du Tourisme de St-Pierre (☎ 02 62 25 02 36; fax 02 62 25 82 76; www.sudreunion.com; 17 Blvd Hubert-Delisle; 8.30am-12.30pm & 2-5.15pm Mon-Fri, 9am-3pm Sat) Information is limited, but you can pick up some useful brochures and a town map here.

Sights

There aren't many sights in town, beyond the occasional colonial-era edifice. One of the best preserved is the 200-year old **Hôtel de Ville** which started life as a coffee warehouse for the Compagnie des Indes. During working hours (8am to 4pm Monday to Friday) you can usually pop upstairs to look at the grand, wood-panelled meeting room running the length of the building. The old colonial-era train station is now occupied by the tourist office. Nearby is the **Bassin de Radout**, a dry dock dating from the 19th century.

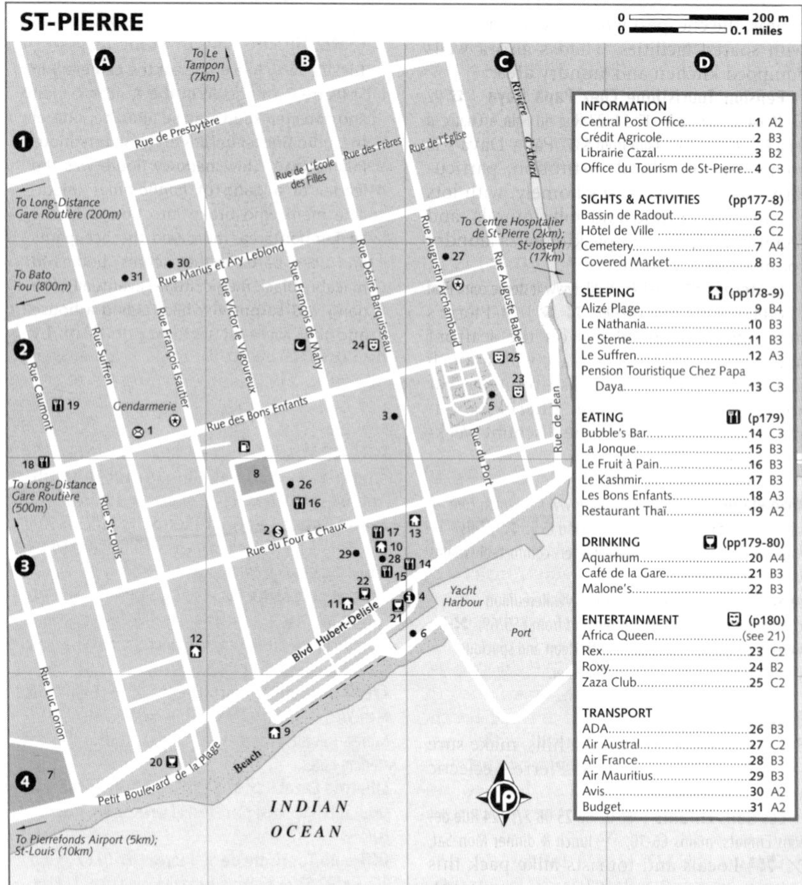

St-Pierre's only real tourist attraction lies in the **cemetery** at the west end of Blvd Hubert-Delisle. The grave of the African sorcerer, Le Sitarane, is still a popular pilgrimage spot for Réunionnais who believe in *gris gris* or black magic (see Le Sitarane, p179). The grave is on the right-hand side at the west end of the cemetery. Other features of the cemetery include some interesting Hindu graves, marked by yellow headstones in the shape of Sanskrit letters; a number of Chinese marble vaults; and Christian graves crowded with crosses and dried flowers.

St-Pierre's **main market** takes place on Saturday morning (7am to noon) spread out along the seafront at the west end of Blvd Hubert-Delisle. During the week (8am to 6pm Monday to Saturday) there's a smaller **covered market** (Rue Victor le Vigoureux) under a hall in the town centre. Alongside fresh fruit and vegetables, stalls sell souvenirs such as local spices and herbs, *vacoa* bags and the usual assortment of Malagasy crafts.

Sleeping

St-Pierre has a variety of hotels that cater for a range of budgets. Most are concentrated down towards the seafront.

Le Nathania (☎ 02 62 25 04 57; hotel.le.nathania@wanadoo.fr; 12 Rue François de Mahy; s/d from €20/25; ✖ P) The nicest choice overall is this friendly and well-run hotel just back from the seafront. It has a range of tidy rooms, the cheapest with a TV and fan, but with shared facilities. There's also a well-equipped kitchen and laundry area.

Pension Touristique Chez Papa Daya (☎ 02 62 25 64 87, 02 62 25 11 34; 27 Rue du Four à Chaux; d from €25, d with bathroom from €35) Papa Daya's is something of a local institution, particularly among walkers. It's homely, with lots of greenery around and jolly murals, and facilities include a simple kitchen, a laundry room and a TV lounge.

Le Sterne (☎ 02 62 25 70 00; www.lesterne.com; Blvd Hubert-Delisle; s/d from €67/90;) St-Pierre's most upmarket hotel lies on the seafront boulevard. It's a modern place with a touch of Creole atmosphere, stylish rooms, a bar and a poolside restaurant offering good-value buffets. Ask about the discount weekend rates.

Other recommendations:

Alizé Plage (☎ 02 62 35 22 21; www.ilereunion.com/alizeplage.htm; Blvd Hubert-Delisle; d €75;) This two-star place right on the beach offers comfortable rooms with a private terrace.

Le Suffren (☎ 02 62 35 19 10; www.ilereunion.com/suffren.htm; 14 Rue Suffren; s/d from €55/69;) A welcoming mid-range place with clean and spacious rooms, if somewhat lacking in character.

Eating

Before heading off into the hills, make sure you make the most of St-Pierre's eclectic array of restaurants.

Les Bons Enfants (☎ 02 62 25 08 27; 124 Rue des Bons Enfants; mains €6-10; lunch & dinner Mon-Sat;) Locals and tourists alike pack this unpretentious Creole-Chinese restaurant. You can choose a meal at the canteen-style counter for around €7 or opt for something from the menu in the slightly smarter dining room.

Restaurant Thaï (☎ 02 62 35 30 95; 54 Rue Caumont; mains €6-12; lunch Tue-Sun, dinner Tue-Sat) The walk here is rewarded with authentic Thai curries laced with lemongrass, ginger or coconut milk, and chillies hot enough to knock your socks off. For a terrace table, get here early or phone ahead.

Le Kashmir (☎ 02 62 35 38 21; 18 Rue François de Mahy; mains €9-18; lunch Tue-Sun, dinner Tue-Sat;) This tiny, north Indian restaurant is another popular choice, particularly for its €10 set lunch. Dishes include a creamy aubergine curry and chicken with almonds. It also sells snacks and takeaways. No alcohol is served.

LE SITARANE

Tucked away in a corner of the cemetery in St-Pierre is the grave of the African bandit and sorcerer known as Le Sitarane, one of the more sinister heroes of the superstitious Réunionnais. This shadowy figure was the leader of a gang of *bonhommes* (medicine men) who broke into homes in the Le Tampon area, murdered the occupants and used parts of the victims' bodies in macabre black-magic rituals! Eventually, the gang was surprised while raiding a house and they were all sentenced to death by hanging in 1911.

Today, the grave of Le Sitarane is covertly used for black magic rites by Réunionnais looking to bring misfortune upon others. The grave is usually covered with offerings, from glasses of rum, candles and pieces of red cloth to neat and tidy rows of cigarettes and even the occasional beheaded rooster!

La Jonque (☎ 02 62 25 57 78; 2 Rue François de Mahy; mains €7-11; lunch & dinner except Tue;) Popular Chinese serving the usual favourites at very reasonable prices. No complaints as to quantity and quality, but the service could be more cheerful. Head upstairs for a touch more ambience.

Other recommendations:

Alizé Plage (☎ 02 62 35 22 21; Blvd Hubert-Delisle; restaurant/brasserie mains €15-24/8-15; lunch & dinner;) The hotel's main restaurant offers gourmet dining and sea views. There's also a simpler brasserie.

Bubble's Bar (☎ 02 62 25 21 90; 38 Blvd Hubert-Delisle; mains €9-30, tapas per plate €3 ; lunch & dinner;) Fun – and very trendy – seafood restaurant and tapas bar.

Le Fruit à Pain (☎ 02 62 35 63 50; 14 Rue Victor le Vigoureux; lunch & dinner except Tue & Sun) Behind the café is a pleasant garden-restaurant serving couscous and paëlla alongside local dishes.

Drinking

Malone's (☎ 02 62 25 02 22; 36 Blvd Hubert-Delisle; 8am-2am;) An ever-popular bar-cum-café and restaurant with regular theme evenings. Things can get pretty lively after midnight.

Café de la Gare (☎ 02 62 35 24 44; 17 Blvd Hubert-Delisle; 7am-midnight Tue-Sun) One of the nicest spots for a quiet coffee is the back terrace of this cafe in the old train station. In the evening it transforms into a popular bar.

RÉUNION

Other happening places include the club-like **Aquarhum** (☎ 02 62 96 341 2; 18 Petit Boulevard de la Plage; 6pm-2am Tue-Sun;) and the ultra-chic **Bubble's Bar** (☎ 02 62 25 21 90; 38 Blvd Hubert-Delisle; 8am-2am;). The latter's electric-blue lighting and Philippe Stark décor wouldn't be out of place in St-Tropez.

Entertainment

Bato Fou (☎ 02 62 25 65 61; bato.fou@wanadoo.fr; 15 Rue de la République; tickets €6-15) To the west of town, this is one of Réunion's prime concert venues and is a good place to catch up-and-coming bands.

There are two cinemas in St-Pierre: the **Roxy** (☎ 02 62 35 34 90; 53 Rue Désiré Barquisseau) and the **Rex** (☎ 02 62 25 01 01; Rue Auguste Babet).

If you fancy a bop, see what's happening at Malone's, Aquarhum or Bubble's Bar (above) or try one of the town-centre discos: the **Africa Queen** (17 Blvd Hubert-Delisle; admission free; 11pm-5am Fri & Sat), next to the Café de la Gare, goes in for Polynesian décor and '80s music; the more intimate **Zaza Club** (☎ 02 62 96 40 61; 16 Rue Méziaire Guignard; men/woman €8-10/free; daily 10pm-4am) attracts a younger crowd with its techno, house and dance playlist.

Getting There & Away

AIR

Air Mauritius and Air Austral operate daily flights between **Pierrefonds Airport** (☎ 02 62 96 77 66; www.grandsudreunion.org), 5km west of St-Pierre, and Mauritius. Since there are few facilities for arriving visitors at Pierrefonds, you're generally better off flying into St-Denis.

BUS

Car Jaune's long-haul buses stop at the long-distance *gare routière* beside the junction of Rue Presbytère and Rue Luc Lorion, west of town. Regular and express buses to/from St-Denis (€7.10) run frequently along the west coast via St-Louis and St-Gilles-les-Bains. There are also two or three services a day to St-Benoît via Plaine-des-Palmistes (€7.60) and the same number around the south coast through St-Joseph and Ste-Philippe (€7.10). From Monday to Saturday buses operate between St-Pierre and Cilaos (€2.50); on Sunday they start from St-Louis.

CAR RENTAL

For car rental, try **ADA** (☎ 02 62 21 59 01; 18 Rue Victor le Vigoureux), **Avis** (☎ 02 62 35 00 90; 82 Rue Marius et Ary Leblond) or **Budget** (☎ 02 62 25 45 40; 90 Rue Marius et Ary Leblond). They can all arrange airport pick-ups.

TAXI

A taxi from the long-distance *gare routière* into the centre of St-Pierre costs about €8. From the airport, you're looking at around €15. Call **Taxi St-Pierrois** (☎ 02 62 38 54 84) if you can't find a taxi on the street.

AROUND ST-PIERRE

St-Louis

You may have to travel to St-Louis to catch the bus to Cilaos but there's really no other reason to visit this predominantly industrial town.

The *gare routière* is located on the south side of town near a couple of snack bars and the church, which is the oldest on the island, dating from 1733.

About 1.5km west of St-Louis, the chimneys of the **Sucrerie du Gol** (☎ 02 62 91 05 47; visitesucrerie@gqf.com; adult/child €5/3) dominate the plain. You can tour this old sugar refinery, one of only two on the island still functioning, during the cane harvest (July to December). Visits take place daily (except Sunday and Monday) with prior reservation.

Entre-Deux

This sweet little village high in the hills 18km north of St-Pierre got its name (which means 'between two') because it is situated between two rivers – the Bras de Cilaos and the Bras de la Plaine, which join to form the Rivière St-Étienne. Most visitors come here for the tough hike up the slopes of Le Dimitile to a super view over the Cirque de Cilaos.

Even if you're not a walker, Entre-Deux is a delightful place to stay and get a taste of rural life. It boasts a wealth of *cases créoles*, traditional country cottages surrounded by well-tended and fertile gardens, many of which are being restored. There's also a strong tradition of local crafts, including natty slippers made from the leaves of an aloe-like plant called *choca*.

INFORMATION

Tourist office (☎ 02 62 39 69 80; ot.entredeux@wanadoo.fr; 9 Rue Fortuné Hoareau; 8am-5pm Mon-Sat, 9am-1pm Sun) Entre-Deux's tourist office occupies a pretty *case créole* on the road into the village. Staff give

RÉUNION

guided visits (usually in French) of the village (adult/child €9/5) and can provide leaflets on walks in the region (including climbing Le Dimitile) and on local artisans.

ACTIVITIES

If you leave at dawn, the ascent and descent of **Le Dimitile** (1837m) can be done in a single day. You should plan on at least eight hours, however, and unless you're superhuman it's preferable to stay at one of the two *gîtes d'étape* near the summit. The longer but slightly easier climb takes you along the Sentier du Bord, a footpath which starts to the north of the village, branching right off the Route de Bras Long. The tourist office can provide information and sketch maps detailing the various routes.

SLEEPING

Auberge de Jeunesse (☎/fax 02 62 39 59 20; 120 Rue Défaud; dm €13, breakfast €2) This youth hostel is 1.5km northeast of Entre-Deux in Ravine des Citrons (on one of the paths to Le Dimitile). At the time of writing it wasn't offering evening meals.

Mme Gilette Seznec (☎ 02 62 39 66 44; danielseznec@wanadoo.fr; 55 Rue Maurice Berrichon; d €40, dinner €17) Signed from the road to the youth hostel, this welcoming *chambre d'hôte* is one of the closest options to Entre-Deux. It consists of three spacious rooms in a lovely old Creole house.

Mme Nicole Vienne (☎ 02 62 39 64 03; lesdurentas@wanadoo.fr; Les Durentas, 35 Rue Défaud; s/d €27/39, meals €15; 🖳 🏊) Another friendly place, in this case right opposite the youth hostel, with just two good-sized rooms.

Mme Lucienne Clain (Mirest; ☎ 02 62 39 65 43; 1 Chemin Source Raisin; s/d €39/55, meals from €17) A *chambre d'hôte* about half way along the road to the youth hostel offering three comfortable rooms and excellent *table d'hôte* meals.

M Patrice Lavocat (Ranch Kikouyou; ☎ 02 62 39 60 62; 6 Rue Cinaire; dm/s/d €11/30/35, breakfast/dinner €4/16) In an unbeatable location 2km north of Entre-Deux, you can choose between one of the two *chambres d'hôte* or a bed in the *gîte d'étape*.

Up on Le Dimitile, **Gîte Émile** (☎ 02 62 39 66 42, 02 62 57 43 03; r incl half board per person €30) run by M François Payet offers basic accommodation or there are slightly more comfortable surroundings at the *gîte d'e'tape* run by **Mme Francia Bardil** (☎ 02 62 39 60 84, 02 62 57 64 29; dm €14; breakfast/table d'hôte meals €4/15).

EATING

Le Longani (☎ 02 62 39 70 56; Rue du Commerce; meals €6-10; ⏰ lunch daily, dinner Fri & Sat) Opposite the post office, this place is good for snacks and light lunches, which you can take away or eat on the terrace in fine weather.

Le Malina (☎ 06 92 61 33 25; Rue Hubert Delisle; set menus from €9; ⏰ lunch Tue-Sun) A slightly more formal restaurant near the church serving Creole favourites.

GETTING THERE & AWAY

Car Jaune operates a bus service between Entre-Deux and the *gare routière* in St-Pierre (€1.60). There are five buses a day from Monday to Saturday and two on a Sunday.

WEST COAST

Immediately southwest of St-Denis is Réunion's resort strip, with the best of the island's beaches and a huge variety of organised activities laid on for visitors. You could be forgiven for thinking that a piece of the south of mainland France had been transplanted to the Indian Ocean. The main part of this sunshine coast lies between St-Gilles-les-Bains and Étang-Salé-les-Bains.

The countryside back from the coast is also worth exploring. Here you'll find some engaging museums and two excellent botanical gardens. There's also good walking and biking in the hills and, if you're lucky and the weather's clear, dizzying views from lookout points teetering on the rims of the cirques. This back country also boasts some very appealing places to stay. With your own transport, you can easily nip down to the coast for the day and then escape to rural calm at night.

As elsewhere in Réunion, getting about by public transport is a mixed affair. There are good connections between the coastal towns, which are linked by Car Jaune services between St-Pierre and St-Denis. Destinations in the hills are more of a problem, however, as local services – where they exist – tend to be fairly sporadic.

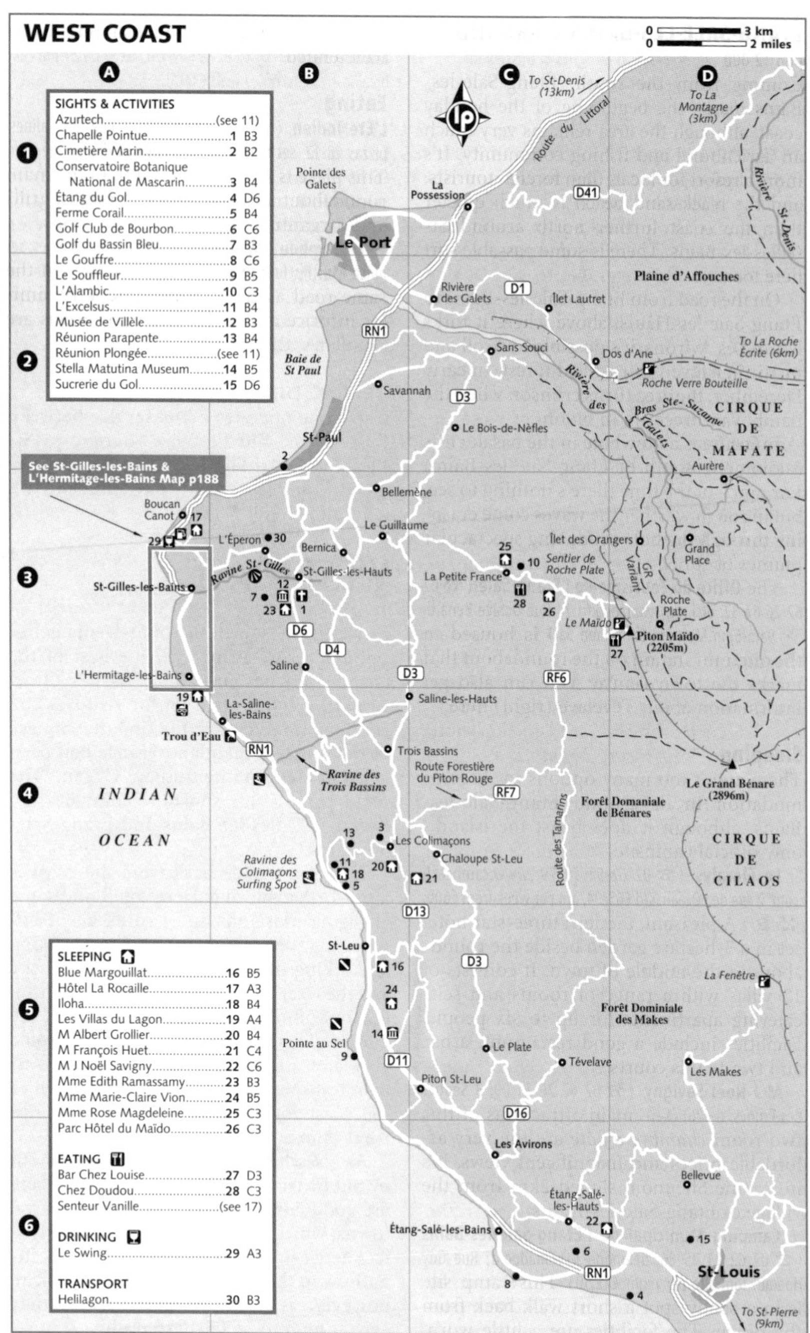
WEST COAST
0 3 km
0 2 miles
SIGHTS & ACTIVITIES
Azurtech.....(see 11)
Chapelle Pointue.....1 B3
Cimetière Marin.....2 B2
Conservatoire Botanique National de Mascarin.....3 B4
Étang du Gol.....4 D6
Ferme Corail.....5 B4
Golf Club de Bourbon.....6 C6
Golf du Bassin Bleu.....7 B3
Le Gouffre.....8 C6
Le Souffleur.....9 B5
L'Alambic.....10 C3
L'Excelsus.....11 B4
Musée de Villèle.....12 B3
Réunion Parapente.....13 B4
Réunion Plongée.....(see 11)
Stella Matutina Museum.....14 B5
Sucrerie du Gol.....15 D6
SLEEPING
Blue Margouillat.....16 B5
Hôtel La Rocaille.....17 A3
Iloha.....18 B4
Les Villas du Lagon.....19 A4
M Albert Grollier.....20 B4
M François Huet.....21 C4
M J Noël Savigny.....22 C6
Mme Edith Ramassamy.....23 B3
Mme Marie-Claire Vion.....24 B5
Mme Rose Magdeleine.....25 C3
Parc Hôtel du Maïdo.....26 C3
EATING
Bar Chez Louise.....27 D3
Chez Doudou.....28 C3
Senteur Vanille.....(see 17)
DRINKING
Le Swing.....29 A3
TRANSPORT
Helilagon.....30 B3
See St-Gilles-les-Bains & L'Hermitage-les-Bains Map p188
To St-Denis (13km)
To La Montagne (3km)
Route du Littoral
Rivière St-Denis
Pointe des Galets
La Possession
Le Port
D41
Plaine d'Affouches
Rivière des Galets
D1
Îlet Lautret
RN1
Sans Souci
Dos d'Ane
To La Roche Écrite (6km)
Roche Verre Bouteille
Baie de St Paul
Savannah
D3
Rivière des Galets
Bras Ste-Suzanne
CIRQUE DE MAFATE
Le Bois-de-Nèfles
St-Paul
Aurère
Bellemène
Boucan Canot
Le Guillaume
L'Éperon
Bernica
Îlet des Orangers
Grand Place
Ravine St-Gilles
St-Gilles-les-Hauts
La Petite France
Sentier de Roche Plate
GR Variant
St-Gilles-les-Bains
Roche Plate
Le Maïdo
Piton Maïdo (2205m)
D6
D4
Saline
L'Hermitage-les-Bains
RF6
Saline-les-Hauts
La-Saline-les-Bains
Trou d'Eau
Trois Bassins
Ravine des Trois Bassins
Route Forestière du Piton Rouge
RF7
Le Grand Bénare (2896m)
INDIAN OCEAN
Forêt Domaniale de Bénares
Route des Tamarins
Les Colimaçons
Ravine des Colimaçons Surfing Spot
Chaloupe St-Leu
CIRQUE DE CILAOS
D13
St-Leu
D3
La Fenêtre
Forêt Dominiale des Makes
Pointe au Sel
D11
Le Plate
Tévelave
Les Makes
Piton St-Leu
D16
Les Avirons
Bellevue
Étang-Salé-les-Hauts
Étang-Salé-les-Bains
RN1
St-Louis
To St-Pierre (9km)

ÉTANG-SALÉ-LES-BAINS & AROUND

pop 12,000

Coming from the south, Étang-Salé-les-Bains marks the beginning of the holiday coast, although the area remains very much an agricultural and fishing community. It's more a resort for locals than foreign tourists, and the black-sand beach is much quieter than the coast further north around St-Gilles-les-Bains. There is some passable surf here too.

On the road from Étang-Salé-les-Bains to Étang-Salé-les-Hauts, above where it forks left to Les Avirons, it's possible to stroll and picnic in a lovely, bird-filled forest. In early December, the area turns crimson when the flamboyant trees are in bloom.

Le Gouffre is a blowhole in the basalt cliffs a kilometre south of Étang-Salé-les-Bains. For much of the time there's nothing to see, but in rough weather the waves come crashing through the hole producing spectacular plumes of spray.

The **Office du Tourisme de l'Étang-Salé** (☎ 02 62 26 67 32; otsi.run@wanadoo.fr; 74 Rue Octave Bénard; 9am-5pm Mon-Fri, 9am-noon Sat) is housed in the old train station on the roundabout that marks the town centre. You can also get information about Tévelave (right) here.

Sleeping

There aren't too many options for accommodation in or around Étang-Salé-les-Bains, although it does boast the island's only official campsite.

Le Floralys (☎ 02 62 91 79 79; www.carobeach.com; 2 Ave de l'Océan; s/d €68/94, apt per week from €600;) A pleasant, modern three-star hotel set in a 3-hectare garden beside the roundabout in the middle of town. It consists of 12 villas with a range of rooms and self-catering apartments for up to six people. Facilities include a good restaurant, a bar and two tennis courts.

M J Noël Savigny (☎ 02 62 26 31 09; 3 Sentier des Prunes; d €26) The main attractions of this two-room *chambre d'hôte* are the very affordable prices and magnificent views. It's in Ravine Sheunon, signed 2km from the village of Étang-Salé-les-Hauts.

Camping Municipal de l'Étang-Salé-les-Bains (☎ 02 62 91 75 86; delongprez@wanadoo.fr; Rue Guy Hoarau; tent site per night €12.50) This camp site is in a shady spot a short walk back from the beach. The facilities are a little worn, but there's hot water and it's all reasonably well tended.

Eating

L'Été Indien (☎ 02 62 26 67 33; 1 Rue des Salines; pizzas €8-12, set lunch €10; lunch & dinner Tue-Sun) This place is a short walk south of the main roundabout and specialises in pizzas, grills and gargantuan ice-cream concoctions.

Le Bambou (☎ 02 62 91 70 28; Rue des Salines; set lunch €10; lunch & dinner daily except Tue) On the same road as L'Été Indien and very similar in price and style. The mini pizzas are popular with kids.

TÉVELAVE

pop 1500

Ten kilometres up an impossibly twisty road in the hills above Les Avirons, the village of Tévelave offers a real taste of rural life and is a great base for walkers and mountain bikers. At the top of the village is the starting point for Route Forestière 6 (RF6), more poetically known as the Route des Tamarins. This road leads through the Forêt Domaniale des Bénares and emerges 36km later below Le Maïdo.

Sleeping & Eating

Auberge Les Fougères (☎ 02 62 38 32 96; fax 02 62 38 30 26; 53 Route des Merles; s/d from €31/48, set menu €14; lunch & dinner Tue-Sun) Right at the start of the forestry road, this is a homey rural hotel offering a warm welcome and bright and breezy rooms; the best are those on the front with panoramic views. The restaurant specialises in traditional Creole cuisine cooked over wood fires.

Le Camphrier (☎ 02 62 22 09 29; perso.wanadoo.fr/camphrierhotel; 2 Route du Tévelave; s/d from €35/43, half board €55/85) If the Auberge Les Fougères is full, this new two-star hotel on the D16 at the entrance to Tévelave makes a reasonable alternative. It has just 14 rooms and a small restaurant open for dinner only.

Mme France-May Boyer (Chez Mamie; ☎ 02 62 38 00 39; fmayboyer@yahoo.fr; 65 Route des Vacoas; s/d €33/38, dinner €17) The kindly 'Mamie' Boyer runs a *chambre d'hôte* on the D16 just below Le Camphrier with a handful of tidy rooms, all with private bathroom. She'll also treat you to her heavenly home cooking.

M Olivier Idmond (Le Jasmin de Nuit; ☎ 02 62 38 07 55; olivier.idmond@wanadoo.fr; 25 Rue du Camphrier; s/d €34/40, dinner from €17) On a sideroad below

Le Camphrier, this *chambre d'hôte* offers four nicely decorated rooms (each taking a different 'ethnic' theme) in an attractive Creole house.

ST-LEU

pop 25,000

St-Leu used to be a major centre for the sugar industry, but the town fell on hard times in 1978 when the Stella sugar refinery closed down. These days, St-Leu depends largely on tourism. It's not an unattractive town and will be a lot quieter when the new bypass is completed. It has a smattering of handsome stone buildings dating from the French-colonial era, such as the *mairie* (town hall) and the church opposite. Other attractions are the shady park along the seafront and a protected beach that is popular with families.

Historically, St-Leu has had its share of problems, including a violent slave rebellion in 1811 and devastating cyclones in 1932 and 1989. However, it was spared the cholera epidemic that destroyed St-Denis and St-Louis in 1859, an event commemorated in the town's historic chapel, Notre Dame de la Salette.

Information

Internet access is available at **Le Bureau** (☎ 02 62 34 87 72; 14 Rue du Commandant Legros; 8.30am-noon & 1.30-6pm Mon-Fri, 8.30am-noon Sat), behind the Apolonia hotel, and at the bar **Namasté** (☎ 349241; 2 Rue Haute; 10am-midnight Tue-Sat, 5pm-midnight Sun) on the roundabout at the north end of town.

The helpful **Office du Tourisme de St-Leu** (☎ 02 62 34 63 40; ot.stleu@wanadoo.fr; 1 Rue Le Barrelier; 1.30-5.30pm Mon, 9am-noon & 1.30-5.30pm Tue-Fri, 9am-noon & 2-5pm Sat) is at the north end of the main road passing through the centre of town. It has brochures galore and helpful, English-speaking staff.

Notre Dame de la Salette

Perched on the side of the hill to the east of town is this little white chapel, built in 1859 as a plea for protection against the cholera epidemic sweeping the entire island. Whether by luck or divine intervention, St-Leu was spared from the epidemic, and thousands of pilgrims come here each year on 19th September to offer their thanks.

Ferme Corail

Following the international ban on the trade of turtle products, the **Ferme Corail** (☎ 02 62 34 81 10; www.tortuemarine-reunion.org; adult/child €5.50/3; 9am-6pm) turtle farm, 2km north of St-Leu has had to reinvent itself as a research-and-development centre. You get a close-up look at the five different varieties of turtle found in the waters around Réunion, but seeing the distressingly small pens in which these magnificent creatures are kept is likely to undermine the experience.

Sleeping

Blue Margouillat (☎ 02 62 34 64 00; www.blue-margouillat.com in French; Impasse Jean Albany; r from €123; dinner €35;) This delightful, small hotel on the southern outskirts of St-Leu has the feel of a French country house, with its mix of antiques and modern art, its elegant dining room and just 14 luxurious rooms.

Iloha (☎ 02 62 34 89 89; www.iloha.fr; Pointe des Châteaux; s/d from €55/76;) This is a very nice three-star place just north of town, with mature gardens, great views and a decent restaurant and pool. Also on offer are a variety of self-catering bungalows for up to six people. You'll need to book well ahead.

Apolonia (☎ 02 62 34 62 62; www.hotel-apolonia.com; Blvd Bonnier; s/d €71/114;) This large, modern hotel just back from the seafront in the centre of St-Leu is a good mid-range option. The rooms aren't large but are perfectly adequate. In the middle is a rather cramped pool area, restaurant and bar with a stage for evening entertainment. Other facilities include a kids' club (during the métro school holidays only), free water sports, a tour desk and car rental.

Eating

Self-caterers should visit the well-stocked **Super-U** (Rue Général Lambert) supermarket of St-Leu for provisions.

Chez Stephanie (☎ 02 62 34 89 30; 135 Rue Général Lambert; curry €10; lunch & dinner Tue-Sun) The motherly Stephanie prides herself on her home-made Creole curries cooked in a time-honoured fashion over a wood fire. Her restaurant is equally unpretentious – look for the green-and-white building with a grilled-chicken stand out front, across from the Super-U.

Casa San Fermin (☎ 02 62 34 90 58; 1 Rue de la Salette; mains €15-26; lunch & dinner Tue-Sun) Beside the turning for Notre Dame de la Salette, this bodega-style restaurant offers delicious Spanish dishes such as paella, tortilla and salt cod with peppers.

Le Lagon (☎ 02 62 34 79 13; 2 Rue du Lagon; mains €10-15; lunch & dinner except Tue & Wed) Attractive surroundings and a good choice of reasonably priced drinks, snacks and main meals make this beachfront place across the road from the Apolonia hotel a reliable choice.

Other recommendations:

Chez Lulu (☎ 02 62 34 89 53; 57 Rue Général Lambert; mains around €8; lunch & dinner Mon-Sat) Lulu is a kindly soul who rustles up tasty Creole dishes in a tiny outlet next to the tourist office.

La Varangue (☎ 02 62 34 79 26; 36 Rue du Lagon; mains €18-26; lunch Tue-Sun, dinner Tue-Sat) An upmarket restaurant specialising in grills and seafood. Find it on the seafront to the south of the Apolonia hotel.

Entertainment

Le Drugstore (☎ 02 62 34 72 72; Rue Général Lambert; 5.30pm-midnight Mon-Sat) This trendy wine bar, with an intimate terrace out back, is near the Super-U. It offers more than 60 different wines and a good range of beers, with cheese and cold-cut platters to soak it up. Local bands play here most weekends.

Namasté (☎ 02 62 34 92 41; 2 Rue Haute; 10am-midnight Tue-Sat, 5pm-midnight Sun) Another happening place in St-Leu, in this case a cocktail bar which puts on a varied programme of live music on Friday. During the day it serves drinks, snacks and light meals and doubles as an Internet café. It's located on the roundabout near the tourist office.

AROUND ST-LEU

The region around St-Leu holds more of interest than the town itself. The former sugar refinery now houses an engaging museum and there's whole raft of sporting activities to choose from, notably surfing but also diving, paragliding and mountain biking. Above the village of Les Colimaçons, the Route Forestière du Piton Rouge (RF7) runs east up into the Forêt Domaniale des Bénares, connecting with the forestry road between Tévelave and Le Maïdo.

On the cliffs at Pointe au Sel, between St-Leu and Étang-Salé-les-Bains, **Le Souffleur** (The Blowhole) is a rocky crevice that spurts up a tower of water as the waves crash against it. It's only worth making the journey, however, if the sea is pretty rough.

Many of the villages in the hills above St-Leu, including Piton St-Leu and Les Colimaçons, lie on the Car Jaune bus route 'E' from St-Pierre to Chaloupe St-Leu.

Stella Matutina Museum

This quirky but well-designed **museum** (☎ 02 62 34 16 24; www.stellamatutina.com in French; 10 Allée des Flamboyants; adult/child €6.50/2.30; 9.30am-5.30pm Tue-Sun) 4km south of St-Leu on the D11 to Les Avirons, tells the agricultural and industrial history of Réunion. It's dedicated primarily to the sugar industry, but also provides insights into the history of the island and has exhibits on other products known and loved by the Réunionnais, such as vanilla, orchids, geraniums and vetiver. Allow at least two hours to do it justice.

Conservatoire Botanique National de Mascarin

At Les Colimaçons, on the slopes north of St-Leu, is the **Conservatoire Botanique National de Mascarin** (☎ 02 62 24 92 27; cbnm@cbnm.org; adult/child €5/2; 9am-5pm Tue-Sun), an attractive garden in the grounds of the unusual Creole mansion built by the Marquis of Chateauvieux in the 1850s. You can easily spend half a day exploring the site, which spreads over seven hectares and contains an impressive collection of native species, all neatly labelled, as well as many from around the Indian Ocean.

Activities

DIVING

The dive spots off Pointe au Sel to the south of St-Leu offer some of the best underwater landscapes in Réunion, while the lagoon closer to St-Leu is good for coral. For details of dive centres in the area and more about diving in Réunion, see p39.

PARAGLIDING

With consistent but not overly strong winds, this region is particularly good for paragliding. Flights start at €65 for 20 minutes over the lagoon. The two companies following also offer various combinations of flights with diving, mountain biking and other activities.

Bourbon Parapente (☎ 02 62 34 18 34; www.bourbonparapente.com; Rue Général Lambert, St-Leu)

Réunion Parapente (☎ 02 62 24 87 84; www.parapente-reunion.fr in French; 103 Montée des Colimaçons, St-Leu)

RÉUNION

SURFING

Surfers should head for the mouth of the Ravine des Colimaçons, at the northern edge of St-Leu. There is a break in the reef that generates an impressive left-handed wave regarded as one of the best in the Indian Ocean. It's a tricky wave to master and amateurs are probably better off sticking to La-Saline-les-Bains or St-Gilles-les-Bains further up the coast. Local surfers had a reputation for intimidating new arrivals who wanted to try the wave, but things have calmed down recently and the fire coral below is likely to be more of a threat.

For all board-related problems and advice on the local scene, head to Aussie-owned **Mickey Rat** (☎ 02 62 34 79 00), behind the tourist office in St-Leu.

Sleeping & Eating

There are several peaceful villages within 10km of St-Leu that offer accommodation in a relaxed, rural setting. All the places listed below boast bird's-eye views down to the coast.

Mme Marie-Claire Vion (Bardzour; ☎ 02 62 34 13 97; www.bardzour.com in French; 22 Chemin Georges Thénor, Piton St-Leu (postal address); d €41, gîte per week from €317, dinner €18;) Three pretty and well-equipped *chambres d'hôte* and four *gîtes* set among orchards, where the evening meals are particularly good value. To find it, take the D11 towards Stella and Piton St-Leu, then continue to the very end of the lane.

M François Huet (☎ 02 62 54 76 70; 202 Chemin Potier, Bras Mouton; d from €35, table d'hôte from €17) Further uphill from the botanical garden, surrounded by a flower-filled garden, the four rooms here are sparkling and spacious. It's worth paying a little extra for a sea view.

M Albert Grollier (À l'Univers III; ☎ 02 62 24 94 27; www.univers111.com; 396 Rue Georges Pompidou, Les Colimaçons; s/d €51/55;) Just beyond the botanical gardens, a friendly couple offer two airy *chambres d'hôte* in an immaculate blue-and-white Creole-style house.

Entertainment

In a converted tobacco-drying shed in Piton St-Leu, **Le Séchoir** (☎ 02 62 34 31 38; le.sechoir@wanadoo.fr; Rue Adrien Lagourgue, Piton St-Leu) is one of Réunion's venues for contemporary theatre, dance and music, as well as puppet shows, circus acts and other cultural activities. Tickets and information are available from its St-Leu **office** (Le K, 209 Rue Général Lambert). The organisers also put on open-air concerts and film shows in the area.

LA-SALINE-LES-BAINS & AROUND

pop 2750

Heading north from St-Leu along the coast, the first town you come to is La-Saline-les-Bains. It's effectively a suburb of St-Gilles-les-Bains, but the atmosphere here is more mellow and there's a nice strip of beach.

The area is popular for windsurfing, especially for beginners. Boards can be rented from a couple of outfits along the beach: **Planch Alizé** (☎ 02 62 24 62 61) and **Club Nautique de l'Ouest** (☎ 02 62 33 95 62). The former also has canoes, pedalos and snorkelling gear for rent.

To the south of La-Saline, surfers gather at the mouth of the Ravine des Trois Bassins, where the waves are generally easier and more consistent than around St-Leu. A number of operators park their vans on the clifftop and offer board rental and lessons for adults and children.

Sleeping & Eating

Hôtel Swalibo (☎ 02 62 24 10 97; www.swalibo.com in French; 9 Rue des Salines; s/d from €86/109;) The nicest place to stay in La-Saline is this quiet three-star hotel with well-appointed rooms overlooking a garden and secluded pool. There's a restaurant and water sports are available. It's in the middle of La-Saline-les-Bains, across the main road from the beach.

Le Nautile (☎ 02 62 33 88 88; www.hotel-nautile.com; 60 Rue Lacaussade; s/d from €92/122;) For those that simply must be on the beach, the best option is this three-star hotel signed off the highway by the Champion supermarket. It's a bit expensive for what you get, however.

Copacabana (☎ 02 62 24 16 31; 20 Rue des Mouettes; mains €11-22; lunch daily, dinner Fri & Sat) This relaxed café-restaurant on the beach provides a varied menu of snacks and main meals and offers special deals including lunch and a sun lounger – so that you can sleep it off. There's occasionally a DJ or some sort of event on Friday or Saturday night.

ST-GILLES-LES-BAINS & L'HERMITAGE-LES-BAINS

pop 6000

Réunion's premier beach destination comes across as either a lively party place or an overhyped tourist trap, depending on your perspective. Certainly at the weekends St-Gilles-les-Bains can be ridiculously overcrowded, with packed restaurants, cramped beaches and all-day traffic snarls.

During the week, however, you shouldn't have to fight for a space to lay your towel, and the atmosphere is much more relaxed. As well as a nice beach, St-Gilles (as it's usually known) boasts an excellent selection of rest-aurants. There are numerous water activities on offer, from diving to deep-sea fishing. The surf here isn't bad either; many amateurs hone their skills in St-Gilles before attempting the more challenging swells at St-Leu.

If you find the scene in St-Gilles a little too much, there is a pleasantly uncrowded beach with good snorkelling at L'Hermitage-les-Bains, immediately to the south.

Orientation

Almost everything of interest in downtown St-Gilles is on Rue du Général de Gaulle, the former coastal highway. The main beach is Les Roches Noires. South of the centre at the mouth of the river is Port de Plaisance, a modern harbour complex with some expensive restaurants, water-sports operators and a good aquarium.

Information

For the widest choice of newspapers, guides and maps, go to **Point Presse** (☎ 02 62 24 23 77; Rue du Général de Gaulle) on the main road above the port.

You can log on to the Internet at **Cyberwave** (☎ 02 62 24 04 04; 37 Rue du Général de Gaulle; 10am-7pm Mon-Sat).

As for money, **Crédit Agricole** (Rue du Général de Gaulle) has an ATM and can change cash and travellers cheques in major currencies. There are also ATMs outside the **post office** (Rue de la Poste) and in L'Hermitage outside the casino and at the Score supermarket.

St-Gilles' **office du tourisme** (☎ 02 62 44 07 07; odt-saintpaul@wanadoo.fr; 1 Pl Paul-Julius Bénard, St-Gilles-les-Bains; 10am-6pm) is one of the most helpful on the island.

Sights & Activities

AQUARIUM DE RÉUNION

In the modern Port de Plaisance complex, the **aquarium** (☎ 02 62 33 44 00; fax 02 62 33 44 01; adult/child €7/5; 10am-6.30pm Tue-Sun) houses a series of excellent underwater displays, including tanks with lobsters, barracudas, groupers and small sharks. You should probably avoid the special exhibit on shark attacks if you're planning on taking a swim!

LE JARDIN D'EDEN

The name, which means Garden of Eden, may be selling it just a bit strong, but this unusual **botanical garden** (☎ 02 62 33 83 16; adult/child €6/3; 10am-6pm Tue-Sun) across the main highway from L'Hermitage is definitely worth an hour or so for anyone interested in tropical flora. Sections of the gardens are dedicated to interesting concepts such as the sacred plants of the Hindus, medicinal plants, edible tropical plants, spices and aphrodisiac plants. It's also a haven for birds and butterflies.

WATER ACTIVITIES

The attractive beach of Les Roches Noires, on the north side of town, is obviously the biggest pull at St-Gilles, closely followed by the surf scene.

If you fancy taking on the surf, various outlets here rent out longboards and bodyboards. Try the Rip Curl Pro Shop **Glissy** (☎ 02 62 33 13 13; b.glissy@guetali.fr; 15 Rue de la Plage) or nearby **High Surf** (☎ 02 62 24 24 24; 15 Rue de la Plage), both of which can also help with information about local surf clubs and any surf-related queries.

Fans of more equipment-intensive water sports should head to the harbour complex, where numerous operators offer diving, boat charter, deep-sea fishing and other watery activities (see p212).

Several glass-bottomed boats depart from the jetty beside the aquarium. **Visiobul** (☎ 02 62 24 37 04; www.visiobul-reunion.com in French; adult €12, child €7-10; 8-11am) offers a popular half-hour tour in an extraordinary little 'bubble boat' with a totally submerged viewing chamber; reservations are recommended. **Le Grand Bleu** (☎ 02 62 33 28 32; www.reunioncroisieres.com in French; adult/child €16/9.50; 8.30am-5pm) is a much larger glass-bottomed boat that runs hour-long cruises along the coast towards St-Leu or St-Paul (see p40 for more information on diving operators).

Tours

St-Gilles is a popular take-off spot for helicopter tours around the island (for details,

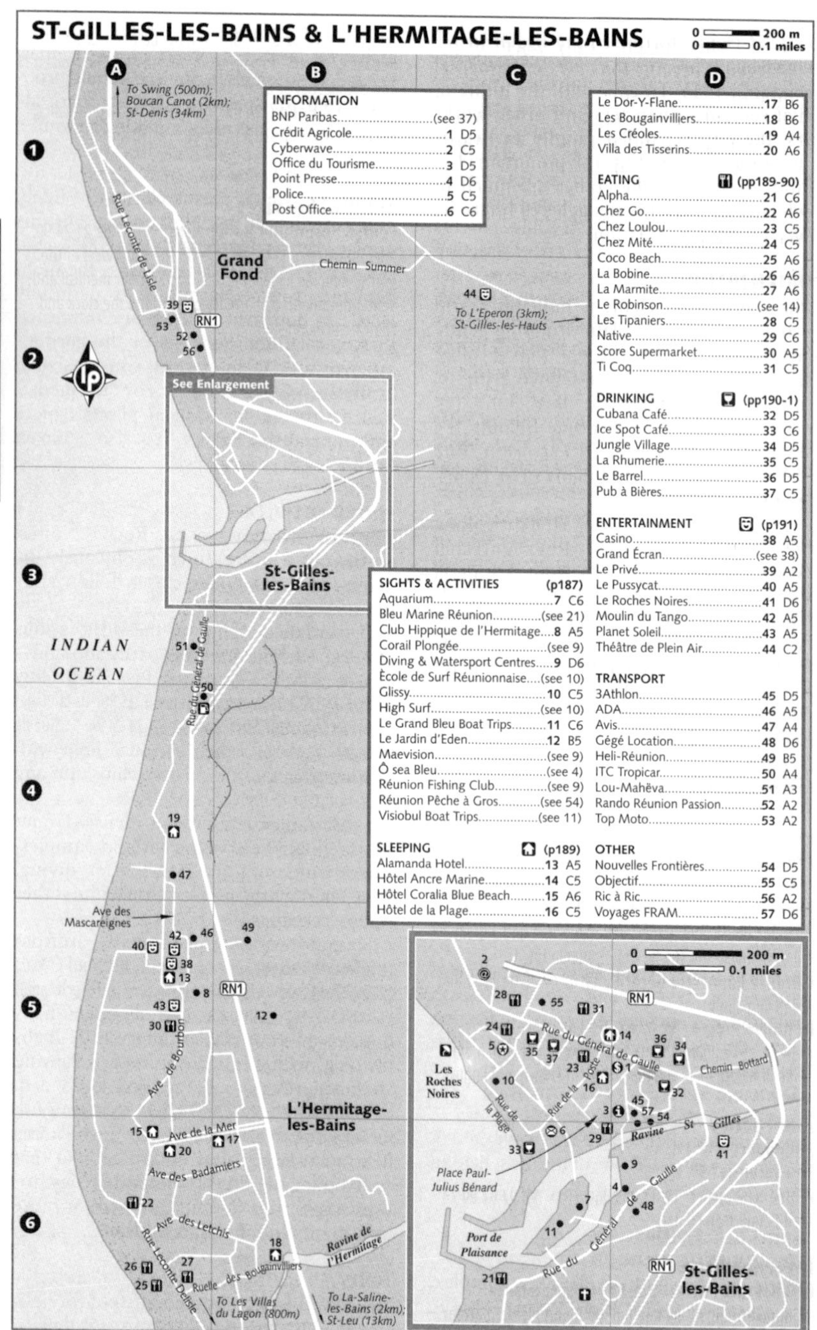
ST-GILLES-LES-BAINS & L'HERMITAGE-LES-BAINS
0 200 m
0 0.1 miles
To Swing (500m); Boucan Canot (2km); St-Denis (34km)
Rue Leconte de Lisle
Grand Fond
Chemin Summer
To L'Eperon (3km); St-Gilles-les-Hauts
See Enlargement
St-Gilles-les-Bains
INDIAN OCEAN
Rue du Général de Gaulle
Ave des Mascareignes
Ave de Bourbon
L'Hermitage-les-Bains
Ave de la Mer
Ave des Badamiers
Ave des Letchis
Rue Leconte Delisle
Ruelle des Bougainvilliers
Ravine de l'Hermitage
To Les Villas du Lagon (800m)
To La-Saline-les-Bains (2km); St-Leu (13km)
RN1
INFORMATION
BNP Paribas (see 37)
Crédit Agricole 1 D5
Cyberwave 2 C5
Office du Tourisme 3 D5
Point Presse 4 D6
Police 5 C5
Post Office 6 C6
SIGHTS & ACTIVITIES (p187)
Aquarium 7 C6
Bleu Marine Réunion (see 21)
Club Hippique de l'Hermitage 8 A5
Corail Plongée (see 9)
Diving & Watersport Centres 9 D6
Ècole de Surf Réunionnaise (see 10)
Glissy 10 C5
High Surf (see 10)
Le Grand Bleu Boat Trips 11 C6
Le Jardin d'Eden 12 B5
Maevision (see 9)
Ô sea Bleu (see 4)
Réunion Fishing Club (see 9)
Réunion Pêche à Gros (see 54)
Visiobul Boat Trips (see 11)
SLEEPING (p189)
Alamanda Hotel 13 A5
Hôtel Ancre Marine 14 C5
Hôtel Coralia Blue Beach 15 A6
Hôtel de la Plage 16 C5
Le Dor-Y-Flane 17 B6
Les Bougainvilliers 18 B6
Les Créoles 19 A4
Villa des Tisserins 20 A6
EATING (pp189-90)
Alpha 21 C6
Chez Go 22 A6
Chez Loulou 23 C5
Chez Mité 24 C5
Coco Beach 25 A6
La Bobine 26 A6
La Marmite 27 A6
Le Robinson (see 14)
Les Tipaniers 28 C5
Native 29 C6
Score Supermarket 30 A5
Ti Coq 31 C5
DRINKING (pp190-1)
Cubana Café 32 D5
Ice Spot Café 33 C6
Jungle Village 34 D5
La Rhumerie 35 C5
Le Barrel 36 D5
Pub à Bières 37 C5
ENTERTAINMENT (p191)
Casino 38 A5
Grand Écran (see 38)
Le Privé 39 A2
Le Pussycat 40 A5
Le Roches Noires 41 D6
Moulin du Tango 42 A5
Planet Soleil 43 A5
Théâtre de Plein Air 44 C2
TRANSPORT
3Athlon 45 D5
ADA 46 A5
Avis 47 A4
Gégé Location 48 D6
Heli-Réunion 49 B5
ITC Tropicar 50 A4
Lou-Mahëva 51 A3
Rando Réunion Passion 52 A2
Top Moto 53 A2
OTHER
Nouvelles Frontières 54 D5
Objectif 55 C5
Ric à Ric 56 A2
Voyages FRAM 57 D6
Les Roches Noires
Rue du Général de Gaulle
Rue de la Poste
Rue de la Plage
Chemin Bottard
Ravine St Gilles
Place Paul-Julius Bénard
Port de Plaisance
St-Gilles-les-Bains

see p219). A half/full day's tour prices start at around €30/60.

Tickets for Souprayenmestry coach tours (p219) are available from Chez Loulou (see Eating below). Travel agents in St-Gilles offer various coach tours of the island. Cilaos, Salazie and Piton de la Fournaise are popular destinations.

Objectif (☎ 02 62 33 08 33; objectif.reunion@wanadoo.fr; 28 Chemin Summer)

Nouvelles Frontières (☎ 02 62 33 11 95; www.nf-reunion.com in French; 31 Pl Paul-Julius Bénard)

Voyages FRAM (☎ 02 62 24 58 45; pdebiasi@fram.fr; Pl Paul-Julius Bénard)

Sleeping

There's plenty of accommodation in the area, but it tends to be quite pricey and almost everything is booked out during holiday periods and on weekends. There are a couple of cheapish places in St-Gilles itself which aren't too bad, but the more appealing hotels and guesthouses are in the countryside just north of town (see p192) or to the south in L'Hermitage-les-Bains.

ST-GILLES-LES-BAINS

Hôtel Ancre Marine (☎ 02 62 24 31 32; ancre.marine@wanadoo.fr; Le Forum, Rue du Général de Gaulle; d €43, apt from €57;) Above the mall in the middle of town, this nautical-themed hotel is better than it looks from the outside. It has a choice of good-value air-con rooms and two-bedroom self-catering apartments that sleep up to four people.

Hôtel de la Plage (☎ 02 62 24 06 37; fax 02 62 33 20 05; 20 Rue de la Poste; r from €30, with bathroom from €39;) This fairly hip place on the road down to the beach has marine murals on the walls and a range of rooms from rather pricey boxes with shared facilities to more acceptable rooms with bathroom and TV. The upstairs terrace is a bonus

L'HERMITAGE-LES-BAINS

Budget

Villa des Tisserins (☎/fax 02 62 33 15 23; 25 Ave de la Mer; r from €35;) A laid-back guesthouse on the main road down to L'Hermitage beach with a garden and good-sized pool. There's a choice of rooms for two to four people and a self-contained bungalow.

Le Dor-Y-Flane (☎ 02 62 33 82 41; fax 02 62 33 98 52, 21 Ave de la Mer; r €31, with bathroom €38;) Near the Villa des Tisserins, this is a popular budget option, though it's worth paying the extra for your own bathroom. Guests can use the communal kitchen.

Les Bougainvilliers (☎ 02 62 33 82 48; www.bougainvillier.com; 27 Ruelle des Bougainvilliers; r from €37;) This cheerful guesthouse on the east side of L'Hermitage-les-Bains offers nine rooms. Those upstairs are more basic (no air-con or toilet) and some cop a bit of road noise from the highway. Kitchen facilities are available.

Mid-Range & Top End

Alamanda Hotel (☎ 02 62 33 10 10; www.alamanda.fr; 81 Ave de Bourbon; s/d from €50/64;) With its Creole architecture, garden and bright, modern rooms (all with TV, phone and air-con), this two-star provides for a very agreeable stay, though make sure you're overlooking the garden, not the car park. It has a decent restaurant with some form of entertainment most weekends.

Les Villas du Lagon (☎ 02 62 70 00 00; www.villas-du-lagon.com in French; 28 Rue du Lagon; s/d from €120/140;) At the very south end of the beach at L'Hermitage, this luxury hotel with its verandas, cane chairs and colonnaded villas set among the palms plays the colonial card. Three restaurants, a big pool and all sorts of activities, including a kids' club, round out the picture.

Les Créoles (☎ 02 62 33 09 09; sehb@oceanes.fr; Ave de Bourbon; s/d from €85/120;) This is a small and attractive three-star place with airy rooms in little Creole villas. Facilities include a good-sized pool, a restaurant (dinner only) and a bar.

Hôtel Coralia Blue Beach (☎ 02 62 24 50 25; H1126@accor-hotels.com; Ave de la Mer; s/d from €98/130, apt from €182;) While this hotel feels a bit cramped, with buildings completely encircling the pool, the rooms aren't bad. An added attraction is access to facilities at the big Novotel Coralia across the road: these comprise water sports, spacious grounds, entertainment and kids' club.

Eating

St-Gilles is well endowed with eating places, and new restaurants are constantly opening up. As a result of the continuous flow of hungry tourists, standards tend to be more variable than elsewhere on the island.

Good areas to browse include Pl Paul-Julius Bénard, with its cafés and *crêperies* (pancake houses), the beach end of Rue de la Poste, and around the harbour. For cheap eats, try the snack vans along Rue du Général de Gaulle and on the seafront behind Les Roches Noires beach. Self-caterers will find most of what they need in the supermarkets along Rue du Général de Gaulle in St-Gilles and in the big Score supermarket in L'Hermitage. A few market stalls are set up on St-Gilles' Pl Paul-Julius Bénard on Wednesday morning.

ST-GILLES-LES-BAINS

Chez Loulou (☎ 02 62 24 40 41; Rue du Général de Gaulle; 7am-1pm & 3-7pm) This bakery sells tasty samosas, cakes and sandwiches as well as takeaway meals.

Ti Coq (☎ 02 62 33 22 98; 79 Rue du Général de Gaulle; mains €10-27; lunch & dinner Mon-Sat) Tucked off the main road, this garden restaurant is the best choice all-round for atmosphere, value and a warm welcome. Though you can opt for more pricey métro dishes, it would be a shame to miss out on a curry served on a banana leaf with all the trimmings. For afters, try the platter of Creole cakes.

Chez Mité (☎ 02 62 24 22 92; 6 Rue de la Plage; meals around €7; lunch & dinner Mon-Sat) This spick-and-span canteen-style restaurant has a choice of very affordable salads and curries. It's best to eat there on fine days when you can sit in the little garden.

Les Tipaniers (☎ 02 62 24 44 87; 58b Rue du Général de Gaulle; mains €12-26; lunch Mon & Wed-Fri, dinner daily except Tue;) Also known as Chez Dante after its charismatic patron, Les Tipaniers is full of arty clutter and makes a good choice for an intimate dinner. The food is a cut above the norm, well presented and innovative, ranging from fresh fish through Creole to métro dishes.

Native (☎ 02 62 33 19 24; Pl Paul-Julius Bénard; mains €11-20, set lunch €10; lunch & dinner daily except Tue) This classy place, which doubles as an interior-design shop, offers upmarket métro fare, such as frogs' legs with honey or apricot, and pistachio tart, and an atmosphere to match – teak tables and mellow music, with candles at night.

Other recommendations:

Alpha (☎ 02 62 24 02 02; Port de Plaisance; mains around €13; lunch & dinner Tue-Sun) Good fish restaurant down by the port. Ask what the catch of the day is.

Le Robinson (☎ 02 62 24 21 79; Le Forum, Rue du Général de Gaulle; mains €7-9; 10am-2am) Friendly and good-value café-restaurant in the shopping mall.

L'HERMITAGE-LES-BAINS

La Marmite (☎ 02 62 33 31 37; 34 Blvd Leconte de Lisle; buffet €15; dinner Mon-Sat) La Marmite is well known among locals for its excellent buffet of traditional Creole dishes – you'll need a hearty appetite to do it justice. The setting, in a plant-filled courtyard lit by candles and fairylights, adds a romantic touch.

Coco Beach (☎ 02 62 33 81 43; Blvd Leconte de Lisle; mains €12-22; lunch & dinner) Right on the beach, this happening restaurant-cum-bar offers a tropical garden atmosphere and an eclectic menu, from salads and grills to Creole curries and 'tapas' (platters of local tidbits, served evenings only). Although prices are a little above average, the quality is good.

La Bobine (☎ 02 62 33 94 36; Blvd Leconte de Lisle; mains from €10; lunch & dinner) This is another popular beachfront choice with a varied menu, including a wide range of salads. Its grills and ultra-fresh fish get most people's vote. The couscous, usually served on Sunday, is a bit of a treat.

Chez Go (☎ 02 62 33 82 61; 7 Blvd Leconte de Lisle; mains €11-15; lunch & dinner Wed-Sun) Though not big on atmosphere, Chez Go serves reasonable Chinese and Creole fare in its main restaurant, while at lunch time beach-goers queue up for sandwiches and other takeaway meals.

Drinking

As one would imagine, St-Gilles is relatively flush with cafés and bars. You'll find them concentrated along Rue du Général de Gaulle, on Pl Paul-Julius Bénard and around the harbour. There's also a clutch of cafés overlooking Les Roches Noires beach.

Ice Spot Café (☎ 02 62 33 26 77; Rue de la Plage; daily) A great spot for an ice cream or a sunset drink while checking out the Roches Noires surf scene.

Jungle Village (☎ 02 62 33 21 93; Rue du Général de Gaulle; 7pm-4am Tue-Sun) It's hard to miss the log-cabin exterior – not to mention the monkey mannequin – of this hugely popular bar on St-Gilles' main drag. The ground-floor bar is young and cool with a disco ambience. Upstairs is far more mellow.

Cubana Café (☎ 02 62 33 24 91; 122 Rue du Général de Gaulle; 9am-2am Mon-Sat) Across the road from the Jungle Village, the terrace here is a popular meeting place. There are events most nights; it's always worth dropping by to see what's on.

Le Barrel (129 Rue du Général de Gaulle; 6pm-2am) Cosy little bar that's worth a look for its bizarre mix of gothic mirrors and surfer memorabilia.

Coco Beach (☎ 02 62 33 81 43; Blvd Leconte de Lisle) This beachside restaurant in L'Hermitage is packed on Sunday evening, when there's live music.

Other recommendations:

Le Rhumerie (☎ 02 62 24 55 99; 68 Rue du Général de Gaulle; 7.30am-9pm) Old-fashioned, down-to-earth bar serving a mean *rhum arrangé*.

Pub à Bières (☎ 02 62 33 16 65; 80 Rue du Général de Gaulle; 4pm-2am) Fifty different Belgian beers, billiards and a youngish crowd.

Entertainment

St-Gilles is by far and away the capital of Réunion's disco scene. In addition, there's a cinema, theatre and casino. For details about what's currently happening in town, ask locals or at the tourist office.

CASINO

Casino de St-Gilles (☎ 02 62 24 47 00; 7 Ave des Mascareignes; admission to gaming tables €10; slot machines 10am-2am, gaming tables from 9pm) St-Gilles' casino is at the north end of L'Hermitage and offers blackjack, American roulette and poker.

CINEMA

Grand Écran (☎ 02 62 24 46 66; Ave des Mascareignes;) Two to three screenings a day of mainstream releases in French.

DISCOS

This area has a greater density of discos than anywhere else on the island. Check the flyers posted around town or ask the locals to find out which clubs are the flavour of the month.

Le Privé (☎ 02 62 24 04 17; www.le-prive.fr in French; 1 Rue du Général de Gaulle; 11pm-5am) Le Privé is *the* party place in Réunion; very lively, a very young crowd and with events most nights, such as ladies night on Tuesday (free admission and drinks for women) and half-price drinks and '80s music on Thursday.

Moulin du Tango (☎ 02 62 24 53 90; www.moulin-du-tango.fr; 9 Ave des Mascareignes; admission €13; 10pm-5am Wed, Fri & Sat) This self-styled 'retro' dance club in L'Hermitage aims for an older clientele. It's a big place with two open-air dance floors and three bars and hosts a wide range of events.

Planet Soleil (☎ 02 62 33 15 00; Ave de Bourbon; admission €13; 11pm-5am Fri & Sat) Another crowd-puller in L'Hermitage, again with two dance floors (one open-air) but a more eclectic play list.

Other recommendations:

Le Pussycat (☎ 02 62 24 05 11; Ave de Bourbon; admission men/women €14/free; 10.30pm-5am Fri & Sat) Indoor dance floor and mainly techno on the turntable.

Le Roches Noires (☎ 02 62 24 44 15; 151 Rue du Général de Gaulle; admission €10; 10.30pm-5am Sat) Popular with the local crowd.

Le Swing (☎ 02 62 24 45 98; Grand-Fond; admission men/women €11/13; 10pm-5am Fri, Sat & Sun) Big club to the north of St-Gilles.

THEATRE

On the road between St-Gilles-les-Bains and St-Gilles-les-Hauts, the modern open-air **Théâtre de Plein Air** (☎ 02 62 24 47 71) is styled after Greek amphitheatres, and has the sky and ocean as a backdrop. The St-Gilles tourist office can provide the programme and make bookings for you.

Getting There & Away

Car Jaune's nonexpress buses between St-Denis and St-Pierre (lines B and C) run though the centre of St-Gilles, stopping along Rue du Général de Gaulle and along the main highway behind L'Hermitage. Buses run about every half-hour in either direction from 5am to 6pm. The trip to St-Denis takes at least one hour and costs around €3.

Getting Around

CAR & MOTORCYCLE

Of the big international car-rental agencies, both Avis and ADA have outlets in St-Gilles; see p221 for details. There are also numerous local operators. Those listed below have reasonable prices and a good reputation.

Gégé Location (☎ 02 62 24 59 77; gege.location@wanadoo.fr; 167 Rue du Générale de Gaulle)

ITC Tropicar (☎ 02 62 24 01 01; www.itctropicar.com; 207 Rue du Générale de Gaulle)

Lou-Mahëva (☎ 02 62 24 40 96; 208 Rue du Générale de Gaulle)

As for motorbike rental, **Top Moto** (☎ 02 62 24 25 78; www.topmoto.fr in French; 2 Rue du Général de

RÉUNION

Gaulle) is a helpful place offering a range of bikes from 125cc to 750cc.

BOUCAN CANOT

pop 2000

Just north of St-Gilles-les-Bains, the village of Boucan Canot (the final 't' is pronounced) boasts a great beach and good surf. It's become a very chic place for day-trippers to hang out, so you may struggle to find a parking spot on weekends. There are a number of exclusive hotels here, but few budget places to stay or eat.

Sleeping

Hôtel La Villa Du Soleil (☎ 02 62 24 38 69; www.lavilladusoleil.com; 54 Route de Boucan Canot; s/d from €39/46;) This cheerful, family-run hotel on the southern skirts of Boucan Canot and St-Gilles is the cheapest in town. It has small but well-kept rooms with a private bathroom for one or two people.

Résidence Les Boucaniers (☎ 02 62 24 23 89; www.les-boucaniers.com in French; 29 Rue du Boucan Canot; studio/apt from €69/93;) Overlooking the beach, this complex offers a variety of well-maintained self-catering studios (for up to three people) and apartments (for up to five). They all have a sea view from a terrace or balcony.

Le Boucan-Canot (☎ 02 62 33 44 44; www.boucancanot.com; 32 Rue du Boucan Canot; s/d from €120/146;) A very stylish hotel at the north end of the beach mixing Creole and contemporary design. The rooms boast all the three-star comforts you'd expect and it has two restaurants and a bar with entertainment most nights.

Senteur Vanille (☎ 06 92 78 13 05; www.senteurvanille.com; Route du Théâtre; bungalow/chalet from €60/72;) Away from the hubbub of the coast, this working farm offers a number of very well-equipped self-catering chalets set deep among orchards, and older but rather sweet Creole bungalows surrounded by flowers. You have to stay a minimum of three nights. It's signed down a lane beside the Total petrol station.

Hôtel La Rocaille (☎ 02 62 33 29 29; www.hotellarocaille.com; 45 Chemin des Lantanas; s/d from €62/69;) On the same lane as Senteur Vanille, La Rocaille is a modern hotel with a quiet garden and rooms that are smallish but nevertheless well kept and perfectly comfortable. There's the option of self-catering. Rooms upstairs with a sea view are the most sought after.

Eating

There's a clutch of snack stands and laid-back café-restaurants along the seafront promenade.

Bambou Bar & Grill (☎ 02 62 24 59 29; Rue du Boucan Canot; mains €10-30; lunch Wed-Sun, dinner Tue-Sun) Boasting a touch more ambience than the competition, this place on the promenade is best known for its grills, but also does a good range of Creole and métro mains.

Le Victory (☎ 02 62 24 47 74; 29 Rue du Boucan Canot; mains €8-17; lunch & dinner) The restaurant at Résidence Les Boucaniers (left) is a more ordinary place. It serves up everything from pizzas to seafood and has a range of good-value set menus; the cold buffet lunch (€9.70) is a popular choice.

ST-GILLES-LES-HAUTS & AROUND

pop 2000

If beaches aren't really your thing, there are several attractions up in the hills around St-Gilles-les-Hauts. This peaceful village, 6km above St-Gilles-les-Bains, offers a refreshing break from the commercialism of the coast. It also makes a good base for an early-morning start up to Le Maïdo (opposite). There are several options for accommodation in the small hamlets that dot the hillside above St-Gilles-les-Hauts.

The villages of St-Gilles-les-Hauts, Villèle, L'Éperon and Bernica can all be reached by fairly infrequent minibuses operated by **Réseau Pastel** (☎ 02 62 22 54 65) out of St-Paul.

Musée de Villèle

South of St-Gilles-les-Hauts on the D6, this **museum** (☎ 02 62 55 64 10; admission €2; 9.30am-5.30pm Tue-Sun) is set in the former home of the wealthy and very powerful Madame Panon-Desbassyns (the name originated because the family's turf surrounded the *bassins*, or lakes, above St-Gilles-les-Bains). She was a coffee- and sugar-baroness who, among other things, owned 300 slaves. Legend has it that she was a cruel woman and that her tormented screams can still be heard from the hellish fires whenever Piton de la Fournaise is erupting. She died in 1846 and her body lies in the **Chapelle Pointue**, a pretty little chapel she had built a few years earlier; it stands on the D6 by the entrance to the museum.

The house itself, which is only accessible on a guided tour (in French only), was built in 1787 and is full of elegant period furniture. Exhibits include a clock presented to the Desbassyns by Napoleon; a set of china featuring *Paul et Virginie*, the love story by Bernardin de St-Pierre (p85); and, last but not least, a portrait of Madame Panon-Desbassyns in a red turban looking surprisingly impish.

After the tour, you're free to wander the outbuildings and the 10-hectare park, which contains the ruins of the sugar mill.

Village Artisanal de L'Éperon

Housed in a picturesque old grist mill in the village of L'Éperon, the Village Artisanal de L'Éperon is home to a small community of artists and artisans. Among the more interesting is the sculptor Guy Trichet, who hosts exhibitions of local artists at his **Galerie Noir et Blanc** (☎ 02 62 22 96 57; galerienoireetblanc@cheminements.org) at the top end of the village. There are also a number of boutiques selling ceramics, locally tanned leather and other *objets d'art*.

Sleeping & Eating

Mme Edith Ramassamy (☎ 02 62 55 55 06; ramassamy.anthony@wanadoo.fr; 100 Chemin des Roses; s/d €23/31, meals €18) Signed from opposite the Chapelle Pointue is this welcoming *chambre d'hôte* with five spick-and-span rooms. It offers good-value *table d'hôte* meals. M Ramassamy, who also acts as a mountain guide, is a mine of information on the local area.

Mme Marie-Thérèse Ramincoupin (☎ 02 62 55 69 13; 18 Chemin Bosse; d €41, meals from €15) Just off the main road in Bernica, Madame Ramincoupin is a motherly soul who has two sweet *chambres d'hôte* and also offers *table d'hôte* in the evening.

Auberge de Jeunesse (☎ /fax 02 62 22 89 75; Rue de l'Auberge; dm €13, breakfast/dinner €2/8.50) A modern youth hostel in the centre of Bernica with 29 dorm beds.

L'Imprevu (☎ 02 62 55 36 34; 72 Rue Joseph Hubert; mains €10-15; 🕑 lunch Mon-Fri, dinner Mon-Sat) The best place to eat in St-Gilles-les-Hauts itself is this jolly little restaurant on the main road. It serves excellent Creole meals as well as salads, pizzas and other métro fare.

LE MAÏDO & AROUND

Far above St-Gilles-les-Bains on the rim of the Cirque de Mafate, Le Maïdo is one of the most impressive viewpoints in Réunion. The lookout is perched atop the mountain peak at 2205m and offers stunning views down into the cirque and back to the coast. As with other viewpoints, you should arrive early in the day – by 7am if possible – if you want to see anything other than cloud.

The name Le Maïdo comes from a Malagasy word meaning 'burnt land', and is most likely a reference to the burnt appearance of the scrub forest at this altitude. The peak is the starting point for the tough walk along the cirque rim to the summit of Le Grand Bénare (2896m), another impressive lookout (allow at least six hours for the return trip). Hikers can also descend from Le Maïdo into the Cirque de Mafate via the Sentier de Roche Plate, which meets the GR R2 variant that connects the villages of Roche Plate and Îlet des Orangers (allow three hours to reach Roche Plate). Ambitious walkers can head in the direction of Îlet des Orangers and down to the hamlet of Sans Souci near Le Port for a very long day's walk (at least eight hours).

There are a few attractions for nonwalkers in the area too. On the way down the mountain you could stop off at the Begue family's **L'Alambic** (☎ 02 62 32 47 66; admission free; 🕑 7.30am-6pm Mon-Sat, 10.30am-6pm Sun) in La Petite France to see a traditional distillery producing essential oils from geranium, cryptomeria and vetiver leaves.

Further down again is the **Centre Équestre du Maïdo** (☎ 02 62 32 49 15; fax 02 62 32 43 10; horse riding per hour €16; 🕑 Wed, Sat & Sun school term, daily school holidays). Among various horse-riding treks, the most popular outing is a full day's excursion up to Le Maïdo and along the crest.

Sleeping & Eating

Parc Hôtel du Maïdo (☎ 02 62 32 52 52; www.hotelmaido.com; Route du Maïdo; s/d €64/83) Six kilometres below Le Maïdo on the road to St-Gilles, this appealing hotel provides an excellent base for walkers. It offers accommodation in cosy bungalows with panoramic views of the coast. The restaurant offers good Creole and European dishes from around €12 and a popular buffet lunch on Sunday (€22); it's best to reserve.

Mme Rose Magdeleine (☎ 02 62 32 53 50; Chemin de l'École; s/d €23/34, gîte per week €300, meals €15) Just off the main road in La Petite France you'll find this smart, well-run place with four *chambres d'hôte* and a *gîte* for up to four people.

Chez Doudou (☎ 02 62 32 55 87; 394 Route de Maïdo; set menus €16 & 22; ⏰ lunch daily except Wed) 'Doudou' is a jovial character who is passionate about his food. He produces magnificent Creole curries slow-cooked over a wood fire and served with all the traditional accompaniments. The restaurant is on the main road in Le Petite France. Phone ahead to be sure of a table.

Bar Chez Louise (⏰ 7am-4pm) This snack stand in the car park at Le Maïdo is a boon for walkers. You can get sandwiches and hot drinks and it even does breakfast.

Getting There & Around

The sealed Route Forestière du Maïdo winds all the way up to the viewpoint from Le Guillaume in the hills above St-Gilles-les-Bains, offering a long but scenic drive. If you're walking from here, it's not recommended that you leave your car at Le Maïdo overnight.

Réseau Pastel runs three buses a day (Monday to Saturday) taking walkers from St-Paul to the start of the Sentier du Maïdo, the footpath into the Cirque de Mafate, which strikes off the road about 4km below the summit. The first bus up the hill leaves at 6am and the last one down is at 5.20pm. The journey takes one hour and costs €2.60.

Cycling enthusiasts can whoosh down to the coast by mountain bike along special biking trails. Various companies offer packages including bike hire and transport to the start; some also include a guide. Try **Rando Réunion Passion** (☎ 02 62 24 25 19; www.vttreunion.com; 13 Rue du Général de Gaulle) or **3Athlon** (☎ 02 62 24 55 56; www.3athloncycles.com in French; 1 Pl Paul-Julius Bénard) in St-Gilles-les-Bains, or contact **Télénavette** (☎ 06 92 21 11 11; www.descente-vtt.com in French). Packages cost around €35 to €40.

ST-PAUL

pop 20,000

St-Paul is Réunion's second-largest *commune* after St-Denis. Although it was once the capital of Réunion, these days it is merely a lively shopping centre and a place for locals rather than for tourists.

> **PERFUMED ISLE**
>
> In keeping with the French love of perfume, Réunion has long been the garden of the great fragrance houses of Paris. Essential oils, which are used as a fixative in perfumes, are extracted from roots or leaves. The mainstays of the essential-oil business are vetiver (an Asian grass), geranium and the evocative ylang-ylang, which you can often smell in the night air all over the island. All are cultivated in the hills, and the oils are extracted in traditional distilleries that look like they could also be used for moonshine whisky! It is still a cottage industry, concentrated mainly around Le Maïdo and Le Tampon. The cultivation of these plants is in slow decline, but certain Parisian perfumiers still insist on the best oils from Réunion for their fragrances.

Most tourists who do come here simply visit the Cimetière Marin, which lies on the highway at the south end of St-Paul, but for those with time to spare the centre is worth a quick wander to soak up a bit of local atmosphere. There are a few relics from the town's past on the seafront promenade, which is also the venue for a huge market all day on Friday and on Saturday morning.

Cimetière Marin

The only real attraction in St-Paul is the bright and well-kept cemetery at the southern end of town, which contains the remains of various famous Réunionnais, including the poet Leconte de Lisle (1818–94). The graves are clearly marked and signposted, making them easy to find.

The cemetery's star guest, however, is the pirate Olivier 'La Buse' Levasseur (The Buzzard), who was the scourge of the Indian Ocean from about 1720 to 1730, when he was captured, taken to St-Paul and hanged. His biggest catch was the Portuguese treasure ship *La Vierge du Cap*; people are still searching for the location of La Buse's treasure in Mauritius, Réunion and the Seychelles (see Pieces of Eight, p252).

The grave is marked by the pirates' trademark skull and crossbones, and it is sometimes covered with *remerciement* (thank you) plaques, cigarettes and glasses of rum, deposited by superstitious Réunionnais as part of black-magic rituals.

Another interesting grave is that of Eraste Feuillet (1801–30), who died because he took a sense of remorse too far. The young sea captain accidentally struck a passer-by with an empty toilet-water bottle that he threw from his hotel room window (perhaps forgetting he was on dry land). The irate passer-by challenged Feuillet to a duel, but fortunately, his pistol jammed. Less fortunately, Feuillet had a sense of honour and offered his own weapon as a replacement – and the bugger accepted it! Feuillet's epitaph reads very simply *'Victime de sa générosité'* ('Victim of his generosity').

Eating

There are snack stands around the bus station but a nicer option is the snack bar **La Bergère** (☎ 02 62 45 13 07; Pl Foraine; mains around €7 lunch & dinner) on the seafront market place, which serves decent sandwiches, salads and quick meals. For something smarter, head a couple of blocks inland to **La Proue** (☎ 02 62 45 01 80; 93 Rue Marius & Ary Leblond; mains €7-12; lunch & dinner;). This cheerful little café-restaurant specialises in build-your-own sweet and savoury pancakes and salads, and offers a good choice of children's menus.

Getting There & Away

St-Paul lies on Car Jaune's bus route between St-Denis (€2.70) and St-Pierre (€4.30). There are express buses every one to two hours in either direction (fewer on Sunday) and much more frequent nonexpress services. If you just want to go to the cemetery, there's a bus stop immediately by the main entrance.

The local bus company **Réseau Pastel** (☎ 02 62 22 54 65) operates fairly infrequent services to villages up in the hills such as Bernica, Petite France, Villèle and L'Éperon. There's also a special bus for walkers up to the start of the footpath into the Cirque de Mafate (the Sentier du Maïdo) daily except Sunday.

DOS D'ANE

The isolated village of Dos d'Ane, in the hills above Le Port, is an excellent base for hikes in the interior. From here you can walk to the Plaine d'Affouches and La Roche Écrite, as well as into the Cirque de Mafate via the Rivière des Galets route. An easy day's walk from Dos d'Ane will get you to the *gîte de montagne* at Grand Place, while a magnificent but more challenging route will take you up the beautiful Bras des Merles to Aurère. For a shorter ramble, there are superb views to be had from the Roche Verre Bouteille lookout, less than an hour's walk from the Cap Noir car park above Dos d'Ane.

SLEEPING & EATING

M Axel Nativel (Les Acacias; ☎ 02 62 32 02 34; fax 02 62 32 06 51; Rue Germain Elisabeth; dm/r €14/38, breakfast €4, dinner from €17) Offering two *chambres d'hôte* and a 15-bed *gîte d'étape*, this is a good cheap option for hikers. The hearty evening meals go down well after a day's tramping.

Mme Raymonde Pignolet (Le Cap Noir; ☎ 02 62 32 00 82; 3 Allée Pignolet; d €40, meals €18) A short walk up the road to Cap Noir from Dos d'Ane is this welcoming *chambre d'hôte* with four spacious rooms and great views. It also serves excellent homecooking.

Le Ben Île (☎ 02 62 32 01 39; 4 Chemin du Cap Noir; 2-course meal €12.20; lunch) There's no menu at this spick-and-span little restaurant by the turn off for Cap Noir. Just sit down and you'll get fed. A typical meal consists of cold meats, salad, a choice of main dishes (such as roast chicken or *rougail saucisses*) and home-made cakes to follow. The kindly owners also sell sandwiches, hot meals and drinks from their snack van in the Cap Noir car park from 8am to 4pm daily.

GETTING THERE & AWAY

To get to Dos d'Ane by public transport you'll have to change buses in Le Port. All nonexpress and some express buses between St-Pierre and St-Denis stop at the Le Port bus station. From there, Bus No 8a operated by **Bus Fleuri** (☎ 02 62 75 22 22) will take you to Dos D'Ane. There are six buses a day from Monday to Saturday but only three on Sunday.

THE INTERIOR

Like the leaves of a three-leaf clover, the cirques of Cilaos, Salazie and Mafate dominate the interior of the island. The whole island was once the dome of a vast prehistoric shield volcano, centred on Piton des

Neiges, but the collapse of subterranean lava chambers formed the starting point for the creation of the cirques. Millions of years of rainfall and erosion did the rest, scouring out the amphitheatres that are visible today.

Evidence of the forces that shaped the island can still be seen around Piton de la Fournaise, a volcano which rumbles away in the southeast corner of Réunion and which regularly spews lava down its flanks. Between the volcano and the cirques lies the region known as Les Hautes Plaines (the High Plains). The plains present a much gentler scene of dairy herds and rolling meadows and provide the corridor for the only road across the island.

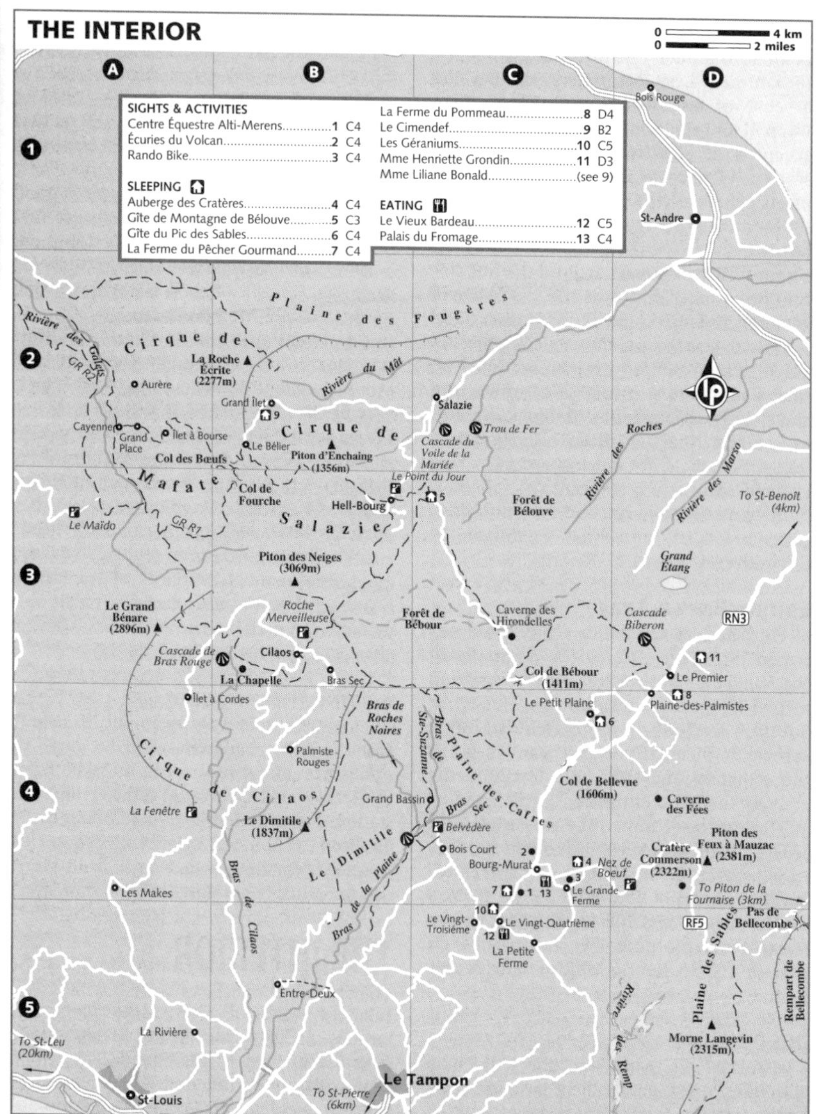

Until recently, however, the interior was a largely inaccessible and hostile place. It first began to be settled by runaway slaves or *marrons* in the 18th century, and their descendants still inhabit some of the wild remote villages of the cirques. If the coast seems a little too close to mainland France, the cirques are where you'll find the real identity of Réunion.

The whole region is a tremendous hiking ground, with breathtaking mountain scenery and the opportunity to indulge in any kind of adventure sport taking your fancy. It's up to you how far you take the thrills and spills; if abseiling down a waterfall seems too much like hard work, there are dozens of easy walks where you can just soak up the awe-inspiring environment around you. (For detailed information on hiking in the Interior, see p224. For information on the other adventure activities on offer, see p212)

Even if you don't fancy hiking through the cirques, it's worth taking a road trip through these amazing amphitheatres just for the views. Whether you come by bus or private car, you will have to negotiate corkscrew turns, narrow tunnels and precarious viaducts. The locals treat these roads like mountain motorways, so be prepared to pull over and let others whiz past.

The landscape here is other-worldly and surreal, sometimes revealed in all its breathtaking splendour and other times hidden by swirling banks of cloud. If you see a photo opportunity, snap it up immediately; the chances are it will be enveloped in cloud if you wait even a few minutes.

MARRONS

Perhaps from a sense of shame, until recently there has been little mention made in Réunion of the earliest settlers of the rugged interior of the island. During the 18th century, a number of resourceful Malagasy and African slaves escaped from their owners and forged the first inroads into this unforgiving environment. Some of them established private utopias in inaccessible parts of the cirques, while others grouped together and formed organised communities with democratically elected leaders.

Sadly this sense of liberty was to be short-lived. Most of the renegades or *marrons* were hunted down and captured or killed by bounty hunters such as François Mussard, lending their names to the locations where they made their last stands, such as Mafate and Enchaing.

The Maison du Peuplement des Hauts in Cilaos and Salazie's Ecomusée provide excellent introductions to these sensitive subjects, tracing the history of slavery and '*marronage*' and celebrating the achievements of these unsung heroes of the cirques.

CIRQUE DE CILAOS

Cilaos

pop 6000

The largest settlement in any of the cirques is Cilaos, high in the cirque of the same name, which developed as a spa resort at the end of the 19th century. The town's fortunes still rest on tourism, and particularly hiking, backed up by agriculture and the fast-growing bottled mineral water industry. The area is known for the production of lentils, embroidery and increasingly palatable red and white wines.

The name, pronounced 'see-*la*-oos', is thought to be derived from the Malagasy term *tsy laosana* (place from which one never returns). These days, most people come to Cilaos to leave the town, on foot, to climb Piton des Neiges and hike over into the cirques of Mafate and Salazie. There are also plenty of shorter walks in the area and a number of museums and other attractions for nonwalkers. In any case, it's worth lingering in Cilaos at least a couple of days to make the most of the laid-back atmosphere and the wealth of accommodation and eating options.

ORIENTATION

Rue du Père Boiteau, which runs to the tourist office, is the main shopping street, with grocery stores, a pharmacy, a post office and several restaurants. At the far end the white bell tower of Cilaos church provides a useful landmark. Accommodation is widely scattered; unless you've got your own transport, choose somewhere central.

INFORMATION

There aren't any banks in Cilaos. There is an ATM which accepts Visa and MasterCard at the post office, but don't rely on it

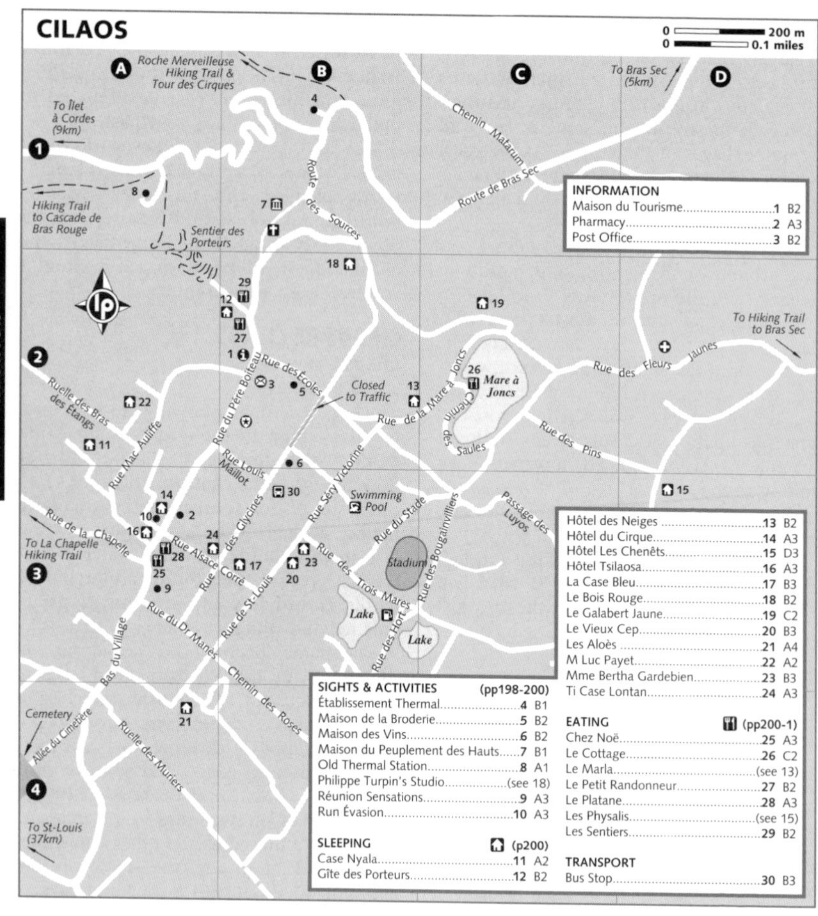

completely: it occasionally breaks down or runs out of euros.

Maison du Tourisme (☎ 02 62 31 71 71 71; mmocilaos@wanadoo.fr; 2 Rue Mac Auliffe; 🕑 8.30am-12.30pm & 1.30-5.30pm Mon-Sat, 9am-noon Sun) The tourism office is particularly helpful, with multilingual staff who provide reliable information about local and long-distance walks and dispense lists of accommodation, restaurants and activities. You can also book *gîtes de montagne* here. A free slide presentation about Cilaos is held here every evening except Sunday.

SIGHTS

Maison du Peuplement des Hauts

Close to Cilaos church, this informative **museum** (☎ 02 62 31 88 01; fax 02 62 31 81 56; 5 Chemin du Séminaire; adult/child €5.50/3.20; 🕑 10am-noon & 2.30-6.30pm Mon-Sat, 9.30-11.30am & 1.30-4.30pm Sun) is dedicated to the escaped slaves who first settled the hostile landscape of the cirques. The displays are imaginative and provide a much-needed monument to the unsung Creole heroes of Réunion (see Marrons p197). Although visitors can wander on their own, it's well worth taking a guided tour (at no extra charge); the staff are knowledgeable and enthusiastic.

Maison de la Broderie

The originator of Cilaos' embroidery tradition was Angèle Mac Auliffe, the daughter of the town's first doctor of thermal medicine. Looking for a pastime to fill the long, damp days in the cirque, Angèle established the first embroidery workshop with 20 women producing what later evolved into a distinctive Cilaos style of embroidery.

Nowadays, the **Maison de la Broderie** (☎ 02 62 31 77 48; fax 02 62 31 80 38; Rue des Écoles; admission €1; 9.30am-noon & 2-5pm Mon-Sat, 9.30-noon Sun) is home to an association of 30 or so local women dedicated to keeping the craft alive. They embroider here and sell children's clothes, serviettes, place settings and tablecloths. It's laborious work: a single place mat takes between 12 and 15 days to complete.

Sources Thermales

The *sources thermales* (thermal springs) of Cilaos were first brought to the attention of the outside world in 1815 by a goat hunter from St-Louis, Paulin Técher. A track into the cirque was constructed in 1842, paving the way for the development of Cilaos as a health spa for rich colonials. The spring is heated by volcanic chambers far below the surface, and the water contains bicarbonate of soda with traces of magnesium, iron, calcium, sulphur and weak radioactivity. It's said to relieve rheumatic pain, among other bone and muscular ailments.

The old thermal station was opened in 1896, but the spring became blocked in a cyclone that occurred in 1948. The project was revived in 1971, only to close in 1987 because of damage to the buildings from the chemicals in the spa water. The latest incarnation of the Cilaos spa is the **Établissement Thermal** (☎ 02 62 31 72 27; thermes-cilaos@cg974.fr; Rte de Bras-Sec; 9am-6pm Mon-Sat, 9am-5pm Sun) at the north end of town.

All manner of health treatments are offer-ed, from *aérobains* (spas) and hydromassage (with jets of spring water) to traditional hands-on shiatsu. A 15-minute shiatsu massage costs €11, a hydromassage is €17, or you can pay €81 for the full monty, with massages, water therapy and a sauna. This is a perfect way to relax after your hike and rejuvenate tired and sore muscles.

Maison des Vins

Not to be deprived of their wine, the French brought vines with them to Réunion in the 17th century. They were originally grown along the west coast, but in the late 19th century settlers introduced vines into the cirques, cultivating them on trellises outside their houses or on tiny terraces hacked out of the hillside. For years, the wines they produced were sugary sweet whites, reminiscent of sherry and tawny port. In the late 1970s, however, a few enterprising growers in Cilaos upgraded their vine stock and began producing something far more palatable.

You can learn more about Cilaos wine at the association's **Maison des Vins** (☎ 02 62 31 79 69; lechaidecilaos@wanadoo.fr; 34 Rue des Glycines; 10.30am-noon & 1-6pm Mon-Sat). A short film (in French) is followed by a guided tour of the modern vinification plant and one tasting (€2). In addition to sweet and dry whites, growers now produce red and rosé wines. It's by no means the best claret, but not bad nevertheless. A bottle sells for €8.

RHUM LUCK

Up in the hills, almost everyone will have their own family recipe for *rhum arrangé*, a heady mixture of local rum and a secret blend of herbs and spices. In fact, not all are that secret. Popular concoctions include *rhum faham*, a blend of rum, sugar and flowers from the faham orchid; *rhum vanille*, made from rum, sugar and fresh vanilla pods; and *rhum bibasse*, made from rum, sugar and tasty *bibasse* (medlar fruit). The family *rhum arrangé* is a source of pride for most Creoles; if you stay in any of the rural *gîtes* or *chambres d'hôte* you can expect the proprietor to serve up their version with more than a little ceremony.

Philippe Turpin's Studio

Philippe Turpin's studio (☎ 02 62 47 57 57; www.ilereunion.com/leboisrouge in French; 2 Route des Source; 9am-6pm) is open to the public (see p153 for more information).

ACTIVITIES

In addition to hiking, Cilaos is also a centre for mountain biking, rock climbing and canyoning. A couple of local adventure specialists sell and rent out equipment and can help with arrangements.

Run Évasion (☎ 02 62 31 83 57; www.runevasion.fr in French; Rue du Père Boiteau)

Réunion Sensations (☎ 02 62 31 84 84; www.reunionsensations.com; 28 Rue du Père Boiteau)

See p224 for more about hiking and p212 for other activities.

SLEEPING

Cilaos has an ample choice of accommodation options, but it can become crowded at weekends and during the tourist season – for peace of mind, you're advised to book ahead. If you get really stuck, the tourist office might be able to recommend likely places to try.

Budget

Ti Case Lontan (☎ 02 62 31 80 30; 9 Rue Alsace Corré; dm/d €10/26, breakfast/dinner €3/15) A cheerful and well-run *gîte d'étape* with a choice of dorm beds or private rooms, all with shared bathroom, and a communal kitchen.

La Case Bleu (☎ 06 92 65 74 96; fax 02 62 31 77 88; 15 Rue Alsace Corré; dm €13.50, breakfast €4.50) Under the same ownership as Run Évasion, this youth-oriented *gîte d'étape* now spreads into two buildings. Facilities are a bit worn, but it's fine as a place to crash.

Gîte des Porteurs (☎ 02 62 31 82 88; gitedesporteurs@wanadoo.fr; 1 Rue des Thermes; dm/d €12.50/25, breakfast/dinner €3/4) Another welcoming *gîte d'étape* in an attractive Creole house with both dorms and basic double rooms.

Le Galabert Jaune (☎ 02 62 31 88 60; 11 Rue des Platanes; s/d €31/39, dinner €14) An attractive location, a warm welcome and four spotless rooms (all with private bathroom) make up for this *chambre d'hôte* being out of the centre. The energetic owner, Marie-Joëlle Hoarau, is an excellent cook.

Other recommendations:

Mme Bertha Gardebien (☎ 02 62 31 72 15; 50 Rue St-Louis; s/d €23/30.50, dinner €14) A *chambre d'hôte* with three simple rooms (with communal bathroom) set in a pretty garden.

M Luc Payet (Le Panoramique; ☎ 02 62 31 77 79; 1 Ruelle des Artisans; s/d €35/39) Five slightly aged *chambres d'hôte* close to the centre offering great views from the terrace.

Mid-Range & Top End

Case Nyala (☎ 02 62 31 89 57; www.case-nyala.com; 8 Ruelle des Lianes; s/d from €50/65; ✻) On a quiet backstreet close to the centre, you can't miss this sweet little Creole place with its lemon-yellow walls and electric green shutters. Inside is a clutch of cosy, contemporary rooms and a well-appointed communal kitchen.

Hôtel des Neiges (☎ 02 62 31 72 33; www.hotel-des-neiges.com; 1 Rue de la Mare à Joncs; s/d from €41/51; 💻 🏊) A very pleasant and good-value two-star hotel with a range of appealing rooms. All are equipped with bathroom, phone and heating; more expensive rooms come with terrace and TV. The hotel has a good restaurant, Le Marla (see Eating opposite), and a sauna among other facilities.

Hôtel Tsilaosa (☎ 02 62 37 39 39; su.dijoux@outremeronline.com; Rue du Père Boiteau; s/d €76/90) A genteel place offering good value for three-star comforts, including jacuzzi baths as standard. The 15 rooms are beautifully decked out in Creole style; those upstairs boast mountain views.

Le Vieux Cep (☎ 02 62 31 71 89; www.levieuxcep-reunion.com; 2 Rue des Trois Mares; s/d €77/83; 🏊) This is a friendly, family-run hotel surrounded by flower-filled gardens. Rooms in the older block are more rustic; newer rooms have less character, but better bathrooms. Facilities include a smallish heated pool, a sauna and a good, old-fashioned restaurant.

Hôtel Les Chenêts (☎ 02 62 31 85 85; h1674-gm@accor-hotels.com; Rue des Trois Mares; s/d €97/118; 🏊) Cilaos' most luxurious hotel is a big, colourful place with a touch of a hunting lodge about its foyer. The rooms are spac-ious and come with gleaming bathrooms. There's a heated pool, a sauna, a bar and a good restaurant, Les Physalis (see Eating opposite).

Other recommendations:

Hôtel du Cirque (☎ 02 62 31 70 68; fax 02 62 31 80 46; 27 Rue du Père Boiteau; d €45) Functional but acceptable rooms on the main drag.

Le Bois Rouge (☎ 02 62 47 57 57; www.ilereunion.com/boisrouge_lien.htm; 2 Route des Sources; d from €85) A handful of rooms beautifully decorated by artist-owner Philippe Turpin.

Les Aloès (☎ 02 62 31 81 00; www.hotelaloes.com in French; 14 Rue St-Louis; s/d €51/64) Friendly two-star hotel on the edge of town; rooms upstairs get a bath and views.

EATING

Cilaos is noted for its lentils, grown mainly around Îlet à Cordes, and its wines. Lentils come with most meals at the *chambres* and *tables d'hôte*, and a sip of the wine too.

Self-caterers will find bakeries and grocery stores along the main street. On Sunday morning a small market takes place on Rue des Écoles, near the tourist office.

Les Sentiers (☎ 02 62 31 71 54; 63 Rue du Père Boiteau; mains €10-15; 🕐 lunch daily except Wed, dinner daily except Tue & Wed) This jolly restaurant does a brisk business with its tasty Creole and métro dishes served in generous portions. Daily specials might include lamb with Cilaos lentils, *cabri massalé* or entrecôte with green pepper sauce.

Le Petit Randonneur (☎ 02 62 31 79 55; Rue du Père Boiteau; mains €8-10; lunch daily except Wed) No-nonsense traditional fare such as sausages with lentils, vanilla chicken and *boucané* (smoked pork) is the order of the day at this friendly place with tables out under the sunshades.

Chez Noë (☎ 02 62 31 79 93; 40 Rue du Père Boiteau; mains €11-24; lunch & dinner Tue-Sun) This cosy restaurant is packed to the rafters most evenings. It offers Creole favourites such as *carri poulet* (chicken curry) and home-made sausages. On the whole, the atmosphere is better than the food.

Le Marla (☎ 02 62 31 72 33; 1 Rue de la Mare à Joncs; 2-course menu €15; lunch & dinner) The restaurant at the Hôtel des Neiges (see Sleeping, opposite) offers homey Creole meals such as chicken curry with *bois de songe* (a local vegetable with stems of a vine-like plant) followed by sweet-potato cake smothered in chocolate for dessert.

Les Physalis (☎ 02 62 31 85 85; Rue des Trois Mares; mains €8-25, 3-course menu €23; lunch & dinner) Gastronomic French and Creole cuisine and excellent service at the Hôtel Les Chenêts (see Sleeping, opposite) make this Cilaos' top address. Treat yourself to *cassoulet*, a hearty bean stew, or succulent duck breast flavoured with tarragon.

Other recommendations:

Le Cottage (☎ 02 62 31 70 38; 2 Chemin des Saules; mains €15-20; lunch daily except Tue, dinner Mon-Sat) In a picturesque location on the Mare à Joncs, serving upmarket but affordable Creole cuisine.

Le Platane (☎ 06 92 63 20 64; 46 Rue Père Boiteau; pizzas €6-10, Creole mains from €10; daily except Tue) Passable pizzas plus Creole daily specials.

Hôtel Tsilaosa (☎ 02 62 37 39 39; Rue du Père Boiteau; cakes €2.50-3; 11am-8pm) Treat yourself to a tea and home-made cakes beside the fire in the hotel's tea room (see Sleeping opposite).

Le Vieux Cep (☎ 02 62 31 71 89; 2 Rue des Trois Mares; mains €12-28; lunch & dinner) The restaurant of this hotel (see Sleeping, opposite) serves tasty traditional fare.

GETTING THERE & AWAY

Cilaos is 112km from St-Denis by road and 37km from the nearest coastal town, St-Louis. The road through the cirque is magnificent, but hair-raising in sections, particularly when you see the way the locals drive it! Before the road was built (in 1936), visitors to the cirque had to walk from Le Pavillon, where the road crosses the Bras de Cilaos (wealthier visitors were carried up the valley in palanquins!).

Buses from St-Pierre to Cilaos run via St-Louis, so you can save time if you're coming from St-Denis by changing here. There are about six buses daily, with four on Sunday; the journey costs €2.50 and takes up to two hours. The last service up to Cilaos leaves St-Pierre at 5.15pm; going down again, the last bus leaves Cilaos at 4pm, but this terminates at St-Louis.

GETTING AROUND

Adventure specialists **Run Évasion** (☎ 02 62 31 83 57; www.runevasion.fr in French) and **Réunion Sensations** (☎ 02 62 31 84 84; www.reunionsensations.com), both on Rue du Père Boiteau, rent out mountain bikes for about €15/20 for a half/full day.

Around Cilaos

There are some excellent day and half-day walks starting from Cilaos. The tourist office produces a sketch map detailing the more popular paths.

The following walks are shown on the Tour des Cirques map (p233). For information on longer hikes around the cirques, see p224.

CASCADE DE BRAS ROUGE

This pretty waterfall is a popular picnic stop less than 1½ hours' walk from Cilaos on the GR R2 to the Col du Taïbit and Mafate. To pick up the path follow signs from beside Les Sentiers restaurant, down past the Old Thermal Station, then up again to join the GR R2 proper near the Îlet à Cordes road.

LA CHAPELLE & ÎLET À CORDES

A cave known as La Chapelle is just downriver from the Cascade de Bras Rouge, but you have to go the long way round to get here. The trail begins on Rue de la Chapelle at the southwest end of Cilaos. After about 1.5km, the trail to the cave branches off to the right. Allow four hours for the return trip.

You can also use this route to get to Îlet à Cordes; the trail continues straight ahead at the junction to La Chapelle and crosses the Ravine de Bras Rouge. Allow at least four hours one way to reach Îlet à Cordes if you include La Chapelle; three hours otherwise.

ROCHE MERVEILLEUSE

This airy viewpoint lies close to the GR R1 from Cilaos to Hell-Bourg. The path starts behind the church, passes to the right of the Établissement Thermal Cilaos and climbs up to the Plateau des Chênes, where you take the right fork. Allow an hour each way.

BRAS SEC & PALMISTE ROUGE

These two pretty villages near Cilaos offer a taste of rural life in the cirques. The trail starts near the hospital on Rue des Fleurs Jaunes, then descends to cross the Ravine du Bras de Bejoin before climbing through dense cyrptomeria forest to Bras Sec. It takes about 1½ hours to reach Bras Sec, from where you can take the bus back to Cilaos.

From the southern end of Bras Sec, the Sentier des Calumets runs south to the village of Palmiste Rouge, passing behind the Bonnet de Prêtre (Priest's Bonnet), the obvious peak southeast of Bras Sec. Allow about 1½ hours one way. Again, you can catch a bus back to Cilaos from Palmiste Rouge.

SLEEPING & EATING

Staying in the middle of Cilaos is handy for the restaurants and activities in town, but for hikers who want to get a head start, Îlet à Cordes or Bras Sec make good bases.

Bras Sec

M Christian Dijoux (Le Vieux Pressoir; ☎ 02 62 25 56 64; fax 02 62 25 49 87; 40 Chemin Saül; d €34, dinner €16) is on the main road coming into Bras Sec. It offers five simple *chambres d'hôte* all with private bathrooms. Home-produced ducks, chickens and wine feature at dinner.

M Jean-Paul Benoît Dijoux (Les Mimosas; ☎ 02 62 96 72 73; 29 Chemin Saül; dm €15, meals €16) is located a bit further south, just beyond the church. This is a spick-and-span *gîte d'étape* and offers *table d'hôte* meals to satisfy hungry walkers.

Îlet à Cordes

Mme Hélène Payet (☎ 02 62 35 18 13; 13 Chemin Terre Fine; s/d €31/34, dinner €16) offers tidy *chambres d'hôte* with private bathrooms in a friendly environment. It's on the bus route, at the south end of the village.

Mme Solange Grondin (Gîte de l'Îlet; ☎ 02 62 25 38 57; 27 Chemin Terre Fine; dm/s/d €14/34/36, dinner €18) runs a nearby welcoming *chambre d'hôte* with wood-panelled rooms which also double as dorms. Traditional meals are served in the large communal dining room.

Le Reposoir (☎ 02 62 25 38 57; Chemin Terre Fine; 🕑 7am-7.30pm) is across the road from Mme Solange Grondin and run by the same family. It is a café-bar where you can get sandwiches and other snacks.

GETTING THERE & AWAY

There are eight buses a day (four on Sunday) from Cilaos to Bras Sec (€1) between 7.30am and 7pm. The last bus back to Cilaos leaves at 3.30pm, but it's only an hour's walk back to Cilaos if you miss it.

For Îlet à Cordes (€1) there are buses every two hours (only one on Sunday) from 7.20am to 7pm, with the last bus back just after 3pm. Another option for Îlet à Cordes is the minibus service offered by the **Société Cilaosienne de Transport** (☎ 02 62 31 85 87), which costs €23 for up to four people.

The same outfit provides transport from Cilaos to Le Bloc on the GR R1 to Hell-Bourg (€10 for two people) and to the trailhead for the Col du Taïbit on the GR R1/GR R2 to Mafate (€12 for two people), saving you about an hour's walking time in each case.

CIRQUE DE SALAZIE

The Cirque de Salazie, accessed by road from St-André on the northeast coast, is busier and more varied than the Cirque de Cilaos. It's a bit 'flatter' (although 'flat' is not the first word that will spring to mind when you see it!), but the scenery as you approach is nearly as awesome. The vegetation is incredibly lush and waterfalls tumble down the mountains, even over the road in places – Salazie is the wettest of the three cirques and has the dubious distinction of holding several world records for rainfall. The name is thought to derive from the Malagasy word *salaozy*, which means 'good camping ground'.

For detailed information on the Tour des Cirques, a hiking route that takes in the Cirque de Salazie, see p231.

Salazie

The town from which the Cirque de Salazie takes its name lies at the eastern entrance to the cirque. You'll have to change buses here if you're heading further up into the cirque, but there's not much to see. Most people press on to Hell-Bourg.

INFORMATION

The post office, opposite the hotel, has an ATM (the only one in the cirque) which accepts major international credit cards. There's also an Internet café, **Cyber Salazie** (☎ 06 92 05 62 24; 9am-10pm Tue-Sun), just up the road.

The **Office du Tourisme de Salazie** (☎ 02 62 47 75 39; pat.salazie@wanadoo.fr; 9am-5pm Mon-Fri, 9am-4pm Sat & Sun) occupies a small office on the main road opposite the Mairie (town hall) in Salazie.

SLEEPING & EATING

Hôtel Le Bananier (☎ 02 62 47 57 05; fax 02 62 47 51 65; s/d €35/50) is on the main road in Salazie. The place offers comfortable rooms, with private bathroom and TV, and a decent restaurant (main dishes €10 to €16). If you're a light sleeper, ask for a room at the back.

Restaurant Le P'tit Bambou (☎ 02 62 47 51 51; mains €9-16; lunch & dinner daily except Wed), up from the tourist office, serves delicious Creole and Chinese cuisine in rustic surroundings.

GETTING THERE & AWAY

The road alongside the gorge of the Rivière du Mât from St-André to Salazie winds past superb waterfalls. In places, swinging bridges cross the chasm to small farms clinging to the slopes. The road to Grand Îlet turns off the Hell-Bourg road just south of Salazie.

There are seven buses daily from St-André to Salazie (€1.60) between 6.10am and 5.45pm (in the reverse direction, buses run from 5.30am to 4.40pm). On Sunday buses leave St-André at 8.40am, 1.30pm and 5.45pm (8am, 12.40pm and 2.40pm from Salazie).

Buses from Salazie to Hell-Bourg (€1.10) run about every two hours from 6.45am to 6.20pm. In the reverse direction, there are services from 6.15am to 5.45pm. There are four buses in each direction on a Sunday.

Services to Grand Îlet (€2.20) run from 6.45am to 6.20pm (9.15am to 6.20pm on Sunday).

Hell-Bourg

Hell-Bourg is the main community in the Cirque de Salazie, with an unusual wealth of Creole houses and a beautiful setting in the centre of the natural amphitheatre. A sign on the road into town proclaims that Hell-Bourg is *l'un des plus beau villages de France* (one of France's most beautiful villages). It takes its curious name from the former governor Amiral de Hell; the town itself is anything but!

Hell-Bourg served as a thermal resort until a landslide blocked the spring in 1948. Visitors can still see the Hôtel des Salazes, which once accommodated the thermal crowd and is now earmarked for a museum, and the ruins of the old baths. While Cilaos is known for its lentils, Hell-Bourg is synonymous with *chou chou*, a green, pear-shaped vegetable imported from Brazil in 1834. There's also a trout farm just outside town.

Popular day hikes from Hell-Bourg include Trou de Fer via Bélouve, and Piton d'Enchaing. The town makes a pleasant alternative to Cilaos if you're planning to hike up to Piton des Neiges or in to the Cirque de Mafate. Hikers doing the Tour des Cirques route will have to pass through Hell-Bourg as they cross the Cirque de Salazie. For detailed information on all of these hiking possibilities, see p224.

The helpful **Maison du Tourisme** (☎ 02 62 47 89 89; pat.salazie@wanadoo.fr; 47 Rue Général de Gaulle; 9am-5pm Mon-Fri) is the local tourist information centre and can also arrange bookings at the *gîtes de montagne*. There is also a **post office** on Rue Général de Gaulle.

SIGHTS

Creole Buildings

The resort of Hell-Bourg always attracted a rather well-heeled crowd, and they left numerous appealing Creole buildings, which date back as far as the 1840s. The tourist office, the museum and some local shops sell *Le Circuit des Cases Créoles* (€5), an excellent booklet which guides you around the most interesting and important structures. Alternatively, you can go on a guided tour (in French) organised by the tourist office; it takes about an hour and costs €4.

One of the loveliest of Hell-Bourg's Creole houses is **Maison Folio** (☎/fax 02 62 47 80 98; 20 Rue Amiral Lacaze; admission €4; 9am-11.30pm

& 2-5pm), a typical 19th-century, bourgeois villa almost engulfed by its densely planted garden. The owners show you around, pointing out the amazing variety of aromatic, edible, medicinal and decorative plants, and give insights into local culture – unfortunately, only in French.

Ecomusée Salazie

This small **museum** (☎ 02 62 47 89 28; ecoumsee-salazie@wanadoo.fr; admission €2; 9am-4pm) on the north side of town is part of a much larger project to preserve local history and culture. For the moment there are just a couple of rooms, one showing videos about the region, but it's worth dropping by to find what else is happening.

Thermal Bath Ruins

The ruins of the old spa are found in the ravine a short walk west of town. From the end of the main street, follow the road down and then up again, bearing right in front of the *gendarmerie* (police station). The track leads down towards a stream, where you'll see the remnants of the old baths. There's not much left now, but it's a quiet and leafy spot. Cross the stream and climb the hill and you'll connect with the Îlet à Vidot road.

ACTIVITIES

The adventure specialist **Ric à Ric** (Map p188; ☎ 02 62 33 25 38; www.canyonreunion.com) organises canyoning and rock-climbing trips in the area. You can contact them direct or locally through the shop **Maham** (☎ 02 62 47 82 82; www.randoneereunion.com; Rue Général de Gaulle), beside the tourist office. Maham also offers accompanied hikes. For a couple of suggested hikes around Hell-Bourg, see p232.

SLEEPING

Mme Madeleine Parisot (☎ 02 62 47 83 48; fax 02 62 47 83 40; 16 Rue Général de Gaulle; s/d €16/32, meals €16) Mme Parisot runs a homely *gîte d'étape* spread over several old Creole houses in the centre of town.

La Mandoze (☎ 02 62 47 89 65; 14 Chemin de l'École; dm/d €13.50/30, breakfast/dinner €4.50/15) With neat and tidy doubles and six-person dorms, each with its own bathroom, this is another attractive choice.

Relais des Gouverneurs (☎ 02 62 47 76 21; calouboyer@wanadoo.fr; 2 Rue Amiral Lacaze; dm €18.50, d from €45, dinner €18) This smart, new place on the edge of town offers *gîte d'étape* accommodation a cut above the norm and six equally stylish *chambres d'hôte* combining elegant colonial touches with Creole colour.

Salaozy (☎ 02 62 47 82 82; www.randoneereunion.com; Rue Olivier Manès; dm/d €13.50/31, breakfast/dinner €4.50/14) A friendly welcome, nice surroundings and good food make up for rather basic accommodation.

Auberge de Jeunesse (☎ 02 62 41 15 34; fax 02 62 41 72 17; 2 Rue de la Cayenne; dm €13, breakfast/dinner €2/8.50) Hell-Bourg's newly renovated youth hostel occupies a huge colonial edifice. A touch institutional, nevertheless it's good and clean.

Le Relais des Cimes (☎ 02 62 47 81 58; fax 02 62 47 82 11; 67 Rue Général de Gaulle; s/d €51/64, mains €15-30) The only hotel in town has well-appointed rooms and a good restaurant although some people say the service here can be a little indifferent.

EATING

You can stock up on basic provisions at the grocers and other food shops along the main road.

Chez Alice (☎ 02 62 47 86 24; 1 Rue des Sangliers; mains €10-14; lunch & dinner Tue-Sun) This excellent restaurant serves hearty regional dishes including Hell-Bourg trout and *chou chou* at very affordable prices. You'll need to get here early for lunch, especially if you want a table on the vine-covered terrace.

Ti Chou Chou (☎ 02 62 47 80 93; 42 Rue Général de Gaulle; mains around €11, menus €14-22; lunch & dinner) Although this convivial little place does serve other dishes, *chou chou* fanatics come here to feast on their favourite vegetable. It comes in salads, gratins and as *chou chou* gâteau to finish.

Le Relais des Cimes (☎ 02 62 47 81 58; 67 Rue Général de Gaulle; mains around €23; lunch & dinner) Treats such as the local *truites* (trout) with vanilla flambéed in rum are in store at the hotel restaurant (above). It's packed on Sunday, when it offers good-value set menus at €15 and €19.

GETTING THERE & AWAY

Buses run between Salazie and Hell-Bourg (€1.10) about every two hours from 6.45am to 6.20pm. In the reverse direction, there are services from 6.15am to 5.45pm. There are four buses in each direction on Sunday.

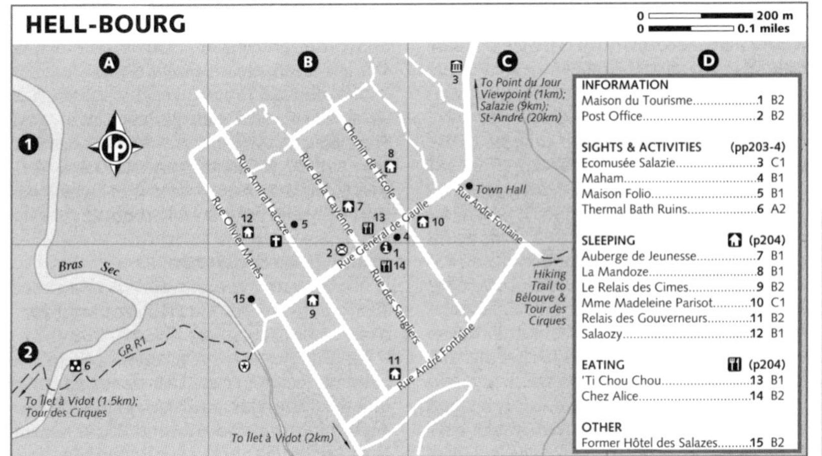

Around Hell-Bourg

A kilometre below Hell-Bourg on the road to Salazie is a superb viewpoint known as **Le Point du Jour**. From here you have a stunning view over the peaks of Salazie, or, alternatively, a view of dense cloud, depending on the weather.

Further along the same route, just north of the turn-off to Grand Îlet, is the **Cascade du Voile de la Mariée** (Bridal Veil Falls). These towering falls drop in several stages from the often cloud-obscured heights into the ravine at the roadside. You get an even better view from the Grand Îlet road.

Grand Îlet & Around

Grand Îlet lies about 17km west of Salazie, at the base of the ridge separating the Cirque de Salazie and the Cirque de Mafate. Above the village are the mountain passes of Col des Bœufs and Col de Fourche, which form the main pedestrian routes between the two cirques; access is via the village of Le Bélier, 3km above Grand Îlet.

While there's nowhere to stay in Le Bélier, several *chambres d'hôte* in and around Grand Îlet make good starting points for walks. This isolated village is slowly being geared up for tourism, and now boasts its own **Office du Tourisme** (☎/fax 02 62 47 70 01; pat.salazie@wanadoo.fr; 9am-5pm Mon-Fri), where staff can provide useful information about walks in the area and can book *gîtes de montagne*. The office is in the centre of Grand Îlet, beside the appealing old Creole church and the post office; you'll also find a few shops here selling basic foodstuffs.

SLEEPING & EATING

Le Cimendef (☎ 02 62 47 73 59; fax 02 62 47 63 69; Route du Bélier; s/d €33/38, dinner €16) A very agreeable *chambre d'hôte* 1km above Grand Îlet, offering modern, wood-panelled rooms for up to three people.

Mme Jeanine Grondin (☎/fax 02 62 47 70 66; Rue de l'Église; s/d €22/30, meals €14) Near the church in the middle of Grand Îlet, this place is popular with walkers for its four simple *chambres d'hôte* (with shared bathroom) and traditional *table d'hôte* meals.

Mme Liliane Bonald (☎ 02 62 41 71 62; fax 02 62 47 73 34; Chemin Camp Pierrot; s/d €30/38, dinner €16) Up a little sideroad about 300m above Grand Îlet on the road to Le Bélier is this welcoming *chambre d'hôte*. The rooms are a touch aged but clean and perfectly acceptable.

Restaurant Le Grand Îlet (☎ 02 62 47 71 19; mains €8; 8am-8pm) This friendly café-restaurant is a life-saver: it's the only place around where you don't have to reserve. It offers a couple of daily dishes, such as the ubiquitous *rougail saucisses* or *cabri massalé*, sandwiches and snacks. Find it just northwest of Grand Îlet's main square, at the start of the path to La Roche Écrite.

GETTING THERE & AROUND

There are seven buses a day (five on Sunday) from Salazie to Grand Îlet and Le Bélier (€2.20) between 6.45am (9.15am on

Sunday) and 6.20pm. Heading back to Salazie services depart from Le Bélier between around 5.45am and 5pm (7am to 5.20pm on Sunday), calling at Grand Îlet 10 minutes later.

If you're coming here to hike and have your own car, you can leave it in the guarded **car park** (☎ 06 92 11 97 37; parking 1/2 days €2/10) at Le Petit Col, 6km up the *route forestière* and only 20 minutes' walk below the Col des Bœufs; the attendant also runs a 24-hour snack kiosk.

RÉUNION

CIRQUE DE MAFATE

Despite its remoteness, the Cirque de Mafate is populated and there are several villages large enough to support shops and other minor enterprises. Not much happens in these sleepy little places but they provide a few trappings of civilisation if you're walking through the cirque. There are no roads into the cirque (although a *route forestière* runs right up to the pass at Col des Bœufs), so the villages of La Nouvelle, Roche Plate, Marla, Îlet à Bourse, Îlet à Malheur, Grand Place and Aurère are accessible only on foot.

The cirque was named after a runaway slave, the chieftain and sorcerer Mafate, who took refuge among its ramparts. He was hunted down and killed in 1751 by François Mussard, a hunter of runaway slaves whose name is now remembered only because it has been given to a dank, dark cave near Piton des Neiges.

For information on hiking in the area, and on the settlements of Marla, La Nouvelle and Roche Plate, see the chapter Hiking in Réunion on p224, which details a four-day walk in the Cirque de Mafate. The map in that section shows the settlements of Îlet à Bourse, Aurère, Grand Place and Cayenne.

Îlet à Bourse

This pleasant village has an awesome view down the cirque and makes a convenient first night stop if you're coming over Bord Martin from Le Bélier.

The only place to stay is the 16-bed **Gîte de Montagne** (☎ 02 62 43 43 93; dm €13.50, breakfast /dinner €4/13.50).

Aurère

Undoubtedly the grottiest of the Mafate communities, Aurère is nevertheless well positioned, perched Machu–Picchu like above the precipitous canyon of the Bras Bémale and beneath the Piton Cabris.

Accommodation is available at two *gîtes de montagne*: the **Auberge Piton Cabris** (☎ 02 62 43 36 83; dm €13.50, breakfast/dinner €4/13.50) and that run by **M George Boyer** (☎ 02 62 55 02 33; dm/d €13.50/31, breakfast/dinner €4/13.50), which has dorms and private double rooms.

Grand Place & Cayenne

These two tiny communities lie above the rushing Rivière des Galets near the cirque's main outlet.

Of the three *gîtes de montagne* in the area, the newest is the **Cœur de Mafate** (☎ 02 62 55 01 68; dm €13.50, breakfast/dinner €4/13.50) in a superb location above Grand Place. Nearby is **Le Pavillon** (☎ 02 62 43 66 76; dm €13.50, breakfast/dinner €4/13.50), while the **Gîte de Montagne de La Cayenne** (☎ 02 62 43 85 42; dm/d €13.50/31, breakfast/dinner €4/13.50) is down in the valley at Cayenne and offers the option of private double rooms.

LES HAUTES PLAINES

Réunion's only cross-island road passes through the Plaine-des-Palmistes and the Plaine-des-Cafres, collectively known as Les Hautes Plaines (the High Plains). These relatively large open areas actually form the saddle that separates the massif (comprised of the three cirques) from the volcano, Piton de la Fournaise. Because there's a road from here that approaches within a few kilometres of the summit of the volcano, nearly all visitors approach it from this side. If you're feeling particularly energetic you can also hike from Les Hautes Plaines into the Cirque de Salazie and the Cirque de Cilaos. For detailed information on hiking in the volcano area and the cirques, see the chapter Hiking in Réunion on p224.

Plaine-des-Palmistes

There were once large numbers of palm trees on the Plaine-des-Palmistes (hence the name), but as a result of heavy consumption of palm-heart salad, few now remain (see Have a Heart, opposite). The town itself is spread out along the highway. Its only specific sight is the **Domaine des Tourelles**, a lovely 1920s Creole building just south of the town centre which now houses the tourist office, the **Maison**

HAVE A HEART

The Plaine-des-Palmistes was once covered in palmiste palms, but early settlers developed a taste for salads made from the bud of the tree, known as the 'heart of the palm'. The palm dies once the bud is removed, earning this wasteful salad delicacy the title 'millionaire's salad'. The Plaine-des-Palmistes was stripped almost bare in a few generations, but the tree is protected these days, and the palm-heart on offer in restaurants is commercially grown.

du Tourisme des Hautes Plaines (☎ 02 62 51 39 92; pat.hautesplaines@wanadoo.fr; 260 Rue de la République; 8am-noon & 1-5pm Mon-Thu, 8am-noon & 1-4pm Fri), and a shop selling local crafts and produce. The number of good accommodation possibilities around Plaine-des-Palmistes make it a convenient base.

WALKS AROUND PLAINE-DES-PALMISTES

Fôret de Bébour-Bélouve

This magnificent tamarind forest lies to the northwest of Plaine-des-Palmistes. It is accessible via a surfaced forestry road which begins at La Petite Plaine, just southwest of Plaine-des-Palmistes, and finishes 20km later, 400m from the **Gîte de Montagne de Bélouve** (p231), from where there is a superb view over the Cirque de Salazie.

The forest is crisscrossed by footpaths of varying levels of difficulty, from a one-hour *sentier botanique* (nature trail) to a 3.5km walk to the magnificent horseshoe-shaped falls known as the Trou de Fer. The path to the falls is signed from the Gîte de Montagne de Bélouve at Bélouve; it's an easy walk on the whole, but can get muddy after a lot of rain.

A leaflet outlining these and other walks in the area are available from the tourist office in Plaine-des-Palmistes.

Note that the forestry road is closed to traffic 2.5km below the Gîte de Montagne de Bélouve from noon on Friday to 7am on Monday.

Cascade Biberon

Cascade Biberon is a 240m-high waterfall and natural swimming lake situated a half-hour stroll away to the north of Plaine-des-Palmistes. It's signposted from the highway near the Azalées hotel. The falls are less than 2km along an obvious track; when you cross the Ravine Sèche, just follow the electricity wires to find the next stretch.

SLEEPING

La Ferme du Pommeau (☎ 02 62 51 40 70; www.lepommeau.com; 10 Allée des Pois de Senteur; s/d €50/70) The all-round nicest place to stay in the area is this well-run hotel in a quiet location on the eastern edge of town. The rooms are immaculate and stylish, if not huge, and the restaurant is also excellent.

Mme Henriette Grondin (Les Héliotropes; ☎ 02 62 51 33 79; 43 Rue Doreau; d €30, dinner €16) The best option at the budget end is this *chambres d'hôte* with three simple rooms (with shared bathroom) and good food – the kindly Mme Grondin ensures her guests don't go hungry. It's signed to the left as you come into Plaine-des-Palmistes from St-Benoît.

Gîte du Pic des Sables (☎ 02 62 51 37 33; Route de la Petite Plaine; dm €14, breakfast/dinner €5/15) This cheery *gîte d'étape* near the start of the forestry road is popular with walkers and canyoning groups. If you phone ahead, the owner will collect you from the bus stop in Plaine-des-Palmistes.

Hôtel des Plaines (☎ 02 62 51 35 67; fax 02 62 51 44 24; 156 Rue de la République; s/d €49/61) On the main road in the centre of town, this small two-star hotel occupies an attractive Creole building. The rooms are nothing special, but they're spacious and nicely old-fashioned, with big baths, and there's a decent restaurant.

EATING

La Ferme du Pommeau (☎ 02 62 51 40 70; 10 Allée des Pois de Senteur; mains €13-25; lunch & dinner Mon-Sat; ☒) This hotel (above) has a delightful restaurant where you can feast on superb Creole cuisine at prices that won't break the bank. Dishes include local delicacies such as *boucané* with *baba figue* or a quiche of *bois de songe*. Watch out for the *rhum arrangée*!

Café Grègue (☎ 02 62 51 30 36; 175 Rue de la République; mains €12-16; 8am-4pm; ☒) Set back from the main road slightly and surrounded by gardens, this is a jolly café-restaurant which serves traditional Creole dishes, as well as surprisingly fancy fare – venison with vermouth and guinea-fowl with *combava* (an aromatic citrus fruit), for example.

Hôtel des Plaines (☎ 02 62 51 35 67; 156 Rue de la République; mains €11-30; ⏰ lunch & dinner) The restaurant of this hotel (see p207) is slightly expensive but the setting is good, especially in the evening with an open fire, and the service attentive. It serves upmarket French and Creole cuisine.

GETTING THERE & AWAY

Plaine-des-Palmistes lies on the cross-island highway between St-Benoît and St-Pierre. There are three buses a day (two on Sunday) in each direction. The fare from St-Pierre is €4.90. From St-Benoît it's €3.30.

Plaine-des-Cafres

The Plaine-des-Cafres, once a refuge for runaway slaves from the coast, offers a gently rolling, almost European landscape, hemmed in between the cirques and Piton de la Fournaise.

Approaching from the north, the Plaine-des-Cafres begins at Col de Bellevue, at the top of the winding road from Plaine-des-Palmistes, and ends at the big and decidedly humdrum regional centre of Le Tampon (the name is derived from the Malagasy word *tampony*, which refers to a small hill). North of Le Tampon on Route Nationale 3 (RN3; the cross-island road) are numerous small settlements which are named for their distance from the sea – Le Vingt-Quatrième (24th), for example, is 24km from the ocean.

BOURG-MURAT

The most interesting place on the Plaine-des-Cafres from a visitor's perspective is Bourg-Murat, where the Route Forestière du Volcan turns off to Piton de la Fournaise; for information on getting to the volcano and hiking around its crater, see p234. The town and the surrounding area present several accommodation and dining choices, making it a handy base.

Bourg-Murat is also the location of the informative Maison du Volcan museum and of the well-organised Plaine-des-Cafres **Office du Tourisme** (☎ 02 62 59 09 82; Route du Volcan; ⏰ 1.30-5.30pm Mon, 8am-12.30pm & 1.30-5.30pm Tue-Sat, 8.30am-12.30pm Sun), which is located about 400m east of the Maison du Volcan along the Route du Volcan (the road to the volcano).

SIGHTS & ACTIVITIES

Maison du Volcan

If you wish to know more about the behaviour of volcanoes in general and Piton de la Fournaise in particular, it's well worth visiting the **Maison du Volcan** (☎ 02 62 59 00 26; www.maisonduvolcan.com in French; adult/child €6.50/2.29; ⏰ 9.30am-5.30pm Tue-Sun), a museum and monitoring centre in Bourg-Murat. Unfortunately, most of the information is in French, but some interactive displays are in English and the videos of eruptions are self-explanatory. In the lobby you can see footage of Piton de la Fournaise's most recent tantrum in 2003. There's also a live TV link showing the actual conditions at the summit – don't be surprised to see a somewhat unexciting shot of cloud!

Grand Bassin

This picturesque valley, only accessible on foot, is known as *la vallée perdue* (the lost valley). It is formed by the confluence of three rivers: the Bras Sec, the Bras de Ste-Suzanne and the Bras des Roches Noires. Near where they join is a lovely waterfall and a quiet agricultural village with a handful of *gîtes*. To get there, follow the road to Bois Court from Vingt-Troisième village. At the end of the road you can look down into the valley from the Belvédère viewpoint.

The path down to Grand Bassin begins on Rue Thomas Payet, 800m south of the Belvédère. It plunges almost straight down to the river 600m below; allow 1½ hours for the descent and at least 2½ hours to get back up again.

Mountain Biking

Bike trails lead from the volcano down to Bourg-Murat. You can hire bikes through **Rando Bike** (☎ 02 62 59 15 88; ⏰ 8.30am-4pm) on the Route du Volcan; a package including bike hire, transport to the top and a picnic lunch costs €35.

Riding Centres

The pastoral Plaine-des-Cafres makes for great riding country. In addition to one-day treks, it's possible to organise longer excursions around the volcano through **Écuries du Volcan** (☎ 06 92 66 62 90; fax 02 62 35 54 45), a riding centre just north of Bourg-Murat on the main road. Or you could try the **Centre**

Èquestre Alti-Merens (☎ 02 62 59 18 84; Route Nationale 3) to the south of town. The cost is around €16 for an hour and €100 per day including meals and accommodation.

SLEEPING

Auberge des Cratères (☎ 02 62 27 30 66; aubergedescrateres@wanadoo.fr; dm/d €13.50/31, breakfast/dinner €4.50/14.50) This new and welcoming *gîte de montagne* has a choice of dorms or private rooms. It's on the Route du Volcan about 2km from the centre of Bourg-Murat and you can arrange transport from here up to the volcano (€54 for up to eight people).

La Ferme du Pêcher Gourmand (☎ 02 62 59 29 79; corinne.combelles@wanadoo.fr; d €40, dinner €17) The restaurant (right) to the south of Bourg-Murat now offers six simple but appealing rooms. The views down to the coast are magnificent.

Mme Madeleine Robert (Les Zakacias; ☎ 02 62 59 20 59; gite-les-zakacias@wanadoo.fr; d €40, gîte per week from €303) In La Petite Ferme, to the south of Bourg-Murat, you'll find this haven of peace with two pretty *chambres d'hôte* and a *gîte* for up to four people.

Hôtel Le Volcan (☎ 02 62 27 50 91; fax 02 62 59 17 21; s/d €28/37) The Auberge du Volcan (right) offers 10 rather characterless rooms in a newish annex across the road. On the plus side, the price is good and it is very convenient.

Hôtel l'Ecrin (☎ 02 62 59 02 02; www.hotel-ecrin.fr.st; s/d from €56/72) Although it doesn't look promising, the rooms in this modern hotel on the crossroads smack-bang in the middle of Bourg-Murat are bright and well equipped and the restaurant serves decent food. There are also self-catering apartments for €95 a double.

Les Géraniums (☎ 02 62 59 11 06; hotelgeranium@wanadoo.fr; s/d €62/78, half board €68/112) More immediately attractive than Hôtel l'Ecrin, rooms here are rather ordinary for the price, although they are gradually being renovated. The restaurant has a good reputation. The hotel is located in Le Vingt-Quatrième on the main road south of Bourg-Murat.

There are several *gîtes d'étape* in Grand Bassin. Two pleasant options as you come into the village are the **Auberge de Grand-Bassin** (☎ 02 62 59 21 99; half board per person €24), and a bit further on, the smaller, quieter **Paille-en-Queue** (☎ 02 62 59 03 66; fax 02 62 59 20 08; half board per person €23).

EATING

Auberge du Volcan (☎ 02 62 27 50 91; mains €11-22; ⏰ 6.30am-late) For more than 20 years this welcoming country inn (left) in the centre of Bourg-Murat has been serving traditional home-cooking. You'll find all the usual Creole favourites and a sprinkling of métro dishes served in hearty portions. Not surprisingly, it's often packed.

Relais Commerson (☎ 02 62 27 52 87; mains €8-12; ⏰ 9am-7.30pm daily except Wed) Near the tourist office in Bourg-Murat, this friendly place is popular for its cheap-and-cheerful Creole and Chinese dishes and grills.

La Ferme du Pêcher Gourmand (☎ 02 62 59 29 79; set menu €17; ⏰ lunch & dinner) Reservations are required to eat at this delightful *ferme-auberge* (farm restaurant) on the main road south of Bourg-Murat (opposite). Most of the food comes from the farm: duck pâté, guinea-fowl with *combava*, chicken flavoured with vanilla. Guests are welcome to wander around the farm.

Le Vieux Bardeau (☎ 02 62 59 09 44; mains €13-22; ⏰ lunch & dinner daily except Thu) Duck cooked in beer and *carri 'la misère'* (poor man's curry), featuring eggs, sardines and tinned beef, are some of the unusual dishes you can sample at this upmarket Creole restaurant. It's easy to find – in a lemon-yellow Creole building beside the main road in Le Vingt-Quatrième.

Bourg-Murat has several grocery stores, but for dairy produce you're best going to the **Palais du Fromage** (☎ 02 62 59 27 15; ⏰ 10am-6pm Thu-Sun) past the tourist office on the Route du Volcan. It sells a mouthwatering range of local cow's cheese – laced with herbs, *combava* or pepper, for example – as well as yoghurts and fresh milk and its own bread, perfect for a picnic.

GETTING THERE & AWAY

There are three buses daily (two on Sunday) each way between St-Benoît and St-Pierre via Plaine-des-Cafres and Plaine-des-Palmistes. From St-Pierre to Bourg-Murat, the fare is €2.70. Coming from St-Benoît, it's €5.40.

RÉUNION DIRECTORY

The following section contains practical information for visitors to Réunion arranged in alphabetical order. For relevant information to the entire region, see the Regional Directory (p277).

ACCOMMODATION

While accommodation in Réunion might not reach the stellar heights of Mauritius and Seychelles, there is still plenty of choice. The smarter hotels tend to be concentrated around the coast and in the attractive mountain towns of Cilaos and Hell-Bourg. In the mid-range, there's a smattering of small, family hotels and lots of *chambres d'hôte* (B&Bs), the best of which offer excellent value for money. Budget travellers will find it hard to keep costs down in St-Denis and the coastal towns around St-Gilles-les-Bains, but elsewhere youth hostels, *gîtes de montagne* (mountain lodges) and the cheaper *chambres d'hôte* fit the bill. A general idea of what you'll pay for budget, mid-range and top-end accommodation is under €40, €40-100 and over €100, respectively. Rates include all government taxes and are for double rooms.

It is wise to book accommodation well in advance, particularly in high season (the métro and local school holidays, particularly July and August and around Christmas), when the best places fill up weeks, if not months, ahead. Budget travellers should plan ahead at any time of year; some of the better and more convenient places seem permanently packed out. Otherwise, it's usually possible find a room with a day or two's notice as long as you're not too fussy about where you stay; it widens the choice enormously if you have your own transport and speak at least a little French.

Camping

Réunion's only official campsite is on the southwest coast at Étang-Salé-les-Bains. In theory, there's no reason why you shouldn't put up your tent at any secluded spot around the coast, but there are an increasing number of signs warning *camping interdit* (camping forbidden).

You can camp for free in some areas in the cirques, but only for one night at a time. Popular spots in the Cirque de Mafate include Trois Roches on the GR R2 between Marla and Roche Plate; Le Grand Sable on the GR R1 near Le Bélier; Plaine des Tamarins on the GR R1 near La Nouvelle; and at the *gîte de montagne* at Bélouve. Setting up camp on Piton de la Fournaise (the volcano) is forbidden for obvious reasons.

There are also emergency shelters along some of the main hiking paths, but they provide only a roof.

Chambres d'Hôte

A *chambre d'hôte* is a small family-run bed and breakfast. They are normally tucked away in the hills and offer a window into a more traditional way of life. The best offer excellent value. You may be treated like a member of the family in some places; in others you'll definitely be aware that you are a paying guest. B&B rates are from around €30 for a double room. Hearty traditional meals cost about €17 per person, but must be reserved in advance.

Many *chambres d'hôte* are members of Gîtes de France and are listed (with photos and full information) in the association's booklet *Île de la Réunion* (€11). Updated annually, this is available in Réunion from the **Relais Départemental des Gîtes de France** (☎ 02 62 90 78 90; www.itea.fr GDF/974 in French; 10 Pl Sarda Garriga, 97400 St-Denis), local tourist offices and some newsagents. In France, contact the **Maison des Gîtes de France** (☎ 01 49 70 75 75; www.gites-de-france.fr; 59 Rue Saint-Lazare, 75009 Paris). You can reserve a room by telephoning the owner direct, or by booking through Gîtes de France.

Gîtes de Montagne

Gîtes de montagne are basic mountain cabins or lodges, operated by the government through the Maison de la Montagne. It is possible to organise a walking holiday using the *gîtes de montagne* only. Cirque de Mafate, inaccessible by road, has *gîtes de montagne* at Aurère, Grand Place, Îlet à Bourse, Îlet à Malheur, La Nouvelle, Roche Plate and Marla. There are also useful *gîtes de montagne* at Cilaos, Hell-Bourg, Piton des Neiges, Bélouve, Plaine-des-Cafres and Piton de la Fournaise.

The *gîtes de montagne* in Réunion are generally in pretty good condition. Thanks to solar power, they all now have electricity, although not all get as cushy as providing warm showers. The Caverne Dufour gîte at Piton des Neiges is the most basic: it has no hot water, but there are now inside toilets.

Gîtes de montagne must be booked and paid for in advance, and charges are not refundable unless a cyclone or a cyclone alert prevents your arrival. You can book through the **Maison de la Montagne head office** (Map p158; ☎ 02 62 90 78 78; www.reunion-nature.com in French; 10 Pl Sarda Garriga, 97400 St-Denis) or through affiliated tourist offices, including those in Cilaos, Salazie, Hell-Bourg, St-Gilles-les-Bains, St-Pierre, St-Leu and Bourg-Murat (see individual town entries for contact details). In France, contact the Maison des Gîtes de France (see Chambres d'Hôte). It's highly recommended that you book well in advance, especially during the busy tourist seasons. One night's accommodation without food costs around €14 per person.

When staying in a *gîte de montagne*, you have to call the *gîte* at least two days ahead to book your meals (or you can ask for this to be done for you when you make the original booking). Dinner costs from €13.50 to €15, and usually consists of *carri poulet* (chicken curry), *rougail saucisses* (sausages in tomato-sauce) or *boucané* (smoked pork) with vegetables, plus the usual rice, *brèdes* (local spinach), *grains* (lentils or other beans) and *rougail* (spicy chutney). Many places throw in a glass of *rhum arrangé* (local rum with herb and spices) or local wine as well. Breakfast costs around €5 and normally consists of coffee, bread and jam.

Sleeping arrangements usually consist of bunk beds in shared rooms, so be prepared for the communal living that this entails, although the newer *gîtes* usually have a few private rooms. Sheets and blankets are provided, though you might want to bring a sheet sleeping bag (a sleep sheet).

It's not a bad idea to also bring along toilet paper and a torch. It can get quite chilly at night, so warm clothing will be in order. Some places will let you cook, but many kitchens are so basic – and sometimes grimy – that you probably won't bother.

On arrival and departure you must 'book' in and out with the manager, who will collect your voucher and payment for meals. In theory, you're not meant to occupy a *gîte* before 3pm or remain past 10am. For more information about these *gîtes* and for hiking-related information, see the chapter Hiking in Réunion on p224.

Gîtes d'Étape

Gîtes d'étape are privately owned and work in roughly the same way as the *gîtes de montagne*, offering dorm beds and meals. One main difference is that you can book these places directly with the owners. There are several *gîtes d'étape* in the Cirque de Mafate, and numerous others dotted around the island; most are in the vicinity of walking trails. The host will often offer meals or cooking facilities.

You'll find a number of *gîtes d'étape* listed in the Gîtes de France booklet, *Île de la Réunion* (see Chambres d'Hôte, opposite). Local tourist offices should be able to provide lists of others in their area.

Gîtes Ruraux

Gîtes ruraux (often referred to simply as *gîtes* and mentioned in the text) are private houses and lodges that families and groups can rent for self-catering holidays, normally by the week or weekend. There are dozens of *gîtes ruraux* scattered all over the island.

Most offer lodging for four or more people, with facilities of varying standards; you may have to bring bed sheets in some cases. Costs vary from around €300 to €400 per week and from €150 to €250 for a weekend (note that not all offer bookings for just a weekend).

Again, you'll find many listed in the Gîtes de France booklet (see Chambres d'Hôte, opposite) and they can be booked either through Gîtes de France or by phoning the owners direct. A deposit of some sort is usually required in advance.

Hotels

Réunion isn't flush with hotels, so getting a room can sometimes be difficult. Primarily, they're found in St-Denis and around the beach resorts of the west coast, especially St-Gilles-les-Bains, though you'll also find some scattered in the interior. Most hotels on the island are rated as one-, two- or three-star, and lots are unclassified. There is only a sprinkling of four-star hotels.

Many of the mid-range hotels attract businesspeople and can get booked out quite quickly. It's wise to make reservations well in advance so that your choices are not limited. If you will be staying for more than a week in one place, it's worth asking for a discount when making your booking. Keep an eye open for special deals offered by hotels, particularly during the low season. Most room rates include breakfast, but check when booking to be sure.

Youth Hostels

Réunion has three *auberges de jeunesse* (youth hostels): at **Bernica** (☎ 02 62 22 89 75), **Entre-Deux** (☎ 0262 395920) and **Hell-Bourg** (Map p205; ☎ 02 62 47 41 31). They are operated by the **Fédération Réunionnaise des Auberges de Jeunesse** (☎ 02 62 41 15 34; www.ajoi-reunion.com; 10 Pl Sarda Garriga, 97400 St-Denis), which is an affiliate of the Ligue Française pour les Auberges de la Jeunesse (French Youth Hostels League). Booking can be done direct with the hostel or through the central organisations.

Officially, the hostels are only open to Hostelling International (HI) card holders. You can purchase an HI card at the office in St-Denis for €15.25 (€10.70 for those under 26 years). Married couples are entitled to a 'family' card (€18), which also includes any kids.

Guests over 18 years of age pay €13 per night and an additional €2 for breakfast. Evening meals are usually available for €8.50 per person.

ACTIVITIES

Réunion is a paradise for anyone in search of an activity holiday. Given the extremes of the landscape, it's not surprising that much of what's on offer involves some element of adventure, usually accompanied by strenuous effort. To some, it might seem the emphasis is less on enjoyment than on blood, sweat and tears. The logical conclusion of this quest for endurance is the Grand Raid, an incredible race right across the middle of the island (see Cross Country for Crazies, right).

There are established clubs for just about every sort of activity you can imagine: flying, parachuting, sailboarding, hang-gliding, canyoning, equitation, mountain biking, diving, deep-sea fishing, water-skiing, sailing and numerous competitive sports. Water activities are concentrated around St-Gilles-les-Bains, which is the holiday and leisure centre of Réunion.

Inquiries about what's on offer should be directed to the operators listed below (those without addresses only take phone or email enquires) and to local tourist offices. Another good source of information is the *Guide de Loisirs*, a booklet listing selected operators for each activity. It's available free from tourist offices, hotels and other outlets around the island.

THE CROSS-COUNTRY FOR CRAZIES

The tortuous topography of Réunion is the setting for one of the world's most challenging cross-country races, the Grand Raid, held every October or November. The route roughly follows the path of the GR R2 hiking trail which traverses the island from St-Denis to Mare Longue, near St-Philippe, taking in parts of the Mafate and Cilaos cirques, the Plaine-des-Cafres and the lunar landscape around Piton de la Fournaise.

Covering some 130km, the Grand Raid would be a challenging race over level ground, but runners also have to negotiate a total of some 7000m of altitude change, hence the race is nicknamed the 'Cross-Country for Crazies'! The pack leaders can complete this agonising run in 18 hours or less, but contestants are allowed up to 60 hours to finish.

If you feel like entering, contact the **Association Le Grand Raid** (☎ 02 62 20 32 00; www.grandraid-reunion.com in French; 168 du Général de Gaulle, St-Denis), though you need to apply early since numbers are limited.

Canyoning, Rafting & Rock Climbing

For real thrill seekers, there's the exhilaration of canyoning, which challenges you to abseil down the steep walls of canyons using natural watercourses. The most popular canyons are along the Fleurs Jaunes valley in the Cirque de Salazie, which is suitable for all levels, while classic venues for experienced canyoners include Takamaka and Trou de Fer. The sport, however, is very vulnerable to the vagaries of the weather, so venues change according to the time of year. The canyoning specialist Ric à Ric produces an excellent guide to Réunion's 39 best canyons (€21).

White-water rafting takes place on the turbulent rivers of the south and east, notably the Langevin, Marsouins and Mât rivers, while rock climbing is on offer around Cilaos and Salazie among other places.

The price for all these activities (with a guide and equipment) usually starts at around €50/70 per person for a half/full day.

Austral Aventure (☎ 02 62 32 40 29; www.creole.org/austral-aventure/index.html)
Run Aventures (☎ 06 92 64 08 22; www.runaventures.com)
Run Évasion (Map p198; ☎ 02 62 31 83 57; www.runevasion.fr; Rue du Père Boiteau, Cilaos)
Réunion Sensations (Map p198; ☎ 02 62 31 84 84; www.reunionsensations.com; 28 Rue du Père Boiteau, Cilaos)
Ric à Ric (Map p198; ☎ 02 62 33 25 38; www.canyonreunion.com in French; 13 Ave du Général de Gaulle, St-Gilles-les-Bains)

Cruises

La Compagnie des Alizés (☎ 06 92 65 60 00; www.voile-reunion.com in French; 1 Rue Berthier le Forban, Le Port) runs cruises around the island and further afield. A day trip in a modern catamaran costs around €100 per person, or €380 for the whole boat (up to eight people). Better still, you can cruise the island in a glorious old yacht. Prices are €80 per person or €640 for the whole boat (up to 13 people).

Deep-sea Fishing

As elsewhere in the Indian Ocean region, the season for deep-sea fishing is tied to the feeding habits of bait-fish species; you stand the best chance of hooking a monster marlin from January to March. A boat with crew costs roughly €400/700 per half/full day (maximum of six people). This usually includes soft drinks and a light lunch. If you intend spending several days fishing, you should negotiate a discount. Some operators offer individuals rates of around €90 per person.

The main operators are based in St-Gilles-les-Bains.

Alpha Centre de Pêche (☎ 02 62 24 02 02; Port de Plaisance)
Maevasion (Map p188; ☎ 02 62 33 38 04; www.maeva-fishing.com in French; Port de Plaisance)
Réunion Fishing Club (Map p188; ☎ 02 62 24 36 10; www.reunionfishingclub.com; Port de Plaisance)
Rèunion Pêche au Gros (Map p188; ☎ 02 62 33 33 99; www.reunion-pecheaugros.com in French; Pl Paul-Julius Bénard, Port de Plaisance)

Diving

Réunion's dive sites are concentrated along the lagoon-fringed west coast. See the chapter Underwater Worlds on p39 for further information.

4WD Excursions

For a guided day's tour by 4WD expect to pay upwards of €100 per person. Popular destinations include Piton de la Fournaise and Le Dimitile, or you could try creek-bashing in the Rivière des Remparts. Contact **Kréolie 4x4** (☎ 02 62 39 50 87; www.kreolie4x4.com in French; 4 Impasse des Avocats, Entre-Deux) for further information.

Golf

There are three golf courses on the island: a nine-hole course at La Montagne and two 18-hole courses. For nine holes, fees start at around €14/20 on weekdays/weekends; for 18 holes you pay €20/30. Club hire costs around €11.

Golf Club de Bourbon (Map p182; ☎ 02 62 26 33 39; www.golf-bourbon.com; 140 Les Sables, Étang-Salé-les-Bains)
Golf du Bassin Bleu (Map p182; ☎ 02 62 55 53 58; club@golfbassinbleu.com; Villèle, St-Gilles-les-Hauts)
Golf du Colorado (☎ 02 62 23 79 50; Zone de Loisirs du Colorado, La Montagne, St-Denis)

Hiking

No visitor to the island should miss the volcano and the superb rugged cirques of Cilaos, Salazie and Mafate, even if you only get to visit the towns of Cilaos or Hell-Bourg. To see the best of the cirques, of course, you'll need to hike through the peaks and valleys of the Cirque de Mafate. For the less energetic, the volcano climb makes a manageable day trip and offers some of the most unusual and impressive scenery on the island. (For more detailed information, see the chapter Hiking in Réunion on p224).

Horse Riding

If the idea of exploring the countryside on horseback appeals to you, contact one of the following organisations. Most places charge around €16 per hour, or €40/100 for a half/full day including lunch.

Centre Équestre Alti-Merens (Map p196; ☎ 02 62 59 18 84; RN3, Bourg-Murat)
Centre Équestre du Maïdo (☎ 02 62 32 49 15; fax 02 62 32 43 10; 352 Route du Maïdo, Le Guillaume)
Club Hippique de l'Hermitage (Map p188; ☎ 02 62 24 47 73; fax 02 62 33 00 48; Chemin Ceinture, St-Gilles-les-Bains)
Écuries du Volcan (Map p196; ☎ 06 92 66 62 90; fax 02 62 35 54 45; Domaine de Bellevue, Bourg-Murat)
Ferme Équestre du Grand-Étang (Map p168; ☎ 02 62 50 90 03; riconourry@wanadoo.fr; RN3, Pont-Payet, St-Benoît)

Mountain Biking

In recent years Réunion has seen an explosion of interest in the *vélo tout terrain* (VTT) or mountain bike. The Fédération Française de Cyclisme has established more than 1400km of special biking trails winding through its forests and scooting down its mountainsides. They are graded according to level of difficulty (like ski-runs, from green for the easiest up to black for the most demanding), numbered and divided into 10 areas (called 'VTT stations'), including Cilaos, Entre-Deux, Volcan, Salazie and Maïdo. Laminated cards with maps for each station are available from the **Maison de la Montagne** (☎ 02 62 90 78 78; www.reunion-nature.com in French; 10 Pl Sarda Garriga; 9am-5pm Mon-Thu, 9am-4pm Fri, 9am-noon Sat) and tourist offices.

You can rent bikes from any of the organisations listed below; prices for a half/full day start at around €10/12, rising to €30 for a specially adapted descent bike *(tout-suspendu)*. The same organisations also offer packages including bike rental, transport to the start of the trail and guided bike rides. A half-/full-day's outing will cost in the region of €40/70.

Rando Bike (Map p196; ☎ 02 62 59 15 88; 100 Route du Volcan, Plaine-des-Cafres)

Rando Réunion Passion St-Gilles-les-Bains (Map p188; ☎ 02 62 24 25 19; www.vttreunion.com; 13 Rue de Général de Gaulle); St-Leu (☎ 02 62 34 44 53; 84 Rue Général Lambert)

Run Évasion (Map p198; ☎ 02 62 31 83 57; www.runevasion.fr; Rue du Père Boiteau, Cilaos)

Réunion Sensations (Map p198; ☎ 02 62 31 84 84; www.reunionsensations.com; 28 Rue du Père Boiteau, Cilaos)

3Athlon (Map p188; ☎ 02 62 24 55 56; www.3athloncycles.com; 1 Pl Paul-Julius Bénard, St-Gilles-les-Bains)

For more on biking and renting bikes in Réunion, see p221.

Paragliding & Hang-Gliding

The main centre for these two activities is St-Leu on the west coast. Local companies offer everything from short flights over the lagoon for beginners to longer outings soaring over the cirques. Prices range from €65 to €130 depending on the length of the flight.

Azurtech (Map p182; ☎ 02 62 34 91 89; www.azurtech.com; 3 Impasse des Plongeurs, St-Leu)

Bourbon Parapente (☎ 02 62 34 18 34; www.bourbonparapente.com; Rue Général Lambert, St-Leu)

Réunion Parapente (Map p182; ☎ 02 62 24 87 84; www.parapente-reunion.fr in French; 103 Montée des Colimaćons, St-Leu)

Surfing

The prime surfing spots are located off St-Gilles-les-Bains and St-Leu. Two good locations are at the mouths of Ravine des Colimaçons and Ravine des Trois Bassins, both to the north of St-Leu. Les Roches Noires beach, at St-Gilles-les-Bains itself, is another popular spot.

If you're keen to ride the waves but could do with a few pointers, contact one of the following organisations. Private lessons for beginners cost around €25; group classes are considerably cheaper. Glissy and High Surf also sell surfing gear and rent out boards from around €7 per hour.

École de Surf des Roches Noires (☎ /fax 02 62 24 63 28; www.web-soleil.com/ecolesurf in French)

École de Surf Réunionnaise (Map p188; ☎ 06 92 68 00 83; High Surf Shop, 15 Rue de la Plage, St-Gilles-les-Bains)

Glissy École de Surf (Map p188; ☎ 02 62 33 13 13; b.glissy@guetali.fr; 15 Rue de la Plage, St-Gilles-les-Bains)

LES DENTS DU MER

Swimmers should think twice before diving headlong into the waters around Réunion. Attacks by *les dents du mer* (the teeth of the sea) are a part of life on the island, and while the risks are statistically very low, most years see a shark attack on a surfer, diver, swimmer or spear fisherman.

You should avoid any water sports after storms, when dead animals and debris washed out of the ravines attract the sharks closer to land. The mouths of rivers and ravines are risky spots at any time as the mix of fresh water and salt water turns the ocean cloudy – sharks prefer an element of surprise. They also tend to be more active at dawn and dusk. Swimming or surfing at night in general is not advisable.

The safest place for water sports is the coral lagoon along the west coast, while the exposed east coast is regarded as a higher-risk zone. Surfers who paddle out beyond the reef break may be at risk anywhere along the coast. The locals know their ocean, so it's best to seek their advice before entering the water.

Swimming

The best beaches for swimming are all on the west coast within the protective barrier of the lagoon. The main tourist beaches include those at St-Gilles-les-Bains, Hermitage-les-Bains, Saline-les-Bains and Étang-Salé-les-Bains. *The* beach as far as locals are concerned is Boucan Canot. All these beaches have lifeguards and designated safe swimming areas. Elsewhere around the coast there are dangerous currents, so take advice before plunging in.

BOOKS

There is a fine range of French-language guides and books about Réunion, but almost nothing in English. For general reading matter, the best chance of finding books in English is in the bookshops in St-Denis (p157), but it's advisable to bring some with you.

(Remember that a bookshop is *une librairie*. The French term for a library is *une bibliothèque*.)

For a general introduction to the island, you can't beat Catherine Lavaux's classic *La Réunion: Du Battant des Lames au Sommet des Montagnes*. It covers everything from the geography, fauna and flora of Réunion to its history and cultural traditions.

The best of the locally produced French-language guide books is Daniel Vaxelaire's *La Réunion: Le Guide Touristique et Encyclopédique*. Written by a long-term resident, journalist and historian, it provides a brief but comprehensive overview of the island and is packed with illustrations.

Taking the empahsis off the French text, Serge Gélabert's *La Réunion: Histoire d'une Île Déserte* is essentially a photo book but includes a good, brief historical introduction. In the same vein, his *Reunion, J'Aime ton Nom*, is not quite so lavish, but with the text in both English and French. *Scènes de la Re'union Vue d'en Haut* by Roland Bénard contains magnificent aerial shots.

Réunion is a fascinating place for the magically minded. Creole beliefs and potions have spawned a number of books on voodoo-style sorcery. Daniel Honorés books *Légendes Créoles* (in two volumes) and *Kroyans* are particularly good on local culture and superstitions.

Roger Lavergne has produced a number of beautifully illustrated books on the island's indigenous medicinal plants, including *Tisaneurs et Plantes Médicinales Indigènes de la Réunion* and *Les Plantes Médicinales de Père Raimbault*.

For a very brief introduction to the island's music, try *Les Musiques à la Réunion* by Xavier Filliol. Those in search of a weightier tome will be better satisfied by *Musiques Traditionelles de la Réunion* by Jean-Paul La Selve.

The bible of Creole cookery is the six-volume *Les Délices de la Cuisine Créole* by Francis Delage, regarded as the *crème de la crème* of cookbooks. For those more interested in a simple taster, the *Grand Livre de la Cuisine Réunionnaise* by Marie-France *et al* contains a range of easy-to-follow traditional recipes. *La Cuisine Ŕeunionnaise* by Carole Iva covers similar ground, with the added benefit of colour plates.

For hiking guides, see p226.

BUSINESS HOURS

As in mainland France, lunches are long, relaxed affairs in Réunion, and most shops and offices close for at least two hours.

In general, the banks are open from 8am-4pm Monday to Friday. The Government offices are open from 8.30am-noon and 2-5pm Monday to Thursday, 8.30am-noon and 2-3pm Friday. Shops are open from 8.30am-noon and 2.30-6pm Monday to Saturday (some close Monday).

CHILDREN

In most respects travelling with children in Réunion is similar to mainland France. Few hotels offer kids' clubs, but on the other hand even quite young children can participate in a huge array of sports activities, from paragliding to scuba diving, and from rock climbing to pony trekking. There's a whole network of footpaths suitable for children *(sentiers marmailles)* while older and more adventurous kids will be able to tackle some of the longer hikes – just make sure you allow plenty of time and don't try to cover too much ground in a day.

For more about travelling with children in the region, see p278.

ELECTRICITY

The electric current in Réunion is 220V AC at 50Hz. Outlets take continental two-pin plugs, so non-European visitors will need to use an adaptor for their appliances.

RÉUNION

EMBASSIES & CONSULATES

French Embassies & Consulates

Countries in which France has diplomatic representation:

Australia (☎ 02-6216 0100; www.ambafrance-au.org; 6 Perth Ave, Yarralumla, Canberra, ACT 2600)
Canada (☎ 613-789 1795; www.ambafrance-ca.org; 42 Promenade Sussex, Ottawa, Ontario K1M 2C9)
Germany (☎ 030-590 03900; www.ambafrance-de.org; Pariser Platz 5, 10117 Berlin)
Ireland (☎ 01-277 5000; www.ambafrance.ie; 36 Ailesbury Rd, Dublin 4)
Mauritius (☎ 230-2021100; www.ambafrance-mu.org in French; 14 Rue St Georges, Port Louis)
Netherlands (☎ 70-312 5800; www.ambafrance-nl.org in Dutch; 1 Smidsplein, The Hague 2514 BT)
New Zealand (☎ 04-384 2555; www.ambafrance-nz.org in French; 34/42 Manners St (PO Box 11-343), Wellington)
Seychelles (☎ 38 25 00; www.ambafrance-sc.org in French; Victoria House, Independence Ave, BP 478, Victoria)
UK (☎ 020-7201 1004; www.ambafrance-uk.org; 58 Knightsbridge, London SW1X 7JT)
USA (☎ 202-944 6195; www.info-france-usa.org; 4101 Reservoir Rd NW, Washington, DC, 20007)

Embassies & Consulates in Réunion

Since Réunion isn't independent, only a few countries have diplomatic representation:

Belgium (☎ 02 62 97 99 10; chatel@runnet.com; 72 Ave Eudoxie Nonge, BP 32, 97491 Sainte-Clotilde)
Germany (☎ 21 62 06; fax 02 62 21 74 55; 9c Rue de Lorraine, 97400 St-Denis)
Italy (☎ 02 62 22 28 89; fax 02 62 22 28 89; 12 Rue Rouget-de-l'Isle, Résidence La Taniers, 97419 La Possession)
Norway (☎ 02 62 43 30 48; fax 02 62 43 22 48; 43 Rue Paul Verlaine, BP 111, 97823 Le Port)
Seychelles (☎ 0262 57 26 38; fax 02 62 25 20 42; 67 Rue de Kerveguen, 97430 Le Tampon)
Spain (☎ 02 62 34 90 58; fax 02 62 34 83 04; 1 Rue de la Salette, 97436 Saint-Leu)

See the Regional Directory (p281) for information about what to expect from embassies and consulates.

FOOD

You can expect to pay under €10 for a meal in a budget restaurant in Réunion. Eating in a mid-range place should come in at between €10 and €20, while at the top end the bill will be from around €20 up.

Many restaurants offer a set menu consisting of a starter, main course and dessert. Often there is no choice but in some cases there will be perhaps one or two different dishes per course to choose between. If what's on offer appeals, set menus can represent very good value, particularly at lunch time.

FESTIVALS & EVENTS

Major festivals in Réunion involve street parties, exhibitions, sports events, music, dancing and various other activities. Towns and villages across the island take turns at celebrating over a week or weekend; the excuse is to honour their primary product, which can be anything from *chou chou* (a green squash-like vegetable) to sugar cane. The atmosphere is generally commercial rather than celebratory, with plenty of market stalls selling the fêted produce. Beauty pageants are a popular feature, usually featuring loud rock music.

Abolition of Slavery Day (a national holiday) is taken very seriously, particularly among the Creole population, who still occupy a disadvantaged position in society. The celebrations usually involve street parties with live reggae and *séga* music, dancing and other lively activities.

The Indian community is principally made up of Tamil Hindus and they hold some amazing rites, including *Cavadee* (in which pilgrims practice self-mutilation) and fire-walking ceremonies. The Hindu temple in St-André is the most popular location for these events. (See p134 for more about these festivals.)

To find out what's happening during your stay contact any of the tourist offices or the *mairie* (town hall) in the relevant town.

Festivals in Réunion:

JANUARY

Fête du Miel Vert (Festival of Honey) Plaine-des-Cafres.
Fête des Vendanges (Wine Harvest Festival) Cilaos.
Fire-walking ceremonies Various locations.

FEBRUARY

Cavadee (Tamil procession) St-André.
Chinese New Year Various locations.

APRIL

Tamil New Year (dance displays) Various locations.

MAY

Fête du Chou Chou (Festival of Chou chou) Hell-Bourg.

Fête du Choca (Festival of Choca; crafts made from choca leaves) Entre-Deux.

JUNE

Fête des Goyaviers (Festival of Guava) Plaine-des-Palmistes.
Le Tempo (one week of theatre and street events in June or July) St-Leu.

AUGUST

Foire du Bois (Festival of Wood) La Rivière, St-Louis.
Fête du Vacoa (Festival of Vacoa; crafts made from screw-pine fronds) St-Philippe.
Pèlerinage à la Vierge au Parasol (Pilgrimage to the Virgin with the Parasol) Ste-Rose.

SEPTEMBER

Florilèges (flower show in late September or early October) Le Tampon.
Fête de Notre Dame de la Salette (Festival of Notre Dame de la Salette; fair street events over 10 days) St-Leu.

OCTOBER

Fête de l'Ail (Festival of Garlic) Petite Île.
Fête des Bichiques (Festival of Bichiques) Bras-Panon.
Fête du Safran (Festival of Saffron) St-Joseph.
Kabaréso (music festival) St-André.
Semaine Créole (Créole Week; a week of cultural events) various locations.
Grand Raid (cross-country race in October or November) St-Philippe to St-Denis.
Divali (or Dipavali; Tamil festival of light in late October or early November) St-André and other locations.

NOVEMBER

Fête du Curcuma (Festival of Curcuma) St-Joseph.
Fête des Lentilles (Festival of lentils) Cilaos.

HOLIDAYS

Most of Réunion's offices, museums and shops are closed during *jours fériés* (public holidays), which are as follows:

New Year's Day 1 January
Easter Monday March/April
Labour Day 1 May
Victory Day 1945 8 May
Ascension Day late May or June
Bastille Day (National Day) 14 July
Assumption Day 15 August
All Saints' Day 1 November
Armistice Day 1918 11 November
Abolition of Slavery Day 20 December
Christmas Day 25 December

See p281 for more about holidays.

INTERNET RESOURCES

There are several useful sites covering Réunion though unfortunately most of the information is in French.

Clicanoo (http://vacances.clicanoo.info in French) A fair number of interesting articles, listings and links put together by the newspaper *Journal de l'Île Réunion*.
Communauté de Communes de Sud (www.reunion-sud.com in French) Information-rich bilingual site covering the south of the island.
Île de la Réunion (www.iledelareunion.net in French) This huge, colourful site is packed with practical information and useful links. It also includes interesting news snippets and background articles.
La Réunion (www.la-reunion-tourisme.com) The official site of Réunion's tourist board is well organised, easy to use and informative. It's also in English.
RUNweb (www.runweb.com in French) This portal site offers a broad range of tourism-related links.

MAPS

For most purposes the **IGN** (Institut Géographique National; www.ign.fr in French) 1:100,000 map, which covers the island in one sheet, is perfectly adequate. The most detailed and accurate maps for hiking are the six-sheet 1:250,000 series (see p225).

MEDIA

Newspapers & Magazines

The two most popular daily newspapers are the conservative **Journal de l'Île de la Réunion** (JIR; www.clicanoo.com in French) and the more liberal *Le Quotidien*. Each costs around €1 and carries local, métro, regional and world news. They're both good for features and events listings, while the *JIR* also has a large Sunday edition with a section devoted to local history and culture.

You can pick up English-language newspapers at a few places, including the major bookshops in St-Denis and newsagents in St-Gilles-les-Bains. But by far the best range of newspapers and magazines in English, French and several other languages is at Le Rallye Presse in St-Denis (p157).

A magazine of interest to visitors is *Réunion Magazine*, published every three months in Paris, which contains in-depth features on tourist destinations in Réunion and France's other tropical islands. The bimonthly *Cascavelle* is published locally and is of more general interest. It covers local news and personalities and has interesting, in-depth articles on the island's history, its arts and so forth.

TV & Radio

Television viewers have the choice of two government channels (Télé Réunion and Tempo) as well as the independent Antenne Réunion. Most of the programming on the public channels does come from mainland France.

There are also two government-run radio stations, and scores of 'free' stations such as Radio Free-DOM and Radio Arc-en-Ciel; these cover the island and satisfy a range of creeds and tastes. Because of the mountainous landscape, radio reception can be very variable.

MONEY

As in France, the unit of currency is the euro (€), which is divided into 100 cents. Euro coins come in denominations of one, two, five, 10, 20 and 50 cents and one and two euros. Banknotes are issued in denominations of five, 10, 20, 50, 100, 200 and 500 euros.

ATMs

Most banks and post offices have an ATM (known as a *guichet automatique de banque* or GAB) which honour major international credit cards. Visa and MasterCard are the most widely accepted. If you're heading off into the cirques, it's wise to stock up with euros beforehand. There is only one ATM in Cilaos and one in Salazie and neither can be relied on.

Credit Cards

Visa and MasterCard are the most useful cards to carry, followed by Amex. You should have no problem using plastic in larger shops, hotels and restaurants. Smaller places, however, sometimes refuse cards for small amounts (typically under €10 or €16) and it's rare for *chambres d'hôte* and *gîtes d'étape* to take credit cards.

Moneychangers

Changing money in Réunion is a bit of a problem. Few banks have foreign-exchange facilities and those that do (the most likely being Crédit Agricole and PNB Paribas) generally accept only British pounds and US dollars cash, rarely travellers cheques. In any case, banks charge punitive commission rates on all foreign-exchange transactions. Euro-denominated travellers cheques don't attract commission, nor do you pay commission if you change cash (British pounds and US dollars only) at the main post offices in Réunion.

There are no exchange facilities at either Roland Garros International Airport or the ferry terminal in Le Port, though the airport does at least have an ATM.

As a general strategy, it's sensible to bring a fair supply of euros with you and to top it up from the ATMs.

TELEPHONE

Réunion's telephone system is efficient. There are numerous public telephones scattered around the island and you can directly dial international numbers on them. They only accept *télécartes* (phonecards), not coins. Phonecards are available at post offices and shops; they cost €6.72 for 50 units and €12.40 for 120 units of call time.

Alternatively, there are several prepaid calling cards which require you to dial a free number and enter a personal identity number before you place your call; the compensation for the inconvenience is reduced rates for international calls. Options include France Télécom's Ticket Alizés and Outremer Télécom's Pass.

Local calls cost roughly €0.02 per minute. Calls to France are €0.20 per minute; to the UK €0.55 per minute; to Australia and New Zealand €0.87 per minute; and to Canada and the USA €0.50 per minute. Charges are slightly higher during peak times (ie during business hours).

When making a call to Réunion from abroad, you'll need to dial the international code for Réunion (262), followed by the local number minus the first 0. The code for a mobile number is 0692. There are no area codes in Réunion.

Mobile Phones

If you have a GSM phone and it has been 'unlocked', it is possible to buy a SIM card with either of the two local network operators: Orange (France Télécom) and SFR. The starter pack costs €30, which includes a certain amount of credit. Re-charge cards are widely available.

Local calls cost between €0.16 and €0.35 per minute, depending on whether you're calling someone on the same network or a fixed phone.

TOURIST INFORMATION

Tourist services in Réunion have the full backing of the French government, so the information and assistance available is generally excellent. Most of the *offices du tourisme* (tourist offices) have at least one staff member who speaks English and other languages.

For information on hiking, refer to the sources described in the chapter Hiking in Réunion on p224. Other queries should be taken to the **main tourist office** (☎ 02 62 41 83 00; fax 02 62 21 37 76; 53 Rue Pasteur) in St-Denis or one of the local offices scattered around the island. There's also a useful information and welcome counter at **Roland Garros International Airport** (☎ 02 62 48 81 81); the counter is open to meet international arrival flights.

Tourist office staff can generally offer plenty of advice and information. They also provide maps, brochures and the monthly magazine *GuideRUN*, which is a useful directory of hotels, restaurants, discos, travel agencies and other places of interest to visitors. The associated *Guide de Loisirs* gives an overview of the various activities on offer and lists the principal operators.

If you want to obtain copies before you arrive in Réunion, contact the **Comité du Tourisme de la Réunion** (☎ 02 62 21 00 41; www.la-reunion-tourisme.com; Pl du 20 Décembre 1848, 97472 St-Denis), or the **office** (☎ 01 40 75 02 79; www.la-reunion-tourisme.com; 90 Rue de la Boétie, 75008 Paris) in mainland France. You can also contact the French tourist office in your home country; these are listed on www.franceguide.com.

TOURS

Coach Tours

Souprayenmestry (☎ 02 62 44 81 69; transports-souprayen@wanadoo.fr) runs a regular programme of coach tours to the major sites: on Tuesday there's a tour of the Cirque de Salazie, on Thursday there's a tour all around the coast road, on Friday the tour goes to Piton de la Fournaise and on Saturday it's the Cirque de Cilaos. All tours cost €15/8 per adult/child. The coach has designated pick-up and drop-off points in towns along the west coast from St-Denis down to St-Pierre.

A few travel agents in St-Denis and St-Gilles-les-Bains offer similar tours; see below for contact details. These tours are more expensive; however you're likely to be travelling with a smaller group. Prices start at around €30/60 for a half/full day's tour. If you fancy something less regimented, the same agencies will happily put together tailor-made itineraries.

Comète Voyages Réunion (Map p159; ☎ 02 62 21 31 00; comete.voyages@wanadoo.fr; cnr Rue Jules Auber & Rue Moulin à Vent, St-Denis)

Objectif (Map p188; ☎ 02 62 33 08 33; objectif.reunion@wanadoo.fr; 28 Chemin Summer, St-Gilles-les-Bains)

Nouvelles Frontières (Map p188; ☎ 02 62 33 11 95; www.nf-reunion.com in French; 31 Pl Paul-Julius Bénard, St-Gilles-les-Bains)

Voyages FRAM (Map p188; ☎ 02 62 24 58 45; pdebiasi@fram.fr; Pl Paul-Julius Bénard, St-Gilles-les-Bains)

Helicopter & Light Aircraft

Helicopter tours of the magnificent cirques and the volcano are understandably popular, although not with the walkers on the ground who have their peace and quiet disturbed every few minutes by the whirring of rotor blades. The tours certainly offer an exhilarating and sensational view of the landscape, and while they aren't cheap, most travellers rate such a trip as a highlight of their visit to Réunion.

Helilagon (Map p182; ☎ 02 62 55 55 55; www.helilagon.com) is based at L'Éperon, in the hills above St-Gilles-les-Bains. A 45-minute tour of all three cirques and Piton de la Fournaise costs €260 per person, or €220 without the volcano. To visit Salazie and Cirque de Mafate with a stop in Mafate costs €180. For an extra €82 you can be dropped off in Mafate at the end of a tour and be picked up again in the afternoon. Prices include transfers to the heliport from hotels in St-Gilles-les-Bains and tours leave between 7am and 9am in the morning.

Heli Réunion (Map p188; ☎ 02 62 24 00 00; www.heli-reunion.com in French) is a smaller outfit offering similar tours for similar prices. For example, a tour of the three cirques and the volcano costs €240 (€200 without the volcano). A 25-minute tour over the cirques of Salazie and Mafate costs €160. Flights leave from the heliport at Hermitage-les-Bains.

As well as in helicopters, it's possible to make a tour of the cirques in a light aircraft. While the planes can't get you as close to the scenery, they are more affordable than the helicopter tours; prices start at around €110 per hour for two people. Contact the

Aéroclub du Sud (☎ 02 62 25 03 80; fax 02 62 57 27 47) based at Pierrefonds airport near St-Pierre for further information.

For the ultimate aerial experience, **Felix ULM** (☎ 02 62 43 02 59; www.felixulm.com in French) and **Papangue ULM** (☎ 06 92 08 85 86; www.fransurf.com/papangue-ulm in French) will take you up in an ultralight aircraft where you are exposed to all the elements. Tours of the three cirques cost around €150.

All flights are dependent on the prevailing weather conditions, and may be cancelled at the last minute if there is heavy cloud over the cirques.

VISAS

The visa requirements for entry to Réunion are the same as for France. There are no restrictions on nationals of the EU. Citizens of Australia, the USA, Canada, New Zealand and a number of other countries do not need visas to visit as tourists for up to three months. Check with the French embassy or consulate nearest your home address to find out if you need a visa.

Except for EU citizens, those who don't need a visa and wish to stay for longer than three months need to apply for a *carte de séjour* (residence permit). Contact the **Service Étrangers** (☎ 02 62 40 75 90; 6 Rue de la Messageries) at the Préfecture in St-Denis. You could always pop across to Mauritius and then re-enter Réunion to get around this requirement.

It is difficult to get a tourist visa extension except in the case of an emergency (eg medical problems). Again, if you have a visa extension query, contact the Service Étrangers.

TRANSPORT

GETTING THERE & AWAY

The following section covers transport between the three islands of Réunion, Mauritius and the Seychelles. For information about getting to the region from elsewhere, see the Regional Directory (p277).

Air

There are several flights a day between Mauritius and Réunion operated by Air Mauritius and Air Austral. Low-season fares start at around €250 for a one-month return. The flight takes around 45 minutes. Air Mauritius also has two weekly flights from Rodrigues; a one-month return fare costs €350. From the Seychelles, there's a choice between Air Seychelles and Air Austral. They operate one flight a week each and tickets cost around €440 for a one-month return. The flight takes 2½ hours. All three carriers have a good safety record.

Réunion has two international airports. The vast majority of flights come in to **Roland Garros International Airport** (code RUN; ☎ 02 62 28 16 16; www.reunion.aeroport.fr in French) about 10km east of St-Denis. Coming from Mauritius, you have the option of landing at **Pierrefonds Airport** (code ZSE; ☎ 02 62 96 77 66; www.grandsudreunion.org), in the south of the island near St-Pierre.

AIRLINES FLYING TO & FROM RÉUNION

Air Austral (airline code UU; ☎ 02 62 90 90 91; www.air-austral.com in French; 4 Rue de Nice, St-Denis; hub Roland Garros International Airport, Réunion)

Air Mauritius (airline code MK; ☎ 02 62 94 83 83; www.airmauritius.com; 13 Rue Charles Gounod; hub SSR International Airport, Mauritius)

Air Seychelles (airline code HM; ☎ 02 62 40 39 63; www.airseychelles.net; hub Seychelles International Airport, Mahé)

Sea

The most comfortable way to travel between Mauritius and Réunion by sea is the smart, new *Mauritius Trochetia*, which operates several times monthly from Port Louis in Mauritius to Le Port in Réunion. The cheapest berth in a second-class cabin costs around Rs 3750/4350 in low/high season for a return trip from Mauritius and €165/200 from Réunion. One-way tickets are about 35% less.

The *Mauritius Pride*, which also sails several times a month, is older, but has the option of slightly cheaper reclining seats. These cost roughly Rs 3000/3600 for a low/high season return from Mauritius, while a berth in a two-person cabin is Rs 4350/5259. Departing from Réunion, you'll pay €135/160 for a reclining seat and €195/230 for a berth. One-way tickets cost roughly 30% less. Prices include meals.

In either case the journey takes around 11 hours. Tickets and information are available in Réunion through travel agents or direct from **SCOAM** (☎ 02 62 42 19 45; passagers@scoam.fr; 4 Ave du 14 Juillet 1789) in Le Port. Note that

Raffia baskets, St Paul's Market, St-Paul (p194)

OLIVIER CIRENDINI

OLIVIER CIRENDINI

Tamil temple (p216), Réunion

Indian festival (p216), St Louis

JEAN-BERNARD CARILLET

JEAN-BERNARD CARILLET

Hiking trail, Forêt de Bélouve (p207)

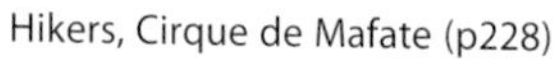

Hikers, Cirque de Mafate (p228)

JEAN-BERNARD CARILLET

Canyoning (p199), Cirque de Cilaos

JEAN-BERNARD CA

during the cyclone season (October to March), services may be cancelled.

GETTING AROUND

Air

See p286 for information regarding air travel in Réunion and around.

Bicycle

The traffic, the haste of most motorists and the steep and precarious nature of the mountain roads means that those considering cycling as a form of transport in Réunion should be prepared for some hair-raising and potentially dangerous situations.

The coastal roads are far too busy for casual cycling and the cirque roads are too steep, but the back roads and rugged terrain of the interior are ideally suited to *vélos tout terrain* (mountain bikes). In recent years a network of challenging dirt trails has been established on the island. For more about these trails and a list of rental outlets, see p214.

When renting a bike, prices start in the region of €12 to €15 per day (including a helmet), less if you take it for longer periods. A deposit of €250 or more depending on the type of bike is usually required; most places will take an imprint of your credit card.

Bus

The Réunion bus service **Car Jaune** (☎ 06 92 12 39 74), which has distinctive yellow buses, covers most parts of the island with several main routes. The main *gare routière* (bus station) is on Blvd de l'Océan on the St-Denis seafront. There's an **information counter** (⏰ 4.30am-7.45pm Mon-Fri, 6.45am-noon & 1pm-5.45pm Sat & Sun) where you can buy tickets and get *horaires* (timetables) for the different routes. You can also pick up timetables at the St-Denis tourist office.

Buses on most routes run between about 5am and 7pm, with a limited number of services on Sunday. For a few sample fares, you'll pay €7.10 from St-Denis to St-Pierre, €3.30 from St-Denis to St-Benoît and €7.60 from St-Benoît to St-Pierre via Plaine-des-Cafres. You can pay the driver as you board. To get the bus to stop, you ring the bell or clap your hands twice loudly.

Car Jaune provides regional minibus services for several towns on the island; these services are known as Ti' Car Jaune (from *petit*). Ti' Car Jaune buses run from St-Benoît, Ste-Rose, St-Leu and Entre-Deux. Regional bus companies fill in the gaps between the Ti' Car Jaune services, but these convoluted local routes can be fairly confusing, particularly if you don't speak much French. Of most use to travellers are the buses from Salazie to Hell-Bourg, Grand Îlet and Le Bélier, and the buses from St-Pierre to Cilaos, Îlet à Cordes and Bras Sec.

Car

The road system on the island is excellent and well signposted. Route Nationale 1 (RN 1), the main road around the island, approaches international motorway standards in parts.

Heading into the mountains via the cirque roads – especially the route into Cilaos – is a magnificent experience. The superbly engineered roads snake through hairpin bends, up steep slopes and along sheer drops, surrounded all the while by glorious – and distracting – scenery.

The experience is likely to be marred somewhat by the local drivers, who insist on driving these roads at breakneck speeds. If you suddenly encounter an irate local inches away from your rear bumper, pull over and let them overtake rather than driving faster to appease them. Beware, too, of the cavernous storm drains which take the place of a verge on the already narrow mountain roads.

RENTAL

With most attractions located in the hills, *location de voitures* (car hire) is extremely popular in Réunion, and rates are very reasonable, particularly if you stick to small hatchbacks. Most companies stipulate that the driver must be at least 21 (sometimes 23) years of age, have held a driving licence for at least a year, and have a passport or some other form of identification. EU citizens can drive on their national driving licence; from elsewhere, you'll need an international driving licence.

Prices and regulations don't vary much between the main international companies. Rates start at €50 to €60 per day (including insurance and unlimited mileage) and drop rapidly for longer hire periods. The total amount is normally payable in advance. Most policies specify that you are liable for

BUS TIMETABLE IN RÉUNION

Route no	Route name	Frequency	Duration	Main stops
Line A	St-Denis to St-Pierre Express	Roughly every hour	1½ hr	Limited stops on the highway in St-Paul, Boucan Canot, L'Hermitage-les-Bains, St-Leu, Étang-Salé-les-Bains and St-Louis
Line B	St-Denis to St-Pierre, via the coast	Roughly every 1½ hr	2½ hr	Frequent stops in downtown Le Port, St-Paul, St-Gilles-les-Bains, St-Leu, Étang-Salé-les-Bains, St-Louis etc. Some only go as far as St-Louis
Line C	St-Denis to St-Pierre, via the hills	Roughly every hour	2¾ hr	As for Line B to St-Leu, then Piton St-Leu, Les Avirons, Étang-Salé-les-Bains and St-Louis
Line D	St-Denis to St Paul	Roughly hourly	1 hr	La Possession and Le Port
Line E	St-Pierre to Chaloupe St-Leu	3 daily (2 on Sunday)	2 hr	Colimaçons, Piton St-Leu, Les Avirons, Étang-Salé-les-Bains and St-Louis
Line F	St-Denis to St-Benoît Express	Roughly hourly	1 hr	Ste-Marie, Ste-Suzanne, St-André and Bras Pranon
Line G	St-Denis to St-Benoît	Every 30 min	1½ hr	Frequent stops in downtown Ste-Marie, Ste-Suzanne, St-André and Bras Pranon
Line H	St-Benoît to St-Pierre, via the plains	3 daily (2 on Sunday)	2 hr	Plaine-des-Palmistes, Plaine-des-Cafres and Le Tampon
Line I	St-Benoît to St-Pierre, via St-Philippe	Every 2 hr	2½ hr	Ste-Anne, Ste-Rose, Piton Ste-Rose, St-Philippe, Vincendo, St-Joseph and Petite Île
Line J	St-André to Salazie	7 daily (3 on Sunday)	30 min	
Line L	St-Pierre to Entre-Deux	5 daily (2 on Sunday)	30 min	

at least the first €300 of damage in the event of an accident; companies usually take an imprint of your credit card to cover the refundable deposit.

International companies with offices at the airport include **Avis** (☎ 02 62 48 81 85; fax 02 62 29 29 11), **Budget** (☎ 02 62 28 01 95; budget-reunion.com in French), **Europcar** (☎ 02 62 28 27 58; europcar@runnet.com), **Hertz** (☎ 02 62 28 05 93; www.hertzreunion.com) and **Sixt** (☎ 02 62 29 79 79; sixt-reunion@sogerent.fr). Most of these companies also have representatives in St-Gilles-les-Bains and St-Pierre.

There are plenty of cheaper independent operators around the island. Rates can drop as low as €30 per day or €25 if you rent for several days, but be aware that in peak season most of these bargain cars are booked up in advance from mainland France.

Reliable independent car rental companies include the following at the Roland Garros Airport:

Au Bas Prix (☎ 02 62 22 69 89; aubasprix@wanadoo.fr; Roland Garros International Airport)

Rent A Car (☎ 02 62 53 22 70; rentacar-lareunion.com; Roland Garros International Airport)

See individual towns for local companies (p165; p191).

ROAD RULES

Like mainland France, Réunion keeps to the right side of the road. Speed limits are clearly indicated and vary from 50km/h in towns to 110km/h on dual carriageways. Drivers and passengers are required to wear seat belts. The alcohol limit is 0.5 grams per litre.

Motorcycle

With its well-maintained roads and glorious scenery, Réunion should be a motorcyclist's dream. Sadly the adage 'hell is other people' certainly holds true on Réunion's roads. Car drivers show little consideration for motorcycles and beginner riders should think carefully – and have a good insurance policy – before setting out on two wheels.

If that doesn't put you off, there are a couple of reliable rental outlets on the island. Both offer bikes from 125cc to 750cc or bigger, but for these roads the best all-purpose bikes are 600cc or 650cc machines (for which you'll need a motorbike licence). The price is around €70 to €80 a day, dropping to €50 or €60 if you rent for a week. See p165 and p191 for local companies listed.

Hiking in Réunion

CONTENTS

When to Hike	225
What to Take	225
Costs & Money	225
Reading Up	226
Tours	226
Sleeping & Eating	226
Responsible Hiking	227
Cirque de Mafate	228
Tour des Cirques	231
Piton de la Fournaise	234

For many visitors, hiking is the *raison d'être* of a trip to Réunion. The island boasts more than a thousand kilometres of hiking trails, the best of which take you through an awe-inspiring landscape of jagged mountain crests, forested valleys, tumbling waterfalls and surreal volcanic tuff. Vast swathes of the interior of the island are accessible only on foot. As a result, the natural environment is remarkably intact, with a huge variety of flora, from tropical rainforest to gnarled thickets of giant heather. Formed from one mighty dead volcano (Piton des Neiges) and one very alive volcano (Piton de la Fournaise), the island is a paradise for hikers, adventure-sports enthusiasts or indeed anyone who is receptive to the untamed beauty of a wilderness environment.

There are two major hiking trails, known as Grande Randonnée Route 1 (GR R1) and Grande Randonnée Route 2 (GR R2), with numerous offshoots. The GR R1 does a tour of Piton des Neiges, passing through Cilaos, the Forêt de Bélouve, Hell-Bourg and the Cirque de Mafate. The GR R2 makes an epic traverse across the island all the way from St-Denis to St-Philippe via the three cirques, the Plaine-des-Cafres and Piton de la Fournaise.

Thanks to the Office National des Forêts (ONF), the trails are well maintained, but the tropical rainfall can eat through footpaths and wash away steps and handrails. Even experienced hikers should be prepared for tortuous ascents, slippery mud chutes, and narrow paths beside sheer precipices. The routes are well signposted on the whole, but it's essential to carry a good map and you should check locally on the current situation; trails are occasionally closed for maintenance, especially following severe storms.

The trails described in this section are popular hikes, though there are countless variations, and they should be well within the capabilities of any reasonably fit adult; children with a sense of adventure and a good head for heights should be able to do the walks with a little extra time. The hiking times given are for an average hiker carrying a light daypack and taking only brief breaks. (For more information on the towns and villages that you may pass through, such as Cilaos and Hell-Bourg, see The Interior p195).

HIKING TIPS

Safety is basically a matter of common sense and being prepared. Make sure you

- use a detailed and up-to-date map
- double-check the state of the paths before setting out
- check the weather report before setting out
- leave early enough to reach your destination before dark
- take plenty of water and energy-rich snacks
- wear comfortable hiking boots
- take wet-weather gear
- carry a basic medical kit
- tell people where you're going if you are hiking alone.

WHEN TO HIKE

The best time to hike is during the dry season, from around late April to the end of October; May and June are probably the best months of all. The weather is extremely changeable from one part of this small island to the other. For example, you can leave Col des Bœufs shrouded in mist and arrive at the village of La Nouvelle under a blazing sun.

The weather in Réunion has a tendency to become worse as the day goes on. As the hours pass, the island's uplands seem to delight in 'trapping' any cloud that happens to come their way. An early start is therefore one of the best defences against the vagaries of the elements.

The next day's weather forecast is shown on the two main television channels after the evening news (generally around 8pm). You can also get the forecast by telephoning the **Météo France voice service** (☎ 08 92 68 08 08; per min €0.30). Cyclone bulletins are available on ☎ 08 97 65 01 01 (per min €0.51). Both these services are in French.

WHAT TO TAKE

Good shoes are essential for hiking the trails of Réunion, which are of gravel and stone and often very steep, muddy or slippery. Hiking shoes with good ankle support are better than sneakers. If you're overnighting, take a pair of sandals for the evening – your feet will thank you.

Be sure to carry water (at least 2L for a day's hiking), wet-weather gear, a warm top, a hat, sunscreen, sunglasses, insect repellent, a whistle, a torch and a basic medical kit including plasters (Band-Aids), elastic bandages and muscle balm for blisters and minor muscle injuries. If you intend sleeping out at altitude, you'll need a decent sleeping bag, as temperatures in the cirques can fall rapidly at night. Although the *gîtes de montagne* (mountain lodges) provide sheets and blankets, a sheet sleeping bag (sleep sheet) wouldn't go amiss.

You will be able to buy most last-minute supplies at a sporting-goods store or one of the big supermarkets in Réunion. Cilaos has a couple of excellent outdoor suppliers (p199).

Réunion is covered by the six 1:25,000 scale maps published by the **Institut Géographique National** (IGN; www.ign.fr in French). These maps are reasonably up-to-date and show trails and *gîtes*. Map number 4402 RT is one of the most useful for hikers, since it covers Cirque de Mafate and Cirque de Salazie as well as the northern part of the Cirque de Cilaos. It also covers the whole of the GR R1. The maps are sold all over the island, including at the Maison de la Montagne in St-Denis (p157). They cost around €12 apiece.

COSTS & MONEY

The cost of a dorm bed in a *gîte de montagne* is a standard €13.50 per night (€9.50 to €11.50 for children); this must be paid for in advance (see p226). Meals, which have to be paid for on arrival at the *gîte*, cost

INFORMATION

Hiking information is provided by the headquarters of the **Maison de la Montagne** (☎ 02 62 90 78 78; www.reunion-nature.com in French; 10 Pl Sarda Garriga; 9am-5pm Mon-Thu, 9am-4pm Fri, 9am-noon Sat) in St-Denis and by associated tourist offices, including those in Cilaos, Salazie, Hell-Bourg, St-Gilles-les-Bains, St-Pierre, St-Leu and Bourg-Murat. All these offices organise bookings for *gîtes de montagne* (mountain lodges) and can give advice as to which paths are currently closed. They also provide guides and arrange hiking tours.

EMERGENCIES

In a real emergency out on the trail, lifting both arms to form a 'V' is a signal to helicopter pilots who fly over the island that you need help. If you have a mobile phone, call the emergency services on ☎ 112 or ☎ 02 62 93 09 30. *Gîtes de montagne* (mountain lodges) have telephones with which you can contact emergency services.

between €13.50 and €15 (€7.50 to €11.50 for children) for dinner and €4 to €6 for breakfast. Private *gîtes d'étape* (privately run walkers' lodge) tend to charge about the same, while at a *chambre d'hôte* (B&B) you can expect to pay around €30 for a double room. In all cases, payment will be expected in cash.

If you'll need to buy provisions along the way, make sure you carry plenty of cash with you. The only places to get euros in the cirques are the ATMs at the post offices in Salazie and Cilaos, and these can't be depended on.

Fully qualified mountain guides can be contacted through the Maison de la Montagne and local tourist offices. Rates are negotiable and vary according to the length and degree of difficulty of the hike; an undemanding one-day outing should start at around €100.

READING UP

Several excellent route guides are available at the Maison de la Montagne. Though only in French, they are still useful for their maps.

The definitive guide to the GR R1 and GR R2 is the Topo-guide *L'île de la Réunion*, published by the Fédération Française de la Randonnée Pédestre. It uses 1:25,000 scale IGN maps and includes eight one-day hikes of varying lengths and degrees of difficulty.

52 Balades et Randonnées Faciles (published locally by Orphie) is designed with children in mind and describes outings that can be covered in less than four hours.

A broader range of walks is covered by *62 Randonnées Réunionnaise* (also by Orphie). The loose-leaf format, with one walk per page, is extremely practical.

Sur les Sentiers de Mafate, published by the ONF, details hikes in the Cirque de Mafate. This high-quality guide also describes the flora, fauna and history of Mafate, but unfortunately it's a touch heavy to pop in your rucksack.

For map recommendations, see What to Take (p225).

By far the most useful website for hikers is that of the **Maison de la Montagne** (www.reuion-nature.com in French). It allows you to book *gîtes de montagne* online and buy maps and guides, and also has general information about hiking in Réunion, including brief details of the most popular walks, places to buy food in the cirques and so forth. The information is not always up-to-date, however, so double-check on the ground.

TOURS

Réunion's hiking trails are well established and reasonably well signposted, but you may get more information about the environment you are walking through if you go with a local guide. The Maison de la Montagne publishes *La Réunion: une île grandeur nature*, which lists organised adventure trips on the island. Alternatively, contact one of the following operators.

Simple guided walks start at €40/150 per person for one/two days, while a seven-day hike costs upwards of €650, including meals and accommodation. More-expensive itineraries that include adventure activities such as mountain biking and canyoning are also available. Further information is available from the Maison de la Montagne in St-Denis and from local tourist offices (see p225).

Austral Aventure (☎ 02 62 32 40 29; www.creole.org/austral-aventure/index.html)

Maham (☎ 02 62 47 82 82; www.chez.com/maham in French; Rue du Général de Gaulle, Hell-Bourg)

Rando Run (☎ 02 62 26 31 31; www.randorun.com in French)

Réunion Sensations (☎ 02 62 31 84 84; www.reunion-sensations.com; 28 Rue du Père Boiteau, Cilaos)

SLEEPING & EATING

Most of the accommodation for hikers consists of *gîtes de montagne* (mostly found in isolated locations on the trails themselves) or of small, family-run B&Bs known as *chambres d'hôte* (mostly found in the villages at the ends of the hiking trails). Some of the *gîtes de montagne* on the walking trails are more accurately described as *gîtes d'étape*, which are privately run and offer dorm beds and meals. There's often very little to separate the two types of *gîte* in terms of comfort or facilities. Showers are often solar heated and are rarely piping hot; some places can be downright cold at night. Your choice of where to stay will most likely be based on where you can find a room. There are also a few hotels in Hell-Bourg and Cilaos for that last night of luxury (and central heating) before you set out on your hike.

Many visitors from mainland France book their accommodation before arriving in Réunion, so don't make the mistake of leaving it to the last minute. During July and August and around Christmas it's hard to find a bed in the cirques for love or money. At other times it's best to book at least a couple of months in advance, particularly for popular places such as the *gîtes* at Caverne Dufour (for Piton des Neiges) and Piton de la Fournaise.

The *gîtes de montagne* are managed by the Maison de la Montagne and must be booked and paid for in advance. This can be done at the Maison de la Montagne in St-Denis (or through its website) and at certain tourist offices (see p225 for details). Most of these offices accept credit cards, though check beforehand to be sure. When you pay, you will receive a voucher to be given to the manager of the *gîte*. You must call the *gîte* to book your meals at least two days in advance; this can be done at the same time as the original booking if you'd rather, but meals still have to paid for on the spot.

If all this organisation doesn't fit in with your idea of adventure, camping is permitted in most areas, but for one night at a time. You can usually pitch a tent somewhere near a village or a *gîte*, though be sure to ask first. Camping is strictly prohibited around Piton de la Fournaise.

Most *gîtes* offer Creole meals, which are normally hearty, though a little rustic for some palates. The standard fare is *carri poulet* (chicken curry), *boucané* (smoked pork) or *rougail saucisses* (sausages in tomato sauce), often with local wine or *rhum arrangé* (rum punch) thrown in. Breakfast usually consists of just a cup of coffee with bread and jam.

If you plan to self-cater, you'll need to bring plenty of carbohydrate-rich food. Instant noodles are light and filling, while chocolate and other sugary snacks can provide the energy necessary to make that last mountain ridge. There are cooking facilities at a few *gîtes*, but you are best off bringing a camping stove; note that you are not allowed to light fires anywhere in the forest areas. Some villages in the cirques have shops where you can purchase a very limited variety of food; few places stock anything more wholesome than biscuits, processed cheese and canned sardines.

RESPONSIBLE HIKING

The popularity of hiking is placing great pressure on the natural environment of Réunion. Please consider the following tips when hiking, and help preserve the ecology and beauty of Réunion.

Rubbish

Carry out *all* your rubbish. Don't overlook easily forgotten items such as silver paper, orange peel, cigarette butts and plastic or paper wrappers. Empty packaging should be stored in a dedicated rubbish bag. Make an effort to carry out rubbish left by others.

Never bury your rubbish: digging disturbs soil and ground cover and encourages erosion. Buried rubbish will likely be dug up by animals, who may be injured or poisoned by it. The buried rubbish may also take years to decompose.

Minimise waste by taking minimal packaging and no more food than you will need. Take reusable containers or stuff sacks.

Sanitary napkins, tampons, condoms and toilet paper should be carried out despite the inconvenience. They burn and decompose poorly.

Human Waste Disposal

Contamination of water sources by human faeces can lead to the transmission of all sorts of nasties. Where there is a toilet, please use it. Where there is none, bury your waste. Dig a small hole 15cm (6in) deep and at least 100m (320ft) from any watercourse. Cover the waste with soil and a rock.

Washing

Don't use detergents or toothpaste in or near the watercourses, even if they are biodegradable.

For personal washing, use biodegradable soap and a water container (or even a lightweight, portable basin) at least 50m (160ft) away from the watercourse. Disperse the waste water widely to allow the soil to filter it fully.

Wash cooking utensils 50m (160ft) away from watercourses and use a scourer instead of detergent.

Erosion

Hillsides and mountain slopes are prone to erosion. Make sure you stick to existing trails and avoid short cuts.

If a well-used trail passes through a mud patch, walk through the mud so as not to increase the size of the patch.

Avoid removing the plant life that keeps the topsoil in place.

CIRQUE DE MAFATE

HIKE AT A GLANCE

Duration four days
Distance 25km
Difficulty moderate
Accommodation *gîtes de montagne, gîtes d'étape*
Start Le Petit Col
Finish Le Petit Col

Surrounded by ramparts, crisscrossed with gullies and studded with narrow ridges, Mafate is the wildest and most remote of Réunion's cirques (see p206). The cirque is only accessible on foot, but a forestry road runs up to the pass at Col des Bœufs between Cirque de Mafate and the Cirque de Salazie. The other main routes into Mafate are from Cilaos via the Col du Taïbit (2082m); along the banks of the Rivière des Galets from Dos d'Ane or Sans Souci; and via Le Maïdo, which involves a precipitous descent into Roche Plate. Most people take the easy option and hop over the ridge at Col des Bœufs.

The following itinerary takes you through some of the most interesting and scenic parts of Mafate in four days. Numerous other options exist; staff at the Maison de la Montagne will be able to make recommendations. This hike can also be combined with the Tour des Cirques (see p231).

Secure parking is available at **Le Petit Col car park** (☎ 06 92 11 97 37; parking per 24hr €10). Buses from Salazie and Grand Îlet drop you at the bottom of the hill in Le Bélier (p205). From there, **Titine Nourry** (☎ 02 62 47 71 84), who runs a small grocery store, offers minibus transport to Le Petit Col for €30 for up to 10 people; phone the day before to reserve.

The walk into the cirque traditionally begins in Le Bélier, but it's a long, tedious trudge up the Haut Mafate forestry road to Le Petit Col car park, so most people choose to begin the walk from the car park.

Day One: Le Petit Col Car Park to La Nouvelle

The trail to La Nouvelle (about two hours) starts at the car park. From here, it takes only 20 minutes to reach the Col des Bœufs, from where you'll get your first glimpse of the Cirque de Mafate. Ahead, GR R1 plunges steeply down to the forested Plaine des Tamarins. The *tamarin des Hauts* (mountain tamarind trees) are cloaked in a yellowish lichen called *barbe de capucins* (monks' beard), and the low cloud often creates a slightly spooky atmosphere like something from Tolkien's *The Lord of the Rings*.

Follow the path signposted to La Nouvelle (the other branch heads south to Marla), which meanders through the forest in a fairly leisurely fashion before dropping rapidly to the village of La Nouvelle. There are some fabulous views of Le Grand Bénare on the cirque rim to the south as you descend.

La Nouvelle used to be a cattle-raising centre, but tourism has very much taken over as the village's main source of income. There are only about 200 inhabitants, but the numbers are swelled daily by the jetsetters who drop out of the sky by helicopter for lunch. The village has several shops, a school, an interesting shingle-roofed chapel and, unique in the cirque, a (solar-powered) payphone; you'll need a phonecard to use it.

SLEEPING & EATING

There are two *gîtes de montagne* in La Nouvelle. The first you come to is the **Relais de Mafate** (☎ 02 62 43 61 77; dm/d €13.50/31, breakfast/dinner €6/15), near the school, with a choice of dorm beds and private rooms; meals appear pricey but you get plenty to eat. The alternative is that run by **Maxime Oréo** (☎ 02 62 43 58 57; dm €13.50, breakfast/dinner €4/13.50) further down the hill by the football ground.

There are also a number of private *gîtes d'étape*. A good option is the red-roofed *gîte* belonging to **Joseph Cuvelier** (☎ 02 62 43 49 63; dm €12, breakfast/dinner €5/13) which is signposted down a narrow trail on your right as you enter the village.

La Nouvelle boasts a bakery and no fewer than three groceries where you can buy basic provisions.

Day Two: La Nouvelle to Roche Plate via Le Bronchard

The trail to Grand Place, Cayenne and Roche Plate (four to five hours) via Le Bronchard turns downhill just after the La Nouvelle chapel and heads into the maize fields before plummeting into the valley of the Rivière des Galets. This steep and often treacherous descent is not for the faint-hearted, though reassuring handrails are provided for some of the steeper sections.

To make up for the risk, the views are to die for (figuratively speaking!) and an exhilarating two hours or so will get you to the bottom of the cirque, where you can take a well-deserved splash in the river. When you've recovered your energies, ford the river and start the arduous ascent up the far side of the valley.

When you reach the white metal cross at Le Bronchard, the worst is over. The final stretch descends not into the ravine as it first appears, but slowly down to the village of Roche Plate. Ignore the turn-off to Marla, Trois Roches and La Nouvelle, which branches off to the left as you enter the village. The village of Roche Plate sits at the foot of the majestic Le Maïdo (2205m).

SLEEPING & EATING

The nice, tidy **Gîte de Montagne de Roche Plate** (☎ 02 62 43 60 01; dm €13.50, breakfast/dinner €4/13.50) is a short distance uphill from the school, and has hot water, a kitchen and a fine view over the cirque.

Further along is the village grocery and another *gîte de montagne*, the **Auberge de Bronchard** (☎ 02 62 43 83 66; dm €13.50, breakfast/dinner €4.50/14).

Day Three: Roche Plate to Marla via Trois Roches

The trail to Marla (five to six hours) via Trois Roches begins where the trail from La Nouvelle enters Roche Plate. The first section rises steadily through a dry landscape with *choka* (an agave species). Towering overhead are the peaks of Le Grand Bénare and Le Gros Morne. Apart from one significant drop, the path stays fairly level before descending in earnest to the waterfall at Trois Roches (at least 2½ hours from Roche Plate).

This curious waterfall drops through a narrow crack in a bed of grey granite that has been perfectly polished into ripple patterns by aeons of erosion, and is a popular camping spot. The falls are named for the huge boulders (there are actually seven, not three) that were deposited here by prehistoric torrents.

Marla is about 2½ hours beyond the falls. The trail crosses the river and then follows the left bank, passing through a rather arid landscape of eroded volcanic cinders from Piton des Neiges. After recrossing the river just downstream from a pile of vast alluvial boulders, the trail then climbs the far bank to Marla in about an hour.

At an altitude of 1640m, Marla is the highest village in Cirque de Mafate. Its name is said to be derived from a Malagasy term meaning 'many people', but these days, the town consists of only a few houses. You can elect to end your hike here by crossing the Col du Taïbit to Cilaos (see Day Five of Tour des Cirques, p234).

SLEEPING & EATING

Marla has several good places to stay and eat: the new *gîte de montagne* run by **Fanélie César** (☎ 06 92 03 26 15; dm €14, d €32, breakfast/dinner €4.50/14), with a choice of dorms or double rooms; the **Gîte de Montagne de Marla** (☎ 02 62 43 78 31; dm €13.50, breakfast/dinner €4.50/13.50); and the slightly more basic *gîte d'étape* belonging to **Mme Giroday** (☎ 02 62 43 83 13; dm €10, breakfast/dinner €5/13.50). A third *gîte de montagne* comprising six double rooms will be opening in Marla in 2005, managed by **Sylvio Bègue** (☎ 06 92 23 38 37; d €35, breakfast/dinner €5/14).

There's also a well-stocked village shop.

Day Four: Marla to Le Petit Col Car Park

This easy last day (about three hours) picks up the GR R1 at the north end of the village. The trail is signposted to La Nouvelle, Col de Fourche and Col des Bœufs, and should get you to Maison Laclos within about

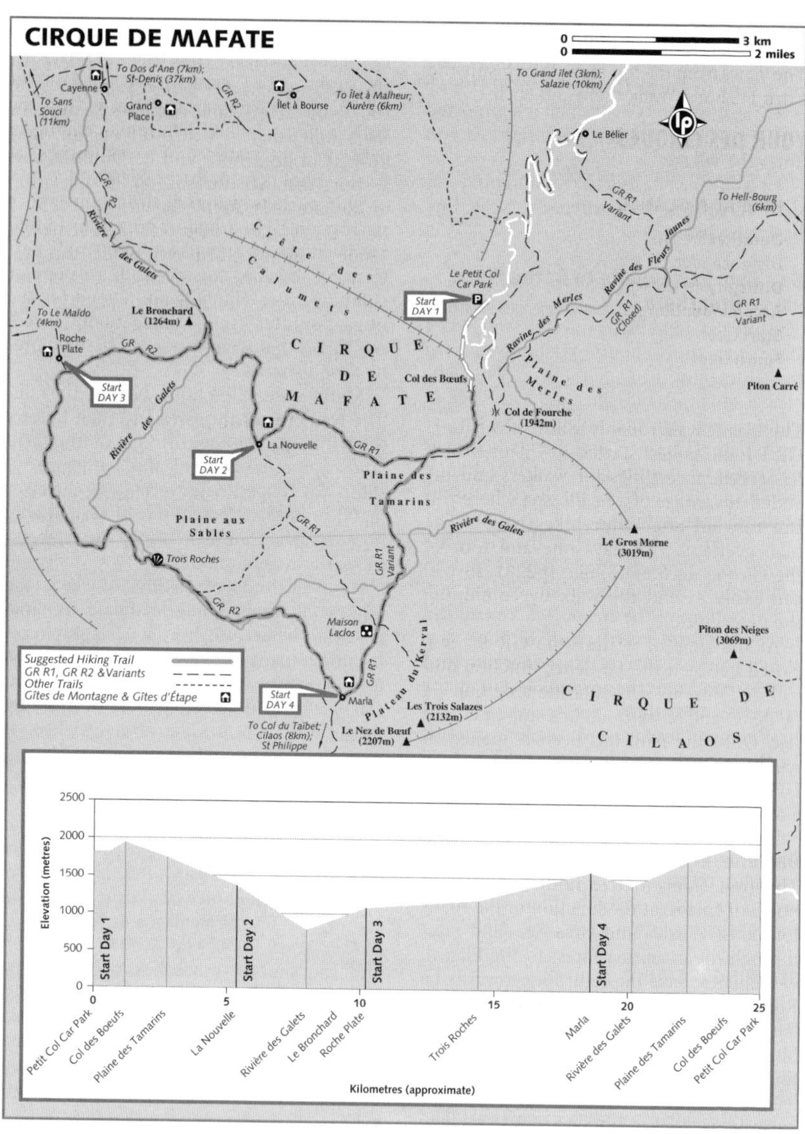

20 minutes. This traditional dwelling – said to be one of the oldest in the cirque, was abandoned in the aftermath of Hurricane Hyacinthe, which came through in 1980, and is now a ruin. From there, the main GR R1 trail returns to La Nouvelle, but you can cut out some distance by taking the right-hand fork, a GR R1 variant, which cuts straight back up (northward) to the Plaine des Tamarins (allow about one hour). This trail connects with the main GR R1 trail into the cirque, from where it's roughly an hour back over the Col des Bœufs to the car park at Le Petit Col.

If time allows, you can extend the walk by adding a side trip from the Maison Laclos up to the beautiful Plateau du Kerval (1768m). The views from the top more than justify the extra 1½ hours' walk there and back.

TOUR DES CIRQUES

HIKE AT A GLANCE

Duration five days
Distance 50km
Difficulty demanding
Accommodation *gîtes de montagne, gîtes d'étape*
Start Cilaos
Finish Cilaos

This classic walk roughly follows the path of GR R1 and is best started in Cilaos, which has excellent facilities for walkers and the added advantage of a health spa where you can unwind after your hike (p199). The hike overlaps with days one and four of the Cirque de Mafate hike (p228), so you can easily extend the walk by combining the two routes.

At the time of writing the GR R1 was closed between the Le Bélier junction and Col de Fourche, necessitating a detour via Le Bélier and an extra night's stop in Grand Îlet. Once the path has been reopened, it will be possible to walk from Hell-Bourg to La Nouvelle in a very long day, making this a four-day hike.

Day One: Cilaos to Caverne Dufour

The trail (four to five hours) starts just north of Cilaos, at the junction of the roads for Îlet à Cordes and Bras Sec, and rises through the casuarina forest to the Plateau des Chênes. Take the right fork towards La Roche Merveilleuse (Marvellous Rock); the left fork leads along the ridge to Col du Taïbit. The trail crosses the forestry road several times before it reaches La Roche Merveilleuse (avoid the Sentier de Découverte, a circular nature trail around the rock), and then descends to meet the Bras Sec road.

The trail follows the Bras Sec road for about 500m, then branches off to the left at Le Bloc. If you like, you can skip this first hour's walk by getting a bus up to Le Bloc from Cilaos (see p201).

From Le Bloc, the path climbs steadily through a forest of cryptomeria (a cedar-like tree) to the Plateau du Petit Matarum, where the forest changes to stunted giant heather bushes (known as *branles* or *brandes*), cloaked in wisps of lichen. It's uphill all the way from here to the *gîte*. Once you gain the saddle, there's a turn-off on the right to the Col de Bébour and Le Dimitile, and a short distance further on, you'll come to the **Gîte de la Caverne Dufour** (☎ 02 62 51 15 26; dm €13.50, breakfast/dinner €4.50/13.50) at nearly 2500m. Though still pretty rustic, this *gîte de montagne* now boasts inside toilets and (cold) showers. You'll need to bring plenty of warm clothes and remember to book well in advance; even with 51 beds, it's often packed out.

Day Two: Caverne Dufour to Hell-Bourg via Piton des Neiges

Because the summit of Piton des Neiges is usually cloaked in cloud by mid-morning, most people choose to stay overnight at the Gîte de la Caverne Dufour, starting out for the peak at, or even before, dawn. The path begins directly opposite the *gîte* and is clearly marked in white on the rock face, but you should bring a torch (flashlight) if you start out before dawn. The climb takes three hours return.

The landscape becomes increasingly rocky the higher you climb, and the final section rises steeply over shifting cinders that make for slippery footing. At the summit there are few traces of vegetation, and the red, black and ochre rock leaves little doubt about the mountain's volcanic origins. On a clear day, the whole island is spread out beneath you. If you didn't beat the cloud to the summit, you may just be confronted by an enveloping cloak of white.

Back at the Caverne Dufour, the trail to Hell-Bourg (six hours) runs north across the saddle and skirts the rim of the Cirque de Salazie, passing through giant heather forest. It's a bit of a mud chute, so watch your footing. After 1½ hours you'll reach a white-painted cross at Cap Anglais, from where there are excellent views over the Cirque de Salazie. If you just want some creature comforts, you can take the GR R1 variant straight downhill from here to the southern end of Hell-Bourg (3½ hours), emerging near the stadium and the trout farm.

More interesting is the walk along the cirque rim through the lush Forêt de Bélouve. Just beyond the turn-off, the trail begins a series of slippery ascents and descents through a marshy area of heather forest. Anchored metal ladders and wooden boardwalks are provided to help you over the boggiest sections. Once you start to see ferns among the trees, the worst is over.

From here, the trail enters an enchanted tropical forest, with primordial ferns and huge trees draped in sheets of moss. The woods suddenly seem to come alive with the sound of birdsong. Walking is easier through this lush area, and plaques describe some of the wildlife you are seeing and hearing. Around four hours from Cap Anglais you'll reach a radio antenna on the lip of the cirque. This point offers spectacular views over Hell-Bourg and plenty of photo opportunities.

Following the gravel forestry road for another kilometre, you'll come to the comfortable and beautifully situated **Gîte de Montagne de Bélouve** (☎ 02 62 41 21 23;, dm/d €13.50/31, breakfast/dinner €4.50/14). Campers can set up for free (one night only) by the lookout in front of the *gîte*. If you've got the time, you could overnight here and the following day take a side trip to the Trou de Fer (below) before hitting the bright lights of Hell-Bourg.

The final descent to Hell-Bourg from the Gîte de Montagne de Bélouve takes around two hours. Cut through the garden of the *gîte* and bear left at the lookout. You emerge in Hell-Bourg by the park on Rue Général de Gaulle. Treat yourself to a meal and a hot shower when you arrive! (For information on places to stay and eat in Hell-Bourg, see p204).

Day Three: Hell-Bourg to Grand Îlet

Start this day's walk (about six hours) by taking the track at the end of Rue Général de Gaulle in Hell-Bourg to the thermal-bath ruins; this track connects with the Îlet à Vidot road, which will take you to the car park in Îlet à Vidot.

From the car park, a dirt road descends into the valley, reaching a turn-off on the left to Trou Blanc after about 500m. Ignore this turn-off (the trail is currently closed) and continue straight ahead, passing a turning on the right to Piton d'Enchaing. The track ascends rather uneventfully for the next 1½ hours, crossing several ravines, before skirting along the edge of a large plantation of casuarina trees at Le Grand Sable. The trail then drops down to cross one of the tributaries of the Rivière des Fleurs Jaunes. There's an excellent bivouac on the far bank where the trail to Le Bélier (a GR R1 variant) strikes off to the right through the woods. Allow about three hours from Hell-Bourg to reach this point.

Since the GR R1 onwards to the Col de Fourche is currently closed at this point, you will have to take the GR R1 variant, following signs down to Le Bélier. You should reach the road at Le Bélier after

TOUR DES CIRQUES – SIDE TRIPS

If you have time and energy to spare on your tour of the cirques, you could incorporate one of the following side trips along the way.

Trou de Fer

This trail starts beside the Gîte de Montagne de Bélouve (see Day Two, p231) and takes you across a plateau covered in tamarind forests to a magnificent viewpoint overlooking the lost valley of Trou de Fer. It makes an easy three-hour return trip from the *gîte* or a more challenging hike from Hell-Bourg (allow 6½ hours total walking time). The path is well signed but after heavy rain it can get very muddy across the plateau.

Piton d'Enchaing

This enticing 1352m peak is a popular but very challenging day hike from Hell-Bourg (see Day Three, above). The peak was named after an escaped slave who used this lofty vantage point to keep an eye on the movements of bounty hunters in the Cirque de Salazie (see Marrons, p197).

To get to the peak, follow the GR R1 through Îlet à Vidot and fork right when the trail divides (the left fork for Trou Blanc is currently closed). A short distance further on, the trail to Piton d'Enchaing branches off to the right. Allow about 2½ hours each way from Hell-Bourg.

HIKING IN RÉUNION

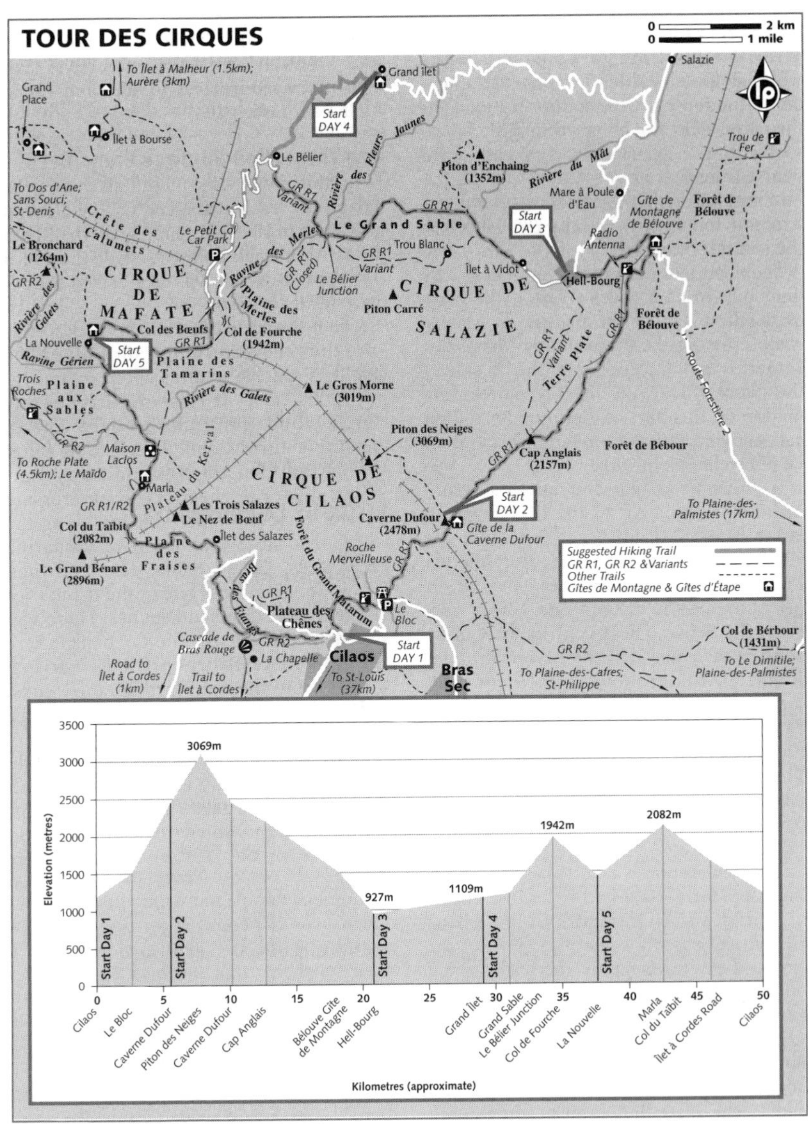

1½ to two hours. From there it's less than an hour's walk downhill to Grand Îlet, where you'll find grocers, a bread shop and overnight accommodation. For a very comfortable night's stay try **Le Cimendef** (☎ 02 62 47 73 59; fax 02 62 47 63 69; s/d €33/38, dinner €16), a *chambre d'hôte* on the road 1km before you come into Grand Îlet. Among a clutch of more basic *chambres d'hôtes* signed to the right a little further down, **Liliane Bonald** (☎ 02 62 41 71 62; fax 02 62 47 73 34; Chemin Camp Pierrot; s/d €30/38, dinner €16) provides a warm welcome, or there's that of **Jeanine Grondin** (☎/fax 02 62 47 70 66; Rue de l'Église; s/d €22/30, meals €14) near the church in the middle of Grand Îlet.

Day Four: Grand Îlet to La Nouvelle

The day (about five to six hours) begins with a slog back uphill to Le Bélier and then on up the *route forestière* (forestry road) to the Col des Bœufs; allow around 3½ hours to the top. Alternatively, you can spare yourself the first hour's walk by taking the bus from Grand Îlet to Le Bélier, or even get a ride up to Le Petit Col car park just below the summit (see p228).

From the Col des Bœufs it's an easy 2½-hour hike to La Nouvelle. This is the same as the first day of the Cirque de Mafate walk, crossing the atmospheric Plaine des Tamarins and descending on the far side to the village of La Nouvelle. (For more information on this part of the route, including a rundown of accommodation options in La Nouvelle, see p228).

A more attractive, but also more demanding alternative to the hike from Le Bélier to the Col des Bœufs is to take the GR R1 variant signed to 'La Nouvelle via Col de Fourche'. The trail branches left off the *route forestière* about one hour's walk above Le Bélier. The ascent to the Col de Fourche takes about 2½ hours, and it's then another half-hour's walk to where you meet the path from the Col des Bœufs.

Day Five: La Nouvelle to Cilaos

This final day (about six hours) will take you back to the modern comforts of Cilaos, passing through some stunning countryside on the way.

The first section is a fairly easy two-hour walk to Marla via Maison Laclos, beginning with a steep descent into the Ravine Gérien and passing some nice views of the cirque. Be sure to ignore the trails signed off to Marla par passerelle and to the Plaine aux Sables.

Marla consists only of a few houses, but the village shop sells snacks and drinks. Ignore paths off to the right for Trois Roches and Roche Plate, but keep heading south towards the reservoir. The trail ascends steadily towards the obvious low point on the ridge, reaching Col du Taïbit in about 1½ hours. If you reach this viewpoint early in the morning, there are magnificent views over the Cirque de Mafate, and down the Cirque de Cilaos to St-Louis and the coast.

The trail (GR R1/R2) descends slowly to the plateau at Îlet des Salazes, before dropping steeply through drier country to cross the Îlet à Cordes road after about two hours. You could always pick up a lift or a bus to Cilaos here, but die-hards should continue across the road and descend into the valley. The trail divides just beyond. The easier and prettier option is to take the right fork, following the GR R2 along the west bank of the Bras des Étangs. It crosses the river near the Cascade du Bras Rouge and then climbs gradually to come out at the ruined thermal baths on the outskirts of Cilaos. From there you can take a short-cut up the Sentier des Porteurs for the final ascent into town.

Depending on how you feel, you could stop off at the spa in Cilaos for a massage, or hit one of the restaurants in town for a well-earned Bourbon beer!

PITON DE LA FOURNAISE

HIKE AT A GLANCE

Duration five hours
Distance 14km
Difficulty moderate
Accommodation *gîtes de montagne*
Start Gîte du Volcan
Finish Gîte du Volcan

Piton de la Fournaise is a smouldering volcano that is probably Réunion's most renowned feature. The walk to the summit can get very busy, but the fascinating tortured landscape more than makes up for the crowds of people. Most people simply walk up to the two central craters, along their northern rims and back again (three hours), but it's worth continuing all the way round to appreciate the monster in its full grandeur (allow an extra two hours).

While the volcano walk is popular, it shouldn't be taken lightly. The landscape here is harsh and arid, despite the mist which can drench hikers to the skin. The chilly wind whips away moisture, leaving walkers dehydrated and breathless. At times it can feel like you are walking on Mars, with only the dry crunch of the cinders underfoot for company.

Early morning is the best time to climb the volcano, as you stand a better chance of clear views, but this is when everyone else

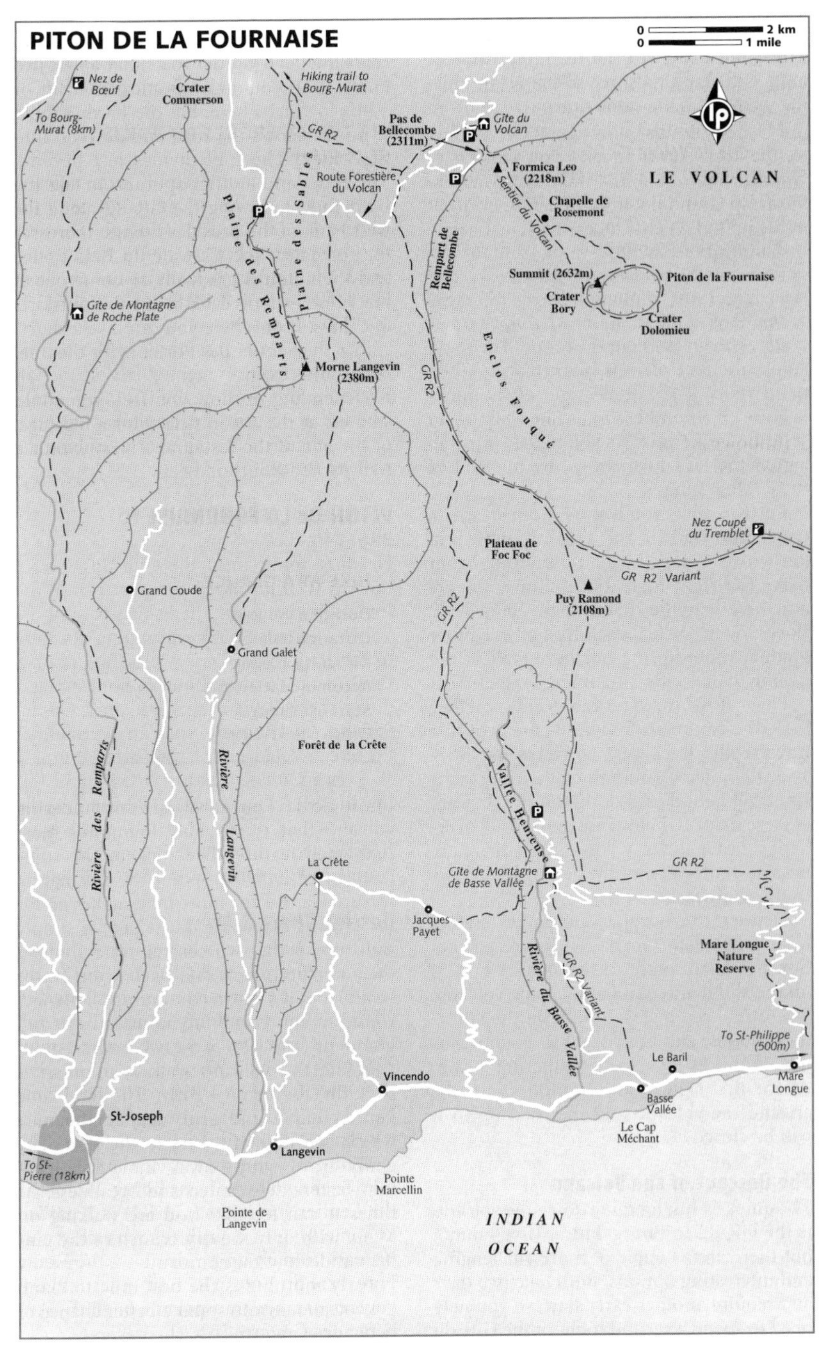

HIKING IN RÉUNION

hits the trail as well. The path from the ridge across the lava plain can resemble a trail of ants, with hundreds of walkers all heading for the peak at the same time.

Many people get a head start by staying at the **Gîte du Volcan** (Gîte de Bellecombe; ☎ 02 62 51 17 42; fax 02 62 51 18 29; dm €13.50, breakfast/dinner €4.50/14.50) and leave at the crack of dawn, so be sure to book well in advance.

The *gîte* is a 15-minute walk from the Pas de Bellecombe, where the Sentier du Volcan starts in earnest by plunging *down* 527 steps to the floor of the immense U-shaped outer crater, known as Enclos Foucqué. The route across the lava plain is marked with white paint spots. The liquid origin of the rocks is quite apparent here – it's like walking on solidified cake-mix. As you make your way across the lava formations, be mindful of the endless snags.

On the way, you'll pass a small scoria cone, Formica Leo, and a cavern in the lava known as Chapelle de Rosemont. From here, the right-hand path climbs steeply and directly to the 2632m-high, 200m-wide Bory Crater, while the left fork takes a more gradual route up the northern wall of the gaping 900m-wide Dolomieu Crater.

Once at the top, you can decide whether to do the circuit around both craters or just traverse the track that connects the Bory and Dolomieu Craters along their northern rims. While walking along the rim, beware of large fissures, holes and, most of all, overhangs. Leave the way you came – there are no safe routes across the recent lava flows to the southeast.

Neither the Bory or Dolomieu craters have erupted for years. All the recent action has taken place in the smaller craters on the south and east flanks of the volcano. Scientists keep a close watch on the volcano's moods, and are poised to issue warnings if things look to be gathering steam. At the first sign of an eruption, the paths around the volcano and the road up to it will be closed.

The Descent of the Volcano

The quickest hiking route down the volcano is the GR R2 to Bourg-Murat (five hours), but there are a couple of more challenging and interesting options. Both take two days and require another early start, so you may need to spend a second night in the Gîte du Volcan. For more information about these trails, consult the Maison de la Montagne or the tourist office at Bourg-Murat.

VIA THE RIVIÈRE DES REMPARTS TO ST-JOSEPH

The most dramatic descent of the volcano takes you down the stunning gorge of the Rivière des Remparts to St-Joseph. The total walking time is about 10 hours, but you can break the journey halfway at the excellent **Gîte de Montagne de Roche Plate** (☎ 02 62 59 13 94; dm €13.50, breakfast/dinner €4.50/15).

The trail starts just north of the Nez de Bœuf viewpoint, branching left off the GR R2 some 8km west of the Gîte du Volcan. The initial descent is precipitous, but once past Roche Plate, it's a gentle hike along the river to the sea.

VIA THE VALLÉE HEUREUSE TO BASSE VALLÉE

Heading south from the Gîte du Volcan, the GR R2 runs along the west rim of the Enclos Foucqué and then skirts west of the Vallée Heureuse before dropping abruptly to the Riviére du Basse Vallée (6½ hours). From here it's only about an hour straight down the valley to the coast on a GR R2 variant. Alternatively, you can overnight at the **Gîte de Montagne de Basse Vallée** (☎ 02 62 37 36 25; dm €13.50, breakfast/dinner €4/13.50) and follow the GR R2 eastwards to descend via the dense woods of the Mare Longue Nature Reserve (four hours). It brings you out a couple of kilometres west of St-Philippe.

Getting There & Away

For those with a vehicle, getting to the volcano couldn't be easier because of the all-weather Route Forestière du Volcan, which climbs 25km from Bourg-Murat all the way to Pas de Bellecombe on the crater's outer rim. On the way it passes a superb lookout over the Rivière des Remparts just below Nez de Bœuf (2135m) and crosses the Martian landscape of the Plaine des Sables.

Without your own car, the 5½-hour hike to the volcano from Bourg-Murat via the Sentier Josémont (GR R2) is regarded as something of a walk for masochists, as it's easy to pick up a ride along the Route Forestière du Volcan instead. Alternatively, you can arrange transport through the Auberge des Cratères (p209).

Seychelles

JOHN HAY

Seychelles

CONTENTS

Highlights	239
Climate & When to Go	239
History	240
The Culture	242
Religion	243
Arts	243
Environment	245
Mahé	**247**
Victoria	247
Beau Vallon & Around	251
North Mahé	253
South Mahé	255
Ste Anne Marine National Park	257
Silouette Island	257
Praslin & Around	**258**
Praslin	258
Curieuse Island	263
Cousin Island	263
Aride Island	264
La Digue & Other Inner Islands	**264**
La Digue	264
Félicité Island	267
Bird Island	267
Denis Island	268
Outer Islands	**268**
Amirantes & Alphonse Groups	268
Aldabra Group	268
Seychelles Directory	**269**
Transport in Seychelles	**274**

SEYCHELLES

FAST FACTS

- **Area** 455 sq km
- **Capital** Victoria
- **Country code** ☎ 248
- **Main religion** Catholicism
- **Major exports** canned tuna, frozen fish, cinnamon, bark
- **Money** rupee; €1 = Rs 6.40
- **Official languages** English, French, Creole
- **Official name** Republic of Seychelles
- **Population** 81,000
- **Unemployment** approximately 10%

Among the 115 coral islands that make up the Seychelles are some of the most idyllic island getaways in the Indian Ocean, or indeed the world. Here you will find the luxuriant, tropical paradise that appears in countless advertisements and glossy travel brochures. But however seductive the images, they simply can't compete with the real-life dazzling beaches and crystal-clear waters of Praslin and La Digue, or the cathedral-like palm forests of the Vallée de Mai. There are more shades of blue and green in the Seychelles than it is possible to imagine.

There's no denying, however, that the Seychelles is an expensive destination. To make the most of your sojourn in paradise, you really do need to indulge in visits to at least a couple of the smaller islands and in some of the amazing snorkelling and diving on offer. When you tire of beaches there are national parks to explore and one or two reasonably challenging hikes. Bird-watchers will have a field day among the wheeling clouds of sooty terns and frigate birds, and watching white-tailed tropicbirds gracefully riding the thermals. For divers, these islands boast some of the world's largest coral atolls and the seas are inhabited by a rainbow array of marine life.

Forming a backdrop to the relaxed tropical image of the Seychelles are the rhythms and flavours of Africa, including *gris gris*, the local brand of black magic. Further in the shadows lurks an intriguing and occasionally dangerous political background. Things have calmed down nowadays, but the Seychelles still remains a beguiling tropical destination.

HIGHLIGHTS

- **Best beach** Check into paradise at Anse Lazio (p260)
- **Natural wonders** Encounter erotic nuts in the Vallée de Mai (p258)
- **Photo opportunity** Get shutter happy at Anse Source d'Argent (p264)
- **Adrenaline rush** Dive with the big guys at Shark Bank (p41)
- **Chill-out spot** Take the slow lane on La Digue (p264)
- **Off-beat experience** Marvel at the feathered frenzy on Cousin Island (p263)
- **Green spaces** Mug up on botany in Victoria (p247)
- **Seafood extravaganza** Have a blowout at Beau Vallon Beach (p251)
- **Remote adventure** Cast yourself adrift on Aldabra (p268)

CLIMATE & WHEN TO GO

The seasons in the Seychelles are defined by the trade winds. These bring warmer, wetter airstreams from the northwest from October to April. From May to September the southeast trades usher in cooler, drier weather but the winds whip up the waves and you'll want to find protected beaches. The turnaround periods (March to April and October to November) are normally calm and windless.

The rain generally comes in sudden, heavy bursts. Mahé and Silhouette, the most mountainous islands, get the highest rainfall. January is the wettest month by far, and July and August the driest. Temperatures range between 24°C and 32°C throughout the year, and humidity hovers around 80%.

Although the Seychelles lies outside the cyclone zone, cyclone activity elsewhere in the Indian Ocean can still bring unseasonably grey, windy weather between December and March.

Hotel prices shoot up and accommodation can be hard to find during the peak seasons from December to January and July to August. Easter can also get busy.

See p279 for the climate chart for Victoria, the capital of Mahé.

HOW MUCH?

- Cup of coffee Rs 10
- Sandwich Rs 30-50
- Meal in a cheap restaurant Rs 50-80
- Meal in a good restaurant Rs 150-200
- Scuba dive (including gear) Rs 300

LONELY PLANET INDEX

- Litre of petrol Rs 8
- Litre of bottled water Rs 8
- Small bottle of Seybrew beer Rs 20
- Souvenir T-shirt Rs 75
- Street snack – samosa Rs 2

HISTORY

Until the 18th century the Seychelles was uninhabited, though there are ancient tombs on Silhouette Island which are attributed to shipwrecked Arab sailors. The islands were first spotted by Portuguese explorers, but the first recorded landing was by a British East India Company ship in 1609. Pirates and privateers used the Seychelles as a temporary base during lulls in their maraudings. It is believed that the famous French pirate, Olivier 'La Buse' Levasseur, hid his treasure somewhere in the islands, possibly around Bel Ombre on Mahé (see Pieces of Eight, p252).

The First Colonisers

In 1742, the great Mahé de Labourdonnais, the governor of what is now Mauritius, sent Captain Lazare Picault to investigate the islands. Picault named the main island after his employer (and the bay where he landed after himself) and laid the way for the French to claim possession of the islands 12 years later. To do this they simply shouted 'long live the king', fired off a few canons and left behind a stone with the king's flag flying above it. You can still see the Stone of Possession in Victoria's National History Museum. Henceforth, the islands were to be known as the Seychelles in honour of the finance minister to Louis XV, Jean Moreau de Séchelles.

It took a while for the French to do anything with their possession. It wasn't until 1770 that the first batch of 21 settlers and seven slaves arrived on Ste Anne Island. After a few false starts, the settlers began growing spices, cassava, sugar cane and maize, at the same time munching their way through the population of giant tortoises.

British Rule

In the 18th century, the British began taking an interest in the Seychelles. Rather than risking life and limb to fend off British attacks, the French governor Queau de Quinssy lowered the French flag and surrendered to the British frigates, raising the French flag again as soon as they departed! The 'great capitulator', as de Quinssy became known, was to repeat this manoeuvre about a dozen times before the Seychelles became a British dependency in 1814.

The British did little to develop the islands except increase the number of slaves. After abolition in 1835, freed slaves from around the region were also brought here. Because few British settled, however, the French language and culture remained dominant.

Over the years the islands have been used as a holding pen for numerous political prisoners and exiles – not a bad place to be exiled! As recently as 1956, the rebellious Archbishop Makarios of Cyprus was housed in the former governor's lodge on Mahé. He later described his exile as more of a 'vacation' and tried to buy the house; his offer was rejected.

In 1903 the Seychelles became a crown colony administered from London. It promptly went into the political and economic doldrums until 1964, when two political parties were formed. France Albert René, a young lawyer, founded the Seychelles People's United Party (SPUP). A fellow lawyer, James Mancham, led the new Seychelles Democratic Party (SDP).

Independence

Observers in the 1960s noted that the Seychellois showed little interest in politics, and even the locals joked that they are so laid-back the clocks chime twice for the sake of those who were not awake the first time. However, the next 20 years transformed these sleepy, forgotten islands, with events that would wake up the world.

Mancham's SDP, made up of businesspeople and planters, won the elections in

1966 and 1970. René's SPUP fought on a socialist and independence ticket. In June 1975 a coalition of the two parties gave the appearance of unity in the lead up to independence, which was granted a year later. Mancham became the first president of the Republic of Seychelles and René the prime minister.

The flamboyant Sir Jim (as James Mancham was known) – poet and playboy – placed all his eggs in one basket: tourism. He jet-setted around the world with a beautiful socialite on each arm, and he put the Seychelles on the map.

The rich and famous poured in for holidays and to party, party, party. Adnan Khashoggi and other Arab millionaires bought large tracts of land, while film stars and celebrities came to enhance their romantic, glamorous images. The film *Goodbye Emmanuelle* was filmed on La Digue.

According to René and the SPUP, however, the wealth was not being spread evenly and the country was no more than a rich person's playground. René stated that poor Creoles were little better-off than slaves.

René Takes Over

In June 1977, barely a year after independence, René and a team of Tanzanian-trained rebels carried out an almost bloodless coup while Mancham was in London attending a Commonwealth Conference. As Mancham said at the time, 'It was no heroic deed to take over the Seychelles. Twenty-five people with sticks could seize control.' René brought in Tanzanian and North Korean soldiers to make sure that any opposition would need more than that to oust him.

An attempt to do so came in 1981, when a band of mercenaries, led by ex-Congo 'dog of war' Colonel Mike Hoare, bungled a coup attempt. The group posed as a South African rugby club on an annual binge, but a customs officer discovered weapons in their luggage. Two people died in a shootout at the airport before the mercenaries beat a hasty retreat by hijacking an Air India plane back to South Africa. Five mercenaries and the advance guard were rounded up, tried and sentenced to death, though they were eventually deported. In 1992 the South African government paid the Seychelles government eight million rupees as compensation for the attempted coup.

In the following years, René consolidated his position by deporting many supporters of the outlawed SDP. Opposed to René's one-party socialist state, these *grands blancs* (rich whites) set up 'resistance movements' in Britain, South Africa and Australia.

The country fell into disarray as the tourist trade dried to a trickle. The 1980s saw a campaign of civil disruption by supporters of the SDP, two army mutinies and more foiled coup attempts. In 1984 Gerard Hoareau, the leader of the Seychelles resistance movement in Britain, was machine-gunned to death outside his London home.

Towards a Multiparty State

Facing growing international criticism, and the threatened withdrawal of foreign aid, René pulled a political about-face in the early 1990s; he abandoned one-party rule and announced the return to a multiparty democracy.

Elections were held in 1992 under the watchful eye of Commonwealth observers. René and his renamed Seychelles People's Progressive Front (SPPF) won 58.4% of the votes; Mancham, who had returned to the Seychelles with a hefty Special Air Force (SAS) security team from the UK, fielded 33.7% for his SDP and claimed the results were rigged.

Since then René has maintained his grip on power, while the SDP's star has continued to wane. Even Mancham himself abandoned the SDP in favour of the centrist Seychelles National Party (SNP) in 1999. In the 2002 elections, the SNP, led by Wavel Ramkalawan, an Anglican priest, confirmed its stand as the main opposition party by winning over 42% of the vote. It now holds 11 seats in the National Assembly, though still lags far behind the SPPF with the remaining 23.

The Seychelles Today

While René has been much criticised over the years, there's no denying that the Seychelles has come a long way since independence. Overall standards of health, education and housing have improved, and annual per capita income has grown from around US$1000 in 1976 to close on US$7000 today. With the influence of the former Soviet Union on the wane, René has steered the country slowly towards privatisation and a free-market economy. He has also loosened his grip slightly on the media. There is now at least a choice of newspapers, of which the most outspoken is the opposition paper *Regar;* it regularly gets sued by the government for libel.

Tourism continues to play a significant role. It now contributes as much as 18% of gross domestic product and employs at least 20% of the labour force, with luxury hotels replacing the spice and coconut plantations. Despite the worldwide downturn in tourism, arrivals in the Seychelles are holding up reasonably well at around 120,000 per year. To maintain this high level of interest, the Seychelles Tourism Marketing Authority (STMA) is very active in promoting the islands' tropical image around the world.

The other mainstay of the economy is industrial fishing, which actually overtook tourism as the country's biggest foreign exchange earner in 2002. The huge Indian Ocean Tuna plant in Victoria is the world's second largest tuna cannery, capable of processing up to 400 tonnes of fish per day.

Nevertheless, the economy remains extremely vulnerable to external events. Despite attempts to strengthen its agricultural base and use more locally manufactured products, the Seychelles continues to import 90% of its needs. As a result, even a slight dip in export earnings causes major ructions in the economy. By 2002 the Seychelles had accumulated debts of some US$170 million, with repayments totalling a massive US$20 million each year – to be paid in foreign exchange. The government has promised to reduce spending and in 2003 imposed a whopping 12% Goods and Services Tax (GST) on all imported goods except for a few basic foodstuffs such as rice, vegetables and oils. This extremely unpopular tax is causing concern in the tourist sector, where there are already fears that the Seychelles is pricing itself out of the market.

Whatever happens, the chronic foreign exchange shortage and levels of inflation hovering at around 6% look set to continue for the foreseeable future. Not that Albert René will be around to worry about it. In April 2004, René finally relinquished the presidency to the former vice president, James Michel, who has stood by René through thick and thin. No-one is anticipating any radical shifts in policy, but there could be interesting times ahead as the Seychelles enters a new political era.

THE CULTURE

The vast majority of Seychellois people are friendly and helpful. There's not much anticolonial feeling evident – it has long been replaced with a sense of national pride that developed after independence. There's even a lingering fondness for such British institutions as afternoon tea, while French cultural influence has waned somewhat, mainly because it is regarded as rather elitist.

The National Psyche

As in Mauritius and Réunion, it is the Creole language, cuisine and culture which help bind the Seychelles society. Over 90% of the population speak Creole as their first language, though most also speak English – the language of government and business – and French. Since 1982, when Creole was made the language of education, literacy rates have risen to nearly 90%.

The government has worked hard to promote social cohesion. As a result, racism is extremely rare, though there are concerns that the number of immigrant workers, particularly Indian labourers brought in to work on construction sites, may upset the balance.

On the whole, however, the Seychellois are pretty relaxed and traditional work patterns are very different from Western ones.

Despite the apparently easy-going existence, the living standards of many Seychellois is lower than you might expect, mostly because of the disproportionately high cost of living. The islands may seem very Westernised, but the minimum wage is around Rs 2000 (€325) per month. As prices creep up and more people struggle to make ends meet, so burglaries and petty theft are also on the rise. Crime levels are still extremely low, but it's a favourite topic of conversation among islanders.

Lifestyle

The Seychellois are quite traditional, and society continues to be largely male dominated. Fortunately for women, the tourism industry is regarded as an equal-opportunity employer.

Most Seychellois are Catholic, but marriage is an unpopular institution. The reasons cited are that it's a relic of slavery, when marriages simply didn't take place, and that it's expensive. As a result an estimated 75% of children are born out of wedlock. There's no taboo about illegitimacy, however. Though the children tend to stay with the mother, fathers are legally obliged to support their offspring.

Since the age of consent is only 14 years, there are a large number of teenage mothers. Pregnant girls are not allowed to attend school and after the birth, few bother to return. This obviously has a negative impact on education levels and job options for a certain number of women.

The Seychellois are generally tolerant of gay and lesbian relationships as long as couples don't flaunt their sexuality. Indeed, there are few rules and regulations to be followed, beyond respecting local attitudes towards nudity and visiting places of religious worship (see p48).

Population

The population of the Seychelles is more strongly African than in Mauritius or Réunion, but even so you'll see almost every shade of skin and hair imaginable, arising from a mixture of largely French and African genes, together with infusions of Indian, Chinese and Arab blood. Distinct Indian and Chinese communities make up only a tiny proportion of the ethnic mix, however, the rest being Creole. Most of the *grands blancs* were dispossessed in the wake of the 1977 coup.

About 90% of Seychellois live on Mahé and nearly a third of these are concentrated in and around the capital. This trend will continue as new housing developments go up on the reclaimed land along the northeast coast. Most of the remaining 10% live on Praslin and La Digue, while the other islands are either uninhabited or are home to tiny communities.

Although birth control was frowned on in the past for religious reasons, education and social welfare programs have seen a gradual decline in the number of births. The population growth rate is stable at around 0.5%.

RELIGION

Nearly 90% of Seychellois are Roman Catholic, 7% Anglican and 2.5% belong to the rapidly expanding evangelical churches. The remainder belong to the tiny Hindu, Moslem and Chinese communities largely based in Victoria.

Most people are avid churchgoers. On a Sunday, Victoria's Catholic and Anglican cathedrals and the smaller churches scattered around the main islands are full to bursting.

There is also a widespread belief in the supernatural and in the old magic of spirits known as *gris gris*. Sorcery was outlawed in 1958, but a few *bonhommes* and *bonnefemmes di bois* (medicine men and women) still practise their cures and curses and concoct potions for love, luck and revenge. Victoria's National History Museum contains a small display devoted to *gris gris*.

ARTS

Since these islands were originally uninhabited, the Creoles are the closest the country has to an indigenous population. Many aspects of their African origins survive, including the *séga* and *moutia* dances.

The government formed the National School of Music and the National Cultural Troupe (NCT) to foster Creole cultural identity and tradition. These organisations have produced some fine singers, dancers and writers. Creole culture is also promoted through the colourful Festival Kreol (see boxed text, p244). The National Arts Council is responsible for the promotion of art in all its forms. As part of its remit it organises an arts festival each April.

For more information about arts events, contact the Ministry of Culture's **information office** (☎ 321333; National Library, Francis Rachel St, Victoria).

Literature

The **Kreol Institute** (☎ 376351; 8am-4pm Mon-Fri), near Anse aux Pins on Mahé, was set up to research and promote Creole language and literature. It publishes a few books each year in Creole by local authors as well as translations of foreign works; these are available at the Institute.

Among the most important local authors writing in Creole are the poet-playwright Christian Sevina, short-story author and playwright Marie-Thérèse Choppy, and mystery writer Jean-Joseph Madeleine. Unfortunately, their works are not yet available in English.

In fact there is surprising little English-language fiction about these islands. Most authors go in for travelogues and autobiographies (see p270). The one exception is long-time resident Glynn Burridge, who mixes fact and fiction in his short stories. They are published locally in two volumes under the title of *Voices: Seychelles Short Stories* and are available in the bookshops in Victoria.

Music & Dance

The Indian, European, Chinese and Arabic backgrounds of the Seychellois are reflected in their music. The accordion, banjo and violin music brought to the islands by the early European settlers has blended with that of the *makalapo*, a stringed instrument with a tin sound-box; the *zez*, a monochord sitar; African skin drums; and the *bom*, a bowed instrument.

You may also come across roving *camtole* bands, which feature fiddle, banjo, accordion and drums. They sometimes accompany the *contredanse*, a dance similar to the quadrille. European influences are also evident in the *mazok*, which is reminiscent of the French waltz, and the *kotis*, which has its roots in Scottish country dancing.

It is the sombre *moutia*, however, with its strong African rhythms that is the traditional dance of the Seychelles. The slow, repetitive dance routines were originally accompanied by prayers that the slaves turned into work chants, similar to the early black gospel music of the USA. The *moutia* is normally danced around an open fire and serves as the primary evening entertainment.

The Seychelles version of the *séga* differs little from that of Mauritius. Many of the large hotels hold *séga* dance displays at least one night a week.

Patrick Victor and Jean-Marc Volcy are two of the Seychelles' best-known musicians, playing Creole pop and folk music. Other local stars are Emmanuel Marie and the late Raymond Lebon, whose daughter Sheila Paul recently made it into the charts with an updated rendering of her father's romantic ballads.

David André's *Esper Sa Sanson*, some of which is sung in English, and Jean Ally's *Welcome* (an entirely English-language recording of *séga*) are both good introductions to local music.

FESTIVAL KREOL

The vibrant **Festival Kreol** (www.seychelles.net/festivalkreol) aims to preserve and promote Creole culture. Held every year during the last week of October, it is an explosion of Creole cuisine, theatre, art, music and dance. Creole artists from other countries are invited to participate, and the festival provides young artists with a platform on which to unleash their creative talent. There are various Creole handicrafts and foodstuffs on sale and many hotels and restaurants join in the fun with special meals and activities. Events take place on Mahé, Praslin and La Digue.

Visual Arts

Over recent decades, more and more artists have settled in the Seychelles and spawned a local industry catering to souvenir-hungry tourists. While shops are full of stereotypical scenes of palm trees and sunsets, there are also some innovative and talented artists around.

Michael Adams is the best-known and most distinctive contemporary artist. He has a studio near Baie Lazare in South Mahé.

George Camille is another highly regarded artist who takes his inspiration from nature. He has a gallery on Praslin and also exhibits at the Sunstroke shop in Victoria.

Other notable artists are Barbara Jenson, who has a studio on La Digue, and Nigel Henry at Beau Vallon.

Look out, too, for works by Leon Radegonde, who produces innovative abstract collages; Andrew Gee, who specialises in fishy watercolours and silk paintings; and the sun-drenched paintings of Christine Harter. The painter and sculptor Egbert Marday produces powerful sketches of fisherfolk and plantation workers, but is perhaps best known for the statue of a man with a walking cane, situated outside the courthouse on Victoria's Independence Ave.

Lorenzo Appiani was responsible for the sculptures on the roundabouts at each end of 5th June Ave in Victoria. The Freedom Sq monument known to locals as Twa Zwazo (meaning 'three birds') is said to represent the continents of Africa, Europe and Asia, each of which has played a part in the development of the Seychellois.

ENVIRONMENT

The Seychelles is a haven for wildlife, particularly birds and tropical fish. Because of the islands' isolation and the comparatively late arrival of humans, many species are endemic to the Seychelles. Some are plentiful, some are rare and some are now extinct.

The government has traditionally tried to balance tourist developments with the protection of the natural assets that attract the tourists (and therefore revenue) to the islands. The rising population and the demands of tourism, however, are putting a strain on that policy.

Much of the marine life in the Seychelles is protected, but that doesn't stop unscrupulous operators offering souvenirs made from coral and other marine species. It's best not to buy anything made out of turtle shell or to buy or collect seashells. For more tips on responsible travel see p16. For further information on marine life, see Underwater Worlds on p33.

The Land

The Seychelles lies about 1600km off the east coast of Africa and just south of the equator. It is made up of 115 islands, of which the central islands (including Mahé, Praslin and La Digue) are granite and the outlying islands are coral atolls. The granite islands, which do not share the volcanic nature of Réunion and Mauritius, appear to be peaks of a huge submerged plateau that was torn away from Africa when the continental plates shifted about 65 million years ago.

Wildlife

ANIMALS

Common mammals and reptiles include the fruit bat or flying fox, the gecko, the skink and the tenrec (a hedgehog-like mammal imported from Madagascar). There are also some small snakes, but they are not dangerous.

Insect life is represented by more than 3000 species. Among the more interesting are the lumbering rhinoceros beetle, whose larvae cause considerable damage by feeding on the young shoots of coconut palms; the giant tenebrionid beetle of Frégate Island; and various wasps, which excel in creating mud pots attached to vegetation, rocks or walls. Despite an impressive appearance, the giant millipedes, palm spiders and whip scorpions are not life threatening, but you can expect a nasty reaction if you handle them.

Giant tortoises, which feature on the Seychelles coat of arms, are now found only in the Seychelles and the Galàpagos Islands, off Ecuador. The French and English wiped out the giant tortoises from all the Seychelles islands except Aldabra, where happily more than 100,000 still survive. Many have been brought to the central islands, where they munch their way around hotel gardens, and there is a free-roaming colony on Curieuse Island. Perhaps the biggest daddy of all is on Cousin Island (although Bird Island's owners also claim that distinction for Esmeralda; see p267).

Almost every island seems to have some rare species of bird: on Frégate, Cousin, Cousine and Aride are magpie robins (known as *pie chanteuse* in Creole); on Cousin, Cousine and Aride you'll find the Seychelles warbler; La Digue has the *veuve* (paradise flycatcher); and Praslin the black parrot. The bare-legged scops owl and the Seychelles kestrel live on Mahé, and Bird Island is home to millions of sooty terns.

PLANTS

The coconut palm and the casuarina are the Seychelles' most common trees. There are a few banyans and you're also likely to see screw pines, bamboo and tortoise trees (so named because the fruit looks like the tortoises that eat it).

There are about 80 endemic plant species. Virgin forest now exists only on the higher parts of Silhouette Island and Mahé, and in the Vallée de Mai on Praslin, which is one of only two places in the world where the giant coco de mer palm grows wild. The other is nearby Curieuse Island.

In the high, remote parts of Mahé and Silhouette Island, you may come across the insect-eating pitcher plant, which either clings to trees or bushes or sprawls along the ground.

On the floral front, there are plenty of orchids, bougainvilleas, hibiscuses, gardenias and frangipanis.

The Botanical Gardens in Victoria provide a pleasant and interesting walk. The Vallée de Mai on Praslin is a must. For chance discoveries, get away from the beach for a day and head into the hills on Mahé, Praslin or La Digue.

National Parks

The Seychelles currently boasts two national parks and seven marine national parks, as well as several other protected areas under government and NGO (nongovernmental organisation) management. In all, about 46% of the country's total landmass is now protected and some 45 sq km of ocean, providing an invaluable resource for scientific investigation and species protection.

The most important protected areas include those listed in the table below.

Environmental Issues

Overall the Seychelles has a pretty good record for protecting its natural environment. As early as 1968, Birdlife International set the ball rolling when it bought Cousin Island and began studying some of the country's critically endangered species. This was followed in the 1970s with legislation to establish national parks and marine reserves.

The Seychelles was also the first African country to draw up a 10-year environmental management plan, in 1990, which ushered in a more integrated approach. Under the current plan the government wants 80% of protected areas to be under private management by 2010. This is partly for financial reasons (someone else bears the cost) and partly to increase the involvement of local communities in decision making and day-to-day management. The plan also sets strict guidelines for all new building and development projects.

Not that the government's record is entirely unblemished. In 1998 it authorised a

SEYCHELLES NATIONAL PARKS

Park	Features	Activities	Best time to visit	Page
Aldabra Marine Reserve	raised coral atoll, tidal lagoon, birdlife, marine turtles, giant tortoises	diving, snorkelling, scientific study	Nov, Dec & mid-Mar – mid-May	p268
Aride Island Marine Nature Reserve	granite island, coral reef, seabirds, fishlife, marine turtles	bird-watching, snorkelling	Sep-May	p264
Cousin Island Special Reserve	granite island, natural vegetation, hawksbill turtles, seabirds, lizards	bird-watching	all year	p263
Curieuse Marine National Park	granite island, coral reefs, coco de mer palms, giant tortoises, mangrove swamps, marine turtles, fish life	diving, snorkelling, walking	all year	p263
Morne Seychellois National Park	forested peaks, mangroves, glacis habitats	hiking, botany, bird-watching	May-Sep	p254
Praslin National Park (Vallée de Mai)	native forest, coco de mer, other endemic palms, black parrot	botany, bird-watching, walking	all year	p258
Ste Anne Marine National Park	forested islands, coral reef, varied marine ecosystems, marine turtles	glass-bottomed boat trips, snorkelling, diving	all year	p257

vast land-reclamation project on Mahé's northeast coast to provide much-needed space for housing. This has caused widespread silting, marring the natural beauty of this coast indefinitely, though the alternative was to clear large tracts of forest. A difficult choice.

Tourism has had a similarly mixed impact. Hotels have been built on previously unspoilt beaches, causing problems with waste management and increased pressure on fragile ecosystems. On the other hand, tourist dollars provide much needed revenue for funding conservation projects. Local attitudes have also changed as people have learned to value their environment.

Further impetus for change is coming from NGOs operating at both community and government levels. They have notched up some spectacular successes, such as the Magpie Robin Recovery Program, funded by the Royal Society for the Protection of Birds and Birdlife International. From just 23 magpie robins languishing on Frégate Island in 1990, there are now nearly 200 living on Frégate, Cousin and Cousine Islands. Similar results have been achieved with the Seychelles warbler on Cousin, Cousine and Aride Islands.

As part of these projects, a number of islands have been painstakingly restored to their original habitat by replacing alien plant and animal species with native varieties. Several islands have also been developed for ecotourism, notably Frégate, Denis, North and Alphonse Islands, with the likelihood that Aldabra and other outer islands will follow. The visitors not only help fund conservation work, but it is also easier to protect the islands from poachers and predators if they are inhabited. With any luck, this marriage of conservation and tourism will point the way to the future.

To learn more about conservation work in the Seychelles, contact the following groups.

Nature Protection Trust of Seychelles (☎ 323711; members.aol.com/jstgerlach; PO Box 207, Victoria, Mahé) NGO working on Silhouette Island.

Nature Seychelles (☎ 225097; www.nature.org.sc; PO Box 1310, Victoria) Local partner of Birdlife International.

Seychelles Island Foundation (☎ 321755; www.sif.sc; 305 Premier Bldg, Albert St, Victoria) NGO managing the Vallée de Mai and Aldabra Atoll.

MAHÉ

Mahé was named by the French in honour of the 18th-century governor of Mauritius, Mahé de Labourdonnais, and is by far the largest and most developed of the Seychelles islands. It is home to the country's capital, Victoria (no prizes for guessing who that was named after), and to about 90% of the Seychelles' population.

Mahé is only about 27km long and between 3km and 8km wide. A range of granite peaks runs down the island's spine from north to south, including its highest point, Morne Seychellois (905m), which overlooks Victoria. Most of the settlements on Mahé stick to the narrow coastal strips, while the densely forested interior, with its towering granite boulders, has been left relatively undisturbed.

The main highway hugs the coast around most of the island, breaking only at the rugged southern tip and at the Morne Seychellois National Park in the northwest corner. A number of smaller roads cross the interior, linking the east and west coasts. The airport is on the coast at Pointe Larue, about 8km south of Victoria.

Much of the east coast is given over to housing, so there are only a few spots that fit the picture-postcard ideal. The mountainous interior and the more remote beaches to the south and west offer the best chance for a bit of seclusion. On the northwest coast, Beau Vallon beach falls nicely between the two extremes, with a beautiful white sand beach, as well as some excellent restaurants and places to stay.

Most of the industrial development is concentrated on the northeast coast around Victoria. To ease the island's housing crisis, this coast has been given over to a huge land-reclamation project that is altering the appearance of the island forever. Although the majority of the country's tourist accommodation and restaurants are on Mahé, most visitors now head for the quieter and more immediately appealing islands of Praslin and La Digue.

VICTORIA

pop 23,300

Victoria is one of the smallest capital cities in the world. It is the country's main

VICTORIA

0 — 400 m
0 — 0.2 mile

A B C D
1 2 3 4 5 6

INFORMATION

- Airtel.....(see 30)
- Antigone.....(see 14)
- Barclays Bank.....1 B3
- Barclays Bank.....2 C4
- Behram's Pharmacy.....(see 14)
- British High Commission.....(see 28)
- Cable & Wireless.....3 C5
- Central Police Station.....4 B4
- Central Post Office.....5 B4
- Créole Holidays.....(see 46)
- Double Click.....6 B3
- French Embassy.....(see 14)
- Immigration House.....7 C4
- Indian High Commission.....8 C5
- Kokonet.....(see 31)
- Marine Charter Association (MCA)..9 C4
- Mason's Travel.....10 B4
- Memorabilia.....11 B4
- Ministry of Culture.....12 C5
- Net.....13 B4
- Nouvobanq.....14 B4
- Seychelles Savings Bank.....15 C4
- Silhouette Cruises.....16 D3
- Sunsail.....(see 16)
- Tourist Office.....17 C4
- Travel Services Seychelles (TSS).....18 B4
- USA Embassy.....(see 28)
- Victoria Hospital.....19 C6
- VPM Yacht Charter.....(see 41)
- Water World.....(see 9)

SIGHTS & ACTIVITIES (pp249-50)

- Botanical Gardens.....20 C6
- National Museum of History.....21 B4
- Natural History Museum.....22 C4
- Sir Selwyn Selwyn-Clarke Market.....23 B4

SLEEPING (p250)

- Hilltop Guest House.....24 A4
- Hotel Bel Air.....25 A5
- Rose Garden Hotel.....26 B6

EATING (pp250-1)

- Alliance Française Café.....(see 34)
- Lai Lam's Bread Shop.....27 B4
- Mahek Cafeteria.....28 B4
- Marie-Antoinette.....29 A4
- News Café.....30 B4
- Pirates Arms.....31 C4
- Sam's Pizzeria.....32 B4
- SMB Supermarket.....33 B4

ENTERTAINMENT (p251)

- Alliance Française.....34 C6
- Carrefour des Arts.....35 C4
- Deepam Cinema.....36 B3

SHOPPING (p251)

- Antik Colony.....(see 31)
- Camion Hall.....37 B4
- Ray's Music Room.....38 B4
- Sunstroke.....39 B4

TRANSPORT

- Air Austral.....(see 31)
- Air France.....(see 46)
- Air Mauritius.....(see 46)
- Air Seychelles.....(see 14)
- Avis.....(see 14)
- British Airways.....(see 46)
- Bus Terminal.....40 C3
- Cat Cocos Catamaran to Praslin.....41 D3
- Hertz.....42 B4
- Kenya Airways.....43 C4
- Schooner Ferries to La Digue.....(see 41)
- Taxi Stand.....44 B4

OTHER

- Clock Tower.....45 B4
- Kingsgate House.....46 C4
- National Library.....(see 12)
- Seychelles Island Foundation.....(see 38)

Oliver Marandan St
Palm St
Hangard St
Quincy St
Albert St
Huteau La
To Anse Étoile (4km); North-East Point (8km)
Labordonnais St
Lodge St
Market St
Malakoff St
Harrison St
Benezet St
Manglier St
5th June Ave
Flamboyant Ave
Freedom Square
Serret Rd
Revolution Ave
Oceangate House
Independence Ave
Long Pier Rd
Security Gate
Bel Air Cemetery
State House Ave
Francis Rachel St
Stadium
Île Hodoul
To Beau Vallon (2km)
Inner Harbour
Jardin des Enfants
Liberation Rd
Bel Air Rd
Lantanier Rd
Veloutier Rd
To Wharf Hotel & Marina (3km); Airport (8km)
Bois de Rose Ave
Rivière Trois Frères
Canal
Mont Fleuri Rd
Sans Souci Rd
To Port Glaud (10km)

SEYCHELLES

economic, political and commercial centre, and home to about a third of its population, but even so Victoria retains the air of a sleepy provincial town.

It's a pleasant place, set against a backdrop of hills, but aside from a few notable old buildings, the centre of Victoria is too clean and modern looking to have a great deal of atmosphere. The focal point of downtown is a downsized replica of the clock tower on London's Vauxhall Bridge. The replica was brought to Victoria in 1903 when the Seychelles became a crown colony.

The old courthouse beside the clock tower will appeal to fans of Creole architecture, and there are also a few attractive old buildings along Francis Rachel St (named after the lone 'martyr' of the 1977 coup) and Albert St.

Information

BOOKSHOPS

Antigone (☎ 225443; Victoria House, Francis Rachel St) Stocks a reasonable range of English-language novels and books on the Seychelles, plus a few imported newspapers and magazines.

Memorabilia (☎ 321190; Revolution Ave) Gift shop and art gallery with a selection of Seychelles titles.

EMERGENCY

Police (☎ 999)
Fire (☎ 999)
Ambulance (☎ 999)
Central Police Station (☎ 288000; Revolution Ave)

INTERNET ACCESS

Double Click (☎ 610590; Palm St; 🕒 8am-9pm Mon-Thu, 8am-11pm Fri & Sat, 9am-9pm Sun) Great little café open after hours.

Kokonet (☎ 322000; Pirates Arms Bldg, Independence Ave; 🕒 8am-6pm Mon-Fri, 9am-1pm Sat)

Net (☎ 718359; Sham-Peng Tong Plaza, Albert St; 🕒 8.30am-1pm & 2-5pm Mon-Fri, 8.30am-1pm Sat)

MEDICAL SERVICES

Victoria Hospital (☎ 388000; Mont Fleuri) The country's main hospital has an emergency unit and outpatient and dental clinics.

Behram's Pharmacy (☎ 225559; Victoria House, Francis Rachel St; 🕒 8.30am-4.45pm Mon-Fri, 8.15am-12.30pm Sat)

MONEY

All the major banks have ATMs and exchange facilities.

Barclays Bank (☎ 383838; Independence Ave); Market Branch (☎ 383838; Albert St)

Nouvobanq (☎ 293000; Victoria House, Francis Rachel St)

Seychelles Savings Bank (☎ 225251; Kingsgate House, Independence Ave)

POST

Central Post Office (☎ 225222; Independence Ave; 🕒 8am-4pm Mon-Fri, 8am-noon Sat)

TOURIST INFORMATION

Tourist Office (☎ 610800; www.aspureasitgets.com; Independence Ave; 🕒 8am-5pm Mon-Fri, 9am-noon Sat) Helpful staff hand out booklets detailing all the country's accommodation options and decent maps of Mahé, Praslin and La Digue.

TRAVEL AGENCIES

Créole Holidays (☎ 224900; www.creoleholidays.sc; Kingsgate House, Independence Ave)

Mason's Travel (☎ 322642; www.masonstravel.com; Revolution Ave)

Travel Services Seychelles (TSS; ☎ 322414; www.tss.sc; Albert St)

Sights & Activities

The main sights in Victoria are concentrated in the compact town centre. The exception is the botanical gardens, but even they are easily accessible on foot.

BOTANICAL GARDENS

These manicured **gardens** (☎ 224644; admission €5; 🕒 8am-5pm) full of streams and birdsong are about 10 minutes' walk south of the centre. They were established in 1901 and contain some magnificent old trees. This is a good place to mug up on native plantlife before venturing further afield.

It takes about an hour to explore the gardens. Star attractions are the coco de mer palms lining the main alley. There's also a spice grove, a pen of giant tortoises and a patch of rainforest complete with fruit bats. Remember to bring insect repellent.

NATIONAL MUSEUM OF HISTORY

Not to be confused with the Natural History Museum, the **National Museum of History** (☎ 225253; admission Rs 10; State House Ave; 🕒 8.30am-4.30pm Mon, Tue, Thu & Fri, 8.30am-noon Sat) contains a small but well-displayed collection of historical artefacts. In pride of place is the Stone of Possession, which was erected in 1756 by Captain Corneille Nicolas Morphey to indicate French possession of the islands. Other exhibits also relate to the settlement of the islands and to local culture, including musical instruments, games and *gris gris*.

SIR SELWYN SELWYN-CLARKE MARKET

When it first opened, the revamped covered **market** (Market St; 5.30am-5pm Mon-Fri, 5.30am-noon Sat) was something of a tourist gimmick, but over the years it's evolved into quite a lively, bustling place. Early morning is the best time to come, when fishmongers display an astonishing variety of seafood, from parrot fish to barracuda.

NATURAL HISTORY MUSEUM

At the time of writing, the **Natural History Museum** (321333; Independence Ave) was closed for major renovations. When it eventually reopens, it should be worth a quick visit to learn about the islands' curious creatures, such as the Seychelles crocodile and the giant tortoise, both now sadly vanished from the main islands.

Tours

Victoria's three main travel agencies offer the full range of services, including ticketing, car hire, yacht charter and tours around Mahé and to other islands. Their tours are pretty much interchangeable in terms of itineraries and prices: a full-day bus tour of Mahé including lunch costs around €60/35 per adult/child (a half-day tour is €30/20); glass-bottomed boat trips to Ste Anne Marine National Park cost €85/50; and day tours to Praslin and La Digue are €140/90 by boat or €190/145 by plane.

Sleeping

There are a number of guesthouses dotted around the suburbs of Victoria and one business hotel on the road to the airport. On the whole, though, you're best staying elsewhere and visiting the town on day trips.

Rose Garden Hotel (225308; www.seychelles.sc/rosegarden; Sans Souci Rd; s/d from €181/196;) High above the botanical gardens, this serene colonial bungalow has five immaculate suites equipped to a high standard. There's also a good restaurant.

Wharf Hotel & Marina (Map p253; 670700; provide@seychelles.net; d from €200;) This smart new hotel on the road to the airport caters to business travellers and yacht crews, but is a good option for a first or last night's stay. In addition to the marina, there's a dive centre, restaurant and bar.

Hotel Bel Air (224416; www.seychelles.net/belair; Bel Air Rd; s/d €94/125;) Fairly central, on the road to Sans Souci, is this clean and friendly, if somewhat faded, guesthouse; it's a bit expensive for what you get.

Hilltop Guest House (266555; Serret Rd; d from €50) Nothing fancy, but this is the cheapest you'll find in Victoria. It's under the same ownership as the nearby Marie-Antoinette restaurant, off the road to Beau Vallon, and within walking distance of the city centre.

Eating

Victoria is relatively well endowed with places to eat. There are many takeaway outlets offering Creole staples such as grilled fish and chicken curry in the streets around the market. For something more relaxing, try one of the following.

Pirates Arms (225001; Independence Ave; mains Rs 50-65; 9am-midnight Mon-Sat, noon-midnight Sun) Hugely popular with locals and tourists, this open-fronted café and restaurant is *the* meeting place. The menu ranges from breakfast deals to sandwiches, pizzas, salads and catch-of-the-day – all fresh and tasty. On weekdays takeaway lunches are available from the counter around the side.

Marie-Antoinette (266222; Serret Rd, St Louis; set menu Rs 120; lunch & dinner Mon-Sat) An atmospheric Creole restaurant in a beautiful old colonial house on the road to Beau Vallon. The set menu provides an excellent introduction to traditional Seychelles dishes.

Sam's Pizzeria (322499; pizzas Rs 60, other mains around Rs 65; Francis Rachel St; lunch & dinner) Funky marine décor and authentic pizzas make this breezy, 1st-floor restaurant a popular choice. There's plenty of choice for vegetarians and non-pizza eaters too.

Other recommendations:

Alliance Française Café (282424; Bois de Rose Ave; mains Rs 35-40; 9am-7pm Mon-Fri, 9am-noon Sat) Drinks and light lunches in a nice leafy spot above the library.

Double Click (610590; Palm St; salads Rs 32; 8am-9pm Mon-Thu, 8am-11pm Fri & Sat, 9am-9pm Sun;) Internet café with fresh juices, salads and decadent cakes.

Mahek Caféteria (Oliaji Trade Centre, Francis Rachel St; meals Rs 25; 10.30am-4pm Mon-Fri, 10.30am-1pm Sat) Scrummy Indian takeaway.

News Café (Trinity House, Albert St; sandwiches Rs 25, salads Rs 45-50; breakfast & lunch) Fresh, tasty food and great coffee.

SELF-CATERING

Self-caterers should head for the market and the well-stocked **SMB Supermarket** (Albert St). **Lai Lam's Bread Shop** (Benezet St; 8am-5pm Mon-Sat) bakes excellent bread, samosas and other snacks.

Entertainment

The most popular drinking hole is the Pirates Arms, which doubles as a bar and offers live music (a crooner with a guitar) several nights a week.

The **Deepam Cinema** (322585; Albert St; tickets Rs 17-20) screens American and Indian films three times daily.

For more high-brow culture, the **Alliance Française** (282424; Bois de Rose Ave) puts on a varied programme including concerts, French-language films and theatre.

On the second and fourth Fridays of each month, young locals dance up a storm at the **Carrefour des Arts** (6-11pm). These free, open-air concerts featuring local bands take place on a sports ground behind Oceangate House, at the east end of Independence Ave.

Shopping

The majority of craft and gift shops are concentrated in and around the market. **Camion Hall** (Albert St) is a crafts centre with a range of upmarket shops, including Caprice des Îles, which sells fabulous fabrics; Aphrodite Marine, a model-ship manufacturer; Pineapple Studio, which does a nice line of general souvenirs; and the jeweller Kreol'or.

Other souvenir shops worth browsing are **Antik Colony** (321700; Pirates Arms Bldg, Independence Ave) and **Sunstroke** (224767; Market St).

For a wide selection of Creole music, visit **Ray's Music Room** (322674; Premier Bldg, Albert St).

Getting There & Around

Victoria is the main transport hub for buses around Mahé and for boats to Praslin and La Digue. For information about these services and for flights around the islands, see p274.

Coming from the airport, a taxi into town costs around Rs 75 plus Rs 5 per piece of luggage. Alternatively, cross the road and pick up any bus heading north. See p275 for more about local buses.

BEAU VALLON & AROUND

The fine, white sands at Beau Vallon (on Mahé's northwest coast, 2km from Victoria) used to be the most popular beach in the Seychelles, but with most tourists moving directly on to the islands of Praslin and La Digue, Beau Vallon can be surprisingly quiet. Numerous palms and takamaka trees provide shelter for sunbathers. It's also one of the few beaches where the water is deep enough for swimming (watch out for large swells between June and November). There's good snorkelling offshore and this is the main dive centre on Mahé. For more on snorkelling and diving in the Seychelles, see p40.

In Beau Vallon village, where the road from Victoria forks west to Bel Ombre and northeast to Glacis, there is a petrol station, a Barclays Bank ATM, a Cable & Wireless Internet café and the police station. You'll find minimarkets supplying basic foodstuffs and other necessities on the beach road, behind the Beau Vallon Internet Café, and around the junction with the Bel Ombre road.

Sleeping

Beau Vallon offers the widest range of accommodation in north Mahé.

Georgina's Cottage (247016; georgina@seychelles.net; s/d from €55/75) This excellent homey guesthouse is across the road from the beach and just a few minutes' walk north of Beau Vallon village. There's a communal kitchen and a washing machine. The owner is a mine of information.

Coco d'Or Hotel (247331; pleasure@seychelles.net; s/d from €117/156) A small, well-run hotel offering style and facilities a cut above the competition. Most rooms come with private terrace or veranda, plus satellite TV and phone.

Augerine Guesthouse (/fax 247257; s/d from €90/100) On the beach next to the big Berjaya hotel, the nicest rooms at this spick-and-span little place look out across the garden to the sea.

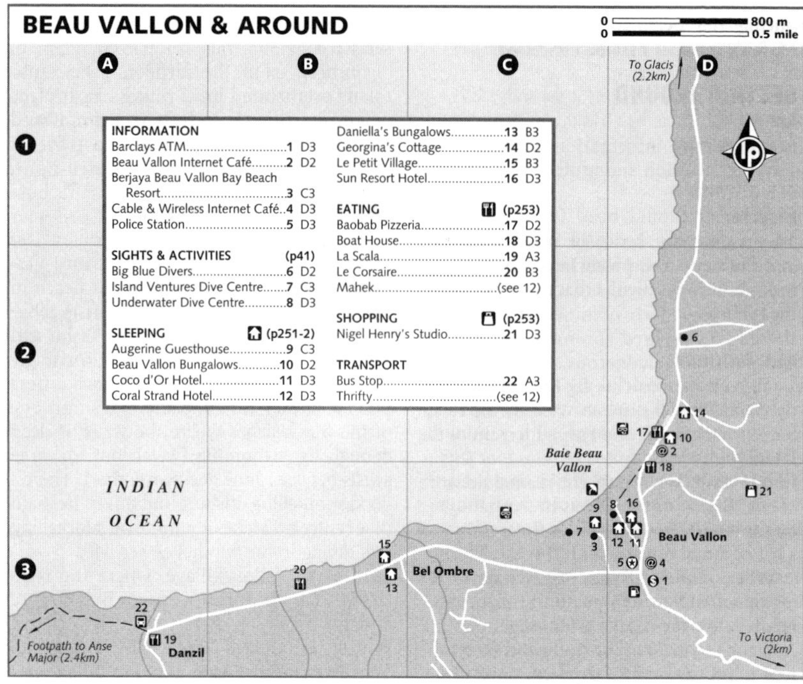

Daniella's Bungalows (☎ 247212; www.daniellasbungalows.com/english/bungalows.asp; s/d €80/100) It's a bit of a trek to the beach from this place in Bel Ombre, but you do get a warm welcome, spacious gardens and well-kept bungalows, decked out in cheerful fabrics. Perfect for a relaxing stay.

Le Petit Village (☎ 284969; www.lepetitvillage.com; studio from €165;) Luxury self-catering accommodation in log cabins overlooking the ocean in Bel Ombre. There's a choice between one-bedroom studios and two-bedroom apartments, all equipped to a very high standard.

Other recommendations:

Beau Vallon Bungalows (☎ 247382; www.seychelles.net/bvbung; s/d €70/90) Guesthouse with airy fan-cooled rooms. The self-catering bungalows by the road can be noisy.

Coral Strand Hotel (☎ 621000; www.coralstrand.com; s/d from €108/120;) The better of Beau Vallon's two big hotels offers lots of facilities and comfortable rooms.

Sun Resort Hotel (☎ 285555; sun@seychelles.net; s/d from €90/100;) Small and welcoming hotel with attractive gardens.

PIECES OF EIGHT

Bel Ombre is one of several possible locations for the treasure trove of the legendary pirate Olivier Levasseur, known as 'La Buse' (the Buzzard). When La Buse was finally caught and hanged in Réunion in 1730, he is said to have tossed a piece of paper into the crowd and shouted 'Find my treasure, he who can'.

A cryptogram belonging to an old Norwegian whaling skipper, and strange markings on the shore rocks at Bel Ombre, have led several treasure seekers to dig up this particular stretch of coast. A retired Englishman, Reginald Cruise-Wilkins, devoted the last years of his life to the search in the 1940s, but found nothing more than a few tantalising coins and pieces of weaponry.

He may, however, have been looking in the wrong place. Poudre d'Or in north Mauritius is just one of several other contenders for the title of final resting place of La Buse's fortune.

OLIVIER CIRENDINI

Big game fishing boat, Flic en Flac (p101)

JEAN-BERNARD CARILLET

Traditional basketware (p125), Port Mathurin

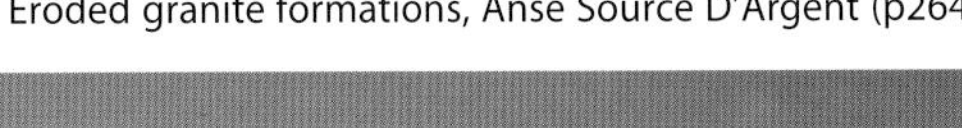

Eroded granite formations, Anse Source D'Argent (p264)

RALPH LEE HOPKINS

RALPH LEE HO

Mushroom atoll (p268), Aldabra Islands

JOHN HAY

Granite rocks (p245), Mahé

Eating

Boat House (☎ 247898; buffet adult/child Rs 115/65; lunch Sun, dinner Tue-Sun) Locals and tourists flock from far and wide for the magnificent all-you-can-eat buffet of salads, curries, barbecued fish and scrummy deserts. It's best to get here early (12.30pm for Sunday lunch; 7.30pm for dinner) or reserve.

Baobab Pizzeria (☎ 247167; mains Rs 32-50; lunch & dinner) This sand-floored restaurant right on the beach is also something of a local legend, offering cheap but tasty pizzas and pasta dishes plus a few salads. It's packed most nights.

Mahek (☎ 621835; mains Rs 60-200; lunch & dinner, closed Tue;) Splash out on top-notch Indian cuisine at this very upmarket restaurant in the Coral Strand Hotel.

La Scala (☎ 247535; mains Rs 90-250; dinner Mon-Sat) At the end of the coast road near Danzil, this long-established Italian restaurant is great for a romantic candlelit dinner. The prices aren't bad for the quality, with interesting dishes such as smoked sailfish tagliatelle and stuffed clams. It has a good wine list and impeccable service.

Le Corsaire (☎ 247171; mains Rs 90-120; dinner Tue-Sun) By the water in Bel Ombre, this is a more formal restaurant than La Scala, offering mostly Italian cuisine plus a few local dishes – adventurous diners could opt for bat in white-wine sauce!

Shopping

Nigel Henry's studio (☎ 715353; www.seychelles.sc/nigdesigncon; 10am-5pm Mon-Sat) Henry's acrylics capture all the life and colour of the local markets.

Getting There & Away

Buses leave regularly from Victoria for Beau Vallon, either straight over the hill via St Louis, or the long way round via Glacis. The last bus to Victoria leaves around 7.30pm; it's a 40-minute trudge or a Rs 70 taxi ride if you miss it.

NORTH MAHÉ

The most developed and populous area of Mahé lies to the north of an imaginary east–west line from the airport to Grande Anse. Indeed, the whole northeast coast

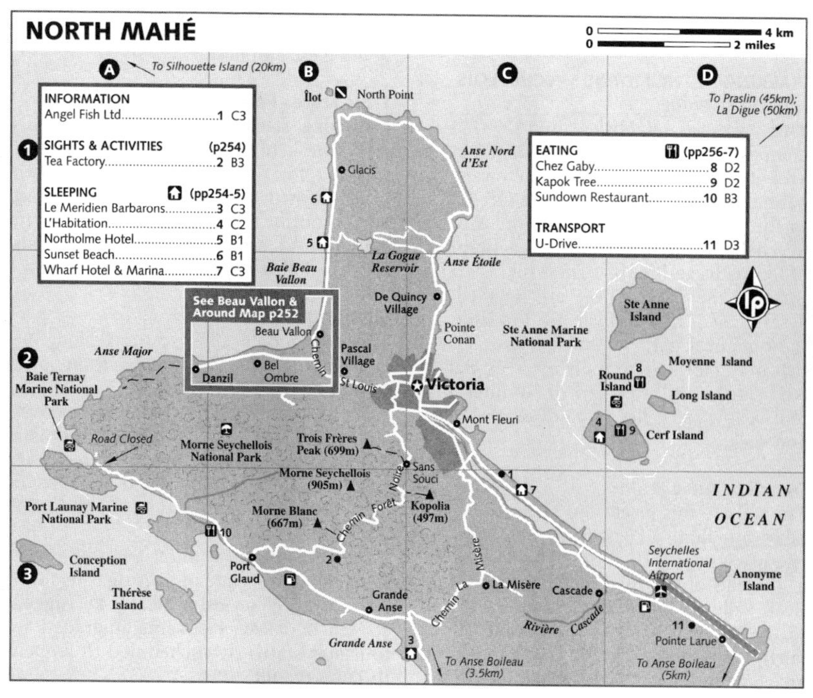

from the airport to Anse Étoile has been marred by a huge land-reclamation project designed to ease the island's housing shortage. However, there are still some lovely spots to be found around Mahé's northern tip and heading down the northwest coast of the island.

Beau Vallon is the main destination on the northwest coast because of its beach and tourist infrastructure, but there's also some great scenery north, up the coast to Glacis and on the road over the mountains from Victoria to Port Glaud, which cuts through the Morne Seychellois National Park. Follow the road north of Port Glaud and you'll find yet more idyllic beaches around Port Launay.

Sights & Activities

TEA FACTORY

This working **tea factory** (☎ 378221; admission with/without guided tour Rs 20/10; 10am-4pm Mon-Fri) is on the Sans Souci road about 3km above Port Glaud. It's best to visit before noon, when you can see the whole process from drying to packing. The estate produces about 45 tonnes of organic tea per year for export.

WALKING IN THE MORNE SEYCHELLOIS NATIONAL PARK

This park was established in 1979. It encompasses an impressive 20% of the land area of Mahé and contains a wide variety of habitats, from coastal mangrove forests up to the country's highest peak, the Morne Seychellois (905m). There are a number of footpaths and more serious hiking trails through the park. These are detailed in a series of leaflets which are available at the botanical gardens and the tourist office in Victoria. The trails are reasonably well signed and are marked by intermittent yellow splotches of paint on the trees and rocks.

Danzil to Anse Major

The walk to this lovely and secluded beach takes you along a coast fringed by impressive glacis rock formations. The path starts at the end of the road heading west from Beau Vallon. Though the last stretch down to the beach is a bit of a scramble, it's a fairly easy romp. Unless you happen to arrive at the same time as a tour group, the beach is blissfully quiet, and is good for swimming, though there can be strong currents. You'll have to return by the same route, a total of roughly 5km.

Tea Factory to Morne Blanc

The imposing white bulk of Morne Blanc and its almost sheer 500m face make a great hiking destination. Although the track is only 600m long, it is quite steep – climbing 250m from start to finish. Unless you're pretty fit, plan on roughly an hour for the ascent. The reward is a tremendous view over the northwest coast and the sight of tropicbirds circling below you.

The path starts 250m up the road from the tea factory on the cross-island road from Victoria to Port Glaud. You have to descend the same way.

Kopolia Peak

This is the easier of two walks to the peaks overlooking Victoria and the Ste Anne Marine National Park. The trail starts on the cross-island Chemin Forêt Noire about 5km above Victoria. It's only just over 1km to the top of Kopolia (497m), but the final section is quite steep; allow roughly two hours there and back.

Trois Frères Peak

It's a long, steep climb to the top of Trois Frères Peak (699m), behind Victoria, but worth it for panoramic views. The path is well signed from the Sans Souci Forest Station on the Chemin Forêt Noire, about 4km from Victoria, although the final leg is tricky to follow. Allow four hours in total.

Sleeping

There are good options scattered along the west coast. The list below moves from north to south.

Sunset Beach (☎ 261111; www.sunset-beach.com; Glacis; s/d from €266/308;) Perched on a little headland among rocks and trees, this small hotel offers understated elegance. It has a good restaurant and lots of attractive nooks and crannies.

Northolme Hotel (☎ 261222; northolm@seychelles.net; Glacis) At the time of writing, this famous old hotel set on a pleasantly rugged stretch of coast was being upgraded to four-star status. It's scheduled to reopen in January 2005.

SEYCHELLES

Le Meridien Barbarons (☎ 378253; www.lemeridien.com; Grande Anse; s/d from €190/250;) Popular resort hotel set around an impressive pool in lush gardens. The rooms aren't huge but have some Creole colour; the superior rooms are more airy and better equipped. Evening entertainment, mini-golf, tennis courts and various water sports round out the facilities.

Eating

Sundown Restaurant (☎ 378352; Port Glaud; mains Rs 60-100; noon-9pm Mon, Wed & Fri, 11am-6pm Tue, Thu & Sat) Despite its laid-back atmosphere, this waterfront restaurant offers surprisingly upmarket dishes such as sea snails in white-wine sauce as well as more standard curries and fresh seafood.

SOUTH MAHÉ

The southern half of Mahé is less mountainous and less populated than the north. There are one or two sights to aim for, but it's the beaches and coastal scenery that are the star attraction.

On the southeast coast, the best strips of sand are found at Anse Bougainville, Anse Parnel, Anse Forbans and Anse Marie-Louise. Around the headland, the currents are too dangerous for swimming, but the beaches are great places to watch the surf: Anse Intendance and Police Bay, right at the tip, are both splendid spots.

Coming up the west coast, Anse Takamaka, Anse Gaulettes and Anse à la Mouche all vie for the 'best beach' accolade, though most people plump for the idyllic little beach of Anse Soleil. The walk to it from the bus stop by Harvey's Café (see p256) takes about 30 minutes.

Sights

LE JARDIN DU ROI

Located 2km up in the hills above Anse Royale, **Le Jardin du Roi** (☎ 371313; admission Rs 27; 10am-5.30pm) is a lush spice garden that owes its existence to Pierre Poivre, the French spice entrepreneur. There is a self-guided walk around the 35-hectare orchard-cum-forest, and you can help yourself to star fruit and other tropical delights as you wander around.

The planter's house contains a one-room museum and there's a pleasant café-restaurant (p256) with views down to the coast.

CRAFT VILLAGE

The rather contrived **craft village** (☎ 376100; admission free; 9.30am-5.30pm) at Anse aux Pins consists of 12 craft shops grouped around the Domaine de Val des Près, an old plantation house with a few bits of memorabilia. The rather motley assortment of crafts on offer includes model boats, pottery and products fashioned from the hugely versatile coconut tree.

You can also eat here in the Vye Marmit restaurant (see p256).

Sleeping

Accommodation in south Mahé ranges from modest guesthouses and self-catering apartments to big resort hotels with everything laid on. The recommendations following head down the east coast and then back up the west coast.

EAST COAST

Lalla Panzi (☎ 376411; fax 375633; s/d from €45/60;) This cheap and friendly guesthouse at Anse aux Pins is close – but not too close – to the airport. It offers four absolutely spotless rooms and a garden leading down to the sea. Though on the main road, it's quiet enough at night.

La Roussette Hotel (☎ 376245; www.seychelles.net/larousse; s/d €77/102;) Opposite the Lalla Panzi and set back from the road in gardens, this is a surprisingly attractive complex of neat and tidy bungalows.

Fairyland (☎ 371700; fairyland@seychelles.net; s/d from €75/100) A sweet little hotel tucked under the rocky outcrop of Pointe au Sel. The rooms are homey and have big balconies; there are only six, so book well ahead.

Allamanda (☎ 366266; www.the-seychelles.com/allamanda; s/d €158/172;) In another lovely quiet spot on the beach at Anse Forbans, this charming and well-run hotel makes an excellent mid-range option. It has just 10 spruce and well-appointed rooms and a good restaurant (see p256).

WEST COAST

Lazare Picault Hotel (☎ 361111; www.lazarepicault.net; s/d from €99/125;) On the hillside overlooking Baie Lazare, these whitewashed chalets contain unexciting but comfortable rooms with sea-view terraces.

Anse Soleil Resort (☎ 361090; fax 361435; s/d from €35/70;) Though nothing fancy, these

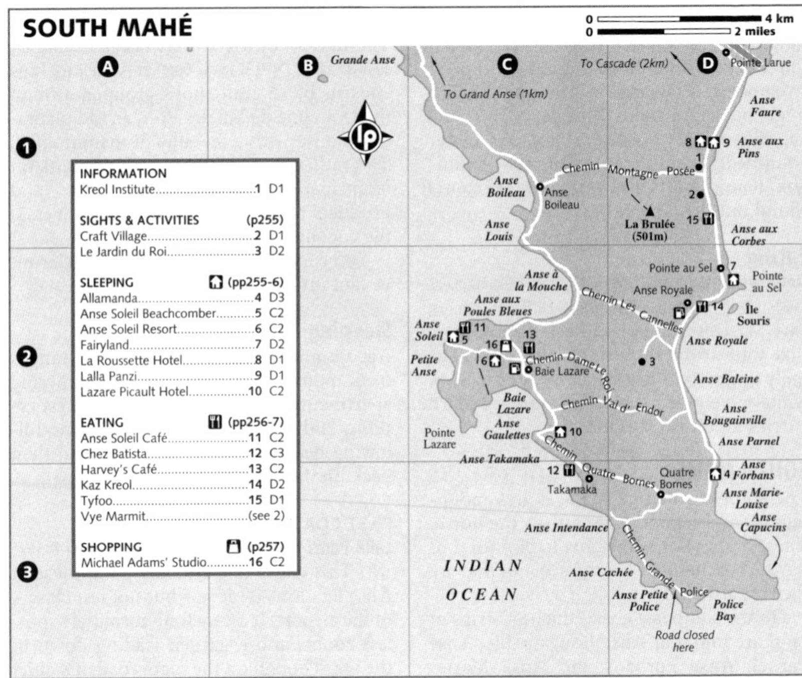

four self-catering apartments on the road to Anse Soleil are in a great location, with wonderful views over Anse à la Mouche.

Anse Soleil Beachcomber (☎ 361461; www.beachcomber.sc; s/d from €110/130; ❄) Among rocks on the secluded cove of Anse Soleil, this small, welcoming hotel is a perfect hideaway. The rooms are clean and simple with private terraces.

Eating

EAST COAST

Kaz Kreol (☎ 371680; mains Rs 60-100; 🕑 lunch & dinner Tue-Sun) Good, crispy pizzas, curries and fresh seafood are the order of the day at this rustic beachside restaurant at Anse Royale. Fish and palm-tree murals add to the tropical atmosphere, and a singer cranks it up on Friday and Saturday evenings.

Le Jardin du Roi (☎ 371313; mains Rs 75-100; 🕑 10am-4.30pm) The café-restaurant at the spice garden (see p255) serves fresh fruit juices and dishes using home-grown herbs and spices. There's a three-course 'plantation lunch' on Sunday (Rs 100); reservations are required.

Allamanda (☎ 366266; mains Rs 80-130; 🕑 lunch & dinner; ❄) This hotel restaurant at Anse Forbans is usually full for both lunch and dinner on Sunday when it lays on a superb Creole buffet (Rs 120). There's a smaller, but still excellent, buffet on Wednesday evenings (Rs 100). At other times the cooking has a French twist, offering such delicacies as smoked swordfish with ham mousse, and giraffe crab with ginger sauce.

Other recommendations:

Tyfoo (☎ 371485; mains from Rs 40; 🕑 lunch & dinner) Cheap and cheerful Chinese in a garden setting.

Vye Marmit (☎ 376155; mains Rs 75-95; 🕑 11am-9pm Mon-Sat) Traditional Creole cuisine in the Craft Village (p256).

WEST COAST

Chez Batista (☎ 366300; mains around Rs 100; 🕑 9am-10pm) This easy-going eatery on the beach at Anse Takamaka offers grilled fish, salads and so forth. The prices are high, but it's the location you're paying for.

Harvey's Café (☎ 713535; dishes Rs 40-90; 🕑 9.30am-5.30pm Tue-Sun) This cheerful little café at the turn for Anse Soleil serves great filter coffee and is perfectly placed for a quick snack (sandwiches, salads and hot dishes) while you're waiting for the bus.

Anse Soleil Café (☎ 361700; mains Rs 75-175; lunch & dinner) The nicest place to eat on the southwest coast is this rustic beachfront restaurant at Anse Soleil. The menu revolves around ultra fresh seafood served in generous portions; the lobster is superb.

Shopping

Michael Adams' studio (☎ 361006; www.seychelles.net/adams; 10am-4pm Mon-Fri, 10am-noon Sat) Adams' silk-screen prints burst with the vivid life of the forests. They are irresistible and highly collectable, so bring plenty of rupees if you're thinking of buying.

STE ANNE MARINE NATIONAL PARK

This park off Mahé's east coast consists of six islands. Of these, day-trippers are permitted to land on Cerf, Round and Moyenne Islands. Though the scenery and the islands themselves merit a trip and the marine life is still impressive, the coral in the park is no longer as awesome as it was. Silting from the land-reclamation project in the bay has led to significant coral damage, compounded by several episodes of coral 'bleaching' (see p33 for more about bleaching).

The national park is primarily visited on glass-bottomed boat tours offered by the main tour operators (see p249). The cost of a full day's outing including snorkelling and lunch starts at €85/50 per adult/child. However, you can get a much cheaper deal at the **Marine Charter Association** (Map p248; ☎ 322126; mca@seychelles.net) in Victoria, which offers day trips to Cerf and Round Islands for Rs 150 per person, excluding lunch. Alternatively, if there's enough demand the restaurants on Round and Cerf Islands usually offer a package including transport and lunch at weekends.

Note that the park authorities charge a fee of €10 per person (free for children under 12 years) to enter the marine park. Tour operators usually include this in their prices, but private operators may not; remember to check when fixing a price.

Moyenne Island

Moyenne is the most interesting island. The native fauna and flora have been carefully regenerated and everything is neatly labelled, giving it the air of a botanical garden. It is now owned by Brendon Grimshaw, who has spent the last 40 years hacking back the jungle to create his own tropical paradise. You'll discover something of the island's history during the visit and can learn more about Grimshaw's labour of love in his autobiographical *A Grain of Sand*.

Day tours are organised solely through TSS (p249) and include snorkelling and lunch at the island's Jolly Roger restaurant.

Round Island

This island, like Curieuse Island near Praslin, was once home to a leper colony, but these days it's better known for the offshore snorkelling and its restaurant **Chez Gaby** (Map p253; ☎ 322111; lunch). The restaurant is famous for its melt-in-the-mouth tuna and the amazing Creole spread it lays on for the Sunday buffet (Rs 150). Afterwards, a quick tour of the island takes all of 30 minutes, maximum.

In addition to the regular organised tours, on Sundays you should be able to get a lift over on a charter boat for around Rs 60 per person; phone the restaurant to check on availability.

Cerf Island

About 60 people live on Cerf Island, including Wilbur Smith, the South African novelist. As with Moyenne and Round Islands, there is good snorkelling and a restaurant, the **Kapok Tree** (Map p253; ☎ 322959; lunch), which offers another fine Creole buffet. A package including transport and lunch costs Rs 170 per person.

You can also stay on the island at a comfortable little colonial-style hotel, **L'Habitation** (Map p253; ☎ 323111; habicerf@seychelles.net; s/d from €165/177, s/d/half board from €200/234;), just a 10-minute boat ride from Victoria. One slight disadvantage is the occasional plane passing overhead.

SILHOUETTE ISLAND

This imposing island 20km from Mahé is named not for its moody profile at sunset, but for an 18th-century French minister. With steep forested mountain peaks rising from the ocean above stunning palm-shaded beaches, Silhouette is a truly magnificent island hideaway.

Sadly, the romance is reserved for guests of the exclusive **Silhouette Island Lodge** (☎ 224003;

sillodge@seychelles.net; s/d full board from €290/470) but you may be able to stop off at one of the beaches if you charter a fishing boat. The best person to talk to is **Jimmy** (☎ 510269), who can generally be found through the Boat House restaurant (p253) at Beau Vallon. A full day's fishing, including barbecue lunch on the island, costs around €100 per person plus landing fees. The big tour companies might also be able to help.

PRASLIN & AROUND

Northeast of Mahé is a group of islands dominated by Praslin and including Curieuse, Cousin and Aride Islands. On Praslin you can see wild coco de mar palms, while the smaller islands are noted for their wildlife.

PRASLIN

Praslin is the second-largest island in the Seychelles, and lies about 45km northeast of Mahé. In terms of development and tourism, it falls somewhere between the relative hustle and bustle of Mahé and sleepy La Digue. The landscape is lush and tropical and the mood slow and easy, as befits such a tropical island paradise.

Like Mahé, Praslin is a granite island, with a ridge of mountains running east–west along the centre. The island measures 12km long and 5km across at its widest point. It's named after the Duc de Praslin, a French minister of state who was guillotined in the French Revolution.

The main attraction here, apart from some splendid beaches, is the Vallée de Mai. This forest reserve is one of the few places where the unusual coco de mer palm grows wild (see Lovely Bunch of Coconuts on p260).

The 5000 inhabitants of Praslin are scattered around the coast in a series of small settlements. The most important from a visitor's perspective are Anse Volbert (also known as the Côte d'Or) and Grand Anse. At the southwest tip of the island is Baie Ste Anne, Praslin's main port.

Information

INTERNET ACCESS

Verimedia (☎ 232157; Anse Volbert; 10am-7pm Mon-Sat) Praslin's only Internet café is a pricey €3 for 10 minutes.

MONEY

All the major banks have ATMs and exchange facilities.

Barclays Bank (☎ 233344; Grand Anse); Baie St Anne Branch (☎ 232218; Baie St Anne)
MCB (☎ 233940; Grand Anse); Anse Volbert Branch (☎ 232602; Anse Volbert)
Seychelles Savings Bank (☎ 233810; Grand Anse)

POST

Central Post Office (☎ 233212; Grand Anse; 8am-noon & 1-4pm Mon-Fri) Next to the police station in Grand Anse.

TOURIST INFORMATION

Praslin's two tourist offices can provide maps and basic information and help with accommodation bookings.

Airport Tourist Office (☎ 233346; Amitié; praslin@seychelles.sc; 8am-5pm Mon-Fri, 8am-3pm Sat, 8am-1pm Sun)
Baie St Anne Tourist Office (☎ 232669; Baie St Anne; praslin@seychelles.sc; 8am-12.30pm & 2-5pm Mon-Fri, 8am-1pm Sat)

TRAVEL AGENCIES

Créole Holidays (☎ 233223; Grand Anse)
Mason's Travel (☎ 233211; Grand Anse)
Travel Services Seychelles (TSS; ☎ 233438; Grand Anse)

Sights & Activities

The single most popular sight in the whole of the Seychelles is the magnificent Vallée de Mai forest reserve in Praslin National Park. Other than that, most people come here for the beaches and to explore the surrounding islands. There's also some superb snorkelling and diving around Praslin. For more information, see Underwater Worlds on p40.

VALLÉE DE MAI

Praslin's World Heritage–listed **Vallée de Mai** (admission €15, children under 12 free; 8am-5.30pm) is one of only two places in the world where you can see the rare coco de mer palms growing in their natural state (the other being nearby Curieuse Island). If the entry price seems steep, remember this is a unique chance to experience a slice of Eden. On a more practical level, your money also goes towards conservation work here and on Aldabra Atoll.

Three trails lead through the park, of which the longest takes around three hours. Signs indicate some of the other endemic trees to

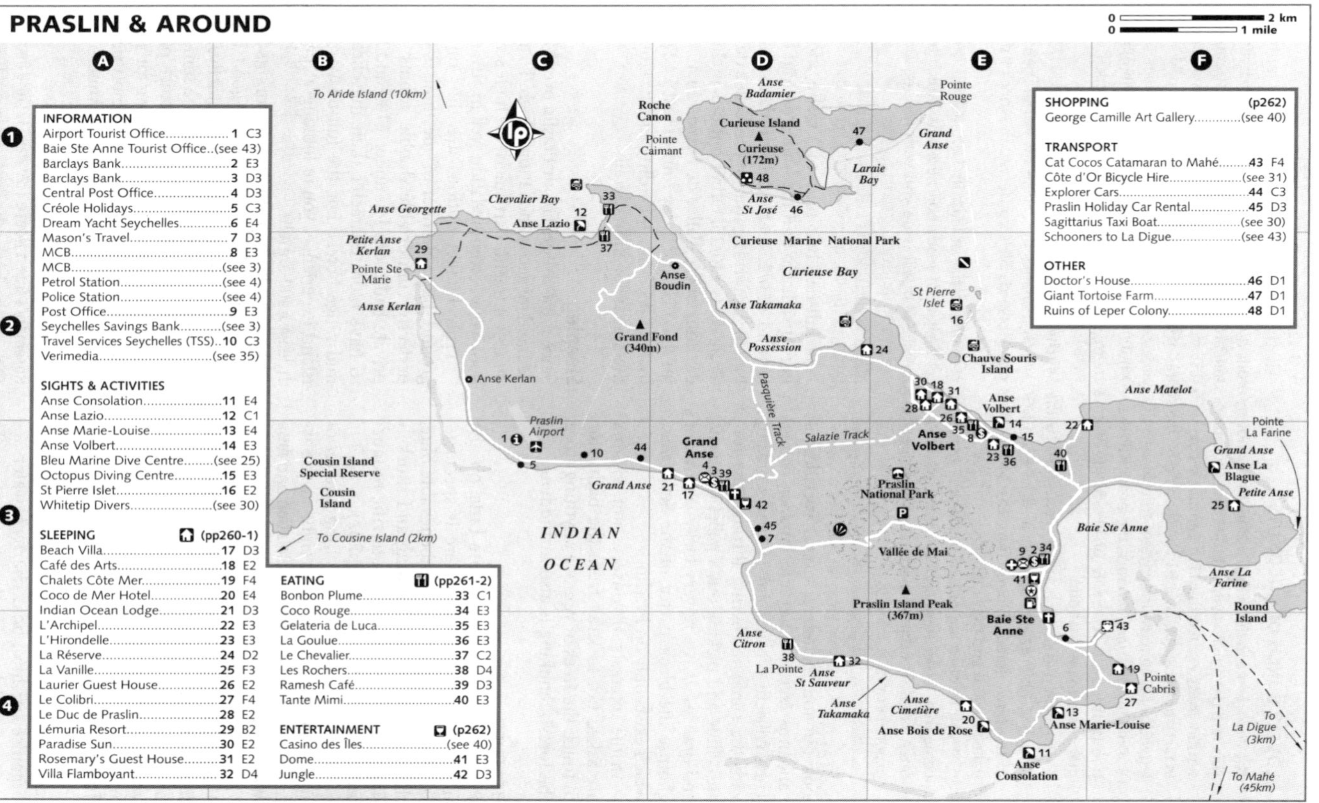
PRASLIN & AROUND
0 2 km
0 1 mile
A
B
C
D
E
F
1
2
3
4
INFORMATION
Airport Tourist Office.....1 C3
Baie Ste Anne Tourist Office..(see 43)
Barclays Bank.....2 E3
Barclays Bank.....3 D3
Central Post Office.....4 D3
Créole Holidays.....5 C3
Dream Yacht Seychelles.....6 E4
Mason's Travel.....7 D3
MCB.....8 E3
MCB.....(see 3)
Petrol Station.....(see 4)
Police Station.....(see 4)
Post Office.....9 E3
Seychelles Savings Bank.....(see 3)
Travel Services Seychelles (TSS)..10 C3
Verimedia.....(see 35)
SIGHTS & ACTIVITIES
Anse Consolation.....11 E4
Anse Lazio.....12 C1
Anse Marie-Louise.....13 E4
Anse Volbert.....14 E3
Bleu Marine Dive Centre.....(see 25)
Octopus Diving Centre.....15 E3
St Pierre Islet.....16 E2
Whitetip Divers.....(see 30)
SLEEPING (pp260-1)
Beach Villa.....17 D3
Café des Arts.....18 E2
Chalets Côte Mer.....19 F4
Coco de Mer Hotel.....20 E4
Indian Ocean Lodge.....21 D3
L'Archipel.....22 E3
L'Hirondelle.....23 E3
La Réserve.....24 D2
La Vanille.....25 F3
Laurier Guest House.....26 E2
Le Colibri.....27 F4
Le Duc de Praslin.....28 E2
Lémuria Resort.....29 B2
Paradise Sun.....30 E2
Rosemary's Guest House.....31 E2
Villa Flamboyant.....32 D4
EATING (pp261-2)
Bonbon Plume.....33 C1
Coco Rouge.....34 E3
Gelateria de Luca.....35 E3
La Goulue.....36 E3
Le Chevalier.....37 C2
Les Rochers.....38 D4
Ramesh Café.....39 D3
Tante Mimi.....40 E3
ENTERTAINMENT (p262)
Casino des Îles.....(see 40)
Dome.....41 E3
Jungle.....42 D3
SHOPPING (p262)
George Camille Art Gallery.....(see 40)
TRANSPORT
Cat Cocos Catamaran to Mahé.....43 F4
Côte d'Or Bicycle Hire.....(see 31)
Explorer Cars.....44 C3
Praslin Holiday Car Rental.....45 D3
Sagittarius Taxi Boat.....(see 30)
Schooners to La Digue.....(see 43)
OTHER
Doctor's House.....46 D1
Giant Tortoise Farm.....47 D1
Ruins of Leper Colony.....48 D1
To Aride Island (10km)
Roche Canon
Pointe Caïmant
Anse Badamier
Curieuse Island
Curieuse (172m)
Anse St José
Grand Anse
Laraie Bay
Pointe Rouge
Curieuse Marine National Park
Curieuse Bay
St Pierre Islet
Chauve Souris Island
Anse Georgette
Chevalier Bay
Anse Lazio
Petite Anse Kerlan
Pointe Ste Marie
Anse Kerlan
Anse Boudin
Anse Takamaka
Anse Possession
Grand Fond (340m)
Pasquière Track
Salazie Track
Praslin Airport
Cousin Island Special Reserve
Cousin Island
To Cousine Island (2km)
Grand Anse
INDIAN OCEAN
Anse Volbert
Praslin National Park
Vallée de Mai
Praslin Island Peak (367m)
Baie Ste Anne
Anse Matelot
Pointe La Farine
Anse La Blague
Petite Anse
Anse La Farine
Round Island
Anse Citron
La Pointe
Anse St Sauveur
Anse Takamaka
Anse Cimetière
Anse Bois de Rose
Anse Consolation
Anse Marie-Louise
Pointe Cabris
To La Digue (3km)
To Mahé (45km)

LOVELY BUNCH OF COCONUTS

The coco de mer palm, which produces a famously erotic nut, grows naturally only in the Seychelles. This rare palm may seem a little tame by today's standards, but you can see why these strange, sensual fruits excited the 17th-century sailors who first stumbled upon them after months at sea. In fact, the occasional nut had washed up on the shores of distant continents long before, sparking legends of a curious underwater tree (hence the name coco de mer, or coconut of the sea).

Only female trees produce the erotically shaped nuts, which can weigh over 30kg. The male tree possesses a decidedly phallic flower stem a metre or more long, adding to the coco de mer's steamy reputation.

Harvesting the nuts is strictly controlled by the **Seychelles Island Foundation** (SIF; ☎ 321735; www.sif.sc; 305 Premier Bldg, Albert St, Victoria), an NGO which manages the Vallée de Mai on behalf of the government. Money from the sale of nuts goes towards SIF's conservation work in the Vallée de Mai and on Aldabra.

If you want to lug one of these nuts home, be prepared to pay at least Rs 1200 (€200). They come in a husky state and will need to be polished; beware of ready-polished nuts, which are often fakes. The safest place to buy is directly from SIF, who will issue you with the required export permit.

look out for, including several varieties of pandanus (screw pine) and latanier palms. Their collective fronds are an artist's dream, with the sunlight filtering through the forest ceiling and picking out a pallet of greens and oranges. If you're very lucky you might glimpse the black parrot of the Seychelles, which exists only on Praslin.

In the interests of conservation, visitors are asked not to stray from the paths nor to touch the trees or remove anything from the forest. Smoking is also forbidden.

BEACHES

Praslin's best beach is **Anse Lazio** on the northwest tip. The sand here is spectacular and the lagoon is an unbelievable blue; there is also good swimming and snorkelling offshore. Also here is a terrific restaurant called Bonbon Plume (p262).

There is another lovely, long stretch of sand at **Anse Volbert**, while right at the island's southern tip, **Anse Consolation** and **Anse Marie-Louise** are also pretty spots.

The waters around **St Pierre Islet**, off Anse Volbert, are good for snorkelling and sloshing around. Boat trips to St Pierre organised by hotels and private operators cost upwards of €20 per person.

Tours

Praslin's travel agents (p258) all offer similar excursions at similar prices and can organise car hire, boat charters, water activities, air tickets and the like.

A full-day bus tour of Praslin including Anse Lazio and the Vallée de Mai costs around €50/25 per adult/child, excluding lunch. A morning tour of the Vallée de Mai alone costs €40/25. Other options include a day tour of the Vallée de Mai and La Digue for €100/50 and a day tour of just La Digue for €85/45, both including lunch. Contact the agents for more details.

Sleeping

Since most visitors favour Praslin over Mahé, demand for accommodation is high. To avoid disappointment, particularly in high season, book your accommodation well in advance.

Truly budget options are thin on the ground, but a number of guesthouses offer perfectly comfortable double rooms with private bathroom for under €100 and tend to have more character than the cheapest mid-range hotels. For the full-on paradise island experience, you're looking at paying at least €400 a night.

Anse Volbert, with its restaurants and other tourist facilities, makes a good base. Grand Anse is busier and less attractive, but handy for the airport, and there are some decent options within walking distance of the Baie St Anne jetty. If you're looking for a real hideaway, head for the wild and empty promontories to either side of Baie St Anne.

BUDGET

Rosemary's Guest House (☎/fax 232176; d from €75) One of the better budget deals on Praslin,

Rosemary's is a homely place right on Anse Volbert beach. It offers simple, fan-cooled rooms around a small garden.

Beach Villa (☎ 233445; www.the-seychelles.com/beachvilla; d €88) At Grand Anse you'll find this a friendly guesthouse with a handful of comfortable rooms in bungalows overlooking the beach.

L'Hirondelle (☎ 232243; www.seychelles.net/hirondelle; s/d €80/95) With bright, spacious and neat one-bedroom self-catering apartments, this German-run guesthouse makes a fine place to stay at Anse Volbert.

Chalets Côte Mer (☎ 232367; www.chaletscotemer.com; d/apt from €80/90;) Set among gardens at Pointe Cabris, this guesthouse has a choice between smart air-con rooms and self-catering apartments. It's excellent value and handy for the boat jetty.

MID-RANGE

Café des Arts (☎ 232170; www.café.sc; d from €173) This very stylish small hotel run by two artists represents one of the best mid-range options on the island. It's a stone's throw from the beach in Anse Volbert and has just four rooms, each one beautifully decked out with pristine white linens and rattan furnishings. It's also home to a small art gallery.

Coco de Mer Hotel (☎ 233900; www.cocodemer.com; s/d from €212/236;) At the top of this category, but good value considering the level of service and facilities provided: two pools, two restaurants, a bar, water sports and free shuttle boats to Anse Lazio. It is perched above a secluded but ordinary beach at Anse Bois de Rose.

La Vanille (☎ 232178; http://lavanille.free.fr; s/d from €100/150;) Set on a lovely secluded beach at Anse La Blague, to the north of Baie Ste Anne, this small, relaxed hotel is a great hideaway. It has just nine rooms in the hillside bungalows, a decent restaurant and a dive centre.

Indian Ocean Lodge (☎ 233324; hmcom@seychelles.net; s/d from €206/226;) This beachfront hotel at Grand Anse has been refurbished with great attention to detail. From the flower-filled reception and elegant restaurant to the colonial-style bedrooms with four-poster beds, it's all very welcoming.

Le Duc de Praslin (☎ 232252; www.leduc-seychelles.com; s/d from €150/170;) A friendly little hotel just off the beach at Anse Volbert. The rooms are well appointed, with lots of wood and colourful fabrics, and there's a restaurant and a decent size garden full of orchids.

> **AUTHOR'S CHOICE**
>
> **Laurier Guest House** (☎ 232241; www.laurier-seychelles.com; s/d €80/100;) In the centre of Anse Volbert, this family-friendly guesthouse has a handful of cheerful rooms. It's not as close to the beach as other hotels, but has an excellent restaurant.

Other recommendations:

Le Colibri (☎ 232302; colibri@seychelles.net; s/d €83/106) Attractive wooden villas in a tranquil setting at Pointe Cabris, just south of Baie Ste Anne.

Villa Flamboyant (☎ 233036; hmcom@seychelles.net; s/d from €110/160) A lovely quiet retreat at Anse St Sauveur, on the southwest coast.

TOP END

Lémuria Resort (☎ 281281; www.lemuriaresort.com; s/d from €473/630;) Praslin's top hotel lives up to its tropical paradise image. It occupies the whole northwest tip of the island, where the buildings blend in among the rocks and water features. Facilities include three restaurants, four bars, a health spa and an 18-hole golf course. Nonguests are allowed access to the beaches, including the gorgeous Anse Georgette, but have to get permission first at the gatehouse.

L'Archipel (☎ 284700; www.larchipel.com; s/d from €448/520;) Much smaller than the Lémuria, this place is in a lovely secluded location at the eastern end of Anse Volbert. The villas are well spread out and surrounded with flowery gardens; most rooms have views across to St Pierre and Curieuse. It has a fine restaurant and offers free water sports and snorkelling expeditions.

Other recommendations:

La Réserve (☎ 232211; www.lareserve-seychelles.com; d half board from €373;) Child-friendly place on a good beach at Anse Petite Cour, west of Anse Volbert. The pool-side rooms are overpriced.

Paradise Sun (☎ 293293; www.southernsun.com; s/d half board €335/475;) Good facilities, spacious gardens and a nice strip of sand but no air-con.

Eating

Since most people eat in their hotels or guesthouses, there are relatively few independent restaurants on Praslin. You'll find takeaways at Grand Anse, Baie Ste Anne and Anse Volbert and a clutch of smarter places scattered around the coast.

If you're dying for an ice cream, hot-foot it to **Gelateria de Luca** (11am-9pm), at Anse Volbert, which serves suitably tropical concoctions.

BUDGET

Laurier Guest House (232241; buffet Rs 180; dinner Sun) The Sunday buffet here is not to be missed; make sure you reserve. The tables groan with fresh and tasty salads, curries, grills and luscious deserts.

La Goulue (232223; mains Rs 50-75; breakfast, lunch & dinner Mon-Sat) A sweet little café at Anse Volbert which serves Creole home cooking in addition to sandwiches and European standards such as chicken and chips.

Ramesh Café (233742; meals Rs 25-35; lunch & dinner Mon-Sat) This spick-and-span takeaway near the church in Grand Anse offers the usual curries and fish dishes.

Coco Rouge (meals Rs 25; lunch & dinner) Another popular takeaway serving standard fare, this time in Baie Ste Anne.

Le Chevalier (560488; mains around Rs 65; 11.30am-4pm) This has OK food and a nice relaxed atmosphere on Anse Lazio's glorious sands.

MID-RANGE & TOP END

Bonbon Plume (232136; mains around Rs 120-200; lunch) A palm-thatched seafood restaurant located on the gorgeous beach at Anse Lazio is never going to be cheap, but it's definitely worth a splurge. Reservations are recommended.

Tante Mimi (232500; mains Rs 100-200; lunch Sun, dinner) The classy restaurant at the casino in Anse Volbert serves mostly traditional Creole dishes, all beautifully presented. The Sunday buffet lunch is very reasonable at Rs 100, and the restaurant also offers free transport.

Les Rochers (233034; mains from Rs 170; dinner Tue-Sat) On the southwest coast at La Pointe, this place has a slightly high opinion of itself, but it does serve excellent Creole food and the atmosphere at night is magical.

SELF-CATERING

Self-caterers can choose from the small supermarkets and grocery stores in Grand Anse, Anse Volbert and Baie Ste Anne. Buy your fish straight from the fishermen.

Entertainment

Nightlife is pretty limited on Praslin and most people seem to like it that way.

The exception is Saturday, when locals hit the dance floors at the **Jungle** (512683; admission Rs 50; 10pm-4am Fri & Sat) in Grand Anse, which is generally thought to have the best music, and the more flashy **Dome** (232800; admission Rs 50; 10pm-4am Sat) at Baie Ste Anne.

Other than that, most large hotels put on their own entertainment programs, or you can try your luck at the **Casino des Îles** (232500; slot machines noon-2am, gaming tables 7.30pm-3am) at Anse Volbert. Call ahead and you will be picked up from your hotel.

Shopping

George Camille Art Gallery (Casino des Iles, Anse Volbert) Camille's work is inspired by the beauty and nature around him, incorporating stylised fish, geckos and coco de mer palms in his works, as well as more conventional scenes of rural life.

Getting There & Away

Praslin's **airport** (284666) is 3km from Grand Anse and has flights every hour or so from Mahé. For further information, see p274.

It's almost as quick to take the Cat Cocos catamaran from Victoria, or you can save money by hopping on a cargo boat from Mahé to La Digue and then getting a schooner on to Praslin. See p275 for routes, times and prices.

Getting Around

Praslin has a decent bus service as well as the usual pricey taxis. For more information, see p275.

A car is a great way to see the island. For details of car rental outlets, see p275.

You can hire bikes through your accommodation or from **Côte d'Or Bicycle Hire** (232071) in Anse Volbert for Rs 50 per day.

Hopping around the small islands off Praslin is done by chartered boat; trips are usually organised through the hotels or tour operators. See p258.

SEYCHELLES SEA BIRDS

Cousin and Aride Islands support huge colonies of lesser (black) noddies during the southeast monsoon. During the birds' elaborate courtship, the male bird offers his mate leaves until he finds one to her satisfaction (she indicates her approval by defecating on it!). This leaf then forms the keystone of the nest for the season.

Another prevalent species is the wedge-tailed shearwater, which breeds in burrows from May to October. The noise of shear-water colonies has to be heard to be believed; the bird mates for life and when its companion, who hasn't been seen for the past year, turns up all hell breaks loose. The birds have a large wingspan and their 'runways' are well defined; you may see them lined up for their predawn departure for the day's fishing.

CURIEUSE ISLAND

This granite island 1km off Praslin's north coast was a leper colony from 1833 until 1965. As part of a curious reciprocal arrangement, lepers from Mauritius were traded for mentally ill Seychellois. The idea was that leprosy could be more easily contained on an island. However, that wasn't the origin of the island's name, which comes from a French ship, *La Curieuse*.

Curieuse is used as a breeding centre for giant Aldabra tortoises. The wardens at the **giant tortoise farm** show visitors round the pens, after which you're free to explore the rest of the island. The **doctor's house** at Anse St José now contains a small historical museum. The displays aren't hugely interesting but the charming Creole house itself is worth the walk. On your way, look out for coco de mer palms. This is the only place apart from Praslin where they grow naturally.

Getting There & Away

Most visitors to Curieuse Island arrive on an organised tour arranged through their hotel or a tour operator. Day trips cost around €90/50 for an adult/child including lunch, snorkelling at St Pierre Islet and the marine park entry fee of €10.

The alternative is to charter your own boat from Anse Volbert. **Sagittarius Taxi Boat** (☎ 232234), on the beach beside the Paradise Sun hotel, offers day trips to Curieuse for €25; Curieuse with St Pierre costs €30.

COUSIN ISLAND

About 2km southwest of Praslin, Cousin Island is run as a nature reserve by **Nature Seychelles** (☎ 225097; www.nature.org.sc). Seven species of sea bird nest here, including fairy terns, white-tailed tropicbirds and two varieties of shearwater. The bird population is estimated to exceed 300,000 on an island measuring just 1km in diameter. It's an amazing experience to walk through thick forest with birds seemingly nesting on every branch.

Cousin is also home to five species of endemic land birds. In 1968 the population of the Seychelles warbler, a small songbird, had dropped to under 30. Thanks to conservation efforts, there are now over 300 warblers on Cousin and populations have been established on nearby Cousine and Aride Islands. A colony of critically endangered Seychelles magpie robin has also been established on Cousin.

The island is also an important nesting ground for hawksbill turtles. As many as 100 turtles nest here between September and February. At any time of year you're bound to see lizards; Cousin boasts one of the highest densities of lizards in the world. Keep an eye open, too, for George, a very elderly Aldabra tortoise who plods after visitors hoping to have his leathery neck scratched.

To minimise disturbance to the wildlife, Cousin can only be visited as part of an organised tour from Tuesday to Friday. You can get close enough to the birds to photograph them, but flashes and tripods are not allowed.

Getting There & Away

Half-day tours of Cousin can be arranged through Praslin's hotels and tour operators (see p258) for around €70/35 per adult/child. The adult price includes a €25 landing fee, which goes towards conservation efforts.

Since there is no jetty on the island, visitors have to transfer to a smaller boat for landing. It's a good idea to carry valuables in a watertight bag.

ARIDE ISLAND

The most northerly of the granite islands, Aride lies 10km north of Praslin. It was purchased for the Royal Society for Nature Conservation in 1973 by Christopher Cadbury (of chocolate fame) but is now owned by the local Island Conservation Society. The nature reserve supports the greatest concentration of sea birds in the area, including large colonies of lesser noddies, roseate terns and frigate birds.

Aride can be reached by boat between September and May only, as landing can be difficult and dangerous at other times. During the season, the island is open to visitors on Sunday, Monday and Wednesday.

Getting There & Away

Weather permitting, you can organise a tour from Praslin with one of the tour operators (see p258) or through hotels and guesthouses. A day trip costs in the region of €100/50 per adult/child, including lunch and a guided tour of the island. The price includes a €30 landing fee (free for under 16s), which goes towards conservation efforts.

LA DIGUE & OTHER INNER ISLANDS

If any one single image conjures up the magic of the Seychelles, it is the emerald waters, the sugar-white sands and the great, sea-smoothed glacis rocks of La Digue's Anse Source d'Argent. This world-famous beach puts La Digue on most visitors' itineraries. Though the majority of visitors come on day trips from Praslin or Mahé, you really need to stay at least one night to appreciate the island at its best. The relaxed atmosphere, where life still moves at the pace of an ox cart, makes it very hard to leave.

The other main islands making up the Inner Islands group include Félicité, Bird and Denis Islands. These widely scattered islands are all important bird and nature reserves. Unfortunately, they are all run as exclusive island retreats.

LA DIGUE

La Digue is easily the least developed of the main islands, though it's certainly not undiscovered. Most tourists to the Seychelles make a stop on the island, so you'll have to make that little bit more effort to find a quiet place in the sun. There are some lovely isolated beaches on the southeast coast, where you can escape the crowds and indulge your Robinson Crusoe fantasies.

La Digue is only about 5km from Praslin, and regular schooners ferry day-trippers between the two islands. For the moment, accommodation is cheaper than on either Mahé or Praslin, and the island has a quieter, more laid-back feel. Tourist developments have thus far been fairly subtle affairs, though the new casino has brought some protest from locals anxious to preserve the island's traditional way of life. Most of the 2000 or so inhabitants are involved in fishing, agriculture or tourism.

Information

MONEY

Barclays Bank (☎ 234148; 🕑 10am-2.30pm Mon-Fri) Opposite La Digue Island Lodge.

MCB (☎ 234560; 🕑 8.30am-12.15pm & 1-3pm Mon-Fri) Opposite the pier in La Passe.

Seychelles Savings Bank (☎ 234135; 🕑 8.30am-2.30pm Mon-Sat, 9am-11pm Sat) Opposite the hospital in La Passe.

POST

Post office (☎ 234036; 🕑 8am-noon & 1-4pm Mon-Fri) Near the pier in La Passe.

TOURIST INFORMATION

Tourist office (☎/fax 234393; La Passe; 🕑 8am-5pm Mon-Fri, 8.30am-noon & 3-4.30pm Sat, 9am-noon Sun) Provides basic information and helps organise tours.

TRAVEL AGENCIES

Mason's Travel (☎ 234227; La Passe; 🕑 8am-4.30pm Mon-Fri, 8am-noon Sat)

Travel Services Seychelles (TSS; ☎ 234411; La Passe; 8am-noon & 1-4pm Mon-Fri, 8am-1pm Sat)

Safari Club (☎ 234757; www.seychelles.net/safariclub; La Passe; 🕑 9am-6pm)

Sights & Activities

BEACHES

Most new arrivals head straight for the beach at **Anse Source d'Argent**, a classic white-sand beach backed by naturally sculpted

SEYCHELLES

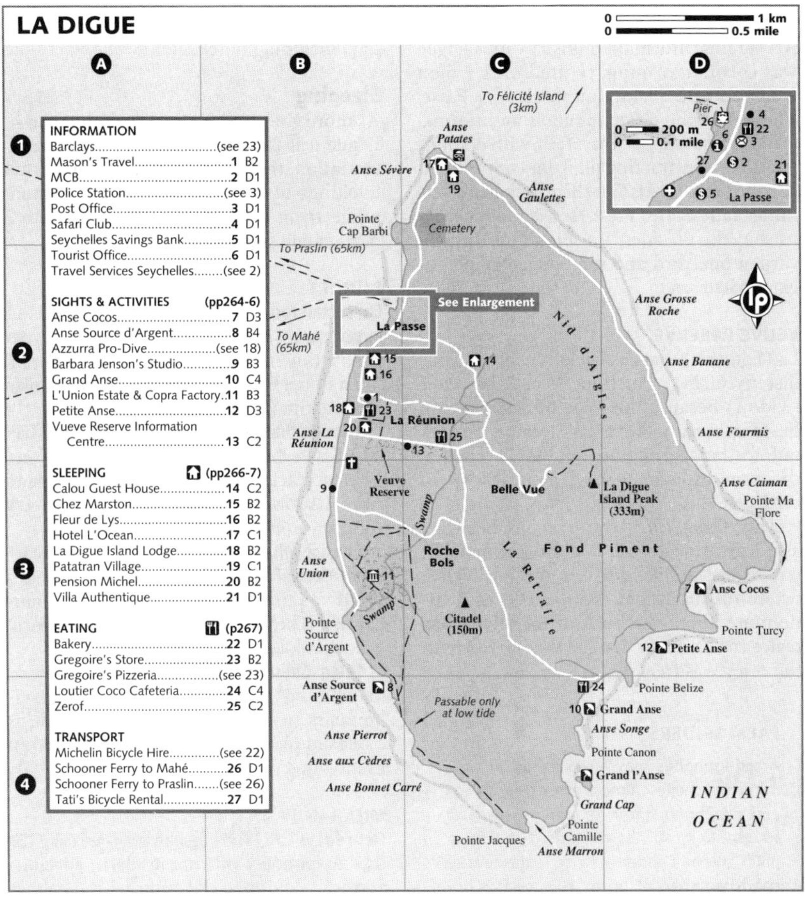

granite boulders that would have made Henry Moore proud. Although the scenery is superb, it can get pretty crowded here, especially at high tide when the beach virtually disappears. If possible, it's best to come in the late afternoon when the crowds begin to thin out and the colours are at their most intense. The path down to the Anse Source d'Argent runs through the old L'Union coconut plantation, which is run as a museum, but at low tide you can walk along the beach and save yourself the €3 entry fee.

On the southeast coast, **Grand Anse** is a stunning beach, and it sees fewer visitors because of the effort required to get there (though you can easily walk or cycle the 4km or so from La Passe). Take care when swimming because of the strong offshore currents. There's a good little restaurant (Loutier Coco Caféteria; p267), where you can get light refreshments.

Beyond Grand Anse, two of the island's quietest beaches are **Petite Anse** and **Anse Cocos**. To reach them, take the path heading northeast from Grand Anse. Watch out for giant millipedes, huge land crabs and palm spiders as you cross over the headland. Petite Anse is palm-fringed and idyllic, though there are strong currents here too. Anse Cocos is reached by a rather vague track at the north end of Petite Anse. Diving, snorkelling and deep-sea fishing are popular activities (see p33).

L'UNION ESTATE & COPRA FACTORY

At one time, the main industry on La Digue was coconut farming, centred on L'Union Estate coconut plantation south of La Passe. These days the estate is run as an informal **museum** (admission €3; 8am-6pm), with demonstrations of extracting oil from copra (dried coconut meat). Also in the grounds are the rather tatty State Guest House (supposedly used by the President), a colonial-era graveyard, a boatyard and the obligatory pen of giant tortoises.

VEUVE RESERVE

La Digue is the last refuge of the black paradise flycatcher, which locals call the *veuve* (widow) because the male bird appears to be in mourning with its streaming black tail feathers. Endemic to the Seychelles, there are thought to be a mere 300 or so birds left.

This small forest reserve has been set aside to protect their natural habitat, but you're just as likely to see the birds elsewhere on the island. You can learn a little more about the birds at the **information centre** (☎ 234353; 8am-4pm Mon-Fri). Entry to the reserve is free.

PALM SPIDERS

Arachnophobes may have a difficult time in the Seychelles. Almost every tree branch and telephone wire is draped in sheets of tough sticky silk belonging to the huge palm spider. Despite its size – the female has a leg span of up to 10cm – this obtrusive arachnid is harmless to humans. Its web silk is extremely strong, however, as you will soon discover if you stray off the beaten track anywhere in the Seychelles. Look closely at the web and you may see the tiny male who spends his whole life avoiding the female, only approaching to mate when she is distracted by a meal.

Organised Tours

Most guesthouses and hotels on La Digue can arrange island tours and snorkelling trips to nearby islands such as Cocos, Marianne, and Petite and Grande Sœur. Alternatively, you could contact one of the travel agencies (see p264). Safari Club, for example, offers guided walks from €30/20 per adult/child and boat charter at €55 per day, including lunch.

Sleeping

As more guesthouses and hotels open on La Digue it is becoming easier to find accommodation, though it's still not wise to leave bookings to the last minute. The options range from self-catering apartments to a moderately smart resort hotel.

BUDGET

Chez Marston (☎ 234023; mars@seychelles.sc; s/d €60/80, s/d half board €70/100) The kindly owner runs a tidy little guesthouse and restaurant in La Passe. He offers five simple, fan-cooled rooms with a small kitchen area.

Villa Authentique (☎/fax 234413; s/d €33/85, s/d half board €50/105;) This is another very homey place on the road heading inland from La Passe. It has a handful of cheery rooms around a small garden.

Pension Michel (☎/fax 234003; s/d €80/95, s/d half board €95/130) Heading south of La Passe, signs point you to these pretty, Creole-style bungalows. The furnishings are a little worn, but it's a lovely quiet spot.

Calou Guest House (☎ 234083; www.calou.de; s/d half board €80/123) Tucked among glacis boulders to the east of La Passe, Calou is a relaxed place offering accommodation in rustic bungalows.

MID-RANGE

Fleur de Lys (☎ 234459; fleurdelysey@yahoo.com; €120;) A complex of four modern, spacious and well-equipped self-catering bungalows in trim gardens to the south of La Passe. The owners are exceptionally helpful and cook up excellent evening meals (Monday to Friday, on request only).

Patatran Village (☎ 234333; www.the-seychelles.com/patatran; s/d from €137/200, s/d half board from €155/250;) This romantic little hotel offers chalets in a tranquil location overlooking the sea at Anse Patates. Though not huge, the rooms are nicely decorated and have lovely views of the nearby islands. There's also a decent restaurant which puts on a popular Creole buffet with *séga* music on Saturday night (Rs 150).

Hotel L'Ocean (☎ 234180; hocean@seychelles.net; s/d €135/170, s/d half board €180/210;) Beside the Patatran Village, the rooms here are not quite so smart, but they are spacious and comfortable and have good-size terraces. It's very welcoming and has a fine restaurant (see Eating, below).

La Digue Island Lodge (☎ 292525; www.ladigue.sc; s/d half board from €190/300;) On the beach at Anse La Réunion is this large, resort-style hotel consisting of A-frame chalets packed rather close together, though the garden setting is attractive. Facilities include three bars, two restaurants, free boat excursions and a dive centre.

Eating

The range of eating options on La Digue is fairly limited since most visitors eat in their hotels and guesthouses. If eating out in the evening, remember to take a torch as there are few street lights, and note that most restaurants close around 9.30pm.

Chez Marston (☎ 234023; mains Rs 55-75; lunch & dinner) The cheerful restaurant at Marston's guesthouse (see Sleeping) is popular with locals and tourists alike for serving standard fare at very reasonable prices. You can opt for salads and sandwiches, omelettes, pasta or fresh fish cooked Creole style.

Loutier Coco Caféteria (☎ 514762; buffet Rs 110; 9am-5pm) It's worth going over to Grand Anse just for the buffet at this rustic café-restaurant which is tucked behind the dune. The spread on offer includes grilled fish, traditional Creole curries and salads, fruit and coffee.

Hotel L'Ocean (☎ 234180; set menu Rs 140; lunch & dinner) The terrace restaurant of this hotel (see Sleeping, p266) is a fine place to treat yourself to spicy fish cooked traditional style in a banana leaf, or crab curry with coconut milk. Diners are serenaded by a local guitarist on Mondays and Wednesdays, and on Saturday night there's a full Creole buffet with live entertainment (Rs 150).

Other recommendations:

Gregoire's Pizzeria (☎ 292557; mains Rs 45-70; lunch & dinner;) Bright, breezy pizza joint beside Gregoire's store.

Zerof (☎ 234439; mains Rs 60-70; 11am-8.30pm). Creole cuisine in a garden setting.

SELF-CATERING

For self-caterers, **Gregoire's Store** (☎ 234024; 8am-7.45pm Mon-Sat, 8am-1pm Sun) near La Digue Island Lodge is the best-stocked supermarket on the island. A small bakery near the pier sells fresh bread.

Shopping

Barbara Jenson Studio (☎ 234406; Anse Réunion; www.barbarajensonstudio.com; 9am-6pm Mon-Sat) Barbara's work reflects the unique landscape and ethnically diverse people of the Seychelles.

Getting There & Around

You can reach La Digue by boat and helicopter from both Mahé and Praslin. See p274 for details.

Although there's now, sadly, a stretch of surfaced road running through La Passe on the west coast, elsewhere on La Digue the 'roads' are still just sandy tracks. This, coupled with the fact that the island is less than 5km from north to south, means by far the best – and most enjoyable – way to get around is on foot or bicycle. There are loads of bikes to rent. Operators set up by the pier waiting for arrivals, or you could try **Michelin** (☎ 234304) or **Tati's Bicycle Rental** (☎ 234346), both with outlets near the pier. Most places charge around Rs 25/50 per hour/day.

Ox carts are an easy-going mode of transport. There are usually a few waiting by the pier. It costs around Rs 300 to rent a cart for half a day. A one-way journey to L'Union Estate costs Rs 25 per person.

There are only a handful of taxis on La Digue, as most people get around on bicycle or on foot. A one-way ride from the pier to Grand Anse costs around Rs 75; to Anse Patate it's Rs 40. There is a surcharge of Rs 5 per item of luggage.

FÉLICITÉ ISLAND

This mountainous island, 3km northeast of La Digue, has good walking trails and excellent snorkelling sites. It is run as an extremely luxurious resort by **La Digue Island Lodge** (☎ 292525; www.ladigue.sc; island package €1000;) on La Digue. The maximum number of guests is 16 and the minimum stay is five nights. Once a reservation has been confirmed, that's it; the whole island is yours.

If you can't afford to stay here, you can at least snorkel around it. Guests staying at La Digue Island Lodge get free snorkelling trips to Félicité Island.

BIRD ISLAND

True to its name, this tiny coral island 96km north of Mahé, is dominated by birds. Sooty terns, fairy terns and common noddies descend here en masse between May and October. A visit is an awesome experience, but it takes a while to become accustomed to the sights, smells and noises of the bird world.

Hawksbill turtles breed on the island's beaches between October and February, while their land-bound relatives lumber around the interior. One of these giant tortoises, Esmeralda, is in *Guinness World Records* as the oldest tortoise in the world. She is actually a he, and is believed to be over 150 years old.

The island is open only to guests of the **Bird Island Lodge** (☎ 323322 or 224925; www.birdislandseychelles.com; s/d full board from €335/430). Reservations can be made in person at the office in **Kingsgate House** (Map p248; Independence Ave, Victoria). Apart from being an obvious magnet for ornithologists, it is also good for snorkelling, swimming and simply lazing around.

DENIS ISLAND

Ideal for the well-heeled ornithologist, the privately owned Denis Island, 85km north of Mahé, is similar to Bird Island, but is even more exclusive. It was named after the French navigator Denis de Trobriand, who discovered it in 1773. Nowadays it belongs to the **Denis Island Lodge** (☎ 321143; denis@seychelles.net; s/d full board from €630/770;), which offers guests a range of activities such as scuba diving and deep-sea fishing.

OUTER ISLANDS

The majority of the Seychelles islands are scattered over hundreds of kilometres to the southwest of the main Mahé group. They fall into four main groups – Aldabra, Amirantes and Farquhar. The main industry is copra, used in the production of coconut oil, and there are also fledgling attempts at aquaculture. Sadly, most of these islands are accessible only to yachtsmen and those who can afford to stay at the extremely exclusive resorts.

AMIRANTES & ALPHONSE GROUPS

The largest of the three groups, the Amirantes, lies about 250km southwest of Mahé. Its main island is Desroches, which is now reserved for guests of the luxury **Desroches Island Resort** (☎ 229003; desroches@7south.net; s/d full board from €483/635;).

Another 200km further south, the Alphonse Group is another cluster of coral islands that provide some of the best saltwater fly-fishing in the world. The largest of the group, the 1.2km-wide Alphonse Island, is home to the **Alphonse Island Resort** (☎ 229030; www.alphonse-resort.com; s/d full board €546/696;), which offers the full paradise-island experience.

ALDABRA GROUP

This is the most remote and most interesting of the outer island groups. It is also the best known, thanks to the Aldabra Atoll, the world's largest raised coral atoll, which is a Unesco World Heritage Site and nature reserve. The atoll stretches 34km east to west and consists of four major islands enclosing a huge tidal lagoon. Aldabra lies more than 1000km from Mahé – in fact it is closer to Madagascar (400km) than to its own capital. It is thought to have been discovered around the 9th century by Arab seafarers, who called it Al Khadra; through the centuries and various European pronunciations, the name evolved into Aldabra.

Aldabra Atoll is home to about 110,000 giant tortoises. Green and hawksbill turtles lay their eggs here, and flocks of migratory birds, including crab plovers, flamingos, herons and frigate birds, fly in and out in their thousands. Other notable species include the white-throated rail, the sole remaining flightless bird species in the Indian Ocean, and the giant robber crab, which supposedly climbs coconut trees and cuts down the nuts with its pincers!

Aldabra is managed by the **Seychelles Island Foundation** (SIF; ☎ 321735; www.sif.sc; 305 Premier Bldg, Albert St) in Victoria. Anyone wishing to visit must first get SIF's written permission. Until now the islands have only real-ly been accessible to scientists and a very small number of tourists. However, SIF is considering building a few chalets and tapping in to the lucrative ecotourism market in order to raise funds. Any development will be subject to an Environmental Impact Assessment and, whatever happens, the only access to the atoll will be by boat. The nearest airstrip is on Assomption Island, 27km to the south.

Getting There & Away

The **Indian Ocean Explorer** (☎ 345445; www.ioexplorer.com) offers two-week trips to Aldabra:

one week to get down there and a week cruising around the atoll, then a flight back from Assomption Island (around €4100 including full board). Alternatively, you can fly both ways and meet the boat for the week's cruise (around €3200). The boat only operates during November, December and from mid-March to mid-May.

If you have masses of time, you may be able to wrangle a passage on the government supply vessel which calls at Aldabra every couple of months. Contact SIF for further information.

SEYCHELLES DIRECTORY

The following section contains practical information for visitors to the Seychelles, arranged in alphabetical order. For information relevant to the entire region, see the Regional Directory (p277).

ACCOMMODATION

All accommodation in the Seychelles is registered and regulated by the Ministry of Tourism. This ensures a certain standard of service and facilities, but you might feel that you don't get a lot for your money, particularly at the bottom end of the market. Options include private island resorts, hotels, self-catering apartments and guesthouses. Camping is forbidden anywhere on the islands.

For a double room, you can expect to pay under €100 for budget accommodation, €100 to €350 for mid-range and over €350 for top-end rooms. Rates include all government taxes, and also breakfast unless otherwise stated.

Even in the cheapest guesthouse you can expect to get a room with a private bathroom and a fan. Moving up the scale, there are now some very attractive family-run guesthouses and small hotels offering local colour; it's these that arguably represent the best value for money in the islands. If you want the full range of services, though, you'll need to opt for one of the larger hotels, which generally provide tour desks, evening entertainment and a range of sports facilities. Standards have improved dramatically at the top end and some of the newer hotels now rival those in Mauritius for levels of service and all-round luxury. Best of all are the private island resorts where you really are buying into the dream.

Virtually all the hotels and a few guesthouses charge higher rates during peak periods: Christmas–New Year, Easter, and July and August. Some may insist on a minimum stay at Christmas.

You are strongly advised to book well ahead, particularly during peak periods and at any time of year on Praslin and La Digue, where accommodation is more limited. You can contact the hotels direct, or make online bookings through **Seychelles European Reservations** (www.seychelles-resa.com), which specialises in the 'cheaper' end of the market.

ACTIVITIES

Water Sports

The main draw is undoubtedly the water activities – snorkelling, diving, windsurfing, sailing and the like. Big hotels usually offer at least some water sports to their guests for free. Otherwise, there are plenty of independent operators around; the main centres are Beau Vallon on Mahé and Anse Volbert on Praslin. The water sports centres at the **Coral Strand Hotel** (Map p252; ☎ 621000) and the **Berjaya Beau Vallon Bay Beach Resort** (Map p252; ☎ 287287) in Beau Vallon are open to nonresidents. As an indicator, windsurfing usually costs about €40 per hour, while water-skiing is a steep €30 or so for a couple of laps.

For detailed information on diving and snorkelling in the Seychelles, see the special section Underwater Worlds on p42.

Cruises

The best months for cruising are April and October; the worst are January, July and August. You can charter schooners, yachts and motor cruisers through tour agents or the **Marine Charter Association** (MCA; Map p248; ☎ 322126; mca@seychelles.net) in Victoria. Prices start at around €600 for a day trip. Tours to islands should include landing fees – make sure you ask when booking.

For the romantics, **Silhouette Cruises** (☎ 324026; www.seychelles.net/cruises), based near Victoria's interisland ferry terminal, owns the delightful SV *Sea Shell* and SV *Sea Pearl*, a pair of old Dutch schooners that offer live-aboard cruises around the inner islands with activities such as deep-sea fishing and scuba diving thrown in.

Other charter companies include the following:

Angel Fish Ltd (Map p253; ☎ 344644; PO Box 1079, Victoria; www.seychelles-charter.com)

Dream Yacht Seychelles (Map p259; ☎ 232681; Baie St Anne, Praslin; www.dream-yacht-seychelles.com)

VPM Yacht Charter (Map p248; ☎ 225676; PO Box 960, Victoria; www.vpm-boats.com)

Sunsail (Map p248; ☎ 225700; PO Box 1076, Victoria; www.sunsail.com)

Water World (Map p248; ☎ 514735; PO Box 735, Victoria; www.seychelles.net/wworld)

Fishing

The Seychelles supports extremely rich fisheries for big game fish such as giant barracuda, sailfish and marlin. There is also excellent saltwater fly-fishing around the Alphonse islands for the dedicated – and wealthy – angler.

A number of operators have jumped on the boat, so to speak, offering all-inclusive trips where they do everything for you but put the fish on the hook. They can be contacted through the **Marine Charter Association** (Map p248; ☎ 322126; fax 224679) in Victoria. Alternatively, most yacht charter companies (p274) and tour companies (p249) also offer fishing expeditions. Expect to pay in the region of €600/800 for a half/full day's outing. 'Tag and release' is widely practised.

Hiking

Because the islands are relatively small and the roads little travelled (away from north Mahé), walking is a pleasurable activity just about anywhere in the Seychelles. There are still lots of wild, hilly and mountainous areas where you can escape the crowds, appreciate the islands' natural scenery and enjoy some of the many alternatives to beach-oriented activities.

The Ministry of Environment produces a good set of leaflets detailing individual hiking routes (with maps) in Mahé's Morne Seychellois National Park. They are available for between Rs 5 and Rs 10 each from the tourist office (p254) and the botanical gardens (p249) in Victoria.

If you prefer to try a guided walk, contact **Basil Beaudoin** (☎/fax 241790 or 514972), who leads hiking and bird-watching trips into the Mahé back country. Basil knows his stuff and charges Rs 350 for an informative day walk with lunch.

None of the routes is more than a few kilometres long, but you should still carry more water than you expect to need – you'll sweat buckets climbing in this humidity. Take sunscreen and a hat, but be prepared also for the frequent tropical downpours that occur throughout the year. Footwear with good tread is essential since the almost perpetually muddy mountain tracks turn to ski slopes after rain.

For tips on responsible hiking, see p227.

BOOKS

There are a number of books on the Seychelles worth reading before visiting the islands.

For a broad historical overview, you can't beat William McAteer's *Rivals in Eden* and *Hard Times in Paradise*. These highly readable books trace the islands' history from the first French landing in 1740 up to 1919. Deryck Scarr brings things up to date in *Seychelles Since 1770*, which covers the ups and downs of the twentieth century.

Not surprisingly, the island's recent political history has spawned some lively books. The Seychelles first president, James Mancham, tells of his rise and fall in *Paradise Raped*, while 'Mad Mike' Hoare, the leader of the 1981 coup attempt, writes a novelistic version of events in *The Seychelles Affair*.

Sir James Mancham may have fallen out of favour in the Seychelles, but his mum's recipe book, *The Mancham Family Cookbook*, remains a bestseller. Traditional Seychelles cuisine is the focus of *Dekouver Marmit*, compiled by the Ministry of Local Government, Sports and Culture.

There's no shortage of books for fauna-and-flora buffs. One of the earliest records of the islands' exotic plant life was made by artist Marianne North in 1883. Her travel memoirs are set out in *A Vision of Eden* along with a selection of her paintings. One of the best everyday reference works is *The Beautiful Plants of Seychelles* by Adrian and Judith Skerrett.

Adrian Skerrett is also a passionate ornithologist. The *Field Guide to the Birds of Seychelles*, by Adrian Skerrett, Ian Bullock and Tony Disley, offers the most comprehensive and informative guide to local bird life. For the amateur enthusiast, Skerrett's

SEYCHELLES

The Beautiful Birds of Seychelles details only the more common species.

BUSINESS HOURS

You need to be up early to catch the banks in the Seychelles, as in general they are open only from 8.30am to 2pm Monday to Friday, and 8.30am to 11am on Saturday. Government offices usually open from 8am to 4pm Monday to Friday. Shop hours are typically 8am to 5pm Monday to Friday, and 8am to noon on Saturday.

CHILDREN

The Seychelles is a very child-friendly place. The big hotels cater for all age groups, offering baby-sitting services, kids' clubs and activities laid on especially for teenagers. While children will happily spend all day splashing around in the lagoon, boat trips around the islands should also appeal. Communing with giant tortoises is a sure-fire hit and, with a bit of creativity, visiting some of the nature reserves can be fun.

Finding special foods and other baby products can be difficult, especially outside Victoria, so you might want to bring your favourite brands with you. For more about travelling with children in the region, see p278.

ELECTRICITY

The power supply is 240V AC. The plugs in general use have square pins and three points, though most hotels and guesthouses provide adaptors. You'll probably experience at least one power cut during your stay, so be sure to keep a torch (flashlight) or a candle handy.

EMBASSIES & CONSULATES

Seychelles Embassies & Consulates

The Seychelles has diplomatic representation in the following countries:

Australia (☎ 03-9796 4010; seychelles@barallon.com; 18 Dansu Court, Hallam, Victoria 3803, Melbourne)
Canada (☎ 514-2843 322; connsey@cam.org; 67 Rue Ste Catherine Ouest, Montreal, Québec H2X1Z7)
France (☎ 01 42 30 57 47; ambasey@aol.com; 51 Ave Mozart, 75016 Paris)
Germany (☎ 30-3190 7660; rasudhoff@t-online.de; Bleibtreustrasse 51 A, D-10623 Berlin)
Mauritius (☎ 211 16 88; gfok@intnet.mu; 616, St James Court, St Denis St, Port Louis)
Netherlands (☎ 35-694 0904; p.c.t.van.schaardenburgh@palm.a2000.nl; Oud Bussummerweg 40A, 1272 PW Huizen)
UK (☎ 020-7224 1660; seyhclon@aol.com; 2nd fl, Eros House, 111 Baker St, London W1M 1FE)
USA (☎ 212-972 1785; seychelles@un.int; 800 Second Ave, Suite 400C, New York, NY 10017)

Embassies & Consulates in the Seychelles

Countries with embassies and consulates in the Seychelles include the following:

British High Commission (Map p248; ☎ 225225; www.bhcvictoria.sc; PO Box 161, Oliaji Trade Centre, Francis Rachel St, Victoria)
France (Map p248; ☎ 382500; BP478, Victoria House, Francis Rachel St, Victoria)
Germany (Map p253; ☎ 261222; northolm@seychelles.net; Northolme Hotel, Glacis)
Indian High Commission (Map p248; ☎ 610301; Le Chantier, Mont Fleuri Rd)
Mauritius (☎ 225097; birdlife@seychelles.net; Room 202, Aarti Chambers, PO Box 1310, Mont Fleuri)
Netherlands (Map p253; ☎ 261111; sunset@seychelles.net; PO Box 372, Sunset Beach Hotel, Glacis)
USA (Map p248; ☎ 225256; fax 225189; PO Box 251, Oliaji Trade Centre, Francis Rachel St, Victoria)

FESTIVALS & EVENTS

The Seychelles may lack the range of festivals found in Mauritius and Réunion, but there are some lively cultural bashes during the year and a whole raft of fishing competitions and other sporting events. The local newspapers usually have details of what's on, or you can ask at the tourist office. Both the **Kreol Institute** (Map p256; ☎ 376351; 🕑 8am-4pm Mon-Fri) near Anse aux Pins and the **Alliance Française** (Map p248; ☎ 282424) in Victoria put on various cultural events. For more information about arts events, contact the **Ministry of Culture** (Map p248; ☎ 321333) at the National Library in Victoria.

JANUARY

Sunday of Bygone Days Celebration of old traditions and foods.

MARCH

Semaine de la Francophonie French culture takes over Mahé for a week of song recitals, films and art exhibitions.

APRIL

Arts Festival Five days of exhibitions, dance, theatre and other cultural events at various locations on Mahé.

MAY

FetAfrik The Seychelles celebrates its African origins with a weekend of music and dance.

AUGUST

La Digue Festival Religious procession followed by three days of traditional dance and music.
Dekouver Vye Marmite Festival of traditional recipes.

SEPTEMBER

Coconut Evening Open-air buffet comprised entirely of dishes made from coconut.

OCTOBER

SUBIOS Underwater Festival (www.subios.sc) Week-long underwater photography competition at Beau Vallon.
Festival Kreol Week-long festival of Creole culture.

FOOD

In the Seychelles, a meal in a budget restaurant will cost up to Rs 80; in a mid-range place between Rs 80 and Rs 150 and upwards of Rs 150 at the top end.

HOLIDAYS

Public holidays in the Seychelles are observed as follows:
New Year 1 & 2 January
Good Friday March/April
Easter Day March/April
Labour Day 1 May
Liberation Day 5 June
Corpus Christi 10 June
National Day 18 June
Independence Day 29 June
Assumption 15 August
All Saints' Day 1 November
Immaculate Conception 8 December
Christmas Day 25 December

INTERNET RESOURCES

There are a number of sites worth browsing for a spot of pretrip planning.
Atlas Seychelles (www.seychelles.net) The local Internet service provider carries a useful list of members' home pages.
Seychelles Magic (www.sey.net) Tour operator offering good background information on the country, including activities, events and island hopping.
Seychelles Tourism Marketing Authority (www.aspureasitgets.com) This well-organised site gives an excellent overview of what's on offer and provides masses of useful information.
Virtual Seychelles (www.virtualseychelles.sc) Though it presents the official line, this government site is a good place to find out what's happening around the islands.

MEDIA

Newspapers & Magazines

The only daily paper is the government-controlled **Nation** (www.nation.sc), which contains international and local news in English, French and Creole, and carries cinema, TV and radio schedules.

The other papers are the *People*, also government backed, and the two opposition papers: **Regar** (www.regar.sc) and the *Seychelles Weekly*. They are all published weekly, mainly in English, and tend to focus on local news.

The Seychelles boasts its very own 'current affairs and lifestyle magazine', *Seychelles Today*. Printed monthly, it features articles on local culture and history as well as various tourist activities.

TV & Radio

The **Seychelles Broadcasting Corporation** (SBC; www.sbc.sc) provides TV broadcasts from 6am to around midnight in English, French and Creole. The news in English is at 6pm. Many programs are imported from England, America or France.

SBC also runs the main radio station, which broadcasts daily from 6am to 10pm in three languages, as well as a 24-hour music station, Paradise FM. The frequencies of these stations vary depending on where you are on the islands.

MONEY

The unit of currency is the Seychelles rupee (Rs), which is divided into 100 cents (¢). Bank notes come in denominations of Rs 10, Rs 25, Rs 50 and Rs 100; there are coins of Rs 1, Rs 5, 1¢, 5¢, 10¢ and 25¢.

There are some complex rules governing foreign exchange in the Seychelles. By law visitors must pay for all accommodation (including meals and drinks), excursions, marine park fees, diving, car hire and transport in a major foreign currency, either in cash or by credit card. Prices for these services are therefore nearly always quoted in euros, UK pounds and US dollars.

When changing travellers cheques or withdrawing money from an ATM, however, you will receive the money in rupees, not in foreign currency. Even when you pay for something in foreign currency, you will often receive the change in rupees. You can use rupees in shops, cafés and restaurants outside the hotels and for taxi and bus fares, but they can be quite hard to spend, so only change small amounts at a time.

The best strategy overall is to use a credit card wherever possible and to bring plenty of cash with you as a backup.

If you want to change rupees back into foreign currency at the end of your stay, you must go back to the same bank (not necessarily the same branch, but it doesn't hurt) with the original exchange receipt or ATM slip. The maximum you can convert is Rs 800 and it is illegal to take more than Rs 2000 out of the country. If possible, don't leave it until the airport because the bank you need may not be open or may claim not to have sufficient currency; it's better to do it in Victoria.

ATMs

There are ATMs, which accept major international cards, at the airport and at all the major banks in Victoria. You'll also find ATMs at Beau Vallon on Mahé and on Praslin and La Digue. American Express card holders can only obtain money through **Travel Services Seychelles** (TSS; p258; ☎ 322414); you have to buy travellers cheques which can then be changed in a bank.

Credit Cards

Major credit cards including Visa, MasterCard and American Express are accepted in most hotels, restaurants and tourist shops.

Moneychangers

The four main banks are Barclays Bank, Seychelles Savings Bank, Nouvobanq and Mauritius Commercial Bank (MCB). All have branches in Victoria while Barclays Bank and Nouvobanq have desks at the airport that are open for all flights – in theory at least. There are also banks on Praslin and La Digue. None of the banks charges commission for changing cash but some do so for travellers cheques, generally a flat rate of Rs 25.

You may occasionally find someone willing to change money on the black market, or offering cheaper prices or room rates if you pay in cash in a foreign currency, but it is illegal and you run the risk of being caught.

TELEPHONE

The telephone system is efficient and reliable. There are public payphones (both coin and cardphones) on the three main islands from which you can make local and international calls. They are operated by either Cable & Wireless or Airtel, though so far Airtel only has phones on Mahé. Prices work out roughly the same.

Local calls within and between the main islands cost around Rs 0.90 for up to three minutes. For an idea of international rates, calls to America, Australia and the UK with Cable & Wireless cost roughly Rs 8 per minute. Cheaper rates apply all weekend and from 7pm to 7am on weekdays.

If you are tempted to phone from your hotel room, remember that hotels often add a hefty mark-up.

Mobile Phones

If you have a GSM phone and it has been 'unlocked', you can use a local SIM card purchased from either **Cable & Wireless** (Map p248; ☎ 284000; Frances Rachel St, Victoria) or **Airtel** (Map p248; ☎ 610610; Trinity House, Albert St, Victoria). A starter pack, including the card and a certain credit allowance, costs between Rs 150 and Rs 200.

Phonecards

Telephone cards are available from Cable & Wireless and Airtel offices and from most retail outlets. They come in various denominations between Rs 30 and Rs 200, but note that for international calls you need at least Rs 100; anything smaller hardly gives you time to say hello.

VISAS

You don't need a visa to enter the Seychelles, just a valid passport, an onward ticket, booked accommodation and sufficient funds for your stay. On arrival at the airport, you will be given a visitor's visa for up to a month, depending on the departure date printed on your onward ticket.

If you wish to extend your visa, apply with proof of funds and your onward ticket at the **Immigration Office** (Map p248; ☎ 611100; info@immigration.gov.sc; Independence House, Independence Ave, Victoria; 🕑 8am-noon & 1-4pm Mon-Fri). Processing takes about a week. The first three-month extension is free of charge. Thereafter the cost is Rs 200 per three-month extension up to a maximum of one year.

TRANSPORT IN SEYCHELLES

GETTING THERE & AWAY

The following section covers transport between Mauritius, Réunion and the Seychelles. For information about getting to the region from elsewhere, see the Regional Directory (p277).

Air

There are roughly 10 flights a week between Mauritius and the Seychelles operated by Air Mauritius and Air Seychelles. Low-season fares start at roughly €250 for a one-month return ticket. The flight takes around 2½ hours. From Réunion, there's a choice between Air Seychelles and Air Austral, each with one flight a week each. Tickets cost around €440 for one-month return. All three carriers have a good safety record.

Seychelles International Airport (code SEZ; ☎ 384400) sits on an area of reclaimed land about 8km south of Victoria.

Airlines serving Seychelles:

Air Austral (airline code UU; ☎ 323262; Pirates Arms Bldg, Independence Ave, Victoria; www.air-austral.com; hub Roland Garros International Airport, Réunion)

Air Mauritius (airline code MK; ☎ 322414; Kingsgate House, Independence Ave, Victoria; www.airmauritius.com; hub SSR International Airport, Mauritius)

Air Seychelles (airline code HM; ☎ 381300; Victoria House, Francis Rachel St, Victoria; www.airseychelles.net; hub Seychelles International Airport, Mahé)

GETTING AROUND

Air

Air Seychelles (☎ 381300; www.airseychelles.net) takes care of all interisland flights, whether scheduled or charter. The only scheduled services are between Mahé and Praslin, with around 20 flights per day in each direction. The fare for the 15-minute hop is €50; a return costs €100.

Check-in time is 30 minutes before departure and the luggage limit is only 10kg (€1 per kilo for excess luggage) – you may be able to stretch the rules if you are connecting with an international flight, but don't bet on it. Fortunately there is a free luggage storage facility at the international airport. Alternatively, if you are returning to a hotel on Mahé, the hotel may be able to store your bags for you.

Helicopter Seychelles (☎ 385863; www.helicopterseychelles.com), based at Seychelles International Airport, operates shuttle flights between Mahé and Praslin (€170 per person one way), Mahé and La Digue (€170), and Praslin and La Digue (€85). Flights must be booked 72 hours in advance. It also offers transfers to resort islands (bookings should be made through the hotel) and scenic flights. A 30-minute buzz over Mahé, La Digue or Praslin costs €525 for up to four people.

Bicycle

Bicycles are the principle form of transport on La Digue. On Praslin you can rent bikes at Anse Volbert or through your accommodation. Mahé is a bit hilly for casual cyclists and most visitors rent cars, so bike hire is hard to find.

The Seychelles isn't really substantial enough to justify bringing your own bike. One poor traveller had his bike impounded by customs for most of his stay while he waited to get a licence and a bell!

Boat

There are regular ferries between Mahé, Praslin and La Digue. Boats leave from the interisland ferry terminal in Victoria, from Baie Ste Anne on Praslin and from La Passe on La Digue. For all other islands you have to charter a boat, take a tour or hitch a ride on a government vessel or fishing boat.

MAHÉ TO PRASLIN

The **Cat Cocos catamaran** (Map p248; ☎ 324843; catcocos@seychelles.net) makes two return trips daily between Mahé and Praslin. Departing from Victoria, the journey takes one hour (not that much longer than the plane, if you include check-in time) and the fare is €40 one way (€45 in the upper, air-con lounge); children over two pay full fare. Tickets should be booked at least a day in advance with the ferry company or through a travel agent.

MAHÉ TO LA DIGUE

The schooner **Clarté** (☎ 234254) and the **Dauphin Noir** (☎ 234013) are cargo boats which run between Mahé and La Digue from Monday to Friday and which carry passengers if there is room. If you don't mind a bit of discomfort it's a fun and cheap way to travel. The boats generally depart mid-morning from Mahé, and return around 5pm, but check when making the booking. The three-hour crossing costs just €12/6 per adult/child.

PRASLIN TO LA DIGUE

The **Inter-Island Ferry Co** (☎ 232329) operates a schooner service between Praslin and La Digue. There are at least seven departures daily between 7am and 5.15pm (5.45pm on Sunday) from Praslin and between 7.30am and 5.45pm (6.15pm on Sunday) from La Digue. The 30-minute trip can be a rocky one, sometimes spraying unsuspecting passengers with water – make sure your valuables are well protected.

The one-way/return fare is €10/19 per adult and €6/10 per child under eight. It's a good idea to book ahead – most hotels will do this for you.

Bus

An extensive bus service operates throughout Mahé, with a more limited service on Praslin. Destinations and routes are usually marked on the front of the bus. There is a flat rate of Rs 3 whatever the length of journey; pay the driver as you board. Bus stops have signs and shelters and there are also markings on the road. When you want to get off, ring the bell or shout *'Devant!'*.

On Mahé, timetables and maps of each route are posted at the terminus in Victoria, where you can also pick up photocopied timetables at the **information office** (☎ 518339; 🕑 7am-4pm Mon-Fri). The principal destinations are Beau Vallon, Anse aux Pins (for the airport), Port Launay (for the Morne Seychellois National Park) and Baie Lazare. There's a bus roughly each hour on most routes from around 6am until 7pm (slightly later heading into Victoria). Check the time of the last bus or you may face a long walk home.

On Praslin, the basic route is from Anse Boudin to Mont Plaisir via Anse Volbert, Baie Ste Anne and Grand Anse. Buses run in each direction every hour (every half-hour between Baie St Anne and Mont Plaisir) from 6am to 6.30pm. Timetables are available at the two tourist offices.

Car

Most of the road network on Mahé and Praslin is sealed and in good shape. More of a worry are the narrow bends and the speed at which some drivers, especially bus drivers, take them.

Drive on the left, and beware of drivers with fast cars and drowsy brains – especially late on Friday and Saturday nights. The speed limit is supposed to be 40km/h in built-up areas, 65km/h outside towns and 80km on the dual carriageway between Victoria and the airport. On Praslin the limit is 40km/h throughout the island.

If you run over something that explodes like a pistol shot while driving at night, you've probably hit a giant African snail. These huge molluscs were imported as a delicacy by the French and have overrun the islands.

RENTAL

While you will still see the occasional Mini Moke, most rental cars these days are regular hatchbacks and saloon cars or open jeeps – more sturdy, secure and comfortable, but not nearly so much fun.

There are any number of car-hire companies on Mahé and quite a few on Praslin, but little to choose between them as regards prices. The cheapest you're likely to get on Mahé is around €65 a day for a small hatchback with air-con and €70 for a jeep (less for longer periods). Rates on Praslin are about €15 more expensive.

Drivers must be over 23 years old and have held a driving licence for at least a year, sometimes three years. Though it's wise to bring an international driver's licence, most companies accept a national licence.

Because of the difficulty (and expense) of getting spare parts in the Seychelles, breakdowns are common and parked cars are pillaged for anything remotely removable – never leave your vehicle in an isolated spot.

Options include the following:

Austral Car Rental (☎ 232015; www.seychelles.net/austcars; Anse Volbert, Praslin)

Avis (Map p248; ☎ 224511; www.avis.com.sc; Victoria House, Francis Rachel St, Victoria, Mahé)

Explorer Cars (Map p259; ☎ 233311; explorer@seychelles.net; Grand Anse, Praslin)

Hertz (Map p248; ☎ 322447; hertz@seychelles.net; Revolution Ave, Victoria, Mahé)

Praslin Holiday Car Rental (Map p259; ☎ 233219; pracars@seychelles.net; Grand Anse, Praslin)

Thrifty (Map p252; ☎ 247052; Coral Strand Hotel, Beau Vallon, Mahé)
Tropicar (☎ 373336; tropical@seychelles.net; Providence Industrial Estate, Mahé)
U-Drive (Map p253; ☎ 373171; udrive@seychelles.net; Anse des Genets, Mahé)

TAXI

Taxis operate on Mahé and Praslin and there are even a handful on La Digue. Though taxis are metered you often have to insist pretty hard to get the driver to use it. In most cases you'll have to negotiate; make sure you fix a price before setting off. As a guideline, the official rate is Rs 15 for the first kilometre on Mahé (Rs 18 on Praslin and La Digue) and Rs 5 for each additional kilometre; rates are slightly higher at night. Drivers can also charge Rs 5 per piece of luggage.

Regional Directory

CONTENTS

Accommodation	277
Activities	277
Children	278
Climate	279
Customs	279
Dangers & Annoyances	280
Disabled Travellers	280
Embassies & Consulates	281
Gay & Lesbian Travellers	281
Holidays	281
Insurance	281
Internet Access	281
Legal Matters	282
Maps	282
Money	282
Photography & Video	282
Post	283
Shopping	284
Solo Travellers	284
Telephone	284
Tourist Information	284
Visas	285
Women Travellers	285

This chapter contains information relevant to the whole region. For destination-specific information for the three countries, see also the Mauritius Directory (p129), the Réunion Directory (p209) and the Seychelles Directory (p269).

ACCOMMODATION

Although Mauritius and the Seychelles have traditionally been playgrounds of the rich and famous, there are cheaper accommodation alternatives. Mauritius is perhaps the best destination for those seeking the tropics on a budget, with a choice of inexpensive guesthouses and self-catering apartments. The cheapest places in the Seychelles can seem poor value for money, but both Mauritius and the Seychelles have plenty of small, family-run hotels catering to the middle market and world-class luxury establishments at the top end.

Réunion is short on top-end hotels, but has a fine selection in the mid-range as well as numerous cheaper options, including youth hostels, self-catering *gîtes ruraux* (usually known simply as *gîtes*), *gîtes de montagne* (mountain lodges), *gîtes d'etape* (walkers' lodges) and *chambre d'hotes* (B&Bs).

Camping is possible on Réunion and Mauritius, although it tends not to be encouraged. It is not an option in the Seychelles.

In all three destinations, tariffs at many mid-range and top-end hotels vary according to the season. Prices shoot up during peak periods, which are generally the European summer holidays (July and August) and around Christmas and New Year. At these times some of the smarter places offer rooms on a full-board basis only (including breakfast, lunch and dinner). If you intend staying in upmarket hotels, it's worth investigating package rates and special deals by booking from abroad. Be warned that it can be difficult finding accommodation in high season – book well ahead to avoid disappointment.

Mauritius offers the best chance for bargaining in the low season. Some smaller hotels offer discounts, but guesthouses and self-catering accommodation are the most likely candidates, especially for stays longer than a week. Cheaper guesthouses in the Seychelles may also be willing to bargain if you stay several days.

For more information about the different options available locally and price definitions for accommodation, see p129 for Mauritius, see p210 for Réunion and p269 for the Seychelles.

ACTIVITIES

Water activities are the focus in Mauritius and the Seychelles, while land-based adventure sports are Réunion's forte. On the waterfront, diving, snorkelling, surfing, fishing and sailing are just some of the activities on offer. Tours in glass-bottomed boats are extremely popular – see p130 for Mauritius, p187 for Réunion and p250 for the Seychelles. A highlight in Mauritius is the undersea walks (you don a weight belt and a diving helmet supplied with air from the surface; see p131).

In addition to hiking, land-based activities include mountain biking, golf, tennis and horse riding. In Réunion, thrill-seekers can also indulge in canyoning, rock climbing and paragliding.

For more information see p130 for Mauritius, p212 for Réunion and p269 for the Seychelles.

Deep-sea Fishing

Deep-sea fishing is popular throughout the region, but there is growing concern about its environmental impact. The Indian Ocean supports huge fisheries, and deep-sea angling has far less impact than commercial fishing, but the sport takes the healthiest individuals from the population, and little is known about the breeding cycles of the large predators that are the traditional targets of the sport. However, 'tag-and-release' is widely available, which allows anglers to take home the trophy photograph as well as the knowledge that the fish will live another day.

The main centres are St-Gilles-les-Bains (p187) in Réunion and Grande Rivière Noire (p107) in Mauritius. The prime season is November to April, when the warm water brings marlin and other large predators close to the shore. Other species such as tuna, sharks and wahoo can be found all year.

Diving & Snorkelling

The Seychelles is the prime destination for underwater exploration; the variety of fish and the range of dive sites are outstanding. Nevertheless, Mauritius also offers excellent diving and snorkelling and has the added advantage of more affordable prices. Réunion is geared more towards the novice diver, but has some great snorkelling spots. In all three places the shallow lagoons are perfect for learning to dive.

For full coverage of diving and snorkelling, see Underwater Worlds, p33.

Hiking

Top billing here goes to Réunion, which offers sensational hiking opportunities (see Hiking in Réunion, p224). You could spend weeks exploring the island's rugged interior, while there are also plenty of gentler walks to suit all age groups and levels of fitness.

In Mauritius, the Black River Gorges National Park (p86) is a popular destination for hikers, while Rodrigues (p126) also offers several excellent trails and sees surprisingly few visitors.

Hikes in the Seychelles tend to be short, but lead to magnificent viewpoints. The Morne Seychellois National Park (p254) in Mahé boasts the greatest number of trails. Walking around the sandy tracks of La Digue is also a great pleasure.

In general, the most favourable time to hit the trail is during the cool, dry winter (roughly May to September). It also pays to start early in the day before the clouds build up.

Surfing

The tricky, left-handed wave off St-Leu in Réunion (p186) is rated among the best surf spots in the Indian Ocean. The island's west coast also provides plenty of easier waves to master. There's no particular season; the winds are pretty consistent all year.

By comparison, the surf scene in Mauritius is a low-key affair. The main centre is Tamarin (p105) on the southwest coast, with other popular spots dotted around the Morne peninsula and along the south coast. The season lasts from May to September.

CHILDREN

Travelling with children should pose no particular problems in any of these destinations. Indeed, having kids along can be a great icebreaker as locals generally make a huge fuss of children. Mauritius and Réunion offer the broadest range of activities and the best facilities for children, while in the Seychelles such things tend to be concentrated in the big hotels. The star attraction from a kid's point of view is undoubtedly the beach and simply splashing around in the lagoon.

Practicalities

Réunion offers the best facilities in terms of what's available in the shops, highchairs in restaurants, car safety seats and so forth. The Seychelles makes the least provision (although international car-rental companies

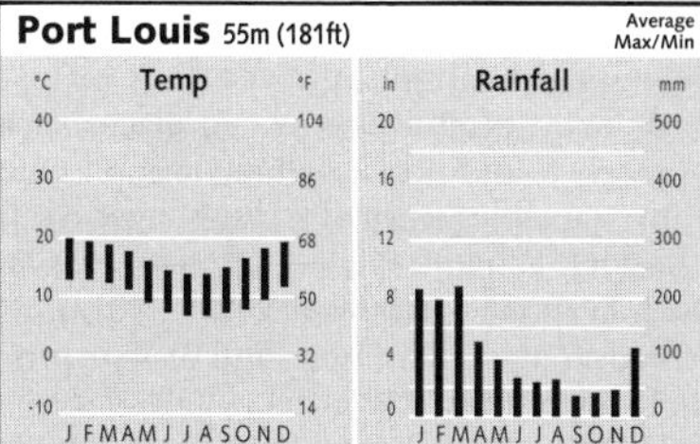

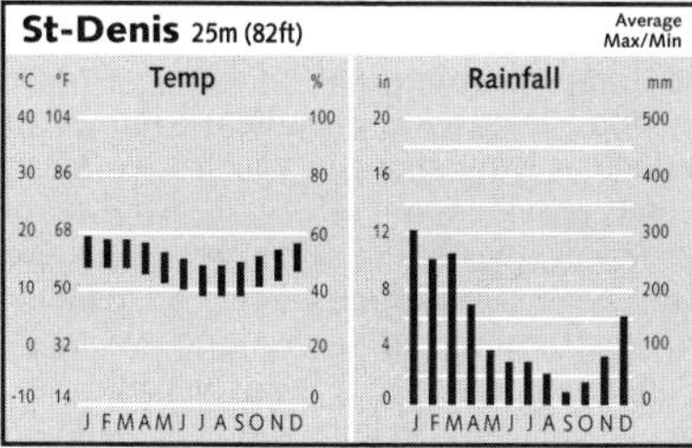

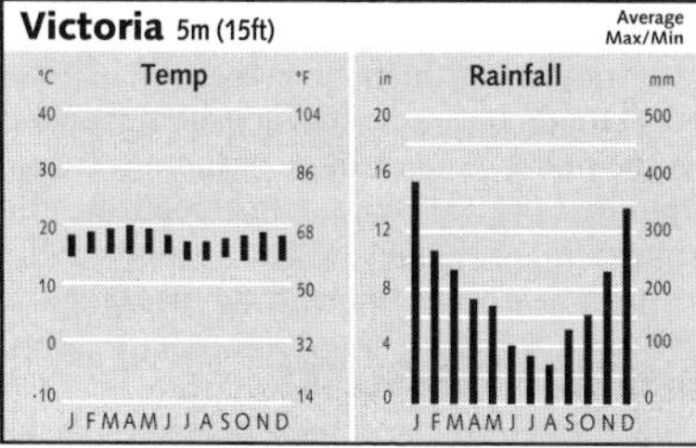

should provide safety seats and the big hotels should have highchairs), while Mauritius comes somewhere in between. Few hotels in Réunion have kids' clubs, whereas there are many excellent 'miniclubs' in Mauritius and the Seychelles.

Most hotels and guesthouses should be able to provide cots and upmarket hotels usually have baby-sitting services. Ask about the extent of facilities when you make your reservation.

Remember to bring along plenty of sun protection for your kids, and take extra care to prevent sunburn. Keep in mind that children are more likely to be affected by unaccustomed heat, and need time to acclimatise. Be prepared also for the minor effects often brought on by a change of diet or water, disrupted sleep patterns, or even just being in a strange place. Avoid giving your children street food, as it can sometimes bring on tummy upsets.

Nappies, lotions and baby foods are available, but the choice is somewhat limited, especially in the Seychelles. If there is a particular brand you swear by, it's a good idea to bring it along with you.

On the financial side, quite a few hotels and tour operators offer discounts for children – usually around 50% of the adult rate for children under 12 years old; those below two years are often not charged at all.

For practical advice and information on how to make travel as stress-free as possible, for children and parents alike, consult Lonely Planet's *Travel with Children*.

CLIMATE

As the charts below show, Mauritius, Réunion and the Seychelles share the same basic climate: a hot, wet summer (roughly November to March) and a cooler, drier winter (May to September). Within this overall pattern, temperatures in the Seychelles remain fairly stable throughout the year. Because of the mountains, the climate in both Mauritius and Réunion varies from one part of the island to another; see p45 for Mauritius, p147 for Réunion and p239 for the Seychelles. For the best time to visit the region, see When to Go on p13.

CUSTOMS

Duty-free limits on arrival are basically the same throughout the region. In Mauritius, visitors aged 16 years and over may import 200 cigarettes or 250g of tobacco; 1L of spirits; 2L of wine, ale or beer; 250mL of eau de toilette; and up to 100mL of perfume. In Réunion, the limits are 100 cigarettes, 250g of tobacco, 2L of alcohol under 22% and 1L over 22%, 2L of still wine, and 50g of perfume. In the Seychelles, visitors can bring in up to 400 cigarettes or 500g of tobacco, 2L of spirits or wine, and 200mL of perfume or eau de toilette.

In all cases there are restrictions on importing food, plants and animals, for which import permits are required. Other prohibited and restricted articles include spear guns and items made from ivory, shell, turtleshell or other materials banned under the Convention on International Trade in Endangered Species (CITES); it is also illegal to take such items out when you leave.

With regards to currency, visitors to Mauritius may import a maximum of Rs 700 in local currency, and take out Rs 350. Anyone entering or leaving Réunion must declare sums in excess of €7600. You are allowed to carry up to Rs 2000 in local currency in to or out of the Seychelles, but there are no restrictions on foreign currency.

DANGERS & ANNOYANCES

Mauritius, Réunion and the Seychelles are relatively safe places to visit and with any luck the most you'll have to worry about is falling coconuts. Lying under a coconut palm may seem like a tropical idyll, but there have been some tragic accidents. Take care when walking under coconut trees and don't lie (or park your car) beneath them.

The Indian Ocean is a warm tropical ocean, so there are several aquatic nasties to watch out for. Fortunately, few travellers encounter anything more serious than the odd coral cut. For more information, see Dangerous Marine Life on p34.

All beaches below the high-tide line are public property, so you are entitled to plop your towel down on the sand, whatever some over-officious security guard might tell you.

Cyclones

Mauritius and Réunion lie within the cyclone belt. Most cyclones occur between December and March. While direct hits are relatively uncommon, storms miles away can bring very strong winds.

As soon as a cyclone is detected, a system of alerts is used to inform the public of the level of danger. In Réunion there are three levels of alert (see Cyclone Warning on p148), in Mauritius four, but the principle is the same. The alerts and then regular bulletins are broadcast on radio and television. There are also special phone numbers you can call for the latest update (see the inside front cover).

Theft

Petty theft is not a major problem in this region, but one that you should be aware of. Favourite haunts for thieves are the beaches. Île aux Cerfs in Mauritius is a particular hot spot (see p133). The best strategy is not to take any valuables to the beach – and never tempt a passing thief by leaving your belongings unattended.

Be extra careful in crowded places such as markets and avoid walking around with your valuables casually slung over your shoulder. When travelling on public transport, keep your gear near you.

If you hire a car, it's best not to leave anything valuable in it at all. If you must do so, hide everything well out of sight. Wherever possible, park in a secure car park or at least somewhere busy – never park in an isolated spot, especially at night.

Don't leave vital documents, money or valuables lying about in your room. Many hotels provide room safes. Otherwise, leave your valuables in the safe at reception and get a receipt. While most hotels are reliable, to be extra sure, pack everything in a small, double-zippered bag that can be padlocked, or use a large envelope with a signed seal which will reveal any tampering. Count money and travellers cheques before and after retrieving them from the safe.

If you do have something stolen, report it to the police. The chances of them recovering anything are remote, but you'll need a statement proving you have reported the crime if you want to claim on insurance.

DISABLED TRAVELLERS

Overall, Réunion and then Mauritius make the best provision for those with a mobility problem. Modern buildings in both places conform to international standards for disabled access, while Réunion performs better with regard to lifts in older buildings, ramps, accessible public toilets etc. Even some guesthouses in Réunion offer specially adapted rooms. The Seychelles makes least provision, although as in Mauritius and Réunion, most top-end hotels have wheelchair access, lifts and specially equipped bathrooms. In big hotels, there are always plenty of staff around to help and it is often possible to hire an assistant if you want to go on an excursion or a boat trip. With a bit of extra warning, some riding stables, dive centres and other sports operators can cater for people with disabilities.

None of the public transport systems offer wheelchair access. Anyone using a wheelchair will be reliant on taxis and minibuses.

EMBASSIES & CONSULATES

It's important to realise what your own embassy – the embassy of the country of which you are a citizen – can and can't do to help you if you get into trouble. Generally speaking, it won't be much help if the trouble you're in is remotely your own fault. Remember that you are bound by the laws of the country you are in. Your embassy will not be sympathetic if you end up in jail after committing a crime locally, even if such actions are legal at home.

If you have all your money and documents stolen, the embassy should issue some sort of temporary passport, but a loan for onward travel is out of the question – you would be expected to have insurance.

For embassies' and consulates' contact information, see p133 for Mauritius, p216 for Réunion and p271 for the Seychelles.

GAY & LESBIAN TRAVELLERS

Réunion is the most liberal of the three destinations when it comes to homosexuality, and follows French law whereby the age of consent for both homosexuals and heterosexuals is 15 years. The gay male scene is more developed than the lesbian one, but don't expect the same liberal attitudes you might find in mainland France. Overt displays of affection between members of the same sex may still be viewed with disdain, particularly away from the capital.

In Mauritius and the Seychelles, homosexuality is still illegal, although generally tolerated; one of Mauritius' most popular politicians, Sir Gaetan Duval, was openly bisexual for much of his tenure. The Seychelles offers more secluded situations where you don't have to feel inhibited, but Mauritius is probably the more liberal society. Open affection in public is likely to attract stares and possibly jeers in both countries.

HOLIDAYS

There are no major festivals or holidays in any of these destinations which should affect your travel plans. Indeed, if your visit happens to coincide with a festival, it's usually worth popping along. For local festivals, see p134 for Mauritius, p216 for Réunion and p271 for the Seychelles.

More important are outside factors such as the European – and particularly French – school holidays. The dates vary each year but the main French school holidays are two weeks over Christmas and New Year, two weeks at Easter and all of July and August. During these periods (especially the Christmas and summer holidays) flights, accommodation and car hire tend to be booked up months in advance. Prices also go up.

It's also worth being aware of the school holidays in Réunion as local families increasingly take holidays in Mauritius and, to a lesser extent, the Seychelles. It's also busier in Réunion itself, of course, during these times. Réunion's school holidays are roughly two weeks in March, one week at Easter, a month from mid-July to mid-August, two weeks in October and a month over Christmas and New Year.

Dates of French school holidays (including in Réunion) are posted on the **Ministry of Education website** (www.education.gouv.fr) under *calendrier scolaire*.

INSURANCE

A travel insurance policy to cover theft, loss and medical problems is a good idea. Some policies specifically exclude dangerous activities, which can include scuba diving, motorcycling and even hiking. Always check the small print.

You may prefer a policy that pays doctors or hospitals directly rather than having to pay on the spot and claiming later. If you have to claim later ensure you keep all documentation.

Check that the policy covers ambulances or an emergency flight home.

For more information on health insurance see p291.

INTERNET ACCESS

Most travellers make constant use of Internet cafés and free Web-based email such as **Yahoo** (www.yahoo.com) or **Hotmail** (www.hotmail.com). If you need to access a specific account of your own, you'll need three pieces of information: your incoming (POP or IMAP) mail server name, your account name and your password. Your Internet Service Provider (ISP) or network supervisor will be able to give you these. With this information, you should be able to access your Internet mail account from any Net-connected machine in the world, provided it runs some kind of email software (remember that Netscape and Internet Explorer both have mail modules).

In line with its ambition to become a 'cyberisland', Mauritius is the most wired-up of the three destinations. There are Internet cafés in Port Louis and the main tourist centres, where you'll pay around Rs 10 for 15 minutes. Though it's catching up fast, Réunion is slightly less well provided and rather more pricey at between €2 and €4 per half-hour. In the Seychelles, you'll find a few cybercafés on Mahé and one on Praslin; prices range from €2 to €3 for 15 minutes. In all three destinations, some hotels and even a few guesthouses offer Internet connections. Connections are reasonably fast and reliable throughout.

The other option is to bring your own portable computer, in which case be aware that your modem may not work outside your home country. The safest option is to buy a reputable 'global' modem or, if you're spending an extended time in any one country, a local PC-card modem. It's also worth investing in a universal AC adaptor to cope with the different power supplies and you'll need the right plug to connect to the local phone system. In Mauritius and the Seychelles an RJ-11 will do the trick; in Réunion you'll need an adaptor to convert from the RJ-11 to a French plug. For more information on travelling with a portable computer, see www.teleadapt.com.

For Internet resources see p15.

LEGAL MATTERS

Foreigners are subject to the laws of the country in which they are travelling and will receive no special consideration because they are tourists. If you find yourself in a sticky legal predicament, contact your embassy (see p133 for Mauritius, p216 for Réunion, and p271 for the Seychelles). You should carry your passport with you at all times and keep a photocopy of the first page of your passport (with your personal details and photograph), as well as a copy of your visa (if applicable), in a safe place.

MAPS

The best maps of Mauritius and Réunion are those produced by the **Institut Géographique Nationale** (IGN; www.ign.fr). They are widely available locally. There's nothing so detailed for the Seychelles, though GeoCenter's *Seychelles Holiday Map* isn't a bad option.

For further information about the best maps and where to find them, see p135 for Mauritius and p217 for Réunion.

MONEY

If you are visiting all three destinations, the most useful currency to carry is the euro. It is the local currency in Réunion, while euro cash and travellers cheques can easily be changed in Mauritius and the Seychelles, and in the Seychelles euros are also accepted as legal tender. However, if you are only visiting Mauritius and/or the Seychelles, any major currency, but particularly the euro, British pound or the US dollar, will be fine.

Throughout the region there are ATMs that give cash advances in the local currency, and credit cards are widely accepted by shops, hotels, restaurants and tour operators.

Changing travellers cheques and even major foreign currencies can be a problem in Réunion. The best strategy is to bring plenty of euros with you, and then use your credit card to withdraw cash as needed from the ATMs. In Mauritius and the Seychelles, banks will change cash and travellers cheques in any major currency without much ado.

Although it is illegal, there is a black market of sorts in the Seychelles. It usually takes the form of a guesthouse or a vendor offering cheaper prices if you pay in a foreign currency.

For further information on money matters, see p136 for Mauritius, p218 for Réunion and p272 for the Seychelles. For information on costs refer to p14. Exchange rates for major currencies are given on the inside front cover.

Tipping

Tipping is not expected anywhere in the region. However, it is much appreciated if you feel the service has been out of the ordinary.

PHOTOGRAPHY & VIDEO

The Indian Ocean islands are the very image of paradise, and many photographers strive to capture that image on film. For the most comprehensive guide to taking photographs on the road, get a copy of Lonely Planet's *Travel Photography*.

Print and slide film are widely available locally and there are decent developing studios in the three capital cities. The average cost for a 36-exposure film is Rs 100 in Mauritius, €6 in Réunion and Rs 45 in the Seychelles; slide film costs around Rs 200/€10/Rs 55 for 36 exposures. With regards to processing, you'll pay around Rs 220 for 36 exposures in Mauritius, €25 in Réunion and Rs 125 in the Seychelles for the express service.

Blank video tapes and discs are widely available in the main tourist centres in Réunion. They are harder to come by in Mauritius, however, and very scarce in the Seychelles, so bring plenty with you.

Technical Tips

Take into consideration the heat, humidity, tropical sunlight and equatorial shadows. If you're shooting on beaches, it's important to adjust for glare from water or sand, and to keep sand and salt water well away from your equipment.

PHOTOGRAPHY

The best times to take photographs on sunny days are the first two hours after sunrise and the last two before sunset. This brings out the best colours. At other times, the harsh sunlight and glare washes everything out, although filters help counter the glare.

VIDEO

As well as filming the obvious things – sunsets, spectacular views – remember to record some of the ordinary details of everyday life. Often the most interesting things occur when you're actually intent on filming something else.

Video cameras have amazingly sensitive microphones, and you might be surprised how much sound they pick up. This can be a problem if there is a lot of ambient noise – filming by the side of a busy road might seem OK when you do it, but you might hear only a deafening cacophony of traffic noise when you view it back home.

One good rule for beginners is to try to film in long takes, and don't move the camera around too much. Otherwise, your video could well make your viewers seasick!

Restrictions

Don't photograph or film airports or anything that looks like police or military equipment or property. Photography is generally not permitted in Hindu temples and mosques – usually there is a sign warning against photography. If you're not sure, don't be afraid to ask.

It may be insensitive to take photos at certain religious ceremonies, so again, it's best to ask first.

Photographing People

Although there are no cultural taboos about photographing people in this region, you should still ask their permission first as a matter of politeness.

A zoom lens is a relatively unobtrusive means of taking portraits – even if you happened to have obtained permission, a reasonable distance between you and your subject should reduce your subject's discomfort, and result in more natural shots.

Underwater Photography

Photographs taken underwater can be startling – at depth, flash photography reveals colours that aren't there for the naked eye. Nowadays, reasonably priced and easy-to-use underwater cameras are available. For souvenir snapshots, disposable underwater cameras are a good option.

If you're serious about underwater photography, it's worth investing in a good flash. As you descend, natural colours are quickly absorbed, starting with the red end of the spectrum. In other words, the deeper you go, the more blue things look. To put the colour back in you need a flash.

In general, 28mm or 35mm lenses work best underwater. Even with these you have to get close to achieve good results, which requires patience when photographing fish. With experience and the right equipment, the results can be superb.

POST

In general, the postal systems throughout the region are quick and reliable. Postcards and minimum-weight letters sent by airmail cost between Rs 7 and Rs 9 from Mauritius, €0.90 from Réunion and between Rs 3 and Rs 4.50 from the Seychelles depending on the destination.

Poste restante is available at central post offices in all three destinations. You usually have to pay a small fee to collect letters and may be asked for your passport.

SHOPPING

The shopping mecca in this region is Mauritius, which produces top-quality clothes, knitwear and leather goods for next to nothing prices. It's also famous for its beautifully crafted model ships – they're not cheap, but the detail is unbelievable. For more on shopping in Mauritius, see p137.

The standard souvenirs throughout the region are sugar, tea, spices, essential oils, vanilla, soaps and basketry. Local foodstuffs, such as *achards* (vegetable pickle) and preserved fruits, and the ever-popular *rhum arrangé* (rum flavoured with herbs and spices), also make good mementos.

You'll also find eye-catching wrap-around skirts called *pareos*, which are great for the beach. Seychelles *pareos* come in particularly bright, tropical designs. There's also great jewellery in the Seychelles, and a number of world-famous artists. Mauritius also boasts some excellent painters. An original work of art makes an unusual and evocative souvenir.

Local markets are full of Malagasy handicrafts, too, such as embroidery, colourful basketware, wooden carvings and solitaire sets made of semiprecious stones (check carefully to be sure).

Bargaining

Bargaining is a way of life in Mauritius, but throughout the region it's normal to bargain in markets and anywhere prices aren't marked. Shop around or ask a local to get an idea of the going price. Keep the negotiations light-hearted and remember that, as a tourist, you're unlikely to get much of a discount.

SOLO TRAVELLERS

There are no particular problems for solo travellers in this region, even for women on their own (see Women Travellers on p285 for more).

The main difficulty is that activities such as diving, snorkelling and surfing should never be practised solo. It's also not recommended to hike on your own; if you do, always let someone know where you are going and when you expect to return. Whatever the activity, it's usually possible to hook up with other people, so there's no need to miss out.

TELEPHONE

The telephone systems throughout the region are efficient and reliable. There are public phones pretty much everywhere and you can use them to make direct-dial international calls without difficulty. Although coin phones do still exist in Mauritius and the Seychelles, it's generally best to use a phonecard and essential for calling abroad. Phonecards are widely available from post offices, newsagents, supermarkets and many other outlets.

For further information about telephoning, including the cost of calls, see p138 for Mauritius, p218 for Réunion and p273 for the Seychelles.

Mobile Phones

The mobile networks in all three destinations use the European GSM system. This means that if you have a GSM phone and a 'roaming' account (set this up with your service provider before leaving home), you will be able to use it locally – at a price, however, since such calls are usually charged at premium rates. Remember, too, that anyone calling you from within the country will have to make an international call.

If you're going to make and receive a lot of local calls, it might be worth buying a local SIM card and a prepaid phonecard. The main benefit is that this gives you a local number. Local calls should also be cheaper than those made using your home service provider. 'Starter packs' including a SIM card are available from phone companies in the country concerned. For your phone to work with a local SIM card, however, it must be 'unlocked'; contact your service provider for assistance before leaving home.

TOURIST INFORMATION

Considering how important tourism is in the region, the amount of information available to visitors is surprisingly poor. Réunion is the best of the bunch. It has the greatest number of tourist information offices and the staff are generally well informed and helpful, though not all speak English. Most offices are well stocked with brochures, flyers and suchlike, but, again, there is little available in English.

Mauritius is woefully lacking in tourist offices, with just one in Port Louis and a desk at SSR International Airport that keeps erratic hours. Staff are helpful, if not always well informed. The saving grace is Mauritius Telecom's 24-hour tourist information phone service (see p139). The Seychelles is not much better off, though there are now tourist offices on Mahé, Praslin and La Digue.

Fortunately, in all three destinations, local people are generally helpful and reasonably reliable sources of information.

VISAS

There are no visa requirements to enter the Seychelles, and citizens of the EU, the USA, Australia, Canada and New Zealand, among other countries, do not need visas to enter either Mauritius or Réunion.

Citizens of other countries should check with the nearest embassy or consulate of the country they intend to visit to find if a visa is required. It will be much easier to get one before you leave home.

For more visa information see p139 for Mauritius, p220 for Réunion and p273 for the Seychelles.

WOMEN TRAVELLERS

In general, women can expect courteous treatment throughout the region. These are fairly conservative societies, so revealing attire is best reserved for the beach. Mauritius follows Indian traditions and women tend to swim fully clothed; bikinis are fine on hotel beaches, but can cause offence elsewhere. You should cover your shoulders and wear trousers or a knee-length skirt when visiting temples or other religious places. (Men should also dress modestly in these places; for more information, see Responsible Travel on p48.)

As most visitors to these islands are couples, a woman travelling alone may be quizzed on the whereabouts of her husband. If you don't want to have to answer a lot of questions about why you choose to travel alone, one possibility is to invent a mythical husband or boyfriend who can't get away from his work.

While the older generation will generally be respectful to women, some younger local males may regard female travellers as candidates for 'romantic' attention (as elsewhere, much of the blame lies with imported films that depict Western women as having 'loose morals'). Things are unlikely to go beyond long stares, catcalls or an inquisitive (or suggestive) *bonjour*, but most would-be suitors will back down if you state firmly – but politely – that you are not interested.

Women are advised to go out in groups if partying in the evening and never to hitch or walk alone after dark.

Regional Transport

CONTENTS

Getting There & Away	**286**
Entry Requirements	286
Air	286
Sea	290
Getting Around	**290**
Air	290
Boat	290

THINGS CHANGE...

The information in this chapter is particularly vulnerable to change. Check directly with the airline or a travel agent to make sure you understand how a fare (and ticket you may buy) works and be aware of the security requirements for international travel. Shop carefully. The details given in this chapter should be regarded as pointers and are not a substitute for your own careful, up-to-date research.

GETTING THERE & AWAY

ENTRY REQUIREMENTS

Entering Mauritius

When entering Mauritius you must have a passport valid for at least six months from the date of entry, a visa for Mauritius if necessary and a ticket out of the country (together with a visa if necessary for your next port of call). If you do not have an onward ticket, you could be invited to buy one on the spot.

Immigration authorities will also want to know where you are staying in Mauritius and may ask for proof that you have a booking. They may also grill you on your finances, especially if you are staying more than the standard two weeks; possession of a valid credit card is usually fine.

Entering Réunion

Entering Réunion is straightforward, especially for EU citizens. All visitors must possess a passport valid for at least three months from the date of entry, a visa for Réunion (if required) and a return or onward ticket (plus a visa if necessary for your next destination).

Entering the Seychelles

Entering the Seychelles is pretty painless. Visas of up to one month are issued free on arrival. You just need to present a passport valid for at least six months from the date of entry, a return or onward ticket (with a visa for your next destination if required) and evidence of booked accommodation at least for your first few nights. You may also be asked for evidence of sufficient funds to cover you during your stay; possession of a valid credit card is usually fine.

AIR

Expensive flights have always been the biggest deterrent to travellers to this region. The good news is that a few airlines, such as Air Mauritius and Air Seychelles, are beginning to offer better deals from the UK and France. It's always worth checking if they've got any special offers. The only other way to cut the cost of flights is to include the region in a round-the-world (RTW) or other intercontinental fare, or to take a package deal with hotel accommodation. A vast number of travel agents offer tour packages to these destinations; shop around for the best bargains.

The principal hubs for airlines flying to this region are Paris and London. In general, prices are lowest on the Paris–Réunion route. Depending on where you are coming from, it may work out cheaper to fly via Paris and Réunion and then take an onward flight to Mauritius or the Seychelles. If you intend visiting all three islands, it's worth investigating the Indian Ocean Pass (p290), which must be purchased outside the region.

Airlines

Air Austral (airline code UU; in Mauritius ☎ 202 6677, in Réunion ☎ 02 62 90 90 91, in Seychelles ☎ 323262;

www.air-austral.com; hub Roland Garros International Airport, Réunion)
Air Bourbon (airline code BUB; ☎ 02 62 31 20 00; www.air-bourbon.com; hub Roland Garros International Airport, Réunion)
Air France (airline code AF; in Mauritius ☎ 208 7070, in Réunion ☎ 02 62 40 38 38, in Seychelles ☎ 322414; www.airfrance.com; hub Roissy Charles-de-Gaulle International Airport, Paris, France)
Air Madagascar (airline code MD; in Mauritius ☎ 203 2156, in Réunion ☎ 02 62 21 05 21; www.air-madagascar.com; hub Antananarivo International Airport, Madagascar)
Air Mauritius (airline code MK; in Mauritius ☎ 207 7070, in Réunion ☎ 02 62 94 83 83, in Seychelles ☎ 322414; www.airmauritius.com; hub SSR International Airport, Mauritius)
Air Seychelles (airline code HM; in Mauritius ☎ 202 6655, in Réunion ☎ 02 62 40 39 63, in Seychelles ☎ 381300; www.airseychelles.net; hub Seychelles International Airport, Mahè)
Air Zimbabwe (airline code UM; in Mauritius ☎ 241 1573; www.airzim.co.zw; hub Harare International Airport, Harare, Zimbabwe)
British Airways (airline code BA; in Mauritius ☎ 202 8000, in Seychelles ☎ 224910; www.britishairways.com; hub Heathrow International Airport, London, UK)
Condor (airline code DE; in Mauritius ☎ 207 3034, in Seychelles ☎ 322642; www.condor.com; hub Frankfurt International, Germany)
Corsair (airline code SS; in Réunion ☎ 02 62 94 82 82; www.corsair.fr; hub Orly International Airport, Paris, France)
Kenya Airways (airline code KQ; in Seychelles ☎ 322989; www.kenya-airways.com; hub Jomo Kenyatta International Airport, Nairobi, Kenya)
South African Airways (airline code SA; in Mauritius ☎ 213 0700; www.flysaa.com; hub Johannesburg International Airport, Johannesburg, South Africa)

Tickets

The main point to remember when buying your air ticket is to start early. Mauritius, Réunion and the Seychelles are popular destinations and some flights are booked months in advance. It's well worth consulting a specialist travel agent who can advise on special deals, routing options and packages.

If you are after a simple return ticket within fairly fixed dates, then the Internet provides a useful resource. Some of the better international online ticket sites:

Expedia (www.expedia.com) Microsoft's US travel site, with links to sister sites in Canada, the UK and Germany.
Flight Centre International (www.flightcentre.com) A respected operator for direct flights, with sites for the UK, US, Canada, Australia, New Zealand and South Africa.
Flights.com (www.tiss.com) Global site for flight-only tickets; cheap fares and a user-friendly database.
STA (www.sta.com) World leader in student travel, but not only restricted to students. Has links to worldwide STA sites.
Travelocity (www.travelocity.com) This US site allows you to research flights from/to practically anywhere.

INTERCONTINENTAL TICKETS

It is possible to include Mauritius, Réunion and the Seychelles as part of a RTW ticket. These can be bought through one of the three big airline alliances (Oneworld Alliance, Sky Team and Star Alliance) or through a travel agent. RTW tickets put together by travel agents tend to be more expensive but allow you to devise your own itinerary. In general RTW tickets are valid for up to one year and are calculated on the basis of either the number of continents or the distance covered.

Oneworld Alliance also offers a Visit Africa pass, which covers eight African countries including the Seychelles. Fares are calculated according to the number of flights taken and you must fly to and from Africa with one of the alliance members.

Another option is to fly from A to Z with as many stopovers as you want going in one direction, rather than buying individual tickets; this is especially worth investigating for the Seychelles. If you choose this option, always do it through a knowledgeable travel agent and not the airlines. That way, the fare may be calculated on the basis of mileage rather than the sum of your journey's parts.

Online ticket sites for intercontinental tickets:

Airbrokers (www.airbrokers.com) US company specialising in cheap RTW deals.
Airtreks.com (www.airtreks.com) Website that allows you to build your own RTW ticket.
Oneworld Alliance (www.oneworldalliance.com) Airline alliance including Aer Lingus, American Airlines, British Airways, Cathay Pacific and Qantas.
Sky Team (www.skyteam.com) Airline alliance including Air France, Alitalia and Delta Airlines.
Star Alliance (www.staralliance.com) Airline alliance including Air Canada, Air New Zealand, BMI, Lufthansa, Singapore Airlines, Thai Airways and United Airlines.

Note that departure tax for all three destinations is now included in the ticket price.

Africa

You can fly to Mauritius direct from a number of cities in Africa, including Johannesburg, Cape Town and Durban (South Africa), Antananarivo (Madagascar), Moroni (Comoros) and Nairobi (Kenya). Airlines serving these routes include Air Mauritius, Air Madagascar and South African Airways (SAA). Return fares from Johannesburg, for example, start at around R4000.

The Seychelles is not particularly well connected with Africa. The only direct flights are to and from Johannesburg and Nairobi with Air Seychelles and Kenya Airways. Again, the cheapest return trip from Johannesburg costs around R4000.

Réunion can be reached direct from Johannesburg, Madagascar, Comoros and Mayotte with Air Austral and Air Madagascar. A Johannesburg return flight costs upwards of R5000.

Rennies Travel (www.renniestravel.com) and **STA Travel** (www.statravel.co.za) have offices throughout southern Africa. Check their websites for branch locations.

Australia

The cheapest flights from Australia to this region are usually via Singapore or some other Southeast Asian hub. Another option is to fly via Europe or Africa. Look in the travel sections of the weekend newspapers, such as the *Age* in Melbourne and the *Sydney Morning Herald*. Two well-known agencies for discount fares with offices nationwide are **STA Travel** (☎ 1300 733 035; www.statravel.com.au) and **Flight Centre** (☎ 133 133; www.flightcentre.com.au).For online bookings, try www.travel.com.au.

Air Mauritius operates reasonably competitively priced direct flights from Sydney, Melbourne and Perth to Mauritius. Return fares from the west/east coast of Australia start at around A$1600/2000.

The cheapest way to get to Réunion is to fly to Mauritius and pick up the boat for St-Denis. A quicker alternative would obviously be to fly from Mauritius to St-Denis; the total cost for a round trip from west-/east-coast Australia would start at around A$2500/3000. Another option would be to fly via Paris and buy a separate Paris–Réunion return (see France, right).

Return flights to the Seychelles from Melbourne and Sydney via Singapore start at around A$1890 with both Air Seychelles (flying via Singapore) and Air Mauritius (flying via Mauritius).

Canada

All flights to the Indian Ocean from Canada connect through London or Paris. The *Globe & Mail*, *Toronto Star*, *Montreal Gazette* and *Vancouver Sun* carry travel agents' ads and are a good place to look for cheap fares.

Low-season return fares from Montreal/Vancouver to Mauritius should start at around C$6200/6600. You'll pay upwards of C$6200/6600 to Réunion and C$5500/6000 to the Seychelles.

A cheaper option is to take a discount flight to London or Paris and buy the onward ticket separately. Low-season return fares start at around C$560 from Montreal to London and C$800 to Paris. From Vancouver you'll pay upwards of C$750 to London and C$1200 to Paris.

Travel Cuts (☎ 800-667-2887; www.travelcuts.com) is Canada's national student travel agency. For online bookings try www.expedia.ca and www.travelocity.ca.

Continental Europe

Most visitors from Europe arrive on hotel-flight package holidays. Air Mauritius and Air Seychelles fly to a number of European destinations, including Paris, Zürich, Geneva, Rome, Munich, Frankfurt, Brussels and Vienna. Because of the French colonial connection, however, fares are generally cheaper from Paris than from other European cities. All flights from Europe to Réunion go via Paris. Note that prices shoot up during July and August and over the Christmas and New Year holidays.

FRANCE

Air Mauritius and Air France operate frequent flights from Paris to Mauritius. Round-trip fares with either airline start at roughly €800/1500 in the low/high season. Another alternative is to look for special offers between Paris and Réunion and then take the boat or a return flight to Mauritius from Réunion.

There's more competition – and consequently lower fares – on the Paris–Réunion route. Air France, Air Austral, Air Bourbon and Corsair (belonging to tour operator Nouvelles Frontières) all fly to St-Denis. Prices start in the region of €570/830 in the low/high season.

Air Seychelles and Air France cover the Paris–Seychelles route. Here you'll pay upwards of €800/1000 in the low/high season. Again, it's worth investigating the possibility of a cheap Paris–Réunion fare and then a return Réunion–Seychelles flight.

Recommended agencies:

Anyway (☎ 0892 893 892; www.anyway.fr)
Lastminute (☎ 0892 705 000; www.lastminute.fr)
Nouvelles Frontières (☎ 0825 000 747; www.nouvelles-frontieres.fr)
OTU Voyages (www.otu.fr) This agency specialises in student and youth travellers.
Voyageurs du Monde (☎ 01 40 15 11 15; www.vdm.com)

GERMANY

Condor flies direct from Frankfurt to Mauritius and the Seychelles, and from Munich to Mauritius. Prices are a steep €1180/1300 in the low/high season to Mauritius and €1150/1260 to the Seychelles. A slightly cheaper option for Mauritius is to fly via Paris on Air France: return fares from Frankfurt to Mauritius, for example, cost upwards of €1020/1230. Air Seychelles operates direct flights from Frankfurt, with fares starting at around €800/1000. And keep your eyes peeled for special discounts and promotions, which pop up from time to time.

Recommended agencies:

Expedia (www.expedia.de)
Just Travel (☎ 089 747 3330; www.justtravel.de)
Lastminute (☎ 01805 284 366; www.lastminute.de)
STA Travel (☎ 01805 456 422; www.statravel.de)

UK & Ireland

Both Air Mauritius and British Airways operate direct flights between London and Mauritius. Return fares come in at around UK£650/850 in the low/high season. A cheaper option, especially off season, is to fly Air France via Paris, which costs upwards of UK£500/830.

Flights for Réunion generally connect through Paris. The return London–Réunion fare with Air France is UK£660/860 in the low/high season, but you can get a cheaper deal by flying with one of the discount airlines on the London–Paris leg and buying a separate Paris–Réunion return.

Air Seychelles and British Airways cover the London to Seychelles route. In the case of British Airways, however, you have to change planes in Nairobi and the Nairobi–Mahè leg is operated by the Kenyan airline Regional Air (a franchise of BA) on a codesharing basis. A London–Mahè return ticket with Air Seychelles costs around UK£550/800 in the low/high season. Keep an eye out for special deals; fares sometimes drop as low as UK£500 return.

Discount air travel is big business in London. Advertisements for many travel agencies appear in the travel pages of the weekend broadsheet newspapers, and in *Time Out*, the *Evening Standard* and the free magazine *TNT*.

Recommended travel agencies:

Bridge the World (☎ 0870 444 7474; www.b-t-w.co.uk)
Flightbookers (☎ 0870 010 7000; www.ebookers.com)
Flight Centre (☎ 0870 890 8099; flightcentre.co.uk)
North-South Travel (☎ 01245 608 291; www.northsouthtravel.co.uk) North-South Travel donates part of its profit to projects in the developing world.
Quest Travel (☎ 0870 442 3542; www.questtravel.com)
STA Travel (☎ 0870 160 0599; www.statravel.co.uk)
Trailfinders (www.trailfinders.co.uk)
Travel Bag (☎ 0870 890 1456; www.travelbag.co.uk)

USA

The majority of flights to the Indian Ocean from the USA connect through London or Paris. A through ticket from New York to Mauritius, for example, will cost upwards of US$1300/1700 in the low/high season. Expect to pay in the region of US$1700/2300 for Réunion and US$1600/2200 for the Seychelles.

Rather than getting a through ticket, however, it's usually cheaper to take a discount flight to London or Paris and buy the onward ticket separately. A return ticket from New York to London costs around US$250 to US$300 in the low season; from New York to Paris around US$400. From Los Angeles you'll pay upwards of US$450 to London and US$550 to Paris.

The *New York Times*, the *LA Times*, the *Chicago Tribune* and the *San Francisco Examiner* all produce weekly travel sections in which you'll find any number of travel agents' ads. Council Travel and STA Travel have offices in major cities nationwide. The magazine **Travel Unlimited** (PO Box 1058, Allston, Mass 02134) publishes details of the cheapest airfares and courier possibilities for destinations all over the world from the USA.

Discount travel agents in the USA are known as consolidators (although you won't see a sign on the door saying 'Consolidator'). San Francisco is the ticket consolidator capital of America, although some good deals can be found in Los Angeles, New York and other big cities.

The following agencies are recommended for online bookings:

Cheap Tickets (www.cheaptickets.com)
Expedia (www.expedia.com)
American Express (www.itn.net)
Lowest Fare (www.lowestfare.com)
Orbitz and Go (www.orbitz.com)
STA Travel (www.sta.com)
Travelocity (www.travelocity.com)

SEA

Opportunities for sea travel to Mauritius, Réunion and the Seychelles are limited. There's just one passenger-carrying cargo boat, the *Mauritius Trochetia*, which sails from Tamatave in Madagascar to Réunion (28 hours) and Mauritius (47 hours) twice a month. Return fares to Réunion start at €150 for a 2nd-class cabin. The equivalent fare for Mauritius is €217. For bookings and information contact **Auximad** (☎ 020 222 2502; auxiship@dts.mg; 18 Rue JJ Rabealrivelo, 101 Antananarivo) in Madagascar. For contacts in Réunion and Mauritius refer to p220 and p140.

The only other alternatives are passing cruise liners, yachts and the occasional cargo-passenger ship. The cost is high, unless you can work your way as a crew member. Cruise liners usually only stop for a day or two in each destination, but cruises do offer the opportunity of seeing the outer islands in the Seychelles group.

Companies offering Indian Ocean cruises:

African Safari Club (www.africansafariclub.com)
La Compagnie des Alizés (www.voile-reunion.com)
Seabourn (www.seabourn.com)
Silversea (www.silversea.com)
Swan Hellenic (www.swan-hellenic.co.uk)

GETTING AROUND

AIR

Air Mauritius, Air Austral (based in Réunion) and Air Seychelles operate a comprehensive network of flights within the region. Services are frequent and generally reliable and there should be no problem getting a seat outside the peak holiday periods (see p281). For information about fares and schedules, as well as airline contact details, see p139 for Mauritius, p220 for Réunion and p274 for the Seychelles.

Air Passes

If you are going to be island-hopping around the region, you can cut the cost of individual fares by buying an Indian Ocean Pass. The pass covers Air Mauritius, Air Austral and Air Seychelles flights between Mauritius (including Rodrigues), Réunion and the Seychelles (including Praslin) and also their services to Madagascar, Mayotte, Comoros and the Maldives. The pass, which is valid for two months, must be purchased outside the region. You must make a minimum of three flights and the price is calculated accordingly; Réunion to Mauritius, for example, is around €90 one way; Mauritius to the Seychelles around €180; and the Seychelles to Réunion around €230. For details of prices and other restrictions contact the participating airlines.

BOAT

There are two passenger services between Mauritius and Réunion: the fast, new *Mauritius Trochetia* and the *Mauritius Pride*. For details of schedules, fares and local contact details, see the Transport Directories for Mauritius (p139) and Réunion (p220).

Health by Dr Caroline Evans

CONTENTS

Before You Go	**291**
Insurance	291
Medical Checklist	291
Internet Resources	292
Further Reading	292
In Transit	**292**
Deep Vein Thrombosis (DVT)	292
Jet Lag & Motion Sickness	292
In Mauritius, Réunion & Seychelles	**292**
Availability & Cost of Health Care	292
Infectious Diseases	292
Travellers' Diarrhoea	294
Environmental Hazards	295

As long as you stay up to date with your vaccinations and take some basic preventive measures, you'd have to be pretty unlucky to succumb to most of the health hazards covered in this chapter. Mauritius, and to a lesser extent Réunion and the Seychelles, certainly have a fair selection of tropical diseases on offer, but you're much more likely to get a bout of diarrhoea or a sprained ankle than an exotic disease.

BEFORE YOU GO

A little planning before departure, particularly for pre-existing illnesses, will save you a lot of trouble later. Before a long trip, get a checkup from your dentist and from your doctor if you have any regular medication or chronic illness, eg high blood pressure or asthma. You should also organise spare contact lenses and glasses (and take your optical prescription with you); get a first aid and medical kit together; and arrange necessary vaccinations.

Travellers can register with the **International Association for Medical Advice to Travellers** (IAMAT; www.iamat.org). Its website can help travellers to find a doctor who has recognised training. You might like to consider doing a first aid course (contact the Red Cross or St John's Ambulance) or attending a remote medicine first aid course, such as that offered by the **Royal Geographical Society** (www.wildernessmedicaltraining.co.uk).

If you are bringing medications with you, carry them in their original containers, clearly labelled. A signed and dated letter from your physician describing all medical conditions and medications, including generic names, is also a good idea. If carrying syringes or needles be sure to have a physician's letter documenting their medical necessity.

INSURANCE

Find out in advance whether your insurance plan will make payments directly to providers or will reimburse you later for overseas health expenditures (in many countries doctors expect payment in cash). It's vital to ensure that your travel insurance will cover the emergency transport required to get you to a good hospital, or all the way home, by air and with a medical attendant if necessary. Not all insurance covers this, so check the contract carefully. If you need medical help, your insurance company might be able to help locate the nearest hospital or clinic, or you can ask at your hotel. In an emergency, contact your embassy or consulate.

Membership of the **African Medical and Research Foundation** (AMREF; www.amref.org) provides an air evacuation service in medical emergencies in some African countries, sometimes including Mauritius, Réunion and the Seychelles, as well as air ambulance transfers between medical facilities. Money paid by members for this service goes into providing grass-roots medical assistance for local people.

MEDICAL CHECKLIST

It is a very good idea to carry a medical and first aid kit with you, to help yourself in the case of minor illness or injury. Following is a list of items you should consider packing.

- antidiarrhoeal drugs (eg loperamide)
- acetaminophen (paracetamol) or aspirin
- anti-inflammatory drugs (eg ibuprofen)
- antihistamines (for hayfever and allergic reactions)

- antibacterial ointment (eg Bactroban) for cuts and abrasions (prescription only)
- steroid cream or hydrocortisone cream (for allergic rashes)
- bandages, gauze, gauze rolls
- adhesive or paper tape
- scissors, safety pins, tweezers
- thermometer
- pocket knife
- DEET-containing insect repellent for the skin
- sunblock
- oral rehydration salts
- iodine tablets (for water purification)
- syringes and sterile needles (if travelling to remote areas)

INTERNET RESOURCES

There is a wealth of travel health advice on the Internet. **LonelyPlanet.com** (www.lonelyplanet.com) is a good place to start. The World Health Organization publishes a superb book called *International Travel and Health*, which is revised annually and is available online at no cost at www.who.int/ith/. Other websites of general interest are **MD Travel Health** (www.mdtravelhealth.com), the **Centers for Disease Control and Prevention** (www.cdc.gov) and **Fit for Travel** (www.fitfortravel.scot.nhs.uk).

You may also like to consult your government's travel health website, if one is available:

Australia (www.dfat.gov.au/travel/)
Canada (www.hc-sc.gc.ca/pphb-dgspsp/tmp-pmv/pub_e.html)
UK (www.doh.gov.uk/traveladvice/index.htm)
USA (www.cdc.gov/travel/)

FURTHER READING

A Comprehensive Guide to Wilderness and Travel Medicine by Eric A Weiss (1998)
Healthy Travel by Jane Wilson-Howarth (1999)
Healthy Travel Africa by Isabelle Young (2000)
How to Stay Healthy Abroad by Richard Dawood (2002)
Travel in Health by Graham Fry (1994)
Travel with Children by Cathy Lanigan (2004)

IN TRANSIT

DEEP VEIN THROMBOSIS (DVT)

Blood clots can form in the legs during flights, chiefly because of prolonged immobility. This formation of clots is known as deep vein thrombosis (DVT). Although most blood clots are reabsorbed uneventfully, some might break off and travel through the blood vessels to the lungs, where they could cause life-threatening complications.

The chief symptom of DVT is swelling or pain of the foot, ankle or calf. When a blood clot travels to the lungs, it may cause chest pain and breathing difficulty. Travellers with any of these symptoms should immediately seek medical attention.

To prevent the development of DVT during flights, walk about the cabin, perform isometric compressions of the leg muscles (ie contract the leg muscles while sitting), drink plenty of fluids, and avoid alcohol.

JET LAG & MOTION SICKNESS

If you're crossing more than five time zones you could suffer jet lag, resulting in insomnia, fatigue, malaise or nausea. To avoid jet lag, try drinking plenty of fluids (nonalcoholic) and eating light meals. Upon arrival, get exposure to natural sunlight and readjust your schedule (for meals, sleep, etc) as soon as possible.

Antihistamines such as dimenhydrinate (Dramamine) and meclizine (Antivert, Bonine) are usually the first choice for treating motion sickness. The main side effect of these drugs is drowsiness. A herbal alternative is ginger (ginger tea, biscuits or crystallised ginger).

IN MAURITIUS, RÉUNION & SEYCHELLES

AVAILABILITY & COST OF HEALTH CARE

Health care in Mauritius and Réunion is generally excellent; the Seychelles is pretty good by African standards, but some travellers have been critical of the standard of the public health system. Generally, public hospitals offer the cheapest service, but may not have the most up-to-date equipment and medications; private hospitals and clinics are more expensive but tend to have more advanced drugs and equipment and better trained medical staff.

INFECTIOUS DISEASES

It's a formidable list but, as we say, a few precautions go a long way...

RECOMMENDED VACCINATIONS

The **World Health Organization** (www.who.int/en/) recommends that all travellers be covered for diphtheria, tetanus, measles, mumps, rubella and polio, as well as for hepatitis B, regardless of their destination.

Although no vaccinations are officially required, many doctors recommend Hepatitis A and B immunisations just to be sure; a yellow fever certificate is an entry requirement if travelling from an infected region (see p294).

Cholera

Cholera is usually only a problem during natural or artificial disasters, eg war, floods or earthquakes, although small outbreaks can also occur at other times. Travellers are rarely affected. It is caused by a bacteria and spread via contaminated drinking water. The main symptom is profuse watery diarrhoea, which causes debilitation if fluids are not replaced quickly. Most cases of cholera can be avoided by paying close attention to the drinking water available and by avoiding potentially contaminated food. Treatment is by fluid replacement (orally or via a drip), but sometimes antibiotics are needed. Self-treatment is not advised.

Diphtheria

Diphtheria is spread through close respiratory contact. It usually results in a temperature and a severe sore throat. It is more of a problem for long stays than for short-term trips. The vaccine is given as an injection alone or with tetanus, and lasts 10 years.

Hepatitis A

Hepatitis A is spread through contaminated food (particularly shellfish) and water. It causes jaundice and, although it is rarely fatal, it can cause prolonged lethargy and delayed recovery. If you've had hepatitis A, you shouldn't drink alcohol for up to six months afterwards, but once you've recovered, there won't be any long-term problems. The first symptoms include dark urine and a yellow colour to the whites of the eyes. Sometimes a fever and abdominal pain might be present. Hepatitis A vaccine (Avaxim, VAQTA, Havrix) is given as an injection: a single dose will give protection for up to a year, and a booster after a year gives 10-year protection. Hepatitis A and typhoid vaccines can also be given as a single dose vaccine, Hepatyrix or Viatim.

Hepatitis B

Hepatitis B is spread through infected blood, contaminated needles and sexual intercourse. It can also be spread from an infected mother to the baby during childbirth. It affects the liver, causing jaundice and occasionally liver failure. Most people recover completely, but some people might be chronic carriers of the virus, which could lead eventually to cirrhosis or liver cancer. Those visiting high-risk areas for long periods or those with increased social or occupational risk should be immunised. Many countries now routinely give hepatitis B as part of the routine childhood vaccination. It is given singly or can be given at the same time as hepatitis A (Hepatyrix).

A course will give protection for at least five years. It can be given over four weeks or six months.

HIV

Human immunodeficiency virus (HIV), the virus that causes acquired immune deficiency syndrome (AIDS), is an enormous problem throughout Africa, but is most acutely felt in sub-Saharan Africa. The impact of the virus on South Africa's health system is devastating. The virus is spread through infected blood and blood products, by sexual intercourse with an infected partner and from an infected mother to her baby during childbirth and breast-feeding. It can be spread through 'blood to blood' contacts, such as with contaminated instruments during medical, dental, acupuncture and other body-piercing procedures, and through sharing used intravenous needles. At present there is no cure; medication that might keep the disease under control is available, but these drugs are too expensive for the overwhelming majority of Africans, and are not readily available for travellers either. If you think you might have been infected with HIV, a blood test is necessary; a three-month gap after exposure and before testing is required to allow antibodies to appear in the blood.

Malaria

The risk of malaria in Mauritius and Réunion is extremely low; there is no risk in the Seychelles. The disease is caused by a parasite in the bloodstream spread via the bite of the female *Anopheles* mosquito. The early stages of malaria include headaches, fevers, generalised aches and pains, and malaise, which could be mistaken for flu. Other symptoms can include abdominal pain, diarrhoea and a cough. Several different drugs are used to prevent malaria, and new ones are in the pipeline – up-to-date advice is essential as some medication is more suitable for some travellers than others. There are antimalaria pills available and it is best to ask your doctor for further advice.

Meningococcal Meningitis

Meningococcal infection is spread through close respiratory contact and is more likely in crowded situations, such as dormitories, buses and clubs. Infection is uncommon in travellers. Vaccination is recommended for long stays and is especially important towards the end of the dry season. Symptoms include a fever, severe headache, neck stiffness and a red rash. Immediate medical treatment is necessary.

Poliomyelitis

Poliomyelitis is generally spread through contaminated food and water. It is one of the vaccines given in childhood and should be boosted every 10 years, either orally (a drop on the tongue) or as an injection. Polio can be carried asymptomatically (ie showing no symptoms) and could cause a transient fever. In rare cases it causes weakness or paralysis of one or more muscles, which might be permanent.

Rabies

Rabies is spread by receiving the bites or licks of an infected animal on broken skin. It is always fatal once the clinical symptoms start (which might be up to several months after an infected bite), so post bite vaccination should be given as soon as possible. Post bite vaccination (whether or not you've been vaccinated before the bite) prevents the virus from spreading to the central nervous system. Three preventive injections are needed over a month. If you have not been vaccinated you will need a course of five injections starting 24 hours after being bitten or as soon as possible after the injury. If you have been vaccinated, you will need fewer post bite injections, and have more time to seek medical help.

Tuberculosis (TB)

TB is spread through close respiratory contact and occasionally by infected milk or milk products. BCG vaccination is a live vaccine and should not be given to pregnant women or immunocompromised individuals.

TB can be asymptomatic, only being picked up on a routine chest X-ray. Alternatively, it can cause a cough, weight loss or fever, sometimes months or even years after exposure.

Typhoid

Typhoid is spread through food or water contaminated by infected human faeces. The first symptom is usually a fever or a pink rash on the abdomen. Sometimes septicaemia (blood poisoning) can occur. A typhoid vaccine (Typhim Vi, Typherix) will give protection for three years. In some countries, the oral vaccine Vivotif is also available. Antibiotics are usually given as treatment, and death is rare unless septicaemia occurs.

Yellow Fever

Although not a problem in Mauritius, Réunion or the Seychelles, travellers should still carry a certificate as evidence of vaccination if they have recently been in an infected country. For a list of these countries visit the **World Health Organization website** (www.who.int/wer/) or the **Centers for Disease Control and Prevention website** (www.cdc.gov/travel/blusheet.htm). A traveller without a legally required, up-to-date certificate may be vaccinated and detained in isolation at the port of arrival for up to 10 days or possibly repatriated.

TRAVELLERS' DIARRHOEA

Although it's not inevitable that you will get diarrhoea while travelling in the region, it's certainly possible. Sometimes dietary changes, such as increased spices or oils, are the cause. To avoid diarrhoea, only eat fresh fruits or vegetables if cooked or peeled, and be wary of dairy products that might contain unpasteurised milk. Although freshly cooked food can often be a safe option, plates or serving utensils might be dirty, so you should be highly selective when eating food from street vendors (make sure that cooked food is piping hot all the way through). If you develop diarrhoea, be sure to drink plenty of fluids, preferably an oral rehydration solution containing water (lots), and some salt and sugar. A few loose stools don't require treatment, but if you start having more than four or five stools a day, you should start taking an antibiotic (usually a quinoline drug, such as ciprofloxacin or norfloxacin) and an antidiarrhoeal agent (such as loperamide) if you are not within easy reach of a toilet. However, if diarrhoea is bloody, persists for more than 72 hours or is accompanied by fever, shaking chills or severe abdominal pain, you should seek medical attention.

Amoebic Dysentery

Contracted by eating contaminated food and water, amoebic dysentery causes blood and mucus in the faeces. It can be relatively mild and tends to come on gradually, but seek medical advice if you think you have the illness, as it won't clear up without treatment (which is with specific antibiotics).

Giardiasis

Giardiasis, like amoebic dysentery, is also caused by ingesting contaminated food or water. The illness usually appears a week or more after you have been exposed to the offending parasite. Giardiasis might cause only a short-lived bout of typical travellers' diarrhoea, but it can also cause persistent diarrhoea. Ideally, seek medical advice if you suspect you have giardiasis, but if you are in a remote area you could start a course of antibiotics.

ENVIRONMENTAL HAZARDS

Heat Exhaustion

This condition occurs following heavy sweating and excessive fluid loss with inadequate replacement of fluids and salt, and is particularly common in hot climates when taking unaccustomed exercise before full acclimatisation. Symptoms include headache, dizziness and tiredness. Dehydration is already happening by the time you feel thirsty – aim to drink sufficient water to produce pale, diluted urine. Self-treatment is by fluid replacement with water and/or fruit juice, and cooling by cold water and fans. The treatment of the salt-loss component consists of consuming salty fluids as in soup, and adding a little more table salt to foods than usual.

Heatstroke

Heat exhaustion is a precursor to the much more serious condition of heatstroke. In this case there is damage to the sweating mechanism, with an excessive rise in body temperature; irrational and hyperactive behaviour; and eventually loss of consciousness and death. Rapid cooling by spraying the body with water and fanning is ideal. Emergency fluid and electrolyte replacement is usually also required by intravenous drip.

Insect Bites & Stings

Mosquitoes in the region rarely carry malaria or dengue fever, but they (and other insects) can cause irritation and infected bites. To avoid these, take the same precautions as you would for avoiding malaria, including wearing long pants and long-sleeved shirts, using mosquito repellents, avoiding highly scented perfumes or aftershaves etc. Bee and wasp stings cause major problems only to those who have a severe allergy to the stings (anaphylaxis), in which case carry an adrenaline (epinephrine) injection.

Leeches may be present in damp rainforest conditions; they attach themselves to your skin to suck your blood. Salt or a lighted cigarette end will make them fall off. Ticks can cause skin infections and other more serious diseases. If a tick is found attached, press down around the tick's head with tweezers, grab the head and gently pull upwards.

Water

As a general rule, tap water in Mauritius, Réunion and the Seychelles is safe to drink, but always take care immediately after a cyclone or cyclonic storm. Never drink from streams as it might put you at risk of waterborne diseases.

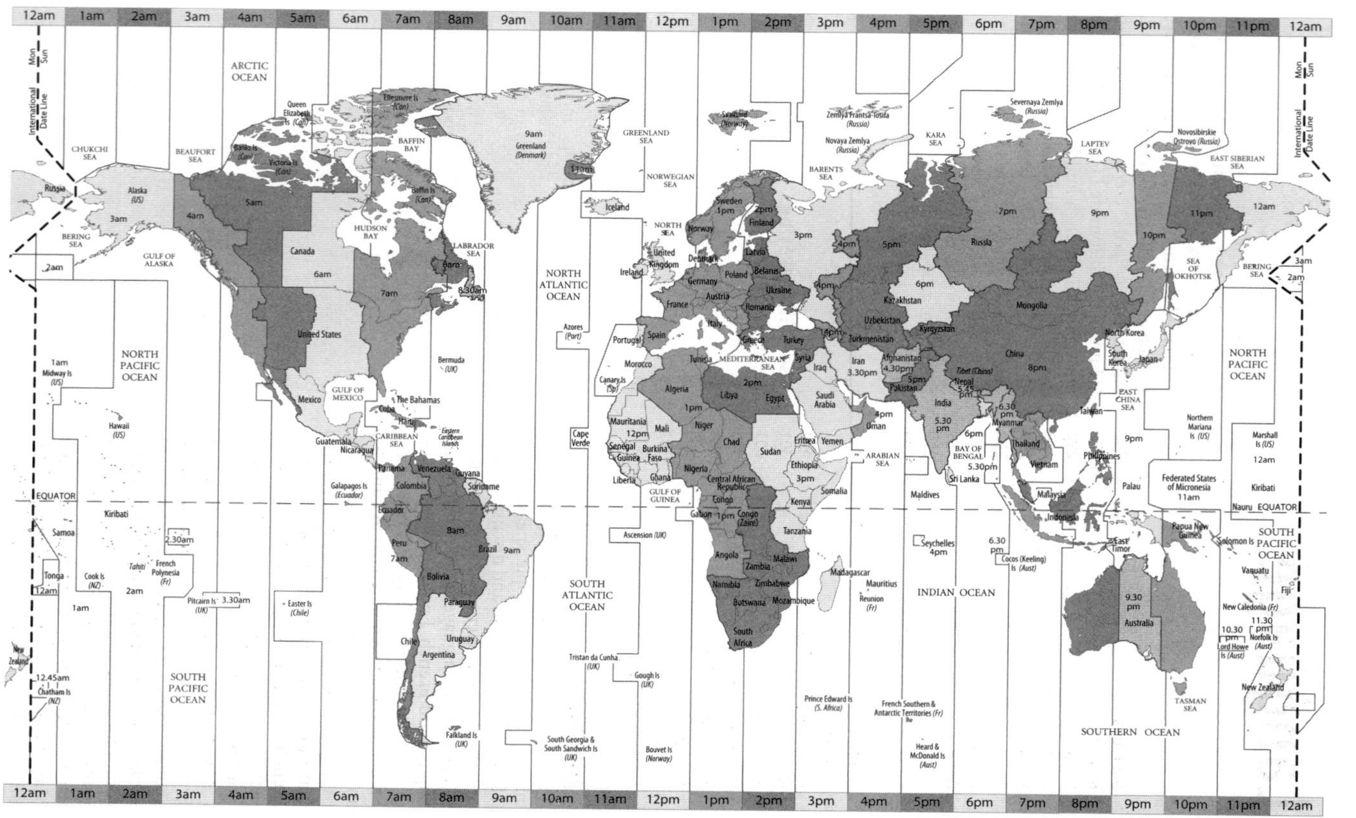
12am
1am
2am
3am
4am
5am
6am
7am
8am
9am
10am
11am
12pm
1pm
2pm
3pm
4pm
5pm
6pm
7pm
8pm
9pm
10pm
11pm
12am
International Date Line
Mon
Sun
EQUATOR
ARCTIC OCEAN
NORTH PACIFIC OCEAN
SOUTH PACIFIC OCEAN
NORTH ATLANTIC OCEAN
SOUTH ATLANTIC OCEAN
INDIAN OCEAN
SOUTHERN OCEAN
CHUKCHI SEA
BERING SEA
GULF OF ALASKA
BEAUFORT SEA
HUDSON BAY
BAFFIN BAY
LABRADOR SEA
GULF OF MEXICO
CARIBBEAN SEA
GREENLAND SEA
NORWEGIAN SEA
NORTH SEA
BARENTS SEA
KARA SEA
LAPTEV SEA
EAST SIBERIAN SEA
SEA OF OKHOTSK
EAST CHINA SEA
BAY OF BENGAL
ARABIAN SEA
MEDITERRANEAN SEA
GULF OF GUINEA
TASMAN SEA
Alaska (US)
Canada
United States
Mexico
Greenland (Denmark)
Iceland
Brazil
Argentina
Russia
China
India
Australia
New Zealand

Language

CONTENTS

Mauritius	297
Réunion	297
Seychelles	298
What's a Creole?	298
French	**298**
Pronunciation	298
Be Polite!	298
Gender	299
Accommodation	299
Conversation & Essentials	300
Directions	300
Health	300
Emergencies	301
Language Difficulties	301
Numbers	301
Paperwork	301
Question Words	301
Shopping & Services	302
Time & Dates	302
Transport	302
Travel With Children	303

MAURITIUS

It's said that when Mauritians have a community meeting, the people speak Creole, take minutes in English and discuss the outcome with government officials in French.

The official languages of the country are English and French. English is used mainly in government and business literature. French is the spoken language in educated and cultural circles, and is used in newspapers and magazines. You'll probably find that most people will first speak to you in French and only switch to English once they realise that you don't understand a word they're saying.

Creole, the common bond, derives from French and has similarities with creoles spoken elsewhere. Ironically, the Creole spoken in Mauritius and Seychelles is more comprehensible to French people than the patois of Réunion, even though Réunion itself is thoroughly French. Most Indo-Mauritians speak Bhojpuri, derived from a Bihari dialect of Hindi.

There are major differences between the pronunciation and usage of Creole and standard French, but if you don't speak any French at all, you're doubly disadvantaged. *Parlez créole/Speak creole*, by Rose Hill (Mauritius: Editions de l'Océan indien) is a phrasebook in French and English.

For Mauritian Creole starters, you might like to try the following phrases:

How are you? *Ki manière?*
Fine, thanks. *Mon byen, mersi.*
I don't understand. *Mo pas comprend.*
OK. *Correc.*
Not OK. *Pas correc.*
he, she, it *li*
Do you have ...? *Ou éna ...?*
I'd like ... *Mo oulé ...*
I'm thirsty. *Mo soif.*
Phoenix beer *la bière zarnier* (literally 'spider beer' – the label looks like one)
Cheers! *Tapeta!*
Great! *Formidabe!*

RÉUNION

French is the official language of Réunion, but Creole is the most widely spoken. Few people speak English.

The Creole of Réunion is beyond the comprehension even of most French people. A word that means one thing in French can mean something completely different in Creole, and where a word does have the same meaning, it's usually pronounced differently in Creole.

Creole has quite a number of *bons mots* and charming idioms, which are often the result of Hindi, Arab and Malagasy influences or misinterpretations of the original French word. *Bonbon la fesse* (bum toffee) is a suppository, *conserves* (preserves) are sunglasses, the *bazaar* is the market, and *coeur d'amant* (lover's heart) is a cardamom seed. *Coco* is your head, *caze* is your house, *marmaille* is your child, *baba* is your baby, *band* means 'family', *le fait noir* means 'night', and, if the stars are out, remember that *mi aime jou* means 'I love you'.

In Creole pronunciation there are two basic rules: **r** is generally not pronounced (when it is, it's pronounced lightly); and the soft **j** and **ch** sounds of French are pronounced as 'z' and 's' respectively. For example, *manzay* for 'manger' (to eat), *zamais* for 'jamais' (never) and *sontay* for 'chanter' (to sing).

There are French-Creole dictionaries for sale in Réunion, but unfortunately there are no English-Creole dictionaries.

SEYCHELLES

English and French are the official languages of the Seychelles. Most people speak both, although French Creole (known as Kreol Seselwa) is the lingua franca. Kreol Seselwa was 'rehabilitated' and made semi-official in 1981, and is increasingly used in newspapers and literature. These days, most Seychellois will use English when speaking to tourists, French when conducting business, and Creole in the home.

Seychelles Creole is similar to that of Mauritius and Martinique, but differs remarkably from that of Réunion. In the local patois, the soft pronunciation of certain French consonants is hardened and some syllables are dropped completely. The soft **j** becomes 'z', for example. The following Creole phrases may help get you started:

Good morning/ Good afternoon.	*Bonzour.*
How are you?	*Comman sava?*
Fine, thanks.	*Mon byen, mersi.*
What's your name?	*Ki mannyer ou appel?*
My name is ...	*Mon appel ...*
Where do you live?	*Koté ou resté?*
I don't understand.	*Mon pas konpran.*
I like it.	*Mon kontan.*
Where is ...?	*Ol i ...?*
How much is that?	*Kombyen sa?*
I'm thirsty.	*Mon soif.*
Can I have a beer, please?	*Mon kapa ganny en labyer silvouplé?*

WHAT'S A CREOLE?

When people of differing native languages come into contact and develop a simple mode of communication that is based in both languages, the product is known as a pidgin. Once this 'neo-language' has become established to the point where it possesses a defined grammatical structure and writing system, and children learn it as a first language, it becomes a creole.

The creoles of Mauritius, Réunion and Seychelles are a blend of French and assorted African languages, but there are a number of regional variations; Seychelles Creole is fairly similar to that of Mauritius, but differs significantly from the Creole spoken in Réunion.

FRENCH

Along with the local creoles, French is spoken in all three destinations. You'll find that menus on the islands are mostly in French, with English variations in some cases.

For a more comprehensive guide to the French language, pick up a copy of Lonely Planet's *French Phrasebook*.

PRONUNCIATION

Most letters in French are pronounced more or less the same as their English counterparts. Here are a few that may cause confusion:

j	as the 's' in 'leisure', eg *jour* (day); written as 'zh' in our pronunciation guides
c	before **e** and **i**, as the 's' in 'sit'; before **a**, **o** and **u**, it's pronounced as English 'k'. When underscored with a 'cedilla' (ç), it's always pronounced as the 's' in 'sit'.
r	pronounced from the back of the throat while constricting the muscles to restrict the flow of air
n, m	where a syllable ends in a single **n** or **m**, these letters are not pronounced, but the preceding vowel is given a nasal pronunciation

BE POLITE!

An important distinction is made in French between *tu* and *vous*, which both mean 'you'; *tu* is only used when addressing people you know well, children or animals. If you're addressing an adult who isn't a personal friend, *vous* should be used unless the person invites you to use *tu*. In general, younger people insist less on this distinction between polite and informal, and you will find that in many cases they use *tu* from the beginning of an acquaintance.

The polite form is used in all instances in this guide unless indicated by 'inf' (meaning 'informal') in brackets.

LANGUAGE

GENDER

All nouns in French are either masculine or feminine and adjectives reflect the gender of the noun they modify. The feminine form of many nouns and adjectives is indicated by a silent **e** added to the masculine form, as in *ami* and *amie* (the masculine and feminine for 'friend').

In the following phrases both masculine and feminine forms have been indicated where necessary. The masculine form comes first and is separated from the feminine by a slash. The gender of a noun is often indicated by a preceding article: 'the/a/some', *le/un/du* (m), *la/une/de la* (f); or one of the possessive adjectives, 'my/your/his/her', *mon/ton/son* (m), *ma/ta/sa* (f). With French, unlike English, the possessive adjective agrees in number and gender with the thing in question: 'his/her mother', *sa mère*.

MAKING A RESERVATION

(for phone or written requests)

To ...	*A l'attention de ...*
From ...	*De la part de ...*
Date	*Date*
I'd like to book ...	*Je voudrais réserver ...* (see the list under 'Accommodation' for bed and room options)
in the name of ...	*au nom de ...*
from ... (date) **to ...**	*du ... au ...*
credit card	*carte de crédit*
number	*numéro*
expiry date	*date d'expiration*
Please confirm availability and price.	*Veuillez confirmer la disponibilité et le prix.*

ACCOMMODATION

I'm looking for a ...	*Je cherche ...*	zher shersh ...
camping ground	*un camping*	un kom·peeng
guesthouse	*une pension (de famille)*	ewn pon·syon (der fa·mee·ler)
hotel	*un hôtel*	un o·tel
youth hostel	*une auberge de jeunesse*	ewn o·berzh der zher·nes

Where is a cheap hotel?
Où est-ce qu'on peut trouver un hôtel pas cher?
oo es·kon per troo·vay un o·tel pa shair

What is the address?
Quelle est l'adresse?
kel e la·dres

Could you write it down, please?
Est-ce que vous pourriez l'écrire, s'il vous plaît?
e·sker voo poo·ryay lay·kreer seel voo play

Do you have any rooms available?
Est-ce que vous avez des chambres libres?
e·sker voo·za·vay day shom·brer lee·brer

I'd like (a) ...	*Je voudrais ...*	zher voo·dray ...
single room	*une chambre à un lit*	ewn shom·brer a un lee
double-bed room	*une chambre avec un grand lit*	ewn shom·brer a·vek un gron lee
twin room with two beds	*une chambre avec des lits jumeaux*	ewn shom·brer a·vek day lee zhew·mo
room with a bathroom	*une chambre avec une salle de bains*	ewn shom·brer a·vek ewn sal der bun
to share a dorm	*coucher dans un dortoir*	koo·sher don zun dor·twa

How much is it ...?	*Quel est le prix ...?*	kel e ler pree ...
per night	*par nuit*	par nwee
per person	*par personne*	par per·son

May I see the room?
Est-ce que je peux voir la chambre? es·ker zher per vwa la shom·brer

Where is the bathroom?
Où est la salle de bains? oo e la sal der bun

Where is the toilet?
Où sont les toilettes? oo·son lay twa·let

I'm leaving today.
Je pars aujourd'hui. zher par o·zhoor·dwee

We're leaving today.
Nous partons aujourd'hui. noo par·ton o·zhoor·dwee

air-conditioned
climatisée klee ma·tee zay

a shower
une douche oon doosh

a washbasin
un lavabo un la·va·bo

hot water
eau chaude o shod

a balcony
un balcon un bal·kon

a window
une fenêtre oon fe·netr

a terrace
une terrace oon tay·ras
a sea view
une vue sur la mer oon vue sewr la mair
full board
pension complète pon·syon kom·plet
half board
demi-pension day·mee pon·syon
dining room
la salle à manger la sal a mon·zhair
kitchen
la cuisine la kwee·zeen
television
une télévision ewn tay·lay·vee·zyon
swimming pool
une piscine ewn pee·seen
towel
une serviettes ewn sair·vyet
(not) included
(non) compris (non) kom·pree
on request
sur demande sewr der·mond
price/tariff
le prix/tarif ler pree/ta·reef

CONVERSATION & ESSENTIALS

Hello.	*Bonjour.*	bon·zhoor
Goodbye.	*Au revoir.*	o·rer·vwa
Yes.	*Oui.*	wee
No.	*Non.*	no
Please.	*S'il vous plaît.*	seel voo play
Thank you.	*Merci.*	mair·see
You're welcome.	*Je vous en prie.*	zher voo·zon pree
	De rien. (inf)	der ree·en
Excuse me.	*Excuse-moi.*	ek·skew·zay·mwa
Sorry. (forgive me)	*Pardon.*	par·don

What's your name?
Comment vous appelez-vous? ko·mon voo·za·pay·lay voo
Comment tu t'appelles? (inf) ko·mon tew ta·pel
My name is ...
Je m'appelle ... zher ma·pel ...
Where are you from?
De quel pays êtes-vous? der kel pay·ee et·voo
De quel pays es-tu? (inf) der kel pay·ee e·tew
I'm from ...
Je viens de ... zher vyen der ...
I like ...
J'aime ... zhem ...
I don't like ...
Je n'aime pas ... zher nem pa ...
Just a minute.
Une minute. ewn mee·newt

DIRECTIONS

Where is ...?
Où est ...? oo e ...
Go straight ahead.
Continuez tout droit. kon·teen·way too drwa
Turn left.
Tournez à gauche. toor·nay a gosh
Turn right.
Tournez à droite. toor·nay a drwat
at the corner
au coin o kwun
at the traffic lights
aux feux o fer

behind	*derrière*	dair·ryair
in front of	*devant*	der·von
far (from)	*loin (de)*	lwun (der)
near (to)	*près (de)*	pray (der)
opposite	*en face de*	on fas der

beach	*la plage*	la plazh
bridge	*le pont*	ler pon
church	*l'église*	lay·gleez
island	*l'île*	leel
lake	*le lac*	ler lak
museum	*le musée*	ler mew·zay
sea	*la mer*	la mair
tourist office	*l'office de tourisme*	lo·fees der too·rees·mer

SIGNS

Entrée	Entrance
Sortie	Exit
Renseignements	Information
Ouvert	Open
Fermé	Closed
Interdit	Prohibited
Chambres Libres	Rooms Available
Complet	Full/No Vacancies
(Commissariat de) Police	Police Station
Toilettes/WC	Toilets
Hommes	Men
Femmes	Women

HEALTH

I'm ill.	*Je suis malade.*	zher swee ma·lad
It hurts here.	*J'ai une douleur ici.*	zhay ewn doo·ler ee·see

I'm ...	*Je suis ...*	zher swee ...
asthmatic	*asthmatique*	(z)as·ma·teek
diabetic	*diabétique*	dee·a·bay·teek
epileptic	*épileptique*	(z)ay·pee·lep·teek

LANGUAGE

EMERGENCIES

Help!
Au secours! o skoor

There's been an accident!
Il y a eu un accident! eel ya ew un ak·see·don

I'm lost.
Je me suis égaré/e. (m/f) zhe me swee·zay·ga·ray

Leave me alone!
Fichez-moi la paix! fee·shay·mwa la pay

Call ...!	*Appelez ...!*	a·play ...
a doctor	*un médecin*	un mayd·sun
the police	*la police*	la po·lees

I'm allergic to ...	*Je suis allergique ...*	zher swee za·lair·zheek ...
antibiotics	*aux antibiotiques*	o zon·tee·byo·teek
aspirin	*à l'aspirine*	a las·pee·reen
bees	*aux abeilles*	o za·bay·yer
nuts	*aux noix*	o nwa
peanuts	*aux cacahuètes*	o ka·ka·wet
penicillin	*à la pénicilline*	a la pay·nee·see·leen

antiseptic	*l'antiseptique*	lon·tee·sep·teek
aspirin	*l'aspirine*	las·pee·reen
condoms	*des préservatifs*	day pray·zair·va·teef
contraceptive	*le contraceptif*	ler kon·tra·sep·teef
diarrhoea	*la diarrhée*	la dya·ray
medicine	*le médicament*	ler may·dee·ka·mon
nausea	*la nausée*	la no·zay
sunblock cream	*la crème solaire*	la krem so·lair
tampons	*des tampons hygiéniques*	day tom·pon ee·zhen·eek

LANGUAGE DIFFICULTIES

Do you speak English?
Parlez-vous anglais? par·lay·voo ong·lay

Does anyone here speak English?
Y a-t-il quelqu'un qui parle anglais? ya·teel kel·kung kee par long·glay

How do you say ... in French?
Comment est-ce qu'on dit ... en français? ko·mon es·kon dee ... on fron·say

What does ... mean?
Que veut dire ...? ker ver deer ...

I understand.
Je comprends. zher kom·pron

I don't understand.
Je ne comprends pas. zher ner kom·pron pa

Could you write it down, please?
Est-ce que vous pouvez l'écrire? es·ker voo poo·vay lay·kreer

Can you show me (on the map)?
Pouvez-vous m'indiquer (sur la carte)? poo·vay·voo mun·dee·kay (sewr la kart)

NUMBERS

0	*zero*	zay·ro
1	*un*	un
2	*deux*	der
3	*trois*	trwa
4	*quatre*	ka·trer
5	*cinq*	sungk
6	*six*	sees
7	*sept*	set
8	*huit*	weet
9	*neuf*	nerf
10	*dix*	dees
11	*onze*	onz
12	*douze*	dooz
13	*treize*	trez
14	*quatorze*	ka·torz
15	*quinze*	kunz
16	*seize*	sez
17	*dix-sept*	dee·set
18	*dix-huit*	dee·zweet
19	*dix-neuf*	deez·nerf
20	*vingt*	vung
21	*vingt et un*	vung tay un
22	*vingt-deux*	vung·der
30	*trente*	tront
40	*quarante*	ka·ront
50	*cinquante*	sung·kont
60	*soixante*	swa·sont
70	*soixante-dix*	swa·son·dees
80	*quatre-vingts*	ka·trer·vung
90	*quatre-vingt-dix*	ka·trer·vung·dees
100	*cent*	son
1000	*mille*	meel

PAPERWORK

name	*nom*	nom
nationality	*nationalité*	na·syo·na·lee·tay
date/place of birth	*date/place de naissance*	dat/plas der nay·sons
sex/gender	*sexe*	seks
passport	*passeport*	pas·por
visa	*visa*	vee·za

QUESTION WORDS

Who?	*Qui?*	kee
What?	*Quoi?*	kwa
What is it?	*Qu'est-ce que c'est?*	kes·ker say
When?	*Quand?*	kon
Where?	*Où?*	oo
Which?	*Quel/Quelle?*	kel (m/f)

Why?	*Pourquoi?*	poor·kwa
How?	*Comment?*	ko·mon

SHOPPING & SERVICES

I'd like to buy ...
Je voudrais acheter ... zher voo·dray ash·tay ...
How much is it?
C'est combien? say kom·byun
I don't like it.
Cela ne me plaît pas. ser·la ner mer play pa
May I look at it?
Est-ce que je peux le voir? es·ker zher per ler vwar
I'm just looking.
Je regarde. zher rer·gard
It's cheap.
Ce n'est pas cher. ser nay pa shair
It's too expensive.
C'est trop cher. say tro shair
I'll take it.
Je le prends. zher ler pron

Can I pay by ...?	*Est-ce que je peux payer avec ...?*	es·ker zher per pay·yay a·vek ...
credit card	*ma carte de crédit*	ma kart der kray·dee
travellers cheques	*des chèques de voyage*	day shek der vwa·yazh

more	*plus*	plew
less	*moins*	mwa
smaller	*plus petit*	plew per·tee
bigger	*plus grand*	plew gron

I'm looking for ...	*Je cherche ...*	zhe shersh ...
a bank	*une banque*	ewn bonk
the hospital	*l'hôpital*	lo·pee·tal
the market	*le marché*	ler mar·shay
the police	*la police*	la po·lees
the post office	*le bureau de poste*	ler bew·ro der post
a public phone	*une cabine téléphonique*	ewn ka·been tay·lay·fo·neek
a public toilet	*les toilettes*	lay twa·let
the telephone centre	*la centrale téléphonique*	la san·tral tay·lay·fo·neek

TIME & DATES

What time is it?	*Quelle heure est-il?*	kel er e til
It's (8) o'clock.	*Il est (huit) heures.*	il e (weet) er
It's half past ...	*Il est (...) heures et demie.*	il e (...) er e day·mee
in the morning	*du matin*	dew ma·tun
in the afternoon	*de l'après-midi*	der la·pray·mee·dee
in the evening	*du soir*	dew swar
today	*aujourd'hui*	o·zhoor·dwee
tomorrow	*demain*	der·mun
yesterday	*hier*	yair

Monday	*lundi*	lun·dee
Tuesday	*mardi*	mar·dee
Wednesday	*mercredi*	mair·krer·dee
Thursday	*jeudi*	zher·dee
Friday	*vendredi*	von·drer·dee
Saturday	*samedi*	sam·dee
Sunday	*dimanche*	dee·monsh

January	*janvier*	zhon·vyay
February	*février*	fayv·ryay
March	*mars*	mars
April	*avril*	a·vreel
May	*mai*	may
June	*juin*	zhwun
July	*juillet*	zhwee·yay
August	*août*	oot
September	*septembre*	sep·tom·brer
October	*octobre*	ok·to·brer
November	*novembre*	no·vom·brer
December	*décembre*	day·som·brer

TRANSPORT

Public Transport

What time does ... leave/arrive?	*À quelle heure part/arrive ...?*	a kel er par/a·reev ...
boat	*le bateau*	ler ba·to
bus	*le bus*	ler bews
plane	*l'avion*	la·vyon

I'd like a ... ticket.	*Je voudrais un billet ...*	zher voo·dray un bee·yay ...
one-way	*simple*	sum·pler
return	*aller et retour*	a·lay ay rer·toor

I want to go to ...
Je voudrais aller à ... zher voo·dray a·lay a ...
The bus has been delayed.
Le bus est en retard. ler bews et on rer·tar
The bus has been cancelled.
Le bus a été annulé. ler bews a ay·tay a·new·lay

the first	*le premier* (m)	ler prer·myay
	la première (f)	la prer·myair
the last	*le dernier* (m)	ler dair·nyay
	la dernière (f)	la dair·nyair
ticket office	*le guichet*	ler gee·shay
timetable	*l'horaire*	lo·rair

Private Transport

I'd like to hire a/an...	*Je voudrais louer ...*	zher voo·dray loo·way ...

ROAD SIGNS

Cédez la Priorité	Give Way
Danger	Danger
Défense de Stationner	No Parking
Entrée	Entrance
Ralentissez	Slow Down
Sens Interdit	No Entry
Sens unique	One-way
Sortie	Exit

car	*une voiture*	ewn vwa·tewr
4WD	*un quatre-quatre*	un kat·kat
motorbike	*une moto*	ewn mo·to
bicycle	*un vélo*	un vay·lo

Is this the road to ...?
C'est la route pour ...? say la root poor ...

Where's a service station?
Où est-ce qu'il y a une station-service? oo es·keel ya ewn sta·syon·ser·vees

Please fill it up.
Le plein, s'il vous plaît. ler plun seel voo play

I'd like ... litres.
Je voudrais ... litres. zher voo·dray ... lee·trer

petrol/gas	*essence*	ay·sons
unleaded	*sans plomb*	son plom
leaded	*au plomb*	o plom
diesel	*diesel*	dyay·zel

(How long) Can I park here?
(Combien de temps) Est-ce que je peux stationner ici? (kom·byun der tom) es·ker zher per sta·syo·nay ee·see?

Where do I pay?
Où est-ce que je paie? oo es·ker zher pay?

I need a mechanic.
J'ai besoin d'un mécanicien. zhay ber·zwun dun may·ka·nee·syun

Also available from Lonely Planet:
French Phrasebook

The car/motorbike has broken down at ...
La voiture/moto est tombée en panne à ... la vwa·tewr/mo·to ay tom·bay on pan a ...

The car/motorbike won't start.
La voiture/moto ne veut pas démarrer. la vwa·tewr/mo·to ner ver pa day·ma·ray

I have a flat tyre.
Mon pneu est à plat. mom pner ay ta pla

I've run out of petrol.
Je suis en panne d'essence. zher swee zon pan day·sons

I had an accident.
J'ai eu un accident. zhay ew un ak·see·don

TRAVEL WITH CHILDREN

Is there a/an ...?	*Y a-t-il ...?*	ya teel ...
I need a/an ...	*J'ai besoin ...*	zhay ber·zwun ...
baby change room	*d'un endroit pour changer le bébé*	dun on·drwa poor shon·zhay ler bay·bay
car baby seat	*d'un siège-enfant*	dun syezh·on·fon
child-minding service	*d'une garderie*	dewn gar·dree
children's menu	*d'un menu pour enfant*	dun mer·new poor on·fon
disposable nappies/diapers	*de couches-culottes*	der koosh·kew·lot
formula	*de lait maternisé*	de lay ma·ter·nee·zay
(English-speaking) babysitter	*d'une baby-sitter (qui parle anglais)*	dewn ba·bee·see·ter (kee parl ong·glay)
highchair	*d'une chaise haute*	dewn shay zot
potty	*d'un pot de bébé*	dun po der bay·bay
stroller	*d'une poussette*	dewn poo·set

Do you mind if I breastfeed here?
Cela vous dérange si j'allaite mon bébé ici? ser·la voo day·ron·zhe see zha·lay·ter mon bay·bay ee·see

Are children allowed?
Les enfants sont permis? lay zon·fon son pair·mee

Glossary

aérobains – spa bath
auberge de jeunesse – youth hostel
ayurvedic – herbal medicine

baba figue – the blossom of the banana tree
bagasse – fibrous residue of sugar cane
bassins – small lakes
bibliothéque – library
bom – stringed instrument with a bulbous gourd-shaped body
bonhommes/bonfemmes di bois – medicine men/women
branles, brandes – giant heather bushes

caïmbe – maraca-like instrument
camtole – in the Seychelles, a traditional roving band featuring fiddle, banjo, drums and accordion
carnet – booklet
carte de séjour – residence permit
case – traditional Creole house
Cavadee – Hindu festival featuring self-mutilating devotees
cerfs – stags
chambre d'hôte – family-run B&B
colons – colonial settlers
commune – administrative district
Compagnie des Indes Orientales – French East India Company
contredanse – dance similar to the quadrille
crêperies – pancake houses

dentelles – decorative frieze on Creole houses

ferme-auberge – farm restaurant
filaos – casuarina trees
framboise bushes – thorny local shrubs found in Mauritius

gare routière – bus station
gendarmerie – police station
gîte – self-catering accommodation
gîte d'étape – walker's lodge
gîte de montagne – mountain lodge
grands blancs – rich whites
gris gris – black magic
guichet automatique de banque (GAB) – automated teller machine (ATM)

haute cuisine – high-class cuisine
hôtel de ville – town hall; see also *mairie*
houleur – hide-covered drum

jour férié – public holiday

kanvar – light wooden frame or arch decorated with paper flowers
kotis – dance similar to Scottish dancing

la malaise Creole – Creole people's anger at their impoverished status
lambrequins – ornamental window and door borders
la gastronomie – gastronomy
la métropole – mainland France as known in Réunion
le sud sauvage – wild south (southern part of Réunion island)
librairie – bookshop
location de voitures – car hire

mairie – town hall; whether a town has a mairie or a *hôtel de ville* depends on the local-government status of the town
makalapo – stringed instrument with a tin sound-box
maloya – traditional dance music of Réunion
marmite – traditional cooking pot
marrons – slaves who escaped from their owners
massalé – Indian spice mix
mazok – dance reminiscent of the French waltz
menu du jour – set menu of the day
merle blanc – cuckoo shrike; Réunion's rarest bird
métro cuisine – cuisine of mainland France
moutia – sombre, traditional dance of the Seychelles

Office National des Forêts (ONF) – Réunion's forestry division
office du tourisme – tourist office

paille-en-queue – white-tailed tropicbird
papangue – Maillardi buzzard, a protected hawklike bird
pareo – wraparound skirt of colourful fabric
plat du jour – dish of the day
pension – boarding house
pétanque – game similar to bowls
pie chanteuse – magpie robins
puja – the burning of incense and camphor at the lake shore and offering of food and flowers

ragga – blend of reggae, house music and Indian music, popular in Mauritius
ravanne – primitive goatskin drum which traditionally accompanies the *séga* dance
route forestière – forestry road

séga – dance of African origin
séga tamboun – version of *séga* popular in Rodrigues

seggae – combination of reggae and traditional *séga* music
sentier botanique – nature trail
sentiers marmailles – footpath suitable for children
source thermale – hot spring

table d'hôte – meal served at a *chambre d'hôte*
tamarin des Hauts – mountain tamarind tree
tampony – small hill
tec-tec – bird native to Réunion's highlands; also known as Réunion stonechat
télécarte – telephone card
teemeedee – Hindu/Tamil fire-walking ceremony honouring the gods
ti' cases – homes of the common folk
tout-suspendu – specially adapted descent bike

vacoa – screw pines; also known as pandanus
varangue – veranda
vélo tout terrain (VTT) – mountain bike
veuve – widow (Seychellois name for the paradise flycatcher)
vigilance cyclonique – cyclone watch

zez – monochord sitar
Z'oreilles – name used in Réunion for people from France (literally 'the ears')

Behind the Scenes

THIS BOOK

This is the 5th edition of *Mauritius, Réunion & Seychelles*. The 1st edition of was researched and written by Robert Willox. The 2nd edition was updated by Robert Strauss and Deanna Swaney, and the 3rd edition was updated by Sarina Singh. Joe Bindloss updated the 4th edition. This edition was researched and written by Jan Dodd; Madeleine and Clancy Philippe contributed the Food & Drink chapter, and Dr Caroline Evans wrote the Health chapter.

THANKS from the Author

First, thanks to Jean Alby in Réunion for his friendship, hospitality and for so generously sharing his knowledge of the region. I also owe a big debt of gratitude to Madeleine Philippe, Jean Alby and Farouk Sohawon for providing valuable insights into life in Mauritius, and to Commissioning Editor Hilary Rogers for getting the ball rolling and for her support during the long, hard slog.

In Mauritius, heartfelt thanks to John Chung and Sushita of Mauritius Tourism Promotion Authority, Mr Soojhawon and Mr Chitoo of National Transport Authority for unravelling the buses, Pierre Baissac of Mauritian Wildlife Foundation for insights on local wildlife, and to Heather Chettiar, Nathan, Françoise Baptiste, Robert Barnes, Pierre Louis Ganzagues, Maurice Giraud, Tom Hopper, Naomi, Jocelyn Legallant and Yan Massai for help and friendship along the way. Ben Gontrand deserves a special mention for treating me to an impromptu concert and a big cheer to the police in Flacq – Sherlock Holmes would have been proud.

In Réunion, many thanks are due to Emmanuelle Tayon and Daniel Schneider for providing a home away from home. Sophie ElKharrat and colleagues at Direction Régionale de l'Environnement, Isabelle Nativel, Blandine Maillot and Catherine Dostes of Maison de la Montagne, St-Denis, Eric Le Franc, Chantale, Martine Akhoun of Directions Régionales des Affaires Culturelles, Madame D Ratinet, Michel Escure of Office National des Forêts, Johnny Gill and the staff of Réunion Sensations all went out of their way to help – a big thank you to you all.

In the Seychelles, I received a warm welcome and much assistance from Glynn Burridge, Anthea Hall, Lina Belize and colleagues at Seychelles Tourism Marketing Authority, David Rowat of Marine Conservation Society Seychelles, Flavien Butler-Payette, Greg Dunn and Janet Guntensperger. Elsewhere, June, John and Alison Eckett and Margaret Driver once again deserve medals for taking on the menagerie. I would also like to thank Jo Bindloss, Simon Richmond, Julie Burge, Julie Lister and Marion Kaplan for their help and support. Last, but by no means least, thanks to Steve for adding spice to life in Mauritius in his usual inimitable way.

This book is dedicated to my father.

CREDITS

This title was commissioned and developed in Lonely Planet's Melbourne office by Hilary Rogers, Will Gourlay and Emma Koch. Cartography for this guide was developed by Shahara Ahmed.

Coordinating the production for Lonely Planet were Jenny Jones (cartography), Simon Bracken (cover design), Quentin Frayne (language) and

THE LONELY PLANET STORY

The story begins with a classic travel adventure: Tony and Maureen Wheeler's 1972 journey across Europe and Asia to Australia. There was no useful information about the overland trail then, so Tony and Maureen published the first Lonely Planet guidebook to meet a growing need.

From a kitchen table, Lonely Planet has grown to become the largest independent travel publisher in the world, with offices in Melbourne (Australia), Oakland (USA), London (UK) and Paris (France).

Today Lonely Planet guidebooks cover the globe. There is an ever-growing list of books and information in a variety of media. Some things haven't changed. The main aim is still to make it possible for adventurous travellers to get out there – to explore and better understand the world.

At Lonely Planet we believe travellers can make a positive contribution to the countries they visit – if they respect their host communities and spend their money wisely.

Charles Rawlings-Way (project management), with assistance from Nic Lehman (cover) and David Burnett (editorial production support).

Coordinating the production for Palmer Higgs Pty Ltd were Celia Purdey and Danielle De Maio (editorial), Andrew Seymour (layout design), William Ainger (photo researcher) and Selina Brendish (project management), with assistance from Brigitte Barta (editorial) and Simon Longstaff (editorial production support).

THANKS from Lonely Planet

Many thanks to the travellers who used the last edition and wrote to us with helpful hints, useful advice and interesting anecdotes:

A Serge Abramowski, Hagar Abramson, Karolina Adamkiewicz, Marcus Adams, Myriam Alexowitz, Roberto Arangath, Naomi Axford **B** Kim Seela Ballentyne-Dannau, Ann Barnatt, Elisabetta Beggiato, Bert van den Berg, Patricia Bernard, Iwan Besdomny, Stephen & Christine Bibby, Christoph Bigler, Keith Bond, Axel Braasch, Helen & Richard Brain, John Brett, Andrew Bruton, Adrian Burger, Gordon Burrows **C** Natasha Campbell, Victoria Cameron, Andrew Carr, Jennifer Cassone, Sophie Chandonnet, Anne Chenuet-Barrios, Bobby Collins, Judy Cove, G Cumberpatch **D** Patrick Daman, Uma Dasgupta, Denise, Laszlo & Madeleine De Bethlen, Mausi Digel, Michael Dittenbach, Ronnie Dooley, Sandrine Donnadieu, Dr Derek Drinkwater, Dr RA Duncan **E** Brian W Ellis, Anha & Charlotte Ehnhuus Brodbaek, George Epler, Sara & Yonatan Eyal **F** Ferdinand Fellinger, Estrela Figueiredo, Alan Forbes, Dr Vedran Franciskovic, Peter & Marilynn Freitag, Dario Frigo **G** Michaela A Gabriela, CGL Gleave, Andrew Geraghty, Mike Gilham, Jonathan Gill, Justin Giorgetti, Hazel Grant, Jane Greenham, Greta, Claudia Grieger, Andreas Grotegut **H** Joris Habraken, Guy Hagan, Mirka Hanibalova, Glen Hart, Dr Graham Hocking, Radka Hollisova, Gernot Hubmann, Helmut Hellen **I** John Ide, Trygve & Karen Inda, Alene Ivey **J** Lucy James, Volkmar E Janicke, Sheena Joymungul **K** Nick Kennedy, Philip Edward Kenny, A & A Kershaw, Christoph Kessel, Lars Erik Klemsdal, Leonard Kreuzer, Robert R Krueger, Annette Kwan-Terry **L** Joep van de Laar, Nishir M Lam, John Lam-Po-Tang, Gay Lee, Martina Lincoln, Manuel Lins, Peter F Longhurst, Veronique Louis, Helen Louise, Lukas, Amanda Lyons **M** Uma Mahadevan-Dagsputa, Astride Maier, Magali Malherbe, Satpal Mann, Maria Merry, Peter Michl, Markella Mekkelsen, Jackie Mitchell, Alan Molenaar, Monika & Alex Marion, Judy Mayer, Liza McCarthy, Robert Metzger, Helen Morgan, Michael, Jacqui Morris **N** Anita Newcourt, Chris Nichols **O** John Osman **P** Nick Pace, Sarah Parker, Bonnie Persons, Anne-Lie Pettersen, Alexandra Peyre, Ronit Piso, Dietmar Plagens, Nathan Plowman, Tallia Polatinsky, Raffaela Poretti **R** Ian Reason, Marie Reynolds, Howard Richards, James Robertson, Rom Rombouts Sr, Marcia Rooker, Cyrus Rosenburg IV **S** Knut Sandahl, Jean-Pascal Schaefer, Katrin Schultz, Franziska Schuster, Giles Scofield, Liz & Len Sexon, Manuela Siegert, Heila & Lawrence Sisitka, Adrian Skerrett, S Suzanne Van Skike, Rhona Smith, Anne K Soper, Verena Stammbach, Uli Steinbrenner, Mona Stenroth, Steve, Dorothy de St Jorre, Mark Stober, Elisabeth Stocker, Lynne Stoddart, Jodie Stokol, Eric Su, Heiko Suess, Katalin Szilagyi **T** Ricado Taboada, Martin Taylor, Thomas Thies, Udo Tillmann, Colonel B Thompson, Jaume Tort, Stefanie Toussain, Ilkka Toyryla **U** Emma Ulmer, Doreen Uzice **V** Katrine Van Malderen, Suzanne Van Skike, Mary Varvaras, Nicky Vereker **W** Barbara Waldis, Sepp Weissenboeck, Johannes Wellmann, Roger Williams **Z** Ruth van Zyl

SEND US YOUR FEEDBACK

We love to hear from travellers – your comments keep us on our toes and help make our books better. Our well-travelled team reads every word on what you loved or loathed about this book. Although we cannot reply individually to postal submissions, we always guarantee that your feedback goes straight to the appropriate authors, in time for the next edition. Each person who sends us information is thanked in the next edition – and the most useful submissions are rewarded with a free book.

To send us your updates – and find out about LP events, newsletters and travel news – visit our award-winning website: **www.lonelyplanet.com**.

Note: We may edit, reproduce and incorporate your comments in Lonely Planet products such as guidebooks, websites and digital products, so let us know if you don't want your comments reproduced or your name acknowledged. For a copy of our privacy policy visit www.lonelyplanet.com/privacy.

Index

ABBREVIATIONS

M Mauritius
R Réunion
S Seychelles

A

accommodation 277, *see also individual locations*
  Mauritius 129
  Réunion 210
  Seychelles 269
activites, *see individual activities*
agriculture
  Mauritius 51
  Seychelles 264
air tickets 287
air travel 286-90
  airline offices 286
  to/from Mauritius 139
  to/from Réunion 220
  to/from the Seychelles 274
  within Mauritius 140
  within Réunion 221
  within the Seychelles 274
Aldabra Atoll (S) 258, 268, 12
Aldabra Group (S) 268
Alphonse Groups (S) 268
Amirantes (S) 268
animals, *see also* birds, *individual species*
  Mauritius 54-6, 80, 114-15, 122
  Réunion 154-5
  Seychelles 245, 263, 268
Anse à la Mouche (S) 255
Anse aux Anglais (M) 126
Anse Bougainville (S) 255
Anse Cocos (S) 265
Anse Consolation (S) 260
Anse des Cascades (R) 173
Anse Forbans (S) 255
Anse Gaulettes (S) 255
Anse Intendance (S) 255
Anse Lazio (S) 260
Anse Major (S) 254
Anse Marie-Louise (S) 255, 260
Anse Parnel (S) 255
Anse Royale (S) 255
Anse St José (S) 263
Anse Soleil (S) 255
Anse Source d'Argent (S) 264
Anse Takamaka (S) 255
Anse Volbert (S) 260
aquarium 187
architecture
  Mauritius 53-4
  Réunion 152-3
Aride Islands (S) 263, 264
arts
  Mauritius 51-4
  Réunion 151-3
  Seychelles 243-5
art galleries, *see individual galleries*
Association Parc Marin de la Réunion 36
Assomption Island (S) 268-9
Aurère (R) 195, 206

B

Baie de l'Arsenal (M) 70
Baie du Cap (M) 117, 119
Balaclava (M) 70
Bambous Virieux (M) 115-17
bargaining 284
Bassin Blanc (M) 90
Battle of Vieux Grand Port (M) 111
beaches, *see individual beaches*
Beau Vallon (S) 251-3, **252**
Belle Mare (M) 99-101
Bel Ombre (M) 90, 119
Bérenger, Paul 47-8, 51
Bernica (R) 195
bicycle rental
  Mauritius 140
  Réunion 214, 221
  Seychelles 274
bicycle travel, see cycling
Birdlife International 246-7
birds, *see also individual species*
  Mauritius 54-6, 80, 103
  Réunion 154-5
  Seychelles 245, 247, 263, 267-8
Bird Island (S) 264, 267-8
black magic 178, 243
black market 282
black paradise flycatcher 266
Black River Gorges National Park (M) 56-7, 86, 89, **88**, 8
Blue Bay (M) 113-14
Blue Penny Museum (M) 61
boat travel, *see also* cruises, catamaran tours, glass-bottomed boat tours
  to/from Mauritius 139-40, 290
  to/from Réunion 220, 290
  to/from Seychelles 290
  within Mauritius 140
  within the Seychelles 274-5
Bois Chéri Tea estate (M) 117
books, *see also* literature
  diving 33
  food 29, 30, 32
  health 292
  hiking 226
  marine life 33
  Mauritius 50, 132
  Réunion 215
  Seychelles 270
  travel 14-15
Bory Crater (R) 236
Boucan Canot (R) 192
Bourg-Murat (R) 208, 236
Bras-Panon (R) 171-2
Bras des Merles (R) 195
Bras des Roches Noires (R) 208
Bras de Ste-Suzanne (R) 208
Bras Sec (R) 202, 208, 231
brewery, Mauritius 93
Brissare Rocks (S) 41
British Council (M) 94
business hours
  Mauritius 132-3
  Réunion 215
  Seychelles 271
bus travel
  Mauritius 140-1
  Réunion 221, 222
  Seychelles 275

C

camping 277
  Mauritius 129
  Réunion 210
  Seychelles 269
canoeing
  Réunion 169, 186
canyoning
  Réunion 199, 204, 212
Cap Malheureux (M) 83-4

car rental
Mauritius 142
Réunion 221-3
Seychelles 275-6
car travel
Mauritius 141-2
Réunion 221-2
Seychelles 275-6
Cascade Biberon (R) 207
Cascade de Bras Rouge (R) 201
Cascade du Voile de la Mariée (R) 205
Cascade Niagara (R) 168
Casela Nature Park (M) 103
catamaran tours
Mauritius 75, 107, 114, 132
Réunion 213
Seychelles 274
cathedrals, *see* churches & cathedrals
Caudan Waterfront 66, **9**
cavadee (festival) 134, 170
Caverne Dufour 231
Caverne Patate (M) 127
caves
Caverne Patate (M) 127
Grotte des Premier Français (R) 148
La Chapelle (R) 201
Cayenne (R) 206, 229
Central Mauritius 86-95, **87**
Central Plateau (M) 86, 89
Centre Charles Baudelaire (M) 94
Centre De Flacq (M) 100-1
Cerf Island (S) 257
Chagos archipelago 50
Chamarel (M) 107
chambre d'hôte 210
Champ de Mars Racecourse (M) 63
Chapelle Pointue (R) 192-3
children, travel with 278-9
food 28
Mauritius 133
Réunion 215
Seychelles 271
Chinese Spring Festival 135
cholera 293
churches & cathedrals
Cathédrale de St-Denis (R) 160
Chapelle Pointue (R) 192-3
Notre Dame Auxiliatrice (M) 83
Notre Dame de la Délivrance (R) 161
Notre Dame de la Salette (R) 184
Notre Dame des Anges (M) 111
Notre Dame des Laves (R) 173
St James Cathedral (M) 62
St Louis Cathedral (M) 62
Cilaos (R) 197-202, 231, **198**
cinema
Mauritius 66
Réunion 191
Seychelles 24, 251
Cirque de Cilaos 195-202, 234-6
Cirque de Mafate (R) 193, 195-7, 206, 228-30, 234-6, **230**, **11**
Cirque de Salazie (R) 195-7, 202-6, 228
climate 279
Mauritius 45-6
Réunion 147
Seychelles 239-40
clothing industry 24, 47, 93, 137
Cocos (S) 266
coco de mer palms 245, 249, 258, 260, 263
Coin de Mire (M) 80
Col des Bœufs (R) 205, 228, 234
Col de Bébour (R) 231, 234-6
Col de Fourche (R) 205
Col du Taïbit (R) 231
Colorado (M) 38
coloured earths
Chamarel 107-8
La Vallée des Couleurs 118
consulates, *see* embassies 62
Company Gardens (M) 62
Confédération Mondiale des Activités Subaquatiques (CMAS) 37
Conrad, Joseph (author) 52
Conservatoire Botanique National de Mascarin (R) 185
Convention on International Trade in Endangered Species 35
coral 33, 39
Corps de Garde (M) 89
costs 14
Cousine Island (S) 263
Cousin Island (S) 263-4
country codes, *see inside front cover*
Creole architecture
Mauritius 53
Réunion 152-3, **10**
Creole culture 49
Réunion 150
Seychelles 242-5
cruises, *see also* catamaran tours, glass-bottomed boat tours
Mauritius 75, 132
Seychelles 269
culture
food 29
Mauritius 48-51
Réunion 150-1
Seychelles 242-3
Curepipe (M) 90-3, **91**
Curieuse Island (S) 263
customs regulations 279-80
cycling
Mauritius 140
Réunion 221
Seychelles 274
cyclones 148, 225, 280

D

dance
Mauritius 52
Réunion 152
Seychelles 224
Danzil (S) 254
David, Barthélémy 95
de Chamarel, Charles de Chazal 108
de Chazal, Malcolm (author) 52, 54
de Labourdonnais, Mahé 46, 59, 84, 109, 149, 156, 240, 247
de Souza, Carl (author) 52
de St-Pierre, Bernardin (author) 85
deep vein thrombosis 292
deep-sea fishing 278
Mauritius 71, 75, 107, 130
Réunion 213
Seychelles 270
Denis Island (S) 264, 268
Departmental Office of Architecture and Patrimony (R) 152
d'Épinay, Prosper (sculptor) 54
Desroches Island (S) 268
diarrhoea 294-5
Diego Garcia 50
diphtheria 293
disabled travellers 280
Divali (festival) 134, 170
dive operators
Mauritius 38
Réunion 40
Seychelles 41
dive organisations
Confédération Mondiale des Activités Subaquatiques (CMAS) 37
National Association of Underwater Instructors (NAUI) 37
Professional Association of Diving Instructors (PADI) 37
diving 278
books 33

000 Map pages
000 Location of colour photographs

INDEX

diving *continued*
festival 40
itinerary 22
Mauritius 37-8, 71, 75, 99, 103, 113, 126, 128, 131
responsibly 37
Réunion 39, 185, 187, 213
safety 37, 39
Seychelles 40, 269
dodos 46, 55
Dolomieu Crater (R) 236
Domaine des Tourelles (R) 206
Domaine de l'Ylang Ylang (M) 116-17
Domaine de la Confiance (R) 172
Domaine de St Félix (M) 118
Domaine du Chasseur (M) 116
Domaine du Grand Hazier (R) 169
Domaine Les Pailles (M) 67-8
Dos d'Ane (R) 195
drinks 26-7
driving, *see* car travel
Duncan, James (horticulturalist) 84

E

East Coast (R) 167-74, **168**
East Mauritius 95-101, **96**
Ecomusée Salazie (R) 204
economy
Mauritius 24, 47-8
Réunion 24-5, 150
Seychelles 24, 242
ecotourism
Mauritius 56, 121
Réunion 25
Seychelles 247, 268
eels 33
electricity
Mauritius 133
Réunion 215
Seychelles 271
embassies 281
Mauritius 133
Réunion 216
Seychelles 271
embroidery 198-9
emergencies, *see also inside front cover*
hiking 226
Enclos Foucqué (R) 236
Entre-Deux (R) 180-1
environment
Mauritius 54-7
Réunion 153-4
Seychelles 245-7
environmental issues 25
coral bleaching 33, 37, 257
development 57, 155, 156
land reclamation 247, 254
overfishing 119
tourism 15-16, 247
Étang-Salé-les-Bains (R) 183
Eureka (M) 53, 95
exchange rates, *see inside front cover*
Expédit, St 161

F

Farquhar (S) 268
Félicité Island (S) 264, 267
festivals 15, *see also* special events
Chinese Spring Festival 135
Divali 134, 170
Festival Kreol 244
Grand Raid 212
Holi 134
Maha Shivarati 93, 134
Pére Laval Feast 68, 135
Teemeedee 134, 216
Feuillet, Eraste 195
fish 33-4, 39
fishing, *see* deep-sea fishing
fishing industry 24, 35-6, 119, 242, 264
Flic en Flac (M) 101-4, **104**, 7
Flinders, Matthew 108, 119, 132
Floréal (M) 93
Fock, Michel (musician) 152
food 26, 28-9
customs 29
festivals 27
Mauritius 77, 135
restaurants 27-8
Réunion 216
Seychelles 272
vegetarian & vegans 28
vocabulary 29-32
forest reserves, *see also* nature reserves, national parks
Vallée de Mai (S) 258
Veuve Reserve (S) 266
Fôret de Bébour-Bélouve (R) 207
Fort Adelaide (M) 63
4WD tours 213
Frederik Hendrik Museum (M) 115
French East India Company 95, 148-9, 160

G

Gandhi, Indira 85
Gandhi, Mahatma 47
gardens & parks, *see also* national parks
Botanical Gardens (M) 92
Botanical Gardens (S) 249
Company Gardens (M) 62
Conservatoire Botanique National de Mascarin (R) 185
Domaine de la Confiance (R) 172
Domaine du Grand Hazier (R) 169
Jardin de l'État (R) 160
Le Barachois (R) 160
Le Jardin d'Eden (R) 187
Le Jardin des Parfums et des Épices (R) 174
Le Jardin du Roi (S) 255
Sir Seewoosagur Ramgoolam Botanical Gardens (M) 84
Garros, Roland (aviator) 161
gay travellers 281
geography
Mauritius 54
Réunion 153-4
Seychelles 245
giant tortoises 114, 117, 121, 245, 263, 268
gîtes d'étape 211, 226
gîtes de montagne 210, 226
gîtes ruraux 211
glass-bottomed boat tours
Mauritius 70, 113
Réunion 187
golf
Mauritius 71, 98
Réunion 213
Seychelles 261
Grand Anse (S) 253, 260, 265
Grand Baie (M) 74-80, **76**, 8
Grand Bassin (R) 208
Grand Étang (R) 172
Grand Gaube (M) 84
Grand Îlet (R) 205
Grand Place 212
Grand Raid 253
Grande Anse (S) 253
Grande Montagne (M) 126
Grande Rivière Noire (M) 90, 107, 8
Grande Sœur (S) 266
Gravier (M) 126
gris gris 178, 243
Gris Gris (beach) (M) 118
Grotte des Premiers Français (R) 148
guavas 90

H

hang-gliding
Réunion 214

health 291-5
  books 292
  insurance 291
  Internet resources 292
  vaccinations 293
heat exhaustion 295
heatstroke 295
helicopter tours
  Réunion 219-20
  Seychelles 274
Hell-Bourg (R) 203, 231-2, **205**, 11
hepatitis 293
hiking 278
  Mauritius 88, 131
  Réunion 213, 225-7
  Seychelles 270
hiking equipment 225
Hindu temples 48, 51, 134, 161, 169, 216, 283
historic buildings
  Creole mansion (M) 95
  Domaine de la Confiance (R) 172
  Domaine du Grand Hazier (R) 169
  Hôtel de Ville (M) 92
  Hôtel de Ville (R) 160, 177
  La Résidence (M) 124
  Maison de la Vanille (R) 169
  Maison Deramond 160
  Maison Le Carne (M) 94-5
  Maison Valliamé (R) 169
  Mauritius 53
  Municipality of Beau Bassin-Rose Hill (M) 94-5
  Musée de Villèle (R) 192-3
  Place S Bissoondoyal (M) 62
  St Aubin (M) 117
history 24
  Mauritius 46
  Réunion 148
  Seychelles 240-2
hitching 143
Hiti, Danielle (painter) 54
HIV/AIDS 293
Hoare, Mike 241
Hoareau, Gerard 241
Holi 134
holidays 13, *see also* public holidays
horse riding
  Mauritius 68, 131
  Réunion 172, 193, 208-9, 213
Hôtel de Ville (R) 160, 177

000 Map pages
000 Location of colour photographs

hunting 115, 116

I
Île aux Aigrettes (M) 55, 57, 114
Île aux Cerfs (M) 98
Île aux Chats (M) 128
Île aux Cocos (M) 126
Île aux Cocos Nature Reserve (M) 128
Île aux Serpents (M) 80
Île des Salazes (R) 234
Île Hermitage (M) 128
Île Plate (M) 80
Île Ronde (M) 57, 80
Îlet à Bourse (R) 206-10
Îlet à Cordes (R) 201-2, 231-4
Îlet à Vidot (R) 232
Îlet des Orangers (R) 193
Îlois (M) 50
Îlot (S) 41
Îlot Gabriel (M) 80
independence
  Mauritius 47, 63, 121
  Seychelles 240-1
industries
  clothing 24, 47, 93, 137
  fishing 24, 35-6, 119, 242, 264
  perfume 193, 194
  sugar 24, 46, 47, 48, 68, 85, 100, 103, 118, 149-50, 180, 185
  tea 117, 254
  tourism 24-5, 121, 242, 247, 264
  vanilla 117, 149, 169, 171-2
Institut Géographique National 225
insurance 281, 291
Interior (R) 195-209, **196**
Internet access 281-2
Internet resources 15
  air tickets 287
  health 292
  Mauritius 135
  Réunion 217
  Seychelles 272
itineraries 17-22
  author's favourite trip 23
  diving 22
  Mauritius 17, 20
  Réunion 18, 21
  Seychelles 19

J
Jardin de l'État (R) 160
jet lag 292
Jugnauth, Anerood 47-8, 51
Jugnauth, Pravind 48
Jummah Mosque (M) 62

K
Kali Temple (R) 169
Kaya 47-8, 52
Kreol Institute (S) 243, 271

L
La Buse (pirate) 194, 252
La Chapelle (R) 201
La Cuvette public beach (M) 75
La Digue (S) 264-7, **265**, 12
La Gaulette (M) 107
La Montagne (R) 166-7
La Nouvelle (R) 228, 234
La Passe St François (M) 38
La Preneuse (M) 106
La Résidence (M) 124
La Roche Écrite (R) 167, 195
La Roche Merveilleuse (R) 231
La Roche qui Pleure (M) 118
La Vallée des Couleurs (M) 118
La Vanille (M) 117
L'Artothéque (R) 160
L'Aventure du Sucre (M) 85
L'Éperon (R) 193, 195
L'Hermitage-les-Bains (R) 186-92, **188**
land-reclamation projects
  Seychelles 247, 254
language 297-303
Lauren, Ralph 137
Laval, Père Jacques Désiré 68
Le Barachois (R) 160
Le Bélier (R) 205, 234
Le Bronchard (R) 229
Le Brûlé (R) 166-7
Le Dimitile (R) 181, 231
Le Gouffre (R) 183
Le Grand Bénare (R) 193, 228
Le Jardin d'Eden (R) 187
Le Jardin des Parfums et des Épices (R) 174
Le Jardin du Roi (S) 255
Le Maïdo (R) 183, 193-4, 228, 10
Le Morne Brabant (M) 108
Le Morne Penninsula (M) 108
Le Pétrin (M) 90
Le Pouce (M) 89
Le Quinzième (R) 167
Le Réduit (M) 95
Le Sitarane (sorcerer) 179
Le Souffleur (R) 185
Le Tampon (R) 208
Le Vingt-Quatrième (R) 208
legal matters 282
legends 85, 93, 161, 252, 260

Leguat, François 121
Les Avirons (R) 183
Les Colimaçons (R) 185
Les Hautes Plaines (R) 196, 206
Les Roches Noires (R) 187, 214
lesbian travellers 281
Levasseur, Olivier 194, 252
Lion Mountain (M) 115-16
literature 14-15, *see also* books
  Mauritius 51-2
  Réunion 152
  Seychelles 243-4

M
Mac Aulliffe, Angèle 198-9
Mafate (chieftan) 206
Madame Panon-Desbassyns (R) 192
magazines, *see also* newspapers
  Mauritius 135
  Réunion 217
  Seychelles 272
Magicienne (ship) 111
Mahatma Gandhi Institute (M) 95
Maha Shivaratri (festival) 93, 134
Mahé 247-58, 12
Mahébourg (M) 109-15, **112**
Maison Deramond (R) 160
Maison de la Montagne (R) 225
Maison de la Vanille (R) 169
Maison du Peuplement des Hauts (R) 198
Maison du Volcan (R) 208
Maison Laclos (R) 229
Maison Le Carne (M) 94
Maison Valliamé (R) 169
malaria 294
maloya (music) 152
Mancham, James 240-1
Mandela, Nelson 85
mangroves 115, 116
maps 282
  legend 316
  Mauritius 88, 135
  Réunion 217, 225
Mare Longue Nature Reserve (R) 236
Marianne (S) 266
marine conservation 35-6, 37
  Mauritius 36, 57
  Réunion 36, 155-6
  Seychelles 36-7, 245
Marine Conservation Society Seychelles 36
marine life 33-5
  books 33
  coral 33, 39
  echinoderms 33
  eels 33
  fish 33-4, 39
  molluscs 34-5
  rays 35
  sharks 34, 37, 214
  starfish 33
  symbiotic relationships 34
  turtles 35, 184, 267-8
marine parks & reserves 57, 246
  Aldabra Marine Reserve 268
  Aride Island Marine Nature Reserve 264
  Curieuse Marine National Park 263
  Ste Anne Marine National Park 263
  Blue Bay Marine Park 114
markets
  Port Louis Central Market (M) 60-1, 7
  St-Pierre (R) 178
  Sir Selwyn Selwyn-Clarke Market (S) 250
Marla (R) 229, 234
marrons 149, 197, 198, 232
Martello Tower Museum (M) 106
Mascarin 148
Mauritian Scuba Diving Association 38
Mauritian Wildlife Foundation 55, 57
Mauritius Marine Conservation Society 36
Mauritius Postal Museum (M) 62
Mauritius Pride (ship) 290
Mauritius Scuba Diving Association 36
Mauritius Trochetia (ship) 290
Mauritius Underwater Group 36
medical services 292, *see also* health
Médine sugar factory (M) 103
meningococcal meningitis 294
metric conversions, *see inside front cover*
Michel, James 242
model ships 93, 138
Moka (M) 95
molluscs 34-5
money 14, 282, *see also inside front cover*
  Mauritius 136-7
  Réunion 218
  Seychelles 272-3
monkeys 55, 103
Mont Lubin (M) 126
Morne Blanc 254
Morne Seychellois National Park 254
mosques 48
  Grand Mosquée (R) 161
  Jummah Mosque (M) 62
motion sickness 292
motorcycle rental
  Mauritius 142
  Réunion 223
motorcycle travel
  Mauritius 142
  Réunion 223
Mt Limon (M) 126
Mt Malartic (M) 126
mountain biking 185
  Mauritius 130
  Réunion 183, 185, 194, 199, 208, 214, 226
moutia (dance) 244
Moyenne Island (S) 257
Municipal Theatre (M) 62
Musée d'Histoire Naturelle (R) 160
Musée de Villèle (R) 192
Musée Léon Dierx (R) 160
museums
  Blue Penny Museum (M) 61
  Ecomusée Salazie (R) 204
  Frederik Hendrik Museum (M) 115
  L'Aventure du Sucre (M) 85
  L'Union Estate (S) 266
  Madame Panon-Desbassyns (R) 192-3
  Maison du Peuplement des Hauts (R) 198
  Maison du Volcan (R) 208
  Martello Tower Museum (M) 106
  Mauritius Postal Museum (M) 62
  Musée de Villèle (R) 192
  Musée d'Histoire Naturelle (R) 160
  Musée Léon Dierx (R) 160
  National History Museum (M) 111
  National Museum of History (S) 249
  Natural History Museum (M) 61-2
  Natural History Museum (S) 250
  Photography Museum (M) 62
  Robert Edward Hart Museum (M) 118
  Stella Matutina Museum (R) 185
music
  Mauritius 52
  Réunion 152
  Seychelles 244
Mussard, François 149, 197, 206
myths 85, 93, 161, 252, 260

N
National Association of Underwater Instructors (NAUI) 37
National History Museum (M) 111

National Museum of History (S) 249-50
national parks 56-7, 246
Black River Gorges National Park (M) 56-7, 86, 89, **88**, 8
Morne Seychellois National Park (S) 254
Praslin National Park (M) 258
Ste Anne Marine National Park (S) 257
National School of Music and the National Cultural Troupe (S) 243
Natural History Museum (M) 61-2
Natural History Museum (S) 250
Nature Protection Trust of Seychelles 247
nature reserves, *see also* marine parks & reserves
Aride Island (S) 263, 264
Casela Nature Park (M) 103
Coin de Mire (M) 80
Cousin Island (S) 263-4
Île aux Aigrettes (M) 55, 57, 114
Île aux Cocos (M) 128
Île aux Serpents (M) 80
Île Rond (M) 57, 80
La Vanille (M) 117
Mare Longue Nature Reserve (R) 236
Yemen (M) 103
Nature Seychelles 37, 247
newspapers
Mauritius 135
Réunion 217
Seychelles 242, 272
North Mahé (S) 253-5, **253**
North Mauritius 68-86, **69**
Notre Dame Auxiliatrice (M) 83
Notre Dame des Anges (M) 111
Notre Dame des Laves (R) 173
Notre Dame de la Délivrance (R) 161
Notre Dame de la Salette (R) 184

O
Office National des Forêts (R) 224

P
Palmiste Rouge (R) 202
palm spiders 266
Pamplemousses (M) 84
Panon-Desbassyns, Madame 192-3

000 Map pages
000 Location of colour photographs

paragliding 185, 214
Parc Marin Réunion 156
parks, *see* gardens & parks, national parks
passports 286
Père Laval Feast 68, 135
Père Laval's Shrine (M) 68
Pereybère (M) 80-2, **81**, 9
perfume industry 193, 194
Petite (S) 266
Petite Anse (S) 265
Petite France (R) 195
Phoenix (M) 93
photography 282-3
Photography Museum (M) 62
Piton d'Enchaing (R) 231, 232
Piton des Neiges (R) 154, 197, 224, 229
Piton de la Fournaise (R) 153-4, 196, 206, 208, 224, 234-6, **235**, 10
Piton de la Petite Rivière Noire (M) 90
Piton St-Leu (R) 186
Place S Bissoondoyal (M) 62
Plaine Champagne (M) 90
Plaine d'Affouches (R) 195
Plaine des Tamarins (R) 228, 230, 234
Plaine-des-Cafres (R) 206, 208
Plaine-des-Palmistes (R) 206, 206-8
planning for travel 13-16
plants, *see also individual species*
Mauritius 56, 80, 84-5, 90, 114
Réunion 155
Seychelles 245-6
Plateau des Chênes (R) 231
Plateau du Kerval (R) 231
Plateau du Petit Matarum (R) 231
Pointe au Sel (R) 185
Pointe Coton (M) 126
Pointe d'Esny (M) 113-14
Police Bay (S) 255
poliomyelitis 294
politics
Mauritius 47
Réunion 150
Seychelles 240-1
population
Mauritius 50
Réunion 151
Seychelles 243
Port Louis (M) 57-68, **58-9**, **63**
accommodation 64
entertainment 66
food 64-6
history 59
shopping 66
travel to/from 67
travel within 67
walking tour 63
Port Mathurin (M) 123-6, **125**
Port Sud-Est (M) 126
postal services 283-4
Praslin (S) 258-62, **259**
Praslin National Park (S) 258
Professional Association of Diving Instructors (PADI) 37
public holidays 281
Mauritius 135
Réunion 147-8, 217
Seychelles 272

Q
Quatre Bornes (M) 94

R
rabies 294
radio
Mauritius 136
Réunion 218
Seychelles 272
Ramgoolam, Sir Seewoosagur 47, 84
Ramkalawan, Wavel 241
Ravine de Bras Rouge (R) 202
Ravine des Colimaçons (R) 186
Ravine des Trois Bassins (R) 186
Ravine Gérien (R) 234
rays 35
Registrar of Civil Status 72
religion
Mauritius 51
Réunion 151
Seychelles 243
Rempart Serpent (M) 38
René, France Albert 240-2
reserves, *see* forest reserves, national parks, nature reserves, marine parks & reserves
responsible hiking 227
responsible travel 15-16, 48
rhum arrangé 26, 199
Rivière des Anguilles (M) 117
Rivière des Galets (R) 229
Rivière des Remparts (R) 176, 236
Riviére du Basse Vallée (R) 236
Rivière St-Étienne (R) 180
road rules
Mauritius 142
Réunion 223
Seychelles 275
Robert Edward Hart Museum (M) 118
Roche Merveilleuse (R) 202
Roche Plate (R) 193, 228, 229

INDEX

rock climbing
Mauritius 103
Réunion 199, 204, 212
Rodrigues (M) 119-29, **120**
Rodriguez, Don Diégo 121
Rose Hill (M) 89, 94
Round Island (S) 257
Royal Society for Nature Conservation 264
Royal Society for the Protection of Birds 247

S

St Aubin (M) 117
St-André (R) 169, **170**
St-Benoît (R) 172-3
St-Denis (R) 156-67, **158-9**
accommodation 161-2
drinking 164
entertainment 164-5
food 162-4
history 156
shopping 165
sights 157-61
travel to/from 165
travel within 166
St Expédit (saint) 161
St François (M) 126
St Géran (ship) 111
St-Gilles-les-Bains (R) 186-92, **188**, **11**
St-Gilles-les-Hauts (R) 192
St James Cathedral (M) 62
St-Joseph (R) 176-7
St-Leu (R) 184-6
St Louis Cathedral (M) 180
St-Louis (R) 62
St-Paul (R) 194
St-Philippe (R) 174-6
St-Pierre (R) 177, **178**
Ste Anne Marine National Park 254, 257
Ste-Anne (R) 173
Ste-Rose (R) 173-4
Ste-Suzanne (R) 168
Salazie (R) 203
Sans Souci (R) 193
séga (dance) 52, 79, 128, 152, 244, **8**
semisubmersibles 75, 130
Sentier de Roche Plate (R) 193
Sentier du Volcan (R) 236
Seychelles Island Foundation 37, 247, 260, 268
Seychelles Tourism Marketing Authority (STMA) 242
sharks 34, 37, 214
Shark Bank (S) 41
shipwrecks
Magicienne 111
St Géran 111
Shiva 93, 134
Shoals 36
Shoals Rodrigues 119
shopping 284
Mauritius 137
Seychelles 250
Silhouette Island (S) 257-8
Sir Seewoosagur Ramgoolam Botanical Gardens (M) 84, **7**
Sir Selwyn Selwyn-Clarke Market 250
slaves, *see* marrons
Smith, Wilbur 257
snorkelling 41-2, 278
Mauritius 38, 41, 70, 81, 99, 128, 131
Réunion 42, 187
Seychelles 42, 251, 257, 260, 263, 267, 268, 269
Société d'Études Ornithologiques de la Réunion 155
solo travellers 284
Souillacn (M) 117-18
South Coast (R) 174-81, **175**
South Mahé 255-7, **256**
South Mauritius 109-19, **110**
special events, *see also* festivals
Mauritius 93, 134
Réunion 151, 170, 216
Seychelles 244, 271
spiders 266
stamps, collectable 61
starfish 33
Stella Matutina Museum (R) 185
submarine rides 71
Sub Indian Ocean Seychelles (SUBIOS) 40
sugar industry 24, 46, 47, 48, 149-50
mills 68, 100, 103, 118, 180,
museums 85, 185
Surcouf, Robert 46
surfing 278
Mauritius 105, 119, 131
Réunion 186, 214
Seychelles 269
swimming
Mauritius 38, 75, 81
Réunion 215
Seychelles 251, 254-5, 260, 265, 268

T

Takamaka (R) 172
Tamarin (M) 105
tamarin des Hauts 155, 228
Tamarin Falls (M) 89
taxis
Mauritius 143-4
Réunion 166
Seychelles 276
tea industry 117, 254
Teemeedee 134, 216
telephone services 284
Mauritius 138-9
Réunion 218
Seychelles 273
temples
Hindu (R) 48, 51, 134, 161, 169, 216, 283
Kali Temple (R) 169
Shiv Kalyan Vath Mandir (M) 75
Surya Oudaya Sangam (M) 75
Temple of Colosse (R) 169
Temple of Colosse (R) 169
Tévelave (R) 183-4
theatre, *see also* individual theatres
Mauritius 66
Réunion 153, 165, 186, 191
Seychelles 244
theft 280
thermal springs
Cilaos (R) 199
Hell-bourg (R) 203, 204
time 296
tipping 282
Topize, Joseph 47-8, 52
tortoises 114, 117, 121, 245, 263, 268
tourism industry 24-5, 121, 242, 247, 264
tourist information 284-5
Mauritius 139
Réunion 219
tours, *see* boat tours, catamaran tours, 4WD tours, glass-bottomed boat tours, helicopter
Tour des Cirques (R) 231-5, **233**
treasure hunting
Mauritius 128
Réunion 194
Seychelles 252
trekking, *see* hiking
Trevassa (M) 119
Trevassa Monument (M) 119
Trois Frères Peak 254
Trois Roches (R) 229